EDUCATION
IN THE
UNITED STATES

EDUCATION IN THE UNITED STATES

An Interpretive History

Robert L. Church
and
Michael W. Sedlak

THE FREE PRESS
A Division of Macmillan Publishing Co., Inc.
NEW YORK

Collier Macmillan Publishers
LONDON

The Free Press
A Division of Macmillan Publishing Co., Inc.
866 Third Avenue, New York, N.Y. 10022

Collier Macmillan Canada, Ltd.

Library of Congress Catalog Card Number: 75-22764

Printed in the United States of America

printing number

1 2 3 4 5 6 7 8 9 10

Library of Congress Cataloging in Publication Data

Church, Robert L
  Education in the United States.

  Includes bibliogrpahical references and index.
    1. Education—United States—History.
I. Sedlak, Michael W., joint author. II. Title.
LA212.C53   370'.973   75-22764
ISBN 0-02-905490-7

Contents

Preface   vii

PART I: *Education in the New Nation, 1776–1830*

Chapter *1:* The District School   3

Chapter *2:* The Antebellum College and Academy   23

PART II: *The Quest for Commonality, 1830–1860*

Chapter *3:* The Common School Movement   55

Chapter *4:* The Search for a New Pedagogy   84

PART III: *The Retreat from Commonality, 1840–1920*

Chapter *5:* The Failure of the Common Schools (I): The South   117

Chapter *6:* The Failure of the Common Schools (II): The North   154

Chapter *7:* Training the Hand: The Rise of Special Education   192

Chapter *8:* The Rise of the University: Special Education at the Top   227

PART IV: *School and Community: Progressivism in Education, 1890–1940*

Chapter 9: Educational Reform in the Progressive Era   251

Chapter 10: The High School in the Progressive Era   288

Chapter 11: Progressivism and the Kindergarten, 1870–1925   316

Chapter 12: American Education Between the Wars, 1918–1940   343

PART V: *Redefining Commonality, 1940–1975*

Chapter 13: The Reaction Against Progressivism, 1941–1960   401

Chapter 14: Changing Definitions of Equality of Educational Opportunity, 1960–1975   431

Index   477

Preface

This volume concentrates on one great theme in the history of education in the United States: the varying commitment among Americans to "mass schooling" and equality of education. The United States was the first major Western nation in which local governmental units declared their intention to offer "free" schooling to every child. That declared intention has been a great source of pride to Americans and especially to professional educators. The failure to live up completely to that intention has been a source of continuing frustration and shame to the nation and its teachers. Since notions of what constitutes equality in every phase of American life are under intense and needed reexamination at this time, it seems particularly fitting to focus our interpretation on the ways those concerned with educational development in this country have defined educational equality and the role of mass education in fulfilling the promise of democracy.

This focus has led us to begin our story with the founding of the common schools—the first institutions of mass schooling—in the early decades of the nineteenth century. We have examined the motives behind this commitment to mass schooling in terms of the growing urbanization of American society. As we approach the second half of the nineteenth century, our attention shifts to a number of experiments that appear to have contradicted the earlier commitment to commonality. Special educational tracks were designed for special elements in the population—industrial and vocational education for blacks, immigrants, and other poor people, as well as a university experience for the elite. Those seeking to provide appropriate educational experiences for children from widely varying backgrounds—children who seemed to share few aspirations or abilities—redefined both equality and democracy. During the nineteenth century, control over education was increasingly vested in professionally trained experts. Because educational professionalism with the administrative bureaucracies it spawned and with its infatuation with educational science—most notably in the testing movement in the early twentieth century—significantly influenced, we believe, the ways that educational goods and services were distributed among individuals and groups in American society, the rise of the educational profession and its effects on the delivery of educational services become increasingly important themes in this study.

We look next at the theory and practice of education in the Progressive era (1880–1930), noting both its continuities with the past and how it broke new ground in presenting problems and issues that would remain with education for the remainder of the century. Educational progressivism promised both to contribute to "community" development and to "individual" self-fulfillment. Although some educators were able to achieve consistency in melding those two goals into a coherent program, most found the two goals difficult to define and somewhat at odds. Which community should the school serve—the neighborhood, the town, the nation? Should the individual child be seen as an autonomous, free-floating individual or as a person with deep roots within a specific subculture? What role, in other words, should schools play in relating the individual child to each of the relevant communities in his life? We have structured our discussion of post-World War I educational history in the United States around these questions—by studying the conceptions of the school's responsibilities to the individual and to various communities, first in the 1920s and 1930s, and then after World War II when criticism of progressive education became something of a national sport. We end with an examination of the magnified demands placed on schools after 1960 by movements to eliminate poverty and racism in the United States. These demands brought to the fore, perhaps more starkly than ever, those basic issues of what role schools should and could play in enhancing or attenuating equality in America.

The contribution of schools to equality in America is by no means a new theme. Indeed, education's vital role in fostering equality has been the dominant interpretive theme—one might even call it a myth—in educational history as it was written between the turn of this century and the middle 1960s. With just three or four important exceptions, educational historians suggested that schools were the great engines of democracy. Implied in this view was the conclusion that since Americans were spending ever increasing amounts of money on and time in schools, the United States must be growing increasingly democratic. Since 1960 this viewpoint has sustained increasing attack from a group of historians who contend, following the lead of revisionists in other areas of American history, that schools, through such explicit devices as tracking and more indirectly by supporting capitalist beliefs, for example, actually preserved and fostered inequality in American society. This group's conclusions differ diametrically from those of earlier educational historians. Schools supported and even promoted injustice and inequality; America's increasing commitment to schools was part of the growing rigidity of a stratified American society. These beliefs led some historians of this persuasion to find "deschooling" an attractive concept.

Happily, people and institutions are neither as good nor as bad as these interpretors might lead us to believe. Our volume is an attempt to weigh both sides of this argument and to discuss the school's historic influence on American social structure in all the complexity that inevitably enters into the affairs of men and women. We wish to transmit no myths. We believe that educators and the society they are committed to serve must know as accurately as possible where schools have been, what they have accomplished, and what they have failed to accomplish before they can determine judiciously where education ought to be going. We hope that this volume will offer a foundation on which to build an accurate interpretation of our educational past.

This volume is devoted almost entirely to the history of schools, of institutionalized education. It is widely recognized that "education" is a process that occurs virtually everywhere—in toilet training, in watching television, in playing games. Ministers, reporters, copywriters, actors, politicians are all teachers. All such means of education and kinds of teachers belong in a fully comprehensive study of education in the United States. But such inclusiveness is simply impossible in a volume of this size, perhaps of any size. We focus our efforts on the school because it stands as society's most deliberate mode of educating its young and thus becomes the primary institution through which social groups attempt to use educational efforts to influence American society. Therefore, a study of the role and theory of education in American society almost inevitably focuses on education as carried on in schools.

Our book is an interpretive essay—we wish to stress the interpretive nature of our work. We do not purport to offer here a full catalogue of the "facts" of American educational history nor even to catalogue all the great personalities and institutions which have graced the American educational past. We have tried, rather, to portray the most important, the most illustrative, and the most illuminating aspects of American educational history and to assess the ways in which they speak to the problem of defining the role and purpose and significance of education as an institution within American society. We hope our exercise will spur others to constant rethinking and reinterpretation of the role of education in the United States.

Our intellectual debts in this volume are legion. Our thinking has benefitted enormously from the work of many scholars and we have tried to acknowledge them in each chapter's concluding bibliography. A special and more personal thanks are due to Patricia A. Graham for a sensitive and invaluable reading of the completed manuscript and to Arthur Powell, Marvin Lazerson, David B. Potts, Carl Kaestle, Paul Mattingly, Cherry Collins, Timothy Walch, and Martin Gill for helpful criticisms at various stages of manuscript preparation. We alone are responsible for errors that may remain in the manuscript.

Responsibility for the volume is divided between the authors as follows: Robert Church outlined and drafted all of the chapters of the book. Michael Sedlak revised all of them, strengthening the interpretation greatly and adding to their coherence and readibility. He also prepared the guides to further reading at the end of each chapter.

The senior author would like further to acknowledge his great good fortune to have been introduced to this field of scholarship under the stimulating tutelage of Paul Herman Buck and Daniel H. Calhoun, men whose very different ideas have indirectly had great influence on the shape of this volume.

PART I

Education in the New Nation, 1776–1830

CHAPTER 1

The District School

I

SCHOOLS AND OTHER INSTITUTIONS OF FORMAL TRAINING AND THE EXPECTA-
tions that people have for those institutions change dramatically only
when a society's vision of its own future changes or when conditions for
fulfillment of that vision are perceived to change. Educational institutions
are assumed to shape the lives of children, of future generations; therefore, major changes in educational institutions follow major changes in
society's future aspirations.

This hypothesis helps us understand the timing of major educational
change between 1760 and 1860. Although the American Revolution occurred in the 1770s, the most dramatic changes in American education—
the common school movement, the founding of the public high school,
and the surge in higher education—occurred only after 1820. If society
and education are so closely intertwined, why does the Revolution not
mark a major turning point in education? Deliberate and wholesale re-
modeling of education has been an important tool of other modern
revolutions—classically, in the French and Russian revolutions, the first
nearly concurrent with the American Revolution. In those instances revolutionary leaders called for a new kind of education capable of retraining
the populace to live up to revolutionary ideals. Those leaders believed
that their revolutions' success depended on eradicating the habits, beliefs, and passivity imposed on the masses by generations of civil and
religious tyranny. In France a new education was thought necessary to
counteract the previous teachings of the church and the state. People had

to learn to return to the natural state of goodness that theoreticians of the revolution postulated as the original condition of mankind. The *ancien régime* had surrounded men with a host of artificial institutions which constrained, even perverted, their natural inclinations. Eradication of these artificial barriers was vital to the success of the revolution; education was the principal agent for such eradication.

The American Revolution differed essentially from these other great modern revolutions in that most of its theorists and leaders thought the masses of colonists were virtuous and believed that the revolution would succeed as soon as British influence was removed. Whereas in France revolutionary leaders believed that civil and religious tyranny and corruption had already affected the citizenry illy, leaders of the American Revolution felt that the colonists in the New World had so far successfully resisted the Britishers' evil influence. The French revolted against tyranny in order to redirect the French people toward the natural and good life; the American Revolution was more limited in scope because it sought only to prevent parliamentary tyranny from interfering with the simple and godly life the colonists sought to lead. The issue was not one of changing the people but keeping them from being changed. In a revolution designed to protect a virtue already dominant, education was to play a relatively minor role.

Thomas Jefferson's championing of a comprehensive American school system for his home state of Virginia and for the whole nation was the exception that proves the rule. Jefferson's plan, first enunciated in 1779,[1] called for each local district to establish a three-year school, free and open to all white children between seven and ten years of age, and for each county in the state to establish a higher three-year school to which the best graduating scholar from each of the district schools in the county would come free of charge. On top of this structure, Virginia was to establish a college to which each year it would send the best graduate from each of the county schools. Other students could attend the grammar school and college at their own expense. At times Jefferson suggested a fourth level of schooling—a national university, to be located in Washington—to which each state would send its best graduates each year. Jefferson thought it vital that these institutions, especially at the higher levels, teach not only the traditional classical languages, philosophy, and a smattering of mathematics and natural philosophy but also the more practical, modern subjects such as modern languages, government, history, medicine, physics, and chemistry.

There were echoes of Jefferson's grand plan in a series of essays written in 1797 in response to the American Philosophical Society's offer

---

[1] Thomas Jefferson, "A Bill for the More General Diffusion of Knowledge" (1779), in Julian P. Boyd et al., eds., *The Papers of Thomas Jefferson* (Princeton, N. J., 1950), II, 526–533.

of a prize for the best essay on a "system of liberal education and literary instruction, adapted to the genius of the government of the United States; comprehending also a plan for instituting and conducting public schools in this country, on principles of the most extensive utility."[2] The essayists argued that a democratic government must see that all its citizens could read and write and thus be capable of resisting demagogic appeals, which were thought to succeed only among the ignorant. None produced plans to equal Jefferson's in scope but, like Jefferson, they all insisted that the new nation must look to the careful education of all its citizens if the fragile republic were to survive the many challenges it faced. One or two other plans for expanded public education appeared in the 1790s.

Jefferson's plan came to naught—except for the tardy establishment of the University of Virginia more or less to his specifications in 1825—and the American Philosophical Society's essayists returned to their other concerns after competing for the prize. It is difficult to assess whether the essays urging the new country to expand and make more deliberate its educational services expressed a popular concern of the time or merely reflected their authors' concern for winning the prize.

The fate of Jefferson's proposal lends weight to the latter interpretation. Jefferson, masterful politician, adept leader of men, and perhaps Virginia's most influential and highly regarded leader in the period between the Revolution and his retirement from the presidency in 1809, failed to gather any significant support for his educational plan among fellow politicians and citizens in Virginia. How do we account for this failure? Part of the opposition was traditional—men with money resisted financing more comprehensive services for those with little or no money. In Virginia, already suffering from the early evidences of soil exhaustion, this problem was especially difficult to overcome. But greater opposition focused on the essentially radical aspects of Jefferson's proposal. Jefferson's plan had three essential thrusts: first, it sought to provide mass literacy training for all citizens; second, it sought to use schooling to guarantee that all children, whatever their background, had access to higher education and to positions of social leadership accruing to those with education and that the leadership classes would constantly renew and replace themselves; and, third, it wished to insure that the new country's leadership, however recruited, would receive its education at home rather than in Europe. On the first point, there was general agreement that the idea was a good one, but not so good that a great deal of money should be spent on it. The second point aroused the greatest opposition. Jefferson might be called America's first prophet of meritocracy because he wished to substitute performance in school for birth, breeding, or electoral success as the criterion for choosing society's lead-

---

[2] Frederick Rudolph, *Essays on Education in the Early Republic* (Cambridge, Mass., 1965), xv.

ers. In keeping with his belief that each generation should rewrite the Constitution so as to insure that the present would not be controlled by the ideas of the past and that the present generation could constantly renew its instrument of social contract, Jefferson desired that political and social power would flow, from generation to generation, not into the hands of the sons and grandsons of those who already held the power but, rather, to the best people—as determined by school performance— selected in each generation from the whole body of citizens. Jefferson's school plan was, as he so bluntly put it, designed so that "the best geniusses [sic] will be raked from the rubbish."[3] Jefferson thought this feature of his proposal would make it a peculiarly American plan; indeed, it was the feature that entitled his ideas to the title "plan" at all. In the century following 1830, Jefferson's idea that the educational system should function to select new leaders of American society became pretty widely, if less bluntly, accepted. In Jefferson's day, however, the idea was revolutionary and its implications poorly understood. Men who did understand those implications rejected his idea. The men who set policy in Virginia, men who had achieved the power they held in the more traditional ways—through birth, marriage, or patronage—were not impressed, indeed, were deeply frightened, by Jefferson's proposal for changing the recruiting methods. What was true in Virginia was equally true among most of the articulate leaders of the early United States. These leaders did not consider changing the means of distributing power in the society a goal of the Revolution; Jefferson's idea of constructing an educational system to "open" up American society did not appeal to them. No more than they expected formal democracy to alter traditional deference politics—in which the masses voted habitually for their betters and for policies approved by their betters—did these leaders expect widespread training in literacy to change the structure of American society.

Nor is there any evidence that the inarticulate found Jefferson's ideas —if they knew of them—any more appealing. Jefferson himself made little effort to promote his ideas among the populace. With the understanding that has come from decades of research on social mobility, we can detect many advantages (as well as many disadvantages) for the middle- and lower-class child in Jefferson's proposals, but there is little reason to think that parents in 1800 saw so clearly the relation between attending school and achieving preferment in later life. Deference to a self-perpetuating leadership class was as habitual with them as it was among the leaders themselves; just how schooling could break that pattern (if breaking it were worthwhile) was not clear to anyone in 1800. Education's role in promoting mobility was largely obscured by the many other routes to

[3] Thomas Jefferson, *Notes on the State of Virginia* (1782; London, 1787), Query XIV: Laws.

advancement open at that time. A parent or a young man could look around him and see a variety of ways that some men—whether few or many—had gained an estate higher than their fathers' had been. Empty land lay waiting to be claimed and farmed; the West beckoned for new settlers to come make a new start and grow with new communities; the cities offered a variety of opportunities for the ambitious to join a new enterprise and prosper with it. Education offered little to those expecting to follow these routes to advancement. Attending school just delayed the beginning of one's career. For these reasons it is not surprising that Jefferson's plan attracted little support from the mass of the American people.

The third part of Jefferson's proposal—regarding the teaching of American leaders at home rather than abroad—did strike a chord in the people and led to a great deal of discussion about establishing institutions of higher learning in America of such quality that traveling to Oxford or Cambridge—or to Edinburgh or Leyden if one expected to practice medicine—would no longer be necessary. All through colonial times, the sons of the "best" families had gone overseas, usually combining the "Grand Tour" of the continent with one or more years of schooling in a European university. Even young men who had completed college in the colonies often felt compelled to seek further training in the liberal arts or in the professional subjects. To answer this need for "postgraduate" training, Jefferson and other leaders called for a national university in Washington in which college graduates from the various states could enroll. Supporters believed the national university would strengthen national unity by gathering potential social and political leaders from various sections to study together for a year or two. George Washington left money in his will for establishing such an institution, but neither his support nor much subsequent agitation by prominent leaders overcame the new republic's refusal to view its capital as a significant symbol of national unity or to overcome the widespread belief that schooling should be a matter of local initiative and control. The nation's sense of nationhood was too weak to support the idea of even a single national educational institution.

Efforts to improve and expand higher education in the United States were primarily motivated by the fear that continuing to educate America's leaders in the institutions of Europe would contaminate them and their future decisions with the love of tyranny, luxury, and sin that Americans generally associated with the Old World. Thomas Jefferson, surely one of the most cosmopolitan, tolerant, and cultured men of his era, advised against educating a youth abroad because there he "learns drinking, horse-racing and boxing. He acquires a fondness for European luxury and dissipation and a contempt for the simplicity of his own country; he is fascinated with the privileges of the European aristocrats, and sees with abhorrence the lovely equality which the poor enjoy with the rich [in America]; . . . he is led by the strongest of all human passions into a spirit for female intrigue destructive of his own and others' happiness, or a passion for whores destructive of his health."[4] As Edmund Morgan has so cogently argued,[5] the American Revolution must be understood in part as a rejection of sinful Europe by Americans who felt themselves morally pure. The goals of revolution would not be met, however, if young men of standing, who naturally would assume leadership positions, received their higher education overseas. In Europe they would fail to learn to appreciate the virtues of the American political arrangement. Jefferson, in discussing plans for the University of Virginia, positively banned the appointment of a non-American to the professorship of political science. Although he believed the university would strengthen itself in all the other fields by looking outside the United States for men of learning, Jefferson did not think it could safely do so in such an important field. The proposed national university and Jefferson's proposed university in Virginia were, then, to safeguard the Revolution by giving future leaders a common educational experience and by insuring that future elites would receive all their education in the United States. Even these beliefs about the vital relation between education and revolutionary nationalism were not strong enough to affect existing institutions of higher learning in any significant way or to influence the founding of new ones.

II

The general lack of interest in major educational reform in the revolutionary era and the inability of plans like Jefferson's to create an effective demand for better educational facilities strongly suggests that Americans were generally satisfied with the educational system they inherited from the colonial era. Most Americans, apparently, found that the district schools, despite their manifest inefficiencies and problems, met their own, and by implication, their country's, educational needs satisfactorily. We can best understand this by asking why, in an era of revolution and growing nationalism, American parents and politicians allowed the educational system to function so poorly—poor, certainly, by twentieth-century standards, and poor even by enlightened standards of 1800.

"District school" is a generic term used to denote the one-room rural or village neighborhood school of the eighteenth and nineteenth centu-

---

[4] *Ibid.*

[5] Edmund Morgan, "The American Revolution Considered as an Intellectual Movement," in Arthur M. Schlesinger, Jr. and Morton White, eds., *Paths of American Thought* (New York, 1963), 11–33.

ries. A district was a legal entity for school purposes only, a subdivision of a town or township, limited in size by the distances children could be expected to walk to school. The essence of the district system was the assumption by this extremely small political entity of virtually complete control over the school. This mode of concentrating educational responsibility developed in the eighteenth century and reached its zenith in the first quarter of the nineteenth century. In states north of the Mason-Dixon line settled in the colonial period, responsibility for providing educational services originally lodged in the town or township which generally founded a single elementary school at its center of population. By the middle of the eighteenth century, however, this procedure proved unsatisfactory as within a single town or township other population centers, other villages, sprang up. The school in the original population center could not serve the new village as the two were widely separated —on average, towns and townships were six miles square. This raised a host of problems. For example, Massachusetts law required each town to maintain an elementary school as soon as the town contained fifty families. It was difficult enough for the selectmen to find enough money to maintain a school in any case—people, then as now, were not eager to pay school taxes—but, when the town's fifty families were divided among two or more villages within the town limits, it became virtually impossible to collect money from the village(s) in which the schoolhouse was not located. In towns or townships which contained two or more large villages, selectmen could fairly easily find enough support for a separate school in each village. In most cases, however, the combined population of the town or township was so small that its people found it burdensome to support even a single school. In the colonial era probably the most common solution to this problem was for the town to ignore its educational responsibility and provide no schools anywhere in the town. Slightly more imaginative was the "moving school." The town appointed a single schoolmaster who spent a part of the school year in each of the town's population centers. In this way the families of the town could be enlisted to pay the school taxes and rates because every child had some chance to attend school. This was, on the whole, an unsatisfactory solution because it meant that individual children attended school for a much shorter time than the law intended.

After 1750, as the villages became more populous, towns and townships delegated their responsibility for maintaining schools to each of the villages within their borders. For this purpose the town designated each village a district and the state, at the request of the town or township, gave each village the power to levy, within set limits, school taxes on the residents of the district and to set the school rates. Taxation was, of course, the crucial power and the essential element of decentralization. For a time the towns or townships remained responsible for approving teachers before the district could hire them, for setting the length of the school year, and for guiding the course of study. These quickly proved to be empty powers: teachers were in such short supply that almost anyone who presented himself was appointed; the length of the school year was in reality determined not by a ruling from the town but by the amount of tax money the district chose to raise for running the school; the course of study was so unorganized, teachers so poorly trained, and schoolhouses so primitive that it was difficult to find a *course* of study to guide. By 1800 towns and townships in the northern states had relinquished even these pro forma controls over the districts.

The decentralized district school system predominated almost everywhere from the Revolution until the 1820s and predominated in many areas much longer. The common school movement that began in the 1830s and continued for nearly a half century sought, among other reforms, to overcome problems of the district system by centralizing control at the township, county, and state levels. Its efforts were gradually successful but, as in most cases of educational reform in the nineteenth century, changes occurred in the more populous states long before they occurred in the more sparsely settled and newer states and changes occurred much more rapidly in urbanized areas than they did in the more rural areas of the same states. For example, legal, institutional, and attitudinal changes in education that occurred very early in the nineteenth century in New York City might not appear in an upstate county for several decades and not in a rural Kansas county until late in the century. But the same development might have appeared in St. Louis or Cincinnati before it appeared in upstate New York. Thus, the system of decentralized district control appears most powerful in New England in the first quarter of the century; in the midwestern states, as *The Hoosier Schoolmaster* (1871) suggests, at mid-century; in the plains states during and after the Civil War.

The district school was, then, an extreme example of "community control." The citizens of the district levied their own taxes; a committee of citizens appointed the schoolmaster, set the length of the school year, maintained the schoolhouse, and was the final authority in conflicts between master and children and parents (most often siding, of course, with the children and their parents). Although there were cases in which a single man—a one-man committee—exercised autocratic control over a district's school for long periods of time, hiring his son to repair the schoolhouse and his daughter to teach school, in general large numbers of citizens participated in school affairs. For many citizens discussing school matters was their only opportunity for political participation and they guarded it quite jealously. Hundreds of district schools stood in swamps or awkwardly on high ridges because the district committee had had to place them at the exact geographic center of the district (since the citizens were unable to agree on a location closer to one end of the village than to the other). School affairs enlisted a good deal of citizen interest also because, often enough, the schoolhouse was the only public building in the village and as such housed community meetings, political debates, social gatherings, and even religious services. In sparsely settled midwestern and western districts, the schoolhouse was one of the few facilities where people could relieve the loneliness of isolated settlement. Both literally and symbolically the school and the schoolhouse stood at the center of the community. The school was, in many cases, the community's most expensive and significant creation.

As often as not, the schoolmaster who taught in this community center was not a member of that community. The men who taught in the winter sessions were especially likely to be outsiders; the women or girls who sometimes taught in the summer sessions for the little children were often local girls. The older children of the community attended the winter sessions that ran for two to five months between November and March. In the summer months the younger children—too small to walk long distances in the winter—attended while the older children worked on the farms. The winter session was educationally the most significant but the man who taught it generally had little commitment to his work— the average teaching life of a teacher in New England in the first quarter of the century was two years—or to the community—a master hardly ever stayed in the same school for more than one winter session. Few district schoolmasters could have gotten professional training had they desired it. The first private teacher training or normal school was established only in 1823, the first public ones in 1839, and there were only twelve public normal schools at the time of the Civil War. Attendance at an academy or college was all the preparation most teachers received in the first half of the nineteenth century. The typical district school teacher was an academy or college student on vacation (institutions of higher learning had three-month winter vacations just so their students could earn money by teaching district schools) or a graduate of one of these institutions awaiting opportunity for permanent employment in another profession. His chief concern was discipline; his pedagogy was limited to listening to recitations; his only technical skill—and not every master possessed it—was the knack of carving and sharpening a quill pen.

It is significant that outsiders so often carried out the educational work of the communal schoolhouse. The theme of constant battle between the schoolmaster, on the one hand, and the students and parents, on the other, runs persistently through factual and fictional accounts of the district school. In the first pages of *The Hoosier Schoolmaster* the district school committeeman tells the new teacher in front of his own sons that the stronger older boys in the school had driven the last two masters from the district. His words both challenged the master and encouraged his own children to challenge the master. This incident illustrates the way local communities used schools to confirm their virtue and worth. The master represented outside knowledge which in turn represented outside authority. He represented standards other than those of the local community. Each time the students humiliated the master or drove him from the district, the community's way, its standards and values, symbolically triumphed over those of the outside world. These attacks on the master and his authority, in a smaller theater, reenacted the anticosmopolitanism and antiauthoritarian drama of the American revolt from Europe itself, and they manifested a profoundly anti-intellectual strain in the early American character. This anti-intellectualism, this need constantly to reaffirm that the community's standards were superior to those of the larger world, accounts in part for the people's willingness to tolerate an inferior educational system.

Efficient learning in the district school faced many more barriers than poorly trained teachers and anti-intellectual communities. Physical conditions for teaching were very poor—in the typical one-room school children of all ages sat together. The buildings were poorly constructed and miserably ventilated, even by early-nineteenth-century standards. (One major concern of the common school movement after 1830 was for the proper construction and ventilation of school buildings.) As a single wood-burning stove or fireplace provided the only heat, one end of the schoolhouse was always too hot and the other too cold.

Pedagogical facilities were no better. In most cases even the primitive textbooks were not standardized within a single school; instead, each student learned from whatever book his family happened to own. Thus a teacher might confront the task of teaching grammar or spelling from six or seven different books at the same time. Since paper was expensive and scarce, writing exercises were kept to a minimum. Lead pencils were not used; students had to use quill pens and poor homemade ink. There were no blackboards. These conditions forced teachers to curtail student creative activity in writing or figuring and instead to emphasize memorizing passages from books. Teachers had none of the equipment—pictures, colored paper, maps, and so on—which might have been used to enliven the schoolroom. In sum, the physical and pedagogical facilities of the district school required students to try to learn in a drab and claustrophobic environment.

As far as we can tell, not much learning occurred. There are, of course, exceptions, dearly beloved by those for whom the one-room schoolhouse represents the golden age of American education. These exceptions prove the rule. Almost all of the fond accounts of the one-room school of the nineteenth century have come from men and women who achieved business or intellectual success after undergoing extensive educational preparation beyond the district school level. For them the endless memorization of grammar rules and spelling words in the district school might have provided a good "grounding" upon which their subsequent training could rest. Even these accounts, when they curb their authors' nostalgia, recognize the general intellectual inefficiency of the district school. How much more inefficient the district school curriculum must have been for those who did not go on to further schooling.

The typical American district school of the nineteenth century was open to all children within the district, although in most cases children of the poorest families probably did not attend very frequently for fear of ridicule or because they lacked proper clothing or because their parents hoped that they could earn wages to help support the family. Pupils ranged in age from 3 to about 17 (although children under 7 seldom attended the winter sessions and adolescent males over 12 seldom attended in summer). For the majority of these children the district school provided terminal education; it was the only school they would attend. It sought to teach only basic literacy, a little arithmetic, and little else. Given the number of years that the average child attended the district school, it should have accomplished more.

Several things besides the poor physical facilities, poor teachers, and community ambiguity about learning account for the schools' severely limited objectives. The ungraded nature of the school was the first. Most schools established no criteria of progress. It was, for example, in no way clear when a student had "finished" district school. Students left it to go on to an academy or a tutor to prepare them for college when they or their parents thought they were old enough. There was, especially in the first half of the century, no body of material or method that a youngster had to learn in the district school before he could move into secondary education—except for the most basic English language arts. Essentially, the district school had educational goals so unreasonably low, such as command of the basic English language arts for children who had attended twelve years of school, that it had no incentive for pushing its students to learn. This lack of incentive was demonstrated by the common practice of making a student study the same book from year to year until he had, in a single year, completed that book. For example, if a student began studying a 300-page grammar in December and memorized it for each of the sixty winter-school-term days at the rate of three pages per day, he would have completed only 180 pages. The next term, instead of starting him on page 181 of the grammar so that he could complete it that year, the teacher told him to begin it again. Thus he had to rememorize the first 180 pages before he could begin on new material. In some cases students took five and six years to complete textbooks because of this continuous backtracking. The practice prevailed because, since teachers turned over so rapidly in the district schools and record keeping was primitive at best, a student got credit for completing a book only when he could recite all of it to a single master. No procedure existed whereby one master could record for the benefit of his successor (and for the benefit of the student) what a student had done in that term so that he could continue from there in the succeeding term. In other words, there was so little concern with an individual student's intellectual progress that it seemed unnecessary to keep a record of that progress.

District schools limited their objectives also because they relied almost exclusively on the recitation method. In grammar and arithmetic, the master assigned the individual student a passage—a paragraph or several pages of rules—in the text and the student went to his seat and memorized the passage. When he had done so he returned to the teacher's desk, closed his book, and repeated the passage. This method did not test or encourage the student's understanding of the passage. Students learned to spell by memorizing spelling words without ever learning their meaning. Reading, surprisingly, involved the same method: the student first memorized the passage and then recited it without looking at the book. Large enrollments forced masters to have students recite in unison, a strategy even less likely to increase the student's understanding of what he read.

Just how much the recitation method could restrict or retard understanding can be gathered from the common method of teaching the "rule of three"—thought to be the crowning achievement of a district school education. The rule of three, sometimes known as the rule of "barter," was a formula which students were to use to solve word problems of the following kind: if three apples cost ten cents, how much do nine apples cost? Before he was allowed to tackle this simple problem, the student had to memorize a set of rules for finding the answer. According to an account in one common school reformer's attack on the district school, the student had first to memorize a definition of barter: "Barter is exchanging one commodity for another, and teaches merchants so to proportion their quantities that neither shall sustain loss." Then the student was to memorize the rule of three proper.

RULES

1. *When the quantity of one commodity is given with its value, or the value of its integer, as also the value of the integer of some other commodity to be exchanged for it, to find the quantity of this commodity:*—Find the value of the commodity of which the quantity is given, then find how much of the other commodity, at the rate proposed, may be had for that sum.

2. *If the quantitites of both commodities be given, and it should be required to find how much of some other commodity, or how much money should be given for the inequality of their values:*—Find the separate values of the two given commodities,

subtract the less from the greater, and the remainder will be the balance, or value of the other commodity.

3. *If one commodity is rated above the ready money price, to find the bartering price of the other:*—Say, as the ready money price of the one, is to the bartering price, so is that of the other to its bartering price.[6]

Upon memorizing, but not necessarily understanding, these rules, the student classified a word problem according to which of the three rules applied to it and then followed the rule's formula in solving the problem. He was taught nothing of ratios, nothing about why he performed the operations required by the rule. Another description of district school arithmetic instruction, this time from the late eighteenth century, demonstrates the weakness of a pedagogy that relied on memorization of rules. A child asked permission of the master to learn how to cipher (add and subtract) and received, along with his permission, his first addition problem—find the sum of six five-digit numbers. The student remembered: "All the instruction he gave me was, —add the figures in the first column, carry one for every ten, and set the overplus down under the column. I supposed he meant by the first column, the left-hand column; but what he meant by carrying one for every ten, was a mystery to me. I worried my brains an hour or two. The columns were finally added from the left to right. The master frowned, and repeated his former instruction, —add up the column *on the right,* carry one for every ten, and set down the remainder. Two or three afternoons were spent in this way (I did not go to school in the morning), when I begged to be excused from learning to cipher."[7]

Things need not have been so backward. Better pedagogical techniques were available at the time, and in a few instances district schoolmasters ran schools at a much higher level of efficiency and used quite imaginative techniques to enhance learning. The child-centered methods of Johann Heinrich Pestalozzi, the great Swiss educational reformer, who argued that children learned best by doing, were known in the United States at least after 1806. Learning by doing was surely how most early-nineteenth-century children mastered farming and mechanical skills out of school—but that method was not applied in the district schoolhouse. District schoolmasters who had attended academies or colleges had been introduced to other pedagogical techniques. In that period institutions of higher education relied too heavily on the memorized recitation from a textbook or reader, but their instructors also lectured (an exciting innovation of the period), took time to try to explain texts and rules to students, and in the most progressive institutions gave scientific demon-

[6] Quoted in James G. Carter, *Letters to the Honorable William Prescott on the Free Schools of New England* (Boston, 1824), 109–110.

[7] Honorable Joseph T. Buckingham, quoted in Barnas Sears, "Educational Progress in the United States," *Education,* I (1880), 23–24.

strations. These institutions also gave students opportunities to do some creative work such as writing compositions or classical poetry, declamations, or debates. Occasionally, the documents describing the district school refer to students getting the chance to write compositions of their own or to speak their own lines at one of the school's public programs (where the community gathered to watch the children perform). But such events were apparently infrequent. This lack of opportunity for student creativity and the deadly boredom of constant repetition of the same half-understood texts made the district school a deadening environment for learning.

One event dispelled the deadening atmosphere of the district school; it excited both the students and, in most cases, the community's adults as well. The spelling bee, or spelldown, was the high point of the school throughout early-nineteenth-century America. Two students chose teams from among their fellows and the master, or a leading citizen if the whole community were involved, called out words to be spelled. When someone on one team failed to spell a word correctly, he was eliminated from the game and the other team given a chance to spell that word. The team that had all its members eliminated first lost the contest. The spelling bee seems to have been the only occasion in the school week or term that kindled the student's enthusiasm, which made him eager to participate. Whole communities shared that enthusiasm. Many schools held small spelling bees throughout the term for the students but then, once or twice a term, they held a spelling bee late on a Friday afternoon or in the evening for which the whole community gathered in the schoolhouse—much as they would for corn-husking bees or quilting bees—to participate in or watch the spelling contest. The spelling bee became a major social event in communities that in the early nineteenth century had few social diversions. It provided opportunities for people to see and be seen, for young people to court, for community leaders to preen. The spelling bee itself was attractive just because it was a contest; young and old enjoyed the sense of competitiveness, the struggle between teams. The spelling bee probably served psychological and recreational functions for that generation much like those served by organized athletics in a later era.

The explanation of the spelling bee's popularity is more complex, however. Other subjects could have focused competition in the district school; debates or declamations or "graduation" could have drawn the community closer to the school. Why spelling? Spelling became *the* symbol of educational progress. Noah Webster arranged his "blue-backed speller" (first published in 1782 and immensely popular for several generations) so that it progressed from short words to long and difficult words. People used it as a convenient standard of educational achievement—ranking people according to the pages of Webster they had mastered. In the social strata below that in which most of the men had received classical training, spelling prowess came to indicate educational status. Why was spelling viewed as so important and why did it become the center of competition in school?

Spelling was intimately related to the American people's conceptions of their liberty and their national unity. In the early nineteenth century in England and in the United States the way a man spoke and spelled identified his regional and class background. Differences in ability to manipulate words accentuated class differences. As Americans believed that their nation was morally and politically superior because it was free of class differences, they felt a special concern for eliminating the linguistic evidences of class distinction. If all Americans could read, write, speak, and spell in the same way, it would demonstrate beyond doubt how equal in station they were. The ability to spell words from Webster's speller was a symbol that one held equal rank with everyone else in America. Similarly, spelling related to nationalism. Differences in pronunciation revealed regional background and retarded communication among people from different sections. It was difficult for the middle- or lower-class New Englander, who had not journeyed from his region or studied the standardized accents of the educated English aristocracy in an institution of higher learning, to comprehend the language of a man of similar background from Georgia or Virginia. Such profound differences in regional dialect threatened to lead to regional misunderstandings, to fragmentation of the new nation. The young nation's unity could be greatly strengthened, the belief went, if all Americans learned to pronounce the language similarly. Thus, spelling contests of the nineteenth century emphasized pronunciation as well as orthography—contestants spelled words syllable by syllable, pronouncing each after spelling it and pronouncing the whole word after spelling it. Webster's and most of the other spellers of the time grouped words according to syllables and the placement of the accent—that is, one page would contain words of three syllables with the accent on the first syllable, the next page words of three syllables with the accent on the second, and so on. Such an arrangement, the authors hoped, would lead to standardized pronunciation. Spelling and spelling contests, therefore, symbolized and contributed to the effort to build a national language. Although regional differences greatly overshadowed class differences in language in the early United States, Americans had only to look to the example of England—and to their own emerging cities—to find how important the way one used the language was to identifying one's class status. They considered schoolwork on language manipulation, therefore, very important to maintaining the American dream of a unified and classless nation.

Noah Webster, author of the first American language dictionary and the greatest American word manipulator of his day, made a career of stressing the importance of common linguistic skill to the success of the democratic experiment in the United States. Webster demanded an American revolution at the linguistic level. "As an independent nation, our honor requires us to have a system of our own, in language as well as government. Great Britain, whose children we are, and whose language we speak, should no longer be *our* standard; for the taste of her writers is already corrupted, and her language on the decline."[8] Several themes in this statement merit attention. The United States could fight to secure its independence from the dictates of the British Parliament, but it was more difficult for it to become culturally independent of a country whose language and culture it shared. What was to be America's unique culture upon which its sense of nationhood and distinctiveness was to rest? Webster argued that Americans should make their language as different as possible from that of Englishmen without, of course, surrendering the use of English altogether. Americans must develop their own standards of correct and incorrect usage and pronunciation so that they would no longer need to rely on English criteria. Americans should assume responsibility for guiding the development of their ever changing language—Webster was one of the first theorists to argue that language continually grew and changed under the impact of changing events and usage. Webster's statement also indicated his belief that in language, as well as in all other aspects of life, the Old World was growing more and more corrupt and Americans should keep free of European linguistic developments lest they be corrupted in turn. For Webster the linguistic situation closely paralleled the political one.

Webster thought the European practice of ranking some people over others on the basis of their ability to manipulate language according to "correct" standards especially corrupt. Europeans used language to divide people; Americans should use it to bring them together. "A sameness of pronunciation is of considerable consequence in a political view," Webster wrote in 1789, "for provincial accents are disagreeable to strangers and sometimes have an unhappy effect upon the social affections. All men have local attachments which lead them to believe their own practice to be the least exceptionable. Pride and prejudice incline men to treat the practice of their neighbors with some degree of contempt. Thus small differences in pronunciation at first excite ridicule—a habit of laughing at the singularities of strangers is followed by disrespect —and without respect friendship is a name, and social intercourse a mere ceremony."[9] To strengthen American nationalism, friendship and social intercourse among classes and among regions had to be made more than superficial.

[8] Noah Webster, *Dissertations on the English Language with Notes Historical and Critical* (Boston, 1789), 20–21.
[9] *Ibid.*, 18–20.

Webster set out to facilitate such friendship and intercourse in two ways. First, he promised to publish an American dictionary which would be guided by American standards of usage rather than British ones. He hoped that the dictionary would help Americans develop a single language common to all regions, and he paid particular attention to preparing the dictionary so that it would be useful as a guide to pronunciation. Webster's second strategy was to develop a spelling text for the schools which would be used in all sections and which would teach all children to spell and pronounce words in the same way. His blue-backed speller succeeded beyond his wildest dreams. Distributed all over the country, it was the standard speller in its many editions, up to the Civil War. There can be little doubt of its influence in promoting the adoption of a uniform orthography in the United States. Webster's speller was much less effective in furthering uniformity of pronunciation, more important to national unity than orthography. Because pronunciation was an oral matter, Webster's written directions for pronunciation had little power against the examples of speech that children heard every day. In almost all cases the student learned to pronounce as the master and his parents and friends did rather than as Webster wished him to. The spelling bee in *The Hoosier Schoolmaster* is probably typical: the squire, a New Englander who had assimilated Indiana modes of speech, mispronounced the words he gave the spellers and they, in turn, similarly mispronounced them as they spelled them. That increase in uniformity of pronunciation which did occur in the United States after 1800 must be credited, not to Webster, but to the great geographic mobility of the population which so mixed people from different regions that a "common" speech pattern gradually developed.

A large majority of Americans shared Webster's hopes that improved spelling and pronunciation would strengthen democracy. After the Bible, Webster's speller was the country's most widely distributed book. It and the Bible were commonly the only two books a family owned. The popularity of Webster's ideas was also manifest in the popularity of the spelling bee. Americans found the spelling bee a drama of the classlessness and equality that Webster argued common linguistic skills would strengthen. No matter that the spelling bee successfully dealt only with the least important aspect of language—spelling—in a culture that was still largely an oral one in which sermon, political speech, folk tale, and song were of immensely greater significance to community life and learning than the written word. No matter that spelling, as there conceived, was nothing but an exercise in memory and that most of the participants and most of the audience did not know the meanings of the words spelled. No matter that the exercises served to ingrain regional peculiarities of speech rather than to obscure them. The spelling bee dramatized equality: any person of any background could win and children and their parents could prove their ability to "use" language as well as any person of whatever background. That someone in their community could spell a word from the last pages of Webster's speller assured the people that their village was as good as any other place, whether village, or urban cultural center. It also proved that the promises of democracy were real: the most sophisticated and cultured "use" of language, the possession of only the upper classes in despotic Europe, was available to all in America.

That the patrons of the district school spelling bee could have thought so highly of the efficacy of spelling, as practiced in those situations, suggests how complacent these Americans were with their lot and how isolated they were from the realities of American social structure outside their own communities. Such complacency and isolation explains why parents in many village communities tolerated—indeed, enthusiastically supported—the district school as it was. For them the district school had a very limited function and it performed that function adequately. If we employ the often used distinction between schools that educate children for a known place and those that prepare children for new and unknown opportunities, we find the district school firmly on the side of the former. The district school was supposed to socialize the district's children to the community as it was, generally ignoring the world beyond the community just as it ignored the standards of pronunciation used outside the community. Parents did not expect the district school to provide knowledge or skills that would help their children to rise in the world; there seems to have been almost no pressure for these schools to teach, even the older children, subjects of utilitarian value. Instead, the curriculum and organization of the district school served to blind the community's children to the vastly expanding opportunities in the United States. The transportation revolution of the first half of the nineteenth century, which built the turnpikes, canals, and finally railroads that destroyed the isolation of the countryside, provided young men cheap and easy opportunities to try to improve their luck in several different places within a few years and, by greatly increasing the country's economic growth, created new places for young men in manufacturing, merchandising, and service industries. A widening suffrage offered more and more citizens a chance to influence the nation's policy. Ever accelerating development of the West offered young people scores of different kinds of opportunities to prosper. The district schools, however, made no efforts to help their charges exploit these opportunities.

Instead, the schools sought to socialize children to a changeless community in which ties were tight, in which opportunity was fairly circumscribed, in which power relationships were clearly drawn. Socialization to the community was nearly automatic in the district school. Assuming, for example, that each child attended school between the ages of four and twelve and also assuming conditions of no geographic mobility in or out of the district, each child would have attended school—a one-room school in which all children sat together and heard each other recite and get punished—with all the children of the village who ranged eight years on either side of his age. He went, in other words, to school with a whole generation of the future adult population of the village. In this experience the child would have been introduced to the power relationships between children that surely reflected those between their parents, he would have gotten to know their relative social positions, he would have learned whom to defer to and who deferred to him. Now of course he would have learned these things much more quickly had he moved to the village at age forty. But, in the latter instance, he would have been fully conscious of the gradations and of his efforts to understand and adjust to them. In the former case the schoolboy learned these things so subconsciously at school that upon reaching adulthood his role in the village's social structure would have become so habitual as not to be conscious at all. Such gradual socialization was more than likely to make him content with his social situation and complacent about the village in which he lived. The school was to reaffirm the community's social patterns, to reinforce what the child learned about his place and his responsibilities and his future from all the other institutions within the village. This socialization was the function that the district school—not by any conscious choice on the part of schoolmasters, district committeemen, or district citizens in general—came to play. The complacency of the bulk of the rural and small town population about their society meant that the schools—more the creatures of the immediate community they served than schools would be at any other time in the history of the United States—did little more than socialize children, rather inefficiently, to that complacent and contented world. The schools would change only when that complacency changed.

GUIDE TO FURTHER READING

The ablest introductions to the politics and social structure of the early national period are MARSHALL SMELSER, *The Democratic Republic, 1801–1815* (New York, 1968), JAMES STERLING YOUNG, *The Washington Community, 1800–1828* (New York, 1966), ROBERT H. WIEBE, *The Search for Order, 1877–1920* (New York, 1967), chapter 1, and WIEBE, *The Segmented Society* (New York, 1975).

BERNARD BAILYN, *Education in the Forming of American Society* (Chapel Hill, N. C., 1960), LAWRENCE A. CREMIN, *American Education: The Colonial Experience, 1607–1783* (New York, 1970), and JAMES L. AXTELL, *The School Upon a Hill: Education and Society in Colonial New England* (New Haven, Conn., 1974), explore the colonial heritage.

The character of the American Revolution and its minor educational impact are examined in EDMUND MORGAN, "The American Revolution Considered as an Intellectual Movement," in ARTHUR M. SCHLESINGER, JR., and MORTON WHITE, eds., *Paths of American Thought* (New York, 1963), 11–33, and LOUIS HARTZ, *The Liberal Tradition in America: An Interpretation of American Politics and Thought since the Revolution* (New York, 1955), which suggests that the American Revolution differed from other revolutions whose leaders were obliged to mold revolutionary sentiment among the population through restructured educational institutions.

FREDERICK RUDOLPH, *Essays on Education in the Early Republic* (Cambridge, Mass., 1965), GORDON LEE, ed., *Crusade Against Ignorance: Thomas Jefferson on Education* (New York, 1961), and NOAH WEBSTER, *Dissertations on the English Language with Notes Historical and Critical* (Boston, 1789), are very useful primary sources. The nature of learning in the early national period can be discerned by examining Webster's spellers and the McGuffey readers, which have been recently reprinted in paperback editions. BARBARA M. CROSS, *Horace Bushnell: Minister to a Changing America* (Chicago, 1958), is one of many biographies pointing out the language problems that accompanied the difficult transition from a rural to an urban society.

Early accounts informed our portrait of the structure and activities of the district school. WARREN BURTON, *The District School as It Was by One Who Went to It* (Boston, 1833), EDWARD EGGLESTON, *The Hoosier Schoolmaster* (New York, 1871), EGGLESTON, *The Hoosier School-Boy* (New York, 1883), ORANGE JUDD LAYLANDER, *Chronicles of a Contented Man* (Chicago, 1928), and LUCY LARCOM, *A New England Girlhood* (Boston, 1889), are excellent sources. Useful secondary interpretations are CLIFTON JOHNSON, *Old-time Schools and School-books* (New York, 1904), and GEORGE H. MARTIN, *The Evolution of the Massachusetts Public School System* (New York, 1904). DAVID TYACK fleshes out the meaning of "community control" by recalling the experiences of teachers in district schools in *The One Best System* (Cambridge, Mass., 1974), Part I.

CHAPTER 2

The Antebellum College
and Academy

I

AT THE SAME TIME THAT THE TYPICAL DISTRICT SCHOOL WAS ACTING OUT ITS
rituals of equality in a relatively complacent community, institutions of
secondary and tertiary schooling were being rapidly founded in growing
communities for the purpose of giving their students claims to superiority
in a society increasingly committed, at the rhetorical level at least, to
equality. The academies and colleges shared with the district schools the
same localistic nature—although, because academies and colleges recruited from larger areas, their "communities" were somewhat larger
than a district—in that they were very much creatures of the immediate
community and prepared young people for roles in that community. But,
quite unlike the district school, academies and colleges offered an education whose prime function was to distinguish certain members of the
society as superior to the mass. Although the conferring of such distinction may not have been their primary announced purpose—as we shall
see, they had several—it certainly seems to have been their most significant accomplishment.

In this chapter we will discuss the colleges and academies together,
making little distinction between them, for in essential features and functions the two institutions were fundamentally similar. Both offered postelementary schooling for young people between the approximate ages

of 10 and 40. Most students, however, ranged in age from 14 to 25. Both offered terminal education in that they claimed to provide all the formal schooling that a young person needed for life. Tuition at these private institutions was generally minimal but the student and his family had to bear the burden of the student's refraining from wage-earning employment while he pursued additional years of schooling. These foregone earnings, rather than the cost of tuition and maintenance, generally restricted institutions of higher learning to the middle and upper classes. Additional expense, and additional restrictions, grew from the fact that most students had to live away from home in order to attend these institutions.

The colleges and academies founded after the Revolution were, unlike their predecessors in the colonial period, located in most cases in small towns far from major population centers. The colleges and academies recruited from fairly wide areas surrounding these small towns—colleges, for example, recruited students from areas within a fifty-mile radius. Students came to live in the town housing the institution but, for the most part, they did not live in the institutions themselves. The boardingschool became widespread only after the Civil War. Despite the fact that the students did not live "on campus," their lives were closely disciplined by the colleges and academies. Schools often licensed the boardinghouses in which the students lived and constantly regulated what students could eat, how they should dress, and what they could do with the very little free time that the school program—which usually began with a chapel program at dawn and went straight through a full day to a chapel service at nightfall—left them. In all cases the institutions were expected to stand in loco parentis; discipline, academic and extracurricular, was very tight. Set off in a small town with little entertainment available, faced with seemingly endless and meaningless memorizing of texts, subject to constant faculty interference with their social and religious lives, without the release of organized athletics, students no doubt sometimes found higher education a pretty grim business.

It is little wonder that the pre–Civil War college and academy experienced a series of outbreaks of student violence—outbreaks which ranged from the killing of a professor at Princeton (unpremeditated) and the firing of a cannon into a college building to the more normal harassment of authority and the throwing of food in commons. This violence gradually subsided, especially after 1830; it is not clear why. The advent of organized athletics and the broadening of the curriculum possibly had something to do with it. The rising age of the student body also contributed. Relief was also found in the relaxation of the college's commitment to a rigorous interpretation of in loco parentis—a relaxation that grew from a general softening of nineteenth-century society's view of the sinfulness of children and society's gradual renunciation of force as a means of enforcing personal morals. In the first half of the nineteenth century colleges and academies came more and more to rely, not on physical force, but on the power of religion to control their students. As Frederick Rudolph has so dramatically pointed out, the ideal college experience for every student would include the experience of one revival on the campus in which that student experienced the saving light of the Lord. Masters and students sought to encourage such revivals—and, of course, the conscious effort to do away with sinful behavior was thought one of the most effective means of encouragement. Thus, schoolmasters were able to develop a desire for religious experience among their students and to depend on that desire to make the students themselves enforce a great deal of the institution's disciplinary code. This change made the colleges and academies appear less openly oppressive than earlier when they depended on physical constraints over their students, but whether revivalistic constraints were any less restrictive from the students' point of view is unclear.

The status of women in higher education was a point of much controversy in this period. Academies were most often coeducational while the colleges—with the exception of Oberlin, which, from its establishment in 1833, admitted all comers regardless of race or sex, and a few others—resisted the admission of women well into the second half of the nineteenth century. A large number of academies were opened exclusively for women, several of which offered courses of study equivalent to that offered by most men's colleges. The most famous, perhaps, were Emma Willard's Troy Female Seminary, opened in 1821, and Mary Lyon's Mount Holyoke Seminary, opened in 1837 (it gained collegiate status only in 1893). There women studied the same advanced subjects as men. In teaching women at an equal level with men, Lyon and Willard undermined the assumption that women were intellectually inferior to men that prevailed even among educators of women. The first women's college (Vassar) was not founded until 1865, the next (Smith and Wellesley) in 1875. In most schools women were taught subjects thought likely to improve their performance as housewives, mothers, and elementary school teachers. Their work emphasized English grammar rather than the classics and higher mathematics. The practice in oratory and elocution that was part of the rhetoric course for men was dropped as women were not supposed to speak in public (Lucy Stone refused to write a commencement part at Oberlin in 1842 because a male student would have to read it to the audience). Simple arithmetic, geography, the other elementary school subjects, and work in household arts such as sewing or embroidery rounded out the English course for women. Within the coeducational schools women were often segregated both socially and in the classroom. Contact between the sexes, inside or outside of class, was minimal—or at least was supposed to be minimal.

Whatever its shortcomings, "higher education" for women in the first half of the nineteenth century marked a great improvement on the colonial finishing school for young ladies. And the broadening of women's education greatly influenced education in general in the United States. First, it hastened the day when women would be considered intellectually equal to men. Second, it gave thousands of young women destined to teach the elementary grades some post-elementary-school training. Much of higher education for women in this era grew out of a generally recognized need to recruit better educated members to the steadily feminizing teaching force.

Like the district schools, academies and colleges in this era were community oriented and controlled, but as the colleges and academies recruited from and served far wider communities, the nature of community control was somewhat different. The average man did not have the same sense of control over the academy in his area as he had over the district school (although he might take a good deal more pride in having an institution of higher learning in his community than he did from the existence of a district school). Leadership and control of these institutions generally resided with the social elite of the area—the upper and upper middle classes. Academies and colleges were privately owned by boards of self-perpetuating trustees who appointed the president or master and his subordinate teachers and who had the power to establish educational policy. This form of educational polity was at that time uniquely American, one that had developed in the early colonial era when it was found that traditional ways of governing institutions of learning did not fit the conditions of the country. European precedents suggested either educational institutions governed closely by the church and state or educational institutions largely autonomous from any outside control and governed by the institution's faculty.

The Massachusetts colonists attempted to bring the latter arrangement over from England and established Harvard College on that basis. But the Bay Colony's leaders found that they disliked entrusting their sons and the fate of the college to the young transient "faculty" at Harvard which consisted almost exclusively of young graduates of the college awaiting a "call" from a congregation to take up their proper role as ministers. Furthermore, early American colleges had no steady sources of support like those upon which Oxford and Cambridge could depend. American colleges were from the very start dependent on the gifts of their immediate communities. Community financial involvement, especially when accompanied by the absence of permanent and mature college faculties, inevitably undermined the autonomy of the colleges and led to a system of lay governance whereby community leaders assumed financial and educational responsibility for their operations. At times these lay boards of trustees were composed of community officials and area clergymen—the idea being that those men responsible for maintaining community interests in other areas would be most capable of doing so in the case of educational institutions. At other times boards of trustees of colleges were composed simply of influentials in the community, appointed because they were instrumental in founding the college or in rendering it financial support. This system of governance, which began to emerge from the very first years of Harvard's existence, was pretty well confirmed there by the 1680s when the last Harvard faculty member to serve as trustee (with a brief exception in the 1880s) was forced off the board. The second and third American colleges—William and Mary chartered in 1693 and Yale in 1701—were established with boards of trustees totally distinct—except for the college president—from the teaching body. This pattern has persisted in virtually every American college until the late 1960s when various campus crises brought tentative efforts to give faculty (and students) more "power over their lives" by including them on college boards of trustees. This pattern of governance was, from the first, the one that controlled the development of academies in the United States.

The colleges and academies of the early national period were also similar in that, although they were "private" institutions, they had a public aspect and received a certain amount of public support. Ideally, a college or academy was to apply for a charter from the state before it opened its doors (although hundreds, perhaps thousands, of academies existed for years without a state charter). The chartering process was a hold-over from a period in which the state tightly controlled economic and social life to the extent that no man was allowed to do business until the state had determined that his efforts would help the state. In that mercantilist age the state was supposed to determine or plan its own economic development and virtually assign individuals to the roles necessary for accomplishing that plan. Any group that drew together to manufacture glass or build a bridge or found a school or fight fires (even voluntarily) had to petition either the local or national government for a charter which would grant them the privilege of carrying out their plans. Such a grant of privilege came only when the government had determined that the activity was in the public interest. Charters also often granted monopolies. If the government granted a group the privilege of building a toll bridge in a certain place, it was likely to promise not to allow any other group to build a competing bridge nearby. Monopolies of this kind were granted in order to insure the success of the first venturers on the assumption that, if building a bridge was in the public interest, it was also in the public interest to insure that the bridge builders found the venture profitable enough to continue. In the last half of the eighteenth and the first half of the nineteenth century—the very time

when thousands of colleges and academies were receiving state charters—the chartering system and the system of economic and social control that supported it were being challenged and were breaking down in
England and the United States.

This period in England saw the increasing elaboration of the laissez-
faire theories of Adam Smith and David Ricardo, which held that the
public and state interest is best served by allowing the maximum feasible
individual freedom in economic activity. A state's economy would be
strongest when every individual pursued his own economic self-interest
unimpeded by the state. Thus, Smith could argue that the pursuit of
self-interest was also the pursuit of public interest, and that the public
interest suffered whenever the state interfered with the individual pursuit
of self-interest. Smith's ideas came to dominate nineteenth-century academic thought but became only partially implemented in the economies
of Western Europe in that or any other century. In the United States the
story was somewhat different as the weakness of centralized government
in a sparsely settled country with poor internal communications made
laissez faire a governmental practice long before the classical economists
developed the theory. Colonial governments and early state governments
had neither the enforcement machinery to regulate effectively the economic activities of widely scattered citizens nor the foresight and financial
resources to understand and serve the public interest in a new and rapidly
developing country. So although governments, both colonial and state,
continued to issue charters and grants of privilege, they did so largely
symbolically. Few entrepreneurial ventures were stopped because the
state refused to grant a charter or because it effectively regulated the
venture, once established. Likewise with educational institutions.
Colonial and state governments in almost all cases issued charters to all
who requested them and, once having granted the privilege of establishing an educational institution, the governments interfered in no way with
the running of the institution. Indeed, by a strange piece of irony, freedom from interference became a privilege, made famous in the Dartmouth College case of 1819, that accompanied a state charter. This complex legal case was one of several which arose when state governments,
following the Revolution, had sought either to take control of or to
impose new conditions, more in line with revolutionary democratic doctrine about public control, on "private" colleges originally chartered by
colonial governments. In the Dartmouth College case the Supreme Court
ruled that since the Constitution had explicitly guaranteed that the new
government would honor all contracts made under the colonial governments and that, since a charter was a contract, it was illegal for a state
or local government to interfere in any way with a chartered institution
except insofar as the original charter provided for such interference. In
other words, a charter was a contract in perpetuity and, except under

provisions written into the original contract, the state could not abridge that contract in any way. Although the charter was originally granted in recognition of the public service nature of the institution, it was now interpreted as an assurance of the essential privateness of the institution. Thus the charter was vital because it insured the trustees and potential donors that, despite the election of new governments every few years, the college would continue as planned. In an era when democracy was new and when shifts in European governments had often meant upheavals in all institutions, this kind of assurance was significant; some historians have argued that the assurance given by the Dartmouth College case was the spark which accounts for the ever increasing rate of educational institution founding after 1820. It is doubtful that the Dartmouth College decision "sparked" this movement, but it surely gave the private sector the confidence necessary to sustain the movement.

The charter had another value for an educational institution. It symbolized the fact that the institution carried out a public function—the education of the young, which was in the interest of the society as a whole. The charter symbolized this relation of the private institution to the public interest. As often as not, the charter also brought with it a certain amount of public support for the educational institution. When it chartered a public service institution, the state government would often grant the institution some public land that the school could sell to raise revenue, or a portion of the income from a state or local tax, or sometimes, when the state was feeling especially poor, a guarantee (seldom fulfilled) that the school would have a monopoly on higher education in its region. Thus Harvard College received part of the income from tolls, first on the ferry and then on the bridge across the Charles River, many academies received land in Maine from the Massachusetts legislature upon chartering, academies in many states received money from the liquor tax or from the fines paid by those guilty of certain misdemeanors in their area. Williams College thought the state promised it a monopoly on higher education in western Massachusetts when it was chartered in 1793, and in 1821 angrily and unsuccessfully fought the establishment of Amherst forty-four miles away as a violation of its charter. Thus the charter served both to protect the private nature of the educational institution and to establish its public service character. It is this very ambiguity that is most crucial to understanding the institutional shape of the academy and college in the early nineteenth century; this ambiguity about the publicness of private educational institutions is far from being resolved even in the present day, as we can see in the battles over state support for parochial education and over the issue of the relation of government to the "private" universities.

Another area in which the college and academy resembled each other was curricular. That they should be so similar in this respect is ironic, for the academy was first suggested in America as an alternative form of higher education that was to offer modern and practical subjects—like English, modern foreign languages, navigation, surveying—instead of the classical training of the grammar school and college. The model for the American academy, defined as a secondary institution which combined instruction in the classics with more practical, "modern" subjects, came from the ideas of the poet John Milton as institutionalized in the Puritan dissenting academies in England during the Restoration. Benjamin Franklin had those dissenting academies in mind when he published, in 1749, his *Proposals Relating to the Education of Youth in Pennsylvania*, in which he suggested that Philadelphia needed an institution with a broader curriculum than that of the classical grammar school. He proposed a school where the students would "learn those Things that are likely to be *most useful* and *most ornamental*, Regard being had to the several Professions for which they are intended." Franklin's suggestions for practicality were more radical than most: "While they are reading Natural History, might not a little *Gardening, Planting, Grafting, Inoculating,* &c. be taught and practised; and now and then Excursions made to the neighbouring Plantations of the best Farmers, their Methods observ'd and reason'd upon for the Information of Youth. The Improvement of Agriculture being useful to all, and Skill in it no Disparagement to any."[1] English, mathematics, history and civil government, and natural history were the most important parts of the curriculum; learning foreign languages was also necessary, but Latin and Greek were accorded only equal status with French and German. Franklin's suggestions and arguments were ignored and his planned "English academy" became nothing but a preliminary adjunct to the classically oriented University of Pennsylvania and its attached grammar school.

Franklin's experience was to be repeated time and again in the next hundred years. Proposals for more practical curricula in both colleges and academies and plans for more modern schools were ignored or scrapped in order to meet the demand from faculties and apparently from students (or their parents) for the traditional Latin and Greek. Theoretically, the academy was supposed to be more modern and more practical; in fact, it seems in general to have been about as traditional as the grammar schools and the colleges. Several things may account for this. First, as Franklin found, teachers and parents wanted Latin and Greek taught. These were the subjects of elite education and few parents wanted any less for their own children. Furthermore, it is not clear that Latin and

---

[1] Benjamin Franklin, *Proposals Relating to the Education of Youth in Pennsylvania* (Philadelphia, 1749), quoted in Theodore Sizer, ed., *The Age of the Academies* (New York, 1964), 71, 75.

Greek were such impractical subjects from the point of view of the personal success and mobility of the students in the academies.

The practicality of the practical curricula of those academies that did claim to offer these subjects must be questioned. In most cases the practical and modern subjects in a school's catalogue or advertisements were listed only for advanced students and often it turned out that no students were advanced enough to take them. In other academies the practical subjects received cursory treatment—not through observation and induction, as Franklin suggested, but through memorization and rote recitation from a book. In the early nineteenth century we also find little pedagogical knowledge or concern about the effective teaching of modern subjects such as natural history or trigonometry. Texts in these subjects started to appear only in the thirties and they stressed the memorizable rather than the practical. Botany became the study of the names of the classifications rather than a study of how plants grow. These problems with the "practical" subjects were compounded by the fact that few teachers were even minimally trained to teach these modern subjects. All in all, what practical instruction there was was not likely to be very practical.

So far as historians know, however, most academies made hardly any effort to teach the modern or the practical. It was too expensive. The more subjects a school taught, the more books, equipment, and teachers it needed. And modernity and practicality seemed to call especially for expensive equipment such as surveying instruments and laboratories. Latin and Greek, on the other hand, were fairly cheap to offer. Any man with some college education could teach them since he had learned them in college—and, as "teaching" was largely the hearing of recitations and the grading of papers and tests, special pedagogical training was not very relevant. Furthermore, a school with a traditional classical curriculum could get by with a single teacher as any educated man was expected to know all the classical subjects. But the modern and practical subjects, if they were to be taught at all well, needed specialists at added expense. Had there been a real demand from students and parents for modern and practical subjects, academies would undoubtedly have passed the extra expense on to the students; that so few did so suggests how little effective demand there was. The marginal economic position of most academies prevented them from taking the time and the risk to cultivate a demand for a different curriculum among the communities they served.

These same arguments explain the colleges' experience in this era— the expense and difficulties of teaching modern and practical subjects and the lack of effective demand for that kind of training prevented almost all colleges from departing from the traditional curriculum. Indeed, the colleges argued quite effectively that the traditional curriculum was the most practical teaching that a young person could receive. In 1828 the faculty of Yale College prepared a report to justify that faculty's rejection of an alumnus' suggestion that Yale add several "practical subjects" to its curriculum. The Yale Report argued that the mental discipline that the student received while studying the classics best prepared him to think for himself about other problems that he would encounter. "First exercise the mind and then furnish it," the professors wrote. "Furnishing" would most often come later, on the job or in a special training school like a seminary. The college's function was to exercise the mind and Latin and mathematics were the supreme tools for that purpose. They were pure, abstract, and complete. If a student could master a systematic, ordered, rounded body of knowledge like Latin or mathematics, he then had mastered a system of thought applicable to other, less complete subjects. Study of these traditional and well-ordered subjects gave the student a standard of knowledge, system, and completeness which he could use in seeking knowledge in other subjects. In a sense it was advantageous that Latin was a dead language since it was no longer subject to changes brought about by usage, regional corruptions, and slang. It could safely be treated and studied as a completed, logical, internally consistent, and perfect system—a closed system. Mathematics, of course, possessed the same advantages. Furthermore, the classical languages and mathematics were difficult, and it was thought best to train people on difficult subjects, as it was easier to go from the difficult to the more simple (as the modern subjects were designated). Difficult subjects also had a greater disciplinary value; the harder the subject, the greater disciplining of will power necessary to master it. The Yale Report rested on the faculty psychology and on the assumption of transfer of training— that is, the idea that exercising the mind in the study of one subject would make the mind more adept at studying other subjects, that memorizing Latin would improve the mind's ability to memorize French should the student want to do so at some future date. Thus, according to the Yale Report, disciplines which gave the mind the most rigorous and the most general exercise were the most practical school subjects. And those subjects—happily for the professors—were the traditional Greek, Latin, and mathematics.

The Yale Report came at a critical time for the fate of the classical languages in higher education. From the founding of the universities in Western Europe in the Middle Ages, the classical languages had been recognized as the languages of communication among educated men. Treatises in medicine, law, education, theology, and even science were written in Latin; the "wisdom of the ancients" was constantly called upon and applied in everyday situations. Thus, the most practical education a would-be professional or a well-rounded gentleman could hope for would be one that taught him the language and literature of primary communication. In the eighteenth century the vernacular gradually replaced Latin as the language of communication among even the most educated men. Although scholars and professional specialists still wrote and read Latin in their work, the well-rounded educated man took his ideas and his knowledge of the world from works written in the vernacular. Men still believed in the importance of the wisdom of the ancients—note the constant parallels Americans drew between their own democratic experiment and classical forms of government—but that wisdom was generally thought to be available in translation. Thus, the obvious rationale for the emphasis on the classics in education was undermined. The classics were no longer practical, some argued, and should be replaced with more useful subjects. Had the classics continued to justify their position in the curriculum on the basis of their usefulness as languages of communication and as sources of great classical ideas and ideals, they would surely have been replaced. But the Yale Report subtly but clearly changed the rationale for keeping the curriculum classical; argued, indeed, for a higher form of practicality than did the advocates of the modern subjects.

The ideas of the Yale Report were not original with the professors at Yale, but their report, widely publicized as a statement of positive educational progress (not the reactionary defense of the old that most modern historians term it), set the tone and rationale of higher education for the greater part of the remainder of the century. Although written by college professors as a manifesto about college education, the report had as great an impact on academies as it did on colleges. Here was a report that accomplished everything: it reconciled the financial interests of the schools and the cultural pretensions of the teachers with the practical tendencies of a developing nation and reconciled, perhaps more importantly, the conflict within parents and students between the desire to share the cultural training of the elite and the desire for practical training for the business of life.

There are some exceptions to the generalizations about curriculum made in the preceding pages, just as there are to all the generalizations made in this volume. The most important exceptions were the few technical schools founded for the training of engineers in early America—the United States Military Academy (1802) and Rensselaer Polytechnic Institute (1824) being the most famous. Both, because they were established to deemphasize the classics, took the name of academy or institute in order to distinguish themselves from the colleges. Also exceptional were the normal schools or teacher training academies founded in this period. These schools offered occupationally oriented secondary education (their training was hardly of professional grade, however) and as such carried out the utilitarian mandate of the original academy model. In most cases, however, the normal school was not as advanced as the academy; its curriculum concentrated largely on reviewing the elementary subjects in order to train students to teach in elementary schools.

The colleges and academies in the period 1780–1860, then, largely shaped their curricula according to the traditional classical model. The student occupied the greatest part of his time learning Latin, Greek, and mathematics. Rhetoric and forensics—training in the writing and speaking of English—took up a smaller portion of his day. The lower the level of the school, the more time it devoted to English rather than classical languages. As the period progressed, science—natural philosophy (physics and chemistry) and natural history (geology and biology)— received more attention, especially in the wealthier institutions. Benjamin Silliman gave lectures and laboratory demonstrations in chemistry at Yale in the first decade of the nineteenth century, at least twenty years before the publication of the Yale Report. The colleges and most of the academies conducted some work in mental and moral philosophy—generally in the capstone course in the curriculum where the college president or academy principal guided the graduating class through a book like Francis Wayland's *The Elements of Moral Science* (1835), a treatise that sought to cover the ethical aspects of all phases of an educated man's life. It included discussions of how the mind was formed and how it functioned, of the sources of moral ideas and ideals, of political economy and civil government, and finally of marriage and the family. Here, more than in any other class in the school, the instructor did more than simply listen to and mark recitations. Instead, he discussed and advised his charges on the moral issues of their time.

With this exception, however, pedagogy in institutions of higher learning was not markedly better than it was in the district schools. Rote recitation—in which the student memorized a passage from the text or his translation of a passage from the text and repeated it to the teacher— was a standard practice. Only in rhetoric and forensics was there much student creativity; even the few science laboratories established in the first half of the nineteenth century were used mostly to demonstrate experiments to students, not to let them *do* them. Students' creativity and imagination were stimulated much less by the curriculum and teaching of the schools than by what Frederick Rudolph has called the "extracurriculum"—the network of literary clubs, secret societies, fraternities, debating clubs, and voluntary agencies which students established and ran with a high level of intellectual rigor. Literary and debating clubs, for example, often had larger and better libraries than the colleges or academies—with especially strong collections of modern works, including novels, a class of frivolous books excluded from most college libraries. Whereas college libraries opened perhaps only an hour or two a day and discouraged the circulation of books, the club libraries were much more accessible and consequently much more intellectually influential. As the Yale Report had insisted, the institutions of higher learning were more concerned with disciplining and training the mind than with furnishing it; students turned to the clubs and societies for information about the world around them.

Even on the criteria of grade or level of curriculum and instruction, it is difficult to distinguish the academies from the colleges. Generally, of course, colleges tended to admit a slightly older student and to teach him a bit more advanced and rigorous curriculum. But only slightly and not in all cases. The matter of the age of the students is a very complicated one. We do know that academies often admitted children as young as nine and that colleges matriculated many students under fifteen. And both kinds of institutions registered substantial numbers of students over thirty. But about averages—a statistical picture of the typical student—we know next to nothing. Some colleges kept reasonably full matriculation records from which historians have been able to discover that the average age of freshmen rose steadily from 1800 to the Civil War. The increasing age of college students has also been confirmed in studies of Baptist colleges and of the recruitment patterns of the American Education Society (a group which sent young men to college in return for their promise to become ministers in the West).[2] No similar work has been done with respect to academy matriculants. It is worth noting in this regard, however, that since the academy was not seen principally as a preparation for but as an alternative to college, academy students would not necessarily be younger than those in colleges.

Equally confusing was the college's normal practice of establishing its own secondary school within the college to prepare students for college work. Colleges often sprang up in areas in which there were no secondary schools and had to accept students directly out of district school and offer them a secondary course. Throughout the period some colleges had far more students in their precollege sections than in the colleges themselves; some had no students registered in college courses. Furthermore, less than half—probably fewer—of the students who attended the secondary portion ever went on the register in the college. These colleges were academies in everything but name, as they offered terminal secondary schooling to the majority of their students. While some schools labeled academies gave courses at a level commensurate with those at all but the best colleges, others functioned only as private elementary schools. Academies, especially those located in sparsely settled rural or frontier areas, were desperate for tuition money, and if

[2] David F. Allmendinger, *Paupers and Scholars: The Transformation of Student Life in Nineteenth-Century New England* (New York, 1975), and David Potts, "Baptist Colleges in the Development of American Society, 1812–1861" (Unpublished Dissertation, Harvard University, 1967).

paying students needed elementary work, the academy, however reluctantly, taught it.

Thus, although we can speak in the abstract of varying levels of higher education, we cannot associate those levels firmly with institutional titles. Greek, Latin, mathematics, forensics, rhetoric, natural history, and moral philosophy could be taught at the advanced or the basic level, a distinction corresponding to the tertiary and the secondary levels of schooling. But many institutions labeled colleges taught only at the basic level and many labeled academies taught both the basic and the advanced. Thus the name "college" or "academy" did not necessarily indicate what kind of school existed under that title or what kind of instruction it provided. Specific institutions chose to title themselves as they did, apparently, more in accordance with local prejudices toward the rhetorical "practicality" of the academy or the intellectual elitism of the college than in accordance with the kind of instruction they offered. Many institutions found they had made a mistake and changed their designation—the usual change, as would be expected, from the lower to the higher, from academy to college. Firm demarcation of secondary from tertiary education, however, would not come until the beginning of the twentieth century.

II

Many more colleges and academies were established in the period between the Revolution and the Civil War than were needed to fulfill the demands for higher education among the population of the period. Only by understanding why there was more popular demand for the building of these institutions than there was demand for their educational facilities will we understand the place of higher education in the early American republic.

How many academies were there? We do not really know, for the only way to count is to find copies of academy charters among neglected state legislative records. No one has made this examination as of yet. Moreover, a charter will tell us only that an academy was contemplated; it does not tell us that it was actually founded. Further complicating the statistical picture, there were many more unincorporated (unchartered) academies than incorporated ones. Perhaps the best estimates that we have are those compiled by Henry Barnard in the 1850s.[3] Barnard found that there were over 6,000 academies enrolling more than 250,000 students. He found, on the other hand, that there were 239 colleges enrolling a little over a

---

[3] Henry Barnard, "The Educational Interest of the United States," *American Journal of Education,* I (March, 1856), 368, Table III.

tenth of that number. Albert Fishlow estimates that in 1850 approximately 4 million children were enrolled in public common schools.[4] This attendance figure, according to Fishlow, is equal to approximately 56 percent of the common-school-age population. On the other hand, if we take Barnard's figure of a quarter of a million children attending academies as relatively accurate, which it probably is, and compare it to the estimated total white population in the 15–24 age group—4.1 million—we find that the academies served at any one time approximately 6 percent of the available population. The chances were that about 12 percent of the population coming of age at the time had attended academies for four years during some part of their careers. Perhaps more went to academies, for it is very probable that a majority did not complete a four-year course. These figures help us to understand that the magnitude of the academy movement, in terms of institutions and students, was not insignificant. Moreover, they point out that the academies serviced a far larger proportion of the population than did their predecessors, the Latin Grammar Schools, which were limited in number and located almost exclusively in densely populated areas and which in the colonial era required substantial intellectual achievement and social status for admission. The academy movement saw the founding of literally thousands of institutions devoted primarily to secondary schooling and the spreading of secondary education from cities to the small towns.

The pattern in the growth in numbers of colleges and in numbers of students attending college presents a somewhat different picture. Nine colleges were founded in the American colonies. Between the Revolution and the Civil War the United States saw the founding of 173 colleges that were to survive until the 1920s—when Donald Tewksbury studied and counted antebellum colleges.[5] Actually, many more than 173 were founded, for a majority of these did not survive into the twentieth century—Tewksbury estimates that, for every college that survived, three or four others died.

The figures on the founding of the more hardy institutions reveal a rapidly increasing rate of growth. Only 28 of these colleges were founded before 1820; 12 in the 1820s; but 35 in the thirties, 32 in the forties (there was a steep depression in the late thirties and early forties which slowed down the rate of investment in and the survival capabilities of colleges), and 66 in the 1850s. Another historian has estimated that in 1800, 18 of every 10,000 Americans were college trained (i.e., they had spent some

---

[4] Albert Fishlow, "The American Common School Revival: Fact or Fancy?", in Henry Rosovsky, ed., *Industrialization in Two Systems: Essays in Honor of Alexander Gerschenkron* (New York, 1966), 40–67.

[5] Donald G. Tewksbury, *The Founding of American Colleges and Universities Before the Civil War: With Particular Reference to the Religious Influence Bearing upon the College Movement* (New York, 1932).

time at an American college but had not necessarily graduated) and that in 1830, 17 of every 10,000 were college trained.[6] Although these estimates do not account for European training that some Americans had received, it is probable that no more than two tenths of a percent of the American population was college trained in the first quarter of the century. By mid-century, as Barnard's figures for 1850 suggest, considerable expansion had occurred, yet even then the colleges enrolled less than 2 percent (1.25%) of the population in the 20–24 age group. In terms of enrollments, then, the colleges were small; but their symbolic importance, their wide dispersion over the country, and the prominence of their graduates make them significant for the historian measuring American attitudes toward education and the effects of education on American society.

All the available statistics demonstrate that institutions of higher education greatly expanded in number and enrollment in the first eighty years of nationhood.[7] The most dramatic increase, however, was in the number of institutions, an increase far greater than that necessitated by increasing enrollments. The academies and colleges were seriously overbuilt. This overbuilding—the fact that not enough tuition-paying students existed to fill the numerous institutions to the "breakeven" point —accounts for the extremely high mortality rate among colleges and what seems, so far as we can tell, a similar mortality rate among academies. The cries of educators lamenting the pinch caused by lack of students and their tuition money are universal during the period. At the college and at the academy level, trustees and presidents contemplated desperate schemes to assemble capital to get a school established or over a financial hurdle. One such scheme provided that initial donors to the college received in return a "perpetual scholarship" for their children and *their* children. Some colleges that had financed their beginnings in this manner found in the next generation that all the original contributions had been eaten up by initial building expenditures and that most of their students were descendants of original contributors who attended without charge. Northwestern University was forced to honor such a pledge and admit a student free of charge as late as the early 1970s. Most commonly, however, faculty members were forced to bear the financial burden of overbuilding. There are scores of harrowing tales of faculty members going for years without pay or with greatly reduced pay in order to help their institution stay alive. And of course students bore a consid-

---

[6] Sydney Aronson, *Status and Kinship in the Higher Civil Service: Standards of Selection in the Administrations of John Adams, Thomas Jefferson, and Andrew Jackson* (Cambridge, Mass., 1964), 122–123.

[7] On the relative decline in college enrollment in the nineteenth-century, see Frederick Rudolph, *The American College and University: A History* (New York, 1962), 99, 118–140, and John S. Whitehead, *The Separation of College and State: Columbia, Dartmouth, Harvard, and Yale, 1776–1876* (New Haven, Conn, 1973).

erable burden in consequence of this overbuilding. Although tuition remained surprisingly low—competition for students dictated that—educational quality and educational facilities like libraries suffered greatly because of this underfinancing.

One evidence of the overbuilding is that colleges were often founded right on the frontier line—not a generation after the founding of a town or of a state, but at the same moment as the founding of the town or state. Thus in states like Kentucky, Kansas, and Minnesota, colleges were founded before the population of the states rose above the 100,000 mark—if the 18 in 10,000 figure for college-trained people can be said to apply uniformly across the country, each of these states established colleges before there were 200 college-trained residents in the state. At the 1850 rate of enrollment for colleges in the 20-to-24 age group—less than 2 percent—there were less than 300 students available to go to college in these states. Nor is there any reason to believe that the rate of enrollment in these frontier communities reached nearly as high a figure as 2 percent. The same pattern holds true for academy foundings—Iowa's first appeared in 1836, ten years before statehood and when that territory (which included part of what is now Minnesota) boasted less than 40,000 inhabitants. In 1850 Texas, with a population of only 213,-000, was reported to have 97 academies. Assuming that 6 percent of the young people 15–24 attended an academy and, adjusting for the likelihood that frontier regions would contain a larger cohort of that age group than older locales (young people tended to migrate much more frequently than older, more settled people), each Texas academy could expect about 40 students at a time and Iowa's lone academy had to recruit from a potential 720 students dispersed through the vast territory.[8] And again, as in the case of the frontier colleges, there is every reason to expect that in the frontier areas where young men were especially important in helping families begin new farms and new enterprises fewer youngsters sought higher education than in more settled regions.

The rapidity with which colleges and academies sprang up did not reflect a realistic appraisal of the educational needs of the communities they were designed to serve. Rather, this overbuilding must be seen as a product of the entrepreneurial, cultural, moral, and status aspirations of their founders and patrons. When we come to understand these reasons for overbuilding this kind of institution—there was, we must note, no similar overbuilding at the common or district school level—we will come to understand the underlying functions of higher education in the United States in the first half of the nineteenth century.

---

[8] Twenty-one percent of the national population was aged 15–24 in 1850; we have figured the frontier percentage at 30 percent (which is probably too high). We have made no adjustment for the presence of blacks in the Texas population.

Founding of institutions of higher education was one product of the overoptimistic boosterism that characterized the American development of space in the antebellum period. Daniel Boorstin in the second volume of his trilogy, *The Americans* (1965), describes this booster spirit with great verve and insight.[9] Every settlement, every "wide spot in the road," "claimed the name of 'city,' " he points out. No one seems to have paid any particular attention to the real meaning of the word. "Every place that claimed the honors of a city set about justifying itself by seeking to conjure up suitably metropolitan institutions." Among these metropolitan institutions were a hotel, a newspaper, and, almost as important, an institution of higher learning—whether an academy or a college. Boston, New York, Philadelphia had colleges; why should not Georgetown, Kentucky (1829), and Galesburg, Illinois (Knox, 1837)? And each got a college—when its population had barely reached 1,000.

The efforts to build Athenian cities in the West were somewhat paradoxical. As the founders of these colleges and academies sought to upgrade the towns in which they lived into cities, they brought about a diffusion of culture which would challenge the very definition of a city as a center of culture. The scattering of colleges and similar cultural institutions among hundreds of western towns represented a significant departure from the idea of centralized urban culture which had pervaded Western civilization from its beginning. The founders of colleges and academies were not even content to choose a single town to be the cultural capital of each state. Every town, they seemed to say, should be a cultural center.

The cultural leaders of the West viewed the city ambiguously. On the one hand, they wanted institutions like those located in New York or Boston; on the other, they felt urban environments to be evil. Many westerners thought of Boston and New York in much the same way that Jefferson thought of Paris and London. Noah Webster was but one of many who believed that "large cities [even those in America] are always scenes of dissipation and amusement, which have a tendency to corrupt the hearts of youth and divert their minds from their literary pursuits."[10] Urban educational entrepreneurs agreed with Webster about older large cities, but felt that their own cities—absolutely imaginary as they were— would be free of such corrupting influences and thus safe places in which boys and girls could learn and where a pure culture could be maintained (although they often acknowledged the pervasive distrust of urban influence by placing their institutions on the edge of the city, in a protected place such as on a hill that overlooked the city but was somewhat isolated

[9] Daniel Boorstin, *The Americans: The National Experience* (New York, 1965), especially chapters 16, 17, 20, 21. The sentence quoted below is from p. 152.

[10] Noah Webster in Frederick Rudolph, *Essays on Education in the Early Republic* (Cambridge, Mass., 1965), 52.

from it). Henry Nash Smith has described the American vision of the West as a virgin land, a new Eden, where men could begin all over again in a state of innocence, where men could be reborn. He describes this image as a kind of pastoral vision which saw the West as an agricultural heaven.[11] But the urban boosters of the antebellum period felt that the western cities-to-be could foster this same sense of innocence and rebirth. Establishing educational institutions became one way of insuring that the new urban units would live up to the cultural, moral, and Eden-like aspirations of these boosters.

The building of institutions of higher education in these areas also served to fulfill more mundane aspirations. Among these aspirations, the quest for financial profit dominated. The unflagging preoccupation with land speculation determined educational investment. A school raised the price of nearby land. One frontiersman explained that land developers "are shrewd enough to know that one of the most successful methods to give notoriety to an embryo town, and induce New England settlers, is forthwith to put in operation some institution of learning with a high sounding name." One public elementary school administrator in Madison, Wisconsin, complained that establishment of a female academy "would do more to raise the price of village lots and secure a better class of people for the future city of Madison than any amount of money expended in building school houses and providing teachers for the public schools."[12] This complaint that academies and colleges rather than public elementary schools attracted settlers and investment explains, in part, why higher education was so overbuilt relative to elementary education. It also suggests that settlers were attracted less by the quality of the education offered than by the titles of institutions and their superficial claims to "culture."

The contributions educational institutions made to an area's economic health were well recognized in the antebellum period. Localities actually bid for such institutions—and the institutions chose to locate where they received the best financial guarantees. The University of Missouri was established only when Boone County—where Columbia is located—outbid five other Missouri River counties. The citizens of Boone County raised pledges of $82,000 in cash and $35,000 in land—the contributions coming "from over 900 individuals, of whom nearly a hundred gave five dollars or less."[13] Such patterns of contribution, as Boorstin points out, served to tie the college to the community very closely— the University of Missouri was Columbia's own college because the people of the town and its environs had "bought" it.

[11] Henry Nash Smith, *Virgin Land* (Cambridge, Mass., 1950), *passim.*
[12] Lloyd Jorgenson, *The Founding of Public Education in Wisconsin* (Madison, Wis., 1956), 34.
[13] Boorstin, *National Experience,* 159.

What financial advantages did an institution of higher learning offer a community? It would raise land values by attracting settlers who were interested in sending their children to school. Probably more important to the people who bid for the presence of a college or academy was the fact that these establishments, by attracting students and faculty from the outlying regions and from neighboring towns, would assemble more customers for the local merchants—would pump, in modern parlance, more buying power into the town's economy. Academies and colleges of the period were small, no doubt, but the towns were also small. Thus the influx of forty or fifty students could make a great difference in the town's economy. Before the colleges and academies learned that they could make a profit from renting dormitory rooms to students, the students from the outlying regions were forced to purchase room and board from townspeople. Some colleges deliberately refrained from building dormitories to house their students so that the student board revenue would be distributed throughout the town, convincing the townsmen of the college's importance to the town's economy.

If the overbuilding of higher educational institutions rested on an exaggerated optimism about the development of new areas of the United States, it also rested in large part on an overblown fear that the movement away from the old areas of settlement and their established ways would bring about a barbarism, a lack of community, and a breakdown of culture among those who made the move. Men beginning new communities in new areas felt the need for reassurance that they could maintain, in a new environment, the values and culture they had left behind. Like the erection of a church just like the one they had left behind, the building of a school on the older model served to reaffirm the community's commitment to older values and its capability of achieving traditional standards of morality and culture. This eagerness to affirm that they were still part of civilization, still capable of living up to the old morality and culture, accounts for the rapidity with which communities established institutions of learning. Like the habit of building schools in order to enhance land values, the habit of building schools as symbols of the aspiration to morality and culture and civilization was applicable at all levels. In the earliest years of community settlement, thousands of district schools were founded as just such a symbol. But just as institutions of higher education had greater economic value than the district school, so did they have greater symbolic value as commitments to culture.

While participants in the new community ventures worried about what was happening to them, benevolent groups in the older communities worried about them also. The college president of the early nineteenth century was no less a slave to money-raising responsibility than is his modern counterpart, and part of his obligations included frequent trips to the east coast (and sometimes to England) to raise funds for the college. The educational institution's fund raiser was most successful at home by appealing to the economic interests and community pride of the local community; he was most successful in the East in appealing to the philanthropists' and the churches' concern with the morals and manners of the westerner and frontiersman. When citizens left one community to venture to a new frontier or a new community in a less settled region, they and more particularly those who remained behind felt that the movers were breaking, or at least severely straining, the social code which emphasized loyalty and subordination of self to the interests of the group. Some of the less trusting easterners felt that the pioneers had left "civilized and religious society for the simple purpose of getting out of its restraints." By moving to the West these people had excluded themselves from the community, from "society," and from its control. They had become different and, as such, came to seem more or less dangerous to the settled ways of those living in the traditional communities.

In response to this crisis of "outsiders," several religiously oriented organizations sprang up to supply ministers, schools and Sunday schools, Bibles, and tracts to the outsiders in the hopes of influencing their morals. As the executive committee of the Home Missionary Society, in appealing for funds in 1839, put it: "The Gospel is the most economical police on earth." The most important of these benevolent societies were the American Home Missionary Society (founded in 1826), the American Tract Society (1825), the American Bible Society (1816), the American Education Society (1816), and the American Sunday School Union (1824). These, plus a host of small institutions, individual churches, and individual philanthropists, similarly concerned that the movement away from a settled community effected a deleterious character change in people, provided much of the capital for the overexuberant expansion of higher education in the first half of the nineteenth century. They did so in hopes that such educational institutions would reassert the authority of religion and civilization on a population that seemed to those unfamiliar with it—as the easterners largely were—a dangerous source of disorder and political and social disruption.[14]

Religion and religious instruction were very much a part of the work carried on by most of the academies and colleges founded before the Civil War—as they were of those founded after. This religious orientation manifested the concern many of the supporters of higher education in this period felt for the morals and character of those for whom the institutions were being built. The character of this religious orientation was largely nondenominational, although distinctly Protestant and mili-

[14] The best discussion of these societies is Clifford Griffin, *Their Brothers' Keepers: Moral Stewardship in the United States, 1800–1865* (New Brunswick, N. J., 1960); quotations are from pp. 59–60, 111. Griffin quotes on p. 111 *The Home Missionary*, XII (May, 1839), 9–10.

tantly anti-Catholic. But it is not particularly helpful to describe this period in the history of higher education as one of denominational rivalry in the founding of schools and to attribute the overbuilding of the era to that competition. Each denomination, the argument goes, in adjusting to the voluntarism necessitated by the separation of church and state formalized by the Bill of Rights, sought to gain and keep converts. One important device for furthering this evangelistic enterprise was the denominational school and college. Thus, the argument continues, each denomination rushed to found schools in as many areas as possible so that each school could inculcate the religious dogma of the denomination which controlled it and win for the denomination a much firmer hold on the students who passed through the school. These students, thanks to their training, would be less likely to break the voluntary bonds of denominational membership. Furthermore, it is argued, the various sects sought schools in which to train ministers.

Although this argument from denominational competition has a certain superficial logic, it does not adequately fit the facts of the first half of the nineteenth century. Denominational competition was not an important characteristic or cause of the development of institutions of higher education in that era. The historian of higher education in the antebellum period finds the typical school under a nominal denominational identification, but open to all without tests of religious faith. The school served a geographic rather than a religious community and was attended by students from the surrounding territory, no matter what their religious affiliation—if any. The school engaged in no doctrinal inculcation beyond commonly accepted tenets of Christian morality. Most of the colleges founded before the 1840s took on the denominational coloring of their backers because these backers stipulated that a majority of the institution's trustees must belong to a certain denomination. Often, however, another denomination was given perpetual minority status on the board of trustees in order to secure support for the new venture among town leaders who did not share the denominational affiliation of most of the backers. At the same time, in order to make the college as attractive as possible to all comers, the backers prohibited religious tests for either faculty or students. As Frederick Rudolph has pointed out, the "nineteenth-century American college could not support itself on a regimen of petty sectarianism; there simply were not enough petty sectarians or, if there were, there was no way of getting them to the petty sectarian colleges in sufficient numbers."[15]

On the other hand, there was little likelihood that Americans would maintain nondenominational colleges in this era. Virtually every educational institution established in the nineteenth century set out to instill

[15] Rudolph, *American College and University*, 69.

piety and virtue in students and to explain to them the power and the beauty of God. All the colleges were Christian. But such a designation was hardly enough in that era—a person was, after all, a Christian in a particular way—a Methodist or a Congregationalist or what-have-you. There was no recognized general Christian way of serving God or of worshipping Him. One served and worshipped as a member of a denomination. After all, chapel services had to take some form—a form of communion and a form of the Lord's Prayer had to be agreed upon. "Nondenominational" forms of worship had yet to be invented. Even the ostensibly nonsectarian state colleges, perhaps with the exception of the University of Virginia, were thought to have been "captured" by denominations. But the nature of this "capture" reveals how unimportant denomination affiliation was from the evangelistic point of view. A college was considered captured whenever a majority of the trustees belonged to a single denomination, but the denominational affiliation of the conquerors need not have effected any change in the operation or the personnel of the college.

Denominational identification in the years before 1830 or 1840 seems largely to have been accidental in that the new institution took whatever denominational form that most of its trustees favored. Some denominational identification was virtually necessary to the functioning of the institution, and the natural and simple thing to do was to adopt the religion of the social leaders, the boosters, of the community in which the institution was housed. These were the men who became the trustees. Between 1830 and the Civil War, events become somewhat more complicated. Some academies and colleges, desperate for money, sought to emphasize their denominational leanings in order to convince churches that they merited financial support. These solicitations met with varying success—one college changed its identification three times in as many years in hopes of appealing successfully to some denomination. Also, very gradually after 1830 regional and national administrators of the various denominations grew interested in seeking or building schools in each area with which to affiliate. They took the first steps toward building a network of schools to which members of the denomination could send their children and be sure they were receiving proper religious instruction. But only after the Civil War did the denominations begin to play a central role in organizing, locating, and supporting higher education. By then the spirit of community involvement had weakened considerably. In explaining the overbuilding of colleges and academies in the antebellum period, however, general concern for morality and social control are much more important than denominational competition.

The fourth reason that academies and colleges were so overbuilt in the decades before the Civil War was that local social leaders and their children derived considerable social status from these institutions. Institutions of higher education had economic value for these social leaders in that they increased the wealth of the community. Just as important was the fact that those institutions confirmed (or established) the social leaders' status in that community. The social leaders were, of course, the influentials in the community. They might be like the people responsible for the founding of Phillips Andover and Phillips Exeter, in 1778 and 1783 respectively, or like the founders of Lafayette College in Pennsylvania. Samuel Phillips, Jr., was descended from a long line of Harvard-trained Puritan clergymen; his father was a prominent Massachusetts businessman and politician. Samuel was a member of the General Court of the Massachusetts Bay Colony; he was a member of the convention that framed the constitution of Massachusetts; he became a judge, a state senator, and, at the time of his death, lieutenant governor. Two other members of the family assisted Samuel in establishing the two academies which still bear the family name—one a doctor, the other a leading judge in New Hampshire. The fact that the Phillips family could afford to give the two academies an endowment estimated somewhere between $100,-000 and $150,000—a lot of money at the time—attests to the family's prominence.

In underdeveloped regions, the patterns of influence and leadership were somewhat different. Whereas the Phillipses had both the influence and the money to start their ventures virtually alone, leaders in new towns depended on their ability to mobilize support from others. These leaders, typically, did not have deep social and economic roots in the community. They were men who hoped to establish their wealth and their prestige by developing the communities to which they had recently moved. James Madison Porter, lawyer, canal promoter, and leading citizen-booster of Easton, Pennsylvania, is a case in point. Recently settled in that small underdeveloped community seventy miles north of Philadelphia, Porter took note of the economic stimulus that colleges provided such a small town. In 1824 he published an advertisement calling on all interested citizens to meet to discuss the founding of such a college. The meeting was a success and a board of thirty-nine men was appointed. "This number included several promoters, a number of businessmen, lawyers, a physician, two newspapermen, and two hotelkeepers. Not one of the number had been born in Easton; only one had attended college."[16] The four ministers in the town were excluded so as to prevent any appearance of clerical control. Porter and the other trustees felt that their personal success depended on Easton's growth. In 1824 the town's prospects seemed good. The town, largest in eastern Pennsylvania north of Philadelphia, lay across wagon routes to the West at the confluence of the

---

[16] Boorstin, *National Experience*, 156. A more detailed discussion can be found in David B. Skillman, *Biography of a College* (Easton, Pa., 1932), which confirms Boorstin's account.

Lehigh and Delaware rivers upon which coal and shipbuilding materials were sent to Philadelphia. They expected Lafayette College, as it was called, to draw needed attention to their community. Easton was in an eastern locale but was a town similar in its newness, pretension, and leaders to hundreds of similar towns newly founded in undeveloped regions from Maine to Minnesota.

Status was an important motive in the founding of the academies and colleges. The Phillipses looked on higher education as a way of maintaining the traditional social order and the traditional separation of classes in a society awash with revolutionary theory and paeans to the dignity and equality of all men. Samuel Phillips wholeheartedly supported the revolutionary impulse to secure liberty and purity for Americans, but he did not think that his sons were no better than any other men living in America. He felt that the greatest weakness of the Dummer School, which he had attended between 1765 and 1767, was that it sought to educate charity students along with paying ones.[17] Academy training would give his sons a refinement, an esprit, and a sense of moral character and social responsibility that would make manifest the separation in which he believed. For a man like James Madison Porter, ambitiously trying to carve an upper-middle-class status for himself, sending his offspring to an academy or college would lend them a refinement and a status to help set them (and him) above most of the people living in northeastern Pennsylvania.

Noah Webster noted how differences in language abilities separated people. In one sense, this is what the academies and colleges were all about. The most characteristic feature of their instruction was its emphasis on the classical languages. American educational reformers and theorists from Benjamin Franklin on stressed the need for instruction in more practical subjects in the academies—they argued that the study of English and of the arithmetical skills necessary to the merchant and the engineer should form the core of the academy curriculum. Francis Wayland repeated these injunctions and applied them to the colleges in 1842. But Wayland's efforts at reforming the curriculum in the 1840s came to naught just as Franklin's had one hundred years earlier, and the study of Latin and Greek continued as the most important aspect of instruction in these schools.

Why? Because a knowledge of Latin and Greek, however superficial, gave its possessor something—a skill, but more important a sense of refinement—that his fellow citizens did not have. Speeches and conversations of the period were filled with gratuitous snippets of Latin or Greek

---

[17] Andover's first president preceptor, Eliphalet Pearson, modified Phillips' stand on this issue to the extent that the academy did provide some scholarship funds for indigent students. On Samuel Phillips and his academies, see especially James McLachlan, *American Boarding Schools: A Historical Study* (New York, 1970).

that served to manifest the culture and the refinement of the speaker. Ability to include such quotations served as a kind of badge of status, just as proper pronunciation of English served to separate the classes from the masses. Thus, while the elementary schools, at least in theory, sought to break down class barriers by stressing common training in English, institutions of higher education continued to erect other linguistic separations.

A knowledge of the classics, superficial or not, became a key means of access to the professions and to positions of leadership that society felt should be restricted to educated men. Although the academies and colleges served primarily the children of social leaders, they did not restrict their admissions to these people—they could not afford to. Thus, they afforded a means of mobility to young men bent on bettering themselves. Attendance at these institutions furnished the upwardly mobile youngster with all the patina of culture and refinement that a classical education could give plus the opportunity to mix with and adopt the values of the offspring of social leaders.

A great deal of the mixing, the sharing of values, and the building of cohesion among these upper-middle-class students and those who aspired to that status occurred in the student-organized clubs that appeared in the academies and colleges soon after the turn of the century. At the colleges, Greek letter fraternities appeared in the late twenties and thirties, but literary and debating societies had appeared long before. These societies functioned much as did fraternities in later years. All these clubs, societies, and fraternities carried out some of the most important goals of higher education in this period. The constitution of Phillips Exeter proposed to prepare students for "the Great End And Real Business Of Living" and stressed that "the *first* and *principal* object of this Institution is the promotion of true Piety and Virtue; the *second,* instruction in the English, Latin, and Greek Languages, etc."[18] In the literary and debating clubs, the students gathered to exercise their language skills and to discuss contemporary issues of morality and government—issues affecting the "real business of living." In a curriculum that was dominated by rote memorization, these clubs served an important function by transmitting common social values to students.

Thus, where the elementary schools may have been preparing students to enter comfortably the local power structure in the middling and lower ranks, the colleges and academies were preparing students to enter the local leadership group—to become influentials themselves. They provided badges of status and a sense of cohesiveness among the leaders-to-be. These higher institutions in effect socialized the students to the lead-

[18] Quoted in Elmer E. Brown, *The Making of Our Middle Schools: An Account of the Development of Secondary Education in the United States* (New York, 1903), 195.

ership function and to the values of the local leadership group. They also socialized students to the spirit of local boosterism—there the students were at the very center of the issue, their schooling and their future careers often dependent on whether local promoters could assemble enough money to pay the professors and keep the school in business. They lived in the midst of fund-raising campaigns and all the inevitable huckstering connected with selling the future of the town and its institutions. The schools also socialized the future leaders to the sense of separateness between themselves and others—that they stood somewhat above the common man with special privileges and special responsibilities, with opportunities and duties different from those of the common man. In the early 1840s Isaiah Boott came home from college for summer vacation to visit friends and relatives. "Here for the first time did I begin to feel how perceptibly education separated those of equal age. Tho I had been but two years at college, it seemed that my schoolmates had gone backward half a century. I saw there was a wide difference between us. I supposed that society was becoming rough and going back to heathenism as fast as possible. But the fact was that my comrades were where I left them and I had gone forward."[19] And this, of course, was for many of the students, parents, and founders of institutions of higher learning the whole point of the experience—that these institutions would foster a spirit of separateness, of leadership, and of social responsibility among those lucky enough to attend them.

The academies and colleges were not intent on forming an aristocracy in America; rather, they were contributing to the formation of a broad American middle, or upper middle, class. Their students would become the promoters, the land developers, the lawyers, doctors, ministers, and teachers, the merchants and manufacturers, and the statesmen and politicians of the future. The very diffuseness of the academy and college movement prevented those institutions from assuming aristocratic pretensions. There were too many schools and too many pupils.

Evaluation of the effects of this overbuilding on higher education is very difficult. A number of historians have lamented the fact that the overbuilding of institutions of higher education in the antebellum period caused a serious decline in the quality of education at the secondary and tertiary level. Some historians have seen the antebellum period as the nadir of higher education in which anti-intellectual evangelicals displaced qualified educators and the value of higher education became debased. Much of what these historians say is true—higher education during this period was lamentably bad, for serious overbuilding did cause educational considerations to suffer because of financial and other reasons. And it is possible to argue that, had the money spent on higher education

[19] Quoted in David Potts, "Baptist Colleges" (dissertation draft, chapter 4, p. 29).

been concentrated on a few institutions, the United States would have had colleges and secondary schools ranking with the best in the world.

On the other hand, one must note that the diffusion of cultural and educational institutions and the intertwining of local economic and cultural interests vastly increased the population's interest in cultural activity. For all the superficiality of this interest in culture, for all the interest in form and disregard of content, such diffusion and such stress on the economic and local advantages of education contributed a great deal in teaching Americans to value education. Further, it is quite possible that the diffusion of higher education—however debased—may have played a major role in encouraging the economic growth of the United States in the nineteenth century and in strengthening its institutions. What higher education may have lost in intellectual quality through diffusion of effort, it may have gained in popular support and interest.

GUIDE TO FURTHER READING

FREDERICK RUDOLPH, *The American College and University: A History* (New York, 1962), remains the most thorough analysis of the antebellum college in the United States. His bibliography of institutional histories is the best and most conveniently available. The early chapters of OSCAR and MARY HANDLIN, *The American College and American Culture: Socialization as a Function of Higher Education* (New York, 1970), and more generally their essay on *Facing Life: Youth and Family in American History* (Boston, 1971) examine, with a good deal of perception, the experience of leaving home. RICHARD HOFSTADTER and WALTER P. METZGER, *The Development of Academic Freedom in the United States* (New York, 1955), Part I (published separately by Hofstadter in 1961), is the best account of that topic and a useful introduction to the antebellum academic experience in general. RICHARD HOFSTADTER and WILSON SMITH, eds., *American Higher Education: A Documentary History*, 2 vols. (Chicago, 1961), is a model collection of primary sources. An investigation of the sources of support for antebellum institutions, and an excellent introduction to the concepts of "public" and "private," are included in JOHN S. WHITEHEAD, *The Separation of College and State: Columbia, Dartmouth, Harvard, and Yale, 1776–1876* (New Haven, Conn., 1973). In *Professors and Public Ethics: Studies of Northern Moral Philosophers before the Civil War* (Ithaca, N. Y., 1956), WILSON SMITH examines ethical theorists and public policy in several antebellum institutions. Collegiate innovations based upon student requirements are explored in DAVID F. ALLMENDINGER, *Paupers and Scholars: The Transformation of Student Life in Nineteenth-Century New England* (New York, 1975). DAVID MADSEN, *The National University: Enduring Dream of the U. S. A.* (Detroit, 1966), remains the standard survey.

DONALD G. TEWKSBURY, *The Founding of American Colleges and Universities Before the Civil War: With Particular Reference to the Religious Influence Bearing Upon the College Movement* (New York, 1932), remains the standard introduction to antebellum college founding, but should be supplemented by NATALIE A. NAYLOR's critique, "The Ante-Bellum College Movement: A Reappraisal of Tewksbury's Founding of American Colleges and Universities," *History of Education Quarterly,* XIII (Fall, 1973), 261–274. DAVID POTTS examines the impact that localism had upon the secular nature of denominational institutions before the Civil War in "Baptist Colleges in the Development of American Society, 1812–1861" (Unpublished Dissertation, Harvard University, 1967) and "American Colleges in the Nineteenth Century: From Localism to Denominationalism," *History of Education Quarterly,* XI (Winter, 1971), 363–380. DANIEL BOORSTIN, *The Americans: The National Experience* (New York, 1965), suggests the influence of local "boosterism" upon the antebellum movement to establish institutions of higher learning. GEORGE P. SCHMIDT's volumes on *The Old Time College President* (New York, 1930) and *The Liberal Arts College: A Chapter in American Cultural History* (New Brunswick, N. J., 1957) remain useful.

The American academy and other nonpublic school educational institutions are surveyed in ROBERT MIDDLEKAUFF, *Ancients and Axioms: Secondary Education in Eighteenth-Century New England* (New Haven, Conn., 1963), THEODORE R. SIZER, ed., *The Age of the Academies* (New York, 1964), ROBERT F. SEYBOLT, *The Evening School in Colonial America* (Urbana, Ill., 1925), SEYBOLT, *The Public Schools of Colonial Boston, 1635–1775* (Cambridge, Mass., 1935), and ELMER E. BROWN, *The Making of Our Middle Schools: An Account of the Development of Secondary Education in the United States* (New York, 1903)

PART II

The Quest for Commonality, 1830–1860

CHAPTER 3

The Common
School Movement

THE FORTY-YEAR PERIOD BEGINNING IN 1830 SAW A GREAT REVITALIZATION of interest in public elementary schooling. The causes of this revitalization were complex and its results were ambiguous. The movement occurred in nearly every state in the Union, appearing earliest in New York, Pennsylvania, and New England and spreading westward and into the South somewhat later. The common school movement was a series of state movements for reform of elementary education; it can be considered a national movement only because these individual state movements were roughly congruent in time and in goals and because the various state reform leaders communicated with and learned from each other. As conditions and personalities varied considerably from state to state, each state movement had unique features. In what follows these unique features have been suppressed in an effort to present a general explanation of the causes and effects of the national common school reform movement. Much of the discussion will draw on examples from the Massachusetts reform movement, which was best documented and most influential in other states. The reader must bear in mind that the explanation for antebellum school reform developed here must be altered somewhat when it is applied to any of the specific state reform movements.

The common school movement had three goals. The first was to provide a free elementary education for every white child living in the United States. The second was to create a trained educational profession.

Normal schools or courses for the training of teachers and a codified theory of pedagogy that could be taught in those teacher training institutions had to be established. Reformers also sought to maintain higher standards for appointing school teachers. The third goal was to establish some form of state control over local schools. This last goal was the lynchpin of the movement for, without central control, none of the other goals was possible. As long as the autonomy of the district or town school committees went unchallenged, uniform criteria relating to attendance, the quality of school building, curriculum, and teacher qualifications would be unenforceable. In the early years of the movement, especially, lack of central authority repeatedly stymied the reformers' efforts. The great school reformer Horace Mann, appointed secretary to the Board of Education in Massachusetts in 1837, had to rely only on persuasion and publicity to effect the reform goals he sought. Mann traveled the Commonwealth encouraging change and he published extensive annual statistics on education to "show up" the laggard districts, but he had no power to enforce standards. Only when states began to centralize authority by assuming financial leverage over the local districts could state officials like Mann enforce standards and reform by threatening to withhold money from offending local districts. This centralization of authority and power occurred only to a limited degree and only very gradually over the nineteenth century. The reformers' limited success with centralization meant that other portions of their reform program were carried out haphazardly, or not at all.

I

The most widely advertised and popularly appealing aspect of the reform movement was its effort to increase school attendance. And here is where the results were most ambiguous. The common school movement should not be considered as a transition from few public elementary schools to many public elementary schools. Most communities in the settled portions of the United States had long provided public education of some sort. The common school reformers told their audiences that reform was imperative at the time because there had been a serious weakening of educational resolve in the country since 1800, because newer generations of Americans had refused to carry on the colonial and revolutionary traditions of widespread education for all. School attendance figures for the antebellum period are notoriously difficult to interpret, but it appears fairly clear that the "weakening of resolve" was a figment of the reformers' imagination, or more likely a fictional construct which they used to elicit more immediate support from their audience. The early nineteenth century seems actually to have seen a gradual but steady increase in educational effort at the elementary level. In New York, where the pre-1830 enrollment statistics are the most accurate, Albert Fishlow found no change in the percentage of children aged 5 to 19 enrolled in school between 1795 and 1815. From 1815 to 1823 he found a 25 percent increase, which he attributes to the release of energies following the War of 1812. The enrollment rate then held constant until 1830, when it stood at 73.8 percent. By 1840 Fishlow found that the percentage of school-age children in school (those aged 5–19) had dropped somewhat to 69.4. He noted a similar decline in Rhode Island, Connecticut, and Massachusetts in that decade. Because of faulty statistics this decrease may be more apparent than real, but more likely the decrease reflects the large influx of Catholic immigrants to the industrial areas of those states whose children did not attend school.[1] Another gauge of educational effort is the number of school days provided for each school-age child. Here Fishlow finds, in New York, a slow and gradual increase—from 14 days in 1800 to 20 in 1840. Fishlow feels that his figures represent accurately the curve of educational effort throughout the settled states, if not the absolute percentages from state to state.

Fishlow extended his analysis to 1860. Nationally enrollment increased strongly, from approximately 40 percent of the children aged 5 to 19 in school in 1840, to 50 to 56 percent in 1850, and 57 to 60 percent in 1860. (These percentages, of course, would be higher if historians could work with the normal elementary school-age group of 5–14, but the census did not record the population statistics that way.) These figures indicate, of course, a growth in attendance but how much of that growth can be attributed to the common school movement is problematical. Most of the increase occurred in the West (the Ohio River valley and Michigan and Wisconsin) and South (especially Georgia, Alabama, Mississippi, and Louisiana) rather than in the East. Much of that increase must have been due to continued extension of the district school system and to local boosterism in the developing West and Southwest. Common school reformers were weakest in those sections. In the East, where they were strongest, attendance figures generally leveled off after the 1830s. On the other hand, and probably as a result of the common school movement, the length of the school year significantly increased—in New York from 20 days in 1840 to 40 in 1861.

From 1840 to 1860 expenditures on education in the United States quadrupled while population did not quite double in the same period.

[1] Albert Fishlow, "The American Common School Revival: Fact or Fancy?", in Henry Rosovsky, ed., *Industrialization in Two Systems* (New York, 1966), 40–67. On attendance during the early nineteenth century see Carl Kaestle, *The Evolution of an Urban School System: New York City, 1750–1850* (Cambridge, Mass., 1973), Stanley K. Schultz, *The Culture Factory: Boston Public Schools, 1789–1860* (New York, 1973), and Maris Vinovskis, "Trends in Massachusetts Education, 1826–1860," *History of Education Quarterly*, XII (Winter, 1972), 501–530.

Again it is unclear how much of this increase can be credited to common school reform. Fishlow found that expenditures for education taken as a percentage of estimated Gross National Product equaled .8 percent in 1860. Only Germany exceeded the United States in percentage of GNP devoted to education, spending 1 percent on education. France spent .4 percent and England less. The white literacy figure for the United States of approximately 90 percent in this period was equaled only by the figures for Germany and Scotland. England and France were far behind. But the United States' educational effort in its period of rapid economic development in the nineteenth century appears almost insignificant when compared to the educational efforts of modern developing countries. In the late 1950s, 56 developing countries spent on the average 3.3 percent of their GNP on education; none spent less than 2 percent. The United States did not spend 2 percent of GNP on education until after 1900; 1970 expenditure on education equaled 7.5 percent of GNP in the United States.[2]

II

Whatever the statistics on attendance and length of school year and magnitude of educational effort show, they do not appear to demonstrate any revolutionary changes in the amount of schooling in the United States that can be associated with the common school movement. If anything, the common school movement might be said to have energized an already developing increase in educational effort in the United States. The common school movement had a more profound effect in ways that cannot be measured quantitatively. The rhetoric, efforts, and accomplishments of the common school movement set terms for educational debate and established patterns of professional aspiration and control that have persisted almost without challenge until the present day. The essence of the common school movement was its rhetorical commitment to the deliberate use of education as a tool for social manipulation and social progress. Educational control had to be centralized and educators trained to adhere to a single professional standard in order to accomplish this manipulation of society.

This emphasis on schooling for social manipulation explains the most distinctive element in the common school movement's rhetoric—the im-

[2] It must be noted that the authority with which these figures appear in the text does an injustice to Professor Fishlow and to other econometricians and statistical historians who have so laboriously constructed carefully qualified estimates of educational effort for the early nineteenth century from sparse, conflicting, and sometimes inaccurate statistics. Although stated precisely, these numbers are estimates that illuminate orders of magnitude rather than precise quantitative descriptions.

perative to get all children, and especially urban children, into school. The need for an educated electorate still dominated the speeches of schooling's advocates: If all males have the right to vote, society's interests require that each should be educated. To insure that mothers would correctly nurture children, half of whom were future voters, women should be educated even though they did not vote. But the rhetoric of the common school reformers contained a new urgency, an urgency that sometimes went to the extent of demanding that all children be forced into school. The mere establishment of educational institutions was insufficient; children must attend them if the schools were to accomplish their task of improving society. The idea of compulsory education was anathema to many in the laissez-faire atmosphere of nineteenth-century America and school reformers were very chary of suggesting it, especially before the Civil War. But the reformers' writings are full of hints of a desire to solve the problem by forcing parents to send their children to school. Reformers identified poor parents as the offenders—beginning a tradition in which educators blame poor parents for the failures of the schools—arguing that they kept their children away from school in order that they might work on the farm or in the factory to increase the family income. Industrial states, beginning in the late 1830s, adopted attendance laws which applied only to children working in factories and required them to attend school for three months each year. These laws were aimed at poor parents who were, no doubt, less able to defend themselves against what middle-class parents would have successfully opposed as unwarranted interference with parental prerogative. More honored in the breach than in the letter, these laws foreshadowed those to come mandating statewide compulsory education for all children. Massachusetts and New York, in 1852 and 1853 respectively, adopted the nation's first compulsory education laws. Other states passed laws after the Civil War but the pattern became universal only when Mississippi accepted the principle in 1918.

The common school reformers were also quite concerned with establishing age grading in the common schools and with standardizing textbooks. As we have seen, the absence of grading and of uniform school books had greatly reduced the efficiency of the district schools. School reformers sought vigorously to eliminate these inefficient practices, for there was no hope of financing for all children the leisurely-paced training given in the district schools. The reform movement's economic feasibility required that children move through the common school rapidly so as to free space and teacher time for more children. The reformers considered the widespread establishment of the age-graded school as one of their prime accomplishments.

Another indication of the reformers' concern with getting every child into school and keeping him there until he had learned rudimentary skills and social virtues was their willingness to change the curriculum and the pedagogical approach in order to attract the unschooled. For example, some reformers in New York were so eager to enroll Catholic children whose parents were hostile to the Protestant flavor of the city's schools that they agreed to give the city's Catholic bishop a voice in the appointment of teachers and selection of texts for the Catholic children. Reformers from Horace Mann to E. A. Sheldon were constantly tampering with the curriculum and pedagogical forms in order to make schooling more attractive and more effective. Their discussions suggest that they sought to sell education to children who had so far rejected it.

The capstone of the common school reformers' efforts to enroll all children, and especially those of the lower, "alienated" classes, was the free school. Too often historians of education in the United States have viewed the creation of the free school as the reformers' supreme goal. It is better understood as a means of raising attendance at elementary schools so that those common schools could achieve their major goals of teaching common values to all children. Free schools were meant to eliminate the situation in which the poor did not attend the district or public schools because even the very small "rate" or tuition payment required was beyond their means. In the rural districts poverty was relatively slight and rates might be informally excused for the one or two families that found themselves unable to pay them. In cities and manufacturing and port towns, however, it was a different problem altogether. Here poverty was immense and highly concentrated; whole neighborhoods of families were unable to pay rates and their children were thus excluded from school. In a first attempt to deal with this problem philanthropists financed charity schools or positions for charity scholars in the regular schools. Neither alternative was very effective. Because the poor found the process of declaring themselves impoverished and the stigma of "charity scholar" that their children carried too demeaning, many boycotted the charity schemes. Furthermore, well-to-do parents did not like the idea of paying to send their children to a school when poor children came free. They wished a more exclusive schooling for their money. Paying students tended to withdraw from the schools containing charity scholars leaving those schools exclusively populated by poor children. The free schools, supported entirely by taxation and state grants, solved all of these problems. Everyone went to school "free" so that no child was especially identified as unable to pay. Similarly, the middle and upper classes objected less to mixed economic classes in the same school under these circumstances, especially since they were paying for public education whether their children attended or not. And the free school mechanism provided for a slight redistribution of wealth or income that benefited the poor: taxes derived largely from the property of the middle and upper classes supported schooling for children of all economic classes. The abolition of rates and the establishment of a free school system would, the reformers hoped, remove the last barrier that prevented the poor and the alienated from attending school. As we shall see, the reformers' hopes were too sanguine. Foregone income rather than tuition bills had been the most important economic barrier keeping the poor and the immigrant out of school. Nor were economic reasons the only ones that kept children out of school.

Although it was perhaps the most important single legislative goal of the common school movement, the reformers had a difficult time effecting the abolition of rates. Opposition to raising taxes for schools was widespread. New York State did not abolish rates statewide until 1867; Connecticut, Rhode Island, and Michigan waited even longer. But where it counted the most, the reformers were more successful. In the cities where the poor congregated, rates were abolished much earlier. Most large cities in the United States eliminated rates a full quarter of a century before their states did. New York City, for example, abolished rates in 1832, Buffalo in 1838, and Rochester in 1848. Once the battle for free schools had been won—not without a fight, however—in these cities, the reformers thought rate bills in the rest of the state fairly unimportant. They were committed to free schools less as a democratic principle than as a means of getting the poor into schools. The concern for enrolling the poor that underlay most of the important reforms advocated by the common school reformers grew out of the realization that schools could not be used for social manipulation, for social control, until the vast majority of poor children, who needed the control most, were in attendance.

III

Who were the common school reformers and what kind of reformers were they? Perhaps the best way of comprehending this educational reform movement is in political terms. The desire to use schools for social manipulation or social control was part of the Whig drive to reorder American society. The Whiggish nature of common school reform is evident in the fact that the majority of the reformers—usually conservative, middle class, and often clergymen—identified with the Whig party. Two of the most outstanding of the common school reformers—Mann and Henry Barnard in Connecticut—were themselves Whig politicians before they were appointed to the educational offices that brought them into the center of school reform. Further, more often than not, Whig legislatures passed common school laws and Democrats formed the most vocal opposition, especially to the centralizing features of such legislation.

Educators and educational historians have long comforted themselves with a belief that the common school movement resulted from the democratic sentiments of educators responding to the needs of the working classes who sought improved educational facilities in order to better their lot and take their rightful place in the political and economic life of the nation. Since the Democratic or Jacksonian party is known as the party of the common man, school reform is often vaguely linked with Jacksonian reform and the progress of the Democratic party. But, however much common school reform may have benefited the common man, he was not a leader in its development; and the ideology of common school reform was much closer to Whiggery than to Jacksonianism.

The Whig party was a kind of transition party between the Federalists of the early national period and the Republican party that was established in the 1850s when the Whig party split over the slavery issue. The Whigs came to power nationally in the 1840s and had won power in some states in the thirties. The party's leadership represented the upper and middle classes, industrialists, large bankers, large farmers who sought internal improvements (canals and roads) to enhance their ability to market their products, southern commercial and banking interests and those planters dependent on them, and native American artisans. The Whig party came together in large part as an anti-Jackson party and, as such, contained all manner of men who for personal and/or ideological reasons were unhappy with the policies of the party in power. Broadly speaking, however, the Whigs were the party of the established middle and upper classes, of men who had inherited their high status rather than achieved it. It was the party of the elite and of those who felt their interests to be similar to those of the elite. Whigs were generally economically progressive and socially conservative. The established professions—law, medicine, and religion—were heavily Whig and the party had close ties with organized Protestant religion. It was from this group that most of the common school reformers came.

Despite the diversity within the party and its usual character as an opposition party, it is possible to describe a Whig ideology that was held by the more prominent leaders of the party, if not by the great majority of its followers. The Whig party supported an active role for the government in the stimulation and direction of economic activity, while the Democrats were generally more sympathetic to laissez-faire policies prohibiting governmental intervention. Lee Benson has characterized the distinction between the parties as one between the Whigs' positive liberalism and the Democrats' negative liberalism.[3] The Democrats believed in leaving the individual alone to do as he liked, believing that the max-

---

[3] Lee Benson, *The Concept of Jacksonian Democracy: New York as a Test Case* (Princeton, N. J., 1961), especially 86–109.

imum freedom for the individual would lead to the greatest improvement of the society. They also called for the widest possible decentralization of power, believing that the concentration of power, especially in the hands of the state, inevitably interfered with individual freedom. The Jacksonians were instrumental in seeking to do away with the system of chartering new economic ventures. The Whigs, on the other hand, while not opposed to individual freedom, did wish to subordinate individual economic freedom to higher concerns of social good and economic growth. They wished to retain the charter system and the power of the government to stimulate and guide economic development which that system provided. The Whigs were quite progressive in supporting economic growth and in building economic institutions capable of serving a national economy. Much of the Democratic economic ideology suggests that the Democrats sought to maintain the localistic economy of an earlier day in which each small geographic area was economically independent, and the individual yeoman's farm and the individual artisan's shop were the most important economic units. The Whigs, on the other hand, understood that the nature of the United States economy was changing—that all areas were economically interdependent, that the factory employing hundreds of hands to run complex machinery was replacing the individual farm and shop as the significant economic unit. The Whigs saw that the economy was growing and industrializing, and they welcomed and sought to stimulate those changes.

In a way, Whiggery was a form of national boosterism—the Whigs anticipated a great future for the United States just as the local boosters did for their local areas. Henry Clay, congressman from Kentucky from 1811 until his death in 1852 and three times unsuccessful candidate for the presidency, illustrates Whig support of economic growth. Clay began his career as a booster of Lexington in its fight with Louisville for domination of Kentucky's trade. But then his boosterism went national: he was a leader of the War Hawks, who urged the United States to go to war against Britain in 1812 because Britain refused to honor those portions of the treaty ending the Revolutionary War requiring her to give up her outposts west of the Alleghenies. Clay's national boosterism became even clearer in his advocacy of what he called the American System, a four-point program aimed, in the words of one historian, at "building up the wealth and power of the republic, [at] shaping for the United States a grand destiny that would be carved out in proud independence from old Europe."[4] Clay called for a high tariff that would protect from foreign competition the products of American (home) industry—the theory being that because, in the early stages of industrialization in the United States, American workers and factories were neither as efficient nor as

[4] Glyndon G. Van Deusen, *The Jacksonian Era, 1828–1848* (New York, 1959), 59.

productive as English ones making the same products, a protective tariff must be established to prevent cheaper goods manufactured in England from driving American goods off even the American market. Thus protection to these young industries would keep them viable while they were growing and, Clay argued, once they became mature, they would be as efficient as European industry and no longer need tariff protection. Clay recommended the high tariff in order to encourage the industrialization of the nation. Industrialization, in turn, would provide home markets for the products of American agriculture. Unlike earlier forms of economic organization, industrialization required large numbers of workingmen who needed food grown by others. Clay envisioned an independent United States in which the trading cycle was complete within the borders of the country. Until his time the United States was part of the European trade cycle, sending raw materials and agricultural goods to Europe in return for manufactured goods. Clay hoped that in the future American farmers would sell their products to American workingmen and American factories would sell their goods to American farmers. He also called for nationally financed internal improvements which would improve interregional communication and facilitate interregional trade in the United States. These improvements were to be financed from the sale of public land in the West and from tariff revenues. These internal improvements—chiefly canals, some roads, and harbors—were meant to span the Appalachian mountains and to connect major cities with their hinterlands. Clay saw them as part of the federal government's responsibility to stimulate the economy. The fourth element in the American System was the Bank of the United States. This large central bank was to serve as the place of deposit for government funds and was to control, as much as was possible with the banking techniques of the day, the movement of currency and credit in such a way as to stimulate the economy. The Bank was a very primitive and loosely controlled forerunner of the Federal Reserve banking system. The Bank of the United States was first established in 1797 and was rechartered twenty years later. Congress rechartered it again in 1832 but President Jackson vetoed the recharter and opened the famous and complex bank war of the 1830s. Jackson's views prevailed and the Bank, like the other proposals of the American System, went down to defeat.

The American System violated the tenets of negative liberalism on almost all counts and Jacksonians fought it at every turn. Their opposition had two contradictory thrusts that represented both sides of the ambiguity that Marvin Meyers has located at the heart of "the Jacksonian persuasion."[5] It was opposed by those who opposed all industrialization

[5] Marvin Meyers, *The Jacksonian Persuasion: Politics and Belief* (Stanford, Calif., 1957), and Michael B. Katz, *The Irony of Early School Reform: Educational Innovation in Mid-Nineteenth Century Massachusetts* (Cambridge, Mass., 1968).

and economic growth in favor of retaining an economy of small farms and small shops. And it was opposed by those who favored achieving economic growth by freeing completely the entrepreneurial spirit of individuals and of independent communities to initiate profitable economic schemes. Both groups strongly opposed the American System's threatened interference with local control and local initiative. They based their opposition on the doctrine of states' rights. Everything not entrusted to the federal government in the Constitution was automatically reserved for the states and nowhere in the Constitution were internal improvements, central banking, or the encouragement of manufactures mentioned. Tariff, according to negative liberalism's reading of the Constitution, could be imposed for revenue only. The Whigs were never successful in implementing the American System. Not until the Civil War and the coming to power of the Republican party under Abraham Lincoln were the elements of the American System enacted at the national level. The philosophy of the American System, however, informed the Whigs' evaluation of social problems in the United States between 1830 and the Civil War and their proposed solutions to these problems.

Where did education or schooling fit into the Whig ideology? Clay's vision of the economy made education more vital to economic growth than it had been under earlier forms of economic organization. The older vision of the American economy advocated that the country develop the wealth and resources lying on and in the land, that it should be a land of farmers, loggers, miners, and trappers, and of merchants who helped move these resources to Europe in exchange for manufactured goods. Clay urged intensive investments in nonextractive industry and exploitation of America's population and that population's skills. Many Whigs believed that a population's industrial capabilities were related to its educational level, but they were confused as to just what the relation was. Abbott Lawrence, merchant, textile manufacturer, founder of the first American factory, co-founder of the manufacturing city that bears his name, philanthropist, and Whig congressman from Massachusetts, was typically confused. In 1846 he sought to convince a Virginia congressman of the virtues of the American System, and in doing so expiated on the close relation of education to efficient labor. Lawrence pointed out that when Virginia turned to manufacturing, as he thought it must, it should establish "such manufactures as may be adapted to the peculiar condition of your labor. There are two classes of labor; intelligent, and unintelligent; the former is that kind of labor which requires a considerable amount of mental culture, with active physical power. This combination is capable of applying Science to Art, and of producing results that are difficult, and oftentimes complicated." Tasks suitable for unintelligent laborers, on the other hand, could produce only coarse and common articles. The establishment of manufacturing would itself stimulate a "desire for knowledge" among the workers. "More education, more intellectual cultivation, will be desired by those engaged in the mechanical departments; and with this eagerness for knowledge will follow skill and cleverness in the use of tools, and then will follow the inventive power, for which [the workers of Massachusetts] have become so distinguished in the estimation of the world." In those words Lawrence suggested that industrialization would stimulate education. At other times he implied that education was a necessary stimulus to economic growth. "You cannot, I should suppose, expect to develop your resources, without a general system of popular education; it is the lever to all permanent improvement."[6]

But just how education served as a lever for permanent improvement, or even temporary improvement, is unclear. Every one of the school reformers wrote as if it were obvious that more and better schooling led to economic advance. It seemed so obvious, so much a part of the conventional wisdom, that no one took the trouble to explain just how what children learned in the common schools was going to make them more efficient or more inventive workers. But school reformers always made the claim. Education, Horace Mann wrote, "can raise more abundant harvests, and multiply the conveniences of domestic life; . . . it can build, transport, manufacture, mine, navigate, fortify; . . . a single new idea is often worth more to an individual than a hundred workmen,—and to a nation, than the addition of provinces to its territory. . . . Education has a power of ministering to our personal and material wants beyond all other agencies, whether excellence of climate, spontaneity of production, mineral resources, or mines of silver and gold."[7] Can Mann really have been talking of the district school system before 1840, or the common schools of his own day? Did rote memorization really serve so many functions and teach the youngster industrial skills?

The common school reformers were not arguing, as did the boosters, that the presence of educational institutions would bring wealth to a community through the extra buying power it attracted. Rather, they implied that learning the common school subjects improved a person's potential as a worker. References to Eli Whitney, inventor of the cotton gin and the interchangeable parts method of manufacturing rifles, and to Robert Fulton, inventor of the steamboat, run throughout their writing. Common schooling was supposed to increase greatly the number of inventors of this kind. Yet the reformers did not know how education

[6] Abbott Lawrence to William C. Rives (7 January, 1846) in *Letters from the Honorable Abbott Lawrence to the Honorable William C. Rives of Virginia* (Boston, 1846), 5–7.

[7] Horace Mann, *Fifth Annual Report of the Board of Education; Together with the Fifth Annual Report of the Secretary of the Board* (1842), 82–83. Henceforth, Mann's reports as secretary of the Board will be cited as *Annual Report.*

could accomplish these ends. Listen to Mann again: "An early awakening of the mind," he argued, "is a prerequisite to success in the useful arts." There is no argument there. Moreover, a worker must have the power to take correct mental pictures and to reproduce them. Also, he must be able to revive or reproduce "at will, all the impressions or ideas before obtained, and, also, the power of changing their collocations, of rearranging them into new forms, and of adding something to, or removing something from, the original perceptions, in order to make a more perfect plan or model." Again, few would care to argue with Mann on those points. "Now, every recitation in a school," he continued, in getting to the crucial point of explanation, "if rightly conducted, is a step towards the attainment of this wonderful power. With a course of studies judiciously arranged and diligently pursued through the years of minority, all the great phenomena of external nature, and the most important productions in all the useful arts, together with the principles on which they are evolved or fashioned, would be successfully brought before the understanding of the pupil. . . . When such a student goes out into life, he carries, as it were, a plan or model of the world, in his own mind."[8] Mann sounds as if he were trying to convince himself.

A good deal of recent historical work has been focused on possible relations between education and economic growth in the United States —using insights and conceptual tools from economics, planning, and political science as well as history. These studies have sought to compare the economic growth of the United States in the nineteenth century—a development about which surprisingly little is known—to the experience that nations have had in modernizing and industrializing in the mid-twentieth century. Such comparisons are likely to become one of the most fruitful areas of future research in the history of education in the United States, but as yet their results have been too meager and too conflicting to support any firm conclusions. Some argue that education is a modernization investment that precedes industrial growth—that industrial growth cannot take place until substantial investments in education have been made. Others argue the opposite—that education was something of a luxury, possible for large numbers of people only because of the economic surplus that modernization (and, in the case of the United States, abundant natural resources) made available for educational spending. In this view, education is only a by-product of economic development. The evidence presently assembled does not allow us to choose intelligently between the alternatives.

A smaller but related problem is why industry in the United States was so successful in using new techniques and new methods so rapidly while British industry, for example, was reluctant to adopt new methods.

[8] *Ibid.*, 105–107.

Did education have anything to do with the American capitalist's and workman's ability to discover new processes and to adapt flexibly to rapid change in industrial techniques. The inventiveness and adaptability of American industry and the American worker most impressed foreign visitors to the United States. Those traits explain much of the United States' rapid economic progress in the nineteenth century. One historian explains this trait as resulting from a lack of education. In European apprenticeship systems masters rigorously and carefully taught their apprentices the details of their trades. Their teaching was so careful and effective that trades passed almost unchanged from generation to generation, making it more difficult to introduce new methods or new machines in industry. In the United States apprenticeship was a weak institution in which trades were taught hastily and superficially. Because American workers lacked the careful "education" their European counterparts had received, they were more flexible and adaptable when faced with new problems and new methods.[9] But whether widespread common school education in the United States made any positive contribution to the skill and adaptability of the American workman remains unclear. The school reformers apparently were not clear how education helped, and modern research has not yet solved the problem either. The question remains very much open.

But the Whig school reformers were much more explicit in discussing another area in which education related to economic growth. Education would foster industrialization by teaching future workers to respect property, to work hard, and to accept their lot, if not happily, at least submissively. This aspect of schooling's role is clear in a questionnaire that Horace Mann sent to a group of factory owners and superintendents in 1841 in connection with his fifth report to the Massachusetts Board of Education.

> What . . . has been the effect of higher degrees of mental application and culture upon the domestic and social habits of persons in your employment? Is this class more cleanly in their persons, their dress and their households; and do they enjoy a greater immunity from those diseases which originate in a want of personal neatness and purity? Are they more exemplary in their deportment and conversation, devoting more time to intellectual pursuits or to the refining art of music, and spending their evenings and leisure hours more with their families, and less at places of resort for idle and dissipated men? Is a smaller portion of them addicted to intemperance? Are their houses kept in a superior condition? . . . Are their families better brought up, more respectably dressed, more regularly attendant upon the school and the church; and do their children, when arrived at years of maturity, enter upon the active scenes of life with better prospects of success? . . . [Do the edu-

[9] John E. Sawyer, "The Social Basis of the American System of Manufacturing," *Journal of Economic History,* XIV (1954), 361–379.

cated and uneducated differ in] regard to punctuality and fidelity in the performance of duties? . . . from which [the educated or the uneducated] have those who possess property and who hope to transmit it to their children, most to fear from secret aggression, or from such public degeneracy as will loosen the bands of society, corrupt the testimony of witnesses, violate the sanctity of the juror's oath and substitute as a rule of right, the power of a numerical majority, for the unvarying principles of justice?

To these very leading questions the owners and superintendents answered in kind. Educated workers, one wrote, "have more order and system; they not only keep their persons neater, but their machinery in better condition." Others spoke of greater punctuality, industriousness, and frugality among the educated. All felt their machinery was safer with the educated than with the uneducated.[10]

The superintendents never once spoke of reading, writing, or mathematics as skills that were useful in the factory and that distinguished the educated from those who had not gone to school. Skills taught in school and their possible contribution to economic growth did not concern the managers. They were concerned with the social virtue that they hoped schools would transmit. Mann and the factory managers depended on the schools to serve as the key agent for teaching morality.

Previously, the teaching of morality—regard for the rights of others, respect for property, deference to one's superiors, love of justice, commitment to hard work—had been a principal responsibility of the family, the church, and the community. Morality had not been considered a particularly important part of the school's business when it was thought of as its business at all. But the Whigs found, especially in urban and industrial environments, that the home and the church and the community were not performing their function as inculcators of morality. The Whigs faced the dilemma that the very economic changes that would make the United States a powerful independent nation were also undermining the "quality" of her population—undermining the moral fiber or character of Americans to the point that the nation might be destroyed from within. As Abbott Lawrence reminded his Virginia correspondent in discussing the relation of education and industrialization: "The elective franchise, in the hands of an ignorant and debased population, would very soon place our country in a state of anarchy."[11] The Whigs' search for an agency to inculcate morality testifies to their realization that, under the new economic and social conditions they had done so much to bring about, the family, church, and community had defaulted on their traditional function of socializing the young to the moral codes and values of the society, or at least to what the Whigs thought should be the moral

[10] Mann, *Fifth Annual Report*, 88–89, 90–110.
[11] Lawrence to Rives (7 January, 1846), in *Letters*, 7.

codes and values of the society. A great deal of the motivation behind common school reform in the era after 1830 grew from this Whig desire to establish centralized, efficient agencies that would superintend the moral development of the nation in much the way that the economic institutions they advocated would superintend the development of a flourishing industrial economy. The Whigs were convinced that the two thrusts must occur simultaneously, for they were fearful—indeed, they thought they had ample evidence—that economic change without the reinforcement of social control over the industrial population would spell the doom of the American experiment.

Mann's identification of the moral importance of the common school is typically Whig in its assignment to a centralized institution of the duties previously handled by the family and the community. In his journal he called the common school "the greatest discovery ever made by man." The common schools were preventive and provided antidotes to social ills; other social organizations were merely remedial, dealing with evil only after it had occurred. Mann concluded his journal entry by exclaiming: "Let the common school be expanded to its capabilities, let it be worked with the efficiency of which it is susceptible, and nine-tenths of the crimes in the penal code would become obsolete; the long catalogue of human ills would be abridged; men would walk more safely by day; every pillow would be more inviolable by night; property, life, and character held by a stronger tenure; all rational hopes respecting the future brightened."[12] A few days before Mann left political office to accept the secretaryship of the Massachusetts Board of Education in 1837, a gang of boys set fire to the roof of the building where he lived. He was appalled, and quite probably scared, and his reaction is important as an indication of how men of his background and class thought of education. He confided to his journal the night of the fire that society, "like a mother," should take care of all her children by giving them moral guidance. And, for Mann as for so many Whigs, the common schools were to be society's maternal agent.

The breakdown of traditional community controls that accompanied industrialization, urbanization, and westward expansion frightened the Whigs who, of course, supported these three movements—Mann himself was a principal promoter of state support for railroads and other industrial initiatives when he served in the Massachusetts legislature—and they were not about to cure the social problems caused by industrialization, urbanization, and westward expansion by curbing these movements. By supporting education instead, they hoped to cure the evils and retain the advantages simultaneously. Whigs observed traditional strengths of the

[12] Mary Mann, *Life of Horace Mann* (Boston, 1865), I, 142.

late colonial and early national American community disintegrating on several fronts. Industrialization entailed the expansion of the factory method of manufacturing, a method that required the gathering of large masses of workers in a single place. During English industrialization, an experience with which large numbers of Whigs were familiar, the concentration of industry and people had created filthy industrial cities filled with povertystricken workers who were densely packed in poor and inadequate housing and who contributed to an ever rising crime rate and an ever expanding network of vice. Industrialization appeared to create a socially degraded and vicious population. Americans, like most of the British, were more prone to attribute the final cause of this degradation to the poor moral character of the industrial workers rather than to the conditions under which they lived and worked. But those conditions did serve to emphasize and heighten people's evil traits and to cause them to reveal themselves more readily. Industrialization and urbanization concentrated large numbers of socially vicious people in a single place; where the traditional community controls might have suppressed the major part of this viciousness when such people were widely scattered through the population, those traditional controls had no power in the industrial ghetto. Social viciousness reinforced social viciousness in the urban slum. Industrialism additionally threatened to create a mass of men without property, without the stake in social order that the mass of yeoman farmers and individual artisans had because they owned their farmland or their shops. It had long been assumed that one great strength of republican society in America, one reason why it was relatively free from the disorder and licentiousness thought to mark European populations, was that the mass of Americans were men of property. Industrialization seemed certain to change that condition.

Urbanization threatened additional dangers. It undermined traditional means of social control by greatly increasing the social distance among social classes within the city. In small communities there had not been a great deal of social distance between the rich and the poor. The visible effects of class difference were small because most citizens, as property owners, were economically self-sufficient. Even the wealthy had few means of conspicuous consumption. In the small communities and even in the cities of 1800, the social classes lived close to each other. Often, indeed, their houses were interspersed, with the poor, for example, living on streets behind the homes of the well-to-do. Because there was not much social distance among classes in the traditional communities, personal methods of social control worked fairly well: individual remonstrance by a social leader—with a recalcitrant worker or a husband neglecting his family in favor of drinking at the inn or an adolescent turning to hooliganism—was most often effective and sufficient. But after 1820 or 1830, as the population of cities soared, a new pattern of residential and social segregation appeared. The rich and the poor began to live at opposite ends of town. And, as the towns grew larger, this polarity represented a considerable physical distance and an even greater psychological distance. People felt less and less safe venturing into neighborhoods inhabited by social classes different from their own. Forerunners of modern social workers appeared in American cities during this period, symbolizing the distance between the classes—the well-to-do supported urban missionaries to distribute systematically the charity that had been distributed on a personal basis in earlier times and to report to the upper and middle classes, somewhat in the manner of anthropologists reporting on primitive tribes, on conditions and attitudes in the somewhat mysterious and very distant slums. The personal basis of social control was gone.

Urbanization strained traditional patterns of social control among all people in the city—including the rich and middle class. The small community was filled with formal and informal agencies of social control. The church was a powerful force for inculcating and enforcing habits of obedience, conformity, and morality. Since the open town meeting—for all its alleged contributions to democracy—was run by the community's hierarchy and had no method of secret balloting, a man had to vote publicly before the hierarchy, which was quite likely to punish him if he deviated from acceptable standards. Economic control in the small community was tight. Few sources of credit were open to a man and he knew that they would close to him if he did not conform to the standards of those with financial power. There was a vast amount of informal social pressure on individuals to conform because of the lack of privacy in the small community. Everyone knew everyone else and everyone else's business. In most Protestant churches of the day the individual related the circumstances of his religious conversion publicly; his religion was not a private affair between God and himself but a semipublic concern where the congregation—quite likely to be the majority of adults in his community—judged his piety. Everyone helped everyone with such tasks as barn raising and corn husking, but such mutual dependence extended into such intimate problems as sickness, marital problems, and charity. One did not go to impersonal and professional hospitals or agencies for help in these situations, but to one's neighbors. Neighborliness had great advantages over the impersonality of the professional social agency, but privacy was not one of them. The most intimate aspects of one's life were open to the other families in a small community. Even love was a public affair: an undetected walk in the woods was all two lovers could hope for in the way of privacy for there were no crowded and impersonal public facilities or automobiles in which couples could retreat from the world. Such lack of privacy served to restrain individuals from deviating from the accepted standards of the community. One was too well known by and too dependent on one's neighbors to risk alienating them by behaving in a manner that would outrage their sense of propriety.

People moving to the cities escaped this network almost completely. The person on the move, especially to or within urban areas, could throw off his past and leave his social and economic niche. In moving, he virtually insured that no one was likely to find out about his past; he moved into a world of relative privacy, into what many consider the excessive privacy of urban living. He was free to vote, worship, spend, read, and love as he wished, without a neighbor keeping track of him. The Whigs did not trust people who lived in such privacy to conform to the moral standards of the age. They sought to establish some kind of institutionalized form of social control to substitute for the personal community network of the small town, a form of social control that would insure that individuals living in the impersonal urban world would perform their responsibilities and work so as to promote the general welfare. The Whigs looked to schools as one institution which could efficiently internalize a sense of social control and social duty in the urban population.

Whigs also associated this same breakdown in community networks of social control with expansion westward. Here again individuals were thought to have moved out of their community and out from under its restraints and to be, therefore, in grave danger of turning into dissolute and irresponsible drifters. Timothy Dwight voiced a popular conservative view of westerners in 1826 when he described them as men who led "irregular, adventurous, half-working and half-lounging" lives, who hated "sober industry and prudent economy," and who possessed, furthermore, a "noxious disposition."[13] Westerners acquired these characteristics, according to their critics, because they had moved outside of the community orbit of social control. One unhappy result of their having done so, in the Whig view, was that they grew discontented with their lot and lost respect for their political betters. People in older communities accepted class differences, believing that they served the needs of order and stability by allowing all members of the community to know what to expect of others. Class lines facilitated the distribution of responsibilities and patterns of deference so that the community worked harmoniously. Deference was crucial to the traditional community—men knew their places and respected and deferred to those in superior positions. And those who were deferred to—the social reformers and the forebears of the social reformers of the common school era—liked to think that the lower orders deferred happily and acquiesced cheerfully to the class system. Westerners appeared to the Whigs to have lost all pretense at deference to individuals or responsibility to the general good. Instead, westerners supported "radical," "demagogic" politicians like Andrew Jackson. Whigs did not consider all westerners guilty of such transgressions—Henry Clay was a westerner, after all. But the Whigs saw political

[13] Quoted in Francis S. Philbrick, *The Rise of the West, 1754–1830* (New York, 1965), 345.

radicalism, in the person of Jackson, coming from the West and genuinely feared that the western population, like that in the urban slums, might destroy the nation.

A fourth major social change in the United States during the second quarter of the nineteenth century was the large influx of relatively poor, non-English, and often Catholic immigrants. Vast social and economic changes in Europe, rather than policies fostered by the Whig economic doctrine, caused this increase in the flow and change in the nature of immigration to the United States. This new wave of immigrants—much more "foreign" than earlier immigrants had been—threatened further to destroy traditional modes of social control. The presence of large groups of immigrants, often speaking an alien language, worshipping in different confessions, congregating together in order to maintain their ethnic identity, increased the social distance among peoples in the industrial and urban regions. The Irish immigrants, in particular, driven penniless from their farms in Ireland, arrived on the eastern seaboard without the skills that would make them valuable as laborers in urban and industrial concerns and without the capital to establish farms where they might have used the skills that they did possess. They remained in the cities, a depressed class of ghetto dwellers working for the lowest imaginable wages, the last to be hired and the first to be fired. Their presence greatly increased the problem of urban poverty and vice. "Immigrant" and "poverty and vice" became so synonymous, in fact, that many Americans imagined that only immigrants were poor and lived in degraded slums (much as many Americans today imagine that only blacks are on welfare).

How accurate or justified were the Whigs' fears of urbanization, industrialization, immigration, and western expansion? Superficially, it might seem that they wildly exaggerated the social changes of the common school era. Statistically, those changes do not seem great enough in the period between 1820 and 1840 to have justified the social leaders' great concern for them. Most Americans remained in traditional communities under traditional social controls. For example, in 1840 only about 11 percent of the population lived in cities and towns over 2,500 (the point at which the census divided urban and rural). The figure had already reached 6 percent in 1800. Urban population was to rise five percentage points in every decade after 1840 for the rest of the century, which makes the rise that the common school reformers had experienced seem even less significant. But the statistics must be read another way in order to understand how people perceived urbanization in those years. Because the United States population had been rising so rapidly, nearly six times as many people lived in urban places in 1840 as in 1800, and the percentage growth in urban population reached 82 percent between 1820 and 1830 and 68 percent in the following decade. Urban population was to double between 1840 and 1850 (see table). Three percent of the American population lived in cities over 100,000 in 1840; there was no

Growth of the Urban Population of the United States, 1790–1920
(in thousands)

Year	Total Population	Urban Population	Percent Urban	Percent Growth of Urban Population	Percent Growth of Total Population
1790	3,929	201	5.1		
1800	5,308	322	6.1	60	35
1810	7,239	525	7.3	69	36
1820	9,638	693	7.2	33	33
1830	12,866	1,127	8.8	82	34
1840	17,069	1,845	10.8	68	33
1850	23,191	3,543	15.3	99	36
1860	31,443	6,216	19.8	75	36
1870	39,818	9,902	25.7	59	23
1880	50,155	14,129	28.2	40	30
1890	62,947	22,106	35.1	61	25
1900	75,994	30,159	39.7	36	21
1910	91,972	41,998	45.7	39	21
1920	105,710	54,157	51.2	29	15

From David Ward, *Cities and Immigrants*, 1971, p. 6. Reprinted by permission of Oxford University Press.

city that large in 1810. In 1840 New York City (excluding Brooklyn) contained almost 2 percent of the nation's population, around 300,000 people.

Thirty-three million people immigrated to the United States between 1820 and 1920. Against this figure the 100,000 that came in the 1820s and the 500,000 that came in the 1830s or even the 1.4 million that came in the 1840s seem few indeed, far too few to justify the fear of the immigrant that Americans of the period felt. On the other hand, people living in the 1840s did not have the perspective of a century's experience with immigration. To them the rate of increase was immense and the character of the people arriving radically different from what they had known. Although from 10 to 20 percent of the immigrants each decade before the Civil War came from the United Kingdom—the source of the vast majority of pre-1820 immigrants—from 45 to 73 percent came from Ireland and Germany. And the vast majority of these settled in cities where they were considerably more visible (and threatening) to social leaders already concerned with the moral dangers of urban life than they would have been had they scattered evenly through the nation.

The extent of poverty is even more difficult to determine statistically: there had been poverty, especially urban poverty, in the United States both before and after the Revolution. Its increase in the early decades of the nineteenth century was most probably rather gradual, but at some point in that rise it changed from being an accepted condition with which the community dealt routinely to being a problem calling for special concern. It came to public consciousness dramatized as a new problem calling for new solutions. It is not clear why or how poverty, degradation, and vice became such popular issues at the particular time they did. Probably the early nineteenth-century media—the preacher, the lyceum lecturer, the lady's magazine, and the newspaper—inspired this interest. Also, it is probable that the growing social distance between the financially secure and the poor made conditions among the poor more interesting, more scandalous, and more frightening to the well-to-do than they had been when members of various social classes met each other routinely.

The conservatives' view of the westerner seems, perhaps, the least justifiable. A more hard-working, pious, neighborly, and communal population than that settling the old Northwest is difficult to imagine. The fervor with which the westerners sought to build communities in their new homeland modeled as precisely as possible—down to the details of architecture and ritual—on that of the communities they had left behind suggests that the westerners themselves were troubled enough by their break with the traditional community to seek reinstitution of the network of social control that those communities had provided. Westerners, or at least the community leaders in the West, thought as conservatively on social issues as did the eastern Whigs, and the fervor with which reformers pursued the common school ideal in western areas that contained few immigrants, little industry, and few urban places suggests that westerners did perceive some of the problems in their condition that worried eastern conservatives.[14]

The United States experienced significant social changes in the period after 1820—especially significant when viewed against the background of what had preceded them (as the participants at the time viewed them) rather than against the degree of social change that was to follow. The Whiggish leaders sought desperately to minimize the threat that those changes posed to the social order and stability of their country. Their desperation was evident in the building of the city of Lowell, Massachusetts, in the late 1830s and early 1840s. A group of Boston merchant investors proposed to build a group of textile mills in the countryside at the point where the Merrimac River's fall was sufficient to drive the textile machinery and to build a model town there which would avoid all

[14] Compare this sense of fear with the realities of western conformist communities in T. Scott Miyakawa, *Protestants and Pioneers: Individualism and Conformity on the American Frontier* (Chicago, 1964), and Page Smith, *As a City Upon a Hill: The Town in American History* (New York, 1966), chapters 3, 4.

the evils associated with British industrialization. Lowell was erected from scratch in a rural area far north of Boston and its urban evils. Its labor force was to consist of young women from New England farm families who came to work in the factories in Lowell for only two or three years, long enough to earn a dowry or to support a male relative in school. The young women would live in dormitories under the supervision of house mothers approved by the companies. The factories sought to stand *in loco parentis* for their workers just as the colleges did with students. Lowell's planners overbuilt the city with schools, parks, and churches; in fact, Lowell was a kind of nineteenth-century industrial park trying to hide its true nature under a garden-like mantle.

Industrialism developed in Lowell according to plan for a time, but by 1850 at the latest this plan had been aborted. The factory managers found that the ever increasing pool of immigrant labor provided cheaper and steadier hands; the pursuit of profit squeezed out ideals. Lowell became a typical New England mill town—dirty, shabby, indisputably industrial, and populated by propertyless immigrant laborers who gave every indication that they had already become a permanent working class.

The planners of Lowell had hoped to create conditions under which they could have reaped the advantages of industrialization without suffering any of the evils that accompanied the concentration of industrial workers. Their urban environment was to be pure and isolated; their work force was to be drawn temporarily from the ranks of the property-holding; while living in Lowell the worker would not suffer from the impersonal privacy and lack of social control that typified urban, industrial environments but would be as closely supervised as she would have been at home. The planners' visions for Lowell did not materialize, and even had they, Lowell's scheme was too utopian and expensive to serve as a viable model for easing the dangers of industrialism. More viable and less expensive modes of maintaining social control over industrial and urban and immigrant populations had to be found. Schooling was one such device.

The Whiggish social leaders of the first half of the nineteenth century sponsored a host of educational agencies to meet the need for inculcating social control. They supported the benevolent societies which distributed Bibles and tracts and sent missionaries to the poor and the alien in an effort to persuade them to mend their ways and accept the guidance of the established religions. These were the same benevolent societies that supplied funds and faculty for the western colleges and academies. Easterners of all ranks supported their efforts in the West, which were not limited to the encouragement of higher education. One of Lowell's mill girls remembered that during her stay in the mills, from 1835 to 1845, "the needs of the West were constantly kept before us in the churches. We were asked for contributions for Home Missions, which were willingly given; and some of us were appointed collectors of funds for the education of indigent young men to become Western Home Missionary preachers."[15] Many of these societies sent agents, annually, to the mills in Lowell to recruit teachers for the western elementary schools. Many mill girls felt dutybound to go and civilize the westerner. The Sunday school movement embodied another attempt to teach social control to the poor—in this case the children of the poor. Pioneered in England in the late eighteenth century as a means of teaching young children who worked six days a week their letters and numbers on Sunday, the Sunday school made its way to the United States soon after the turn of the century. Although housed in and supported by churches, the Sunday school's original purpose was to teach intellectual skills—principally reading—and nonsectarian morality to working children. (It took on its present-day religious function only when the expanding common school system made its original function obsolete.) The Sunday school movement flourished throughout the urban United States as a means of combating actual and anticipated social disorder. "There is a growing spirit of libertinism destructive of good order in society and good morals in individuals," an official of the Sunday School Union—the national benevolent society organized in 1824 to encourage the building of Sunday schools—claimed in 1835. "The riots in our cities I know from my observation . . . are sustained by the youths: lads of 16 to 20 years of age." His solution was to teach every child social virtue in a Sunday school.[16]

Whiggish philanthropists supported charity schools for pauper children and scholarships for the poor at regular schools but, as mentioned, these efforts did not succeed in reaching the vast bulk of the children of the poor. Whigs also supported a variety of self-improvement institutions, such as mechanics institutes, which combined a library, scientific cabinet, and reading room with lecture series, in hopes of providing young men the facilities with which they could educate themselves. Many of these institutions turned into lyceums—lecture halls where young and old of all classes gathered to hear touring lecturers discuss in a popular manner current issues, scientific advances, or literary appreciation. Only a few retained their character as hospitable retreats for the working-class boy interested in reading or self-improvement. And these seem to have been used more by the well-trained young man already on the way up rather than by the poor. All of these educative institutions had their successes and their constituencies, but none singly or all in combination effectively rescued the majority of the children of the poor and the alien-

[15] Lucy Larcom, *A New England Girlhood* (Boston, 1889), 256.

[16] Joseph H. Dulles to Frederick A. Packard (20 August, 1835), quoted in Clifford Griffin, *Their Brothers' Keepers: Moral Stewardship in the United States, 1800–1865* (New Brunswick, N. J., 1960), 51–52.

ated. A more systematic and more efficient effort seemed necessary to bring them within the community—to make them conform to the moral and social codes of the majority. The common school—and it is wise to note how closely the words "common" and "community" are related—was to be that effective agency.

The common school appeared even more efficient when school reformers discovered that women could be used to staff the lower grades. Reformers justified the appointment of women in various ways, emphasizing especially the effectiveness of the maternal instinct and the female personality in dealing with young children, especially in schools that were to act as "mothers" to children. Another motivation for choosing women teachers, however, was that they generally commanded less than half of a male's salary for the same work. Although women had taught in the "dame" schools and sometimes in writing schools before 1830 (both schools were for children under seven), the remainder of the teaching force had been male. In the years between 1830 and 1860 the teaching force rapidly feminized, especially in the eastern states where the migration of males to the West left a surplus of women. Women came to predominate in elementary school teaching, a predominance they would maintain to the present day. Although there were many and varied reasons for this change—changing conceptions of child nurture and the abundant supply of unmarried women in the East—economy seems to have been the prime consideration.

Common school reform was primarily an effort to reach down into the lower portions of the population and to teach children there to share the values, ideals, and controls held by the rest of society. The reform also had a lateral aspect, of lesser importance, but still significant. Reformers feared that the children of the social leaders and of the middle class might not be adequately socialized by their families to the norms of the society. The Whig leaders, the school reformers, middle- and upper-class people in general felt some uneasiness about their own behavior during the early nineteenth century. Often they, like the westerner, had moved away from their communities, from their families, and from their religion. Pursuit of the economic and social opportunities open to them had led them to compromise with traditional values. First, those who held leadership positions had made money, often quite a lot of money. On the one hand, such financial success was a warrant of sanctification because fortune smiled only on God's appointed but, on the other hand, financial success challenged the Puritan distrust of riches, the Christian respect for suffering on earth, the Biblical injunctions against accumulating riches on earth. Second, moving to the city, which Whigs did as often as anyone else, caused people to compromise with the ideal of plain living and high thinking. Social status within a small stable community had depended more on the status of a person's ancestors than on the visibility of his wealth. In the impersonal city, where one's inherited status was unknown, one's social rank depended on visible wealth—on the size of one's house, on the gilt on one's carriage, on the number of servants, on the cut of one's clothes, on the lavishness of one's entertainments. Conspicuous consumption became a necessity. Third, the religious piety and orthodoxy that had marked the smaller rural communities of the United States gave way in the cities to less demanding, less dogmatic, and more refined religious practices. As people moved from the smaller to the larger communities they deserted the religious forms of their fathers to adopt the less rigorous and less pious religious habits of the urban elite. Fourth, the well-to-do felt some guilt about what the move to the city had done to family life. Because the kind of work that young children had done on the farm to help the family was not available in the city, children were not economically useful and family size shrank precipitously when families moved to the city. It is not clear how the middle class accomplished family planning in the early nineteenth century but the successful effort to do so imposed tensions on family life and led those families to feel that they were compromising with the values of the traditional community. Where children of poor families in the city found plenty of work in factories, middle-class families in search of status could not let their children face such demeaning work— the ability to support children in idleness was a demonstration of social status.

In sum, members of the middle and upper classes felt that they had compromised with their older values when they moved away from the older network of social controls. They especially worried about the effect of their compromises on their children. Choosing schooling for their children as an antidote to their own compromises allowed parents to appear greatly concerned about their own backsliding without having to alter their own behavior in any way. Such parental concern has often inspired school reform.

The goal of common school reform, then, could be summarized as the effort to find an effective substitute for the mechanisms of social control and socialization that had characterized the preurban and preindustrial small stable community. The common school was common because it taught the common subjects and common values and it was common because it was to enroll every single child in the United States in order to socialize him. Reformers hoped the common school would carry out all the socialization functions that the traditional community had performed with a stable and homogeneous population. Yet the common school was to impose moral and social consensus on a heterogeneous population living in conditions often openly hostile to the influence of organized schooling. However one evaluates the desirability in a free society of the goals that the Whigs set for common schooling, it is clear that Whig hopes for the common school were vastly too high and their goals impossible to achieve. The common school could not help but fail to meet their expectations. The tragedy has been that in the face of common schooling's inevitable failure to fulfill these goals schoolmen and citizens alike have failed, for generation after generation, to reassess either the viability or the desirability of the objectives set for public schooling at the start of the common school movement. The promise behind the commitment to morally oriented schooling for all has not been seriously challenged. Instead, schoolmen and citizens have agreed that success is just around the corner if only the common school system could be made a little larger and a little more powerful.

GUIDE TO FURTHER READING

The best introduction to antebellum American society and politics remains ED-WARD PESSEN, *Jacksonian America: Society, Personality, and Politics* (Homewood, Ill., 1969), which contains a thorough bibliographical essay. LAWRENCE A. CREMIN chronicles educational reform in *The American Common School: An Historic Conception* (New York, 1951). FREDERICK M. BINDER, *The Age of the Common School, 1830–1865* (New York, 1974), HENDRICK D. GIDEONESE, "Common School Reform: Connecticut, 1838–1854" (Unpublished Dissertation, Harvard University, 1963), and SIDNEY L. JACKSON, *America's Struggle for Free Schools: Social Tensions and Education in New England and New York, 1827–1842* (Washington, D. C., 1941), are also useful. A good collection of primary sources is RUSH WELTER, ed., *American Writings on Popular Education: The Nineteenth Century* (Indianapolis, 1971).

Recent statistical research suggests that a rather large percentage of the eligible population before 1830 received some formal instruction and, therefore, the increases in attendance which accompanied the common school movement were more moderate than promoters contended. ALBERT FISHLOW, "The American Common School Revival: Fact or Fancy?", in HENRY ROSOVSKY, ed., *Industrialization in Two Systems* (New York, 1966), 40–67, CARL KAESTLE, *The Evolution of an Urban School System: New York City, 1750–1850* (Cambridge, Mass., 1973), STANLEY K. SCHULTZ, *The Culture Factory: Boston Public Schools, 1789–1860* (New York, 1973), and MARIS A. VINOVSKIS, "Trends in Massachusetts Education, 1826–1860," *History of Education Quarterly*, XII (Winter, 1972), 501–530, agree that participation by middle- and lower-class Americans in the pre-common-school educational enterprise was widespread.

The connections between education and economic growth have been explored in MARIS A. VINOVSKIS, "Horace Mann on the Economic Productivity of Education," *New England Quarterly*, XLIII (December, 1970), 550–571, STUART BRUCHEY, *The Roots of American Economic Growth 1607–1861* (New York, 1965), chapter 8, DOUGLASS C. NORTH, *Growth and Welfare in the American Past: A New Economic History* (Englewood Cliffs, N. J., 1966), and ALBERT FISHLOW, "Levels of Nineteenth-Century American Investment in Education," *Journal of Economic History,* XXVI (December, 1966), 418–436.

Our discussion of the purpose of the common school reformers has drawn on the excellent interpretations by MICHAEL B. KATZ, *The Irony of Early School Reform: Educational Innovation in Mid-Nineteenth Century Massachusetts* (Cambridge, Mass., 1968), CARL KAESTLE, *The Evolution of an Urban School System: New York City, 1750–1850* (Cambridge, Mass., 1973), STANLEY K. SCHULTZ, *The Culture Factory: Boston Public Schools, 1789–1860* (New York, 1973), LAWRENCE CREMIN, *The American Common School: An Historic Conception* (New York, 1951), RUSH WELTER, *Popular Education and Democratic Thought in America* (New York, 1962), and JONATHAN MESSERLI, *Horace Mann: A Biography* (New York, 1972). Also useful are MERLE CURTI, *The Social Ideas of American Educators* (1935; New York, 1959), Part I, LAWRENCE CREMIN, ed., *The Republic and the School: Horace Mann on the Education of Free Men* (New York, 1957), M. J. HEALE, "Humanitarianism in the Early Republic: The Moral Reformers of New York, 1776–1825," *Journal of American Studies,* II (1968), 161–175, and WILLIAM W. CUTLER, "Status, Values, and the Education of the Poor: The Trustees of the New York Public School Society, 1805–1853," *American Quarterly,* XXIV (March, 1972), 69–85. The dilemma of the antebellum reformers is made explicit by MICHAEL B. KATZ, *The Irony of Early School Reform* (Cambridge, Mass., 1968), and MARVIN MEYERS, *The Jacksonian Persuasion: Politics and Belief* (Stanford, Calif., 1957).

The best introductions to the politics of Whiggery are LEE BENSON, *The Concept of Jacksonian Democracy: New York as a Test Case* (Princeton, N. J., 1961), GLYNDON VAN DEUSEN, *The Jacksonian Era, 1828–1848* (New York, 1959), and EDWARD PESSEN, *Jacksonian America* (Homewood, Ill., 1969).

The following studies locate the common school movement within the larger antebellum reform effort. CLIFFORD GRIFFIN, *Their Brothers' Keepers: Moral Stewardship in the United States, 1800–1865* (New Brunswick, N. J., 1960), GRIFFIN, *The Ferment of Reform, 1830–1860* (New York, 1967), WALTER D. LEWIS, "The Reformer as Conservative: Prostestant Counter-Subversion in the Early Republic," in STANLEY COBEN and LORMAN RATNER, eds., *The Development of an American Culture* (Englewood Cliffs, N. J., 1970), 164–191, and RAYMOND A. MOHL, *Poverty in New York, 1783–1825* (New York, 1971), emphasize the conservative nature of the movement, while ALICE FELT TYLER, *Freedom's Ferment: Phases of American Social History to 1860* (Minneapolis, 1944), FRANK TRACY CARLTON, *Economic Influences upon Educational Progress in the United States, 1820–1860* (1908; New York, 1965), and PHILIP CUROE, *Educational Attitudes and Policies of Organized Labor in the United States* (New York, 1926), recall its humanitarian objectives and stress the influence of working people on the reform activity.

On the image of the West as a section desperately in need of order and civilization see HENRY NASH SMITH, *Virgin Land* (Cambridge, Mass., 1950), CONSTANCE ROURKE, *American Humor: A Study in National Character* (New York, 1953), and BERNARD A. WEISBERGER, *They Gathered at the River* (Boston, 1958). PAGE SMITH, *As a City Upon a Hill: The Town in American History* (New York, 1966), chapters 3 and 4, T. SCOTT MIYAKAWA, *Protestants and Pioneers: Individualism and Conformity on the American Frontier* (Chicago, 1964), and DANIEL BOORSTIN, *The*

Americans: The National Experience (New York, 1965), distinguish between this image of rampant individualism and the more accurate reality of the West as a territory in which conformity and consensus were exacted when not offered voluntarily.

A number of authors have suggested that adults, and the nation itself, strayed from old ideals during the early nineteenth century; among the most useful sources are BARBARA CROSS, *Horace Bushnell: Minister to a Changing America* (Chicago, 1958), FRED SOMKIN, *The Unquiet Eagle: Memory and Desire in the Idea of America Freedom, 1815–1860* (Ithaca, N. Y., 1967), JOHN G. CAWELTI, *The Apostles of the Self-Made Man: Changing Concepts of Success in America* (Chicago, 1965), chapters 1–3, OSCAR HANDLIN, *The Americans* (Boston, 1963), and WILLIAM DEAN HOWELLS, *The Rise of Silas Lapham* (Boston, 1884).

CHAPTER 4

The Search for a New Pedagogy

I

THE REFORMERS' DEMAND THAT COMMON SCHOOLS SOLVE SOCIAL, POLITI-
cal, and economic problems forced those reformers to seek new methods,
a new pedagogy, with which the schools could set about the task. When
the major functions of the schools had been to reinforce parental and
community values, symbolize cultural equality in the United States, and
set memory tasks for students, their task was relatively simple. And since
the schools' function was so unspecialized—they simply reinforced what
several other institutions taught—they did not need to be, and were not,
particularly effective. The Whigs, on the other hand, expected the
schools to teach students values and behavior that they did not learn in
their homes or in their community. The Whigs expected the schools to
make immigrant children more like native Americans than like their parents, to make the children of the poor economically ambitious and socially virtuous, to make Catholic children Protestant. Whigs expected the
school to change rather than reinforce the habits that children learned
outside the school.

To accomplish such goals, educational reformers had to substitute for
the haphazard methods of the past a pedagogy that was really capable
of influencing children. The new method or pedagogy had to accomplish
three things. First, it had to make schooling attractive to large numbers

of children who had rejected schooling in the past because idleness and vice were more alluring. Second, the new pedagogy had to insure that once in school children learned certain basic intellectual skills efficiently and in a manner that also contributed to their moral improvement. The new pedagogy had to combine the intellectual with the moral. Third, it had to insure that children learned certain moral values efficiently and permanently. The third task was the most important, as the Whiggish reformers viewed the school's major responsibility as moral rather than intellectual.

The second task—creation of a curriculum that simultaneously trained the intellectual and moral faculties—was the most difficult and the one most imperfectly accomplished in the nineteenth century. Not until William Torrey Harris applied his Hegelian interpretations to the curriculum and John Dewey suggested that the curriculum could be tailored to prepare a child for a socially virtuous life did educators successfully relate skill training in the common branches to moral training. Before that time educators relied almost exclusively on the time-honored device of teaching children to read with didactically moralistic texts. The hornbook used to teach colonial children their letters introduced "A" with the text: "In Adam's fall, we sinned all." Professor William Holmes McGuffey (1800–1873) used the same device in the famous and immensely popular (over 100 million copies have been sold since 1836) series of readers which he edited between 1836 and his death. As they progressed through the grades, children honed their reading skills on McGuffey's graded collections of excerpts from great books and didactic moral tales. Pedagogues in the common schools, like their colleagues in institutions of higher learning, also looked to mental discipline—requiring students to concentrate on difficult subject matter as recommended in the Yale Report of 1828—as a means of transmitting moral values along with academic skills. But pedagogical theorists of the first two thirds of the nineteenth century offered no new devices capable of relating skill training and moral training. In this chapter, therefore, we will concentrate on the reformers' progress in constructing a pedagogy that would attract children to school and change their moral behavior while they attended.

Their efforts occurred in the midst of a crucial change in the religious and social theory of child nurture that swept the United States between 1800 and the Civil War. The new pedagogy would rest upon this changed theory of the child. Traditional teaching methods had followed the Puritan view that the child was born sinful and had to be won—or, as was more common, perhaps, frightened—away from his natural inclination to evil. Children under ten or eleven could not willingly reject sin because they were not mature enough to experience a true conversion experience. They were in an unenviable position—not yet capable of rejecting evil, but treated as if they were responsible for their evil actions. Parents and schoolmasters knew no way of hastening the conversion experience and assumed their job was to protect the young child as much as possible from evil influences from without and from his own evil nature. As he was incapable of inner control, of resisting sin by himself, he had to be disciplined externally. He was exhorted to fear the Lord, flogged and beaten in order to help him overcome the bodily passions which were believed to push him toward sin. Parents and teachers sought to break the child's will, for willfulness in children was the surest evidence of the power of evil over them. From the moral point of view, school was something of a holding action. According to strict Puritan doctrine, a person did not earn God's grace or saving power through the performance of good works or rigorous study or humble prayer. A man's fate was predetermined by God, and nothing a man did on earth could change his predestined fate. Thus, nothing a child learned in school affected his eventual receipt of or failure to receive grace. Adherence to Puritan doctrine was complete in no section of the United States and various compromises with predestination and man's inability to exert any control over his fate appeared quite early. No doubt parents and teachers hoped, even expected, that their efforts to teach children to fear the Lord, control their passions, and submit to the will of others did prepare them for eventual conversion, but such expectations could not become an official rationale for schools.

In the nineteenth century theories of child nature changed, especially among the liberal upper and middle classes and the churches they supported. Evangelist practices and imperatives after 1800 modified the theory of predestination by giving the individual some power to affect his fate before God. Another influence for change grew out of the fact that parents and ministers were discouraged by the low rate at which children of the converted experienced conversion. How to maintain the first generation's fervor for conversion and Christian witness in the second and subsequent generations had always been a serious problem for Calvinist religion. It was also difficult to explain in personal or doctrinal terms why the children of the saved were not saved themselves—yet an explanation was necessary each time a child of converted parents did not convert. These children, reared in Christian homes of converted parents, seemed to constitute a natural source of future church members. Responding to their own needs for building larger congregations and to the parents' need for security about the religious future of their children, the clergy worked out a new doctrine of child rearing that ultimately became known as Christian nurture. Horace Bushnell, a Hartford congregational clergyman, codified the doctrine in a treatise of that name published in 1861, but its major components influenced the conception of childhood held especially by the urban elite much earlier. The doctrine contained three major elements. First, the sudden conversion characteristic of the revival meeting and Puritan literature was not the only kind possible. Some people would, of course, continue to experience the infusion of the light of the Lord all at once and in an instant turn from their evil ways toward righteousness. More commonly, an individual's conversion would be gradual. The maturing child might grow more and more convinced of the extraordinary beauty of God and holiness and gradually find himself more resistant to sin and more capable of submitting to His will. This doctrine of gradualism meant that all influences during childhood and adolescence might further or retard the child's eventual conversion. Parents and educators had vast new powers over the youngster's moral fate. A second component of the doctrine of Christian nurture derived from the Lockean psychological contention that a child's mind at birth was more or less empty, a tabula rasa. John Locke, of course, had referred, in his *Essay Concerning Human Understanding* (1690), to the absence of ideas in the minds of the newborn. He had not considered the presence or absence of the mark of original sin in babies. In the nineteenth century liberal clergymen and social thinkers extended his idea to contend that children were born naturally innocent or at least neutral. Evil existed in the world but was not inherent in individuals at birth. Therefore, Christian nurture required that parents and teachers protect the child from contact with and knowledge of evil. Isolating the child's innocence or neutrality from evil influences until the power of God had had an opportunity to do its work was a key to bringing children into the church. Third, Christian nurture held that the Lord should be introduced to children as a God of Love rather than as a Just and Angry God, as had been traditional. It called for more emphasis on Jesus and the New Testament than on the Old. In this way a child would learn to love the Lord rather than to fear Him, surely a more effective way to win a young person to religion.

This switch from the emphasis on fear to that on love accorded well with early nineteenth-century romanticism about the power of love, especially the power of family love. The move to the city had greatly changed the role of the middle- and upper-class woman. In the country she had been a true economic helpmeet to her husband, sometimes working in the fields, always tending a large garden, making bread, preserving vegetables, slaughtering meat, spinning, weaving, making the family's clothes, and raising a large family. In the city many of these tasks were greatly lightened and some disappeared altogether. Middle-class families were smaller, the husband often worked far from home where his wife could not help him, and food and clothing were purchased ready made. The middle-class woman sought other functions to compensate for the relative idleness in which she found herself. One function she chose was that of moral and spiritual guide for her husband and children. Instead of providing physical and economic help to her family, the woman was to employ her special nature as a woman to protect her family from evil and win them to the Lord. By suffusing the home with the power of her distinctly feminine love, she would make a bastion against the cares and evils of the world outside. The home, under the woman's direction, became an oasis within the evil city. "In the home, hidden from the 'passion-stirring and tumultuous scenes of life,' the divinely meek nature of women redeemed fallen husbands and sons 'reeling from the haunts of dissipation,' " proclaimed, according to Barbara Cross, a treatise on the new function of the urban woman written in 1836.[1] The romanticism of the day often appeared to confuse the mother's role with God's, as in the following celebration, written in 1833, of the power of love to save the fallen. "How often has the profligate son, in the very midst of his dissipation and sin, been led to reflect and repent by a recollection of a mother's prayers and tears!"[2]

Christian nurture and the romantic role assigned to the urban woman made love the most powerful instrument in the moral reform of individuals. Advocates suggested that the judicious use of love in the home could greatly improve society by permanently altering the behavior of children. Of course, in the Whig reformers' view, such promises had gone unfulfilled as they identified the family, of the well-to-do as well as of the poor, as largely responsible for the breakdown in the network of social control. The Whigs sought to build institutions to shoulder the burden of inculcating values that the family had neglected. But in constructing these institutions the Whigs sought to include the family love that was thought to hold such moral power. Thus, in the first half of the nineteenth century, the "family plan" or "cottage system" was introduced in prisons, reform schools, and asylums. Under this system inmates were divided into small groups, each of which lived in a separate building under the supervision of "house parents." The working girls in Lowell were to live in institutions run on the family plan. Reformers supported the feminization of the teaching force because it was cheap but also because it promised to introduce feminine love into the common schools. Much of the school reform of this period must be understood as an attempt to introduce familial relations to mass institutions and to harness those relations to the task of moral and social control.

II

The demands that reformers placed upon the common schools to alter the behavior of large groups of children dictated that the schoolmen

[1] James Matthews, *The Religious Influence of Mothers* (New York, 1836), quoted in Barbara M. Cross, *Horace Bushnell: Minister to a Changing America* (Chicago, 1958), 59.

[2] John S. Abbott, *The Mother at Home: Or Principles of Maternal Duty* (New York, 1833), 15, quoted in Cross, *Bushnell*, 58.

would seek new pedagogies; the age's romantic view of children dictated that that pedagogy would seek to employ methods of gentle and loving nurture. Horace Mann sought to frame such a pedagogy in the 1840s; his experiences testify to the earnestness of the reformers' search and the great resistance they met from conservative educators and parents who did not subscribe to the liberal doctrines of Christian nurture or to the genteel romanticism of the day.

Horace Mann rejected the methods that previous generations and the majority of the schools of his own time used to inculcate morals. He believed that the child was innocent rather than inherently evil. He wanted sectarian dogma eliminated from the school. Nor did he subscribe to the orthodox Calvinism to which Massachusetts residents traditionally adhered. Mann sought, instead, to identify a nonsectarian morality which could be taught to all children without violating anyone's sectarian beliefs. The idea that there might be a nonsectarian morality violated the beliefs of some faiths, but Mann persisted. The leaders of the more conservative denominations who were his critics in Massachusetts constantly charged either that he sought to enforce a Unitarian moral code on the schools rather than a nonsectarian one or that he was simply trying to eliminate religion and impose secularism on the schools. For many Unitarianism and secularism were synonymous. These criticisms had merit: Mann's morality emphasized rationality above piety, it depicted Jesus as an extremely ethical man rather than as part of the Godhead. It was a kind of natural morality, in some ways closer to Deism and pantheism than it was to the more orthodox doctrines of the Calvinist Congregationalists and Baptists who dominated New England numerically. Mann's proclivities are clear in the ordering and relative weight he gave to the various results he expected from the effective teaching of poetry.

> In sentiment, it should inculcate all kindly and social feelings; the love of external nature; regard and sympathy for domestic animals; consideration and benevolence towards every sentient thing, whether it flies, or creeps, or swims; all filial, all brotherly and sisterly affections; respect for age; compassion for the sick, the ignorant, the destitute, and for those who suffer under a privation of the senses or of reason; the love of country, and that philanthropy which looks beyond country, and holds all contemporaries and all posterity in its wide embrace; a passion for duty and a homage for all men who do it; and emphatically should it present such religious views as will lead children to fulfill the first great commandment,—to love the Lord their God with all their heart, and with all their soul, and with all their mind.[3]

Such a separation of kindness, justice, duty, charity, and love from their proper relation to religion additionally marked Mann as a Unitarian.

---

[3] Mann, *Eighth Annual Report* (1845), 132.

Morality, most of his critics agreed, was a function of religious belief and not something that could be taught separately. A religious belief was necessary to ethical living, the critics charged; after all, men without, or who held the wrong, religious beliefs were likely to behave unethically— Catholics, for example, could hardly be expected to be moral when they believed as they did.

It was just because of such attitudes that Mann and the other common school reformers thought it so crucial to find a common nonsectarian morality. The belief that morality was closely tied to a particular religious confession was divisive and, if implemented in the schools in urban and industrial areas, was sure to undermine the goal of enrolling all children in the schools. Sectarian teaching drove children from school; even Bible reading kept Catholic children from attending school. Common school reformers' objectives could not be reached if moral teaching were tied to sectarian, or even religious, teaching. This problem deeply concerned the reformers as they wished to reach just those children whose parents were most likely to be hostile to the sectarian religious teaching offered in the schools. In small communities and in turn-of-the-century cities population had been relatively homogenous in background and in religious belief. "Public" education could be both sectarian and well attended in these communities because the vast majority of a district's citizens usually belonged to the same denomination. In the polyglot cities such neighborhood homogeneity seldom occurred, and the establishment of schools with any denominational coloring was sure to alienate some of the families which the school reformers wished to reach. Sectarianism in the smaller communities had not been particularly divisive; but in the growing cities of the 1830s and 1840s a sectarian common school was a contradiction in terms.

Mann did not—nor did he wish to—abolish the use of the Bible in the public schools. He proudly announced that Bible reading in the common schools in Massachusetts increased while he was secretary to the Board of Education. But he was happy to report in 1844 that only a small fraction of the towns used the Bible as a devotional work; the rest used it as a reader, just as Mann recommended. The Bible was valuable as a history book, he argued, a religious Plutarch, full of "beautiful incidents in the lives of prophets and apostles, and especially, the perfect example which is given to men in the life of Jesus Christ." Mann complimented the Prussian schools for using the Bible in conjunction with courses on secular history. The Bible was also valuable for teaching reading because it so well combined moral example and beautiful prose—although Mann did find that the masters in one town refused to use the Bible as a text because " 'many of the verses [do] not end . . . with a full stop'!"[4] Mann believed that the increase in Bible reading correlated with a decrease in

[4] Mann, *Seventh Annual Report*, 125; *Eighth Annual Report*, 76.

sectarian teaching in the schools; he found less work on catechisms and less Calvinistic emphasis on sin and damnation.

Having rejected sectarian teaching as a means of inculcating morality in children, Mann needed a substitute. The moral stories and examples in the Bible and in the McGuffey readers provided one means of moral instruction, but it was hardly adequate to fulfill the goals of the reformers. The teaching of a rationalized, natural ethics like that of Unitarianism did not appear very promising: Unitarian rationalism had not been very effective in attracting significant numbers of adults to the denomination and it seemed even less likely to influence the moral behavior of large numbers of children. In his efforts to design a pedagogy capable of inculcating an acceptable social morality in children, Mann came to rely more on secular devices than on religious ones. Most important among them were the teaching of vocal music, the psychological theories of phrenology, and the doctrines of Pestalozzi as he found them implemented in Prussia.

Mann described the advantages of teaching vocal music under four headings.[5] His sometimes labored reasoning and his quaint combinations of science and pseudo-science reveal the monumental difficulty school reformers faced in thinking through the new configuration in common schooling and in finding methods adequate to the tasks they had set for those schools. Vocal music's first advantage as a common school subject was that it was the most democratic of the fine arts. Everyone had ears and a voice to use without cost. They were cheaper than any other musical instruments, they were more convenient for the student to carry around with him, and proficiency in singing was not necessary before a person could derive joy from singing. Second, vocal music contributed directly and indirectly to good health. Singing exercised the lungs, thereby helping to prevent consumption (tuberculosis), said by Mann to be the largest killer in Massachusetts. Furthermore, singing expanded the lungs and brought "a greater quantity of air in contact with the blood." Blood is better "vitalized and purified" under such circumstances. "Good blood gives more active and vigorous play to all the organs of absorption, assimilation, and excretion. The better these functions are performed, the purer and more ethereal will be the influences which ascend to the brain." Indirectly, vocal music promoted good health by stimulating "cheerfulness and genial flow of spirits." In outlining the third advantage of vocal music as a common school subject Mann strained hardest to rationalize. Singing trained the intellect because harmonic relations were mathematical and a scientific approach to the study of music could exercise the same portions of the mind that arithmetic did. Mann's argument was correct but meaningless since subjecting music to mathematical anal-

[5] The discussion of vocal music is in Mann's *Eighth Annual Report*, 117–132.

ysis was not a practical possibility in the nineteenth-century common school.

Mann devoted most of his discussion on vocal music to extolling its fourth advantage, its "social and moral influence." Although he did not make the connection, it is clear that he believed music could play an important role in Christian nurture, in promoting love in children and protecting them from the influences of evil. Music, Mann argued, "holds a natural relationship or affinity with peace, hope, affection, generosity, charity, devotion. There is also a natural repugnance between music and fear, envy, malevolence, misanthropy." Music also was revitalizing. It could take over from the intellect when that faculty was overtired or overtaxed, it could "restore the energies that have been wasted by toil, revivify the spirits languishing with care, or cause the dawn of joy to arise upon the long watches of sickness." In 1843 Mann had visited a number of schools in Prussia and was very favorably impressed by what he saw, especially by the orderliness of the Prussian schools and the gentleness of the discipline needed to maintain that orderliness. Music was "not the least efficient among the means by which the schools of Prussia are kept in such admirable order, with so rare a resort to corporal punishment," he claimed. When combined with the amiability of the Prussian teachers, music made the Prussian schoolroom "the abode of peace and love,—a bright spot where the sun of affection is rarely obscured even by a passing cloud." Singing could be just as efficient a guarantor of orderliness beyond the classroom as in it. The director of a particularly orderly Prussian reformatory that Mann visited explained, and Mann repeated this explanation approvingly, that because the children in the institution sang all day, the devil could not corrupt them. Musical training also helped account for the superior order and tranquillity of the German people, according to Mann. Music "adds zest to all social amusements. It saves the people from boisterous and riotous passions. Pervading all classes, it softens and refines the national character."

Mann was not alone in his belief in singing's effectiveness as a mode of inculcating moral virtue. In 1838, five years before Mann visited Prussia, the Boston School Committee established instruction in vocal music in that city's public schools. The committee shared the hope that vocal music would promote morality and good order within and beyond the classroom. Music would help the child to "feel rightly" and "it is of more importance a hundred-fold to feel rightly than to think profoundly." What did "feeling rightly" mean? Schools in which children felt rightly, the school committee reasoned, would be sending forth "happy, useful, well instructed, contented members of society."[6]

[6] Boston School Committee, Musical Tract No. 2 (Boston, 1840); Boston School Committee Minutes, II, 106, quoted in Mary Ann Connolly, "The Boston Schools in the New Republic, 1776–1840" (Unpublished Dissertation, Harvard University, 1963), 274–276.

The significance of this far-fetched faith in singing is that the school-men and reformers evaluated subject matter in terms of its usefulness for moral inculcation, made morality and social control nearly synonymous, and openly sought to make children pliable to the wishes of the teachers. Music is "a moral means of great efficacy," Mann argued, because it "disarms anger, softens rough and turbulent natures, socializes, and brings the whole mind, as it were, into a state of fusion, from which condition the teacher can mould it into what forms he will, as it cools and hardens."[7] That was the point. In order to fulfill the tasks they had set for it, the common school reformers felt it necessary to seek a pedagogy by which the common school could actually remold children to conform to the moral standards the reformers and schoolmen wished to impose. An effective school should have the power, in effect, to melt a child down and build him up again as a different moral being.

Phrenology offered Mann and other reformers that accepted the doctrine another means of remolding the common school student. Phrenology was a psychological doctrine that sought to explain intellectual and emotional development in terms of physical causes. It was a complex faculty psychology designed to give those who understood it the power to alter human nature and behavior. At its most ridiculous extreme, phrenology identified as many as thirty or forty mental and emotional traits or faculties, each of which was controlled by a separate portion of the brain. Some phrenologists mapped the portion of the skull which covered the brain in such a way as to show which faculties lay under which part of the skull and further claimed that a careful feeling of the bumps and depressions in the skull enabled them, with the aid of the map, to diagnose a person's character. The most extreme argued further that they could change a person's character by massaging the skull so as to stimulate areas that corresponded to desirable traits. For example, a phrenologist might argue that the faculty of amativeness (love) was controlled in that part of the brain that corresponded to the portion of the skull two inches above the left ear and that the faculty of combativeness was in a similar position above the right ear. Through massaging the area above the left ear and neglecting that above the right ear the phrenologist claimed that he could change an argumentative person into a friendly agreeable one.

It is quite easy to see how much this extreme form of phrenology would have appealed to educational reformers bent on finding ways to reshape children in conformity with society's moral standards. But few educational reformers accepted the theory that external manipulation of bumps would lead to character change.

[7] Mann, *Seventh Annual Report*, 126–127.

Even stripped of its theory of therapy and the idea that faculties were so precisely localized in the brain, phrenology remained a very useful doctrine for educators concerned with character change. In this guise phrenology should be viewed as a fairly complex faculty psychology not unrelated to the theories of connectionism and behaviorism that were to be so influential in twentieth-century educational theory. For educational reformers phrenology marked a great advance over the other available psychologies—even the traditional faculty psychology—of the day because it considered a host of moral and ethical faculties to be physically controlled in the brain. By taking traits such as obedience, duty, responsibility, kindness, reverence, hopefulness, righteousness, and conscientiousness out of the realm of the spiritual and religious into the realm of science, phrenology helped the reformers separate morals and ethics from religion and sectarianism. These moral traits were brought out in the open where they could be studied, measured, and affected independent of supernatural influence. As such, they, just like intellectual traits of language perception, comparison and causality, and combination, could now become objects for secular education to influence.

Phrenology was also useful because it promised tools to diagnose and classify children's character so that teachers would know how they might best be educated, especially morally. Throughout the United States phrenologists offered the public the opportunity to have their aptitudes tested through head reading, and young men in New York City regularly called on phrenologists to guide them in job seeking. One phrenologist wrote a book specifically for teachers entitled *The Scientific Basis of Education Demonstrated by an Analysis of the Temperaments and of Phrenological Facts, in Connection with Mental Phenomena and the Office of the Holy Spirit in the Processes of the Mind.* In it he urged the use of phrenological testing in the schools. When a teacher is aware that a child has a well-developed faculty for destructiveness, he can appeal to the child's faculty of executiveness (or building); if a child's faculty of combativeness is strong, his teacher should appeal to the child's sense of cautiousness or approbation. In this manner phrenology offered educational reformers and teachers the chance to effect substantial change in students' future behavior.

Because phrenology argued that human beings could become perfect if they allowed all their faculties to develop naturally, it accorded well with the early nineteenth century's romanticization of nature and with the reformers' belief in the natural innocence of the child. Phrenologists suggested that a person's faculties would develop naturally in a harmonious and balanced way, that a person growing up in ideal conditions would have just the right amount of kindness and just the right amount of combativeness. Educational reformers like Mann found this notion compelling and urged the schools to cooperate with nature, including human nature. Superficially, it may seem contradictory that reformers welcomed phrenology because it helped them manipulate children's personalities, and that they used it to justify a belief that the best development for children was to leave their development to nature. They resolved the conflict in arguing that children's character needed manipulation only because careless families and wicked society had interfered with the children's natural development before they came to school. The school had to neglect unnaturally stimulated faculties and to strengthen unnaturally restrained faculties in order to compensate for the unnatural influence of parents and the social environment. The emphasis on natural development encouraged reformers like Mann to argue successfully for changes in the curriculum and in the school's physical plant that did have a significant effect on the school experience. Since the essence of education was balanced development of all the faculties, excessive concentration on linguistic and other forms of intellectual training had to be eased in favor of new activities like art and music and recess. Mann spent much of his time campaigning for better ventilated schoolhouses and school furniture designed to fit young bodies, arguing that cooping youngsters up in overheated buildings on uncomfortable seats was unnatural and therefore inefficient. Effective schooling would always appeal to and encourage the child's natural proclivities and protect him from unnatural influences. As Lydia Sigourney, a genteel poetess of the age, put it: schools must tune the harp so as not to injure its natural harmonies.[8]

III

Mann embodied the findings he made in a six-month tour of European schools in his Seventh Report, published in 1844, that was very critical of educational practices in Massachusetts. In essence he claimed that schools in the United States were ineffective because they sought to force knowledge into children and because, consequently, they devoted so much of their time to physically disciplining children. Mann recommended, instead, that they follow the Prussian model, in turn based upon the ideas of Pestalozzi, by gearing their instruction to the child's level of development and appealing constantly to his natural interests and his natural desire to learn.

Pestalozzianism had been known in America long before Mann's report was published. Indeed, Joseph Neef, who had been one of Pestalozzi's trusted assistants in Switzerland, migrated to the United States in 1806 and taught in a series of schools throughout the country, including that at the New Harmony utopian community, but he seems to have

---

[8] Lydia Sigourney, quoted in Bernard Wishy, *The Child and the Republic: The Dawn of Modern American Child Nurture* (Philadelphia, 1968), 21.

influenced few outside the utopian circle. A Pestalozzian arithmetic text appeared in the United States in 1821. Boston's first vocal music teacher was greatly influenced by Pestalozzi's ideas which he had encountered in Europe. Yet Pestalozzi's reputation in the United States was not high. It suffered because Americans associated him with Rousseau, an educational thinker whom Pestalozzi firmly admired, and the radicalism of the French Revolution. Mann apparently did not expect to win any support by associating his recommendations with Pestalozzi's name. Instead he identified them as Prussian. As has often been pointed out, Mann's description of the Prussian system was inaccurate in the extreme, idealized beyond recognition to enable Mann to criticize American practice more forcefully. What he chose to label as Prussian, however, were largely vestiges of Pestalozzian ideas which Prussia had adopted in revamping its school system after the Napoleonic Wars. Mann's recommendations, then, were clearly rooted in Pestalozzian ideas and should be recognized as such.

Johann Heinrich Pestalozzi (1746–1827) was born in Zurich of economically marginal middle-class parents (his father died when he was a small boy and left him and his mother in very straitened circumstances). Pestalozzi tried several callings, including the ministry, the law, and farming, but failed to make his way in any. The plight of the Swiss peasant of his day, forced to choose between remaining on the farm where productivity was not keeping pace with population growth and taking dehumanizing and debilitating work in a factory, very much moved Pestalozzi. He was particularly concerned at the destruction of the peasant's natural ties with the land and of his family life. Pestalozzi himself bought a farm upon which he attempted a number of agricultural reforms, hoping to set the peasant an example of how to make farmland support more people. He was unsuccessful in this venture, but on the farm he established a school in which poor peasant children would learn the common branches in conjunction with doing useful work on Pestalozzi's farm and spinning mill. Pestalozzi found himself an educator although he had no administrative capabilities. He taught in several different schools, all alike in that they ministered to the needs of children of the disadvantaged. He published several books that described his schools, his methods, and his philosophy. Most of his writings are dull and painfully vague, but in 1781 he published *Leonard and Gertrude* which presented in novelistic form his major educational ideas. A popular success, the novel gave Pestalozzi the beginnings of an international reputation which was confirmed by the success of the school he started at Yverdon in 1804. *Leonard and Gertrude* made two basic points. First, it held that children should begin learning by studying about things they could sense and things they already knew rather than by studying abstractions such as rules of grammar and number. The curriculum should rely on activities with which the child was familiar at home. The teacher should appeal to the senses before he appeals to the reason. In brief, this was the philosophy underlying Pestalozzi's object method. Second, the ideal school should be homelike. Bonds of love between teacher and pupil should replace the normal authoritarian discipline of the school. Pestalozzi's emphasis was on learning by doing, on the natural goodness and curiosity of children, and on the importance of love to the learning process. These were the qualities that Mann identified, incredibly enough, with the Prussian school system in his provocative report of 1844.

That report started a pamphlet war (or, more accurately, a book war, as each "pamphlet" ran to 150 or more pages) between Mann and a group of thirty-one Boston schoolmasters—mostly teachers in upper elementary grade schools. The six heavy pamphlets of charge and counter-charge (Mann's *Report,* the 31's *Remarks on the Report,* Mann's *Reply to the Remarks,* the masters' *Rejoinder to the Reply,* Mann's *Answer to the Rejoinder,* and finally *Penitential Tears; or A Cry from the Dust, by "The Thirty One," Prostrated and Pulverized by the Hand of Horace Mann*) covered a number of topics; three merit discussion in this context.

The first was Mann's recommendation that reading should be taught initially by the "whole-word" method rather than by first teaching students to discriminate the sounds and the shapes of letters. The Prussian system of starting with whole words whose meaning and pronunciation children already knew was the best method because it naturally interested the children and gave them the most pleasure. Mann discouraged the teaching of the alphabet until the pupil had mastered a 1,000-word reading vocabulary. The masters disagreed with Mann's recommendations for several learned technical reasons. "The only philosophical and true" method of teaching, they contended, was to start from the smallest components of a subject and work up. They identified the letters of the alphabet as the smallest components in this case. They also pointed out that Mann's method lost the advantage that English had over Chinese. Since English words represent both ideas and sounds, a reader knows how to pronounce a word by looking at it. But Mann's method, by neglecting phonetics, failed to teach children how to pronounce words with which they were unfamiliar. The masters also mentioned, without comment, that Horace Mann's wife had a financial interest in textbooks which taught the whole-word method.

The masters' real objection did not lie in the realm of technicalities, however. They rejected the whole-word method because it relied on the philosophy that good teaching must relate to the interests and pleasures of the child. The masters were vehement in denouncing this doctrine: "The mere promotion of a child's pleasure should never form the basis of any system of education," they contended.

> To *gratify* the child, should not be the teacher's aim, but rather to lay a permanent foundation, on which to rear a noble and well-proportioned

superstructure. If, while doing *this,* the teacher is successful in rendering mental *exertion* agreeable, and in leading the child from one conquest to another, till *achievement itself* affords delight, it is well; . . . But if, to cultivate pleasure seeking is his aim, he had better, at once, abandon his profession, and obtain an employment in which he will not endanger the welfare, both of individuals and society, by sending forth a sickly race, palsied in every limb, through idleness, and a vain attempt to gratify a morbid thirst for pleasure.[9]

The masters thought that learning should be difficult because hard work in school built character. Further, the experience of having to apply himself to subjects that did not interest him taught the student self-discipline and will power. Teaching students material in which they were interested made them soft and "passive" recipients of knowledge. Moreover, the pursuit of knowledge was difficult and to promise students it could be made "easy" was dishonest. The masters objected to teaching that led

> pupils [to] become accustomed to depend, for their motive to mental effort, upon that excitement alone which is furnished by their teacher. We would have them stimulated to the pursuit of knowledge, by a love of that pursuit for itself, and by a proper appreciation of its results; and not by that temporary interest which is awakened by the pleasing manner or amusing speech of their instructor; for, the former influence, becomes a constant spring of action in the mind, while the latter, depends for its existence upon the presence of the teacher who exercises it. Further, we believe that care is necessary on the part of the teacher, lest the stimulation and excitement, which the pupil experiences under his influence at school, should be so strong, as to produce a reaction, and, when that influence ceases, to leave the mind disinclined to exertion; its energies exhausted, and its faculties deadened. This state of mind must surely be most unfavorable to a perception of those "social, every-day duties and obligations," to which Mr. Mann properly attaches so much importance.[10]

Object teaching would make the child intellectually lazy and thus morally and socially corrupt and pernicious.

The child's moral and intellectual growth depended not only on mental discipline: the masters contended that it also depended on the establishment of adult authority through the use of corporal punishment in the classroom. Mann, of course, disagreed, hailing the Prussian classroom in which parental affection ruled the classrooms and made corporal punishment unnecessary. The Prussian "teacher's manner was better than parental, for it had a parent's tenderness and vigilance, without the foolish dotings or indulgences to which parental affection is prone." In the German classroom "no child was disconcerted, disabled, or bereft

[9] [Boston Association of Masters of the Public Schools], *Remarks on the Seventh Annual Report of the Honorable Horace Mann, Secretary of the Massachusetts Board of Education* (Boston, 1844), 85–86.

[10] *Ibid.,* 46.

of his senses, through fear" of ridicule or physical pain.[11] Mann insultingly criticized American schoolmasters for attempting to rule children through fear. If teachers were more intelligent, he suggested, they would not have to employ corporal punishment. "A teacher who cannot rule by love, must do so by fear. A teacher who cannot supply material for the activity of his pupils' minds by his talent, must put down that activity by force. A teacher who cannot answer all the questions and solve all the doubts of a scholar as they arise, must assume an awful and mysterious air, and must expound in oracles, which themselves need more explanation than the original difficulty."[12] One can wonder if Horace Mann was not trying to rule through ridicule here. But Mann was less worried about the intellectual inefficiency of teaching through the use of fear than in the moral inefficiencies. Teachers who taught with love more effectively altered the behavior of their pupils, he argued, which should be the teacher's primary goal. Corporal punishment made children hard and surly and stifled their natural good will while a teacher's loving and trusting attitude encouraged the child to develop his natural goodness. Mann's report on Prussian education devoted a vastly disproportionate amount of space to analyzing institutions in which children lived all the time—orphanages, reform schools, and schools for the children of prisoners. Mann drew his examples of the effectiveness of institutionalized parental discipline from these institutions but then proceeded to generalize from these examples that his favored method of teaching was everywhere effective and could be used in the regular Massachusetts day school. That he found his model for the ideal common school in institutions which had total control over children is suggestive. To fulfill its objectives, he seemed to feel that the common school must have considerably more power than it then had, a power as great as that possessed by schools which took the child out of society to shape him in isolation.

Again, the masters found little that was persuasive in Mann's arguments. First, they criticized his utopian vision of the all-powerful school and the all-powerful schoolmaster. Men (like themselves) who actually taught (Mann had never taught school) faced children who were, in most of their lives, subject to social influences quite outside the school's control. The common school teacher, unlike the director of an orphanage or reform school, had to battle daily against parental influence. "The practical teacher learns by his daily experience, that the delicate relation of parent and child, will often rise mountain-high before him, when he feels his official duties (in disciplining the child) the most obligatory. The juvenile wanderer often finds the ready apologist in the doting parent."[13] They also pointed out that the German teacher worked in an au-

---

[11] Mann, *Seventh Annual Report,* 137.
[12] *Ibid.,* 127–128.
[13] Masters, *Remarks,* 37.

thoritarian state in which children learned, from all social institutions, to obey; they, on the other hand, had to contend with children raised in a permissive polity. The masters did not advocate frequent use of corporal punishment but did contend that both proper classroom order and correct socialization depended on the threat of corporal punishment and its occasional use. Corporal punishment greatly aided the teacher's ability to counteract the evil influences beyond the school. More important, physical punishment taught children to function properly in the world of law and order beyond the classroom. They must learn to respect authority: "As the fear of the Lord is the beginning of divine wisdom," the masters wrote, "so is the fear of the law, the beginning of political wisdom." Mann, of course, would have disagreed with both halves of this proposition. Love was not enough, the masters argued. Children must be taught to do things they did not enjoy and things for which they did not understand the reason. "Implicit obedience to rightful authority must be inculcated and enforced upon children, as the very germ of all good order in future society."[14] Basically the masters felt that children would not, under any conditions, want to do what was right. Mann, on the other hand, thought they would.

Another issue dividing Mann and the masters was the use of emulation as a goad to student performance in school. The argument was not nearly so vehement as the others described here, but Mann's position revealed a good deal about the kind of citizens Whiggish reformers expected the ideal common school to produce. In some ways emulation was the obverse of physical punishment: when a student did something right the teacher gave him a reward or changed his rank in class in such a way that the student was favorably distinguished from his classmates. Emulation worked in the classroom, its proponents held, because it appealed to the child's competitive instinct and made him work hard to learn in order to outshine his peers. The spelling bee long used in American schools was one form of emulation; Mann sympathetically described another form which he found in a Scottish school. In it, children stood in a row and the master began his questioning. Students exchanged places (passed up or down) according to their relative proficiency and earned chits for passing up past a certain number of their fellows.

When this sharper goad to emulation is to be applied, the spectator will see the teacher fill his hand with small bits of pasteboard, and, as the recitation goes on and competition becomes keen, and places are rapidly lost and won, the teacher is seen occasionally to give one of these tickets to a pupil as a counter, or token, that he has passed up above so many of his fellows; . . . [tickets are] given without any stopping or speaking,—for the teacher and pupil appear to have kept a silent reckoning, and when the latter extends his

14 *Ibid.*, 127–128.

hand, the former gives a ticket without any suspension of the lesson. This gives the greatest intensity to competition; and at such times, the children have a look of almost maniacal eagerness and anxiety.[15]

Interestingly enough, Mann did not object to the psychological pressures engendered by such practices although he admitted that emulation might become too intense. He seems to have believed that the pressure fostered the child's intellectual development. Mann objected to emulative techniques on very different grounds. Emulation introduced the child too early to the competitive pressures of the world and taught him to copy the overly materialistic, competitive, and aggressive manner of adults living in the commercial urban society. It taught children to vie against each other rather than to cooperate in true community fashion. Emulation destroyed the home-like atmosphere appropriate to the classroom and introduced competition in a place where love and acceptance and cooperation should dominate. "I heard no child ridiculed, sneered at, or scolded, for making a mistake," Mann remarked of his experience in the Prussian schools. "On the contrary, whenever a mistake was made, or there was a want of promptness in giving a reply, the expression of the teacher was that of grief and disappointment, as though there had been a failure, not merely to answer the question of a master, but to comply with the expectations of a friend."[16] In emulative practices the teacher displayed no such solicitude, moving on directly to the next student when the first student failed.

The masters did not make much of the emulation issue. As usual, they took the practical view: competition and emulation existed in the world of adults and children naturally copied that world. Since students would be competitive anyway, the masters thought it wise to channel that trait toward useful objectives. They agreed that emulation could be overdone, but otherwise thought that it fully accorded with the objectives of education. Emulation would teach children to internalize the desire to learn, to eschew reliance on outside inspiration. The masters contended that schooling's main objective was to teach independence of thought, self-reliance, and will power, all traits a person would need to live successfully in the United States. Elementary education should, they contended, "discipline and strengthen their [the students'] minds, and prepare them, as far as is possible, for that independent action, which will be required of them in the discharge of the duties of life."[17] Mann's discussion of emulation and of competition suggests that he wished to protect children from the world of commercial competition and the spirit of getting ahead. Self-reliance and independent action were not as important for him as

[15] Mann, *Seventh Annual Report,* 63.
[16] *Ibid.,* 137.
[17] Masters, *Remarks,* 45.

they were for the masters. Mann praised one of the Prussian reform schools because in it "the children are not stimulated by the worldly motives of fame, wealth, or personal aggrandizement. The superintendent does not inflame them with the ambition, that if they surpass each other at recitation, and make splendid displays at public examinations, they shall, in the end, become high military officers, or congress-men, or excite the envy of all by their wealth or fame. On the other hand, so far as this world's goods are concerned, he commends and habituates them to the idea of an honorable poverty; and the only riches with which he dazzles their imaginations are the riches of good works."[18] Although he referred to a school for the disadvantaged, Mann's recommendations against teaching ambition were not limited to that special case. Mann did not regard the Prussian reform schools as a special case but as models of operation for the public schools in his own country. He wished to proscribe the inspiration of ambition and of love of worldly goods in all schools in America. One way the educational reformers wanted schools to solve growing social problems in the United States was by serving as an antidote to the evils associated with materialism, competition, breakdown of community, ambitious consumption, and the substitution of pushiness for deference. Emulation in school would simply foster these undesirable traits. Instead, schools should strive to turn children into socially stable, cooperative, and politically deferent citizens content, if not with honorable poverty, at least with their unexalted place. This was the way that schools were going to foster the social stability for which the Whigs longed.

Unfortunately, Mann's disagreements with the Boston schoolmasters have come down to us as a battle exclusively over corporal punishment —in which Mann led the forces of humanitarianism against the medieval views of the masters.[19] This interpretation has neglected the controversy's considerable significance for the debate on the nature of childhood, the purposes of schooling, and the development of a pedagogy adequate to the new demands being placed on schools. Mann can be said to have won the battle over corporal punishment. Although in Boston that method persisted well into the twentieth century, in most of the United States the arguments of Mann and reformers like him led to a vast reduction in the use of corporal punishment and to the adoption of an apologetic tone by those educators who continued to employ it. On the larger issues of the debate, however, there is little to suggest that Mann's recommendations for more natural pedagogical methods and a more enlight-

[18] Mann, *Seventh Annual Report*, 77.

[19] Michael B. Katz's analysis of the controversy in *The Irony of Early School Reform: Educational Innovation in Mid-Nineteenth Century Massachusetts* (Cambridge, Mass., 1968), Part II, is a conspicuous and insightful exception to this generalization.

ened view of the child were widely heeded. Mann's attempt to implement his vision of Pestalozzianism did not succeed in affecting classroom practice. His ideas—or, perhaps more accurately, a ritualistic homage to his rhetoric—appeared widely in the literature on educational theory in the next several generations. Willingly enough, American educators adopted Mann's rhetoric about humane and gentle teaching that cooperated with the nature of the child rather than fought it, but they failed generally to grasp or implement the spirit lying behind his recommendations.

Several things help account for this failure. By raising the issue of the Massachusetts teachers' intellectual and pedagogical ability in the tone he did, Mann probably damaged any chances his reforms had for implementation in American schools. The masters' many allusions to Mann's lack of classroom experience reveal how defensive Mann's slurs on their abilities had made them. That defensiveness—the typical defensiveness of the professional when he is criticized by outsiders—prevented the masters from understanding some of the merit in and spirit behind Mann's recommendations. The outsider-criticizing-the-professional drama of the Mann and masters imbroglio has been played out many times in the educational history of the United States; reformers' inability to recommend improvements in the schools without throwing educators into a rigidly defensive and unaccommodating position has been a continuing barrier to educational reform in this country. On the other side of the coin, the teaching corps, as Michael Katz has so perceptively pointed out, was most anxious to believe those parts of the reformers' ideas, Mann's especially, which promised to augment the teacher's power, his status, and the general population's belief in the centrality and significance of the teacher's role in American society. Teachers in the United States did not grasp Mann's ideas about cooperating with the natural development of the child, but they understood immediately the favorable implications of his praise of the teacher and the school as crucial to the preservation of American social order and his ideas that the school and the teacher were society's only available means of curbing crime and disorder. Teachers were only too glad to agree that they were the moral bastions of the developing society and that they should be placed in charge of the intellectual and moral nurture of all the children in the United States. When the reformer aggrandized the reputation of the teacher, he was listened to and followed; when he criticized the performance of those teachers, his recommendations fell on deaf ears.

Another cause reduced the influence of Mann's ideas about the schools' obligation to encourage the natural development of the child. Although there is no way of precisely measuring public attitudes on a question such as this, it seems more than likely that the majority of parents agreed more with the masters than with Mann that obedience to authority must be forcibly inculcated in children. The parent in Edward

Eggleston's *Hoosier Schoolmaster* (1871) who demanded that the village schoolteacher "lick 'em and larn 'em" was probably more typical than the common school reformers liked to admit. Mann's admonition that the best way to solve the problems of disorder and lack of social control in society was to loosen the discipline of the school, or to substitute a subtler means of discipline the value of which was untested, seemed inherently wrongheaded to many, many parents. Mann may have had every confidence in the methods he advocated but the fact that he relied on exaggerated evidence from another country to bolster his recommendations suggests that convincing evidence of those methods' effectiveness was not readily available. It is not difficult to see why many would remain unconvinced by his exposition.

IV

Mann's advocacy of Pestalozzian educational ideas failed to change American education practice very much. Another version of Pestalozzianism, however, had a much wider popular and practical success after it was introduced at the Oswego Normal School in 1859. The reasons for this other version's success, when compared to the failure of Mann's version, further explain Mann's failure and illuminate the limits of school reform.

The "object method," as the Oswego version of Pestalozzian reform was called, emphasized a single strand of Pestalozzi's thought to the eventual exclusion of all others. The strand it chose to emphasize, moreover, was the narrowest, most easily codifiable, least crucial to redefining the nature of the relation between teacher and taught, and most easily separated from Pestalozzi's vision of the school as an inculcator of moral values. The object method, essentially, was a means of correlating the curriculum with the development of the child's mental faculties. As the faculty of sense developed well before those of understanding and reason, teachers should first approach children through the senses. "All knowledge is derived in the first instance from the perceptions of the senses, and therefore . . . all instructions should be based upon the observation of real objects and occurrences."[20] Oswego concentrated on teaching young children how to perceive rather than what to think. Teachers were to appeal to the children's senses by bringing into the classroom objects, or pictures of objects—thus the name of the movement—that the students could see and touch. Some objects were familiar, some complex; in all cases the point of the lesson was to have the children describe the objects as fully as possible—thus improving their power of observation. Upon being shown an orange, for example, the perceptive

[20] Edward A. Sheldon, *Autobiography* (New York, 1911), 145–147.

student was to describe it as natural, vegetable, opaque, foreign, impressible, odorous, sapid, edible, wholesome, juicy, refreshing, spherical, rough, reddish yellow, and he was to add that "we must thank God for it." At more complex levels the class might analyze a story or a poem, but the teacher was instructed constantly to draw pictures or provide actual examples of the physical objects discussed in the story, to act out himself or have the students dramatize parts of the story, and to get the children to refer the actions and lessons in the story to the context of their own lives.

Object teaching was based, quite clearly, on Pestalozzi's idea that young children should begin learning about things with which they were already in some way familiar and that they learned best by doing. What is significant is how quickly the Oswego movement lost sight of other aspects of Pestalozzi's ideas about education. Mann had mentioned the object method: his advocacy of the whole-word method of teaching reading had been based on it. For him the object method was simply a strategy; he was more interested in the idea behind it that good teaching appealed to the child's interests and natural desire to learn. He most admired Pestalozzi's emphasis on the power of love and familial relations to enhance the child's natural desires to be cooperative, selfless, and happy. For him Pestalozzi's greatest contribution lay in his insights into moral training. At Oswego the moral implications of Pestalozzi's educational ideas were lost in the effort to define and implement what the movement took to be Pestalozzi's primary pedagogical method.

The Oswego movement had begun with much wider goals: its founder had been as concerned with moral training as any of the Whig educational reformers of his generation. But, where Mann's pedagogical reform attempts had been largely restricted to encouraging schoolmen through writing and public speaking, the founder of the Oswego movement institutionalized his attempts at reform in an urban school system and in a teacher training school. In the process his goals were narrowed and his ideas simplified and rigidified as they were codified for transmission to large numbers of teachers and packaged for implementation in actual classroom situations.

The career of Edward Augustus Sheldon (1823–1897) neatly telescopes the progress of educational reform in the 1830–1870 period. Sheldon believed expanded and more efficient schooling would compensate for the breakdown of other forms of social control. Therefore, he sought to organize and codify the educational practices that he found and to force them upon the children to be reformed. Sheldon was born in rural upstate New York of economically marginal middle-class parents. He found school uncongenial and his work there was unsatisfactory until he experienced an "educational conversion" at the age of seventeen. His conversion led him to apply himself to his studies so assiduously at an academy and then for two years at college that his eyesight failed and he was forced to leave school. He moved to Oswego and entered the nursery business but failed. Here he converted once more—this time to a belief that social control must be imposed on the depressed classes in urban America. Oswego, located on Lake Ontario in upper New York State, was a typical booster city of the period. Two thirds of the way along the Erie Canal and connected to it by a spur, it had visions of becoming a major lake port, but Buffalo and Rochester captured most of the lake-canal commercial traffic. Large numbers of Irish and French-Canadian laborers had been imported to the city to build the canal spur and when that task was complete they remained, unemployed or underemployed, to stagnate in the stagnating city. Oswego enjoyed all the squalor, vice, degradation, and potential instability that belonged to any larger city of the period. It displayed all the problems of urbanization and industrialization that had disturbed Whig reformers in other urban environments. These conditions very strongly affected Sheldon who, as a migrant from the rural regions, found them appalling and somewhat mysterious. In 1848, as he recalled in his autobiography, he decided to investigate the condition of the poor in Oswego. He found 1,500 persons unable to read and write (the population of Oswego in 1850 was 12,205). "As a country boy I had hardly known of such a person, and my astonishment may be well understood on finding such a degree of gross ignorance. To me it seemed like being in the midst of heathendom." He was convinced that reform was imperative. One Sunday, "as I passed through the streets . . . and saw great numbers of ragged, profane children romping the streets, having no idea of the sacredness of the day, my heart was pained within me, and I went to my room reflecting what might be done for these poor children." In 1848 education was an obvious solution and Sheldon, with the help of his roommates, organized a school for which he raised money through appeals at church services and prayer meetings. Through the school he established a program for providing clothing for destitute children, for finding foster homes for orphans and children of especially degraded parents, and for visiting the parents of his students. Sheldon had planned to enroll in a seminary the following year but instead found himself a schoolmaster in a charity school for "one hundred twenty to one hundred thirty wild Irish and French boys and girls." Sheldon's first experience with education beyond his own schooling, then, was as organizer and master of a ragged school designed to elevate poor children out of the wretchedness and immorality of their lot. His typically Whiggish efforts were not confined simply to the ragged school. "During the summer months I occupied my Sundays in distributing religious papers and tracts to sailors and boatmen. I also visited the jail for a similar purpose and for religious conversation and instruction."[21]

[21] *Ibid.*, 74–78, 89.

At the same time Sheldon, sensing the inadequacy of a single ragged school, began campaigning for the city to establish a free school system. The politics of his campaign were quite similar to those in other cities. The city's elite supported the idea but one man whom Sheldon identified as "a politician" urged the city's Catholics to oppose a free school system on the grounds that it was a Protestant plot against Catholic children. The Catholics, with the help of other portions of the population, successfully blocked Sheldon's efforts. When it became clear that the mass of the city's population would not consent to the plan, Sheldon and his influential supporters determined to circumvent the popular will. In 1853 they persuaded the state legislature to pass legislation establishing free schools in Oswego; that legislation contained no provision for a popular referendum on the issue within the city. The law, Sheldon remembered somewhat gleefully, "was, in truth, sprung on the people, as one might say, contrary to their will."[22] The need for reform was so great as to outweigh democratic principle.

Sheldon was appointed superintendent of the new system (he had briefly filled a similar position in Syracuse during the fight for free schools in Oswego) and he set out to placate the people upon whom he had sprung the system. Sheldon set about wiping clean the city's educational slate and erecting a totally new "machine" to educate the populace. He erased the old district lines, planned a thirteen-year graded course and implemented it at once, and fired a large number of teachers, many with friends on the board of education, through the expedient of having the board "blind-grade" a written examination which Sheldon had administered to all the teachers. The board did his firing for him. Sheldon viewed education as a solution to the city's ills and set out in a business-like manner to establish the most efficient and most widespread schooling possible. What took some cities years and generations to accomplish— changing district lines, removing deadwood from teaching staffs, establishing a graded curriculum—Sheldon did within a single year, and he claimed that the reformed system cost the city only $266.83 more than the old one. Almost overnight he created a complete educational system, and he was immensely proud of it. "I have good reason," he remembered, "for believing that I had organized and perfected the most complete educational machine that was ever constructed. By looking at my watch, I could tell exactly what every teacher in the city was doing."[23]

While imposing this educational machine on an initially reluctant citizenry, Sheldon conducted a full-scale community relations program. Just as he had engaged widespread support for his ragged school through public fund-raising activities, he involved the whole community in establishing the free school system. The complexity of his arrangements, he

[22] *Ibid.,* 93.
[23] *Ibid.,* 115.

recalled, made people curious and he took advantage of that curiosity by visiting homes to explain the new system to parents. He also involved the public in evaluating the schools, which devoted the last month of the school year to a series of written examinations designed to test the work done throughout the year. Sheldon claimed he personally prepared the questions for each examination and "I marked the answer to every question, keeping a personal account with each pupil and teacher." Then he tabulated the results and published the school-by-school and grade-by-grade results in his report to the board of education and sometimes in the daily newspapers. "In this way I kept up a high pressure on the schools. The rivalry and competition were something tremendous."[24] Here was emulation with a vengeance. He had the teachers and the pupils striving to outdo each other in front of the whole community. (There are certain parallels to the public competition of the spelling bee.) Thus, Sheldon met the formal objectives of the common school movement— free schools for all, centralized organization, and improved standards of teaching—with efficiency and dispatch. Common school reform occurred as rapidly in Oswego as in any city in the nation; but it was school reform that lacked Mann's concern with humane pedagogy. School reform implemented in the United States after 1830 probably resembled the kind that Sheldon initiated more than it resembled that which Mann recommended.

School reform began in Oswego in 1853; by 1859 Sheldon was aware that, despite its efficiency, it was failing to elevate the morals and character of the poor as it was intended to do. The machinery was perfect, but "there was something wanting to give life, spirit, I may say, soul to the school system," he remarked in his autobiography.[25] The absence of "soul" to which he referred can be interpreted to mean that the schools failed to attract and change the behavior of the poor. The formality, the memorization, the competitiveness drove them away. Seemingly intuitively, like Pestalozzi himself, Sheldon turned to the object method. Although a few of his teachers used objects in scattered parts of the curriculum, Sheldon seemed to have been unfamiliar with the method or the philosophy behind it when he set out, with a friend, to assemble sets of objects with which to teach reading and arithmetic in a systematic way. His efforts rested on a simple-minded Lockean psychology—that all ideas reach the mind through sensation—applied to the teacher-student relation. Since ideas come from sensations, learning should start with sensation, principally with perception. At the same time that he began to assemble his own teaching objects, Sheldon happened, on a visit to the schools in Toronto, to tour the National Museum where he saw objects

[24] *Ibid.*, 114–115.
[25] *Ibid.*, 116.

for teaching that had been designed by the Home and Colonial Infant and Juvenile School Society of London—the organization that pioneered object teaching in England. Sheldon bought the collection of charts, books, balls, cards, pictures of animals, building blocks, cotton balls, samples of grain, and specimens of pottery and glass from the museum— the Toronto schools did not employ object teaching—took them home, and put them to use in the lower grades of his educational machine. When the method seemed to promise eventual success, he set out to show his teachers how to use it. At first he established training classes on Saturday morning (which teachers attended "eagerly" without pay) but found them inadequate. He persuaded the city to establish its own normal school for teachers. The school imported an experienced object-method teacher from England the first year and, when she returned to England, Sheldon became head of the school (he had attended her classes the previous year). One of his most far-reaching reforms was to establish a practice school that closely resembled an actual city school and to require prospective teachers to spend a major portion of their training course practicing there. In a few years the state took over the school so that it could train teachers to go into every part of the state rather than simply train them for the Oswego city system. The object method of teaching taught at the Oswego Normal School became amazingly and almost immediately popular among educators. The National Teachers Association (soon to become the National Education Association) endorsed the method formally in 1865. The school was the most famous and influential teacher training institution in the Reconstruction era; school systems from all over the world sought teachers who had been trained there and its graduates, many of whom considered themselves missionaries spreading the gospel of object teaching, established new normal schools on the same pattern all over the country.

Sheldon seems to have comprehended the wider implications of Pestalozzi's ideas—that encouraging the child's natural development and substituting nonauthoritarian relations between teacher and student for authoritarian ones would increase the moral efficacy of the schools. But his writings subordinated these concerns to narrow explications of the psychology underlying the use of objects and the descriptions of how objects should be used in the classroom. The documents produced by the Oswego Normal School and its followers increasingly reduced complexities of Pestalozzianism to a few simple rules and "cookbook" maxims. As the missionaries of object teaching sought to convince thousands upon thousands of teachers and administrators of the worth of their system and to instruct them on its use, they were forced to simplify and codify its principles and practices. Publishers also played a role in narrowing and simplifying Pestalozzian principles: they could sell packages of texts and objects but not different attitudes between teachers and pupils.

Object teaching became essentially a mechanical rule that required teachers to begin teaching an elementary school subject by appealing to the students' senses. In too many cases teachers simply inserted another step in the traditional memorization process. Material was introduced by an object or a picture of an object, but the children were then expected to go right ahead to learn the old abstractions as if no change had occurred. Charles Dickens' satire in *Hard Times* of the teacher ridiculing the gypsy girl who had spent her whole life around horses when she failed to respond to a picture of a horse by reciting its "description" (that it was a graminivorous quadruped with 40 teeth—24 grinders, 4 eye teeth, and 12 incisors—and hard hoofs requiring to be shod with iron, which sheds its coat in the spring) is apt to the American experience. The object method did make some difference in school practice; it was partly responsible for progressive changes in the teaching of geography, arithmetic, and reading which simplified those subjects by developing curricula that moved from the simple to the complex so that the child himself could synthesize the material. The object method also spurred the introduction of drawing and drawing from memory, activities which were expected to increase the student's powers of observation. The introduction of drawing also revealed the method's chief liabilities. Texts instructed the primary school teacher to introduce her five-to-eight-year-old pupils to drawing by teaching them to identify and define the elements of form—to wit, corners, sides, straight and curved lines, plane and curved surfaces, right, acute, and obtuse angles, equilateral and right-angled triangles, perpendicular, horizontal, and parallel lines, the square, the rhomb, and parallelogram, pyramids, prisms, cubes, circles, semicircles, circumferences, arcs, center, radius, diameter, cylinders, cones, spheres, hemispheres, and ovals. The child was to practice drawing these forms before going on to representational drawing. Oswego's attempt to psychologize education, to correlate instruction to the natural development of the child's faculties, too often simply substituted one kind of abstraction and rote memorization for another.

In sum, object teaching failed to become the comprehensive reform of the common school system that Sheldon had hoped it would be. Sheldon became an institution and a bureaucrat, a crusader for the adoption of a method rather than for encompassing reform. He ended up a tinkerer with classroom practice rather than an advocate of major changes in that system. In all these ways he differed from a reformer like Mann, a prominent politician whose interest temporarily focused on fundamentally changing and vastly expanding educational institutions as one component of a comprehensive program of social reform. Sheldon, although he began by envisioning schooling as part of a more general reform crusade, gradually lost his character as a general reformer and became a professional educator, interested in educational reform for its own sake. With the founding of the normal school Sheldon became an educator's educator.

The educational reform that Sheldon advocated both contributed to and was shaped by the same turning inward. The common school movement generated widespread public interest and support; the Oswego movement's popularity was largely limited to those occupationally engaged in education. Its great attraction among them resulted from the boost it promised to give their professional status and independence as educators. First, it promised to make their efforts more effective, to make them more capable of attracting children to school. These promises of increased effectiveness were especially welcome in the years after the Civil War when outsiders increasingly faulted the teaching profession for failing to meet fully the demands that society had placed on schools and that the schools had willingly undertaken. Furthermore, the object method involved a jargon and a hardware that only those trained to use the method could interpret. This guaranteed educators a certain independence from lay criticism. Further, the method gave teaching the authority of science: the process of observation and then classification that the object method introduced on the elementary level was supposed also to be the method that enabled the natural sciences to advance so rapidly. And object teaching, with its supposedly precise psychological underpinning, gave the appearance of being more scientifically reliable than earlier pedagogies. Another attractive element was that the method clearly distinguished elementary from advanced teaching. Traditionally, the elementary teacher had been supposed to use, at a primitive and unspecialized level, the same methods employed by teachers at higher levels. Her work was merely a simpler version of more advanced techniques of the higher school, and her status among educators was consequently low. The most competent taught in academies and colleges; the less capable in elementary schools. In giving elementary teaching a method unique to itself, the object method allowed elementary teachers to claim a more advanced status without reference to the status of teachers in higher grades. All these advantages derived from the codified and formal aspects of Pestalozzi's ideas. They made object teaching attractive to educators but were not particularly appealing to a larger public. In consequence of its great popularity among educators, the object method was widely implemented in public schools in the second half of the nineteenth century, and it did not lose that popularity until its formalism and underlying psychology came under increasing criticism from educators and laymen alike during the Progressive era. Oswego's version of Pestalozzi's ideas gained wide currency in practice; the attempts to implement his more important ideas failed during the common school era and only after a half-century's hiatus was another attempt made to grasp and implement them.

GUIDE TO FURTHER READING

BERNARD WISHY, *The Child and the Republic: The Dawn of Modern American Child Nurture* (Philadelphia, 1968), remains the best introduction to the nineteenth-century reformulation of the nature of childhood. HORACE BUSHNELL'S *Christian Nurture* (1847; New York, 1861), is representative of a vast literature on modern child-rearing practices. An excellent biography of Bushnell which also offers many wider hypotheses on the period is BARBARA CROSS, *Horace Bushnell: Minister to a Changing America* (Chicago, 1958). CHARLES STRICKLAND, "A Transcendentalist Father: The Child-Rearing Practices of Bronson Alcott," *Perspectives in American History,* III (1969), 5–73, analyzes through autobiographical sources the actual experiences of a New England middle-class family. Similarities to the continental experience in the early nineteenth century can be seen in PHILIPPE ARIES, *Centuries of Childhood: A Social History of Family Life* (New York, 1962). PHILIP J. GREVEN, *Child-Rearing Concepts, 1628–1861* (Itasca, Ill., 1973), is a good collection of primary sources. The importance of women to the inculcation of virtue and character is examined in BARBARA WELTER, "The Cult of True Womanhood: 1820–1860," *American Quarterly,* XVIII (Summer, 1966), 151–174, and MARY P. RYAN, "American Society and the Cult of Domesticity, 1830–1860" (Unpublished Dissertation, University of California, Santa Barbara, 1971).

JONATHAN MESSERLI's volume, *Horace Mann: A Biography* (New York, 1972), is the best analysis of that central figure in mid-nineteenth-century reform. A laudatory work, yet one which contains a useful collection of primary materials, is MARY T. P. MANN, *The Life and Works of Horace Mann,* 5 vols. (Boston, 1891). CARLTON MABEE, "A Negro Boycott to Integrate Boston Schools," *New England Quarterly,* XLI (1968), 341–361, argues that Mann abandoned a definition of "commonality" that included blacks in order to secure and maintain as much white support as possible for the Massachusetts public schools. MICHAEL B. KATZ, *The Irony of Early School Reform* (Cambridge, Mass., 1968), reminds us that Mann sought to use "soft" educational methods to further social goals defined by the middle and upper classes. A more neutral interpretation of the work of Mann is MERLE BORROWMAN and CHARLES BURGESS, *What Doctrines to Embrace* (Glenview, Ill., 1969), chapter 2. The *Annual Reports* of the Massachusetts Board of Education and the Secretary's Report, in which can be found Mann's best published statements, should be read by the interested student. LAWRENCE A. CREMIN, ed., *The Republic and The School: Horace Mann on the Education of Free Men* (New York, 1957), is an excellent collection of Mann's writings.

Phrenology and related mid-nineteenth century psychological theories are surveyed in JOHN D. DAVIES, *Phrenology, Fad and Science: A Nineteenth Century American Crusade* (New Haven, Conn., 1955), and ALLAN S. HORLICK, "Phrenology and the Social Education of Young Men," *History of Education Quarterly,* XI (Spring, 1971), 23–38.

Henry Barnard's educational philosophy is introduced most conveniently by VINCENT P. LANNIE in his collection, *Henry Barnard: American Educator* (New York,

1974). German educational ideals and practices entered the United States through the speeches and publications of VICTOR COUSIN and CALVIN STOWE; see Cousin, *Report on the State of Public Instruction in Prussia,* trans. Sarah Austin (1834; New York, 1835), and Stowe, *Report on Elementary Public Instruction in Europe* (Columbus, Ohio, 1837). On Pestalozzi's influence on utopian communities in America the student should begin with ARTHUR BESTOR, *Backwoods Utopias: The Sectarian and Owenite Phases of Communitarian Socialism in America, 1663–1829* (Philadelphia, 1950), and JOSEPH NEEF, *Sketch of a Plan and Method of Education* (Philadelphia, 1808; reprinted in 1969). On his philosophy see GERALD GUTEK, *Pestalozzi and Education* (New York, 1968), and PESTALOZZI's *Leonard and Gertrude,* trans. and abridged by EVA CHANNING (Boston, 1885). His influence on the American kindergarten is examined in chapter 11.

The best studies of the "object method" and its operation in New York State are H. B. WILBUR, "The Object System of Instruction," National Education Association, *Addresses and Proceedings* (1864), 189–209, and WILBUR, "Object System of Instruction as Pursued in the Schools of Oswego," *American Journal of Education,* XV (March, 1865), 189–208, plus NED HARLAND DEARBORN, *The Oswego Movement in American Education* (New York, 1925), and ANDREW P. HOLLIS, *The Contribution of the Oswego School and Normal School to Educational Progress in the United States* (Boston, 1898). EDWARD A. SHELDON's *Autobiography* (New York, 1911), edited by Mary Sheldon, suggests his contribution to the standardization of the American public schools, and SHELDON's "Object Teaching," in HENRY BARNARD, ed., *Pestalozzi and His Educational System* (Syracuse, N. Y., 1888), acknowledges his reliance upon Pestalozzi. In *The Intelligence of a People* (Princeton, N. J., 1973), chapter 2, DANIEL CALHOUN examines SHELDON's work at Oswego. Normal school preparation is treated in MERLE BORROWMAN, *The Liberal and Technical in Teacher Education: A Historical Survey of American Thought* (New York, 1956).

PART III

The Retreat from Commonality, 1840–1920

CHAPTER 5

The Failure of the Common Schools (I): The South

BY 1880 PERFECTIONISM IN GENERAL WAS ACKNOWLEDGED A FAILURE. THE antebellum effort to purify the nation had won very few victories, and most of these proved hollow. Prisons filled as the level of education increased. Indeed, these institutions filled with educated prisoners. Asylums did not reform their inmates, nor could they make the insane healthy. Drunkenness continued in the face of temperance crusades. The antislavery movement ended with a costly war that never resolved the central problems. Universal schooling did not create order and harmony, and failed drastically its tests in the "reconstructed" South.

The failure of perfectionism taught the American people that human nature could never be made perfect. By the 1870s the enthusiastic and optimistic environmentalism which had fueled the antebellum reform effort was supplanted by a pessimistic hereditarianism. Michael B. Katz has pointed out that reform efforts in this country, as they collapsed in the face of their unrealistic promises, were replaced with hereditarian sentiments not conducive to further enthusiasm or activity. The pattern has been cyclical, Katz maintains, and argues that as the reform activity of the Progressive era deteriorated after 1920, hereditarian doctrines once again became popular as explanations for the failures. And again, in the late 1960s and early 1970s, a feeling of pessimism about the possibility of reforming individuals through improving their environments surfaced as the social programs of the preceding decade appeared to make no dent in the problems of poverty and educational inequality.

117

In the following two chapters we will focus on the failure of the public schools to fulfill the promises made by advocates of the common school movement. Much of the failure was related to the desires and aspirations of various segments of the middle class in particular. A portion of the inability to maintain the spirit of the reform movement, however, can be blamed on weaknesses in the inherent logic of the school crusade. This chapter will concentrate upon the southern experience with public schooling and the inability of that region in particular to define satisfactorily the ideal of "common." While not peculiar to the South, the problem of accommodating a large number of black children forced upon that region, given the nature of its intolerance, a collection of particularly difficult decisions. The causes of the southern failure lay in the sort of educational experience southern whites wanted for their black neighbors, in the type of schooling blacks wanted for themselves, and in the character of the northern white commitment to and aspirations for southern black education. Chapter 6 concentrates upon the northern experience and illustrates how cultural imposition, demands for differentiated schooling, and the mid-century experiment with immature bureaucratic reforms contributed to the disagreeable situation in which urban public education found itself after the Civil War.

I

With the end of the Civil War reformers put the Whig expectations about common schooling's ability to foster social order and community cohesion in a rapidly changing society to the severest test ever. Northerners—as victors, they were primarily responsible for initiating programs to repair wounds left by four years of bitter civil conflict—faced a prostrate South, economically and militarily devastated and riven by virulent race conflict. They were in something of a quandary. Despite President Lincoln's promise of "malice towards none," northerners felt more than a bit vengeful toward the southern whites and felt that some sort of punishment was appropriate. Just what the punishment should be was difficult to determine. Even more difficult, however, was finding a means of reconstructing the quarter of the land area and the third of the population that had just been defeated in a civil war. "Great nations have conquered and subjugated others," one writer observed succinctly in 1862 "but we have to conquer and assimilate half of ourselves."[1] No country's experiences offered analogies for this problem.

Common school reform as practiced in the North did present some-

[1] George W. Curtis to Miss Norton (11 June, 1862), in Edward Cary, *George William Curtis* (Boston, 1894), 155.

thing of a parallel and it seemed almost inevitable that northern leaders and especially northern reformers would hit upon extending common schooling to the South as one means of reconstruction. Schooling would reach the southern rebel, as it was to have reached the urban or western rebel, and would bring the southerners who had excluded themselves from the American community back into it, just as it was supposed to do with the poor and "foreign" in the North. Schooling would discipline the South without actually punishing it; it would exert the same gentle restraints on the southern delinquents that it was supposed to exercise on delinquent youngsters in the North. Schooling was doubly appropriate for the southern situation because its application would largely solve the race problem. Once schooling had alleviated the blacks' ignorance and their reported "lack of civilization," whites would welcome the blacks to an equal position in American society. A common school reform movement in the South seemed a perfect answer to many of the problems of reconstruction and many northerners eagerly and naïvely turned to it. In doing so, they once again demanded of schools far more than those institutions could accomplish. This time the reformers expected more of the schools than ever before. Northern reformers made a heroic effort to provide schooling for both blacks and whites in the South but, both because the educational problems themselves were immense and because the political and economic policies followed during Reconstruction exacerbated rather than relieved instability and race conflict, that effort failed to advance the reconstructing of the South. This failure, dramatically evidenced in the collapse of Reconstruction and reimposition of second-class citizenship on the blacks, severely disillusioned reformers (although not educators themselves) who had believed in schooling's power to solve social problems. This disillusion was so deep that it contributed to the undermining of the faith that the common school reformers' program could effectively impose social control on the population of the industrial and urban North.

In the initial enthusiasm to apply northern Whiggish reform methods to the unreconstructed South, northerners launched what amounted to an educational crusade—in some senses—against the South. Even before the surrender at Appomattox, reformers and educators argued that once the soldier had done his work, the educator must move in and do his. Wendell Phillips argued that "behind every one of Grant's cannons there should be placed a school-house." In 1865 the principal of a Pennsylvania normal school told the National Teachers Association that, now that the troops had been ordered to the rear, the government should "make haste to order school-houses to the front."[2] The educators' and reformers'

---

[2] J. P. Wickersham, "Education as an Element in Reconstruction," *Proceedings of the National Teachers Association* (1865), 292.

faith rested on their belief that the absence of free schools in the South had been responsible for the war between the states. Secession and armed rebellion had occurred, they explained, because southern aristocrats had demagogically enlisted the ignorant southern masses in their policy of defiance of constituted authority. Had the masses of southerners received common schooling, the aristocrats would never have successfully duped them. Further, had there been widespread free schooling in the antebellum South, the class patterns of southern society would have changed radically. The reformers described this class pattern in very oversimplified terms, declaring essentially that southern society comprised aristocrats, poor whites, and blacks. The northern reformers and educators believed that the aristocrats had prevented the establishment of free education throughout the South in order to protect their power and to protect the institution of slavery.

To the extent that these northerners were merely saying that educational effort in the antebellum South had not matched that in the northeast and the Old Northwest, they were accurate enough. Yet their depiction of a simple tripartite class structure in the South and their assertion that the South had experienced no common school movement were false. It is true that from colonial times the South had educated fewer of her people and spent less money on education. Many reasons explain this relative retardation. The southern population was thinly scattered, making it nearly impossible to erect enough district schools within walking distance of every child. Nor did southerners share quite the same degree of Puritan zeal that motivated New Englanders to struggle to educate all their children. Nor did the South develop habits of positive state initiatives in support of economic and social institutions as quickly as did most northern states. Education remained a matter of private philanthropy much longer in the South than in the North. All of these reasons are valid but, taken alone, they tend to make too much of the distinction between southern and northern society in the antebellum period. The South had large plantations, surely, but most southerners did not live on plantations or in plantation regions. There were upland regions of the South just as densely packed as portions of the Old Northwest. Nor were industrialization and urbanization as totally foreign to the southern experience as these reasons implied. Cities grew in the South, and factories were built and internal improvements established. Southern society was undergoing changes similar to those in the North, although on a reduced scale. The South experienced a common school movement in the years after 1830 on a similarly reduced scale.

Before 1830 southern schools were much less widespread than district schools in the North. The only public or semipublic schools were those supported by state and local governments for paupers. Most other elementary education occurred when private tutors taught in individual households (although they might have tutored children from more than one family) or when families in a region would pool their resources to hire a schoolmaster for all their children. These institutions were inadequate: the southern rate of illiteracy for whites was twice that of the North in the antebellum period and the southern schools enrolled a much smaller precentage of school-age youth than did their northern counterparts.

After 1830, however, the South made an educational effort in some ways greater than that of the North. In 1840 the region spent .45 percent of its "Gross Regional Product" on education, quite in line with the rate of spending of other regions excepting New England. The national average in 1840 was .6 percent. By 1860, however, the South had outstripped all but the north central region in percentage of income expended on education, .99 percent. The national average was .8 percent by then. The South tried just as hard as the other regions. But, even so, a smaller percentage of southern children attended school than in the rest of the country because, of course, the South was economically the poorest section of the country—so much poorer, in fact, that, although the South spent more of its resources on education than did the rest of the nation in 1860, it could provide for each child aged 5–19 in her population only 11 days of schooling per year while in the North each child was provided 50 days of schooling.[3] But the significant conclusion to note is that the South, far from being restrained by its aristocratic tradition from establishing schools, made a major educational effort relative to its resources before the Civil War.

This educational effort was launched for reasons very much like those which fueled the drive for common school reform in the North. Well-to-do professionals, businessmen, and owners of small plantations initiated the drive for southern educational reform. All worked within the same economic nexus that included most prominently cotton, commerce, clothmaking, and railroading. Their occupations often overlapped: the planters may have had professional training or even have been part-time practitioners, many of the professionals and businessmen also owned plantations. All were highly successful upper-middle-class men with a high status that still fell distinctly below that of the wealthy aristocratic planter. Most had come from yeoman farmer stock. They all favored state-initiated internal improvements; indeed, their economic position often depended on them. They were boosters who sought to improve the economic growth of their region in order to increase their own economic stature. Although their political affiliations were heterogeneous, they were all Whiggish in their concern for economic nationalism (or national-

---

[3] Albert Fishlow, "The American Common School Revival: Fact or Fancy?", in Henry Rosovsky, ed., *Industrialization in Two Systems* (New York, 1966), 55, 62.

istic regionalism), for powerful state interference in economic and social affairs, and for social control.

This upper middle class felt that the economic growth of their region depended on breaking the stranglehold that the values of the aristocracy had over the southern economy. The reformers viewed these powerful aristocrats as men with a provincial attitude completely isolated from the ideas and values of the nation at large and focused completely on cotton, land, and slaves. They had gained their wealth through traditional patterns of economic organization in the South and saw no reason to change them. Because these aristocrats disdained business and commerce as undignified concerns for wealthy planters, they refused to support commercial development in the South. In Charleston, the South's most aristocratic city, ordinances banned the use of steam engines within the city limits because they were considered too noisy and too dirty. The southern aristocracy shunned business values and instead favored chivalry, honor, and romantic conspicuous consumption.

Men of the upper middle class from which educational reformers came recognized the importance of commerce, business, and internal improvements to the overall economic and social progress of the South. These men understood and wanted to change the South's colonial status vis-à-vis the North. Only if the South built strong commercial and industrial institutions of its own could it break the cycle by which its staple crops were marketed by the North, to northerners' profit (cotton was most often shipped to New York for transshipment to British textile mills), and its manufactured necessities imported from the North, again to the northerners' profit. The balance of payments between the sections ran heavily in favor of the North. In an effort to stimulate commercial and manufacturing growth, these upper-middle-class planter/businessmen sought to overcome the banking monopolies of the aristocracy and to provide cheaper money for southern capital expansion. In Alabama education played a peculiar role in this effort. The reformers used the money gained from the sale of that land which the federal government had deeded to each new state for the support of education under the terms of the Land Ordinance of 1785 to capitalize a new state bank. The bank was intended to loan this money, at reasonable rates, to various commercial and industrial undertakings in the state and to pay the interest derived from these investments to the schools in the various districts. The same funds served both educational and industrial expansion.

Education, the reformers hoped, would serve to break the thralldom in which the values of the aristocracy held the bulk of the southern population. By making the population literate, and able to read information and opinion for themselves instead of depending on the aristocrats' reports, it would break the power that the educated aristocracy had over the average citizen and would lead the masses to adopt a more nationalistic—or at least regionalistic—point of view. Furthermore, education would in some undefined way make the South as progressive economically as the North. These southern educational leaders were no more clear as to the relation of education to economic growth than were Abbott Lawrence or Horace Mann. But their faith was just as strong.

The leaders of southern educational reform also expected schooling to exercise some sort of social control. The southern educational effort, like that in the North, started in cities—in New Orleans, Savannah, Mobile. These cities had a higher rate of immigration than did many in the North. New Orleans had a greater percentage of immigrants in 1850 than did Boston (40% to 36%). Mobile was 24 percent immigrant and Charleston, 30 percent. The immigrants in New Orleans, of course, were not principally Irish and, consequently, were neither as obvious nor as threatening as were the immigrants in Boston. Yet a know-nothing reaction against Catholic immigrants like that of the North occurred in these southern cities. The concern for urban problems—largely immigrant problems—was great enough for Protestant denominations to create and maintain, from 1840 to 1852, a complete system of public schools in Mobile after the tax-supported school system in that Alabama city broke down. In a related event, the Presbyterians of Georgia attempted to establish a statewide system in the late 1840s.

Southern educational leaders also worried about the poor white native southerner. One highly attractive argument used to support establishment of factories in the antebellum South held that such institutions would provide jobs for unproductive and socially undesirable poor whites and would elevate them in every way. Described as "public benefactors" in the southern press, manufacturers who recognized that a large portion of the "poor white population [were] not only unproductive, but [were] actually a burden" on their region, established businesses to hire and redeem that segment of the population.[4] But these social leaders were worried not only about the well-being of the southern poor white. Especially among the classes from which southern educational leaders were drawn, a real fear arose that political demagogues, of aristocratic or of radical background, could too easily influence uneducated poor whites to support nullification and military defiance of the North. These educational leaders came from a class which attempted to steer the South away from such reactions to northern economic domination and northern abolitionism. They were moderate southerners who sought economic and social but not political independence from the North. They hoped education would widen the support for their moderate point of view.

Unfortunately, just as the common school reform was progressing rapidly in the southern states, the slavery issue retarded and ultimately defeated it. In reaction to northern criticism and hostility, southerners

---

[4] Quoted in Herbert Collins, "The Southern Industrial Gospel before 1860," *Journal of Southern History*, XII (August, 1946), 399–402.

retreated more and more into the myth of southern cultural superiority that rested on aristocratic and romantic values. Business and commercial values, because associated with the North, fell into increasing disfavor, and internal criticism of southern economic and social backwardness was suppressed. Militant southern nationalists overwhelmed the moderation of the educational reformers and their supporters among the upper middle class. The bulk of the southern population opted for a military solution to the South's difficult relations with the North.

II

Those who carried the common school crusade to the South after the Civil War did not realize that publicly supported common schools had existed for several decades. In their view, to effect any viable reconstruction of the southern states, educators and reformers from the North had to move in and change the South over, essentially into a carbon copy of the North. This entailed, among other things, the elevation of the poor whites and the newly freed blacks to a station in life roughly equivalent to that of the independent yeoman farmer or independent artisan so celebrated, if somewhat hard to locate in the 1860s, in the North. These educators had little hope for the southern aristocrats. Most were dead, the Pennsylvania normal school principal argued; some would leave the country; "some will atone for their crimes upon the scaffold"; a few would remain, unfortunately. But "they have been already sadly miseducated, and they would scornfully reject all proffers of education at our hands. . . . We must treat them as western farmers do the stumps in their clearings: work around them, and let them rot out."[5] These same educators held out much more hope for the "poor whites" and particularly for the freedmen. Here was the great opportunity: to make these ignorant poor whites and the newly freed blacks into full citizens who could stand up for their own rights and drive the remaining aristocratic traitors out of the land. These poor whites and newly enfranchised Negroes must be educated to see that their real interests lay with the northerners of similar station.

Moreover, educators had a special duty toward the newly freed black. He must be taught to fend for himself in the "rough jostle of American business." Americans had little sympathy for weakness and thriftlessness, one educator pointed out, but the Negro in his present state was just that—weak and thriftless—because of his two centuries of bondage. Therefore, educators must make special pains to protect the Negro from the full rigors of competition until he had had a chance to be educated.

[5] Wickersham, "Education as an Element in Reconstruction," 290.

The normal school principal spoke on the same issue: "Let good men make haste to instruct and care for these new-born children of the Nation. Let teachers and missionaries be sent to them. Let State and church and neighborhood unite in a grand effort to save them from destruction, and give them something like a fair start in the race of life."[6]

The missionary tone of these passages suggests that the educational crusade against ignorance in the South carried much of the flavor and many of the problems of a movement to bring culture to the savages. In facing the problem of making southerners like northerners and blacks like whites, northern educational reformers drew on what seemed the most likely parallels: the experience of urban teachers of the immigrant and of foreign missionaries. The president of the National Teachers Association argued that educators should seek the same objective with the blacks as they had with the immigrants—"assimilating them to the American character." The Pennsylvania normal school principal was explicit: "To reconstruct the Union upon a firm basis, all that is unfriendly to it, or that stands in the way of its success, must be removed; the hostile elements in the south must be reconciled, and the population of the whole country must be made homogenous in interest and sympathy. Of many one must be made." Experience with the immigrants apparently made the work with the freedmen seem somewhat lighter. To one Boston teacher in the sea islands in South Carolina his black pupils looked "wretched and stupid enough" but "to those who were accustomed to many Irish faces, these except by their uniformity, could suggest few new ideas of low humanity."[7] Samuel Armstrong, who founded Hampton Institute in 1868, the first explicitly industrial school for blacks, modeled the program there after the one his parents developed as missionaries to Hawaii two decades previously.

The Civil War crisis, then, was ready made for the common school reformers. They had always touted common school reform as an effective remedy for dislocations and disharmonies brought about by social change, by industrial progress, and by growing class division. Here was the greatest disharmony of all; a part of the nation had become separated from the remainder in values and ideals; the best way to heal this separation, the reformers argued, was through giving southerners common schooling just like that in the North. Here the educational reformer made an extraordinarily broad promise to the American people: that the spread of education would serve to pacify the South, to bring the freedmen and the poor white to northern middle-class levels, and to homogenize the

---

[6] *Ibid.*, 293–294.

[7] Samuel S. Greene, "The Educational Duties of the Hour," *Proceedings of the National Teachers Association* (1865), 238; the Boston teacher is quoted in Willie Lee Rose, *Rehearsal for Reconstruction: The Port Royal Experiment* (Indianapolis, Ind., 1964), 58; Wickersham, "Education as an Element in Reconstruction," 290.

southern population in general to the dominant values represented by the triumphant Republican party in the North. Educational reformers, then, promised that a massive commitment to their reform would solve the most important and the most difficult political problem that the young American nation had faced since the framing of the Constitution. Educational reformers and professional educators were now committed to socializing the southerner, the proletariat, and the immigrant to the American way and had made this commitment on a national scale.

The promises that reformers held out in the name of common schooling were even more significant because the federal government and the American people were reluctant to move forcefully to reconstruct the nation on any but the educational front. Only federal policies that involved economic planning, land redistribution, and long-term federal policing of southern politics could realistically have been supposed capable of changing the southern class structure enough to give the black some chance of gaining a position of even rough equality within that structure. Unless the blacks (and the poor whites) received access to the rich lands held before the war by the wealthy planters (and returned to them during reconstruction by the federal government) and received the chance to farm independently, they could not hope to secure anything but second-class citizenship. Some reformers recognized this and proposed schemes whereby land seized by the government during the war would be divided among the freedmen. They also recognized that the government must commit itself to long-term federal supervision of southern politics in order to enforce the blacks' right to vote. The government, with the support of most northern opinion, refused to take those steps. Northern society and even most northern social reformers, reluctant to interfere with property rights, the individual's economic freedom, and states' rights, turned to the promises of educators gladly, in hopes that schooling would make more sweeping reconstruction policies unnecessary. Schooling did not, of course, and when it was clear that reconstruction through education had failed to reconcile the South to the ideals and values of the North and to raise the black to a position of equality, many came to reconsider the efficacy of mass common schooling. Furthermore, experience with the black during Reconstruction and in the following three decades made many feel that the effort to provide a common educational experience for all Americans no matter what their background or race or probable future career was an inefficient way of meeting social needs. The overall failure of the common school crusade in the South after the Civil War must be seen, then, as playing a significant role in directing educational reform away from its antebellum commitment to commonality and toward a belief that society's needs were best fulfilled by specialized training for different groups within the population—by university training for the elite, industrial training for the poor and for the blacks, and Americanization training for the immigrants.

III

Northern society's faith in and desperate reliance on schooling as a means of solving the problem of reconstruction were boldly evident in the interest that national politicians displayed in common schooling in the South, an interest in elementary education that had never been shown at the federal level before 1865 and would not appear again until well into the twentieth century. For some years before the war, professional educators had sought to nationalize the common school revolution by involving the federal government as an agency of educational reform. Their plan included creation of a federal office of education which would centralize administrative and legal authority over common schools. Their efforts met with no success until 1867 when Congress established, at the height of the crusade against southern ignorance and isolation, the Department of Education (as enthusiasm for education and reform soon waned, in 1869 the department was reduced to a bureau within the Department of the Interior). To politicians and reformers the Department of Education seemed a means of institutionalizing at a national level the effort to revamp the South's culture. Henry Barnard, who had led common school reform in two states and advised it in a third, became the first Commissioner of Education, thereby carrying the state crusade for centralization to the national level. Yet once the promises of the educators began to pall, political interest in the bureau declined, and Barnard's efforts to use it as a lever for change failed. Congress gave the bureau only advisory and statistic-gathering powers and it accomplished very little in this period beyond the gathering of statistics of uncertain accuracy. It had little effect on education in the South.

National politicians did not, however, lose all hope of effecting educational reform in the South. In 1870 Senator Samuel Hoar of Massachusetts introduced a harsh measure threatening that, if any state allowed its educational effort to fall below a certain standard, the federal government would take over the educational system and tax the people to run it adequately. Because it was badly drawn and so harsh, Hoar's bill never came to a vote in Congress. It was an extreme example of the highhandedness with which some wished to impose their will on the defeated South. Senator Henry W. Blair of New Hampshire introduced a much more carefully drawn bill in 1881 which proposed a ten-year program of federal aid to the schools, amounting to $15 million in the first year and decreasing by $1 million each year thereafter. The funds, from surplus tariff revenue, were to be allocated to each state according to the percentage of its population that was illiterate. Although aimed most directly at the South where by far the largest number of the nation's illiterates lived, Blair also sought to provide federal funds for training immigrants in the North who he thought threatened the nation as gravely as did illiterate southerners. "The representative form of government cannot exist unless the people are competent to govern themselves," the senator argued in 1882. Illiterates were "the prey of the demagogue and were the victims of prejudice" and they held "the balance of power in almost every state in the nation at large."[8] Blair's bill came to a vote in the Senate four different times; in 1884, 1886, 1888, and 1890. The first three times it passed the Senate only to be bottled up in a committee by a few powerful House members against the apparent wishes of the majority of the House membership who wished to support the bill. Its opponents in the House were free traders who thought that Blair's proposals to spend excess tariff revenue would guarantee continuation of the protective tariff in the United States. By 1890 when the bill was decisively defeated in the Senate, a combination of forces had gathered to make this attempt at national financing of education for southerners and immigrants unsuccessful. Catholic opposition to the Protestant or secular common school and to state interference in the relationship between church, parent, and child, mounting opposition to the protective tariff among Democrats and liberal Republicans, a growing belief that the South was financially able to solve its own educational problems, and the continuing fear of federal encroachment on state and local powers all undermined Blair's efforts. Blair's attempt in 1890 marked the last serious effort to involve the federal government in financing general common schooling until the New Deal.

The most effective federal initiative in the educational crusade in the South after the Civil War was made when Congress created the Freedmen's Bureau, officially the Bureau of Refugees, Freedmen, and Abandoned Lands, in March of 1865 to ease the transition of the four million newly freed blacks to freedom. When first organized, the Freedmen's Bureau had as one of its major objectives the redistribution of lands that southern owners had abandoned (and failed to pay a federal tax on) when federal troops occupied them. General William T. Sherman's famous Special Field Order Number 15, issued in early 1865, set aside all of the sea islands off the South Carolina and Georgia coasts from Charleston south and all the abandoned rice fields along the rivers for a distance of thirty miles inland, to be redistributed among the thousands of blacks joining his famous march from Atlanta to the sea. According to his order, blacks were to be settled on parcels of land not larger than forty acres and to be given a kind of temporary title until Congress took permanent action. The Freedmen's Bureau moved as soon as it was formed to implement Sherman's orders, but its effort was short lived for President Andrew Johnson late in 1865, ordered all lands seized by federal authority

---

[8] John W. Evans, "Catholics and the Blair Education Bill," *Catholic Historical Review*, XLVI (October, 1960), 274–275.

during the war returned to their original owners. One of the Bureau's major purposes had been cut from under it. Most of its activities were restricted to distributing food, clothing, primitive shelter, and medical care to wandering blacks and whites who came to it for assistance. The Bureau was also charged with supervising relations and mediating conflicts between the races; it was also to oversee labor contracts that blacks signed with their employers to insure that their former masters were not exploiting the blacks. During its three-and-one-half years of existence at full strength, the Bureau, according to one historian, "issued more than twenty-one million rations, established over 40 hospitals, treated nearly half a million cases of illness, provided free transportation to more than 30,000 persons dislocated by war and supervised hundreds of thousands of labor contracts."[9] All these efforts to provide emergency sustenance and to prevent excessive exploitation were clearly stopgap measures: they contributed little to changing the freedmen's place in southern society. Practically the only positive action left to the Bureau was supporting schools for blacks. This it did on a massive scale by cooperating with private missionary agencies in maintaining thousands of schools for blacks and thousands of teachers for those schools. The Bureau's priorities illustrate the government's refusal to deal seriously with the social problems of reconstruction and to depend instead on the panacea of education.

Voluntary rather than governmental organizations carried out most of the northern effort to eliminate southern ignorance and to elevate the freedmen. These voluntary organizations, established by northern philanthropists during and immediately after the war, sent supplies south for the benefit of the freedmen and provided educational facilities for them and for the southern whites. Some were strictly nondenominational and nonsectarian in nature while others were connected with northern churches. The Boston Educational Commission for Freedmen (later renamed the New England Freedmen's Aid Society), the first nonsectarian organization, was founded early in 1862 in response to an appeal from the Treasury agent responsible for supervising the plantations and the blacks on them on the sea islands off South Carolina that northern troops had captured early in the war. Friends in Boston heard the agent's descriptions of the disorganized and destitute state of the blacks living on the sea islands and they organized the Educational Commission which quickly recruited thirty-five New Englanders to go south to teach and supervise the blacks (forty-one more joined within the year) and contributed about $25,000 worth of clothing, blankets, and seeds to the sea

[9] Martin Abbott, *The Freedmen's Bureau in South Carolina* (Chapel Hill, N. C., 1967), 131; see also Martin Abbott, "American Negro Schooling in South Carolina," *South Carolina Historical Magazine,* LVII (April, 1956), 65–81.

islands' black population. In a matter of months societies quite similar to that founded in Boston appeared in New York City and Philadelphia. The constitution of the New York group promised, among other things, to teach the freedmen "civilization and Christianity" as well as "order, industry, economy, and self-reliance; and to elevate them in the scale of humanity, by inspiring them with self-respect."[10] The Port Royal Relief Association of Pennsylvania established a store on the sea islands where the blacks could buy without being exploited by United States Army quartermasters. Thus began the Port Royal Experiment, which Willie Lee Rose has called "the rehearsal for reconstruction" because between 1862 and 1865 this combined public and private missionary effort anticipated all the problems and failures that would occur during full-scale reconstruction. Here the northern reformers and the federal government, unwilling to move forcefully on the economic and political problems of the South and her freedmen, first established education as a panacea.

As federal troops brought more and more land and people under federal control the freedmen's aid societies increased their efforts. They founded schools and recruited teachers for them; they established asylums and distributed provisions to white and black. Despite their titles, these societies also helped provide schools for poor whites.

All the major Protestant denominations eventually organized societies devoted to aiding and educating the freedmen. Denominations found it more profitable not to cooperate with non-sectarian societies. They felt that denominational money and effort ought to be so identified and used to benefit both the church as well as the southerners. As one Methodist minister said, "Methodist hands should have handled Methodist funds, and been appropriated to pay Methodist teachers, to found Methodist schools, and carry on a work for which the denomination should have its due credit." [11] This attitude motivated all the denominations to establish their own missionary societies, organizations which in large part simply duplicated the characteristics of their home mission efforts in northern cities and in the West. The denominational societies operated much as the nonsectarian organizations did except that the former emphasized aid less and teaching and preaching more, showed greater respect for southern traditions of segregation, and sought to harvest religious conversions among the freedmen.

These missionary societies represented a very broad cross-section of northern society including prominent businessmen, professionals, and politicians although ministers and educators predominated as officers, as might be expected. Literally thousands of people contributed money

[10] Rose, *Rehearsal for Reconstruction,* 41.
[11] Quoted in Henry L. Swint, *The Northern Teacher in the South, 1862–1870* (Nashville, Tenn., 1941), 13.

in large and small amounts to support the effort to help the freedmen and to impose northern values on the defeated South. Indeed, the movement was popular to some extent even in Europe: freedmen's aid societies appeared in England, Paris, Holland, and Germany and European philanthropists contributed periodically to the cause.

A survey of the 135 officers of these societies revealed how much the societies represented extensions of the pre–Civil War reform effort. Henry Lee Swint found that 66 of the 135 were "sufficiently prominent in the abolition movement to merit notice in the standard biographical dictionaries as leading abolitionists."[12] He believed that many more had abolitionist connections. Furthermore, these organizations' officers, and presumably many of their supporters, had been closely involved with other aspects of antebellum reform. Many of the officers were prominent in the temperance movement, the women's rights movement, the antitobacco movement, penal reform, and common school reform. Many of these officers combined their interest in education of the freedmen with these other reform interests. J. W. Alvord, the superintendent of schools of the Freedmen's Bureau, was also secretary of the Lincoln National Temperance Association, which sought to have freedmen sign pledges to refrain from the use of strong drink and tobacco.

The Freedmen's Bureau and the voluntary organizations generally worked together to achieve the objective of improving the lot of freedmen. Conflicts, of course, existed between the Bureau and the private efforts just as there were conflicts among the various private organizations. Martin Abbott reports an incident in South Carolina where the Freedmen's Union Commission fought the Bureau over the latter's plan to assist another benevolent society in establishing a school near an already existing Freedmen's Union Commission school.[13] This kind of conflict undoubtedly arose from time to time, but generally the spirit of cooperation was high. As the Freedmen's Bureau had no funds specifically set aside for educating the freedmen, it generally left the recruitment of teachers and their payment to the benevolent and church societies. The Bureau was authorized to spend money for the construction, repair, and rental of school buildings—an authorization that the sympathetic bureau personnel construed quite broadly. Martin Abbott estimates that in the 1866–1867 school year, the Bureau contributed approximately $25,000 of $107,000 spent on black schooling in South Carolina. In the following year the Bureau's portion rose to $57,000 out of $127,-000.[14] For a time the Bureau provided transportation from the North, quarters, and rations to teachers whose wages were paid by the voluntary

[12] *Ibid.*, 26.
[13] Abbott, *Freedmen's Bureau in South Carolina*, 86.
[14] *Ibid.*, 84–89.

organizations. The Bureau also served functions not unlike those that state boards or departments of education performed in the North. Its personnel collected statistics on schools and schooling, publicized the educational effort, directed what educational money the Bureau had where it was most needed, and, where possible, coordinated the efforts of the northern voluntary organizations.

The efforts to educate the freedmen after the Civil War were vastly expensive. We can only estimate from the statistics collected and published by the Freedmen's Bureau and numerous private organizations the magnitude of this effort. Julius H. Parmelee listed 79 major associations concerned with black education in the South and it is assumed that there were many more. Swint estimated that between $5 million and $9 million were spent to support Yankee teachers in the South between 1862 and 1872 and reported that 9,503 men and women taught in freedmen's schools in 1869 alone, the vast majority of them northerners who had gone south to fight ignorance and inequality. The figure on the number of teachers is probably quite conservative. There was probably one school for every teacher recorded: thus, at the height of the northern educational effort in 1868–1869, approximately 10,000 schools sought to teach the freedmen. The number of children that attended these schools is even more difficult to estimate but Martin Abbott, in his careful study of South Carolina freedmen, found that only approximately 25,000 out of 125,000 blacks of school age in the state enrolled in the freedmen's schools between 1865 and 1870. As the quality and duration of the schooling offered varied so greatly from institution to institution, it is nearly impossible to generalize as to how much the freedmen learned as a result of this educational effort.[15] Schooling probably did serve to widen the freedman's experience and to encourage his hopes. Unfortunately, his experiences in the South after 1870 were unlikely to utilize that experience or sustain those hopes.

The benevolent societies did not restrict their efforts to elementary education: they founded numerous colleges for blacks in the South. The American Missionary Association had a hand in founding nine such colleges including Hampton, Fisk, and Atlanta. Almost all the major societies and associations were instrumental in founding at least one such black college. These institutions, like new colleges founded all over the country in the nineteenth century, in their early years functioned more like the high schools, assuming all the educational tasks beyond that of elementary instruction. The national government also participated in this effort when it chartered Howard University—named after the commissioner of the Freedmen's Bureau—in Washington in 1867. Although

[15] Figures from Swint, *Northern Teacher in the South*, 10, 1, 6–7; and Abbott, *Freedmen's Bureau in South Carolina*, 88.

Congress did not fund Howard until 1879, the Freedmen's Bureau helped the university get started by giving it large sums of money. The benevolent societies also made extensive efforts toward adult education for the blacks, establishing hundreds of night schools for adults throughout the South.

The quality of the schools varied enormously from place to place and from year to year. On the whole the schools were quite primitive, they were open for very short periods, and the teachers were generally not very good. Although southern charges that many teachers sent from the North or recruited from the South to teach the freedmen were wholly illiterate or wholly mercenary were surely exaggerated, they undoubtedly contained some truth. The northern teachers' greatest liability, however, was that they were culture bound. As Martin Abbott has pointed out, the northern teachers taught what they knew but unfortunately what they knew and what they taught were not terribly relevant to the needs of the newly freed black. Abbott characterizes their teaching as "more suited to the needs of a socially proficient people than to the needs of one just emerging from slavery; it also failed to recognize that neither in her society, her economy, nor her cultural tradition was South Carolina, the counterpart of Massachusetts."[16] The northern teachers employed a curriculum best adapted to young people preparing for life in a commercial and industrializing society with a population the vast majority of which would necessarily continue to work in agriculture. Henry Swint reported that most schools used the regular northern texts, including McGuffey's readers and Webster's speller, and that some schools used Tate's *First Book in Philosophy,* Tate's *Natural Philosophy,* and Ralph and Gillete's *Philosophy.* J. L. M. Curry, later a prominent supporter of industrial education for blacks and leader of the school crusade after 1890, reported that "a special stress was laid on classics and liberal culture." Many teachers attempted to teach Greek, Latin, and dialectics. Little practical instruction was included, except of course the utilitarian aspects of the three Rs and the sewing and domestic science of one kind and another that was taught to girls.[17]

The northern teachers did not restrict themselves to formal schooling. As the liberal clergyman and reformer Edward Everett Hale put it, the work of the agents and teachers was "founded on the understanding that their work was the construction of civil society on a true basis; that there was no magic in books or slates, or in reading or in arithmetic, by which alone a race not fit for civil government could be made fit. The 'teachers' have been taught, and have understood, that the work of education proposed was the education of savages in to self-governing men; that

---

[16] Abbott, *Freedmen's Bureau in South Carolina,* 91.
[17] Swint, *Northern Teacher in the South,* 81–82.

books and alphabets and figures were of use so far that they tended to
this aim; but that they were to keep this aim in sight all along and in no
way to make the means appear of more importance than the great object."[18] In a few instances northerners acted on the theory that the best
way to teach the freedmen to be free and responsible was to let them be
free. Roanoke, Virginia, missionaries helped establish a town meeting
comprised exclusively of black citizens in the area. At Davis's Bend,
Mississippi, blacks took responsibility for governing a large area that
General Grant assigned for black settlement. Similar experiments occurred elsewhere. In many places the missionaries encouraged the blacks
to arm and protect themselves from their white neighbors. Although
these experiments were no more than qualified successes measured
against northern standards, they greatly encouraged some of the philanthropists. Unfortunately, reformers were unable to expand these experiments in educating the freedman to be a citizen by letting him be a citizen
because the once dominant population was regaining its power and finding more and more effective ways to intimidate the former slaves.

A number of the northern teachers wished to erase the servility and
the marks of second-class citizenship which the freedmen carried over
from their experience as slaves. As an editorial in the *American Missionary*
urged them, "Let Us Make Men." Teachers encouraged the freedmen
to vote, to organize, and to think themselves as good as any other person.
The teachers were not, of course, entirely disinterested; they certainly
expected the blacks to exercise their citizenship rights in support of the
ideas promulgated by the northern teachers rather than in support of the
ideas still held by the majority of southern whites. Northern teachers tried
to achieve these goals in several different ways. Lydia Maria Child edited
a reader called "The Freedman's Book." She included stories about
Ignatius Soncho, a Spanish Negro who had achieved distinction in letters
in Europe during the eighteenth century, about Madison Washington,
and about a slave mutiny in which the slaves on the ship massacred all
the whites, brought the ship into a British harbor, and became free. She
included poems by Francis R. W. Harper, a black; her own account, quite
laudatory, of John Brown's raid on Harpers Ferry; and Wendell Phillips'
eulogy of the Haitian revolutionary Toussaint L'Ouverture. She dedicated the book to the "the loyal and brave Captain Robert Smalls, hero
of the steamboat Planter." Smalls was a free Negro who had taken a ship
out of Charleston harbor during the Civil War and delivered it into the
hands of the federal navy.[19] Teachers urged their students constantly to
repeat such adages as "all men are equal, the negro is as good as the

[18] Edward Everett Hale, "Education of the Freedmen," *North American Review*, CI (October,
1865), 529.

[19] Quoted in Horace Mann Bond, *Negro Education in Alabama: A Study in Cotton and Steel*
(Washington, D. C., 1939), 115.

white." Many of the teachers sought to teach these precepts by example and went out of their way to eat with blacks, sometimes to live with them, and to entertain them in their homes in strict accordance with equalitarian principles. Others helped the freedmen organize political clubs of their own. Many joined the Radical governments which ruled from the late 1860s to the early 1870s and which fought to maintain the blacks' civil rights in the South. It is impossible to know how many of the thousands of northern teachers believed that the black should receive the full rights of citizenship and social equality. Southern researchers have undoubtedly exaggerated the extent to which the northern teachers sought to undermine the social basis of southern biracial civilization. Undoubtedly, a significant portion of the northern teachers did believe in social equality for the Negro, at least in the early years of their stay in the South; but probably a much larger proportion did not. The latter undoubtedly believed that the black should have his economic and social freedom and perhaps a vote, but they did not feel that he deserved or should have as much power as the southern white. These teachers were more interested, naturally, in the black's acquiring discipline and moral habits than they were intent on his gaining a sense of independence and ambition. They were interested in his gaining self-respect but it was a self-respect that was to come, not from independence, but from assuming the responsibilities of his place as a simple farmer or workingman. One missionary enthused that "we shall have as happy and contented a peasantry as the most ardent abolitionist could desire."[20]

As might be assumed, these teachers stressed training in morality, and especially in the performance of moral rituals. Sanctifying the marriage covenant in a church service became one of their favorite reforms. The blacks seldom failed to cooperate because they also wanted their family rituals dignified as the whites' were. Missionaries not only insured that all new weddings were performed before clergymen but encouraged many couples long "married" to solemnize their vows publicly in church. Missionaries struggled valiantly to improve the "quality" of black religious services, seeking to substitute traditional English hymns for Negro spirituals and shouts. Some of the teachers and many of their northern supporters also argued that education of the freedmen should work to make them more efficient laborers so that they could earn higher wages and consume more, mostly northern, goods. What was best for the freedman was also best for the northern economy. Large numbers of northern missionaries, whatever future they proposed for the freedmen, championed the idea that the black males should enter military service, either the Union Army or the state militia, during reconstruction. A military experience would instill discipline in the soldier and discipline was essen-

[20] Quoted in Rose, *Rehearsal for Reconstruction,* 235.

tial to the black's future success. Army service would also teach the blacks to be "manly" and independent and, by proving that blacks were capable of fighting, would convince skeptical whites, north and south, that the black was truly the equal of the white. The educational missionaries to the freedmen combined these motivations in different ways. Each wished to mold the freedmen as he thought best. Few considered that the freedman might have known what was best for himself and fewer still thought to ask him. The educational crusade to elevate the freedmen sought to impose northern cultural ideals on the black and the crusade was ineffectual in large part because those ideals were irrelevant to the conditions of the defeated South and to the needs of the newly liberated blacks.

In terms of numbers, teachers, and money spent, the educational crusade reached its height toward the end of 1868 and then began to wane quite rapidly. One explanation for this was that southern opposition grew more hostile and more effective in blocking the northerners' efforts. At the end of the war white southerners were of at least two minds about how to revitalize their section and how to deal with the freedmen. Many influential southerners advocated educating the black—in separate institutions, of course—so that he would be a good orderly citizen who would use his vote responsibly. These southerners also argued that if the South did not try to educate the freedmen, northerners would move in to do the job in a manner unsuited to southern mores. During presidential reconstruction, when the states were governed by traditional southern elites, black schools were established by state and local authority. Many white southerners taught the freedmen; others donated land, buildings, lumber and equipment, or cash to support freedmen's schools. But, as northern teachers became more numerous and power passed from the traditional elites to the Radical governments, southern opposition to the freedmen's education grew. Some opposition had always existed; there were those who argued from the very beginning that any kind of education would ruin the Negro's willingness to serve as a field hand. Some southerners used physical violence to prevent northern teachers from doing their job and federal troops were often thought necessary to protect the northern teachers from the southern whites among whom they worked. Subtle coercion was not uncommon: "In the little mountain town of Walhalla, for example, the Methodist-Episcopal church had established a school under the direction of a young lady from Vermont. Within weeks local citizens had broken it up and driven the teacher away by hiring a negro vagabond drunkard to attend her classes and to dog her steps daily through the streets." From the very beginning northern teachers remarked on the coolness and hostility they met. "Whites treat us so-so; the men now and then lift their hats while the ladies for variety almost invariably lift their noses," a teacher in North Carolina reported.

"But we pay little or no attention to either and 'the work goes marching on.' " Teachers reported that they could not purchase food or rent living quarters from southern ladies; some teachers were ostracized from southern churches.[21]

The Radical governments' efforts to secure equality for the freedmen and the imposition of the Fourteenth and Fifteenth Amendments (in 1867 and 1869) cemented southern opinion against northern efforts to educate the freedmen. Violence against northerners and against northern schools soared. The Ku Klux Klan, founded in 1866, became quite effective in intimidating black students and, in some cases, white teachers. The Radical governments tried to legislate a new social order in which whites and blacks were nearly equal but failed to change the southern economic structure. Therefore, traditionally powerful groups, even when deprived of formal political power, exerted enough economic leverage to force the blacks back into their traditional subservient role. When these groups determined that freedmen's schools threatened the traditional social order, they sought to destroy them. Although it is doubtful that southern intimidation by itself would have served to halt the experiment in northern education for the freedmen, it certainly, in combination with the other factors to be discussed, contributed to its cessation.

The second major reason for the waning of the northern educational crusade in the South after 1868 was a general decline in enthusiasm and interest in the North. This decline was manifest in the precipitous decrease in funds available for the experiment. Full funding of the Freedmen's Bureau ended in 1868 and it no longer could afford to build, repair, or lease many schoolhouses. At the same time serious crop failures through much of the South in 1868 prevented blacks themselves from continuing the significant financial support they had given to freedmen's schools in previous years. Blacks contributed $17,000 out of $107,000 spent on freedmen's education in South Carolina in 1866–1867. In 1865 and 1866 blacks founded and financed schools of their own.[22] But crop failures and continuing lack of economic advancement among the black population in general made these schools harder to sustain and undermined the blacks' ability to contribute to the effort. Contributions from northern philanthropy and northern churches also dropped off quite sharply after 1868. The first flush of hope had passed and northerners were beginning to despair of ever effecting their goals. From the very start northerners anticipated that the southern states and the blacks themselves would rapidly assume responsibility for educating the freedmen. Edward Everett Hale wrote in 1865, in the first flush of the crusade,

---

[21] Quotations in Abbott, *Freedmen's Bureau in South Carolina,* 93–94, and Swint, *Northern Teacher in the South,* 95–99.

[22] Abbott, *Freedmen's Bureau in South Carolina,* 88–89.

that he looked "forward to the time when they [the blacks] shall build and repair their schoolhouses and bear the general charges of instruction. And that time, according to the best observers, is not distant more than two or three years."[23] By 1868 the time had elapsed and northern philanthropists like Hale began to withdraw, expecting that now the Radical governments would assume the burden. And by 1868 the new Radical governments in the South promised to do so.

This crippling contraction in contributions for the educational crusade reflected a serious decline in enthusiasm for educating the freedmen among northern supporters of the crusade and a good many of the crusaders themselves after 1868. Enthusiasm waned because education failed to fulfill northerners' naïve expectations. Hale's idea that the black schools in the South would become economically self-sustaining within two or three years was but one of many examples of the naïveté with which the goodhearted and otherwise perfectly intelligent northerners viewed education's ability to solve reconstruction problems. The idea that education would enable the southern black to slough off the effects of generations of slavery within two, three, possibly four years was very widespread among northerners, especially those humanitarian reformers who were supporting the educational crusade financially. Under the best conditions it would have been asking too much of education to effect the kinds of changes visualized by the northerners in so short a time; and, of course, conditions in the South right after the Civil War were far from good.

When their hopes for significant and rapid social change through education were dashed, northern philanthropists and especially northern teachers became frustrated and blamed the black himself for not learning fast enough and for not improving conditions in the South. Teachers blamed the freedmen for allowing themselves to be intimidated by the southern whites, for earning a living instead of coming to school, for not voting when their votes were important to maintaining northern hegemony over southern politics. The teachers seemed to say that they had given the black enough common schooling to make him, were he truly comparable to the northern white, perfectly capable of supporting himself and defending his rights in southern society. That the black's condition as a citizen vis-à-vis the whites deteriorated steadily during Reconstruction began to suggest to frustrated northern teachers and philanthropists that, indeed, southern apologists for slavery had a point in arguing that the Negro was essentially inferior to the white. The teachers had given their all but it was not enough. Whom to blame? Or what to blame? Some teachers undoubtedly blamed themselves, more prescient ones probably questioned education's efficacy as an agent for social re-

[23] Hale, "Education of Freedmen," 538.

form, many blamed the southern whites and southern society, some of the most insightful blamed the failure to effect land reform, but a significant number—probably the largest number—refused to blame themselves or their faith in education and turned their frustration, their anger onto the black, blaming him for his failure to live up to the white teachers' expectations. The northerners began to agree with the southerners' assessments of the black and became more receptive to the racial theories of social Darwinism, an increasingly popular social philosophy in the postbellum United States that was based loosely on Darwin's theory of evolution. The theory held that most human characteristics were hereditary and that different races had evolved separately and at different speeds. Social Darwinism lent weight to doctrines of black inferiority by suggesting that the race was behind the Caucasians on the evolutionary time line and that the blacks' disabilities, which northern philanthropists had identified as temporary reactions to slavery, were in fact hereditary and would not disappear when the blacks' condition was altered. Better schools, better wages, and better justice were not sufficient to make the black into a fully responsible citizen.

The northerners' enthusiasm also waned because the irreconcilable contradictions in their motivations for extending common schooling to the South became increasingly clear as the reconstruction period advanced. The reformers had started out to create out of the mass of poor whites and blacks—the powerless classes of the Old South—a harmonious and unified population that conformed to the values of northerners of similar station. They expected to educate this mass of people to support not the aristocrats and demagogues of the Old South but the Republican party and the values of the northern middle class, to work hard and respect property and accept their position in the work force. On the other hand, they were committed to creating out of the mass of poor whites and blacks individuals who would be self-sufficient, self-respecting, and politically, economically, and socially independent of the power groups in the South. They were committed to training the black man to sense his own worth, to consider himself equal to whites, to be strong enough and independent enough to resist both the blandishments and the intimidations of his former masters. The contradiction in the southern educational crusade might therefore be summarized: The northern philanthropists desired to make the poor whites and the freedmen independent and self-sufficient enough to resist the southern leaders but obedient and conformist enough to follow northern leaders.

The reformers found it hard to strike that balance. Northern teachers found to their discomfort that the blacks under their tutelage were growing politically independent and decidedly disobedient. A teacher at Port Royal wrote of the freedmen in 1863 that "with all their subserviency, which I am happy to say is disappearing, they have little idea of obedience." This distinction between subservience and obedience was some-times a rather tenuous one. Those missionaries at Port Royal especially interested in seeing the black become a wage earner were dismayed to see manifestations of labor discontent among them. Workers moved from place to place in search of higher wages, worked harder on their own plots of land than they did for their employers, and even banded together to petition their employers for higher wages. "I do not agree with you in what you say of the *unnatural* dependence of these people," wrote one missionary to a colleague in 1864, "I don't see any people on earth of their rank and civilization who are so independent as they are." The blacks at Port Royal were reported to have organized a certain number of political activities more or less independently of their north-ern tutors and to have acted politically against the advice of the mission-ary teachers.[24] The teachers began to feel that they had wrought too well. Their missionary efforts had taught the blacks independence, self-suffi-ciency, and self-respect. (The reformers assumed that education was the agent primarily responsible for these changes; this assumption accorded well with their hope that students, white and black, could be completely passive personalities in school to be molded totally by the will of the educators. It would undoubtedly have been more accurate to argue that the blacks themselves were responsible for these evidences of independ-ence—that they did not have to wait for white help to be free and human.) The northern teachers feared that they had, in educating the blacks, created the kind of independence in their charges that led to disorder and disrespect. They had not achieved the teaching of stability, content-ment, and deference.

Where the northern teachers may have wrought too well in instilling independence and ambition in the blacks, they failed utterly to fulfill another expectation of the supporters of the educational crusade. Whig-gish common school reformers had placed extremely heavy emphasis on the common school's capacity for assuring social unity, social harmony, and cultural homogeneity within a population growing more diverse in ethnic background and economic status. Racial harmony was one divi-dend expected from the extension of common schooling to the South. The reformers had come south in hopes of effecting a reconciliation between whites and blacks; instead, they kept the conflict burning ever brighter. Attempts to teach the black self-respect and independence served only, it seemed, to exacerbate the antiblack feelings among south-ern whites, and, it must be noted, among most of the northern soldiers and civilians who remained stationed in the South. As northerners ex-pended more effort on educating southern blacks, the influence of the

[24] Elizabeth Ware Pearson, ed., *Letters from Port Royal: Written at the Time of the Civil War* (Boston, 1906), 218; Rose, *Rehearsal for Reconstruction*, 363–367, 311–314; Pearson, ed., *Letters*, 275.

Ku Klux Klan and other white terrorist groups grew stronger. Elevating the black and maintaining social order began to seem antithetical; more and more northern philanthropists and teachers came, as Reconstruction progressed, to share the southern whites' view that the only way to maintain social harmony and order in the South was to keep the black "in his place"—at the expense, of course, of his independence and self-respect.

In order to have fulfilled their goal of achieving equality for the blacks, the educational reformers would have had to seek an economic and social revolution alongside their educational one. Equality required a significantly altered social structure. Some of the humanitarians and philanthropists and missionaries who went south had just this kind of revolution in mind. Most of them, however, were extraordinarily naïve in that they thought such a revolution could occur with very little bloodshed and social hardship—that gentle persuasion of the southern white and common schooling for the southern black would somehow bring about a gradual restructuring of southern society in such a way that the black could take his place as an independent yeoman, welcomed by his white fellow citizens. Because of their naïve faith in schooling, the educational missionaries began their efforts without sensing that achieving equality for the black would destroy whatever chance they had for achieving the other part of their mission, the reconstruction of the South and the reimposition of social unity and social harmony and social order there. Only when they came to recognize that equality for the black could not be won without significant social conflict that would hopelessly set back the cause of harmony and order, did they recognize the contradiction in their goals and back away from the more revolutionary goal of Negro equality. Revealing their essential conservatism, the educational missionaries and their backers ended up on the side of social order and harmony. It was a cruel dilemma and they must not be condemned too readily. Those mid-nineteenth-century humanitarians eagerly sought to help both the black and the defeated South but, as participants in more than a decade of incredibly intense social conflict and five years of extraordinarily brutal (the Civil War was the bloodiest and costliest war fought to that date) fighting, social harmony and order were especially important to them. Already confused between their concern for social harmony and the best interests of the freedmen, these humanitarians faced an entrenched and hostile southern white population with little financial support, without the support of the majority of northerners who, while supporting the war to preserve the Union, did not favor black equality, and without the support of a strong federal apparatus committed to reconstructing the South on the basis of black equality. It is quite easy to imagine why the reformers chose the path they did.

That path led ultimately to the surrender of the principle that all children should go to the same schools to receive the same training. The waning of enthusiasm for common schooling in the South after the war led to a more general deterioration of confidence that giving the same education to all children was an efficacious means of solving social problems. Instead, reformers came to favor the principle of giving special kinds of training to different kinds of children according to their predicted futures, of preparing different groups for different roles. Thus began an era devoted to special education for special groups. In the case of the black, reformers concluded that since the Negro race was inferior in civilization to the white, the black in the United States would for the foreseeable future be a worker and should receive training that would best prepare him for that role in society. For this purpose reformers championed industrial training as defined by Booker T. Washington and northern educational philanthropists of the late nineteenth century. Such training would fit the black into his role in society; such special education would foster social harmony rather than social conflict.

IV

Common schooling in the South quickly became a "whites only" matter. When the next crusade to expand common schooling occurred in the South thirty years after the reconstruction effort, northern philanthropists willingly supported reforms that would curtail the blacks' already severely limited access to education and equality. The northern educational crusade begun in 1862 was supposed to provide seed money and encouragement for the establishment of a public common school system for blacks and whites throughout the South modeled on the northern system. On paper this effort succeeded. In the late 1860s the new Radical constitutions that Congress required from each southern state as a condition for readmission to the Union and the Radical legislatures elected according to the terms of those constitutions established state public school systems open to all children. Although not always required by law, these schools were effectively segregated from the beginning. Very few whites in the South, either unreconstructed Democrats or Radical Republicans, favored the idea of sending black and white children to the same school. The only significant exception seems to have been New Orleans which thoroughly and successfully integrated its schools until 1877.

The common school systems, white and black, were financed through what could be salvaged of the antebellum state literary funds, through steadily declining contributions from the northern philanthropic organizations, and through a statewide property tax collected by the state and redistributed to the counties and through them to the school districts according to the number of school-age children of both races in the county or district. In no state was there provision for local taxation, approved locally, for the support of schools. Under this system of taxation which, on paper, distributed funds equally among white and black, public schooling got off to a rapid and promising start in 1869 and 1870. Although they did not approach northern standards of quality, these state systems offered the best public education that the South would experience before 1900. School terms were short, conditions primitive, and teachers untrained. Literary funds were depleted and taxation was low; there was no money for building new schoolhouses or repairing those which had been neglected for a decade or for establishing desperately needed teacher training institutions. But conditions would get much worse before they improved.

The Radicals soon lost control of southern governments. As southern white dissatisfaction with liberal and pro–black actions of the Radical regimes increased, conservatives, soon to readopt the Democratic party label, grew strong enough to gain majorities in state legislatures as early as 1870 in some states and to elect conservative Democratic governors soon after. The Radical regimes held on longer in some states than in others, but by 1876 Reconstruction had ended and power had shifted from the Radicals to the Democrats, who, it was said, had "redeemed" the south from the vengeful northerner and the newly enfranchised, ambitious black. The great conflict was over and southern society remained pretty much as it had been before the struggle. The redeemers came from the very same leadership class that had dominated the antebellum South, while the black remained at the bottom of society—not indeed reenslaved, but very close to it.

The redeemer governments greatly reduced the financial commitments to public education made by the Radical legislatures but they did not change the liberal education laws that the Radicals had written because they found these laws served their interests well. The redeemers were aristocrats with economic alliances with the railroads and the growing industrial powers in the South, and were neither economically nor socially representative of the vast majority of southern white poor and middling farmers. The redeemers, generally conservative Democrats, faced repeated challenges, both within their party and from third parties, from those more representative of the lower economic strata of the southern white population. The redeemers used the black vote to deflect these challenges. Therefore, they had to protect the freedmen's franchise against those among the lower- and middle-class whites who wished to disenfranchise them. As a simple matter of consistency, they had to protect the freedmen's right to education and a proportionate share of the school tax revenue. Southern conservatives sounded much like the common school reformers in arguing, as did Wade Hampton in 1879, that "as the Negro becomes more intelligent, he naturally allies himself with the more conservative of the whites."[25] Redeemers cajoled and bribed and sometimes intimidated the blacks into voting for the conservative Democrats. The redeemers appointed a few blacks to unimportant jobs in their governments and saw to it that federal patronage from the Republican party went to southern blacks rather than to southern white members of the Republican party. When they could not win the black vote to their side, the redeemers stole it. In the black belt counties, where they were in firm control and where the majority of the blacks lived, the redeemers prevented the blacks from using the franchise they carefully protected for them and counted every black as having voted the redeemer column.

The redeemers also appealed quite subtly to the basic racism in the southern character by using the possibility of black equality to scare poor whites into voting Democratic. Although this device was to be exploited quite openly in the period after 1890 by the "redneck" politicians, it existed in a more restrained and more dignified manner even during the rule of the aristocratic Democrats. Whenever the latter's control appeared threatened, they argued that splitting the Democratic vote would insure victory for a party which would allow Negro domination of the South. Thus, at the same time that they assured the black that they were protecting him from those who wanted to strip him completely of his civil rights, the redeemers urged the poor white to support them because the conservative Democrats would keep the Negro in his place.

The redeemers and the conservative black belt aristocrats found the Negro as manipulable in education as in politics and just as useful. Maintaining the Radicals' education laws enabled the Democrats to provide good public schooling for their children while keeping school taxes to a minimum at a time when low levels of taxation were thought necessary to attract industry and internal improvements to the South. The redeemers' strategy worked something like this although it varied somewhat from state to state. The legal requirement that the state distribute school money to each county according to the size of its white and black school-age population served the redeemers' purposes admirably. It was very simple, once that money had reached the county, to violate the law (the freedmen's northern friends were unlikely to examine county policies and procedures very closely) and assign disproportionate amounts of money to white schools. This the redeemers did from the beginning of their rule. Counties with large numbers of black children had a special advantage because they had more state money to divide among fewer white children. Take North Carolina, which in 1890 distributed $12.00

[25] Quoted in C. Vann Woodward, *The Strange Career of Jim Crow* (1955; New York, 1966), 53.

for every ten children. In a black belt county with nine black children for every white child, $10.80 should have gone to the black schools and $1.20 to the white schools. Being generous, we might say that perhaps the white officials would have divided the money fifty-fifty. Thus in the black belt county the white child received at least $6.00 per year for his education, enough in 1890 to provide a reasonably good common school education, and his aristocratic parents could be satisfied that their child was educated adequately in the public system. On the other hand, in a white county, where nine out of every ten children were white, even the grossest discrimination against the blacks' rights to equal schooling would not significantly increase the state funds available for white schools—in North Carolina in 1890 diverting all the funds that should have gone to black schools in such a county would only add thirteen cents for each white child, hardly enough to make much difference.

Thus the Radical education laws, as implemented during redemption, served the black belt whites while discriminating against the interests of the poorer whites who lived in counties outside the plantation areas. Voters in these counties sought constantly to supplement the state contribution to education by imposing local property taxes or by raising poll taxes and diverting those funds to the schools. The redeemers, eager to industrialize the South, opposed such local initiatives to raise property taxes and redeemer legislatures refused to authorize localities to levy property taxes for the support of schools. In an effort to garner more white support for local property taxes, leaders of the non–black belt counties sought to divide taxes on racial grounds—all taxes raised on property owned by whites would be spent to educate white children and all taxes raised on property owned by blacks to support black schools. North Carolina in 1880 permitted one town to raise taxes locally and divide them racially; this movement spread and in 1883 the legislature authorized other communities to follow this procedure. The redeemers and the blacks, for different reasons, of course, tried to stop this movement in the name of protecting equal rights for the black. The redeemers believed that allowing localities to divide taxes on racial grounds would weaken the resistance to increased taxes because whites, if they believed that all their tax money would support government benefits for whites only, would levy higher taxes. The redeemers successfully appealed to the courts in North Carolina to declare the splitting of taxes along racial lines unconstitutional because it discriminated against blacks.

In addition to the race-related politics of education, economic and demographic problems hindered the growth of public schooling in the South. The region was the poorest in the United States even before the Civil War, and the destruction caused by the war simply made a bad situation much worse. Most of the South's capital, including the capital in the state literary funds, had been invested in Confederate bonds and currency which became valueless at war's end. The physical destruction of battle destroyed much of the section's tax base.

Demographic conditions in the South made adequate support for public education more difficult than in any other section. It had the country's highest dependency rate (the ratio of children dependent on adults to the number of adults in the society); the average southerner had over twice as many children to support and educate as adults elsewhere in the nation. Louis Harlan cites the following figures for 1900: in New York there were 125 male adults to every 100 children of school age, 135 in Massachusetts, and 196 in Nevada. In the South there were more schoolchildren than there were male adults. For every 100 schoolchildren in Virginia, there were 76 male adults. In Georgia there were 68, in North Carolina 66, and in South Carolina 61. As Harlan points out, "This meant that for each dollar provided per school child, the average adult in Massachusetts had to provide 74 cents, the adult in Virginia had to provide $1.31, and in South Carolina $1.64."[26] All rural districts in the country had a high dependency rate; but the South was the most rural section of the country. Thus, in the section with the fewest resources and the smallest tax base, each adult had to spend more money than adults in any other part of the country to provide "equal" education for his children. Another southern demographic pattern that hindered public education was the old problem of scattered population which made it difficult to locate schoolhouses where they could serve conveniently a large enough population to make them financially efficient. Too often only 20 or 30 children lived within walking distance of a school that could more efficiently have served 50 or 60. The scattered nature of its population required the South to spend more per child in order to achieve educational opportunities equal to those provided for the children of the North. The southern decision to provide separate schools for whites and blacks exacerbated these financial and demographic problems. It reinforced the effects of scattered population and required the shrunken tax base to support twice as many school buildings and teachers.

The fact that southerners tended to associate public education with the Yankee, with Radical reconstruction, and with the educational crusade against the South also hindered efforts to expand common schooling. Furthermore, the mass of southerners almost inevitably associated public education with advancing black equality. For one thing, of course, state educational funds were divided, on paper at least, equally between the races, suggesting that the black was getting more than he had before the war. Most southerners probably agreed with the oft-repeated senti-

---

[26] Figures from Louis Harlan, *Separate and Unequal: Public School Campaigns and Racism in the Southern Seaboard States, 1901–1915* (New York, 1968), 32.

ment that education only made the black "uppity" and ruined him as a field hand. If, as most southerners liked to think, the black was to be confined to the lowest, most menial occupations, there seemed no particular reason why he should be educated at white expense. Only in those few instances when reformers could promise these whites that the additional tax money collected from them would go exclusively to white education did these whites support educational reform before 1890.

Between 1890 and 1915 a group of southern progressive reformers, aided financially by a wide range of northern philanthropists, effected a common school revolution in the South. Their goals were various but predominantly conservative, what would have been called Whiggish in an earlier generation. They sought to increase the number of public schools in the South, the length of their school terms, and the number of children enrolled in them. They sought to remove all the political and social barriers that had blocked public school expansion since Reconstruction. They met these objectives with spectacular success. This reform group included progressive politicians of the type that supported Woodrow Wilson and the New Freedom in national politics and supported the curbing of business power in the South, honesty in government, and the uplifting of the poor and the deprived in order to make them more stable and responsible members of the body politic. It also included university professors and administrators, social workers, and other middle-class professionals who held similar views. The reformers were native southerners, but they drew substantial financial support for their educational campaign activities (but never actual money for schools or teachers' salaries) from northern philanthropists, many of whom were literal or spiritual heirs of the families who had supported the reconstruction educational effort. The philanthropists and the southern educational reformers combined in 1901 to form the Southern Education Board to unify the campaign and northern support for it. In its fourteen-year existence, the SEB acted through its agents in each of the southern states, paying them to campaign for and lobby for increased taxation in support of public education. The SEB directed all its expenditures—which were very modest—toward inspiring southerners to help themselves. The northern members of the SEB sought to remain in the background, apparently so as not to seem to be imposing northern values on the South.

The reform movement itself was conducted in the form of a series of campaigns in each state to convince public opinion of the wisdom of expanding common schooling. Whenever a candidate favorable to educational expansion was running for election or whenever tax legislation or referenda affecting schools were to be voted, reformers would lobby in the state capital or harangue white audiences to support educational improvement in revivalistic political meetings. As it happened, a single election in each state focused on the issues of educational reform, and the reformers worked especially hard to fire public support for improved education during these contests. Some of the reformers successfully competed for high office on platforms favoring educational expansion, enacting far-reaching measures when elected. The reform movement was quite successful during that twenty-five-year period in moving southern public education toward parity with public education in the North. It fell short of achieving that parity but made spectacular strides in that direction.

These advances, however, came at the expense of the blacks' rights to equal educational facilities and opportunities. Black access to educational monies had not, in fact, been equitable before 1890, but the fiction had been maintained that whites and blacks shared equal access to education. The progressive school reformers in the South and, more surprisingly, their northern supporters decided quite consciously to dispense with that fiction and to discriminate quite openly against the black. By 1915 all the southern states were openly publishing figures on educational expenditures which clearly outlined the astonishing degree of inequality between facilities for whites and blacks. For example, Georgia, where more than 46 percent of the school-age population was black, spent 5 times more on teachers for whites than on those for blacks, 25 times more on white school buildings than on black ones, 15 times as much for repairing white buildings, 12 times as much for supplies, and 30 times as much for equipment. Black schools "represented only one–thirteenth of the value of publicly-owned school property." The Virginia school report of 1914–1915 revealed that in certain black belt counties expenditures for teachers for white children amounted to $13.46 per child while expenditures for the salaries of teachers for black children totaled only $1.55 per child.[27] The situation was similar throughout the South. What had happened to the educational crusade begun in the 1860s that allowed progressive reformers and northern philanthropists to support this blatant violation of the blacks' educational rights? As was the case with the educational crusaders of the 1860s, the reformers after 1890 faced this dilemma: They could support educational reform in such a way that it would promote, among whites, social unity and stability, economic progress, and the alleviation of the problems arising from poverty or they could fight to insure equal educational opportunity for both races at the cost of increased instability, conflict, and hostility to education. The reformers knew that they could not improve education for whites if they tried, simultaneously, either to improve it for blacks or even to preserve whatever tenuous access to common schooling they had had since Reconstruction.

[27] Figures from *ibid.*, 246, 167.

In essence, the public school reformers in the South sought to convince residents in predominantly white counties to raise taxes for schools in violation of the interests of the wealthy conservatives of the black belt and the conservative businessmen whose property was subject to taxation. The progressives who supported school reform thought that it would improve the lot of the rural southern white and of the textile mill worker in the small industrial towns. They thought that a better educated labor force would enhance the region's economic prosperity. Like northern progressives they wished to reduce government corruption—in the South most often associated with voter fraud and manipulation—and feared the effects of uneducated and unstable voters. At the same time they called for educational expansion, the southern progressives often advocated disenfranchisement of the black and the illiterate white as a means of controlling corruption and irresponsible voting. North Carolina's educational campaign of 1900–1901 was explicitly coupled with the literacy test contained in the new state constitution. That literacy test had a grandfather clause due to expire in 1908 for those coming of age after that date. Thus the progressives pressured the whites from the poor districts to tax themselves more heavily in order to provide the education necessary to enable their children to maintain their right to vote. Charles B. Aycock, soon to be the state's "educational" governor, explained it clearly to some mountain whites during the campaign. "We recognize and provide for the God-given and hereditary superiority of the white man and of all white children now thirteen years of age, but for the future as to all under thirteen we call on them to assert that superiority of which we boast by learning to read and write."[28] Few other states had such restrictive grandfather clauses and the political necessity of education was not so clear cut, but progressives threatened to disenfranchise illiterate whites elsewhere and hoped poor whites would support educational expansion as insurance against disenfranchisement. Progressives also supported educational expansion as part of their general campaign to improve public services in the South by increasing the tax burden on what they considered the unregulated and immoral corporate trusts whose southern investments were hugely undervalued and accordingly too lightly taxed. These northern-owned railroads and mills failed to contribute sufficiently to the South's public welfare; taxing them more heavily for schools would begin to change the pattern. Progressives wished also to restrict child labor. In order to do so, they had to create an appropriate alternative to occupy children's time, for it was widely believed in the South that "idleness was the devil's workshop."

In general, opposition to the public education campaign came from wealthy and conservative businessmen and farmers and from large prop-

[28] Quoted in *ibid.*, 63.

ertyowners. These men knew that improved educational facilities meant higher taxes and that higher taxes would be assessed largely on their property. Moreover, because of the distribution of the black population, they had secured good public schooling for their own children and saw no particular reason to expand the school system in the poorer counties. Nor, as elitists, were they very interested in educating more people to exercise the franchise and, since much of their power had derived from manipulation of votes, an educated and supposedly less corruptible electorate did not appeal to them either. Many employed child labor either in factory or farm and opposed its restriction. Fundamentalist religions which opposed public education as a secular institution resisted the educational campaigns to some extent. Southerners of almost all kinds expressed at one time or another the belief that the South could not afford an expensive system of education. Often this belief coalesced into drives for economy in the school system, drives which sometimes threatened to destroy the public school system in order to balance the state budget. In this southerners greatly resembled the northern public.

All these sources of opposition could not stop the movement, the reformers knew, if the mass of white voters in the white counties could be made to support it. This they refused to do unless they were promised explicitly that the new taxes they voted would be used almost exclusively for white schools. The progressive initiators of school reform and its northern philanthropic supporters began the educational campaign with some limited commitment to providing equal educational opportunity for the black. They found no means, however, of fulfilling that commitment and expanding the public school system at the same time. They chose instead to sacrifice equality for the black in order to achieve better school systems for the southern white. "It is wise and just to help the black man to character and usefulness," the president of Tulane University and a common school reformer rationalized in 1901; "but I cannot reiterate too strongly my belief that the white man is and ought to be and will be the controlling force, and that he will act toward the negro in the light of his training. The education, therefore, of one untaught white man to the point that knowledge and not prejudice will guide his conduct, and that he must deal with these people in justice and kindness, is worth more to the black man himself than the education of ten negroes."[29] Although the campaigns in each of the states involved somewhat different issues, the results were fairly similar. At first many locales and states sought to divide local tax money according to its racial origin, but this division was found basically unworkable because it was difficult to determine where taxes raised from northern-owned corporations should be distributed and because the system required massive record-

[29] Edwin A. Alderman, "Education in the South," *Outlook*, LXVIII (August, 1901), 780.

keeping efforts which were considered inefficient and unwieldy. Soon most of the southern states and locales concluded that the best way to solve the problem was to leave the division of tax revenue to the discretion of the school boards.

Some rewording of the laws governing the distribution of state educational funds gave county and district boards of education the right to divide both state money and money raised locally between the races on the basis of what was called "substantial equality" or on the basis of the board's perception of the general welfare rather than on a strict per capita basis. In 1896 the South Carolina legislature prescribed, as the new constitution allowed it to do, that school tax monies in each district be "distributed and expended by the Board of Trustees [district school board], for the best interest of the school district, according to the Board of Trustees." This language gave almost absolute discretion to the district board: "The best interest of the school district" meant a better education for the whites than for the blacks. Further insuring that the blacks would be short-changed was the fact that in many states all the district school boards were subservient to the state Democratic machines because, rather than being elected locally, they were appointed by county commissioners or justices of the peace who were in turn appointed by the state government. Therefore, even in Republican or black-controlled districts, Democrats controlled the schools. The state machines, committed to depriving the black of educational rights just as they were dedicated to depriving him of his political and social rights, supervised the distribution of even those funds raised at the local level.

What had been the illegal maldistribution of funds between the races was now legal and sanctioned by educational reformers north and south. In most southern states educational leaders sought to raise local taxes on blacks as well as on whites in order to improve school opportunities for white children only. These reformers, in effect, empowered local boards to strip the black schools of any pretensions of adequacy or parity. Although these boards carefully maintained a black school in each district, they kept it open for only a short time, paid its teacher a pitiful wage, and provided almost no equipment for him. While local taxes—paid by white and black—were used to start and rapidly expand a public high school movement for whites, blacks received virtually no high school facilities. Although blacks comprised 35.3 percent of Virginia's school-age population in 1915, blacks comprised only 7.1 percent of the high school pupils, and only 1.9 percent of the high schools in the state were black. In North Carolina the existence of a black high school was first reported in 1917 and in that year only 19 of the state's 15,469 high school students were black. Although some low-level secondary training took place rather clandestinely in black elementary schools and the Rosenwald Fund supported "training schools" for future black teachers which offered some secondary work, white hostility to advanced education at public expense for the black was so great as virtually to exclude blacks from the public high school until well after World War I.[30]

Thus, between 1890 and 1915 the blacks' educational opportunities deteriorated relative to those of whites in that region. The educational crusade designed to elevate the freedmen had come to this. Northern white philanthropists and southern common school reformers supported a drive to expand and improve common schooling in the South that openly discriminated against blacks. At the same time the northern philanthropists were supporting "special," "for blacks only" industrial education in the South. They were making a great exception in the search for a common schooling.

GUIDE TO FURTHER READING

The social and intellectual condition of black Americans after the Civil War is examined in C. VANN WOODWARD, *The Strange Career of Jim Crow* (1955; New York, 1974), C. VANN WOODWARD, *Origins of the New South, 1887–1920* (Baton Rouge, La., 1951), WILLIE LEE ROSE, *Rehearsal for Reconstruction: The Port Royal Experiment* (Indianapolis, Ind., 1964), JOEL WILLIAMSON, *After Slavery: The Negro in South Carolina During Reconstruction, 1861–1877* (Chapel Hill, N. C., 1965), VERNON L. WHARTON, *The Negro in Mississippi, 1865–1890* (New York, 1947), GEORGE FREDERICKSON, *The Black Image in the White Mind: The Debate on Afro-American Character and Destiny, 1817–1914* (New York, 1971), WILLIAM R. STANTON, *The Leopard's Spots: Scientific Attitudes toward Race in America, 1815–59* (Chicago, 1960), and JOHN S. HALLER, *Outcasts from Evolution: Scientific Attitudes of Racial Inferiority, 1859–1900* (Urbana, Ill., 1971).

Black education in the South after the Civil War is examined generally in HENRY BULLOCK, *A History of Negro Education in the South, from 1619 to the Present* (New York, 1967), HORACE MANN BOND, *The Education of the Negro in the American Social Order* (1934; New York, 1966), BOND, *Negro Education in Alabama: A Study in Cotton and Steel* (Washington, D. C., 1939), LOUIS HARLAN, *Separate and Unequal: Public School Campaigns and Racism in the Southern Seaboard States, 1901–1915* (New York, 1968), W. E. B. DuBOIS, *Black Reconstruction in America, 1860–1880* (New York, 1935), final chapter, JAMES ANDERSON, "Education for Servitude: The Social Purposes of Schooling in the Black South, 1870–1920" (Unpublished Dissertation, University of Illinois, 1973), AUGUST MEIER, *Negro Thought in America, 1880–1915: Racial Ideologies in the Age of Booker T. Washington* (Ann Arbor, Mich., 1963), MEIER, "The Rise of Industrial Education in Negro Schools," *Midwest Journal,* VII (Spring and Fall, 1955), 21–44, 241–266, MERLE CURTI, *The Social Ideas of American Educators,* rev. ed. (New York, 1959), chapters 7–8, HENRY L. SWINT, *The Northern Teacher in the South, 1862–1870* (Nashville, Tenn., 1941), MARTIN ABBOTT, *The Freedman's Bureau in South*

[30] Harlan, *Separate and Unequal,* 166, 133–134.

Carolina (Chapel Hill, N. C., 1967), JACK KIRBY, *Darkness at the Dawning: Race and Reform in the Progressive South* (Philadelphia, 1972), HUGH BAILEY, *Edgar Gardner Murphy, Gentle Progressive* (Coral Gables, Fla., 1968), and DANIEL LE-VINE, *Varieties of Reform Thought* (Madison, Wis., 1964), chapter 5.

On educational philanthropy and black opportunity in the late nineteenth and early twentieth centuries, see LOUIS HARLAN, *Separate and Unequal: Public School Campaigns and Racism in the Southern Seaboard States, 1901–1915* (New York, 1968), JAMES MCPHERSON, "White Liberals and Black Power in Negro Education, 1865–1915," *American Historical Review*, LXXV (June, 1970), 1357–1386, LOUIS D. RUBIN, ed., *Teach the Freeman: The Correspondence of Rutherford B. Hayes and the John Slater Fund for Negro Education, 1881–1887*, 2 vols. (Baton Rouge, La., 1959), and the *Reports* of the General Education Board, the Southern Education Board, the George Peabody Fund, and the John Slater Fund.

CHAPTER 6

The Failure of the Common Schools (II): The North

I

BETWEEN 1840 AND 1880 MANY OF THE CHARACTERISTICS WERE INTRO-
duced which have since governed the delivery of educational services in
America. The structure that evolved during the middle few decades of
the nineteenth century distorted the spirit and many of the goals of the
common school movement. This failure in spirit was relative to the promises made by the antebellum reformers; it was not absolute. Many goals
were reached and thousands of children, parents, and teachers benefited
greatly, but much was sacrificed, especially the ideals of commonality,
spontaneity, openness, and individual attention.

We are going to explore this failure through examination of several
of its manifestations. In this chapter we will continue to examine the early
bureaucratization which crippled so many efforts at reform and the growing influence of those who sought to use the schools to differentiate their
children from the talented competition they faced from below and above,
an important and neglected element in the Catholic school controversy
of the early 1840s and in the sort of education sought by the Lowell mill
girls and promoters of the mid-nineteenth-century high school. Historians have popularized an "imposition" model of educational reform. They
argue that through compulsory attendance legislation and overtures to

154

the working class about mobility and the material advantages of character-building instruction, the elite forced the lower classes into schools
where correct values and attitudes were forced upon them. According
to this interpretation, then, social control of the lower classes was the
purpose of universal, free public schools. Much recommends this perspective. Certainly the evidence culled from mid-century theoretical
tracts, school board reports, and promotional literature makes it clear
that one avowed purpose of extending the role of the public schools was
to correct the antisocial behavior of neglected children and to bring
harmony to urban America.

To attract widespread support for this expensive and elaborate task,
however, advocates of this program had to gather the support of a much
larger portion of the population. Much of this support was offered by the
middling classes: parents who grasped the opportunity to differentiate
their children from those of the poorer classes. While the "common"
grammar school introduced the lower classes to the dominant American
values, the earliest high schools and other secondary training classes were
filled by middle-class children whose parents sought to advantage them
in the pursuit of wealth. Secondary schools were not intended for the
lower classes. The curriculum discouraged their attendance and poor
families needed the additional income a working child of twelve could
provide. Through World War I high schools buttressed middle-class
children against lower-class competition for clerical and white-collar employment, and provided many with the skills and credentials to enter the
expanding professions late in the nineteenth century.

Others in the middle class wanted to utilize the expanding public
schools to reinforce traditional patterns of influence, status, and respect.
During this unstable period when mobility and competition threatened
traditional relationships, many segments of the Protestant middle class
wanted confirmation that they were "better" than those socially below
them. Confirmation and recognition of these values kept genteel, down-
wardly mobile Protestants in the middle class. They wanted to believe
it was better to be poor and educated than upwardly mobile and vulgar.

The public schools were loyally supported by the Protestant middle
class. Indeed, this segment of the population was successful in turning
much of the common school movement to its own ends and in this way
captured the public schools. Support of public education by the Protestant middle class was built upon important interests of that group. Parents wanted their children differentiated from poorer children, to have
skills and credentials which could give these middle-class children an
advantage in making their fortunes. These parents wanted their children
to attend school with—to be equals of—wealthier students, not poorer
children. Their definition of equality was quite distant in spirit from the

common schools advocated by the upper-class reformers. The elite common school reformers wanted the public schools to attract and instruct as many children as possible. They were willing to bend to include nearly every child (except those few northern black children who sought a common school education). Their supporters, however, often wanted access to publicly supported schools restricted to their own children and those above them. Gradually, the reformers' desire for a universal common experience was sacrificed to the wishes of the middle-class supporters of unequal opportunities.

Despite the reformers' effort to attract the urban and immigrant masses, the Protestant middle class was able to populate the public schools with their own children. Not everyone was allowed to take advantage of the educational services available, even though everyone was responsible for their share of the tax burden, monies which were eventually used to finance secondary and postsecondary institutions. These groups which captured the schools did so by making them militantly middle class, militantly Protestant, and militantly nativist, as well as ruralistic, antimaterialistic, and impractical. The public schools, before 1880, offered the immigrant and working-class child little that was useful. Concerted effort was made to ridicule and defame the culture and the folkways of the lower-class children. Their religion (predominantly Catholic), their languages, and their foreign habits and values were continually denounced. Whatever pride in their homeland they were able to keep alive after the migration experience was ridiculed and even cursed as evidence of subversive intentions.

By maintaining an inflexible posture toward compromise with the Catholic lower classes over this ridicule and harassment, the Protestant middle classes kept the schools to themselves for several important decades. When immigrant children began to take advantage of the public elementary schools, because of compulsory attendance legislation or their ability to use their political power to reduce the influence of the Protestants, the middle-class patrons turned to the public high school. Tax-supported secondary training remained beyond the lower class as a whole until the first or second decade of this century. The middle class opened the elementary schools to everyone as political pressures forced them and as residential segregation guaranteed that the children of the two classes would not attend the same elementary schools. By the mid-nineteenth century, this segregation was well advanced in the larger cities. The high school, through World War I, was taken as a middle-class refuge, and in subsequent years public colleges and universities have played a similar role. An examination of the Catholic school controversy in mid-nineteenth-century New York City will illustrate the sacrifices which were forced upon the elite common school reformers by the middle classes.

II

Twelve men gathered in New York City in 1805 to survey the educational scene. They found that the city neglected the schooling of the poor, leaving that responsibility to the religious denominations. These schools charged tuition, except to poor members of the denominations. Most poor families, however, were not church members. A number of private fee-charging schools were operated by teachers, either singly or in partnerships, but these enrolled children of more means; only a very few scholarships were available to poor children. Believing that free, nondenominational schooling should be available to poor children, these twelve men, later joined by several others, incorporated themselves into "The Society for establishing a Free School in the City of New York, for the education of such poor children who do not belong to, or are not provided for, by any religious society."

This incorporation, the Free School Society, was established by men of substantial wealth and status; many were Quakers with a tradition of public service. Religious societies provided schools for children whose parents were members of the sect, they admitted, but there remained "a large number living in total neglect of religious and moral instruction." The trustees pointed out that "[c]hildren brought up in ignorance, and amidst the contagion of bad example, are in imminent danger of ruin; and too many of them, it is to be feared, instead of being useful members of the community, will become the burden and pests of society. Early instruction and fixed habits of industry, decency, and order, are the surest safeguards of virtuous conduct; and when parents are either unable or unwilling to bestow the necessary attention on the education of their children, it becomes the duty of the public, and of individuals, who have the power, to assist them."[1] Similar groups who encountered similar problems echoed this rationale for decades in city after city.

Because funds were limited, the Society established only a few schools in its first decade. In 1813 New York State passed a permissive school tax law which allowed individual localities to tax themselves for educational purposes and which established a state school fund to assist those districts which chose to tax themselves. The Free School Society received enough of these funds to operate, by 1825, eleven free schools and to serve nearly 20,000 children, "taken from the most indigent classes."[2]

The Free School Society became the Public School Society in 1825. This changed name symbolized that the Society had broadened its origi-

[1] Quoted in William O. Bourne, *History of the Public School Society of the City of New York* (New York, 1870), 7.

[2] John Griscom quoted in Carl Kaestle, *The Evolution of an Urban School System: New York City, 1750–1850* (Cambridge, Mass., 1973), 84.

nal mandate to include not only those children who could afford no tuition but all the children in the city. The Society began to charge nominal fees, but turned away no child who was without this tuition money. The Public School Society's facilities had become the city's only real "public" schools. The Society called upon the city to provide public education for every child through the Society's auspices and denounced the city's policy of granting tax monies to denominational schools.

> Our free schools have conferred the blessings of education upon a large number of the children of the poor, but still it is to be lamented that a description of public school is wanting amongst us, where the rich and the poor may meet together; where the wall of partition, which now seems to be raised between them, may be removed; where kindlier feelings between the children of these respective classes may be begotten; where the indigent may be excited to emulate the cleanliness, decorum and mental improvement of those in better circumstances; and where the children of our wealthiest citizens will have an opportunity of witnessing and sympathizing, more than they now do, with the wants and privations of their fellows of the same age.[3]

The Society sought a system of schools which would accommodate the wealthy as well as the poor, citing the advantages of a common school experience.

Part of the Society's inspiration apparently came from less altruistic motives. In the early 1820s the Free School Society encountered competition in its effort to school the poor. The Bethel Baptist School Society was also receiving public money to support a small system of schools for poor children. In 1822 the Baptists asked for permission to use a portion of their funds to construct new schools, a right which had traditionally been the Free School Society's alone (the Baptists had used their public monies only for salaries). The Free School Society protested that the Baptists wanted to use public money to build a sectarian school for Baptists rather than for the poor, even though the Baptists pointed out that their facilities were open to all children. The Society also accused the Baptists of wanting to indoctrinate the city's poor children with their denomination's beliefs. The Society argued that to diffuse the fund among each interested denomination (Methodists and Catholics also applied for money in 1822) would lead to chaos and inefficiency and hinder all educational effort in the city. The city, persuaded that the Free School Society could provide the most efficient schooling, denied the Baptist request in 1824.

The Society never addressed the central ethical and political issues. It avoided the question of why state monies should go to one private educational venture and not to another. Why should not the school fund

---

[3] Free School Society, *Annual Report* (New York, 1825), 7, quoted in Kaestle, *Evolution of an Urban School System,* 85.

be divided among those programs dedicated to the same purpose, including the Society's? By offering no viable answer, the Society left itself open to an almost inevitable challenge by the Catholics. Although the various Protestant sects were not too unhappy with the work of the Society—after all, its membership was largely Protestant and its effort was a Protestant one—the Catholics found its thrust antithetical to their own educational ideals. The challenge came in the late 1830s. Their ranks swelled with povertystricken immigrants, the Catholics found themselves less able than most Protestant denominations to support unaided any sort of parochial schooling. In 1834 the Catholic bishop in New York City found across the street from the cathedral a half–empty Society school and asked permission to supervise the teaching and the books used in the school so that all anti-Catholic sentiment might be erased. In turn, he promised to get Catholic children who were not attending school at all to enroll. The Public School Society dismissed the offer and said that sectarianism had no place in public instruction. It did appoint two or three Catholics to its board of trustees, but this attempt at compromise attracted but few Catholic children to the Society's schools.

The Public School Society was quite upset that Catholic children stayed away from school in droves. The trustees shared the views of the Society's founders—that children out of school grew into adults easily corrupted and likely to become the "burden and pests of society." The Catholics, because they were poor and Irish, exacerbated these fears.

The nature of the Irish immigration was fundamentally different from what America had experienced previously. The large non-Irish immigration before the Civil War was primarily composed of men and women who were dissatisfied with their political or legal status, or who were artisans and workers with some skill and status facing displacement by the automation and technology which accompanied the Industrial Revolution; their independence and relatively high status were being eroded. These immigrants were largely from the lower middle class—independent people—not factory operatives or peasants. The Irish, on the other hand, were peasants who existed at the lowest economic and social levels. Unlike other immigrants who left Europe to better themselves or to buttress their declining status in the face of changing conditions, the Irish were driven from their homeland by hunger.

The Irish peasant was struck by a series of disasters which began in the mid-eighteenth century and culminated in the tragic potato famine of the 1840s. Insecure tenantry customs and laws uprooted the Irish peasant. Unlike the English or continental peasant, the Irish farmer had never had a secure inherited tenure on his land. He was mercilessly gouged by absentee English landlords interested only in collecting the rents on their property across the Irish Channel. The peasant rented his land for a short period, as brief as two or three years, and at the end of each term the land passed to the highest bidder. The previous tenant had no preferred position. When the price of grain fell with the end of the Napoleonic Wars, the landlords found that pastureland was more profitable than renting to peasants who grew grain. The landlords tried to drive the peasants from the land.

A shortage of tillable land and a growing population forced peasants to pay rents nearly equal to the value of the crops they could harvest. The Irish peasant raised grain to pay his rent and raised potatoes to feed himself and his family. The great potato famine of the 1840s only made matters worse. These seemingly hopeless conditions bred a debilitating despondency among the peasants and led them to depend upon whiskey, mystical Catholicism, and a complex network of secret societies to give meaning to their lives. The focus of the Irishman's life shifted from the problem of economic betterment to the problems of emotional survival and fulfillment. Along with farm laborers of even less status, the peasants were driven to assume a pattern of life which English, and later American, observers called laziness or shiftlessness.

As they were driven from the land after 1815, the Irish peasants turned to America as a desperate refuge. They did not find it, at least initially, a very receptive refuge. Upon landing in the United States port cities, the Irish found a situation hardly better than that from which they had fled. As Oscar Handlin has noted with regard to Boston, the Irish immigrant encountered a rigid social structure that offered the Irishman little hope of rising and a rather static commercial economy which provided little steady work for the unskilled immigrants. As more immigrants arrived and competition increased, pay scales plummeted. The Irish had neither the capital, the agricultural skills, nor the enterprise to seek out opportunity in the West. Stranded amid conditions not unlike those of his homeland, the Irishman continued to focus on the joys of his mystical religion, the comfort of his liquor, and the security of his secret societies.

Americans, at this time, were particularly worried about the character of their cities and of the people who lived there. With their penchant for blaming environmental difficulties and corruption on individual weaknesses and immorality, concerned Americans found it easy to hold the Irish themselves responsible for the squalor, vice, and shiftlessness that characterized the immigrant slums. Americans believed that if people worked hard they would have no time to patronize saloons, and poverty would disappear. It followed, rather logically, that the health of society depended upon the eradication of the poor immigrant's traditional shiftlessness. Americans argued that these traits were best rooted out through the inculcation of moral values in school and adopted education, then, as an antidote to the urban ills of the 1840s. The reformers contended that this set of moral values was distinctly nonsectarian. Catholics could not agree.

In 1840 the problem of a private sectarian institution dispersing "public" education to the poor, a group which did not share the religious bias of the private institution, boiled to the surface. It boiled in two cauldrons. Not only did the New York City Catholics protest that the public schools were trying to get Catholic children to abandon their religion, but the Whig leadership in the state government, alarmed at the numbers of children going unschooled, demanded that the Public School Society somehow offer an education which would, by respecting the Catholics' religion, attract their children to school. The inability of the two groups to arrive at a mutually acceptable solution indicates several salient characteristics of the process and purpose of Whig educational reform.

In his opening message to the legislature in 1840, Whig Governor William Seward called attention to New York City's unschooled children and advocated establishing schools in which the "children of foreigners" "may be instructed by teachers speaking the same language with themselves, and professing the same faith."[4] Seward retreated from his stand on the language issue in the face of outrage by everyone except the immigrants. He firmly argued, however, that the patrons of an individual school had the right to determine the character of the moral instruction given their children. Seward recognized that the purpose of schooling the poor was to inculcate them with values and habits shared by the rest of society in order to promote harmony and order. He realized that the goal of common values required central control because local communities could not be trusted to contribute to the larger social needs. However, he also understood that if schooling were imposed from above, the children imposed upon were likely to become alienated from and reject the public schools. He did not believe, at least in the case of the Catholics, that central control and large Catholic enrollment were compatible. Some sort of local control was necessary, even at the public's expense, to attract the wayward youngsters to school. He believed that getting the kids into school took priority over controlling exactly which moral values were inculcated in the classroom. It was better, he thought, for the children to learn Catholic morality in school than to roam the streets unattended. It is obvious that Seward did not share the common fear of Catholics and their values; to him, their moral instruction little threatened the safety of society. He and other Whig leaders valued the discipline and socialization to routines transmitted in school more than they prized the specific moral values taught there.

The Public School Society shared Seward's concern for getting the children into school. In the 1830s the trustees had personally snipped out or inked over passages in the Society's library books which were repulsive to the Catholic clergy and appointed several Catholic trustees. Only on one issue did they refuse to compromise—the use of the King

---

[4] Quoted in Bourne, *Public School Society*, 179.

James Bible in the schools. They rejected Seward's localism because it would allow the Catholics to read the Douay version of the Bible. We are not, the trustees wrote, "conscious of a want of sympathy for the oppressed of other lands, who seek an asylum in this; on the contrary, [we] act under a firm conviction that the sooner such persons abandon any unfavorable prejudices with which they may arrive among us, and become familiar with our language, and reconciled to our institutions and habits, the better it will be for them, and for the country of their adoption. [T]he best interests of all will be alike promoted by having their children mingle with ours in the public seminaries of learning."[5] The trustees were, like Seward, eager to get the children into schools, but they were more conscious or more candid about their desire to Americanize the poor immigrants' children when they got them in school. Seward's localism would not have accomplished this purpose, they felt.

While Seward advocated local control from his Whiggish perspective, Catholics were petitioning for a portion of the school fund and state tax revenues in order that they, as a group, could establish their own system of schools. The Catholic petition argued that the Public School Society was using public monies to support sectarian Protestant education. Since that was the case, the Catholic Church deserved public monies to support its own sectarian schools. The Catholic argument was somewhat inconsistent. They blasted the Public School Society's schools as godless *and* Protestant. In order to remove as much evidence of sectarianism from its classrooms as possible, the Public School Society had banned direct moral instruction and explicit dogmatic training. It confined religious instruction to Bible reading and some prayers. Catholics argued that more explicit doctrinaire religious instruction was necessary because, they believed, schools should play an important part in the child's moral upbringing. They could never send their children to the "godless" public schools. On the other hand, Catholics contended that the "public" schools were sectarian because they taught the Bible without authority and commentary (neither the texts nor the teachers told children how to interpret Bible readings) and from the wrong translation. This inconsistency of calling the public schools both godless and sectarian should not obscure the Catholics' fundamental point: a single common school curriculum could not be developed which could inculcate moral and religious values acceptable to both Catholics and Protestants. Therefore, the Catholics concluded, some significant local control over the curriculum was necessary. This would be most easily accomplished by creating, at the public's expense, separate schools for Catholics. We must now turn to the complicated political context of this crisis of the 1840s.

John Hughes, recently appointed bishop of the New York City diocese, led the Catholic cause. A driving, dynamic, and argumentative man

[5] *Ibid.*, 185.

born in Ireland, Hughes found the school controversy useful for several reasons. Of course he wanted to provide adequate education for the children of his See without having them inculcated with Protestant sectarian doctrine. Hughes shared the Whiggish concern that the large number of poor Catholic children not attending school presented a threat to society, as well as to the church. To get all the Catholic children to attend, the church would have to exert strong centralized control from the top. Although he supported localism in relation to the Protestants, Hughes did not advocate localism within the proposed system of Catholic schools.

Indeed, Hughes hoped to use the development of a Catholic school system as a means of enhancing diocesan control of local parishes. In the United States a pattern had evolved of laymen in each local parish holding church property rather than the central diocese, as was the case in Europe. At this time an important struggle was taking place within the Catholic Church in America as the clergy sought to gain control of church property, and the attendant power over religious affairs, from the laymen. Hughes was successful in this quest in Philadelphia and had his program well under way in New York City. His fight for a separate, hierarchically directed system of sectarian schools was but one more tool Hughes hoped to employ against the laymen. If the Catholic petitions were successful, financial resources would begin to flow from the state and local government directly into the hands of the hierarchy which would distribute them to the schools, thus providing Hughes important additional power with which to influence individual parishes.

Bishop Hughes also saw the controversy as a means of unifying New York's badly fragmented Catholic community. Throughout the East, the impoverished and lowly Irish immigrant threatened the status and comfort of those few Catholics who were "native-born Americans." Prior to the 1830s, American Catholics had been fairly well integrated into the nation's social and economic life and were evenly distributed throughout the classes. Therefore, as hordes of Irish entered New York City and people began to associate the word "Catholic" with these shiftless, ignorant immigrants, the native-born Catholics became very unhappy, as these unfortunate associations undermined their own status. This situation made the Irish immigrant no happier. He found himself served by native-born or French priests whose Catholicism was less militant and less mystical than that which had evolved in Ireland. Hughes' predecessor, John Dubois, was a scholarly French intellectual, not a leader of people searching for comfort and courage in the face of difficult, even desperate conditions. His immigrant congregations walked out on his French-accented sermons.[6] The Irish, rapidly becoming a numerical majority in the American Catholic Church, found themselves with less

---

[6] Joseph J. McCadden, "Bishop Hughes Versus the Public School Society of New York," *Catholic Historical Review*, L (1964), 189.

power within the Church than they felt was commensurate with their numbers. Hughes thought that the school controversy might pull the warring factions together.

Hughes began a very interesting correspondence with Seward soon after the governor's 1840 message to the legislature. Hughes apologized constantly that so many of his Catholic parishioners were firmly wedded to the Democratic party and to its urban political machine, Tammany Hall, and implied that he would like to be thought of as a Whig—with the refinement and social position which were commonly associated with that party. Hughes was unhappy that Catholic immigrants in New York City were already identified with boss politics because he felt that that identification exacerbated status problems and confirmed the average American's image of the Catholic as a politically corrupt foreigner. Hughes' friendship with Seward and the bishop's inclination, in these years, toward Whiggery, suggest both his personal desire for social status and his political desire to detach New York City's Catholic residents from the lower-class political party.[7]

Unfortunately for Hughes and Seward, the nature of New York's political parties made it certain that Democrats would more readily support some sort of separate Catholic education than would the Whigs. In New York the parties did not divide on class lines or class issues. The parties disagreed largely over the proper role of government. Lee Benson has shown that New York's Democratic party favored the tenets of the negative liberal state and that the Whigs supported the positive liberal state. While the Whigs promoted governmental intervention to further the general welfare, the Democrats supported a laissez-faire philosophy that distrusted interference and control from outside the local community. This ideological distinction grew rather cloudy in the 1830s as the parties tended to emulate each other in the search for votes. The state Democratic party, under the Albany Regency of the 1830s, flirted with the positive liberal state. However, we must note a significant opposition to this type of interventionary authority that grew within the New York City Democratic party in the 1830s. At times that opposition took the form of a third party but, as the Democratic party lost power statewide, the influence of the opposition increased. By 1840 the philosophy of this opposition group had once more become the philosophy of the state Democratic party. This New York City movement supporting negative liberalism consisted largely of small shopkeepers, small merchants, and skilled artisans. They were not laborers, as is so often argued. One study has shown that the two leading occupations represented were grocers and physicians, with carpenters, shoemakers, printers, and lawyers constituting large numbers. These groups had a common interest in fighting

---

[7] Henry Browne, "The Archdiocese of New York a Century Ago: A Memoir of Archbishop Hughes 1838–1858," *Historical Records and Studies*, XXXIX–XL (1952), 132–190.

vested interests and strong institutions. (Physicians joined the movement because it opposed what was considered to be the monopoly over licensing doctors held by the two leading medical schools in the state.) These men assumed that a person could do best by himself if he were allowed to be free, if the barriers of monopoly were lowered so that every person had the opportunity to compete on equal terms. This was what they called "equal rights."[8]

Democrats who believed in the negative liberal state were sympathetic toward the plight of the Catholics. They needed Catholic votes for, with them, the Democrats were assured of electoral victory in New York City. The Democrats tended to regard the Public School Society as a monopolistic venture, run by unsympathetic aristocrats. Ideologically, the Democratic party was not wedded to a state system of education or to a highly organized common school system; they were willing to support a localistic educational endeavor like that favored by the Catholics and Seward.

The Whig party, on the other hand, was increasingly committed, in the early 1840s, to the positive liberal state ideal, an important part of which was a highly organized system of universal common schooling. Seward, New York's leading Whig, feared an ignorant lower class so desperately that he was willing to surrender state control to get the children into the schools. (The governor almost certainly viewed his policy as a way of undermining Catholic allegiance to the Democratic party.) Whigs closer to the scene regarded the problem somewhat differently. While Seward was able to separate the immigrants' ignorance and corruption from their Catholicism, many of the leaders and most of the followers of the Whig party in New York City made no such distinction. They were certain that the health of their city depended not only on educating the children of the poor but also on converting them to a Protestant faith. Most middle-class urban residents seemed to have assumed that inculcating morality would solve the problems associated with the immigrant ghettos. It was obvious to most that morality depended heavily on reading and studying the Bible. Thus, when trying to salvage the notoriously evil Five Points area of the city, reformers initially established a Methodist mission in the district and counted on its program of prayer meetings, tract distribution, exhortations, and revivals to solve the problems. The Bible, and the tracts written from it, became the staple of those trying to save for society the lower classes, particularly the Catholics. To their dismay, however, they found that Catholics seemed to be opposed to the Bible.

Here lay the root of the problem. Whig Protestants, intent on imposing some kind of educational socialization upon the immigrants, felt that the Bible was crucial to this effort. Catholics, intent on preserving their

[8] Lee Benson, *The Concept of Jacksonian Democracy: New York as a Test Case* (Princeton, N. J., 1961), especially 86–109.

religion, maintained that requiring reading of the King James version was a sectarian act. The Protestants could not believe that reading this book— the basis of all Christian religion—could be a sectarian act. They could not accept—perhaps could not understand—the importance Catholics placed on reading their own translation of the Bible with authoritative interpretations included. School reformers had had considerable experience in compromising sectarian rivalries among Protestants in order to create common schools. In those cases the compromise, whatever else it may have excluded from the curriculum, always retained Bible reading in the classroom. Enter the Catholics, desperately in need, so the Whigs thought, of Americanization and moral training. Yet every possible compromise with the Catholics failed because they objected to Bible reading as the Protestants conceived it. How could Christians object to reading the Bible in school? How could Catholics object to reading the Divine Law that provided the basis of all our moral values, Protestants asked. These questions forced many to conclude that Catholic behavior on this issue only proved that the Pope and his church actually embodied the Anti-Christ, just as orthodox Protestants had insisted since the Reformation.

Whig political leaders encountered an interesting situation in New York. Like Seward, they could work toward detaching Catholics from the Democratic party and thus aid their own electoral cause in that region. It appeared, however, that more votes could be gained for the Whigs by exploiting middle-class fears of, and prejudice toward, the Catholics. By emphasizing the Bible issue, they hoped to force Protestants to break from the Democratic party that supported the Catholics. This latter program seemed to be the most popular among the Whig leadership.

Such was the situation and political context in 1840 when the school controversy finally erupted. Catholics demanded public funds to establish a separate educational system devoted to, among other things, the inculcation of the teachings of Catholicism. Protestants decreed that the children of the immigrants attend the Public School Society's schools wherein they would be introduced to the culture and morality common to "all Americans." The Democratic party, because of its ideology of antimonopoly and localism, was more sympathetic to the Catholic cause, but was also worried about losing Protestant votes. Whigs, generally allied with programs of governmental intervention in the cause of the general welfare and of imposing morality through public education, stood with the Protestants, even though its state leaders expressed a sympathy with the Catholic cause that was certain to lose the party a number of votes in the 1840 elections. As the bulk of the Whig movement separated itself from the Catholic cause, Governor Seward stood almost alone.

The events which followed Seward's address in 1840 and the simultaneous introduction of the Catholic petition for state funds can be recalled briefly. The Public School Society, demanding common schools, fought the Catholic petition. Hughes and a Methodist minister debated before the New York City Common Council over the Bible's relation to any useful system of schooling. Both argued that the Bible was necessary, but could not agree upon which Bible to use. Meanwhile, the lawyer who represented the Public School Society insisted that there should be a system of common schools to which all children could in good conscience go. One suspects that he, and the Society, would have done whatever the minister and the bishop could have agreed upon as a proper common schooling; but, of course, the two clergymen never approached an agreement. It was impossible for the two men to compromise over the issue of Bible reading. "We are sorry that the reading of the Bible in the public schools, without note or commentary, is offensive to them," the Methodist argued, "but we cannot allow the Holy Scriptures to be accompanied with *their* notes and commentaries, and to be put into the hands of children who may hereafter be the rulers and legislators of our beloved country; because, among other bad things taught in those commentaries, is to be found the lawfulness of murdering heretics, and the unqualified submission, in all matters of conscience, to the Roman Catholic Church."[9] The Catholic petition was denied.

Despite significant setbacks for his party in the elections that followed his first recommendation for locally controlled schools, something for which Seward's pro-Catholic stand was held responsible, Seward was courageous enough to call once again for a local solution to the problem of making the schools attractive and acceptable to Catholic parents. In response to Seward's message, the New York Catholics—calling themselves simply citizens of New York—again petitioned the state legislature for a portion of the school monies. The legislature assigned the problem to John C. Spencer, the Whig secretary of state. His subsequent report supported Governor Seward, arguing that compromise was impossible and separate schooling was necessary. The process of schooling itself was sufficient; not every child needed to experience an identical curriculum. Inculcating exactly the same values was neither possible nor necessary. Control over the moral values taught should be left in the hands of the people in the district so that the schools could most effectively attract children from that local community. Spencer recommended that the state's school code, which promoted a district system structure with local taxing authority, be extended to New York City; that the city be partitioned into several districts; and that the residents of each district decide for themselves the kind of religious instruction to be offered. Such a

[9] Bourne, *Public School Society*, 199–200.

system would solve the problems, Spencer concluded, because "each district suits itself, by having such religious instruction in its school as is congenial to the opinions of its inhabitants."[10] While Spencer claimed he could find no objections to this program in all the records of the state school system, the legislature tabled the report to await the outcome of another annual election.

In the New York City campaign of 1841 the school controversy was the central issue. On the eve of the election, Hughes spoke at a Catholic rally. He endorsed ten of the thirteen Democrats nominated for the thirteen state legislative seats from New York City. He urged all Catholics to support these ten and three other candidates who were running on a straight Catholic ticket unendorsed by either major party. The ten Democrats won, but the three not endorsed by Hughes lost to their Whig opponents. The Catholics, by diverting their support from these three Democrats to the three Catholic candidates, gave the Whigs their margin of victory. These results sent new waves of fear through the Protestant community. The Catholic immigrant vote appeared to represent the balance of power in New York City politics.

Statewide, the Democrats won the lower house, but the Whigs regained control of the upper house. New York City Congressman William Maclay, the son of a Baptist minister, designed—in conference with Bishop Hughes—a bill which embodied the recommendations of the Spencer report. The bill, which called for the extension of the district system, with its proviso for local control, to New York City, and for the suppression of the Public School Society in favor of the district system, passed easily through the state lower house as a partisan Democratic measure. The Whig senate, however, pruned out that section of the bill which guaranteed local control over religious instruction before it passed the measure. Enacted in 1842, this law extended to New York City a popularly elected board of education. This board was to receive state school monies, to have a taxing authority of its own, to build its own schools and to distribute the remainder of the state funds to existing schools which met certain requirements. Schools which indulged in sectarian religious instruction were not eligible to receive the funds. This last provision, of course, was directed at the Catholic schools already in existence as well as those planned by Bishop Hughes. In the context of 1842, reading the Protestant Bible in the schools supervised by the Public School Society was not considered sectarian, especially since the Whigs swept the city elections that year and made Bible reading—the King

[10] John C. Spencer, "Report of the Secretary of State upon Memorials from the City of New York, Respecting the Distribution of the Common School Moneys in That City, Referred to Him by the Senate," Document No. 86, *Documents of the Senate* (26 April, 1841), a full discussion of which appears in Vincent P. Lannie, *Public Money and Parochial Education* (Cleveland, 1968), 131–135.

James version—mandatory in any schools sharing these monies. There was nothing left for the Catholics to do but to build their own parochial system with their own money. This Hughes set out to do. This incident has governed the pattern of Catholic educational effort to the present day.

III

Our examination of the Catholic school controversy suggests the complexity of educational change. Several interested groups, the boundaries of which were rarely clear, sought to satisfy through the schools their private aspirations. The conclusion of this controversy reflected an important alignment of interests in the mid-nineteenth century. The common schools became increasingly a manifestation of the values of a segment of middle-class America. This was especially true as the schools became staffed with professionals recruited from this class. The mid-century effort was not simply an attempt, guided by the social elite, to stifle revolution in the lower classes. Much of the support came from segments of the middle class which were concerned, at this particular time, with their position in American society.[11]

In this context, "middle class" depends upon one's perceived social position as well as on economic status. Most professionals—many physicians, lawyers, clergymen, accountants, and military men—were middle class. The middle class, however, also contained the bulk of the merchants and businessmen, those whose wealth and background did not qualify them for membership in the community's social elite. This segment also included thousands of small shopkeepers and men in business for themselves, as well as the more successful artisans. Thus grocers, general store keepers, and independent carpenters and shoemakers were members of the middle class. The lower class was composed of laborers and the unemployed: men who unloaded ships or canal boats or wagons, horsemen, draymen, and seamen, the growing class of factory operatives, and the unskilled in general—men who dug canals and hauled the stones to build the piers.

One distinction should be clear. The difference between an operative in a shoe factory and a man who made shoes in his own small shop was vast. Although the independent shoemaker may have been no more

---

[11] The concept of status concern, or even anxiety, can serve as a reasonably accurate hypothesis with which to explore the social tension which determined the shape of educational change after 1830. It is a concept in need of refinement and clarification, however. We do not wish to appear overly secure in our suggestion of its character and influence. Toward this qualification we will spend some time outlining the structure and context of the mid-nineteenth-century relationships relevant to the concept of middle-class status anxiety.

skilled than the operative, though he usually was, and may have made no more money, though he usually did, he was considered to be of a higher class than the operative. Men with their own shops were independent and "free," and possibly able to hire other men to work for them. As long as they worked in the factories, the operatives were "unfree," and had little chance to become independent. Furthermore, remaining in a factory suggested to many an admission that an operative had not the skills to go it alone. As factories became more efficient and the division of labor more specific within them, the skills required of the factory operative became fewer and fewer. Factory managers took advantage of this fact by hiring workers of less skill because they were cheapest. Thus factory work became associated with poor pay and poor skills. This distinction was true for many trades, wherever the work of artisans was taken over by the more efficient factory system.

Our distinction between the middle and lower classes is one which is most applicable to the urbanized and industrialized regions. In rural America social stratification was less severe; most white people who lived in the country were broadly middle class. Every locale certainly had its squires who thought themselves a part of the elite and most communities had their share of ne'er-do-wells who worked, when inspired, as common farm laborers. In the country, however, men who owned land, farmed it dutifully, belonged to a stable church, and were sufficiently pious were considered members of the proud and independent middle class—the class of republican yeomen.

Urbanization and industrialization threatened the status positions of several segments of the middle class. The movement from the country to the city, an event central to the lives of many Americans of this generation, was cause for much apprehension. Problems arose when people left the stable, well-defined status system of their rural communities for the fluid and indefinite status system of the city. Within rural communities status was a product of one's ancestry, style of work, and mode of worship just as much as it was a product of financial and worldly success. Status was transmitted across generations within the confines of the local community without a great deal of change. The rural system was, relative to the fluidity that came to characterize American urban society, one of inherited status. Within the towns and cities—largely products of geographic mobility, of migration and immigration—inherited status was less important because people could not carry their ancestral and personal reputations with them from the small community to the larger one. In the urban context one had to achieve one's status, usually through some kind of visible accomplishment. Piety, industriousness, and the status of one's forebears were no longer adequate to guarantee respect from one's fellows, for such traits were never easily measured and were difficult to see. (Urban society did not think it was ceasing to value industriousness or piety, of course; but it increasingly assumed that such traits were measured only by one's worldly and monetary success.)

In the city the badges of status could be won and lost more quickly than in the country. Anyone, within a single generation, might be able to acquire monetary success and the status which accompanied it. No one acquired ancestry, breeding, and community roots and the reputation that went with them so quickly. Moving from the rural community to the city endangered inherited status because, however high one's inherited status, one had to compete against everyone else to acquire the badges of worldly accomplishment. Many of the offspring of rural middle-class families, rich in inherited status, moved to the city where they were unable to acquire a commensurate reputation. This sort of strain led much of the middle class to cling to the Protestant and moralistic values of their rural background as a means of emphasizing the status symbols which they controlled and of deemphasizing the urban symbols which they had some trouble acquiring. Even those who succeeded in acquiring the urban badges of status emphasized rural middle-class values in an effort to differentiate themselves from those who had gained acquired status but who lacked inherited status. Both groups, as acquired status became more important, clung to the marks of inherited status which they felt protected their position in the society.

Those whose position on the urban ladder of status was affected by changes in the industrial system felt similar pressures. Artisans, traditionally thought of as proud, independent, and relatively successful pillars of society, found themselves threatened by the specialization of the factory system. Where apprenticeship could no longer restrict entry into a trade, the status of that occupation fell. Small businessmen and entrepreneurs found their social position threatened by widening fluctuations in the patterns of economic boom and bust that characterized the nineteenth century. In this case these men were not concerned that they would fall into the lower class, but that their relative position within the middle class was disintegrating. The middle class was undergoing differentiation. Successful grocers, for example, became even more successful while modest grocery businesses remained modest. This situation created more economic and social distance among men of the same class.

A pattern emerged. Former rural farmers feared that their relative position would decline in the city; artisans were threatened by the increasing division of labor; reputable businessmen feared ruin from depressions; grocers of only moderate success lost ground to an ambitious competition—these groups shared several worries. They were men losing ground, losing status because a new criterion—worldly success— was used to assess their character and accomplishment. They clung to the criteria with which they, and many others, had traditionally been judged—the standards of middle-class acceptability which had been such a large part of the older world. They emphasized piety, moral reform, and symbols of gentility. They wanted the common schools to represent and to inculcate these values.

Some of Charles Bidwell's quantitative research on moral instruction in New York State during this period is very suggestive and can help us clarify how middle-class groups may have influenced educational developments.[12] Bidwell took reading the King James Bible and the use of Protestant texts as his measures of the moral inculcation level in a particular school system. He found their use highest in New York State under the following conditions: in counties which were characterized by a mixed (agriculture and manufacturing) or nonfarm economy; where occupational stratification in monetary terms was advanced; which included large towns; which included large numbers of immigrants; where there were many professionals (clergymen, doctors, and lawyers); where the population had grown at least 25 percent in the preceding decade; where the proportion of residents born outside the county was high; where social mobility was highest; and where the county was bound closely to the outside world (through canal, railroad, newspaper, or institution of higher education). The presence of Roman Catholics pushed the indices only slightly higher and was not a significant causal factor statewide although, as we have seen, it was important in the New York City situation. From these findings we can conclude that in those towns or counties where social complexity and fluidity were highest, the schools strove more ardently to promote the cultural values commonly associated with the middle class by using Protestant texts and the King James Bible. Less effort along these lines was evident in towns where stratification was high but mobility was low. Similarly, those towns with large in-migrations (partly from overseas, but largely from rural areas) displayed the same heavy emphasis on Protestant values; this was especially true when that in-migration was coupled with high stratification and mobility. It seems that fluidity within a complex social structure correlated most highly with the use of the schools to further Protestant cultural values.

[12] Charles Bidwell, "The Moral Significance of the Common School: A Sociological Study of Common Patterns of School Control and Moral Education in Massachusetts and New York, 1837–1840," *History of Education Quarterly*, VI (Fall, 1966), 50–91. Although we rely on Bidwell's statistical analysis and find many of his conclusions useful and convincing, a cautionary qualification should be entered here. His categories and definitions, we find, are overly broad and at times misleading. His equation of Unitarianism in Massachusetts with that state's social elite and of Congregationalism with the middle class, for example, should be held in some suspicion. Further research is needed to determine the composition of these denominations. The concept of "middle class" requires refinement, for it has never been a monolithic entity that imposed its values upon society whenever it felt threatened by "outsiders." It is misleading to think that the middle class, as a whole, is undergoing status anxiety; there is no evidence of this in those cases where it has been examined in the United States, and it is illogical because the middle class has grown in power, size, and wealth. Therefore, for the bulk of the middle class to feel status anxiety at any one time makes little sense.

In a community of high stratification and high rates of mobility—both upward and downward, one must remember—many individuals near the lower levels of the middle class had reason to be aware and concerned about their relative status. Former rural residents who had recently migrated to the larger towns as well as those artisans threatened by industrialization and the increasing division of labor felt themselves falling on the scales of wealth and power. Robert Rantoul reminded an audience in 1841 that, of every ten men who moved from the country to the city to make their fortunes, nine failed within a decade. Rantoul obviously exaggerated his illustration, and his statistic lacks the validity of those collected by Bidwell, but even if Rantoul is far off the mark—and there is little reason to believe he is—this observation suggests the presence of a substantial group who, moving from the secure status of the rural world, slipped in the eyes of their urban neighbors. It was these people— those who felt themselves falling within or out of the middle class in the new social environment—who provided the impetus to make the schools reflect the values of the middle class. Those who lacked the determining badges of middle-class status sought to identify even more vigorously with the values of that class. Those from the country who found themselves unable to compete successfully in accumulating the visible badges of status that were so important in the new context stressed those aspects of middle-class identity which they still possessed—gentility, piety, morality. They tried to get society—through its schools—to reemphasize the importance of character traits they did possess and to deemphasize the importance of wealth and power which they did not possess. They wanted the schools to confirm and refurbish these older rural badges of middle-class status. The power that people attributed to education as a means of preserving status in a world of rapid social and economic change is nicely illustrated by the experience of the Lowell mill girls.

IV

The Lowell mill girls symbolized the attempt by New England manufacturers to secure the advantages of industrialization without any of its disadvantages. In 1821 the leaders of the enormously profitable Boston Manufacturing Company at Waltham—the first manufactory in America, perhaps in the world, to turn baled cotton into cloth in a single factory—began creating a new industrial city in a rural area northwest of Boston at a site where the Merrimack River's thirty-foot drop promised ample water power for a large number of textile mills. When this planned community received its first visit from a president of the United States, in 1833, ten years after the opening of the first mill, the town boasted 19 mills with 84,000 spindles, 3,000 looms, and 5,000 operatives. Nearly

80 percent of these operatives were women and teenage girls—the famous mill girls, 2,500 of whom, gotten up by the managers in white muslin and carrying dainty parasols, paraded two abreast before President Jackson in 1833.[13] The Boston managers liked to show off the mill girls and did so whenever possible, for the girls and the system of paternalistic labor relations of which they were thought to be the product represented one of the most important arguments in favor of the managers' proposition that industrialization could occur without corrupting American natural virtue. The textile magnates of New England pointed to the mill girls to prove that the industrial community they had created was not only a financial but also a moral success.

The factory managers' emphasis on the mill girls was at once idealistic and practical. The early investors in manufacturing were not eager to scar the natural American landscape with ugly factories nor did they desire to transform American yeoman farmers into the kind of landless factory operatives who were so "dangerous" in the English manufacturing cities of Manchester and Birmingham. They thought they found a solution, suggested in part by Robert Owen's paternalistic experiment at New Lanark, in the system of hiring young women from the farms of New England who would come to work briefly in the mills in order to earn money to help their families or to start homes of their own. While living in the factory town, the girls would board in dormitories under the protection of what we would today call housemothers. The girls were to be exposed only to the most wholesome influences—schools, lyceums, and churches. One or two years after coming to Lowell, the theory went, the young women would return home to marry, having in no way suffered from their factory experience. Thus could one of the major drawbacks of English industrialism be avoided.

But the managers' expenditure of time and money on creating a wholesome atmosphere for the operatives was more than idealistic. Where English industrialists could count on an abundant and cheap labor force, American manufacturers found labor scarce. The labor problem was especially acute in Lowell which lay far from any population center large enough to supply 5,000 factory operatives. The availability of opportunity and land to the west and the largely unmechanized economy's

[13] On cotton manufacturing at Lowell, the boardinghouse or Waltham system of labor relations, and the mill girls themselves, see Caroline F. Ware, *Early New England Cotton Manufacture: A Study in Industrial Beginnings* (Boston, 1931), chapter 8, Hannah Josephson, *The Golden Threads: New England's Mill Girls and Magnates* (New York, 1949), Allan Macdonald, "Lowell: A Commercial Utopia," *New England Quarterly*, X (March, 1937), 37–62, Louis Taylor Merrill, "Mill Town on the Merrimack," *ibid.*, XIX (March, 1946), 19–31, Harriet Hanson Robinson, *Loom and Spindle: or Life among the Early Mill Girls with a Sketch of "The Lowell Offering" and Some of Its Contributors* (New York, 1898), Lucy Larcom, *A New England Girlhood: Outlined from Memory* (Boston, 1889), chapters 7–12, and, of course, the volumes of the *Lowell Offering* itself (Lowell, Mass., 1840–1845).

need for skilled workers made attempts to recruit men for jobs as un-skilled mill hands futile. (These conditions and thus the need for farm girls changed with the arrival of the Irish immigrants in the late 1840s.) The managers turned to women. But, in order to employ young unmar-ried women, the mills had to lure them away from the watchful eyes of their parents. Success depended upon persuading parents that Lowell provided a wholesome atmosphere and that factory work would not harm the girls' health or morals. The industrialists had, therefore, a good deal tied up in the success of the mill girl experiment. They constantly adver-tised the advantages which accompanied mill work, a strategy that sug-gests how eager they were to convince themselves that they had suc-ceeded in bringing industry without an industrial proletariat and, in an effort to feed the growing need for labor, to convince more and more New England rural families to part with their daughters for a short time.

If the managers had a good deal tied up in the success of their experi-ment in paternalism, the mill girls, we suggest, had a great deal more. They, after all, were assuming the real risks. In leaving home to work in Lowell, they risked their virtue among the vices and degradations of an industrial town; they jeopardized their standing in their home communi-ties; they, in short, risked a plunge into the proletariat by becoming factory operatives, for however short a time. They were not and could not be satisfied with the guarantee offered their parents and the general public by the mill owners. They had to prove to themselves that a few years spent as factory operatives would not harm them. One of the most important ways that they set out to prove this to themselves was through self-education.

These efforts at self-education culminated in the *Lowell Offering*, a magazine published at Lowell between 1840 and 1845. As each title page proudly announced, "female operatives" wrote and edited all the maga-zine's material. The *Offering* grew out of a classic Franklinesque self-education device, the self-improvement circle. Four or five girls who wished "to improve the few talents God had given them" formed "a society of young ladies for mutual improvement" in 1837.[14] Other groups followed. These circles were devoted almost exclusively to en-couraging literary activity among the girls. According to the usual format, the girls submitted anonymous pieces of poetry and prose which were read aloud and criticized during the meetings of the circle. In 1840 two clergymen suggested that it might be well to bring some of these pieces together into a little book. Published in October of 1840, the book was a success and the *Lowell Offering* was born. For the next two years the *Offering* appeared as an annual; then it became a monthly. It failed in 1845

---

[14] [Maria Currier], "Improvement Circle," *Lowell Offering*, V (January, 1845), 11; Robinson, *Loom and Spindle*, 99–101.

because of declining interest among the mill girls. Several short-lived periodicals written or edited by and for mill girls replaced the *Offering*, but these periodicals emphasized labor reform and spoke to the mill girl as an operative rather than as a middle-class woman.

The articles in the *Offering* and the pieces written for the improvement circles represented only the culmination or distillation of hundreds of single and group efforts at self-education. Lucy Larcom remembered that she and her companions carried poems and passages clipped from their favorite books into the mills and pasted them on the windows near their machines in order to study while working—she worked in a section of the mill where reading while working was not allowed and where overseers confiscated books. Finally she took a lower paying position in a department where she was allowed to read books on the job. This precocious teenager taught herself German so that she could attempt to translate Goethe and Schiller into English. She also joined informal classes in botany and ethics taught by ministers and other adults in the city. Lucy Larcom was more literarily inclined, no doubt, than her companions— she was one of the few we know of who followed anything like a literary career in later life. But her drive for self-education and self-improvement was not exceptional. Lucy Larcom's books were far from being the only ones confiscated; the overseers' desks were often stacked high with Bibles taken from girls who had thought that the Scriptures at least were immune.

The drive for culture that prevaded the mill girls' lives also spilled over into more formal kinds of education. The lyceum was especially popular at Lowell. Several lecturers commented on the girls' attentiveness and interest, and one lecturer remembered entering the hall to find all the girls reading books and that while he lectured they all assiduously took notes. Many of the girls spent six months in the mills and six months attending an academy; more taught school during the summer and worked in the mills during the winter. Many worked to save enough money to continue their formal education; the earnings of a great many sent their brothers to academies and colleges to prepare for the ministry.

The girls' drive for self-education can best be explained as a direct outgrowth of their feelings about being factory operatives. Education played a very special role for them as an antidote to their own perceptions of lost status. Harriet Farley was one of the two editors of the *Lowell Offering* from 1842 to 1845. The story of how she came to Lowell seems typical of the experiences of many girls. She recalled her background in an autobiographical sketch written in 1848: "My father is a Congregational minister, and at the time of my birth was settled in the beautiful town of Claremont, N. H. . . . My mother was descended from the Moodys, somewhat famous in New England history. One of them was the eccentric Father Moody. Another [his son] was Handkerchief Moody, who wore so many years 'the Minister's Veil.' . . . My father was one of the genuine New Hampshire stock, from a pious, industrious, agricultural people; his brothers being deacons, and some of his sisters married to deacons. . . . His mother was a woman of fine character, who exerted herself and sacrificed much to secure his liberal education." Note her emphasis on character rather than material success. However rich the family's background, it had very little material success. Back-country New Hampshire and Massachusetts ministers (Harriet's father moved from village to village in both states) were poorly paid and Harriet was one of ten children. Their life was very hard—so hard that it drove Harriet's mother insane. At fourteen, Harriet began earning money in various home industries and for a time she taught school. Because of her "instinctive dislike" of teaching, she balked at entering it as a lifetime commitment, and left home for the opportunities at Lowell. But she felt guilty about leaving home and attempted to "reconcile" her family to her actions "by a devotion of all my spare earnings to them and their interests. I made good wages; I dressed economically; I assisted in the liberal education of one brother, and endeavored to be the guardian angel to a lovely sister."[15]

Loss of a middle-class father and subsequent lack of means seem to have driven many girls to the mills. Pains were taken to emphasize gentility and old-stock background. Harriet Hanson's father was descended from the family that first settled Dover, New Hampshire, and was himself a fairly successful artisan carpenter. One of her mother's forebears had served on the General Court in the mid-seventeenth century; another was remembered because he sold land to Harvard College in 1705. Another was a noncommissioned captain at Bunker Hill and had participated in the Boston Tea Party. From this background Harriet Hanson suddenly found herself changing bobbins in a Lowell factory.

The plunge from gentility to factory girl was just as abrupt for other girls. Lucy Larcom remembered her first ten years of life in the country town of Beverly where her father, a retired sea captain who owned a country store, was a respected and important member of the community. When he died, he left a family of eight children with no support. The Turner sisters' family had lived in New England for seven generations. Their father had been justice of the peace in Lyme, New Hampshire, for twenty years and a member of the state legislature for two. Tragedy struck him in middle life when he first lost his health and then signed a substantial note for a friend, who quickly decamped. Paying the note bankrupted the Turners. With their incomes sharply reduced and the father either dead or unable to work, the Larcoms and the Turners moved to Lowell. The mothers ran boardinghouses and the children went to work at the mill as soon as they were able. Thus the families survived.

---

[15] Robinson, *Loom and Spindle*, 146–148; see also the contributions by Farley in the *Lowell Offering*, V (July and August, 1845), and her series in vol. II (1842).

The collected biographical sketches of the mill girls reveal a consistent pattern. Almost all of the girls had moved from small villages to the factory city. All came from fairly secure middle-class backgrounds in communities where ancestry and reputation within the community were more important than wealth in determining status. Their parents considered themselves as people of character—steady, property-holding yeomen—who therefore had substantial stature in their communities. The girls' fathers, although far from well-to-do, followed respectable and worthy callings—the ministry, storekeeping, carpentry. Their economic marginality did not seriously affect their status in the village community.

From this kind of status security the girls, and sometimes their families, plunged into the class of factory operatives. It was difficult for the girls to think of this translation as anything but a loss in status. They needed more than the managers' advertisements and promises to overcome their fears of vice, filth, degradation, and coarseness that Americans, recalling the British experience, associated with industrialism. These girls, like most American women of the period, were avid readers of Charles Dickens, and we can be sure that the mill girls did all they could to avoid becoming the kind of laborers that the British novelist depicted. The girls certainly felt the threat—the passages in the *Offering* which contend that manual work is a good thing for young ladies of gentility protested too much. Harriet Farley commended the magazine she edited to the general public and criticized the prejudice against the mill girls.

> All our readers are aware of the prejudice, which has long existed, against the manufacturing females of New England—a prejudice which, in this country, should never have been harbored against any division of the laboring population, and that many circumstances, and the exertions of many different classes of individuals, had contributed to strengthen this prejudice. We were not surprised that, when *The Offering* first appeared, so many were astonished; but we were surprised that so many should, for so long a time, withhold from it their confidence. In spite of these, however, *The Offering* has done much good. The involuntary blush does not so often tinge the faces of our operatives, when mingling with strangers, as when they claimed no place amid the worthy, and the educated.

She returned to the subject in what she thought was to be the last issue of the *Offering* in 1843.

> We wished to do one thing, and that was, to remove aught of stigma which attached to the mere name of factory girl; we wished that *that* alone should be no barrier to her reception into any society for which she was otherwise fitted, and no barrier to her hopes of attaining any other employment or situation. We wished to show the world, that labor which had been thought most degrading, was not inconsistent with mental and moral cultivation.[16]

[16] H. F. [arley], "Editorial: Address to Our Patrons," *Lowell Offering,* III (October, 1842), 24, and Farley, "Editorial: Close of Volume," *ibid.,* III (September, 1843), 284.

A typical volume of the magazine contained, besides numerous regretful pictures of the villages of a simpler era and efforts at romantic poetry, articles on physiology, astronomy, geology, and mineralogy, on New England history, and on temperance. Each issue included descriptions of Lowell and several religiophilosophic homilies on home affections, pleasure and pain, learning and ignorance, and the dignity of labor. The efforts at self-education and self-cultivation that these pieces represented embodied the girls' somewhat desperate rejection of the social abyss that factory labor connoted. The sometimes absurd lengths to which Lucy Larcom went in her German studies or the rather pedantic "research" articles on science that the girls published manifested their desperation. Their successful attempt to model the *Offering* after the scores of ladies' magazines then published in city and hamlet all over England and America represented the girls' refusal to accept the designation of laborer. They chose, rather, to emulate the emerging leisured, middle-class urban woman for whom these magazines were written.

The mill girls did not seek to emulate the idle rich, of course. They filled each waking hour away from the mills with improving activities. Many of the *Offering*'s articles reproached women whose inactivity caused their spiritual or physical downfall. The literary mill girls accepted what Barbara Welter has called the "cult of true womanhood"—the belief that the woman was the vessel of purity, love, piety, and gentility in a masculine world grown increasingly materialistic and crude. In order to maintain their place among such women, however, the girls took particular care to point out that manual work did not interfere with their fulfilling the "true" woman's role. In fact, hard work and sacrifice to help the family seemed to increase a woman's claim to "true womanhood." One story in the *Offering* described Ada who, although forced to leave school and go into the mills because of the death of her father and the illness of her mother, still "escaped the snares spread to allure her feet astray," and assumed the "true" woman's role in the home. She "highly prized her home; it was her delight; in it were those of whom, of all on earth, her heart loved best. She was the idol of that home; and often did her mother gaze in tenderness upon her fair and noble brow. Her sister almost worshipped her for her gentle sweetness, thinking her happiness complete whenever she could have the pleasure of her company. Earnestly did they pray that no false intruder might again enter their peaceful home, to mar its happiness."[17]

[17] On the women's magazines of the era, see Bertha M. Stearns, "New England Magazines for Ladies, 1830–1860," *New England Quarterly*, III (October, 1930), 627–656, Barbara Welter, "The Cult of True Womanhood: 1820–1860," *American Quarterly*, XVIII (Summer, 1966), 151–174, and Barbara Cross, *Horace Bushnell: Minister to a Changing America* (Chicago, 1958); Grace, "The Young Wife," *Lowell Offering*, III (December, 1842), 49; Annaline, "Ada, the Factory Maid," *ibid.*, III (February, 1843), 97–100.

The *Offering* refused to identify itself or the girls connected with it with the interests of the laboring class and refused to support the labor movement which was growing among some of the girls at the mills in the 1840s. Instead, the magazine tended to identify with the interests of the owners. At one point Harriet Farley noticed that some of the superintendents in the Lowell mills had reported that "in times of difficulty" they looked "for sympathy and assistance" to girls who were well educated. "Well educated girls are not more fond of insult and oppression than are the ignorant," she hastened to add, "but they are less under the dominion of passion, and more guided by reason. They would not easily be made the tools of aristocrats or demagogues. They would not be so influenced by prejudice, or so easily led by [those] designing to disgrace themselves by 'showing their spirit.' They would not surround the City Hall in a mob, but, if wronged, would seek redress in some less exceptionable manner." Educated operatives would not "disgrace themselves" as some of the girls at Lowell had done by "striking" in 1834 and 1836 and again in 1842.[18] They were more dependable and dutiful than that. Questions of wages and hours lay beyond the scope of the *Offering*, Miss Farley announced. The *Offering* was concerned with overseeing and defending the moral virtue of the girls, not with securing more material benefits for them. It was as if to say that the girls worked for the virtue and nobility that sacrifice and work gave them, instead of for money or for material gain. It is significant that, just when labor organization came to Lowell and groups of mill operatives began petitioning the legislature for a shorter workday, the mill girls and their ministerial advisers felt called upon to publish a periodical that stressed the girls' identification with middle-class, Victorian values.

In Miss Farley's editorials and in the various articles by the girls themselves, the historian senses both the girls' concern with what was happening to them and their concern with what others might be thinking of them. To help resolve the first problem, they turned to self-education to prove to themselves that manual labor was "not inconsistent with mental and moral cultivation." They published the results of their efforts at self-education to convince others that, despite their economic situation, they remained cultivated, genteel, and proud Americans. In 1842 Miss Farley spoke of her emotions at seeing the first issue of the *Offering* in print two years earlier. She admitted that she had heard all of the articles before in the self-improvement circle, "but they seemed so much better in print. They appeared, to us, as good as any body's writings.

---

[18] H. F.[arley], "Editorial: A Manual Labor School," *Lowell Offering*, III (June, 1843), 215. She is probably referring to the responses to Horace Mann's questionnaire reported in his *Fifth Annual Report*. Labor agitation is treated in Josephson, *Golden Threads*, 231–243. See also Farley, "Editorial: History of the Lowell Offering," *Lowell Offering*, III (November, 1842), 48.

They sounded as if written by people who had never worked at all."[19] This, of course, is the clue. This is what the literary mill girls thought "education was for." They wanted education to become an alternative to wealth and economic position as a means of defining one's status in a changing world. Moving to the city and going to work for wages had destroyed the girls' status security. In reaction, they stressed their relatively advanced education—and the strength of mind and character they claimed that education represented—as an indication that they should be considered as worthy in the new community as they and their families had been in the old.

We would suggest that large numbers of women teachers shared the mill girls' attitudes toward education. Although teaching school did not carry all the evil connotations that accompanied factory work in that period, working for wages, even in teaching, must have carried some stigma for a woman before 1900. Although this stigma might have been slight for those teaching only a year or two, it must have become very important for those who remained in teaching for more than a few years and who thereafter assumed decisive roles in schools. Having to work for a living caused a woman to lose status. Would not these teachers, in order to minimize this loss, have sought to dissociate the world of education from the world of work, to stress its association with culture, with gentility, and with learned accomplishment? And would not these women, like the mill girls, have half believed and half hoped that their identification with education and culture would provide them with an emblem of high cultural status that would counteract their loss of economic status? Would not this association have inclined them to emphasize, as did the mill girls, the more cultural, less practical aspects of education?

V

The establishment and character of high schools in the United States between 1820 and 1860 allows us to speculate further about the influence of the lower middle class. It makes a good deal of sense to view both the creation of a separate educational structure higher than the common grammar school and the elaborate cultural emphasis of its curriculum as devices to meet the needs of people experiencing status anxiety in an increasingly mobile and urban society.

Prior to the Civil War, the newly established public high school provided an extended educational experience for children whose parents did not feel it necessary, or right, to send their children to work before age sixteen or so. High schools were not, as some have argued, designed to

19 Farley, "Editorial: History of Lowell Offering," 48.

open the avenues of social mobility to the lower classes. They were not institutions devoted to furthering equality of opportunity. At a time when child labor laws were virtually unknown, the children of the poor and working classes had to begin work before they reached high school age. One student of high school development in Massachusetts, where most of the early high schools were established, estimated that on the average high schools catered to only about 20 percent of the eligible adolescents. In large towns where a disproportionately large laboring class could be found, this figure dropped to about 15 percent. In the largest cities only 8 percent of the high school students were from the families of industrial workers. The lower class, he emphasized, took almost no advantage of the high schools.[20]

The high schools were almost exclusively urban. Early institutions appeared in Boston in 1821, in Portland, Maine, in New York City, in New Bedford, Salem, and Haverhill, Massachusetts, and in Burlington, Vermont, in the 1820s; in Fitchburg, Lowell, Medford, Cambridge, and Taunton, Massachusetts, in Augusta, Brunswick, and Pittston, Maine, and in Harrisburg, Philadelphia, and Buffalo in the 1830s. Springfield, Massachusetts, New Orleans, Providence, Detroit, Cleveland, Cincinnati, Hartford, and Toledo followed in the 1840s. As Michael B. Katz has pointed out, high school development was more an urban than an industrial characteristic and was most intense in towns undergoing rapid economic and social and demographic change.

The high school was not usually created as a totally new institution; someone did not suggest that extra schooling was needed for certain people and then invent a four-grade high school to place atop the existing eight-grade elementary school. Rather, the high school was created largely through fission. The existing grammar school, much like the district school, tended to serve students from seven to seventeen. If anyone wanted to and could remain in school long enough, the master was prepared to offer special lessons in geometry or accounting, or even in Latin. In the larger areas between 1820 and 1860 citizen pressure forced the school system to formalize this advanced instruction by separating it into an independent unit, and by articulating formal requirements for admission and graduation.

Much of this pressure appears to have come from anxious middle-class people, fearful of their economic and social circumstances, seeking to use the high school as a badge of status which would partially substitute, they hoped, for a lack of firm social status that rested on wealth or inherited place in a stable social structure. The high school developed as a separate unit to facilitate its symbolic value as a badge of status. In

[20] Michael B. Katz, *The Irony of Early School Reform: Educational Innovation in Mid-Nineteenth Century Massachusetts* (Cambridge, Mass., 1968), Part I.

the existing system, the child who spent ten years in school was probably better educated than others who spent only five years there (though certainly not twice as well educated). But the distinction was subtle and not very visible. Placing the child's extended schooling in a separate higher school, however, greatly clarified the distinction. High schools quickly introduced such ceremonies and symbols as graduations and diplomas to further distinguish their patrons. To be able to say that your children were going or had gone to high school said so much more clearly and precisely that you were well enough off to allow them to stay off the labor market and that you valued education and culture and things of the mind than did any statement to the effect that your children had stayed in grammar school for a long time. Middle-class supporters greatly valued the high school's symbolic value in this regard.

The pressure to create a distinct high school appears to have followed the decline in status of the grammar school that occurred when it became open to more children. The Boston case is perhaps indicative. Through most of the colonial period, and until 1818, Boston had a system of public grammar schools which were theoretically open to all. In fact, however, a child could not enter one of these schools, at age six or seven, unless he could read. Yet Boston maintained no lower system of public schools that prepared children to read and write. This effectively restricted the use of the public grammar schools to those who could afford to give their children a few years of preparation in reading and writing at private tuition-charging schools. Boston's lower-class children were thereby effectively excluded from the public schools. In 1818 pressure from social and religious leaders who were certain that community order depended upon educating lower-class children, culminated in the establishment of a system of public primary or reading schools in Boston, thus opening the entire public school system (except the Latin School) to every class of resident. Increased access to the grammar schools was applauded by those anxious to expose urban children to the more conservative American values, but such a step posed a threat to the lower middle class for it removed one more badge of status. Before 1818 attending grammar school had been prestigeful because not everyone could do so; when the grammar school became open to all, the middling classes sought another more exclusive educational structure to distinguish them from the lower classes. Three years after the opening of the public primary schools, Boston English Classical School, or English High School, opened. Many acknowledged that much support for this venture came from the "middling interests"—from mechanics or artisans or small shopkeepers—those people most affected by changes in status brought on by rapid social change. Boston English and other urban public high schools provided children of the middling class with access, at the public's expense, to an education that would serve to distinguish them from those children whose parents could not afford to keep them off the labor market in early adolescence.

Part of the popularity of the idea of the public high school movement rested on the fact that it was seen as an alternative to the "exclusive" and "undemocratic" academies. Here too, we think, we can see the influence of the lower middle class' striving to use educational institutions to relieve status anxiety. They sought to use schools to differentiate their children from those lower on the social scale. But they were also concerned to keep their children from being denied educational opportunities that families higher than they were on the social scale could use to distinguish their children from those of the middling class. The middling classes thought, not without reason, that the social elites were using the academies to accomplish just that. Supporters of both the common school and the public high school constantly denounced private schools, especially academies, because they competed against the public schools for the patronage and support of the wealthiest members of the community. The reformers' rhetoric and purpose suited the middling classes perfectly. Nothing would bolster their sense of status and worth more than to have their children go to school with the children of the elite for that would help confirm their own desperately sought sense of identity with those above them. Thus they followed the reformers in proclaiming that American educational institutions would further democracy only when all children would attend the same schools, where all classes would learn a common sense of values and where all would share a common set of educational experiences. Thus, somewhat paradoxically, we find the middling classes employing the rhetoric of inclusiveness so that their children would be included in the higher levels of education which they supported in order to differentiate themselves from those below them in the social structure.

The transformation of the high school curriculum between 1820 and 1860 was also indicative of the influence of the lower middle class in the formation of the public high school. Although Boston English, founded in 1821 and recognized as the first actual public high school in the United States, purposefully excluded the study of Latin and Greek from its curriculum to prepare its students better for "life," as they—even then—called it, such an exclusion was not typical of most public high schools, especially those begun after 1840. The Boston school had initially been called the English Classical School—surely an attempt by those pressing for its creation to identify it with cultural, rather than useful, education. Latin became an increasingly popular addition to high school curricula and was soon of singular importance to those designing appropriate courses of study. We suggest that the lower middle class, an important constituent in the creation of the high school, wanted more than a practical education for, after all, they hoped to use the high school to confer status upon their children. In a culture which was still thought to be dominated by the learned languages, a Latin education was awarded a higher status than was an English education. The high school curriculum became another device through which the lower middle class hoped to relieve its status apprehension.

We would like to avoid the implication that the lower middle class alone created the public high schools. Many members of the upper classes fought for the existence of such institutions. Their purposes, however, seem to have differed. The upper classes most often saw, or thought they saw, the connection between the upward extension of a practical English education and economic growth. They also conceived of the high school as a means of recruiting talent from below for assistance in managing the burgeoning economic machine of mid-nineteenth-century America. They also worried about social unity and apparently felt somewhat guilty about their patronage of such exclusive institutions as the academies. The elite saw the public high school not as a help to the lower middle class but, rather, as a means of restoring that sense of social harmony and community which their own economic and social endeavors had done so much to destroy irreparably. The public high school, like the common school, would knit together the society by providing all children with a common educational experience and a common set of values. They rarely considered that the most alienated and impoverished classes could no more afford to attend the public high school than they could afford a boarding academy.

Common school reform and the effort to create a system of public high schools would not have succeeded without the electoral and participatory support of the lower middle class. Worried and anxious about its relative social and economic status, the lower middle class sent its children to school enthusiastically and voted for the extension of public educational services. Without this support the Whig reforms would have failed completely; but the lower middle class regularly and significantly perverted the intentions of the Whig leaders. The lower-middle-class demand that education remain in some way exclusive, that it differentiate and distinguish certain students, hampered the drive to extend education to all. The Whig leaders' desire to make schooling attractive to the working class was blocked by lower-middle-class demands that certain values and certain subjects which were important to their sense of well-being and status be taught in the public schools. The lower middle class demanded, in effect, that in return for its support the schools reflect and broadcast values upon which the members of that class thought their importance and their moral superiority to rest.

The antebellum effort for extended educational facilities was beset quite early by a tension over purpose. This resulted in the inability of the schools to inspire social unity and order in America. The attempt by the upper classes to impose education upon the lower classes, when combined with the narrow definition of values and desire to differentiate certain children sought by the lower middle class, made the schools unattractive to the urban poor. The moral exclusivity and curricular irrelevance which resulted from this early confusion of purpose has remained a significant part of the American educational enterprise.

VI

By 1880 the American educational structure was characterized by what appeared to be a rather formal, if still incipient, bureaucracy. While the bureaucracy was not yet tangible or housed at 110 Livingston Street, the procedural and structural drift was evident during the third quarter of the nineteenth century. Throughout most of the United States, the systems evolving during this period were not the bewildering and oppressive organizations many became after 1890. The mid-century drift was a collection of logical responses, given the purposes and functions agreed to by the variety of schooling advocates, to the situation in which education found itself. In many instances there was only a sense, rather than the actual machinery, of bureaucracy. As an organizational form, the bureaucratic revolution had just begun.

But begun it had. By the 1850s superintendents and inspectors were common, especially in the nation's larger cities, and teacher independence was proportionately weakened. Formal curricula obliged teachers and children to work by the book. Our earlier discussion of the Oswego movement, guided by Edward A. Sheldon, illustrates the problem, perhaps peculiar to education, of transmitting to thousands the common school commitment to the ideal of spontaneous teaching which appealed to student imagination and interest. The ideal became narrowed through institutionalization and codification as reformers, superintendents, and teacher trainers called for recipes to give to teachers that would insure educational success.

This new form of institutional organization became an alternative to the casual idiosyncratic procedure common, in the early nineteenth century, to organized groups in the United States. The concept of bureaucratization, its formalized procedure and hierarchical structure, became woven into the language and was adopted by many to deal with the problems of numbers, disorder and confusion, individual preference and whim, and even justice. It is difficult to separate the rhetoric of bureaucracy from the reality of the procedures adopted. Caution should be exercised when discussing the structure of nineteenth–century bureaucratic reform for much of the change was simply talk, and we should understand that the assurance with which advocates treated their procedures was much less than it eventually became. They were trying to evolve a set of mechanisms to accomplish things their organizations had never been called upon to accomplish. Some accepted more easily than others the new forms available to them. A full half century passed before enough were so convinced of the superiority of bureaucracy that it became the dominant organizational alternative. In this section we would like to examine briefly several of the elements of this mid-nineteenth-century drift toward bureaucratization.

The effort toward providing public education for the nation's children, the common school movement, stressed the universal redemptive social purpose of education. Schooling became part of a national campaign, even though most of the reform programs were organized on the state level. States which thought of themselves as participants in the common school movement shared goals and ideals; their inspiration was a common one. Because the effort was shared, a campaign was undertaken to develop, as David Tyack has shown, the "one best system." Of course, one system was never found that satisfied every interest or locale, but a number of organizational procedures and mechanisms were soon shared by many districts. As the educational enterprise was infused with the reform enthusiasm of the common school movement, procedures and methodologies to accomplish common goals were shared by a number of districts, particularly by the larger urban systems facing similar problems. A shared purpose, then, contributed to the adoption of many bureaucratic forms by the developing city school systems.

Families moved often and many bureaucratic reforms were designed and implemented to cope with this inconvenient fact of urban life. The quantitative work of Stephan Thernstrom and Peter R. Knights suggests the pattern of geographical mobility common to the mid-nineteenth-century city.[21] Children could not often remain in one school long enough to complete the entire program. To facilitate transferring, curricula and grading were often standardized, something for which parents and their children were certainly grateful. Relocation became easier for both students and teachers. Children could expect to participate in certain activities no matter where they moved within the city and teachers could be assured that students enrolled in a certain grade would be somewhat similarly prepared. While the expectations that accompanied formal grading often overlooked and even denied individual differences, it was introduced to reflect the progress children were expected to make and to insure that such progress was orderly and convenient for all concerned. Opposition to this sort of grading does not appear to have been great for it made the schooling experience easier. The notion of

[21] See Stephan Thernstrom, *Poverty and Progress: Social Mobility in a Nineteenth Century City* (Cambridge, Mass., 1964), and Peter R. Knights, *The Plain People of Boston, 1830–1860: A Study in City Growth* (New York, 1971).

"progressing" through school was a welcome one, especially to students and their parents. Repetition of coursework was reduced and students' vanity, as well as their employment opportunities, was enhanced when they could point to the number of grades they had completed. Progress through the grades, reflected in the twentieth century in certification requirements for certain jobs, became a goal in itself, something that might have given students an incentive to finish a term or a program.

A third element in the drift toward bureaucratization was the desire to increase justice in the schools. Without standardized procedure, individual teachers could reward and punish their students unrestrained. Standardization made the classroom situation more comfortable; students and teachers had some security in their recourse to the rules. Impartial regulations—behavioral as well as academic—while depersonalizing the classroom experience, were designed to protect children and teachers from the private whims of their superiors, as Carl Kaestle and David Tyack have suggested. These regulations have made many teachers and students unhappy, but for others the guarantees and protection offered by established codes and procedures have made the costs acceptable. It cannot be denied that classroom regulations and standardized procedures have frustrated many in their attempts to secure their rights. We would like to suggest, however, that such a result is not inherent in the implementation of rules and uniform regulations. Under different circumstances, with a different collection of administrators and supervisors, these regulations offered many protection from arbitrary rewards and punishments. These mechanisms are tools used by organizations to accomplish certain goals and are intrinsically neutral. The decisions which have frustrated and made miserable the lives of many teachers and students were made by individuals attempting to accomplish their private ends. Carl Kaestle has reminded us that the cultural intolerance which lay behind the abuses of bureaucratic procedure should be held responsible for many of the apparent biases of organized school systems; organization itself and alone is not guilty. Class and racial bias may have been associated historically with organized educational bureaucracies, but the distinction between bureaucratization and bias is an important one and should be made. Devotion to certain regulations has never been a constant shared among all groups at all times. Many of the overtly biased regulations were often resisted within the school systems and were, therefore, not institutionalized. The historically accurate relationship between larger social imperatives, such as racism and class and ethnic bias, and specific bureaucratic procedures, such as hiring and promotional patterns and disciplinary practices, has not yet been clarified.

Between 1840 and 1880 the enthusiasm and vigor that had marked the early years of common school reform, particularly in the nation's cities, began to wane. The schools began to experience the inflexibility associated with bureaucratization and codification. In the effort to bring order to the urban schools, procedure and system were purchased at the expense of flexibility and attention to the idiosyncratic character of children and neighborhoods. The rigidity and inflexibility which was bred sacrificed the spirit of reform to the letter. The success of the bureaucratic reforms became an "affliction," and in David Tyack's perceptive conclusion, "orderly grooves became ruts."[22] Yet this search for system was not entirely ignoble and crippling. Many bureaucratic reforms were initiated to remove public education from political interference. The desire to be fair to all children, to restrain the whims of individual teachers, was an important element in the establishment of impartial rules and regulations. Established procedure and impartiality can promote individual freedom as well as they can degenerate into a stifling burden on reform and innovation. In the public schools they have done both.

Those who attribute the failure of the common school, and, implicitly, its twentieth-century counterpart, to the organizational structure of education are wrong. Larger imperatives, social prejudices, and group aspirations are responsible. It is clear that certain organizational alternatives, including bureaucracy, have been selected because of these prejudices and aspirations to accomplish individual or group ambitions, but it is misleading and perhaps dangerous to concentrate responsibility upon the internal structure of the schools when the larger social atmosphere is so much more important. That schools serve social interests and respond actively to various pressures and that their failures are not predominantly the fault of their organization is evident in the rise of special education following the Civil War. It is to the beginning of special education that we now turn.

GUIDE TO FURTHER READING

This chapter's examination of the emotional, affective benefits people derive from seeing the institutions they support generalized is similar to and has drawn upon the examples suggested by JOSEPH GUSFIELD and DAVID TYACK; see GUSFIELD'S *Symbolic Crusade: Status, Politics, and the American Temperance Movement* (Urbana, Ill., 1963), and TYACK's forthcoming interpretation of compulsory schooling legislation.

The most comprehensive analysis of the Catholic school controversy is VINCENT P. LANNIE, *Public Money and Parochial Education* (Cleveland, 1968), which should be supplemented with CARL F. KAESTLE, *The Evolution of an Urban School System: New York City, 1750–1850* (Cambridge, Mass., 1973), JOHN W. PRATT, *Religion, Politics, and Diversity: The Church-State Theme in New York History* (Ithaca,

---

[22] David Tyack, "Bureaucracy and the Common School: The Example of Portland, Oregon, 1850–1913," *American Quarterly*, XIX (Fall, 1967), 479.

N. Y., 1967), and DIANE RAVITCH, *The Great School Wars: New York City, 1805–1973* (New York, 1974). WILLIAM O. BOURNE, *History of the Public School Society of the City of New York* (New York, 1870), WILLIAM W. CUTLER, "Status, Values and the Education of the Poor: The Trustees of the New York Public School Society, 1805–1853," *American Quarterly*, XXIV (March, 1972), 69–85, and KAESTLE, *The Evolution of an Urban School System*, detail the work and personnel of the Public School Society. CHARLES BIDWELL, "The Moral Significance of the Common School: A Sociological Study of Common Patterns of School Control and Moral Education in Massachusetts and New York, 1837–1840," *History of Education Quarterly*, VI (Fall, 1966), 50–91, raises the importance of class identification and perception. The forthcoming work by TIMOTHY WALCH on parochial and public education in mid-nineteenth-century Chicago and Milwaukee suggests that excellent reasons existed for extensive cooperation between Catholics and Protestants in cities seeking to attract settlers. OSCAR HANDLIN, *Boston's Immigrants*, rev. ed., (New York, 1968), PHILIP TAYLOR, *The Distant Magnet* (New York, 1971), ROBERT ERNST, *Immigrant Life in New York City, 1825–1863* (New York, 1949), ANDREW M. GREELEY, *That Most Distressful Nation: The Taming of the American Irish* (Chicago, 1972), NEIL G. McCLUSKEY, *Public Schools and Moral Education* (New York, 1958), McCLUSKEY, ed., *Catholic Education in America: A Documentary History* (New York, 1964), and RAY ALLEN BILLINGTON, *The Protestant Crusade, 1800–1860: A Study of the Origins of American Nativism* (New York, 1938), provide relevant comparative information on the experience of the Irish with public education in the United States, and CARROLL SMITH ROSENBERG'S fine study of *Religion and the Rise of the City: The New York City Mission Movement, 1812–1870* (Ithaca, N. Y., 1971) analyzes Protestant social welfare strategies in mid-nineteenth-century New York City. In "Ladies Bountiful: Organized Women's Benevolence in Early 19th-Century America," *New York History*, XLVIII (July, 1967), 231–253, KEITH MELDER examines private charity and the urban immigrant.

The establishment of the Lowell mills and the experience of the young women who labored in them are treated extensively in HANNAH JOSEPHSON, *The Golden Threads: New England's Mill Girls and Magnates* (New York, 1949), HARRIET HANSON ROBINSON, *Loom and Spindle: or Life among the Early Mill Girls with a Sketch of "The Lowell Offering" and Some of Its Contributors* (New York, 1898), MARVIN MEYERS, *The Jacksonian Persuasion: Politics and Belief* (Stanford, Calif., 1957), and MARVIN FISHER, *Workshops in the Wilderness: The European Response to American Industrialization* (New York, 1967). GERDA LERNER, "The Lady and the Mill Girl: Changes in the Status of Women in the Age of Jackson," *Mid-Continent American Studies Journal*, X (September, 1969), 5–15, and BARBARA WELTER, "The Cult of True Womanhood: 1820–1860," *American Quarterly*, XVIII (Summer, 1966), 151–174, suggest the values important to middle-class women before the Civil War.

MICHAEL B. KATZ's excellent analysis of the nineteenth-century New England high school in *The Irony of Early School Reform: Educational Innovation in Mid-Nineteenth Century Massachusetts* (Cambridge, Mass., 1968) proved very useful to our discussion of urbanism and educational change. KATZ and THEODORE SIZER, ed., *The Age of the Academies* (New York, 1964), outline the early arguments over the function of the academy in the United States. A number of traditional studies of the high school proved useful. ALEXANDER J. INGLIS, *The Rise of the High School in Massachusetts* (New York, 1911), EMIT D. GRIZZELL, *The Origin and Development of the High School in New England Before 1865* (New York, 1923), ELMER E. BROWN, *The Making of Our Middle Schools: An Account of the Development of Secondary Education in the United States* (New York, 1903), CALVIN O. DAVIS, *Public Secondary Education* (Chicago, 1917), and ISAAC L. KANDEL, *History of Secondary Education: A Study in the Development of Liberal Education* (Boston, 1930), are worthwhile introductions.

The bureaucratization of the American public schools is attracting an ever increasing amount of historical research. MICHAEL B. KATZ's imaginative hypothetical speculations and detailed local investigations have contributed much to our understanding of inflexibility and codification. His work is the most critical of the process and the personalities. In his essay, "From Voluntarism to Bureaucracy in American Education," *Sociology of Education,* XLIV (Summer, 1971), 297–332, KATZ outlines the alternative forms of organization available to system designers in the mid-nineteenth century, and "The Emergence of Bureaucracy in Urban Education: The Boston Case, 1850–1884," *History of Education Quarterly,* VIII (Summer and Fall, 1968), 155–168, 319–357, details the process in one city. This work should be supplemented with KATZ's *Irony of Early School Reform* (Cambridge, Mass., 1968) and STANLEY K. SCHULTZ, *The Culture Factory: Boston Public Schools, 1789–1860* (New York, 1973). CARL F. KAESTLE, DAVID B. TYACK, and SELWYN K. TROEN have offered a somewhat different interpretation of bureaucratization in KAESTLE, *The Evolution of an Urban School System: New York City, 1750–1850* (Cambridge, Mass., 1973), TYACK, "Bureaucracy and the Common School: The Example of Portland, Oregon, 1850–1913," *American Quarterly,* XIX (Fall, 1967), 474–498, and *The One Best System* (Cambridge, Mass., 1974), and TROEN, *The Public and the Schools: Shaping the St. Louis System, 1838–1920* (Columbia, Mo., 1975).

CHAPTER 7

Training the Hand: The Rise of Special Education

I

By 1880 THE PUBLIC SCHOOLS WERE STRONG AND HAD ATTRACTED WIDE-spread loyalty. Enrollment and attendance statistics rose with each decade. From the perspective of the earlier reform enthusiasts, however, the schools suffered in several critical ways. Reform ideals of commonality, spontaneity, and individual attention had clearly been sacrificed, or at least unwittingly discarded. Many theorists late in the nineteenth century unabashedly advocated replacing common education with special education, as we will call it, as the central purpose of the schools. By "special education" we mean schooling designed for specific groups of children in recognition that the roles they would play in American society would probably be different than those available to other children.

This process began as early as the 1840s when several privileged groups took advantage of the compromises made by elite mid-century reformers, in attracting the support of the middle class, to turn the schools to their private, yet often humanitarian, goals. The effort to define and implement the ideal of common schooling was troublesome, as we suggested in chapters 5 and 6, and was gradually abandoned as the needs of various groups were thought to be dissimilar. Abandonment was not always easy; most of the significant debates and political feuds within the ranks of professional educationists revolved around the concepts of "common" and "differentiated" schooling. Far away from the realm of debate, however, groups with political power, or which were recognized as legitimate stewards of the nation's social standards, organized special programs with a vengeance. By 1920 such programs existed to "serve the needs" of most groups of children. Citizens other than those for whom the programs were designed often defined these needs and how they were to be met, but one must recognize that for more than half a century organized opposition to differentiated schooling was slight and the informal dissatisfaction reflected in nonattendance statistics lessened with each decade. Parents and children, even those of the working class, felt they were getting something from their educational experience. In this chapter we will examine the earliest explicit efforts at designing and organizing special programs for specific groups of children and their families. After this discussion of programs directed toward the lower class, we will treat, in Chapter 8, the simultaneous effort to offer the children of the elite an education tailored to the roles they would play in late-nineteenth-century American society.

Between 1865 and 1900 the training of the hand became an increasingly popular responsibility for the school to assume in the United States. *Hand training* comprehends manual training, dexterity training as done in the kindergarten and primary grades, industrial education, and vocational training. *Manual training* was training in the use of tools and materials without any vocational goal. *Vocational training* was training in the specific tools and materials used in a specific trade or industry—tool and die making, cloth printing, carriage making, or blueprint reading. *Industrial education* was the most complicated for it included educational programs which taught children work habits and discipline by having them work, usually at profit-making enterprises; and educational programs that trained students in the use of tools and materials to prepare students for general categories of work—farming, woodworking, construction, and such. Industrial education was also sometimes used synonymously with vocational training and at other times as a generic term for both vocational and manual training. Meanings overlapped and the people of the late nineteenth century sometimes used the words interchangeably, especially industrial and vocational.

In this chapter we will seek to account for this upsurge in interest in hand training after 1850, striving to advance beyond the simple assertion that the increased interest in hand training resulted from increasing industrialization and weakening apprenticeship systems in the United States. These explanations are certainly true so far as they go but are not entirely satisfactory because, with the exception of vocational training, most hand training in the nineteenth-century United States did not prepare young people to fill skilled vocational roles. The primary motive for the extensive introduction of hand training was the belief that it would improve the schools' efficacy in moral training. The discussion which follows will also seek to give the student a basis on which to judge how much of the late-nineteenth-century enthusiasm for hand training in the school curriculum represented a continuation of the principles and goals of the common school movement and how much it represented a deviation from those principles and goals.

II

Industrial training first appeared in the United States during the 1820s in the reform schools established in the nation's three largest cities. The founding of the New York House of Refuge in 1825, Boston's House of Reformation in 1826, and the Philadelphia House of Refuge in 1828 marked a major turning point in the care of juvenile offenders in this country. Although additional reform schools did not appear until the 1840s, they and most others founded in the nineteenth century followed the pattern established in New York, Boston, and Philadelphia. Before the 1820s all those convicted of a crime, whatever their age or the gravity of their offense, were incarcerated together in a single jail. Such wholesale mixing of children with adults and first offenders with hardened criminals served, according to those interested in reducing urban juvenile delinquency, only to increase the crime rate—those who entered these mixed jails relatively innocent came out considerably toughened and more hostile to social order. Creating a special separate institution for young offenders would solve the problem, at least somewhat, by segregating the "new" criminal from the corrupting influence of the adult criminal. Another advantage of the reform school was that it offered judges sentencing youths a welcome alternative. Frequently, judges simply warned less serious juvenile offenders because they found it so difficult to justify committing these youths to the foul and degraded mixed jails of the time. Such lenient treatment, those concerned with urban social order charged, only convinced youthful offenders that they could get away with more serious crimes and therefore corrupted them almost as rapidly as placing them with adult criminals would have done. Reform schools offered the judge a chance to institutionalize a juvenile delinquent without feeling that the institution and its other inmates would inevitably corrupt him further, and yet children so sentenced would have no sense of having "gotten away" with their crime.

The greatest advantage, however, was that, by restricting their population to the young and least corrupted (reform schools usually transferred incorrigibles and repeaters to jails rather than permit them to corrupt the other, more innocent youngsters), the reform schools created an environment in which young offenders could be taught to be moral and responsible and thus rehabilitated. It is worth noting that only after 1840 did reformatories label themselves as schools, although earlier ones had sought to perform educational functions all along. Only when the common school movement had established moral training as a prime function of formal schooling was the work done by the reformatories considered schooling. To effect moral rehabilitation the refuges and reform schools instituted programs whereby inmates divided their time between working in the school's workshops or on its farm and studying the three Rs at an elementary level. Its founders designed the New York House of Refuge as a place where "boys under a certain age, who become subject to the notice of our Police, either as vagrants, or houseless, or charged with petty crimes, may be received, judiciously classed according to their degrees of depravity or innocence, put to work at such employments as will tend to encourage industry and ingenuity, taught reading, writing, and arithmetic, and most carefully instructed in the nature of their moral and religious obligations, while at the same time, they are subjected to a course of treatment, that will afford a prompt and energetic corrective of their vicious propensities, and hold out every possible inducement to reformation and good conduct."[1] In the normal day in this institution boys and girls, after rising, took one hour of common school instruction, then breakfasted, then performed seven or eight hours of industrial work, had supper, and studied for an hour or two before being locked up in their dormitories for the night.

The industrial training part of the early reform school "curriculum" can hardly be called training at all, since the boys and girls were not taught either skills or a trade. In some cases the reformatories contracted the children's labor out to outside entrepreneurs who set the children, in the reform school workshops, to routine and repetitive tasks like those done by unskilled factory labor—nailmaking, cheap shoemaking, sewing and simple garment making, and the weaving of cane chair seats and straw hats and baskets. Inmates spent some of their industrial training time—sometimes all of it—performing routine tasks for the institution itself: boys constructed new buildings and grew green goods for the institution's kitchen; girls washed, mended, and sometimes sewed the clothes and bedding needed by the inmates. Sometimes the children manufactured goods for the school which the school then sold. The money received either from contracting out the labor of the children or from selling the products of their labor helped defray the costs of maintaining the refuge. Only rarely did the children themselves receive any "pay" for their labor. Reform schools did not emphasize the connection

[1] New York Society for the Reformation of Juvenile Delinquents, *Memorial to the Legislature of New York . . . on the Subject of Erecting a House of Refuge* (New York, 1824), 22–23, quoted in Robert Bremner et al., ed., *Children and Youth in America: A Documentary History* (Cambridge, Mass., 1970), I, 679.

between work and wages. When the children reached a sufficient age, usually between twelve and fourteen, the reform school bound them out to families as apprentices or domestics. Once bound out, they were supposed to learn a trade. Their industrial training in the reform school had been of a more general nature, designed simply to teach them industriousness, good work habits, and good work discipline. Because these goals were so simple and general, it made little difference what tasks the reform school set for the children so long as they forced them to work hard and carefully. The schools chose simple tasks for which they did not need to train the children very much in order that they could receive the greatest and most immediate profit from their labor. Financial profit for the institution took precedence over the improvement in the quality of training for the child.

In this priority the reform schools were simply following the traditional practices of penal and charitable institutions. Prisoners had always been expected to work to help defray the cost of their incarceration. At least since the Elizabethan Poor Law of 1601 those who requested public relief were gathered into poorhouses, almshouses, or workhouses (the names were nearly synonymous) where they were put to work to earn as much of their keep as possible, or bound out to a master or family as a worker, or their labor "sold" to the man or family who agreed to keep them at the lowest price to the government. When one declared oneself a pauper or was convicted of a crime, one gave his labor to the state for it to use as it saw fit. Those institutionalized at others' expense for whatever reason had always worked in America to help reimburse those who maintained the institution. The reform school was no different but, from the very beginning, it did differ in that the work inmates performed was to have both a profit-making and a training effect. In the early years the former was more important, especially among the men who actually ran the institutions as opposed to the reformers who enthused about the moral influence of work; but, as the century progressed, penologists and juvenile workers as well as educational reformers identified the reform school workshop or farm as the key agent in the moral reform of the inmates.

Somewhat tentatively in the 1830s and 1840s, and then quite generally in the 1850s, the belief grew that not only would industrial training and the teaching of workshop habits reform those already begun on a life of crime but they would also prevent many neglected and vagrant children from beginning a life of crime. Charles Loring Brace (1826–1890) advocated most eloquently the establishment of preventive industrial training for vagrant children who had yet to violate the law. Brace's concerns focused on the neglected or vagabond boy and girl—children of vicious parents, or orphans, or children of immigrant parents who had neither the money nor the will to care for their own children. These often homeless and unsupervised boys and girls wandered about the city streets, without adult authority or support and totally dependent on their wits to keep body and soul together. What little work was available to them was unlikely to promote good habits. Brace did not consider hawking newspapers or matches on street corners or shining shoes particularly elevating; the thievery, pimping, prostitution, and begging that commonly occupied the street children of the vice districts were even worse. Growing up under these conditions would fit these children only to join their parents as members of *The Dangerous Classes of New York,* as Brace entitled an 1872 volume recounting his experiences with and views of the urban poor. "It should be remembered," he warned in 1864, "that there are no dangers to the value of property or to the permanency of our institutions, so great as those from the existence of such a class of vagabond, ignorant, ungoverned children. . . . They will vote. They will have the same rights as we ourselves, though they have grown up ignorant of moral principle, as any savage or Indian. They will poison society. They will perhaps be embittered at the wealth, and the luxuries, they never share. Then let society beware, when the outcast, vicious, reckless multitude of New York boys, swarming now in every foul alley and low street, come to know their power and *use it!*"[2]

After serving some years as an urban missionary in New York City's most infamous vice district, in 1853 Brace organized the New York Children's Aid Society, dedicated to saving the children of New York's "dangerous classes." The Society established lodging houses for newsboys and other street children, reading rooms for them, and a series of Sunday meetings where boys were "preached to." Horatio Alger's stories of street waifs who achieve middle-class status through "pluck and luck" celebrated the influence of the Society's Newsboys' Lodging House, where homeless boys could purchase a clean bed and a nourishing meal for a penny or two and receive lectures on thrift (the Society established a savings bank especially for the newsboys), morality, and hard work from the superintendent for free. The Children's Aid Society also proposed to establish a series of "industrial schools" in the city's various slum districts where "the great temptations to the class arising from want of work may be removed, and where they can learn an honest trade."[3] Brace contemplated a program similar to the reform schools': businessmen in the city provided work which the boys could do in the schools, and at age fourteen the school indentured the boys as apprentices. The work provided at the school would promote habits of work and industry; children would learn a trade during their apprenticeship.

[2] Charles Loring Brace, in *Eleventh Annual Report,* New York Children's Aid Society (New York, 1864), 4, quoted in Bremner et al., ed., *ibid.,* 757.
[3] Charles Loring Brace, *The Dangerous Classes of New York* (1872; New York, 1880), 92.

Brace's next initiative in rescuing the neglected boy from the streets of New York revealed his motives for encouraging industrial education. In 1855 the New York Children's Aid Society began sending boys west to live with farm families so that what Brace called their "moral disinfection" would be completed. Its isolation and the variety of chores it provided for children of all ages made the farm an ideal agent of decontamination. The continuous, difficult, yet varied work of the farm taught the child to be industrious and independent in a way that no institution or urban industrial school could. Brace and others argued that institutional life impeded the child's achievement of the sense of self-sufficiency, the trait most necessary to prevent him from becoming a pauper like his parents. "As a poor boy, who must live in a small house, he ought to learn to draw his own water, to split his wood, kindle his fires, and light his candle; as an 'institutional child,' he is lighted, warmed, and watered by machinery."[4] Inculcation of industriousness, whether on a farm or in an industrial school, could break the cycle of dependency.

Brace was not the first or the only reformer in the mid-nineteenth-century United States to suggest the provision of preventive industrial training for neglected and vagrant children in schools or on farms. In 1833 private citizens established a farm school or manual labor school on Thompson's Island in Boston harbor for children between the ages of seven and fourteen "who are growing up in idleness and hastening to crime" because they were the neglected children of widows, or of broken immigrant families, or of "intemperate or profligate" or "ignorant, inefficient and helpless" parents unable to care for them. These children were neither so good that respectable orphanages would accept them nor so bad that the court would sentence them to reform school. They remained on city streets, "exposed to the contagion of vice, and growing up in idle and ruinous habits, from which, perhaps a few may, by fortunate circumstances, be reclaimed before they arrive at manhood, while by far the greater part will be hurried to an early death, the victims of intemperance and want, or live on only to prey upon the community, fill our Almshouses and Prisons, and increase the burthens and crimes of the State."[5] A manual labor school was proposed in Baltimore in the 1840s for children who were merely vagrant—not in any way yet criminal. The New York Juvenile Asylum, opened in 1853 by the Association for Improving the Condition of the Poor, and the Boston Children's Aid Society, founded in 1864, also sent children to the West for placement, but only after keeping them for a year or two in industrial training schools in the cities. Brace and the directors of the juvenile asylum argued heat-

[4] *Ibid.*, 236.
[5] Charles Jackson et al., *Report on the Establishment of a Farm School* (Boston, 1832), 3–4, quoted in Bremner et al., ed., *Children and Youth,* 727.

edly and at length over the advisability of sending unprepared boys, "fresh" off the streets, immediately to the West. Brace was in the minority in believing that no preparation was necessary to make these boys useful and acceptable to farm families or to make them able to profit from their new environment. Several state-supported reform schools included farming among the occupations performed by inmates prior to their being bound out to farmers. Ohio built a state reform farm in 1857 that combined a concentration on agricultural labor with the family system of management, whereby children lived in small groups of forty in cottages each run by a chief or "father" and two assistant chiefs known as "elder brothers." "That all the various kinds of agricultural and a few of the more simple and more generally diffused mechanical trades form the source of employment[,] . . . [that] the establishment grows gradually and chiefly through the labor of the inmates, . . . [that] its discipline is that of a family whose subsistence springs from labor, and officers as well as inmates are employed and work with each other," were the special virtues of the plan.[6] Thus was Brace's ideal of sending children to live with farm families institutionalized.

Despite Brace's low opinion of institutions for the industrial training of children, their number, including those of the New York Children's Aid Society, grew apace. Brace's organization was running twenty-one of them in 1893, three years after he died. Other organizations in New York and other cities opened many more such schools. Philanthropic upper- and middle-class Catholics in New York, organized in the Society for the Protection of Destitute Roman Catholic Children in the City of New York, detected another motive in Brace's industrial schools. They charged that he was using those schools to try to convert children of Catholic immigrants—who comprised a considerable portion of Brace's dangerous and neglected classes—to Protestantism. In 1863 the Catholic organization established its first industrial school in New York, the New York Catholic Protectory, to prevent delinquency among immigrant children without having them subjected at the same time to the blandishments of Protestant teachers. Also it appears that these Catholic philanthropists wished to rescue their fellow Catholics in the lower classes in order to protect their own status in American society. Until the beginnings of large-scale Irish and German Catholic immigration in the 1830s, American Catholics had been accepted and widely respected by the majority of their countrymen. After 1830, however, public opinion began to identify all Catholics with the depressed and degraded immigrants and to ostracize all Catholics as foreign, poor, and potentially dangerous. The faster they could Americanize the new immigrants and destroy the as-

---

[6] Commissioners, Ohio Reform School, *Annual Report* (1856), 618–619, quoted in Bremner et al., ed., *ibid.*, 705.

sociation between poverty and vice and the Catholic religion, the better their status would become. A somewhat similar pattern developed among Jews in New York City in the 1880s and 1890s. The wealthy and religiously liberal German Jews that populated the city after 1848 found their acceptance and status in the larger society slipping because of the influx of Polish and Russian Jews. As these bearded, Yiddish-speaking, poor, religiously conservative, and militantly ethnocentric immigrants crowded into the Lower East Side, the stereotype of the Jew changed radically: he now was viewed as different and dangerous by the majority of Americans. In an effort to alleviate this loss of status through quickening the Americanization process among lower-class Jews, the German Jews in New York established an industrial school in the Lower East Side in 1884. Jews in other cities acted similarly in the 1890s. As with Brace forty years earlier, assimilation to American values meant training in industriousness.

Brace became the most lucid and respected spokesman for preventive industrial education and placing urban vagrants with farm families. His efforts were largely responsible for extending the sway of philanthropy and of industrial training over a much wider class of children than reform school leaders originally contemplated. Instead of restricting itself to those who had already committed crimes, wise philanthropy should, he argued, seek the child who was a potential criminal and train him in such a way as to reduce his proclivity for evil. The New York Children's Aid Society sought not only to gather the homeless off the streets but also to win or lure certain children away from homes and parents that the reformers did not consider sufficiently moral and transfer them to industrial schools or to farm families. Supporters of the children's aid societies hopefully anticipated a time when parents, realizing their inability to handle or care for their children, would sign them over to the societies' care. They also fought to broaden the range of adolescent behavior that was classified as delinquent so that they could more readily use the power of the courts, if necessary, to secure control over "dangerous" children. Truancy and vagrancy became crimes for which a child could be—for his own good, of course—incarcerated in an industrial school.[7]

The movement which Brace represented did much good, helping thousands of children to materially and socially better lives than those of their parents; but that movement also had more ambiguous results. Besides playing somewhat fast and loose with the civil rights of individual children—many were incarcerated for what they *were* rather than for what they *did*—it forced upon certain lower groups in the society a kind of

[7] Robert Mennell, *Thorns and Thistles: Juvenile Delinquents in the United States, 1825–1940* (Hanover, N.H., 1973), 3–77, and Michael B. Katz, *The Irony of Early School Reform* (Cambridge, Mass., 1968), 163–211, remind us of the "crimes" committed by reformatory inmates.

education different from that the majority of American children received. Training in industriousness had begun as a method of reforming the criminal. Brace and his contemporaries applied it to reforming the neglected and potentially vicious. In both these applications two somewhat conflicting premises appeared. One suggested that teaching the dangerous classes to be industrious would elevate them not only morally but economically and relieve the threat to social order posed by the urban poor by eliminating poverty. Brace loved to recount tales of boys he had sent west who became not only upstanding and honorable citizens but also successful businessmen and politicians. The other premise held that those who qualified for industrial training were destined to be the poor in America anyway and that industrial training's primary purpose was the moral—but not the economic—elevation of those people so that they would form an honest, self-sufficient, and stable lower class. The second premise viewed industrial education primarily as a method of social control, a means of stemming the threats from the dangerous classes by improving the morals of these permanently poor and inferior classes. Most of industrial education's advocates held both premises in some balance but, as the century wore on, the balance increasingly tipped toward the latter premise and industrial education became overwhelmingly a matter of controlling the poor rather than a means of rescuing them from poverty.

At the same time the number of people coming under the sway of industrial training steadily increased. Once reformers conceived of industrial training as a way of controlling the potentially dangerous rather than those who had been convicted of being dangerous, they were free to extend its application to ever wider groups of children according to their own subjective definitions of "dangerous." After the Civil War they imposed industrial education on the southern blacks as a class and more and more readily on the whole class of urban poor. The subtle and insidious shift in ideological emphasis from rescue to control and the reformers' proclivity for applying industrial training to ever greater numbers of people are clear in the following passage. In 1867 two reformers appended to a comprehensive survey of reform school activity in the United States their recommendations as to how American society could effect the prevention as well as the reform of juvenile delinquents. First, they demanded compulsory education laws: "It is far better to force education upon the people than to force them into prisons to expiate crimes, of which neglect or ignorance has been the occasion. Deep and broad foundations of moral and religious, no less than of intellectual character must be laid in our common schools, . . . and the children of the state must be there, even by compulsion, if need be, to be so trained." Common schools were not adequate "to stay the current of crime, to turn it back upon itself, and to dry up its fountain-heads." Impressions received in childhood caused most crime, they asserted, and therefore the states should establish nursery schools for children ranging in age from two to six born to pauper or neglectful parents.

> The industrial school, whether called by that name or some other—truant, ragged, or whatever it may be—is the next link, the second agency in the preventive part of the system. The children of parents who neglect their offspring, either because they are vicious or indifferent to their welfare—children who roam the streets and prowl about docks and wharves, and are almost sure in the end to take up crime as a trade—should be gathered into institutions of this class, where they would receive that mental, moral, and industrial training which their own homes would never afford them, and from which they would at length be sent out to good situations in the country, or elsewhere, where they would grow into virtuous and useful citizens, adding to, instead of preying upon, the productive industry of the country. . . . These schools should be open to the voluntary resort of neglected children, whose parents, regardless of their future character and condition, leave them to do for themselves, battling with their hard lot as best they may be able.
>
> The discipline in these industrial schools should be strictly of the family character. All the arrangements should be such as to cultivate industrious habits, and prepare their inmates for the stations they are afterwards to fill. The kitchen, the wash-tub, the sewing and knitting room, the work shop, the farm, and, above all, the school room, together with such recreation as may be suitable to their years, should occupy the time of those who find their home there; and this home should be, though tidy and attractive, yet of the plainest character, partaking as nearly as may be of the nature of the domestic departments of families of moderate circumstances.[8]

Here, then, reformers were predicting the future of children. They recommended the institutionalizing of children because they thought them likely to be criminal or dependent if not institutionalized. They sought to design the institution's program in such a way as to teach them to be independent while remaining poor. The recommendations contained no hint that the children should be prepared to have an equal chance with other children in the society or that their rescue from neglect should be so successful as to place them in the mainstream of American society. These children were going to be poor, and the industrial school's task was to teach them to be poor in a manner most conducive to what the reformers thought was the health of the society. Also revealing is the indeterminacy of the passage's definition of the kind of child to be recruited for these schools. "Neglected children" was extremely vague; its meaning varied as the reformers' fears of the lower classes waxed or waned. The term's vagueness gave reformers the scope to impose an industrial and limiting education on children whose parents the reform-

---

[8] Enoch C. Wines and Theodore W. Dwight, *Report on the Prisons and Reformatories of the United States and Canada* (Albany, 1867), 62–67, quoted in Bremner et al., ed., *Children and Youth*, 751–752.

ers did not like—whether they happened to be southern and eastern European immigrants or blacks or simply poor.

III

The kindergarten also popularized hand training or training in industriousness in the United States in the second half of the nineteenth century. Its development will not be detailed here as the kindergarten will be treated at length in a subsequent chapter. German immigrants introduced the Froebelian kindergarten in the United States as early as 1856 and the first English-speaking, and relatively permanent, kindergarten (founded by Horace Mann's sister-in-law) appeared in Boston in 1860. For some years the kindergarten was largely an upper-middle- and upper-class phenomenon. The rich were attracted to it because its emphasis on play, singing, and gentleness harmonized better with liberal upper-class theories of child nurture than did the more disciplined procedures found in the lower grades in most public school systems. At first the kindergarten provided an alternative to the primary grades for rich children. Soon reformers like Susan Blow in St. Louis and Mrs. Quincy Shaw in Boston began to argue, just as Horace Mann had done in a different context earlier, that gentler and more child-centered methods would be very effective in training the poor and the neglected children of the great cities. After 1870 urban social reformers and private philanthropists established kindergartens in the poorer sections of America's cities. The public schools adopted responsibility for the kindergartens only near the end of the century—after private philanthropy had, through almost two decades of support, proven their popularity.

That kindergartens sought to tame the dangerous classes is clear from the results of a questionnaire inquiring into the background of kindergarten children enrolled in private and charitable kindergartens in the mid-1880s. "The classes reached range from those in 'moderate circumstances' to 'our future criminals,' with a strong majority in favor of the latter. Between these two extremes are 'children of the working classes,' 'the poor,' 'the very poorest,' making the average class those of 'low and degraded parentage.' "[9] These reformers placed great emphasis on the moral value of the hand-training exercises in the kindergarten curriculum. "Weaving wooden strips into varied designs, folding paper into pretty toys and ornaments, . . . constitute a more real education by and for work," one kindergarten advocate argued. Such activities developed deftness of hand and eye, inspired imagination, and strengthened origi-

---

[9] Constance MacKenzie, "Free Kindergartens," in *Proceedings of the National Conference of Charities and Corrections* (Boston, July, 1886), 51.

nality. At the same time "habits of industry are inwrought upon the most plastic period of life, and the child is accustomed to find his interest and delight in work, and to feel its dignity and nobleness." Inculcating such delight in work, such industriousness, would, of course, affect the crime rate as this advocate argued in explaining "The Bearing of the Kindergarten on the Prevention of Crime." Kindergarten studies accustomed the child to and interested him in work and thus prevented future idleness. Less idleness meant there would be less poverty and want; and it was poverty that "leads to very much of the wickedness with which our courts deal. The prevention of suffering will be found to be the prevention of a great deal of sinning."[10] This kindergarten advocate widened the applicability of hand training—it was no longer the children of just neglectful or vicious parents who must be saved from a life of crime through industrial training; now the children's aid societies and the reformers who brought the kindergarten to the slums acted as if all poor children were meant for this kind of training. Industrial training had begun as a method for teaching the criminal and defective; by the 1880s reformers seemed to feel that poverty itself was evidence of crime, a defect to be treated with special education.

IV

Blackness was also apparently a crime and a defect, for industrial training experienced its greatest popularity during the nineteenth century when whites discovered that it was the proper education for the freedmen. Northern and southern whites, whether they considered themselves friends or foes of the black, agreed almost unanimously that industrial training would best fit the vast majority of black youngsters for the roles and positions they should fill in the United States. Industrial training began for the freedmen at Hampton Institute in Hampton, Virginia, in 1868. Established as one of several normal schools that the American Missionary Association founded after the Civil War to train teachers for black elementary schools, Hampton quickly assumed a character entirely different from the other normal schools under the leadership of its dynamic and complex first principal, Samuel Chapman Armstrong. The son of missionaries to the Hawaiian Islands, a graduate of Williams College, he joined the Union Army as a lieutenant and was discharged a brigadier general at war's end. During the war he commanded a regiment of black soldiers and became committed to aiding the black to civilize himself. He became a Freedmen's Bureau officer at Hampton and, when the American Missionary Association began to plan its normal school there, offered

[10] Reverend R. Heber Newton, "The Bearing of the Kindergarten on the Prevention of Crime," in *ibid.*, 53–54.

suggestion after suggestion, support from Freedmen's Bureau funds, and finally himself as leader of the new school. Once appointed to that position, he severed ties with the Association, raised money for the Institute on his own, and in 1872 successfully claimed for Hampton one third of the money that Virginia received under the terms of the Morrill Act, the federal land grant law of 1862 which encouraged states to establish public colleges giving instruction in the agricultural and mechanic arts.

Armstrong identified the blacks' problems as stemming less from an absence of intellectual power than from a lack of moral strength and industrial energy. Blacks were passive, they were lazy. "Deficiency of moral force and self-respect are the chief misfortunes of the race," he wrote in the school's catalogue in 1872. "The plastic character of the race puts them completely under the control of their leaders."[11] Armstrong perceived the freedmen in much the same terms that Brace applied to vagrants in New York—they were equally dangerous to the society because they were lazy and because they would probably vote incorrectly. They needed education in moral character and Armstrong judged industrial training to be the way to accomplish this. As he was more interested in teaching the blacks "self-control" and self-discipline than in teaching them intellectual subjects or in teaching them to control their environment, he rejected the traditional classical and English curricula for the Hampton students. Classical education only stimulated the blacks' egoism and their desire to get ahead without working for it. That blacks who enrolled in the colleges organized for them after the war shed their work clothes, adopted the collar and tie, and pursued the study of Latin and Greek struck Armstrong as a manifestation of their lack of self-control and their unwillingness to acknowledge how hard they must work to advance themselves. He did not recognize or credit the ambition that lay behind their attempts to change their clothing and habits and to master the middle-class whites' culture. He also indicted efforts to apply classical college training to the freedmen because such training would separate the educated blacks from their brethren among whom they must live and work. Armstrong believed that each black's first responsibility lay in working to elevate his race. He argued that no black could claim equal status with the white until the black race as a whole had reached a higher level of moral culture, and he designed Hampton to train blacks capable of working to elevate their fellow freedmen's moral character. Classical education was irrelevant to that goal.

Armstrong's views of the freedmen and of the role of industrial training in their future contained some of the same ambiguities present in the views of supporters of industrial training for the poor and vagrant in the

---

[11] *Catalogue*, Hampton Institute (1872), 21. See also Samuel Chapman Armstrong, *The Founding of Hampton Institute* (Old South Leaflets, vol. VI, No. 149, 1904), and Louis Harlan, *Booker T. Washington: The Making of a Black Leader, 1856–1901* (New York, 1972), chapters 3–6.

North. Armstrong (and other early supporters of industrial education for the black) sometimes wrote as if a program of industrial training would, in time, elevate the black to a position of equality with the white. However, he also seemed to suggest that industrial training might be preparing the black for a permanent, or nearly permanent, place of inferiority. Armstrong certainly did not share the naïve missionary's expectation that the black would gain social equality with whites within a few years. He differed from at least the more liberal missionaries in believing that blacks were mentally and perhaps physiologically inferior to whites. All missionaries recognized a cultural inferiority among blacks, but the more liberal thought it a temporary result of enslavement. Armstrong thought it a symptom of deeper inferiorities. His feeling for the black had come slowly. Early in the war, he justified his decision to finish college rather than to join the holy war against the slaveholders on the grounds that he was an Hawaiian rather than an American and did not feel engaged in the issues that had caused the war. He joined the army after graduation and became increasing committed to the idea that all blacks should be free, although he wrote in December of 1863 that he desired this freedom for the blacks "more on account of their souls rather than their bodies." The buying and selling of human souls was anathema to him but he could not, as he put it in the same letter, learn "to love the negro."[12] As a commander of black troops he grew to like and respect the black much more—in a situation where he was the officer and they the privates. Armstrong believed that blacks were equal to whites in the sight of God but that they were perhaps physiologically inferior and certainly culturally inferior as a race. The practical educator, he contended, had to start from that position and design a program that fit the blacks' qualifications and probable future. But it was just this question of the blacks' future on which Armstrong was so ambiguous.

Armstrong probably did not believe in a permanent subordinacy of black to white, but he was never clear about how long he expected blacks to remain inferior and to require a different education. By failing to define objectively his criteria for cultural and moral equality and to say that once a certain number of the blacks had fulfilled those criteria second-class citizenship and second-class education were no longer necessary and by refusing to emphasize sufficiently that industrial training was a temporary expedient—if that is, indeed, what he really believed —Armstrong opened the way for others later in the century to establish it as a permanent educational restriction on black people. His failure to come to grips with these underlying issues may have resulted from an unconscious attempt to evade the contradictions that underlay the whole

[12] Quoted in Francis G. Peabody, *Education for Life: The Story of Hampton Institute* (Garden City, N.Y., 1918), 66, 73–74.

educational crusade against the South. For others in the educational crusade, at any rate, Armstrong's theory helped postpone, for at least a generation or two, the need to choose whether to use education to achieve justice and equality for the black or to preserve social order and social harmony within the South. Arguing that the black was presently inferior and that he must receive special training to help him improve his own race allowed reformers to educate the black—thus assuaging their consciences—without threatening traditional race relations. Such an explanation may account for the increasing vogue of industrial education for the freedmen among white teachers and philanthropists after 1870. It allowed them to put off the evil day when they must choose between justice and order.

Industrial training at Hampton meant teaching students to be industrious rather than teaching them technical trades. Armstrong called for an education adapted to "the character and needs of the freed people" that "shall be at once constructive of mental and moral worth and destructive of the vices characteristic of the slave." Among the latter were "improvidence, low ideas of honor and morality, and a general lack of directive energy, judgment, and foresight." In order to counter these vices, Armstrong told the trustees in his first report, the school must attempt "to draw out a complete manhood," an effort in which "the needle, the broom, and the washtub, the awl, the plane, and the plow, become the allies of the globe, the blackboard, and the text-book."[13] As in the contemporary reform schools, most of the industrial work at Hampton consisted of routine maintenance tasks at the institution and of producing farm and factory goods that the institution could sell. Armstrong assigned the more technical trades involved in running the institution—such as printing, wheelwrighting, and supervision of the farming— not to regular students but to night school students who worked full days in the institution in return for elementary-level instruction in the evening and the promise of eventual admission to the day school. The work of the regular students was restricted to cooking, sewing, washing, cleaning, and farm labor. The male students worked two days each week on the farms at Hampton and the women were assigned various housekeeping duties. Military drill occupied additional time; students marched in uniform to and from classes.

Students spent most of their time studying English, geography, history, and the natural sciences—a curriculum, except for the absence of languages, not very unlike that of a public high school or normal school for whites. Hampton's 1870 catalogue outlined a three-year course of study that covered the following academic subjects: mathematics,

---

[13] Quoted in *ibid.*, 114–117. See also Albert Shaw, " 'Learning by Doing' at Hampton," *Review of Reviews*, XXI (April, 1900), 417–432.

through algebra and geometry and including bookkeeping; language, all English including spelling, reading, grammar, rhetoric, and composition; natural science, including geography, natural history, outlines of astronomy, physiology, and botany; history, covering the United States and England and some work in "universal history"; civil government; and the moral sciences, something like, apparently, the moral philosophy courses of the antebellum colleges. In addition, the catalogue continued, "instruction is given in mental arithmetic and penmanship, practical instruction in agriculture, in housework and in household industries, and drill in teaching through the course; a course of lectures every winter upon the application of science to agriculture, daily inspection."[14] Hampton's principal purpose in these early years was to prepare teachers, not skilled craftsmen. (Armstrong sometimes claimed the instruction in farming that Hampton offered helped the future teachers because school terms were so short in the South that those teachers would have to do something else to earn money during the vacation months.) What the successful black elementary school teacher needed, according to Armstrong, was not pedagogy (although Hampton did establish a practice school quite early and by 1883 was requiring each senior to teach one day a month in it) but rather the ability to serve as a model of moral character for his or her students. The black graduates of Hampton would elevate their race through teaching by example.

The kind of moral training that Armstrong advocated and the kind of moral character he wished to build are manifest in the recollections of Booker T. Washington, Armstrong's most famous student and the nineteenth century's most influential spokesman for applying industrial training to the black. Washington had been born a slave in 1856, and enrolled in Hampton Institute in 1872 at the age of sixteen, after having picked up the rudiments of formal education—reading and writing—during a few months in a day school organized and financed by the blacks in the town where he lived. Washington's description of his entrance examination captured Armstrong's spirit very accurately. Washington set out to cover the 500 miles from Malden, West Virginia, to Hampton with little money and lots of determination. After experiencing his first bout with segregated public facilities at a hotel along the route, he arrived penniless in Richmond, Virginia, still 100 miles from his destination. He slept under a raised wooden sidewalk and helped unload pig iron from a ship in the harbor there for some days and finally collected enough money to reach Hampton, where he arrived with fifty cents in his pocket. Washington, who had traveled for almost three weeks, slept under a sidewalk, and done heavy labor under the hot Virginia sun, arrived at the school dirty and disheveled, looking more like a loafer and a bum than

[14] *Catalogue,* Hampton Institute (1870).

a prospective student. He applied to Miss Mary F. Mackie, the head teacher, for admission. She made no immediate decision and asked him to wait. He waited for some time and watched many others admitted. After hours had gone by, Washington remembered, Miss Mackie said, "The adjoining recitation room needs sweeping. Take the broom and sweep it." Washington, remembering what he had learned as a houseboy in the home of a white family in West Virginia, went to work with a will.

> I swept the recitation-room three times. Then I got a dusting-cloth and I dusted it four times. All the woodwork around the walls, every bench, table, and desk, I went over four times with my dusting-cloth. Besides, every piece of furniture had been moved and every closet and corner in the room had been thoroughly cleaned. I had the feeling that in large measure my future depended upon the impression I made upon the teacher in the cleaning of that room, . . . she was a "Yankee" woman who knew just where to look for dirt. She went into the room and inspected the floor and closet; then she took her handkerchief and rubbed it on the woodwork about the walls, and over the table and benches. When she was unable to find one bit of dirt on the floor, or particle of dust on any of the furniture, she quietly remarked, "I guess you will do to enter this institution."[15]

Washington was offered the position of janitor in compensation for which he was to receive his room and board. This was one application of what Armstrong meant by industrial education—offering students the chance to work in order to pay for part of their education. Washington described his position: "The work was hard and taxing, but I stuck to it. I had a large number of rooms to care for, and had to work late into the night, while at the same time I had to rise at 4 o'clock in the morning, in order to build the fires and have a little time in which to prepare my lessons." In addition, he apparently also devoted the normal two days of each week to working on the farm. His contact there with "the best breeds of livestock and fowls" he considered a valuable lesson. "No student, I think, who has had the opportunity of doing this could go out into the world and content himself with the poorest grades."[16] Washington received no other industrial training.

He did learn many moral and cultural skills in his three years at Hampton. He considered them the most valuable part of his training there and sought to teach them in every school with which he was connected thereafter. He learned about "having meals at regular hours, . . . eating on a tablecloth, using a napkin, the use of the bathtub and of the toothbrush, as well as the use of sheets on the bed." Of the bathtub, Washington recalled that he "learned there for the first time some of its

[15] Booker T. Washington, *Up from Slavery*, in Louis Harlan, ed., *The Booker T. Washington Papers* (Urbana, Ill., 1972), I, 241; and Harlan's excellent biography, *Booker T. Washington, 1856–1901.*

[16] Washington, *Up from Slavery*, 242, 249.

value, not only in keeping the body healthy, but in inspiring self-respect, promoting virtue. . . . I have always tried to teach my people that some provision for bathing should be a part of every house."[17] Washington credited Hampton with teaching him to use and value the Bible and with improving his ability as a public speaker. Some teachers who recognized his potential as a speaker tailored the instruction in public speaking specifically for him; it was not part of the regular curriculum. Washington took great delight in the debating societies at Hampton and organized a discussion group to occupy profitably the twenty minutes "between the time when supper was over and the time to begin evening study . . . which the young men usually spent in idle gossip."[18] At Hampton he also met northern whites whose attitude toward hard work struck him as quite different from that of the southern whites he had known. He recalled that one time when he returned from vacation early in order to clean up the campus in preparation for the opening of school, Miss Mackie worked right beside him preparing the beds and cleaning the windows and sweeping the floor. Seeing this "member of one of the oldest and most cultured families of the north" working in such a manner was a lesson Washington would never forget.[19] Lastly, he claimed that Hampton made him aware of education's true value for the individual. He remembered that "before going there I had a good deal of the then rather prevalent idea among our people that to secure an education meant to have a good, easy time, free from all necessity and manual labor. At Hampton I not only learned that it was not a disgrace to labor, but learned to love labor, not alone for its financial value, but for labor's own sake and for the independence and self-reliance which the ability to do something which the world wants done brings."[20] Washington had accepted Armstrong's doctrines whole.

Yet when, in 1881, Washington came to implement Armstrong's doctrines, as principal of Tuskegee Institute in Alabama, the situation had already begun to change. Armstrong's rhetoric, at any rate, could be interpreted as containing the view that industrial training would eventually elevate the black to equal status with the white. Most of the supporters of industrial training for the blacks in the 1860s and 1870s probably agreed that it was a temporary measure, however much they may have disagreed on just how temporary it was to be. As the century advanced, however, industrial training came to be seen more as an end in itself than as a means to the future elevation of the blacks to full equality. Washington's views on this subject are almost impossible to decipher because he tailored virtually everything he ever said or wrote to accord with the

[17] *Ibid.*, 244.
[18] *Ibid.*, 249.
[19] *Ibid.*, 252.
[20] *Ibid.*

prejudices of the particular audience he was addressing. Thus his views tended to change with the temper of the times. In all probability Washington believed that the Atlanta Compromise, which he enunciated in 1895 to the effect that blacks and whites would work together "as one hand" to advance the South economically but would remain as "separate as the fingers on that hand" in social affairs, would be temporary. He probably did believe that in time the black would, by achieving success in the economic sphere, earn the respect and social regard of the southern white. However, a politically astute black could not voice such hopes for the future publicly in the late-nineteenth-century South, no matter how distant he expected that future to be. Instead, Washington stressed the blacks' acceptance of segregation and their commitment to working hard to promote the region's economic growth. Moreover, his imagery constantly suggested that the blacks' contribution would come in the more menial occupations rather than in the skilled trades or professions.

Washington's white listeners did not grasp his underlying hopes but instead heard him clearly announce that social equality no longer concerned the blacks and that blacks accepted the role of menial workers in the South's fight to rise economically. Washington did not mean to accept second-class citizenship for his people, nor would anything he could have said or done in the postreconstruction South have prevented the blacks from becoming more and more restricted to such a role in society. The age shaped Washington more than he shaped it. But when the principal of the leading black industrial school spoke as he did, he confirmed for most of his white audience that industrial education's purpose was to prepare blacks for second-class citizenship. In the eyes of most whites by the turn of the century that was exactly what industrial training had become. As William Henry Baldwin, Jr., president of the Long Island Railroad and a member of the Southern Education Board, expressed it, the Negro "will willingly fill the more menial positions and do the heavy work, at less wages" and will leave to the whites the "more expert labor." His advice to the Negro was quite specific: "Avoid social questions; leave politics alone; continue to be patient; live moral lives; live simply; learn to work . . . know that it is a crime for any teacher, white or black, to educate the negro for positions which are not open to him."[21] Edgar Gardner Murphy, and other progressive southern humanitarians prominent in twentieth-century efforts to extend common schools for whites in the South, agreed with Baldwin. An immense change had occurred since Armstrong's day.

The change was reflected in the programs of the black colleges and normal schools as well. Industrial training, for relatively menial positions, had become an end in itself and popular northern interest in industrial

[21] William H. Baldwin, "The Present Problem of Negro Education, Industrial Education," *Proceedings of the Second Capon Springs Conference on Southern Education* (1899), 72, 74.

training shifted from a concern with the development of moral character to a concern for the production of goods, the establishment of specialized training shops and programs, and the stimulation of manual skills. This was evident even at Hampton. In 1875–1876 the catalogue noted that girls would receive instruction in breadmaking and plain cooking. By 1880 Hampton had appointed a special teacher to handle cooking classes. In the late 1880s programs of instruction in specific trades—agriculture, commerce, and mechanics—became a part of Hampton's curriculum. In 1894 the catalogue announced courses in teaching, tailoring, shirtmaking, dressmaking, seamstressing, agriculture, blacksmithing, harnessmaking, carpentry, painting, printing, planing machine work, shoemaking, wheelwrighting, and woodworking. In 1896 Hampton opened a trade school branch quite similar in conception to northern high-school-level vocational schools. This kind of specialization of industrial training and the habit of seeing industrial training as the proper focus of higher education for most blacks increased throughout the South in the last two decades of the century. In this period whites who supported or encouraged the black colleges from the outside directed their efforts almost exclusively at elaborating industrial training programs. Instead of being a part of the effort to uplift the blacks, industrial training appeared increasingly as a means of fitting blacks to inferior social and economic positions.

White support for the industrial education of the black became increasingly munificent as the century progressed and the sources of that support changed. After 1875 most of the money sent south to support black education that did not come through the regular denominational home missionary associations now came from businessmen or philanthropic foundations, most notably the Peabody Fund (founded in 1867) and the Slater Fund (1882). Successful northern businessmen (George Peabody had been born in Georgia, however) looking for an outlet for their charitable impulses established these funds with gifts of $2 million and $1 million respectively. Peabody charged that his gift be used "for the promotion and encouragement of intellectual, moral, or industrial education among the young of the more destitute portions of the Southern and Southwestern States of our Union."[22] That he used "industrial" in this context before Armstrong began his experiments at Hampton suggests that he perceived the children's aid societies' work in the North as applicable to the problem of the southern poor. The Peabody Fund supported programs for both blacks and whites, including common schools, normal schools, and professional associations of teachers. The Slater Fund focused specifically on the improvement of black education,

---

[22] The Peabody will is quoted in R. Freeman Butts and Lawrence Cremin, *A History of Education in American Culture* (New York, 1953), 412.

especially black industrial education. The boards of both funds entrusted their administration to men who believed in industrial education for the blacks and who used the foundation money strategically to encourage black colleges to add industrial training to their programs. Symbolic of the trustees' increasing concern with promoting sectional harmony was the fact that, although the first director of the Peabody Fund was a northern educator, one of Horace Mann's successors as secretary to the Massachusetts board of education, the funds thereafter delegated responsibility for implementing their donors' wishes to southerners who shared the southern belief that the black was, and would remain for the foreseeable future, inferior. The funds worked in such close harmony with each other—in the 1890s J. L. M. Curry directed both simultaneously—that they did not compete to develop alternative modes of supporting black educational interests.

Although they did not have a great deal of money by modern standards, these funds exercised great leverage in the late nineteenth century over the black colleges and normal schools. Like most colleges founded in that century, they were always in financial difficulty. They received little tuition money and, because there were so many colleges and normal schools established and so little governmental support (relative to the amount state governments spent on white higher education), the money that northern churches, black churches, and the southern black community raised was spread too thinly. In this situation whether a college received a $1,000 or $2,000 appropriation from the Slater or Peabody agents determined whether it could maintain itself at a viable level and retain its full faculty. The agents—especially Atticus C. Haygood, a Methodist minister and later president of Emory University, who headed the Slater Fund in the 1880s—used this leverage to coerce the black colleges to adopt industrial education—many against their wills. Haygood would offer a college $1,000 in general operating funds if it would build and maintain with another $1,000 appropriation an industrial training department. All but the strongest had no choice but to agree, and by 1890 almost every black college—with the notable exceptions of Atlanta, Fisk, and Howard—offered industrial training to all their students.

Most of this training was nontechnical preparation for menial labor or for hand crafts that machinery was making obsolescent. Spelman College did not install washing machines in its laundry training shop because its directors believed that, since black women would seldom find positions in mechanized laundries, they should master the old methods. At Tuskegee students made bricks—some for sale but most for the ever growing number of buildings erected at this, the most financially successful of the industrial schools—by hand when most bricks in the country were manufactured by machine. The only skilled trade commonly taught was printing—the schools saved money by printing their own catalogues and newspapers—but even here students learned to set type by hand rather than on the linotype, which had vastly changed the printing trade since its introduction in the early 1880s. Before the twentieth century blacks did not receive real marketable craft training in the industrial schools of the South; but, even had they received skilled training, they would have been unable to use it. White labor unions and white employers refused to allow blacks to hold skilled jobs anyway. Only in specific instances where industry was engaged in union busting did blacks receive skilled training: the Tennessee Coal and Iron Company founded a school in 1907 in Birmingham to give black teenagers certain skills in order to dampen union enthusiasm among whites in the northern Alabama steel mills. Such instances were few, however. In the first quarter of the twentieth century white philanthropic support for the education of southern blacks continued in the same mold. The Anna Jeannes Fund (1907) sought to improve rural education for blacks by sending through the countryside visiting teachers expert in the methods of industrial education to give in-service instruction to the rural black teachers. The Phelps-Stokes Fund (1909) funded and encouraged industrial education for blacks in the South and took an active part in exporting the industrial training movement to several African nations. Only the Julius Rosenwald Fund, which began dispensing money in 1912 for the support of southern education in general, found the intellectual training of blacks as worthy of support as their industrial training.

Many causes contributed, in a complex interaction, to the preservation of the blacks' second-class status in the South and to the use of industrial training to achieve it. Although educational reformers and the initiators of industrial training certainly were not primarily responsible for the use made of their doctrines to restrict black progress, they do bear a certain responsibility because the nature of the doctrine they espoused made it especially susceptible to that kind of misuse. The weaknesses in the doctrine were present whenever special education was prescribed for classes of people whose character did not appeal to the reformers, but the problems are particularly clear in this case. When industrial education was applied to vagrants and blacks as a preventative and as a means of uplift, reformers promised that such training would remedy defects they found in the character of the blacks and the urban poor. That these defects existed was a subjective decision, based more on the reformers' prejudices than on the actual behaviors of the people in question. But, by institutionalizing this defect, by arranging a program specifically to deal with it, the reformers succeeded, in a way, in objectifying what they had subjectively identified as a defect—or at least made it seem so in popular opinion. In arguing that blacks required special education, the reformers gave substance to the popular belief that blacks were inferior.

A second problem with the doctrine of special education, as applied in the case of the black, was that because the identified defect was originally subjective there was no objective basis for reaching agreement as to when that defect had been removed, when special education could have been said to have accomplished its task. When educators identify a special problem or defect—such as a reading problem, for instance—they can devise a program to correct it and determine, in ways convincing to most people in the society, whether a child undertaking that program has corrected his reading problem—whether he can read as well as the "normal" child of his age. Reading is a skill that is fairly easily measured in a relatively objective way. No such objectivity, no such hope of agreement was possible with a topic so complex and subjective as moral character. When educators assumed the responsibility for curing defects in moral character, they could rely on no tests or measurements to indicate that their task was complete, that the defects in moral character had been removed. Such a decision would require a judgment equally as subjective as the original decision to classify certain characteristics as defective.

Powerful interests, both north and south, had too great a stake in maintaining the separateness between white and black that industrial training's early advocates had furthered to make the subjective judgment that the original justifications for industrial training had passed or been eliminated. The first of these groups, of course, comprised the mass of the southern white population. The industrial educators' identification of the black as somehow defective and in need of special remedial training accorded with their views exactly. They had no inclination to believe that the deficiency or inferiority had been relieved or removed—the southerner liked to think of second-class education for the black as a permanent solution. Continued special education for the black also suited the needs of the southern common school reformers after 1890, for it allowed them to rationalize common school reform for whites only.

Northern whites also found comfortable identification of the blacks as a race in need of special education. Such a doctrine allowed them to justify, in their own eyes, their frustration with the black who did not respond to the classical and traditional curricula that the educational crusade first offered him. It confirmed the inferiority which the crusaders had in anger attributed to the blacks. When the northern reformers, by withdrawing aid from the Freedmen's Bureau and from the missionary educational effort, recognized the implicit conflict between their hopes for elevating the black and their hopes for imposing order and stability on the defeated South, they chose the side of social order and backed away from their effort to provide the black with that common schooling supposedly capable of making him equal to the white. Racial peace was more important than racial justice. Yet these northern reformers felt some guilt about this withdrawal and industrial education for the blacks gave them a perfect opportunity to assuage that guilt. Through industrial education they could both "elevate" the black and serve the causes of racial peace and sectional harmony. Special industrial schooling rather than common schooling allowed the northern reformers to feel that they were continuing the educational crusade to better the blacks. Yet at the same time industrial training, because it made the elevation of the black a long-term affair, extending possibly over generations, produced none of the social conflict that had accompanied the reconstruction crusade to extend common schooling to the blacks.

Much has been made of the fact that the philanthropy that forced industrial education on the black colleges was big business philanthropy—different from that which fueled the original educational crusade in Reconstruction. Businessmen founded the Peabody and Slater funds and made individual grants to many of the industrial schools, the argument goes, in an effort to create in the South a docile and submissive black labor force which could be used both to man the factories that northern investors were financing and to break white union activities in these factories. Industrial training would, according to this interpretation, so affect the character of the southern labor market as to increase the yield from northern investments in southern industry. Such a theory has only a limited validity. The Tennessee Coal and Iron Company, of course, established its school for just those purposes. In general, however, it is very difficult to establish a direct relation between the activities of the northern philanthropists and the fate of northern industrial investment in the South. Few business supporters of industrial education had substantial southern holdings. Moreover, blacks did not and were not expected to work in southern industry—most textile and steel mills there employed only whites, and nothing taught in the industrial schools for blacks affected that situation. It might be argued that the existence of a large population of trained blacks would have constantly reminded white laborers that, if they did not accept low wages and poor working conditions, they would be replaced by available black laborers. Yet there was already an oversupply of white labor in the South, effectively dampening union activities anyway. A more convincing explanation of the businessmen's activities is that they supported industrial training for the blacks less out of direct financial self-interest than out of a belief that racial peace within the South and political peace between the sections promoted the economic and social health of the whole nation and as such improved its investment climate. Industrial training for the blacks had few direct practical advantages for its northern white supporters.

Some blacks, especially those whose careers and status within the black and white communities depended on their leadership of the industrial education movement, supported the continuation of industrial training. Booker T. Washington was the most prominent among that group.

As principal of Tuskegee and most eloquent spokesman for the black "accommodationist" position, Washington was immensely powerful in the black and white communities. By the turn of the century national politicians consulted him on all policies and patronage affecting black men (although they did not always follow his advice); philanthropists distributed their largesse among black projects as he advised; he controlled much of the black press by having his white business friends insert or withdraw advertising according to how closely the paper advocated policies of which Washington approved; because he supported the compromise that northerners had made between justice and order, he served as powerful mediator between his race and the whites, north and south. As indicated in his angry reaction to W. E. B. DuBois' criticism that industrial education imposed second-class citizenship on all blacks by refusing to encourage the "talented tenth" to educate themselves as fully as any white man, Washington saw any threat to industrial education as a threat to his own power. Washington was not unique among blacks in the South; many members of the black middle class owed their power among blacks to their ability to mediate between blacks and whites on the basis of the compromise that industrial education represented. They had risen under the old rules of second-class education for the blacks and, as much as they may have wished to change those rules in the abstract, they were disinclined to risk trying to change those rules. Few black leaders in the South were willing to argue either that industrial education to correct black deficiencies had been a mistaken policy to begin with or that, since industrial education had already achieved its goal of strengthening black character, blacks now deserved the same privileges as whites. Too many people, black and white, benefited from the status quo to challenge the emphasis on special remedial education for the blacks.

V

Calvin M. Woodward, an instructor in mathematics at Washington University in St. Louis, introduced manual training at the Manual Training School of Washington University in 1879. Manual training, as Woodward conceived it, differed from industrial training in two important ways: it stressed work with tools and training for work with tools rather than the production of useful and saleable objects, and it was supposed to be an integral part of a general education—rather than a separate special education. Woodward's first interest in manual training came in the late 1860s when, in teaching mechanical engineering, he found students entirely ignorant of the use of tools and thus unable to build models that he thought necessary for his teaching. This lack of skill convinced him that young men were growing up in the United States too oriented toward the intellectual and the genteel and not oriented enough to using their hands and to appreciating the dignity of hand labor. Woodward did not see manual training as vocational training, but he did think its inclusion in the regular high school curriculum would allow boys to make more intelligent occupational choices. It would, in short, increase the number of intelligent people who chose the trades and cut down the oversupply of clerks and other white-collar workers. Woodward expected it to do more because a balanced education would appeal to more students and keep more of them in school longer, thus introducing those already destined for manual labor to the more liberal, intellectual subjects. His system, he wrote, "aims to elevate, to dignify, to liberalize, all the essential elements of society; and it renders it possible for every honorable calling to be the happy home of cultivation and refinement."[23] By extending the laborers' schooling, manual training would also relieve labor problems, the result, according to Woodward, of worker ignorance.

Thus, Woodward was calling for a general broadening of the school curriculum that would include a judicious mixture of intellectual studies and hand and tool training for all young students. Many leading members of the public educational establishment of his day objected vigorously. One argued that the schools should teach children to gather information, mostly from books. "There is no information stored up in the plow, hoe handle, [or] steam engine." William Torrey Harris argued that the essence of education lay in exercising the powers of abstraction, generalization, comprehension. All experience, including tool work, was instructive, he agreed, but claimed that only those experiences especially useful in cultivating the ability to reason, to generalize, to idealize should be part of the school curriculum. Carpentry did not fill the bill.[24]

But the educational establishment was out of step—its commitment to restricting school curricula to the traditional cultural subjects could not be sustained. Manual training became more and more popular and by the middle 1880s manual training began appearing in cities throughout the nation. Most of the original manual training introduced at this time was really vocational education—preparation for the skilled trades. Woodward's Manual Training School offered instruction not only in carpentry and wood shaping but also in the metal crafts used solely in machine shops and forges. Businessmen established private manual training schools; the public school system in Baltimore was the first to open a public, separate manual training school in 1884; other cities followed soon after. Others, especially smaller cities, instituted manual

[23] Calvin Woodward, *The Manual Training School* (Boston, 1887), 239.
[24] Albert P. Marble, quoted in U. S. Bureau of Education, *Report of the Commissioner of Education for the Year 1893–1894* (Washington, D. C., 1894), I, 887, and William T. Harris, quoted in Lawrence Cremin, *The Transformation of the School: Progressivism in American Education, 1876–1957* (New York, 1961), 30–31.

training courses in their public high schools. Much of the interest in manual training at this relatively advanced level came from businessmen, labor unions, and young men seeking skilled jobs. Woodward's enthusiasm for manual training's contribution to general education did not concern these manual training advocates; instead, they were interested in giving students a general familiarity with the trades that might better fit them to serve as foremen, managers, or skilled operatives. In the same period (1880–1900) a number of specifically vocational schools appeared, some run by private interests, some by specific factories, and a few by trade unions. These schools were slightly more restricted in scope than the manual training schools, promising to turn out journeymen bricklayers or steamfitters or typographers rather than young men broadly trained in the trades. All these schools promised to improve the apprenticeship system of the United States and to undermine increasing union control of that system. Many businessmen, and especially their trade council, the National Association of Manufacturers, founded in 1896, came to see manual training and vocational schools as means of breaking union power by supplying a pool of well-trained nonunion labor. Unions suspected as much and at the level of national debate the vocational school idea and the manual training school idea threatened to founder on this labor-management imbroglio. But on the local scene higher level vocational schools flourished under public and private management, and by 1910 unions and management had agreed to support a system of vocational training in the manual trades under the auspices of the public schools in which management and labor would each have an influential voice in determining curriculum and standards.

Nonvocational forms of manual training also became popular in the public schools. As Woodward had hoped, school authorities included manual training in the curriculum because it contributed to teaching the whole child. The growing popularity of neo-Pestalozzian pedagogies that emphasized learning by doing and the value of physical as well as mental activities insured that manual training would flourish in the schools. Schoolmen pushed nonvocational forms of manual training down into the early high school years and even into the upper grades. As it became adapted for lower grades, manual training concentrated more and more on training children to use hand tools on wood when industry in the United States was moving more and more toward manufacturing metal with machines. By the time Woodward's ideal of manual training had been widely applied in the public schools, it had lost its vocational orientation and, like earlier hand-training methods, was focused on character building. Felix Adler, president of New York's Ethical Culture Society, and an advocate of the introduction of manual training in the grades as well as in the high school, defined manual training's influence on character this way:

By manual training, we cultivate the intellect in close and inseparable connection with action. Manual training consists of a series of actions which are controlled by the mind and which always react on it. Let the task assigned be, for instance, the making of a wooden box. The first point to be gained is to attract the attention of the pupil to the object. A wooden box is interesting to a child, hence this first point will be gained. Lethargy is overcome, and attention is aroused. Next, it is important to keep the attention fixed on the object [or goal]. Thus only can tenacity of purpose be cultivated. Manual training enables us to keep the attention of the child fixed upon the object, because the latter is concrete. . . . And, when finally the task is done, when the box stands before the boy's eyes a complete whole, a serviceable thing, sightly to the eyes, well adapted to its uses, with what a glow of triumph does he contemplate his work? . . . [T]his sense of achievement, in connection with the work done, leaves in his mind a pleasant after-taste, which will stimulate him to similar work in the future. The child that has once acquired, in connection with the making of a box, the habits just described, has mastered the secret of a strong will, and will be able to apply the same habits in other directions and on other occasions.[25]

Manual training had become, like industrial training for Charles Brace, a way of teaching children industriousness and clearing up their character problems. Adler and others extended, however, the concern with character from just the vagrant or the poor or the black to the population as a whole. All American children displayed a lack of industriousness. The poor's problems in this regard were surely greater than those of the middle and upper classes, but all classes shared in this declension from the work ethic. Urbanization and the lack of healthy, demanding chores for boys and girls were undermining the industriousness that rural children had learned on the farm. The urban child was in danger of becoming effete and manual training, to which the public schools added domestic science or home economics for girls, would help alleviate the problem. Middle- and upper-class Americans, the reformers argued, were in danger of divorce "from those primal sources of strength from which mankind has always drawn its vitality." Muscular strength was not the only concern—although it was important to Americans at the time as shown in Theodore Roosevelt's prescriptions for the "strenuous life" and the increasing popularity of contact sports as part of the character-building activities of schools and colleges. "We must also preserve that spiritualized strength which we call skill, the tool-using faculty, the power of impressing on matter the shape of the mind."[26] In a similar vein, supporters of manual training for all children argued that it would reduce class conflict. Classes were growing separate and hostile in America not

[25] Felix Adler, "The Influence of Manual Training on Character," *Proceedings of the National Conference of Charities and Corrections* (Boston, 1888), 275–276.
[26] *Ibid.*, 279.

because of the differences in wealth between them but because they "have become so widely separated by differences of interests and pursuits that they no longer fully understand one another, and misunderstanding, as is well known, is the fruitful source of hatred and dissension." This dissension could best be diminished by insuring that all children took manual training in school and thus shared a common interest no matter what their subsequent career.[27] Manual training suggested the possibility of recreating the world of yesterday, when all people worked together, when the poor and the rich trusted each other because they worked with their hands together. Urban Americans found manual training attractive because it promised to recreate some of the noble characteristics of the peaceful, cohesive, ordered, and stable village that had been lost in the rapidly changing cities. Educational reformers like John Dewey would elaborate this meaning of hand training into a new theory of elementary schooling at the turn of the century and call it "progressive education."

VI

Hand training also had less pretty connotations, and these carried over into twentieth-century educational reform just as clearly as did the more genial ones. It is well at this point to prepare for the discussion of twentieth-century educational reform, in which hand training and vocational training were crucial issues, by reviewing the various motivations which account for the increasing popularity of hand training in the nineteenth century.

One of the most significant reasons for hand training's appeal at all levels was the belief that it interested and thus would attract children, especially poor children, to the school so that their morals could be reshaped. Hand training, industrial training, manual training, vocational training were all thought to be more attractive to poorer students—both economically and mentally poorer—than were the traditional intellectual subjects. Felix Adler wrote that manual training was more effective than traditional subjects because "history, geography, and arithmetic are not interesting, as a rule, to young children, especially not to young children of the class with which we are now dealing. These listless minds are not easily roused to an interest in abstractions."[28] At the lower levels the promise that they would work with things rather than memorize books and abstractions would convince poor and degraded children to try school, and at the higher levels shop and tool training would keep children who most required the school's influence from dropping out. In a

---

[27] *Ibid.*
[28] *Ibid.*, 275.

way hand training more accurately implemented the Pestalozzian ideal of having children learn by doing, of engaging the children's interest in their schoolwork, than did the Oswego method. There is no apparent evidence that Pestalozzi's ideas directly affected the introduction of industrial and hand training in America (except in the kindergarten through Pestalozzi's influence on Froebel), but social reformers found hand training so promising for the same reasons that drew Mann to Pestalozzi's ideas.

Hand training, in the same vein, would also effectively solve the educational reformers' third pedagogical problem—that of affecting the future moral behavior of their charges, especially those from the poorer and more dangerous classes. Manual training would teach children to be industrious and prevent the idleness that, by creating poverty, accounted for the ever rising crime rate in the United States. The late nineteenth century saw a vast increase in visible unemployment in the United States and with it a vast increase in the number of tramps and vagabonds. Brace had been appalled and frightened by the number of homeless and idle boys in New York City in the 1850s. By the end of the century the middle class was alarmed by the homeless and jobless adults who appeared seemingly everywhere. Many diagnosed the tramp and unemployment problems as simply manifestations of a refusal to settle down and work hard. Early training in industriousness would eradicate that general laziness among the poorer classes of the population. In the late nineteenth century the United States also experienced a host of labor problems, marked most traumatically by the killing of a policeman in Chicago's Haymarket Square in 1886, the long and bloody Pullman strike of 1894, and the march of Coxey's army of unemployed from the Midwest to Washington to demand labor's rights. Strikes broke out in industry after industry as the workingmen of the nation began to organize to demand higher wages and better working conditions. Middle-class opinion generally sided with the bosses and shared much of management's opinion that labor discontent was simply another symptom of the indolence of the poor. Industrial training in the schools would relieve this problem. In addition, some advocated vocational education in the crafts as a means of creating a pool of trained nonunion labor which would make it less difficult for management to oppose labor organization.

Industrial training could improve the character of poor people by teaching them self-discipline and will power. The sense of accomplishment and seeing a job through that was part of the hand-training experience in the schools would encourage children to learn to concentrate on the job and thus make them more effective workers. Industrial training promised to discipline the will and the hands much as Latin and Greek promised to discipline the mind. Adler thought manual training would increase the child's power to concentrate because it made children active in school rather than passive as they had been in the traditional intellectual curriculum and he thought that, by showing the child the relation of thought and action, of will and results, it would strengthen his will power and ability to discipline his mind and body. Adler also argued that the various forms of hand training served to increase the child's respect for private property. Once the child had made the box that Adler described in the passage quoted above, he would own property of his own and, because he wanted others to respect his property, he would learn to respect theirs. The wooden box gave the child a stake in the social contract.

There were other, sounder theories underlying the move toward more hand training in the schools. One was the idea that training in coordination between the hand and the eye and between the mind and the hand was important to the child's mental development. Another held that hand training would help the child learn to observe more accurately. On the latter point hand-training advocates agreed with the proponents of the Oswego method. Drawing was always a central part of the manual training classes because it was thought to strengthen the observing and recording faculties of the eye (and, one suspects, because pencil and paper were considerably cheaper than tools and wood). In the search for alternatives to memory training of the early-nineteenth-century curriculum, training of the eye's observing power had its place.

In many ways these motives for the popularity of hand training suggest that it was something of a logical continuation of the common school movement—that in hand training the common school reformers or their successors had discovered a pedagogy and curriculum capable of effectively changing moral behavior. But hand training violated the common school ethic in two ways: it was restricted, in that it was almost exclusively directed toward the poor, the outcast, the different; and it was restrictive, in that it limited the future opportunities of students. Hand training was meant in large part for those who were inferior in some way to the "acceptable" social type. It was class education rather than common education. The reformers assumed that they could predict a man's future from the social class into which he was born and design a training program which limited him to that kind of future, which denied him the skills that would have allowed him to pursue the additional higher education even then necessary to social advancement. In the nineteenth century educators and social welfare specialists did not seek to apply their predictive powers to any but the helpless and the institutionalized. They would seek to apply it more widely in the Progressive period.

Too much can be made of the motives that lay behind the welfare enthusiasts' efforts. Some have argued that this movement to offer second-class education to already second-class citizens was a conscious design to keep the poor in their place; that it was a middle-class movement to reduce the threat of social and job competition from the lower class. If we could examine as closely as we would like the politics surrounding the establishment of industrial training in various public institutions to see if those whose status was really threatened by the very poor—the upper lower class, the semiskilled laborer, the skilled laborer—supported movements to segregate the very poor into second-class education, we might find something to the argument that industrial education or hand training was imposed on the poor to protect the economic status of those above them. It is clear, however, that the reformers who instituted and advocated hand training for the poor were in no way economically threatened in a personal sense by the people their industrial training was to serve. Personal economic self-interest cannot explain the increase in the application of hand training to the poor.

The argument that big business imposed hand training on the poor in order to create a more submissive labor force is no more acceptable. As we have seen, most of the hand training given was technologically valueless to American industry. When students were taught skills at all, they were the skills of the home workshop or of personal service (washing, cooking, waiting tables) or hand skills long outdated by the advent of machinery. Nor were graduates of industrial schools useful in breaking strikes, for most strikes occurred among the skilled tradesmen whose number was never great enough to satisfy industry's needs and whose skills were vital to the industrial process. Business was not benefited by industrial training as practiced among the poor or among the blacks. Industry was interested only in high-level hand training that would prepare journeymen craftsmen whose skills could fuel the growing economy (and undermine the powers of unionism). Management derived no advantage from keeping men in their place; it needed schools to turn the sons of the unskilled into skilled craftsmen. (Whether trade schools in fact did encourage mobility, especially with the restrictions placed on them by unions, we simply have not the data to answer at this point.)

What is important to note here is that the development and popularization of hand training in schools resulted from no conspiracy or plot to keep down the poor. The advocates of extending a limiting education to the blacks and the poor and the working classes were motivated by fear of the dangerous classes and by concern for the welfare of the whole society, and they were propelled by an arrogance that they knew what was best for society and for certain individuals in it. These people feared the poor, the black, and the workingmen as a threat to social order and moral order, but not as a threat to their own economic status. They were arrogant because they sought to impose their moral and social values on other people and because they sought to predict the lives of individuals and to force them to follow those paths by limiting their educational opportunities. They were arrogant because they thought that imposing their own moral values on others in school was more important than enabling people to seek their own values in later life. But such traits were not unique to reformers concerned with education in the second half of the nineteenth century. Those traits were prevalent among the common school reformers and would appear still more prominently among educators and educational reformers in the Progressive era.

GUIDE TO FURTHER READING

JOHN GARRATY, *The New Commonwealth, 1877–1890* (New York, 1968), and ROLAND BERTHOFF, *An Unsettled People: Social Order and Disorder in American History* (New York, 1971), provide the context for our discussion of the late nineteenth century.

We have found the following useful for our interpretation of juvenile life and reform: ROBERT MENNELL, *Thorns and Thistles: Juvenile Delinquents in the United States, 1825–1940* (Hanover, N. H., 1973), MICHAEL KATZ, *The Irony of Early School Reform* (Cambridge, Mass., 1968), JOSEPH HAWES, *Children in Urban Society: Juvenile Delinquency in Nineteenth–Century America* (New York, 1971), WALTER TRATTNER, *Crusade for the Children* (Chicago, 1970), JEREMY P. FELT, *Hostages of Fortune: Child Labor Reform in New York State* (Syracuse, N. Y., 1965), ROBERT S. PICKETT, *House of Refuge: Origins of Juvenile Reform in New York State, 1815–1857* (Syracuse, N. Y., 1969), JACK M. HOLL, *Juvenile Reform in the Progressive Era: William R. George and the Junior Republic Movement* (Ithaca, N. Y., 1971), RICHARD WOHL, "The 'Country Boy' Myth and Its Place in American Urban Culture: The Nineteenth-Century Contribution," *Perspectives in American History*, III (1969), 77–156, edited by MOSES RISCHIN, ROBERT BREMNER et al., ed., *Children and Youth in America: A Documentary History* (Cambridge, Mass., 1970), vol. I, and CHARLES L. BRACE, *The Dangerous Classes of New York* (1872; New York, 1880).

On the kindergarten consult our bibliography for chapter 11.

LOUIS HARLAN, *Booker T. Washington: The Making of a Black Leader, 1856–1901* (New York, 1972), is an excellent introduction to Washington and life at Hampton and Tuskegee. WASHINGTON'S *Up from Slavery* (New York, 1901) is a useful personal statement and HUGH HAWKINS' anthology, *Booker T. Washington and His Critics: The Problem of Negro Leadership* (Boston, 1962), contains several exchanges between black leaders, including W. E. B. DuBois' important essay, "Of Mr. Booker T. Washington and Others," originally published in *Souls of Black Folk* (Chicago, 1903). Two recent interpretations of DuBois are ELLIOTT M. RUDWICK, *W. E. B. DuBois: Propagandist of the Negro Protest* (Philadelphia, 1960), and FRANCIS L. BRODERICK, *W. E. B. DuBois, Negro Leader in a Time of Crisis* (Stanford, Calif., 1959). See also our bibliography for chapter 5; most relevant are those works by AUGUST MEIER, MERLE CURTI, LOUIS HARLAN, HENRY BULLOCK, JAMES ANDERSON, and HORACE MANN BOND.

BERENICE FISHER, *Industrial Education: American Ideals and Institutions* (Madison, Wis., 1967), CHARLES A. BENNETT, *History of Manual and Industrial Education up to 1870* (Peoria, Ill., 1926), and LAWRENCE A. CREMIN, *The Transformation of the School: Progressivism in American Education, 1876–1957* (New York, 1961), Part I, are excellent introductions to manual training and vocational education in the nineteenth century. SELWYN K. TROEN, *The Public and the Schools: Shaping the St. Louis System, 1838–1920* (Columbia, Mo., 1975), ARTHUR G. WIRTH, *Education in the Technological Society* (Scranton, Pa., 1971), B. EDWARD McCLELLAN, "Education for an Industrial Society: Changing Conceptions of the Role of Public Schooling, 1865–1900" (Unpublished Dissertation, Northwestern University, 1972), and ROBERT H. BECK, "Progressive Education and American Progressivism: Felix Adler," *Teachers College Record*, LX (1958–1959), 77–89, provide important insights into the personalities and controversies surrounding the shift from manual training to vocational education. MARVIN LAZERSON makes explicit this shift in *Origins of the Urban School: Public Education in Massachusetts, 1870–1915* (Cambridge, Mass., 1971), and has edited an excellent collection with NORTON GRUBB on *American Education and Vocationalism: A Documentary History* (New York, 1974). CALVIN M. WOODWARD, *The Manual Training School* (Boston, 1887), remains the central document.

CHAPTER 8

The Rise of the University: Special Education at the Top

THE FOUNDING AND RAPID EXPANSION OF THE UNIVERSITY IN THE UNITED States in the last third of the nineteenth century is best seen as another aspect of this abandonment of the principle of universal common schooling as the favored solution to America's social problems. Universities embodied principles of specialization and expertise quite different from those which characterized the colleges founded earlier in the nineteenth century, providing, in effect, special education at the top. The original spirit of the university revolution was a response to the failure of mass education in the nineteenth century. Solutions to the grave social problem faced by the United States were beyond the ability, perhaps even the inclination, of the common man. A concentrated effort was necessary, many argued, to train leaders capable of guiding the nation and its people toward proper social goals. The universities, with a curriculum different from that of the antebellum college and a new commitment to the creation and dissemination of research, were to provide the training and knowledge for the formation of such a leadership group.

The "rise of the universities" in the United States dates from the founding of Cornell in 1868, the beginning of Harvard's conversion in 1869 from a college to a research university under Charles William Eliot,

227

and the founding of Johns Hopkins in 1876. The pace of university growth accelerated rapidly in the 1890s with the founding of Stanford (1891) and the University of Chicago (1892) and the dedication of several major land grant institutions, such as Wisconsin, Michigan, and California, to the university ideal. The new universities differed from their collegiate predecessors in several ways. Universities allowed students to elect from an ever widening curriculum those courses which they wished to take; they offered the new teacher-scholars who filled their faculties free time and resources to conduct research which only indirectly affected the students in the university; and they based their faculty members' salary and promotion as much on scholarly research, on their "contribution to knowledge," as on their abilities as classroom instructors. The university's most distinct institutional development was the academic graduate school, with its program leading to the Ph.D., which established scholarly research as a full-time vocation.

These institutional features of the university reflected a purpose and spirit far different from that which had prevailed among antebellum colleges and academies. Universities were more explicitly elitist: they sought to train a more select group for more crucial and more complicated roles in society than had earlier institutions of higher learning. They came to emphasize intellectual rather than social or cultural preparation; thus the content of their curriculum was more important to the function of the universities than it had been in the antebellum institutions. Whereas the college's extracurriculum probably influenced students more than the formal curriculum, the universities sought to make academic coursework the central experience of the student. Universities took a more national view of their task than had the antebellum colleges and academies; they were preparing national, rather than local, leaders. They placed more emphasis on inculcating a sense of social duty and responsibility in their students: the role of the educated man was to further the public welfare—as a statesman, businessman, or research chemist. Concurrently, they placed less emphasis than had academies and colleges on the personal advantages associated with higher education, less stress on higher education's possible contributions to personal mobility and success. The nature of the antebellum institutions was also much more religious than was that of the university. Differences in purpose, structure, and function distinguished the two kinds of institutions. In their rhetoric and in the authority of their ideal, universities reflected their intimate concern for the improvement of society in the United States. This set them apart from earlier institutions of higher education which had lain manifestly outside of the sweeping educational reform effort of their era—the antebellum common school movement.

The rise of the university in no way diminished the momentum of college founding in the late nineteenth and early twentieth centuries.

Communities and religious groups continued, just as they had in the antebellum period, to found small liberal arts colleges throughout the nation (indeed, religious groups were more involved in college founding late in the century than they had been earlier). State and local governments followed the trend. Hundreds of public colleges were founded after the Civil War; although many of these institutions adopted the title of university from the very beginning, they resembled the small private colleges much more than they resembled Harvard, Johns Hopkins, or Columbia or, after 1890, major state universities like those in Michigan or Wisconsin. With a law or medical school attached, these schools technically held university status, but they perpetuated for many years after their founding the narrow classical curriculum of the college. Because they were established in areas where there were no public high schools, many were forced in their early years to concentrate on offering high school training and consequently to neglect collegiate education.

Only after the turn of the century did some of the more prestigious public and private colleges gradually bring their curricula more in line with that found in the universities. In emulating the university, colleges relaxed discipline somewhat, granted students a wider choice of studies, and encouraged innovative classroom methods. Not until the beginning of this century did public institutions begin in large numbers to resemble the modern state and municipal universities with their vast array of courses, their variety of undergraduate programs leading to any number of different vocations, their applied research stations and laboratories where scholars worked directly on regional economic and public welfare problems, and their facilities for pure research. The American university, between 1860 and 1920, was definitely a minority institution, one that in a numerical sense at least was a mere sidelight to the vast expansion of higher education in that period. Until well into the twentieth century most students enrolled in higher education in the United States attended colleges rather than universities. Yet the university, almost from its beginnings in the 1870s, became the pace setter in higher education. Although it enrolled many fewer students, it quickly outshone the college in terms of public attention and respect.

In this chapter we will be concerned almost exclusively with describing that university spirit and the reasons it took hold in the United States in the late nineteenth century. This focus will inevitably exclude our discussing a great number of important facets of higher education. We will examine the motivations of those who organized the universities and joined their faculties; we will not talk about the majority of their students or the parents who sent them. We will describe the few very best universities to the neglect of the hundreds of other institutions of higher education that claimed university status. We will not discuss the beginnings of vocational and professional training in higher education, except in the case of professional scholarship. These are important topics, but we have chosen our focus because we think it most important to understand how the emerging university defined its peculiar relation to society—as an institution that influenced society while remaining isolated from social conflict. This understanding, we believe, will best help the reader comprehend the universities' response to the complaints and the new demands that have been emanating from students and from society since 1964. There is another topic relating to universities before 1920 that we would have liked to have pursued as it too would greatly increase our understanding of the current university crisis. But how a democratic society reacted to the elitist claims of the university organizers or whether that society heard them at all are questions yet unexplored by historians. We hope that our discussion of the motives of university reformers will inspire others to explore that other side of the question: What did a democratic society think it would receive in return for its relatively lavish support of universities?

I

The 1840s, 1850s, and early 1860s saw a good deal of rhetoric and some significant actions in behalf of making higher education more flexible and more relevant or practical. Francis Wayland, while president of Brown, called for a more practical collegiate curriculum (one supposedly more attractive to potential students); several universities founded engineering and scientific schools in the 1840s and 1850s; and in 1862 the Morrill Act granted public lands to each state for the support of higher instruction in the military, mechanical, and agricultural arts. Although some have seen university reform after the Civil War as an extension and culmination of those prewar reform efforts, the university reform movement that began in the late 1860s differed fundamentally from those antebellum efforts. It was elitist; the earlier reforms aimed, instead, at broadening the appeal of higher education to reach everyone—at including, in effect, colleges in the common school movement. Thus Wayland and the supporters of the Morrill Act favored curricula appropriate to future farmers, mechanics, and workingmen. Even the great scientific schools at Yale (Sheffield) and Harvard (Lawrence) had been originally endowed as training schools for future engineers and practical geologists, meant for students without the preparation in the classical languages characteristic of children of socially eminent families. These intentions, however, only briefly delayed the scientific schools' evolution into pure scientific research institutions and the land grant colleges' development into liberal arts colleges.

The motives of these prewar reformers were, of course, mixed. Wayland's proposals grew almost certainly from his desire to attract a wider paying public to colleges like Brown. Those favoring the Morrill Act—which lacked widespread support among those for whom it was intended and became law only because of freakish legislative logrolling and senatorial disinterest—felt that farmers and mechanics in a democracy should have all the facilities and resources accessible to the wealthy. If the rich possessed facilities for higher education, it was the state's duty to provide them for the rest of the society. Many believed that higher education in the scientific and practical arts would improve worker efficiency and thus contribute to the economic growth and prosperity of the United States. Like the common school reformers, they seemed more confident that mass higher education would assure progress than they were clear as to the process by which it would do so. Almost none of these reformers displayed the motive that was primary for most of the university reformers after the Civil War: that improved higher education would better prepare society's elite leaders for their social responsibilities.

University reform after 1860 was not an extension of the common school movement but a product of the disillusion with antebellum reformist ideals among a significant portion of America's social elite. The men and women who directed and financed this reform, especially before 1890, were members of elite families, traditionally centered on the eastern seaboard, whose power and authority had peaked during the late antebellum decades. Since their families had comprised the prewar "establishment," their descendants thought that by right they should play a large role in the nation's politics. In fact, however, because they had lost power and could not match the enormous wealth accumulated by the newly rich in the late nineteenth century, they were, as their bitter and pessimistic reminiscences indicate, politically impotent. They constitute a difficult group to define; indeed, one of their interests in the university was its potential for helping them to define a profitable role for themselves in American society. One such role they discovered was that of cultivated custodians of virtue and responsibility in a country barbaric enough to reject their political leadership. They promoted universities, along with museums and public libraries, to help them protect and nurture the "best" in the United States. While they were very unrepresentative of the population at large, they believed that their actions were always in the best interests of the majority even though the majority may not have understood that to be the case.

While many of their forebears had ardently supported common school reform as a means of bettering the nation, these men and women had lost faith in mass public schooling's ability to alleviate the nation's troubles. When they considered educational reform at the lower levels

at all, they advocated various forms of special education—industrial training, kindergartens, reform schools, and the like. There were four principal causes of their disillusion. First, university reformers as much as any
group in society were discouraged by the common school crusade's manifest inability to solve the social problems over which the Civil War was
fought. Many of these elite families had contributed to the massive relief
effort, the results of which appeared uniformly negative—conflict within
the South and the desperate position of the blacks had worsened over
the reconstruction decade. Second, the reformers felt that, in spite of the
common school's promises to elevate the political virtue and competence
of the American people, national politics had deteriorated markedly in
tone and honesty. University reformers shared Henry Adams' difficulty
in equating evolution with progress when he recalled that Grant was
president after Washington. Overt dishonesty, like the infamous Crédit
Mobilier scandal, exposed during the Grant administration, was rampant
at the national, state, and local levels. University supporters were particularly outraged at the many "immoral," if perfectly legal, policies of the
postwar governments. It was dishonest, they fumed, for the Grant administration to maintain a high tariff and soft money after wartime conditions of financial crisis had evaporated. Catering to the interests of iron-
masters, farmers, and labor—common policy among supposedly
upstanding politicians as well as among demagogues—was disreputable.
The spoils system in government, where with every political victory
competent civil servants were turned out in favor of loyal party members,
whether competent or not, was, for these reformers, the crowning disgrace. Despite the promises of common school reformers that mass public schooling would eliminate these manifestations of demagogy and self-
interest, the practice worsened. A third, related cause of disillusion was
the reformers' perception that the quality of urban life and politics was
growing worse. Social distance within the burgeoning cities was growing;
immigration, temporarily slowed by the Civil War, had reaccelerated, and
as the century closed an increasing number of immigrants came from the
swarthy "races" of southern and eastern Europe—Italians, Portuguese,
Poles, Slavs, Croats, and Russian Jews, peoples whose appearance, habits, and language made them even more "alien" than the Irish. The votes
of these immigrants constituted the balance of power in many cities.
Repeated evidence of political corruption like that revealed in the exposé
of the Tweed Ring in New York City in the early 1870s shattered their
hopes for purified politics and a stable community. The machinations of
Tweed, first of the famous urban bosses, revealed a typical and dangerous
urban pattern. William Marcy Tweed (1823–1878), who bilked the taxpayers of New York of millions of dollars on construction project rakeoffs
and licensing fee kickbacks, stayed in office because he successfully organized—mostly through bribes, Tweed's enemies thought—the support

of the poor and the immigrant voters (men who paid few taxes, the elites noted). The fourth source of disillusion was the growth of irresponsible economic power in the United States. Antebellum businessmen, so the story went, had consciously served the public interest in an honest and forthright manner. After the Civil War a new kind of entrepreneur—denounced as "robber barons" by one spokesman of disillusion—emerged, one who was quite willing to increase his wealth by defrauding the investing and consuming public with watered stock and shoddy merchandise and services. The picture drawn by Henry and Charles Francis Adams of the fraudulent dealings of Cornelius Vanderbilt, Jim Fisk, and Jay Gould in *A Chapter of Erie* (1869) deeply disturbed men who thought that the possession of wealth brought, concomitantly, great social responsibilities. Even worse, these robber barons had the effrontery to squander their ill-gotten wealth on lavish and tasteless personal luxuries rather than using their money to cultivate the arts or to support worthy social causes.

The fact that the generation of 1870 viewed the world of their fathers as a golden age, from which they and their society had been evicted, heightened the contrast they saw between the eras.[1] The antebellum social cohesion had broken down by the mid-1860s and was replaced with a gilded age of economic individualism and political dishonesty, a world in which special interests fought without thought of the general welfare. The decline in cohesion and morality suggested to them that the antebellum reform effort which had sought to extend and strengthen that cohesion and morality had been misdirected. The misery of the blacks' condition had been reduced only slightly since the height of abolitionist enthusiasm, and the same rebellious men continued to control southern society. Urban immigrants were still Catholic, poor, and intemperate. Extending the suffrage had only encouraged political demagoguery and corruption, a declension in public virtue which culminated in the success of the urban boss. Economic growth had led only to the triumph of vulgar wealth. The faith that they had shared that diffusing education among the masses would preserve the good society was shattered. In the postwar period they looked elsewhere for the instruments that would restore the positive characteristics which they thought had pervaded pre-1840 America.

Charles Eliot Norton (1827–1908), Boston Brahmin, esthete, Dante scholar, Harvard professor, art critic, one of Ruskin's most prominent

---

[1] It is difficult from our perspective to judge whether conditions after the Civil War were worse than they had been at the height of the common school movement. Our estimation must rely largely on documents, journalism, and contemporary historical accounts written by the very people who were most disillusioned after the war. Their bitterness at being excluded from the seats of authority to which they thought they were entitled could not but jaundice their assessment of their society.

American followers, and (he hoped) taste setter for the American public, typifies the kind of person who found university reform so appealing after the Civil War. His progress from reformer of the masses to reformer of the elite illustrates perfectly the process which led so many of the early university reformers to see university training as the key vehicle of reform.

Son of Andrews Norton (who was sometimes referred to as the "Unitarian Pope"), Charles Eliot Norton moved in the highest circles of Boston and Cambridge society at an early age. His father shaped the opinion of the social and political leaders of eastern New England. Charles felt no call to the ministry and instead, after college, started out in the 1840s as a merchant in a counting house. He soon discovered that this career was not satisfying and, although he kept his position for some years, his interests turned elsewhere. Soon after leaving college he started a night school for working children in Boston. He worried about poverty and its effect on people's character. This concern led him to support a drive to build model lodging houses for the poor (these tenements, built by private philanthropy, were to be light, sanitary, airy, and cheap). "The character of the population depends," he wrote in 1852, "upon the nature of its habitations." Squalid housing encouraged viciousness; therefore, both humanitarianism and self-interest demanded that the wealthy work to improve the living conditions of the poor. Although he did not play a central role in the common school reform movement, Norton argued for the extension of free schooling to the poor in much the same terms as did Mann. He believed that a comprehensive system of public education and philanthropic investment in good housing would, by altering the environment of the poor, solve many of the impending social problems in the United States.

Norton believed that slavery was morally wrong and supported its abolition, but he did not believe that blacks deserved a place equal to that of whites in the United States. When the conflict over slavery erupted into civil war, Norton delighted in war's capacity to prove that Americans were men of strong character: "We shall come out of this war with . . . new reason for trust in the political instincts and intentions of an instructed and intelligent people. We shall have given proof of the possession by a free popular government of those very qualities which it has been erroneously supposed such a government was incapable of exhibiting."[2] War inspired Norton's pride in the masses and augmented his confidence about the future of democracy. It had shown that the mass of Americans could support a moral principle like the opposition to slavery, Norton argued. (He was probably mistaken; most Americans

[2] Kermit Vanderbilt, *Charles Eliot Norton: Apostle of Culture in a Democracy* (Cambridge, Mass., 1959), 39, 67.

seem to have supported the war to preserve the union and not to abolish slavery.) Furthermore, war submerged individualism in collective action, something Norton always favored. "The little value of the individual in comparison with the principles upon which the progress and happiness of the race depend is a lesson enforced by the analogies of Nature, as well as by the evidence of history and the assurance of faith," he wrote. "Men are nothing in the count;—man is everything."[3] Death in war was man's noblest role. Norton, however, did not join the army; instead, he started a propaganda agency which distributed prowar and Union pamphlets nationwide.

In 1865 Norton helped to organize the New York *Nation,* a weekly journal of opinion founded to uphold the principles of honest government, social unity, and a just fate for the freedman. The *Nation* and the *North American Review,* of which Norton was an editor at times, would become the journalistic outlets for the university supporters in the years ahead. "The *Nation* and Harvard and Yale College seem to me almost the only solid barriers against the invasion of modern barbarism and vulgarity," Norton wrote.[4] At the beginning these journals supported efforts to extend full rights of citizenship to the freedmen and hoped that the ideas and principles they published would guide the public policy makers. Norton expected the public to follow this guidance. In 1867 Norton could still argue that compulsory education was an "indispensable foundation and safeguard of a system of universal suffrage."[5] But Norton and journals like the *Nation* soon soured on the prospects of democracy and civil rights for the freedmen. The problem of establishing a just place for the black while reconstructing the nation seemed intractable, producing only continued instability and national conflict on all sides. Evening schools, public education, and model housing were not, it turned out, improving the character of the poor and the immigrant. The American people who had risen so magnificently to the challenge of war were now supporting Grant and Tweed. Society was hurtling toward destruction or toward radical revolution—neither prospect was welcome to Norton. The *Nation* and its contributors turned from their early optimistic stance toward an elitist and carping position that concentrated on criticizing governmental and business corruption, immorality, irrationality, and failure to follow the guidance of scholarly findings and principles. They lodged their hopes for improvement in the universities and in civil service reform.

[3] Charles Eliot Norton, "The Advantages of Defeat," *Atlantic,* VIII (September, 1861), 363–364.

[4] Charles Eliot Norton to Edwin L. Godkin (3 November, 1871), quoted in Ari Hoogenboom, *Outlawing the Spoils: A History of the Civil Service Reform Movement, 1865–1883* (Urbana, Ill., 1961), 99.

[5] Charles Eliot Norton, "Compulsory Education," *Nation,* V (5 September, 1867), 192.

Norton explained postwar social deterioration in terms that clarify why men of his beliefs thought universities so vital. The worst feature about the United States after the war, he claimed, was that the rich and well born just watched the approach of society's impending destruction without exercising their responsibility to direct society in more constructive ways. Universities were important because the wealthy elite needed education, "in its nature moral,—an education in social duties, and in that enlightened self-interest which sees its advantage, not in a selfish accumulation of wealth regardless of the claims of those who assist in its production, but in such a division of profits as should raise the general standard of comfort." Norton concluded that "unless the ruling classes, upon whom rests the responsibility for remedial effort, are aroused from their selfish inactivity to a new sense of duty and to new exertions, no prophet is needed to foretell the approaching overthrow of social order."[6] Norton, like so many others of his class, turned to the reformation of collegiate education in an effort to make the rich act in accordance with their social duties, to take an interest in the social welfare of all rather than in their personal self-interest, to respect and preserve the traditional moral and cultural values that they were so seriously neglecting. Only in this way would the nation's social crisis be resolved. Efforts at mass reform would forever be ineffective if the quality of the country's leadership were not improved. The creation of better leadership rather than the reform of the commoners seemed the only means of effectively rescuing the American experiment from demagoguery, corruption, and selfishness. Reform depended more on improving the elite than on reforming the masses.

Men like Norton turned to university training to reform the elite with the expectation that the new elite would restore their country's former virtues. They thought the university would train a new generation of leaders who would recognize their social duties, who would know how and would want to act morally, and who would eschew economic individualism. They hoped also that university training would give students the tools with which to regain the legitimate power of their class and to use it effectively.

The initial function of the university was to impress upon a new generation of upper-class youths (and those aspiring to become upper class) their responsibilities to redirect American society. Students fortunate enough to receive the privilege of university training were obligated to use their disciplined skills in the advancement of society. University reformers were convinced that antebellum society had been shepherded by men committed to social and civic responsibility. They recalled, per-

---

[6] Charles Eliot Norton, "Poverty in England," *North American Review*, CIX (July, 1869), 153–154.

haps too naïvely, that the masses had deferred to these responsible leaders. With the passing of that era, the United States was now without leaders who placed the interests of society ahead of their own personal ambitions. University reformers came to blame the kind of training given in antebellum colleges for the present dearth of responsibility among the elite. Charles Francis Adams (1807–1886), ambassador to England during the Civil War, president of Harvard's highest governing body, and an ardent supporter of university reform, thought Harvard's emphasis on classical languages during his matriculation in the 1820s had failed to prepare him to earn the power to which he believed a man of his political lineage was entitled. Since the revolutionary period, Harvard had been contributing less and less to forming a responsible leadership class. While society had changed, Harvard had not altered the training it offered the sons of America's elite, and the elite had lost control. The historian Francis Parkman, another ardent supporter of reform at Harvard, made a similar point. Harvard's classical emphasis had been irrelevant even in the antebellum period, he thought. "The most finished and altogether favorable example of that devitalized scholarship, with many graceful additions," Parkman noted, "was Edward Everett [a Senator from Massachusetts and president of Harvard from 1840 to 1849], and its echoes may still be heard in the halls of Congress, perplexing Western members with Latin quotations, profuse, if not always correct." College men, according to Parkman, were "void of blood, bone, sinew, muscle, and marrow." Harvard must change her curriculum and become a university so that it could train young men to participate in crucial issues or, in Adams' words, "to take efficient part in the treatment of difficult questions connected with the management of public affairs."[7]

There were, of course, many other motives that caused people to support universities and to enter university work. Some wealthy men with pet projects financed universities in order to encourage research on a favorite topic—wealthy Jews funded the development of Semitic studies, for example. Others, particularly the late-nineteenth-century nouveaux riches, sponsored a number of institutional innovations because the association of their name with a university as a donor would improve their public image as stewards of wealth. Other businessmen contributed to universities because they realized that the scientific research carried on there promised direct and indirect benefits to industrial growth: advances in geology made the search for minerals more efficient and discoveries in chemistry suggested whole new arrays of products that American industry could market. But the initial funding of universities was more likely to have come from men, like those we have described, who were disillu-

---

[7] Francis Parkman, "The Tale of the 'Ripe Scholar,'" *Nation*, IX (23 December, 1869), 558–560; and Parkman, "The Failure of Universal Suffrage," *North American Review*, CXXVII (July-August, 1878), 1–20.

sioned with their country's condition and with previous attempts to rectify that situation. They established a pattern that later contributors would follow for a host of other reasons.

The motives of those who worked and studied in the universities were also mixed. Many, as we have suggested, entered the university in order to improve their society and to define a role for themselves. Others entered for the simple love of the work; many scholars' devotion to their research in history or philology or physics needed no ulterior motive. As Donald Fleming has maintained, many entered the universities—especially once it became clear that research and teaching offered a lifelong career—because there one could stand apart from the corruption of the gilded age, from the pressure to accumulate material things in a materialistic culture, and devote oneself to a calling that served mankind. In the university one could put aside the aggressiveness, vulgarity, and materialism of American culture and join a small group of like-minded men in cultivating civilized values in literature and learning. But, again, the pacesetting scholars and university administrators were those who entered this new setting intent upon molding it so that it would facilitate their efforts to improve society.

II

Supporters of the university thought that extensive curricular and pedagogical reform could improve and elevate the educational preparation of America's leaders. The colleges were inadequate to the task because their classical curricula had been too impractical, as well as too easy and superficial. The classical curriculum was impractical, not because it failed to train men for vocational roles, a function that did not concern the reformers, but because it failed to transmit either the kind of mental discipline or the kind of information needed by leaders in the late nineteenth century. When reformers set out to build a curriculum relevant to their ideals of leadership, political economy, political science, and history were obvious choices; engineering was also critical because so much government business was concerned with public works and the need for trained engineers in an industrializing economy was greater each year. Modern languages equipped men for economic and diplomatic contact with other nations. All the sciences had relevance in an industrialized nation with vast resources to be exploited. As important as the specific information transmitted by a subject, however, was the method of inquiry employed in it. The reformers of the last third of the century did not repudiate the Yale Report of 1828 in its entirety. Training the mind was just as important for them as it had been for the Yale professors. But the reformers argued that memorization of languages and mathematical formulae was no longer appropriate to training the society's elite. Leaders needed to know how to search out answers to their problems, and they had to learn to judge public questions by weighing evidence. Future leaders had to be introduced in the university to a method of problem solving which could be applied to political, economic, and social issues they would encounter after graduation. For this, the methods of scientific research were ideal. Happily, university reformers believed in the "transfer of training," a process whereby the discipline acquired in research in one subject could be applied to other subjects without additional training. Researchers in any field learned to weigh and to judge conflicting evidence, to separate the true from the fraudulent, the important from the accidental, and build upon facts toward a solution. These seemed vital skills for future public leaders.

Scientific research had another virtue. For a generation that believed, so seriously and so naïvely, that science was completely objective, scientific research seemed an ideal way of cutting through the conflicting passions and self interests which surrounded most critical public questions to reach an impartial agreement. Solutions for difficult questions would no longer require indecent compromise or political logrolling; research would contribute the true answer, to which all would agree simply because objective scientific assessment identified it as the correct alternative. Reformers assumed that there was a right way to do everything in the public sphere—to organize the economy, to set tariff barriers, to develop natural resources, to balance the claims of capital and labor, to control the currency. This "right way" was unrelated to self-interest —both labor and capital would agree that their conflicting interests would be served best by the "right" solution. Truth and the right way of doing things were independent of opinion; they were something which men, through disciplined inquiry, could discover and apply to the control of social change. Reformers believed that scientific, controlled, impersonal research would reveal the truth and, in their more optimistic moods, understood that once it was found and its validity recognized, it would be implemented immediately because the persuasiveness of the truth would be overwhelming.

The reformers were convinced that public officials should emulate the researcher's commitment to placing the pursuit of truth ahead of personal welfare, his respect for facts rather than opinion, his devotion to constant inquiry in the search for better methods and worthy solutions. Because they believed in the transfer of training, the reformers felt that study of any of the liberal arts or sciences prepared men for public responsibility so long, that is, as students were expected to do research in the subject rather than to memorize a predigested textbook. The entire university curriculum trained students for leadership positions because the intellectual habits of the research philosopher, philologist, and physicist were the same ones the statesman who thought for himself should use.

A second means of improving the curriculum was to make it deeper and more difficult than that of the antebellum colleges. Most universities used some form of the elective system to accomplish these ends. Some universities offered entering students the opportunity to choose among a variety of programs, many of which were vocationally oriented. The courses within each program, however, were rigidly prescribed. Many universities offered one or two years of prescribed studies and an upper division program of electives. Some developed a major and a minor system in which students had to concentrate a portion of their elections in one or two departments. At the extreme Harvard's system of totally free election allowed all students to choose any courses they wished, and in any order they wished, subject only to departmental prerequisites (i.e., a student had to take introductory economics before he could enroll in an advanced course). The elective system, in whatever guise it appeared, offered a variety of advantages to the university reformers. The increase of knowledge in the nineteenth century had severely strained the traditional, prescribed college curriculum where every student completed every course offered. Originally the prescribed college curriculum had been limited to a few basic subjects, but as colleges in the nineteenth century sought, for whatever serious or superficial reasons, to keep pace with the explosion of knowledge, students encountered ten, twelve, fifteen different subjects each year. Students sat through recitations in chemistry and modern history, geology, mental philosophy, political economy, physiology and health, and the United States Constitution, as well as in the traditional classical languages, rhetoric, and mathematics. It was impossible to pursue any subject in depth and students were exposed to only a superficial smattering in any one of them. Yet the reformers wanted to include even more subjects in the curriculum. Under the fully prescribed system, each time an extra hour per week of political economy was included in the curriculum, one less hour could be devoted to some other subject. Such tradeoffs were always a difficult business, and they created great bitterness within faculties and retarded the progress of reform significantly.

The elective system solved these problems by removing the responsibility for collegiate scheduling from the faculty and administration and allowing each student to tailor his own program. Once it was decided that every student did not have to take every course that the college or university offered, new subjects and advanced courses could be added to the curriculum without having to eliminate other courses. It also meant that more intensive and specialized courses in a subject could be offered, for it was now possible for a student to abandon one subject entirely and enroll in several courses in another. The reformers encouraged students to follow just this procedure for, in pursuing a subject in depth, the student came closest to emulating the researcher. The elective system gradually allowed university administrators and faculty members to build the curriculum into a series of disciplinary courses that progressed in scope and in difficulty from the introductory to the most advanced, with advanced coursework introducing students to the methods and fruits of scholarly research. Graduate schools, an important part of the university reform movement, were based entirely on this principle—that the methodology of scholarly inquiry was as important as the informational content of a subject. Students were to learn this method by working closely, either in the laboratory or in the seminar, with an advanced scholar in their field. The content of undergraduate and master's work was necessarily less specialized, but universities tried to insure that everyone being prepared for leadership positions would gain some experience in the scientific research method at an advanced level. (In the late nineteenth century, the scientific method was used in all subjects, even the humanities. The analyst of Greek syntax and the physicist were both "scientists.")

Despite the reformers' ideal, not all undergraduates chose contact with ongoing research. Free election was just that, and undergraduates had a perplexing tendency to stick with the easiest and least demanding survey courses rather than to venture into the advanced courses. This accounts for the increasingly popular requirement of "majors and minors," or disciplinary concentrations. A favorite among university administrators and faculty members after the turn of the century, these systems virtually forced the undergraduate to pursue some subject in depth. But significant numbers of undergraduates and, of course, all graduate students did make use of the advantages that election offered. They took advanced courses in which they acquired information and, more importantly, trained their minds in the methodology of seeking out right answers. There was virulent opposition to the elective system among college professors and administrators who favored retaining control over their students' studies and who feared the effect of student choice on the popularity of their own courses and subjects. This opposition merely retarded the change; it did not stop it. Election became very popular among students and, indeed, became the prevailing symbol of university reform. Free election was commonly associated with democracy; but in fact it was a strategy of intensifying the education of the elite for leadership positions in their society.

University and college reformers shared with preparatory school founders another effort to insure that the experience of higher education would strengthen the character of the children of the rich—an education which would rouse them from what Norton called their "selfish inactivity." The rich were too lazy, too soft, too selfish, too irresponsible to carry out their social duties, the reformers thought. Their educational experience should rectify these deficiencies. Prep schools, founded for the sons of the urban rich, sought through their cloistered grounds, their somewhat spartan life styles and imitation gothic chapels, to overcome the corrosive influences of a childhood spent amidst urban luxury and vice. They sought to redirect their boys' tastes from the material to the spiritual, and toward fulfillment through social service. Schoolmasters and college administrators promoted team sports among their charges —among these young men they celebrated the spirit of cooperation (individual sports like tennis were denounced as selfish). Students exercised and had to prove their strength, stamina, and ability to endure hardship. University faculties and administrators were less enthusiastic about undergraduate devotion to team sports, but many of the universities' financial supporters thought that through their endorsement of organized athletics they were supporting "manly" and "strenuous life" ideals, standards which they expected future leaders to adopt.

Requiring young men to accept responsibility for their actions while attending the universities was also thought an important device for building character. The elective system, for example, taught responsibility by forcing it upon the students. The late nineteenth century witnessed, along with the introduction of the elective system, the overall reduction of restrictions placed by institutions of higher learning on their students' intellectual, moral, and social life. Students were given more free time, and their social life within the university became almost totally unsupervised. Usually living in or near large cities, male university students were expected to learn responsibility by moving freely within that environment. One task of the university was thought to involve the introduction of students to adult responsibility and independence rather than the prolongation of adolescent dependencies. Such training would prepare them to serve society as leaders.

III

The university had originally committed itself to support scientific research as part of its program to train future leaders in the methods of analysis they would need in the public decision-making processes. Within a generation or so the priorities had changed. Scientific research, rather than training, seemed the primary object of the university. Numerically, of course, training remained the principal task: universities have always trained more people intent upon working in the outside world than they have people expecting to pursue careers in conducting and teaching research. Yet, by the turn of this century, the rhetoric of the university builders came to stress research above training; the popular mind associated universities with scientific research rather than with the preparation of public servants. This transition occurred for many complex reasons and the process is not wholly understood at this time.

One source of this change was the elective system. By allowing the curriculum to fragment into more and more courses, it encouraged specialization among university teachers. Professors, no longer bound to introductory level courses, pursued narrower and more specialized subjects in their advanced courses. Soon the ability to specialize became as essential to success in college teaching as the ability to master the breadth of a subject. And specialization required research to sustain it. The specialization of courses under the elective system also led to a vast expansion of faculties, an expansion that far outstripped the dilation of the student body. Each special subject required at least one faculty member who specialized in only that subject area. Universities could not expect one man to teach all its courses in science and mathematics or in philosophy, political economy, and history as liberal arts colleges had done and continued to do. It would be too cynical to argue that research was a task created to keep these specialized teachers busy during their many hours out of the classroom, but surely the rapidity with which research became a major component of university business suggests that faculties and administrators alike were seeking justification for faculty expansion by widening the duties of the professor from merely teaching to a combination of teaching and research. In the early years of the university movement, faculty members had to fight their administrators to get free time and research equipment. As a slowly rising number of students was spread over a vastly increasing number of courses, however, faculty members found that they had some free time and that they had to claim research as a justification for their lightened teaching loads.

The most important reason for the shift from training to research in rhetoric supporting the American university was that research, rather than training, promised to be the most effective means by which the reformers who supported the university revolution could hope to affect social progress. In the nineteenth century the universities failed to establish an association between the training they gave and access to public power. The original university reformers possessed no well-developed theory of how they expected the trained elite to gain power in a democracy. The reformers refused to condone seeking power by soliciting popular favor. Such efforts were certain to destroy a man's independence and his capacity to lead as his knowledge and conscience dictated, for elective office required men to submit to the discipline of political parties. It required a man to act as his constituents wished rather than as he knew he should act, leading him into all sorts of corrupt bargains. The reformers believed that university-trained men should be chosen for responsible positions because they were more knowledgeable about a problem or were more honest in their judgments than were those without such training. They should be chosen because of their competence, of the expertise which they had acquired at the university. The elitist nature of the university reformers, most of whom were political independents, led them to argue that many functions then handled by elected officials should be turned over to the administration of appointed officials and brought to the attention of appointed commissions. Appointed officials and commissions, they reasoned, would be independent of party and therefore exempt from the workings of the spoils system.

The reformers called this process "taking the question out of politics." By this they meant that the question involved—a municipal sewage disposal system or a pure food and drug law—would no longer be subject to party conflict or political logrolling but, instead, would be decided or administered on its own merits. It would be decided by those with scientific knowledge of the problems and with minds trained to make fair detached judgments of complex issues. Such men were trained in universities. Although the movement to remove questions from politics was honestly concerned with improving the administration of public services, there was also an underlying desire to reduce the power of the mass of voters, whom the university reformers did not trust. They sought, instead, to increase the power over public affairs of those who, like themselves, had been trained in the universities. They advocated civil service reform for similar reasons. In setting up criteria of competence that had to be met before a person could receive an appointive public office, they hoped to restrict access to government power to people who shared their values and interests.

In neither case were the university reformers' hopes substantially fulfilled until the mid-twentieth century. "Taking the question out of politics" became a fairly popular activity but it was found that most independent commissions perpetuated political conflict in other contexts, and that the bulk of the commission members were not university-trained experts but politicians and representatives of special interest groups. Civil service reform in the nineteenth century was almost totally restricted to lower level positions for which university graduates were greatly overqualified. As the twentieth century has progressed, however, the reformers have been proven prescient. Governments—national, state, and local—have come to rely more and more on university-trained and university-based experts to guide their decisions. Appointive positions within the government have expanded far more rapidly than have elective positions and, while any man or woman has a chance to be elected, only those with university credentials are eligible for most high-level appointive offices.

The university reformers' difficulties in gaining access to power for university-trained personnel account in part for the tremendous interest of the American reformers in the German university of the mid-nineteenth century. Germany was the home of the first great modern universities and the scientific, philological, historical, and philosophical research conducted there made famous names like Berlin, Heidelberg, and Göttingen. Rather than listening to textbook recitations, German professors lectured to their students. In Germany, students actually worked on their own laboratory experiments and library research, and in seminars illustrious professors transmitted their religious commitment to research and their extensive knowledge of their sources. But what impressed the early reformers most was the close and established relationship between the universities and the German state. Civil service appointments and rights to professional practice were restricted to holders of university degrees. Futhermore, the German government continually solicited from university faculty members advice on political matters of all kinds. Professors, who were technically employees of the state, contributed recommendations on issues such as social insurance, governmental regulations, or the feasibility of industrial research. American university reformers ignored the possible problems associated with such a compromising relationship between university and government. They neglected to consider the restrictions it placed on freedom of inquiry within the university and the narrowness of the training that candidates for various branches of the civil service were required to endure. They dwelt instead on the advantages of university-government cooperation and on its guarantee that scientific methods and university training would affect public policy.

The United States was not Germany. Men trained in the university to apply objective scientific analysis to public affairs found their services in slight demand in the real world of politics. Many found that the university itself was the only place that truly valued objectivity, the commitment to truth, and the discipline of careful research. A number of these men returned to the university to make it their life's career. They did not surrender their desire to affect social progress but hoped to do so through the research they conducted at the university. That the ideas coming out of the universities were going to affect public policy had always been part of the reformers' plans. Originally, however, they had expected those ideas to make their largest impact through students who would carry them from the university into places of great public responsibility. By the end of the century the situation was reversed. The research activities of the university were to affect public affairs directly and its teaching was to affect public affairs only indirectly.

Universities switched from primary emphasis on teaching a method of finding truth to large numbers of potential leaders to an emphasis on finding truth itself and to transmitting those findings directly to the public or, even better, to those in power who could quickly implement any changes suggested by those results. University reformers found that the spirit of scientific research—its objectivity and insulation from self-interest—did not seem to survive outside the academy or to affect the quality or honesty of public debate. The reformers found instead that, whenever scientific advance was to be expected, research would have to be conducted within the university by scholars who felt themselves completely isolated and free from the pressures of self-interest and popular opinion. They found that implementing the university ideal of improving the quality and direction of American politics was possible only by exporting the findings of university researchers to the larger public. It was futile to attempt to teach everyone, or even responsible politicians, to approach public issues as did scientific researchers.

The increasingly popular portrait of the university was of an institution within which disinterested discussion and debate over public issues was undertaken with the results transmitted outside the university for the society to implement. Universities arrogated the role of guiding society and came to deemphasize their earlier purpose of training leaders. Disinterested, objective scientific research provided the method with which all deliberation of public issues should be approached. Only that method would lead to proper results, to society's adoption of the correct policies. Since universities specialized in this research in the theoretical arts and sciences, it was logical, the argument went, for these institutions to conduct research on applied issues, and to circulate their conclusions and recommendations for the society to follow.

Such an arrogation of power was probably an inevitable result of the original reformers' ideal of the university as the place where people could learn to guide society by appearing to shed all self-interest and by adopting an objective scientific stance. People in universities thought more and more that these characteristics described them more accurately than the people they trained to govern society and gradually came to think that they themselves had the major leadership role (that the society had not been completely willing to accept their claims to leadership any more than it accepted those of the university-trained elite of the earlier generation has been a source of much frustration). But they saw it as a peculiar kind of leadership—its authority based not on personality or might or size of constituency but on their scientific access to truth. University people had an access, through research, to truth that no one else had in the society. This self-concept, long a part of university tradition in this country, accounts for the difficulties the American university has had in recent years in responding to demands that it "take sides" or that it analyze the personal and institutional interests it serves or that it respond to social needs as defined by outside groups.

GUIDE TO FURTHER READING

The most comprehensive introductions to the modern American university are LAWRENCE VEYSEY, *The Emergence of the American University* (Chicago, 1965), and FREDERICK RUDOLPH, *The American College and University: A History* (New York, 1962); both contain extensive bibliographies. JOSEPH BEN-DAVID, *American Higher Education: Directions Old and New* (New York, 1972), BEN-DAVID and ABRAHAM ZLOCZOWER,"Universities and Academic Systems in Modern Societies,"*European Journal of Sociology*, III (1962), 45–84, OSCAR and MARY HANDLIN, *The American College and American Culture* (New York, 1970), and DAVID RIESMAN and CHRISTOPHER JENCKS, *The Academic Revolution* (Garden City, N. Y., 1968), are very valuable interpretations. Academic freedom and the influence of social pressure on the direction and structure of higher education are the subjects of WALTER P. METZGER, *Academic Freedom in the Age of the University* (New York, 1955), and two earlier essays, THORSTEIN VEBLEN, *The Higher Learning in America* (New York, 1918), and ABRAHAM FLEXNER, *Universities: American, English, German* (New York, 1930), Part I. Regional and institutional studies were very useful (an extensive bibliography of local histories appears in RUDOLPH, *American College and University*). The most useful are those by SAMUEL ELIOT MORISON, HUGH HAWKINS on Johns Hopkins, THOMAS LE DUC, and MERLE CURTI and VERNON CARSTENSEN. ROBERT A. MCCAUGHEY, "The Transformation of American Academic Life: Harvard University 1821–1892," *Perspectives in American History*, VIII (1974), 239–332, and PAUL BUCK, ed., *Social Sciences at Harvard 1860–1920: From Inculcation to the Open Mind* (Cambridge, Mass., 1965), are two excellent recent studies. Consult HUGH HAWKINS, *Between Harvard and America: The Educational Leadership of Charles W. Eliot* (New York, 1972), for the best biography of a university reformer.

Liberal reform after the Civil War has been thoroughly examined in RICHARD HOFSTADTER, *Anti-Intellectualism in American Life* (New York, 1963), JOHN G. SPROAT, *"The Best Men": Liberal Reformers in the Gilded Age* (New York, 1968), GEOFFREY BLODGETT, *The Gentle Reformers: Massachusetts Democrats in the Cleveland Era* (Cambridge, Mass., 1966), IRWIN UNGER, *The Greenback Era: A Social and Political History of American Finance, 1865–1879* (Princeton, N. J., 1964), ARI HOOGENBOOM, *Outlawing the Spoils: A History of the Civil Service Reform Movement, 1865–1883* (Urbana, Ill., 1961), EDWARD KIRKLAND, *Charles Francis Adams, Jr., 1835–1915: The Patrician at Bay* (Cambridge, Mass., 1965), RICHARD ABRAMS, *Conservatism in a Progressive Era: Massachusetts Politics, 1900–1912* (Cambridge, Mass., 1964), and JAMES MCLACHLAN, *American Boarding Schools: A Historical Study* (New York, 1970). The origins of the "robber baron" figure are explored in JOHN TIPPLE, "The Robber Baron in the Gilded Age: Entrepreneur or Iconoclast?", in WAYNE MORGAN, ed., *The Gilded Age: A Reappraisal* (Syracuse, N. Y. 1963), 14–37.

The politics and operation of the land grant college movement are the subjects of JOHN SIMON, "The Politics of the Morrill Act," *Agricultural History*, XXXVII (1963), 103–111, EDWARD D. EDDY, *Colleges for Our Land and Time: The Land-Grant Idea in American Education* (New York, 1956), ALLAN NEVINS, *The State*

Universities and Democracy (Urbana, Ill., 1962), and EARLE D. ROSS, *Democracy's College: The Land-Grant Movement in the Formative Stages* (Ames, Iowa, 1942).

CHARLES MCCARTHY, *The Wisconsin Idea* (New York, 1912), A. HUNTER DUPREE, *Science and the Federal Government, A History of Policies and Activities to 1940* (Cambridge, Mass., 1957), and JURGEN HERBST, *The German Historical School in American Scholarship: A Study in the Transfer of Culture* (Ithaca, N. Y., 1965), suggest the applicability of university activities to social problems.

The continued attraction of the liberal arts after 1870 is examined in GEORGE E. PETERSON, *The New England College in the Age of the University* (Amherst, Mass., 1964), THOMAS LE DUC, *Piety and Intellect at Amherst College, 1865–1912* (New York, 1946), DANIEL BELL, *The Reforming of General Education* (New York, 1966), and RUSSELL THOMAS, *The Search for a Common Learning: General Education, 1800–1960* (New York, 1962).

Consult OSCAR and MARY HANDLIN, *The American College and America Culture* (New York, 1970) and *Facing Life: Youth and Family in American History* (Boston, 1971), RUDOLPH, *American College and University*, DAVID F. ALLMENDINGER, *Paupers and Scholars: The Transformation of Student Life in Nineteenth-Century New England* (New York, 1975), JAMES MCLACHLAN, *American Boarding Schools: A Historical Study* (New York, 1970), and the novels and periodical literature on collegiate life for an introduction to the students' world between the Civil War and World War I.

The historical discussion of how the university revolution was financed and about the advantages donors, taxpayers, businessmen, and tuition payers sought for their patronage and saw in an expanded sphere for higher education has just begun. Some suggestions can be found in DUPREE, *Science and Federal Government*, LOREN BARITZ, *The Servants of Power: A History of the Use of Social Science in American Industry* (Middletown, Conn., 1960), BARRY KARL, "The Power of Intellect and the Politics of Ideas," *Daedalus*, XCIX (Summer, 1968), 1002–1035, KARL, *Charles E. Merriam and the Study of Politics* (Chicago, 1974), STANLEY COBEN, "The Scientific Establishment and the Transmission of Quantum Mechanics to the United States, 1919–32," *American Historical Review*, LXXVI (April, 1971), 442–466, HOWARD MILLER, *Dollars for Research* (Seattle, 1970), MERLE CURTI and ROBERT BREMNER, *Philanthropy in the Shaping of American Higher Education* (New Brunswick, N. J., 1965), and the essays by CHARLES WEINER, HOWARD MILLER, and CARROLL PURSELL in DAVID VAN TASSEL and MICHAEL G. HALL, eds., *Science and Society in the United States* (Homewood, Ill., 1966).

PART IV

School and Community: Progressivism in Education, 1890–1940

CHAPTER 9

Educational Reform in the Progressive Era

I

EDUCATION IN THE UNITED STATES WAS DEEPLY INVOLVED IN THE PRO-
found debates over the proper future course of American society that
marked the Progressive era between 1896 and 1920. Reformers, social
theorists, and educators in that period rejected Adam Smith's theories
of laissez faire, the nineteenth century's emphasis on individualism, and
the theory that society equaled merely the sum of its parts. They thought
the social organism, the community, had an existence apart from and
greater than the individuals who composed it. Reformers sought to shift
the emphasis in education from individual intellectual and moral achievement to individual social contribution. They repudiated the individualism
or selfishness taught in the nineteenth-century common school where
children worked by themselves to improve their own minds. Instead, they
wanted schools to instill in children a selfless desire to contribute to
community progress. Educators, as ever concerned with using schools
to improve society, accepted the Progressive era's emphasis on community service and sought to establish the school as community agent. The
key words among reformers were "community," "social service," and
"working together." These words pervaded educational debate as well.

Historians have generally considered the Progressive era to have run
from William McKinley's triumph over William Jennings Bryan in 1896
to the United States entry into World War I in 1917. In that era they have

251

identified a "progressive movement" which included the imperialist adventure that began with the Spanish-American War, the trust-busting of Theodore Roosevelt, Roosevelt's New Nationalism and Woodrow Wilson's New Freedom, the Bull Moose party, and a host of "liberal" reforms directed at improving the economic and social lot of the poor, the workingman, and the middle class. The latter ranged from pure food and drug acts and tenement house reform to legislation of the eight-hour day on railroads to enactment of unemployment insurance and workman's compensation. Ongoing historical research has suggested, however, that these events and the impulse behind them were too diverse to be considered as part of a single movement: to do so would impose an order on the past that did not exist. It is wiser to treat the period between 1896 and 1920 as an era in which a number of underlying assumptions about the nature of society changed and in which a number of social issues were raised, debated, and settled, temporarily at least, on the basis of those changed assumptions. To this extent the era has unity. On the other hand, the changing assumptions about social life gave rise to a good number of different and often conflicting practical programs for improving society in the United States. Broadly speaking, two quite different social programs struggled for supremacy in that era. In the end the battle was inconclusive—each side effected parts of its program and failed to enact others. Education was also split by the debate over the conflicting social programs, but there the program that called for greater social control and social engineering to advance society was clearly the victor.

Educational reform in the Progressive period was not the same as "progressive education," a topic which dominated the writings of educators in the 1920s, 1930s, and 1940s. The debates of the 1920s over permissiveness and repression and those of the 1930s over whether the schools dared build a new social order were very different from the prewar debates. Progressive education, although it had roots in the earlier period, became really important only after the founding of the Progressive Education Association in 1919. John Dewey, the great theorist of educational reform in the Progressive era, was also, of course, an influential figure among progressive educators and in that way links the periods and the reform impulses. Each period, however, read Dewey somewhat differently, and we can understand Dewey better if we see him as a product of and shaper of the Progressive era. This chapter will focus, therefore, on the debates over the purposes of education and the efforts to reform education between 1890 and 1920. Progressive education will be a topic of another chapter.

II

The Progressive era experienced a vast outpouring of reform sentiment, reform organizations and writing, and reform projects—a surprisingly large number of which were successfully completed. It was a stirring and exciting time. Several causes lay behind this fervor for social improvement at the beginning of this century and determined the form that the conflicts between different groups of reformers would take. First, the fact that those assuming positions of social responsibility in the period were in the first generation of Americans not to have lived through and to have had their reform energy exhausted by the traumas of the Civil War and Reconstruction explains some of the period's reform exuberance. Progressives had experienced none of that fatigue or disillusion that followed the struggle to abolish slavery and reform the South. The second major determinant of the era's social concern was the tremendous urbanization of the society between 1870 and 1920. In 1870 one quarter of the United States population lived in cities, in 1890 the figure was over one third, and by 1920 more than half of the American people lived in urban places. Tenements, slums, immigrants, boss rule, monopolistic public utilities were now everybody's problems. A third cause of the era's ferment was the increasing public awareness that social and economic institutions were too large and the individual was growing insignificant in the scheme of things. The population of the United States more than doubled between 1880 and 1920; and bulging cities with their new skyscrapers seemed to dwarf the individual.

The most frightening growth, however, was that of business. Through pools, trusts, and mergers, a small number of bankers and managers controlled ever increasing portions of the market in sugar, steel, oil, beef, and money itself. The United States Steel Corporation was formed in 1901 by the merger of almost 200 smaller companies which produced 60 percent of the iron and steel sold in the United States. This was America's first billion-dollar corporation and its domination of the market allowed it to set prices and reap profits almost at will. Even more powerful than the steel monopoly were the investment bankers who provided the needed capital for these vast companies, now far too large to raise their own capital. J. P. Morgan and the House of Morgan symbolized economic power at its zenith. Representatives of Morgan's bank sat in a majority of the country's important board rooms and dictated policy to railroads, manufacturing plants, and other banks on the strength of Morgan's influence over sources of capital. In 1893 the federal government itself had to request the House of Morgan to shore up its financial standing. Beside these powerful giants the individual, even the individual entrepreneur, seemed nothing. Now individuals bought from and dealt with merchants and service representatives who were only middlemen for giant companies that were free to dismiss the individual's desires and complaints cavalierly. Credit was steadily centralized and the individual's relation with his local banker no longer assured him of help in an emergency or in financing a new venture. His loan application was processed "higher up" where personal relations were unimportant. Impersonal factors—in business, in government, in the very tides of population itself —seemed to be overwhelming the individual. Another and much more complex reason behind the rise of the progressive ferment around the turn of the century was a growing impression that Americans had of the fragility of the American experiment. As people grew more self-conscious and knowledgeable about society and its workings, they became fearful that the society might crumble if it were not carefully nurtured. A growing body of social science literature suggested that society could not survive if it were simply left alone. This concern grew in part from a recognition that America offered less opportunity to people than it once had and that its resources were limited. In the nineteenth century many—at least among those not already locked into urban slums and permanent poverty—thought America possessed unlimited resources and offered unlimited opportunity for personal success. In the 1890s that assurance was severely jolted. The historian Frederick Jackson Turner announced in 1893 that with the closing of the frontier a crucial factor in maintaining American democracy and openness was gone. The passing of the frontier suggested that the United States was full. (Actually, of course, the "passing of the frontier" simply meant the retirement of the census category for totally uninhabited land. Plenty of open space remained in the United States. But Turner's essay had struck a responsive chord and Americans talked fearfully about the social problems the end of the frontier would bring.) In this period Americans were also made conservation conscious by those who feared that the United States had wasted its mineral and timber resources and would soon find its mines and forests empty. This accorded well with people's experience—they knew that their economy used lumber and pulp, iron ore, and coal at a fearsome rate. The cut-over forest was a familiar sight. Conservation was especially popular in the East where open recreational land had been steadily depleted. Nature, once thought limitlessly bountiful, seemed to have run out of space and wealth. Her ability to provide a high standard of living to all was endangered. The United States had enjoyed a reputation (historians now think it undeserved) as a place of boundless opportunity in the nineteenth century. America was a classless society. All could and did rise in the United States. Only the most obtuse could accept this myth after the experience of the 1890s when Populists and Bryanites pitted their class interests against those of the "respectable" classes and labor violence soared. Especially in view of the closing of the frontier and the limited resources available to the country, opportunity for those in the bottom segments of the society seemed poor indeed. Social class became an American problem rather than just something that existed in other nations—as the growing literature of an American sociology pointed out.

These limitations on growth and opportunity placed certain strains, reformers realized, on American society. If that society, and the democratic experiment that it represented, were to survive, special steps would have to be taken to manipulate resources in order to preserve a stable democracy. The growing sense of conflict among groups and among individuals would have to be staunched. The belief that resources were limited led to the belief that there would be more conflict over their distribution. This prediction seemed confirmed by the class and bloc conflicts of the 1890s and by the increasing economic struggles among regions, between shippers and producers, between management and labor. Since the economic pie was not growing, conflicts over its division would inevitably grow more intense. Such conflict could destroy the society.

Progressives faced crucial and somewhat grim issues after 1896 but they faced them in a buoyant mood. Part of their optimism came from knowing that the society had survived the 1890s despite that decade's severe depression and its bitter economic and political conflicts. The economy improved radically after 1897, farmers who had fueled the Populist discontent grew prosperous, America swept to victory against a European power (a pitifully weak one), and political conflict subsided considerably. The society had survived the crucible. A new theory of social reform also fostered the reformers' optimism. Social Darwinism, as taught by Herbert Spencer and his myriad followers in the United States after 1860, held that social evolution and change, like biological evolution, was a natural phenomenon beyond the power of men to alter. In the 1890s sociologists and social thinkers, guided and stimulated by the work of Lester Frank Ward, rejected Spencer's analogy between biological and social evolution and his attempt to explain human development in terms of animal development. Man differed from all other animals, Ward argued, because man alone was rational and capable of setting goals. Animals might evolve unconsciously along patterns and towards goals established by God or nature. Man, on the other hand, could apply his brain and consciously choose goals and control his society's evolution toward them. This was exciting doctrine that, after the years of restrictive social Darwinism, seemed to open vast possibilities for social reform. One no longer had to accept society's course fatalistically but could begin to change it. It was just that which the progressives set out to do.

The reforms essayed in the Progressive era—both those passed and those merely attempted—were nearly all directed toward a rejection of laissez-faire policies in favor of expanding state regulation of political, social, and economic processes so as to insure a just and smooth-running society. Two quite different reform persuasions combined in this general search for a more unified society. We can divide reformers into two groups: a smaller group which we may term liberals and a far larger group which we may identify as conservatives. The first group's ultimate goal was social justice; the second's, social order. The liberals, or idealists, and their reforms sprang from Populism, from organized labor, from humanitarians of every stripe. The other group tended to represent the interests of the middle class, of business, and of the social elite. Speaking very generally, liberal progressivism had its roots and support in rural areas and in the West, Midwest, and South, while conservative progressivism was more urban and eastern in orientation. All groups and all regions, of course, produced reformers of both types, but it is possible to detect a trend in which the older and more urban sections of the nation tended to adopt anti-individualist ideas faster than did the western and rural sections and in which the latter sections welcomed reforms that promised to use state power to protect individuals more readily than reforms calling for extensive government interference with individual initiative. These divisions do not correspond to party lines—that Wilson and Roosevelt, the leading political symbols of liberal and conservative progressivism, respectively, represented different parties is more an accident than an indication of a split in party ideology.

Just how to create a strong community was the issue that divided liberal from conservative progressives. For the liberals community would replace conflict when more of the citizens of the republic were allowed to participate in government and the economy. The villains for them were the oligarchic trusts, the corrupt governments, the special interests who sapped the country's resources for personal benefit. When these forces were curbed and regulated and when social justice had been secured for the poor and the workingmen, all men in the society could come together and democratically supervise the development and distribution of the nation's resources. Under this kind of democratic polity, special interests could not grow, class division would disappear, and community would be achieved. The conservatives, on the other hand, thought that conflict would be contained only when responsible, scientifically trained, expert managers who represented the public rather than special interests took control of the society. These managers would eliminate wasteful practices, muting conflict in the society by mediating among interest groups and supervising the distribution of resources—both natural and human. Community, they knew was a complex organism in which many interdependent parts worked in close harmony. The only way they could envisage achieving that kind of harmony and order in a complex twentieth-century society was to impose it. It was necessary to manage the many parts of the complex society so that they would operate in harmony, each fulfilling the role assigned. The achievement of community in the era of bigness was too complex a task to leave to the workings of direct democracy and mass participation. Individuals could not be expected to fulfill their social roles adequately unless they were guided to them and supervised as they performed them.

The liberal progressives supported measures for direct democracy, most notably the initiative, referendum, and recall—measures which allowed voters to intervene in the legislative and judicial process without waiting for scheduled elections—and legislation assuring that a state's voters rather than its legislature would elect United States senators. Conservative progressives, on the other hand, favored measures which centralized political power in the hands of strong executives and measures which circumvented the legislative process by establishing appointive, nonrepresentative commission-type bodies to direct various functions of the state. Like the university reformers, most of whom were counted in the conservative camp, the conservative progressives desired objective, disinterested government by the scientific expert—government unswayed in its commitment to proper policy by the the temporary whims and passions of the mass of voters. Both groups opposed governmental corruption. Liberals, however, attributed corruption to the fact that governments were too large and too subservient to large business interests. Conservatives argued that governments were too small and weak to oppose the forces seeking to corrupt them and that the masses habitually voted for corrupt bosses. The liberal progressives wished to solve the problem of excessive economic concentration by breaking up the large trusts and reducing the size of corporations. In that way they hoped to increase the number of competing firms in any industry, thus reducing the power any single firm or trust exercised over the market and increasing the consumer's power. Antitrust legislation was vital to their program. The conservatives, on the other hand, found dismembering concentrated business firms less appealing—partly because they did not think it would succeed and partly because they saw in big business the model for the big government and powerful social institutions which they favored. Conservatives tended to equate bigness with efficiency, a value that was very important to them. They strove to make society run more efficiently—by which they meant more predictably, more smoothly, and more cheaply. The financial consideration was probably the least important—efficiency meant more than saving dollars and cents. The efficient institution was the one that could get things done quickly and directly without creating conflict. Big business did get things done. Through concentration of power it had reduced conflict with slowed change, and through pooling of resources it had rationalized the processes of production and distribution so as to receive the greatest possible gains from its efforts.

Since bigness was a form of progress, prohibiting economic concentration retarded progress. Instead, conservatives proposed to build a strong government regulatory system expert enough to referee between the interests of the corporations and the public and powerful enough to force corporations to serve the public interest. Theodore Roosevelt's concept of the New Nationalism rested on the idea that big government could balance big business and protect the public from corporate misuse of power. Conservative reformers hoped that the big government they proposed, with its powerful executives and nonpartisan experts, would also get things done quickly and smoothly by rationalizing procedures and controlling conflict. Strong rational government—in other words, efficient government—promised to deliver the most social benefit to the nation. Liberals talked about efficiency much less than the conservatives; speedy implementation of change at the expense of democratic participation did not appeal to them. They challenged the efficiency of bigness and denounced the inhumaneness of much of the bureaucratic rationality that conservatives found so inviting. Yet liberals were not against efficiency—nobody could be in a country that still preserved a puritan abhorrence of waste—but they opted for efficiency that saved not only time and money but also human resources and human comforts.

Liberals tended to support labor causes more enthusiastically than did the conservatives, although both groups increasingly recognized the justice in many of labor's complaints. Liberals supported efforts to limit the hours that women and children could work in industry, to prohibit child labor, and to introduce an eight-hour day for all workers. Many (but not all) liberals supported unionization, believing that organization was the only way the workingman would secure his rights. They also supported legislation requiring industry to install safety devices in factories and to establish insurance programs—under state control—to compensate victims of industrial accidents. Conservatives often supported prolabor legislation, not primarily because it would benefit the laboring man, but because it would increase industrial efficiency and reduce conflict between management and labor. Conservatives supported safety legislation, for example, not because they sympathized with the victims of accidents which proper equipment would have prevented but because they recognized that injuries to employees reduced industry's efficiency. The scales which were established in workman's compensation legislation made predictable the financial payments to be made to injured employees. Many also supported the effort to pass state and federal child labor laws not because they were moved by the horrible conditions under which children worked but because they feared the moral effects of the children's absence from school. Sometimes conservatives backed labor legislation, hoping that if conditions of labor were improved workingmen would show less inclination to organize.

The distinction between liberals and conservatives is also evident in their different attitudes toward immigration. Liberals sought to help immigrants adjust to their new environment without stripping them of their Old World cultures and values. Conservatives were much more eager to impose, rather forcibly, American values (which were, of course, conservative, middle-class values) on the immigrants. Conservatives sustained the Americanization movement that began informally at the turn of the century and became an organized, recognized movement after 1910. Through the imposition of quotas or literary tests, conservatives fostered moves to restrict immigration. They believed that immigrants from southern and eastern Europe, who were arriving in such large numbers at the turn of the century, could not be assimilated into American culture because they were too foreign. The presence of such foreigners threatened the social and moral order of the United States. Sometimes liberals supported restriction, but for very different reasons. Many accepted labor's argument that, because there were so many immigrants and because they were willing to work for such meager wages, management found it easy to drive wages down and oppose labor legislation. Other liberals supported temporary restriction so that the United States might have a breathing spell in which to assimilate and elevate the immigrants already here before new waves arrived (immigrants entered the United States at the rate of nearly 1 million a year between 1900 and 1914).

Conservatives in general were more eager to impose their values— what they thought were the values of all respectable Americans—on their fellow citizens, on immigrants, and on foreigners. They rejoiced that finally the United States had agreed to carry the white man's burden among backward races in Hawaii and the Philippines just as other responsible and powerful nations did in other backward areas. A typical conservative progressive reform was Prohibition, an effort to impose one group's moral beliefs on everyone else. They justified Prohibition on several grounds: excessive drinking on the part of workingmen reduced industrial efficiency, the liquor and saloon interests corrupted state and local governments in order to secure illegal licenses, and drinking led poor people to waste their money and men to desert their families. A less publicized but important cause of prohibition sentiment among the conservative progressives was that public drinking was a treasured pastime of several immigrant communities in the United States.

Both groups supported many of the same measures to improve the public welfare, but their different reasons for doing so revealed the basic differences between their goals. All the reformers agreed that something must be done about the size and sanitation facilities of the urban tenements into which most of the urban poor crowded. The liberals took steps to increase the amount of ventilation and the minimum number of cubic feet required for each resident because they were genuinely concerned for these poor families and about the tenement environment's effect on their family life, their physical well-being, and their happiness. Conservatives, on the other hand, saw tenement conditions as a threat to public health. Disease bred rapidly where so many crowded into so little space with such primitive facilities, and in the urban situation disease could easily spread from neighborhood to neighborhood and endanger the whole urban complex. They also feared that people raised in the tenement environment would be morally dangerous to the rest of society.

Some have argued that the liberals were essentially a backward-looking group, seeking to recreate in twentieth-century America, where bigness was inevitable, the economic organization and ideals of the previous century where individuals and small entrepreneurs dealt personally with each other. Conservatives, on the other hand, looked forward, welcomed bigness, and sought to guide its advance in order to enhance the public interest. In the economic sphere this interpretation makes some sense, although the cyclical nature of public attitudes towards institutional size may make what seemed backward at one point seem more forward looking a generation later. In other spheres, however, this interpretation is less tenable. In their attitudes toward the white man's burden and Americanization of the immigrants and in their drive to prohibit drinking, the conservative progressives clung to nineteenth-century values while liberals were able to accept unionization and some degree of cultural pluralism.

III

Educational reformers joined other progressive reformers in their quest to rebuild community in the United States. John Dewey eloquently expressed the educational reformers' hopes for education as a force in building the community. Dewey was not a "typical" educational reformer in the Progressive era, as no other matched the comprehensiveness of his vision or possessed the mixture of philosophical and psychological insight that informed his work. Yet *The School and Society* (1899) and *The Child and the Curriculum* (1902), two short volumes of lectures in which Dewey explained the philosophy that guided the University of Chicago's Laboratory School, which he headed from its beginnings in 1896 until he left Chicago in 1904, illustrate nicely the relations reformers saw between schooling and the achievement of a healthier community. Because they exemplify the issues of school reform in the Progressive era and because they were so influential among educational thinkers in that and following generations, Dewey's early educational ideas merit extensive consideration at this point.[1]

---

[1] We will be concentrating here on John Dewey's earliest educational writings rather than on the more systematic *Democracy and Education* (New York, 1916) because they are more concrete and more obviously rooted in actual school experience than the later work, and educators seem to have read the earlier work with more frequency and understanding. *The School and Society* (Chicago, 1900; revised in 1915) and *The Child and the Curriculum* (Chicago, 1902) represent, we think, what educators in the twentieth century have meant by "Dewey's ideas."

Education was vital to the proper development of a reformed and conflict-free community, he wrote.

> What the best and wisest parent wants for his own child, that must the community want for all of its children. Any other ideal for our schools is narrow and unlovely; acted upon, it destroys our democracy. All that society has accomplished for itself is put, through the agency of the school, at the disposal of its future members. All its better thoughts of itself it hopes to realize through the new possibilities thus opened to its future self. Here individualism and socialism are at one. Only by being true to the full growth of all the individuals who make it up, can society by any chance be true to itself.[2]

Dewey accepted and developed the pedagogical ideas of Pestalozzi and the German educational thinkers of the nineteenth century such as Friedrich Froebel and Johann Friedrich Herbart. They had taken the position, or were interpreted to have taken the position, that children learned best through doing, through studying material geared to their present state of mental development or readiness, and through studying material which was closely connected to something they had already experienced. Children learned what they needed to use, according to Dewey, who emphasized that "use" should be interpreted broadly and not simply as economic utility. Dewey agreed with the European educational theorists in believing that teachers should teach material that was relevant or interesting to children. "If the subject-matter of the lessons be such as to have an appropriate place within the expanding consciousness of the child, if it grows out of his own past doings, thinkings, and sufferings, and grows into application in further achievements and receptivities, then no device or trick of method has to be resorted to in order to enlist 'interest.' "[3] Dewey also elaborated the principle that a child would learn the basic intellectual skills and symbol systems (language and mathematics) more effectively by engaging in activities which forced him to use them than by memorizing symbols and rules for their use. Dewey also emphasized the idea, adumbrated previously by educational reformers such as Francis W. Parker, principal of the Cook County Normal School, whom Dewey called the "father of progressive education," that both children's minds and the knowledge about the world that they were to learn in school were dynamic and constantly changing, and that any attempt to impose a rigidly classified or graded curriculum distorted the true nature of knowledge and hindered the child's ability to learn.

Dewey was quintessentially progressive in his habit of seeking to repress conflict. His philosophy and educational thought constantly sought to dissolve dualisms—those hoary distinctions that philosophers had stressed between mind and body, body and soul, the individual and

[2] Dewey, *School and Society*, 7.
[3] Dewey, *Child and Curriculum*, 27.

society, and in education between the school and society and between the child and the curriculum. On the latter point, Dewey condemned both the child-centered approach—which made the interest of the child the ultimate standard of what was to be taught in the school—and the curriculum-centered approach—which held that children must master certain defined subjects no matter what. In resolving this dualism, Dewey displayed a typical progressive ambiguity about freedom and authority and about man's power to influence the development of other men and their society. There was no conflict between the child and the curriculum, he contended, because properly interpreted the curriculum—the ordering of the accumulated knowledge of mankind—only provided standards and goals to help teachers guide students in the direction they were naturally intended to go. The curriculum—"the formulated wealth of knowledge that makes up the course of study"—allows the teacher *"to determine the environment of the child,* and thus by indirection to direct," Dewey wrote. But such direction or guidance, Dewey averred earlier in the same essay, "is not external imposition. *It is freeing the life-process for its own most adequate fulfilment. . . .* [D]evelopment is a definite process, having its own law which can be fulfilled only when adequate and normal conditions are provided. . . . The problem of direction is . . . the problem of selecting appropriate stimuli for instincts and impulses which it is desired to employ in the gaining of new experience. What new experiences are desirable, and thus what stimuli are needed, it is impossible to tell except as there is some comprehension of the development which is aimed at; except, in a word, as the adult knowledge is drawn upon as revealing the possible career open to the child."[4] It was in the child's nature, in the life process, that he should master adult knowledge. What adults wanted children to learn and what children really wanted to learn were no different. Dewey, characteristically, did not foresee conflicts over which parts of adult knowledge were most important and which parts children should learn and in what order. Like his progressive colleagues, Dewey opposed conflict and relied on scientific expertise to resolve potential conflict in such a way that disagreement would be impossible. Contention over curriculum content and priorities would be removed by scientific educators and expert curriculum builders. Curriculum, that body of subject matters or sciences which puts "the net product of past experience in the form which makes it most available for the future," was to inform the teacher that "such and such are the capacities, the fulfilments, in truth and beauty and behavior, open to these children" and, of course, the teacher was to guide the students' impulses in those directions.[5] Dewey, like other progressives, expected science to determine values.

[4] *Ibid.*, 31, 17–19.
[5] *Ibid.*, 21, 31.

The second great educational dualism which Dewey wished to dissolve was that between the school and the society. He wanted the school itself to be a community that would reflect the shape and the values of the larger community surrounding it (the vague term "larger" is used here advisably as Dewey never clarified which community he meant—the neighborhood, the city or town, the social class, or the nation as a whole). The school's underlying purpose was social, Dewey contended, for in its very essence mental growth was a social process. Older psychology "regarded mind as a purely individual affair in direct and naked contact with an external world." In that theory the individual's psychological development would have been "exactly the same if there were one mind living alone in the universe." Newer psychological findings—Dewey himself had contributed to these discoveries—conceived the "individual mind as a function of social life—as not capable of operating or developing by itself, but as requiring continual stimulus from social agencies, and finding its nutrition in social supplies . . . mind cannot be regarded as an individual, monopolistic possession, but represents the outworkings of the endeavor and thought of humanity; that it is developed in an environment which is social as well as physical, and that social needs and aims have been most potent in shaping it." As Dewey summarized it, "the chief difference between savagery and civilization is not in the naked nature which each faces, but the social heredity and social medium."[6] Dewey knew the school-age child to be a social creature eager to communicate. How sad, therefore, that teachers had made language teaching so grim when they could have made it enjoyable by appealing to the child's constant desire to tell others about his experiences. Dewey recommended a new kind of recitation—not one in which the individual child recited in isolation to the teacher what he had learned or memorized from a specific portion of a text but one in which the whole class joined, exchanged ideas, and learned to communicate with each other. "From this other standpoint the recitation becomes pre-eminently a social meeting-place; it is to the school what the spontaneous conversation is at home, excepting that it is more organized, following definite lines. The recitation becomes the social clearing-house, where experiences and ideas are exchanged and subjected to criticism, where misconceptions are corrected, and new lines of thought and inquiry are set up."[7] To further community cohesion in and beyond the school, Dewey wished to do away with the selfish competitiveness of the traditional classroom. "The mere absorbing of facts and truths is so exclusively individual an affair that it tends very naturally to pass into selfishness. There is no obvious social motive for the acquirement of mere learning."[8] He poked fun at the

[6] Dewey, *School and Society*, 98–99.
[7] *Ibid.*, 55.
[8] *Ibid.*, 15.

educational values that made mutual assistance among children "a school crime." That would not do for Dewey; children must learn cooperatively. This was all the more important because Dewey wished the school to minimize individualism among future adults. This was the key to moderating social conflict.

Like any good progressive, Dewey included in *The School and Society* a chapter on "Waste in Education." His concern was the waste of human resources, especially of "the life of the children while they are at school, and afterward because of inadequate and perverted preparation." Such waste of lives could be averted by making the parts of the school, the different school subjects, the school, and the society work in greater harmony, each with all the others. "All waste is due to isolation," Dewey asserted, implying once again how much he abhorred the traditional image of the individual child poring over his own book in a silent classroom. He continued in the words of the social or, in this case, educational engineer: "Organization is nothing but getting things into connection with one another, so that they work easily, flexibly, and fully."[9] Later in the chapter he listed the elements and their interrelations that the educational planner would have to supervise.

> Thus I have attempted to indicate how the school may be connected with life so that the experience gained by the child in a familiar, commonplace way is carried over and made use of there, and what the child learns in the school is carried back and applied in everyday life, making the school an organic whole, instead of a composite of isolated parts. The isolation of studies as well as of parts of the school system disappears. Experience has its geographical aspect, its artistic and its literary, its scientific and its historical sides. All studies arise from aspects of the one earth and the one life lived upon it. We do not have a series of stratified earths, one of which is mathematical, another physical, another historical, and so on. We should not be able to live very long in any one taken by itself. We live in a world where all sides are bound together. All studies grow out of relations in the one great common world. When the child lives in varied but concrete and active relationship to this common world, his studies are naturally unified. It will no longer be a problem to correlate studies. The teacher will not have to resort to all sorts of devices to weave a little arithmetic into the history lesson, and the like. Relate the school to life, and all studies are of necessity correlated.
>
> Moreover, if the school is related as a whole to life as a whole, its various aims and ideals—culture, discipline, information, utility—cease to be variants, for one of which we must select one study and for another another. The growth of the child in the direction of social capacity and service, his larger and more vital union with life, becomes the unifying aim; and discipline, culture, and information fall into place as phases of this growth.[10]

[9] *Ibid.*, 64.
[10] *Ibid.*, 91–92.

Total interconnectedness was to replace isolation. School was to prepare students for life, indeed was going to be life itself.

This was a tall order, but Dewey thought that schools could achieve such a harmonious interweaving of knowledge, culture, and discipline with the activities and values of the larger community by introducing large amounts of hand training in the curriculum. Dewey believed, just as Felix Adler did, that work with tools and wood and metal improved the moral nature of children and duplicated some of the advantageous nurturing elements of rural upbringing. But hand training was, for Dewey, in no way the remedial agent it had been for his nineteenth-century predecessors. He favored kindergarten and manual training methods and rejected industrial training that stressed the performance of routine tasks for profit. He recognized and applauded its special attractiveness to those children who were less intellectually inclined. He agreed with its earlier advocates that hand training strengthened the faculties of observation and helped develop coordination between the hand and the eye. These advantages appeared very minor, however, when compared to its capacity to inculcate in children the ability to work together which, after all, was the very essence of the successful community. Dewey encouraged educators and parents to view hand-training activities "as methods of living and learning, not as distinct studies."

> We must conceive of them in their social significance, as types of the processes by which society keeps itself going, as agencies for bringing home to the child some of the primal necessities of community life, and as ways in which these needs have been met by the growing insight and ingenuity of man; in short, as instrumentalities through which the school itself shall be made a genuine form of active community life, instead of a place set apart in which to learn lessons.
>
> A society is a number of people held together because they are working along common lines, in a common spirit, and with reference to common aims. The common needs and aims demand a growing interchange of thought and growing unity of sympathetic feeling. The radical reason that the present school cannot organize itself as a natural social unit is because just this element of common and productive activity is absent. . . . Upon the ethical side, the tragic weakness of the present school is that it endeavors to prepare future members of the social order in a medium in which the conditions of the social spirit are eminently wanting.[11]

The mere process of common productivity in the school would strengthen the child's natural social instinct—where hundreds of reform school children worked together in the same workshop in absolute silence, Dewey expected schoolwork in manual arts to be lively and convivial. There children would not work alone but would help each other

[11] *Ibid.*, 14–15.

and engage in cooperative projects. Such manual activity would also encourage a more effective discipline in children than that of the traditional school. Discipline that "comes from having a part to do in constructive work, in contributing to a result which, social in spirit, is none the less obvious and tangible in form—and hence in a form with reference to which responsibility may be exacted and accurate judgment passed" was a more effective and trustworthy discipline than that which teachers sought to inculcate through assigning moral texts or applying the rod.[12] The process of manual training taught cooperation and social responsibility.

Dewey pointed out another advantage of manual activity: it could inculcate knowledge and virtue simultaneously. He claimed that when a child participated in active occupations in the school he learned the underlying structure of the community and his responsibility in it. Dewey was very much the man of his age in identifying economics or the organization of occupations as the basis of social structure and regarding "work" in the schools as the best means for teaching children to understand that structure. The major problems that progressives addressed had to do with regulating economic power and reducing economic conflicts. American social thinkers after 1890 began to import the economic interpretation of history from Europe and apply it to conditions in the United States. Charles Beard's attempt to reveal the self-interested economic motives behind the writing and passing of the Constitution, long revered as a kind of sacred document written by men but conceived according to natural or religious law, was only the most notable of many such analyses of social change. That era expected to find an economic issue or relation at the bottom of everything.

Dewey contended that the teaching of occupations—so long as that teaching was free of vocational or profit-making aims—led children to understand simple economics which in turn contributed to "the development of social power and insight." In the development of the occupations of man, he contended, the child could best trace human progress and best understand his social or communal heritage. In illustration, he described the Laboratory School's sewing and weaving classes for students between ten and twelve years of age. Whatever practical utility this work might have was entirely secondary. Rather, it "gives the point of departure from which the child can trace and follow the progress of mankind in history, getting an insight also into the materials used and the mechanical principles involved. In connection with these occupations the historic development of man is recapitulated." The class began with newly sheared wool and bolls of cotton and flax and initiated the laborious process of turning these natural resources into first thread, then cloth,

[12] *Ibid.*, 17–18.

and then clothing. Through trial and error the children found that cotton was difficult to separate from its seeds by hand and that, unlike wool which had long nubbly fibers, cotton had short smooth fibers that made it more difficult to spin. Thereby the students "could understand why their ancestors wore woolen instead of cotton clothing." The children also, through trial and error "aided by questions and suggestions from the teacher," followed the development of processes for turning the fibers into thread and thread into cloth, actually, Dewey claimed, reinventing some of the simpler processes themselves. Such activities succeeded in teaching a great deal about science— "the study of the fibers, of geographical features, the conditions under which raw materials are grown, the great centers of manufacture and distribution, the physics involved in the machinery of production." Moreover, Dewey wrote, "you can concentrate the history of all mankind into the evolution of the flax, cotton, and wool fibers into clothing." In sum, manual activities in the school were so valuable because they were so easily and effectively translated into "historic and social values and scientific equivalencies."[13]

More important than the history or the science, however, such occupations made children understand the fact that each person was dependent on every other person in the community. Following the development of the division of labor in the clothing trade from a time when a single family was self-sufficient to the modern era when hundreds of people had a hand in making a single shirt led children to realize, with a clarity impossible to achieve in a text, the communal basis even of complex twentieth-century society.

> The world in which most of us live is a world in which everyone has a calling and occupation, something to do. Some are managers and others are subordinates. But the great thing for one as for the other is that each shall have had the education which enables him to see within his daily work all there is in it of large and human significance. How many of the employed are today mere appendages to the machines which they operate! This may be due in part to the machine itself or to the régime which lays so much stress upon the products of the machine; but it is certainly due in large part to the fact that the worker has had no opportunity to develop his imagination and his sympathetic insight as to the social and scientific values found in his work. At present, the impulses which lie at the basis of the industrial system are either practically neglected or positively distorted during the school period. Until the instincts of construction and production are systematically laid hold of in the years of childhood and youth, until they are trained in social directions, enriched by historical interpretation, controlled and illuminated by scientific methods, we certainly are in no position even to locate the source of our economic evils, much less to deal with them effectively.[14]

[13] *Ibid.*, 20–23.
[14] *Ibid.*, 23–24.

Could Dewey have been suggesting that, if subordinates understood their social significance and responsibilities as subordinates, they would be less likely to fight for higher wages and better conditions, thus reducing social conflict? Doubtless, he was not thinking along such lines, but others certainly read such passages in just that light. Dewey did think that the insights gained from manual training as he conceived it would relieve some of the individual's sense of personal insignificance in an economy dominated by bigness. The individual would feel significant when he understood just how his work fit into the larger structure. The most significant intellectual and moral gain that came from including active occupations in the curriculum was the insight that all members of the community were interdependent, with community survival depending on its members working cooperatively and on each fulfilling his responsibilities to the social whole. Educational reformers before Dewey, especially the common school reformers, had hoped to use the schools to train socially responsible individuals, but Dewey was the first to work out a theory in which the subject-matter curriculum so enhanced moral training, where the actual learning of intellectual skills also instilled social virtue and social ethics.

Dewey summarized the purposes of school reform in the Progressive era when he wrote that it sought "to make each one of our schools an embryonic community life, active with types of occupations that reflect the life of the larger society and permeated throughout with the spirit of art, history, and science. When the school introduces and trains each child of society into membership within such a little community, saturating him with the spirit of service, and providing him with the instruments of effective self-direction, we shall have the deepest and best guaranty of a larger society which is worthy, lovely, and harmonious."[15] There is a fundamental ambiguity in this passage, perhaps one that a man less concerned with resolving conflict and dualism on all fronts would have recognized more clearly. "The spirit of service" and "effective self-direction" were possible to combine harmoniously, but more often they threatened to conflict. Dewey, of course, believed that an individual's self-fulfillment came through his service to the society. Nor did he believe there was any fundamental distinction between the individual and society because, after all, the individual was at bottom a product of social forces. Although in theory such a neat resolution of the conflict between the individual and society may have been convincing, it was of little practical significance. A conflict did exist, or at least many educational reformers came to feel that one did, and in implementing school reform they found themselves forced to choose between stressing social service or self-direction. All agreed that the school was to reflect and prepare children

15 *Ibid.*, 29.

for community life, but the future of educational reform depended on whether educational reformers felt that saturation with the spirit of service or self-direction was the most important element in building communities that were "worthy, lovely, and harmonious."

IV

The "new" education, then, was to prepare children to participate in the community's life. In the Progressive period, however, liberal progressives and conservative progressives held opposing conceptions of the ideal community. Each vision required schools to prepare children somewhat differently. The struggle in the ideological realm was intense but there was almost no contest in the world of the public school where the conservative progressives, far larger in numbers than the liberals and far more powerful in local politics, easily carried the day. To illustrate the struggle and its outcome, we shall contrast the educational ideas and practices of Jane Addams—a liberal progressive who developed the settlement house to embody the community spirit of the new education— with the methods conservative progressives instituted in the urban public schools in order to further their vision of the worthy American community. This chapter will discuss two themes—"socialized" education and the school as community center. The following chapter will discuss the conservative progressives' shaping of the high school during the Progressive era.

The settlement house movement in the United States began in 1886 as an attempt to enrich both the social life of people living in the more depressed areas of America's cities and the social life and awareness of the young middle-class people who would come to live in the settlement houses and socialize with the "neighbors" of the area. Founded by individuals, by groups of college students, or by churches and staffed by college students or young graduates who settled in the houses for a few years, the settlement house was an effort on the part of a new generation of young people to affect the "social problem" by inspiring mutual respect between lower- and middle-class cultures. Although, of course, many young people who settled in the slums harbored condescending attitudes toward the poor, the movement's ideology held that the middle class had as much to gain from understanding the poor and the immigrant as the poor and the immigrant had to learn from the middle class. The movement was somewhat guilty of romanticizing lower-class primitiveness, believing that the poor led a richer, more passionate, more loving life than did the puritanical middle class and that living with them would bring the middle class into contact with real life. Jane Addams remembered that she started Hull House in Chicago in 1889 as a place where "young women who had been given over too exclusively to study might restore a balance of activity along traditional lines and learn of life from life itself."[16] The poor were closer to "life" and, as such, had much to teach the sheltered Victorian young man or woman.

This belief that charitable contact between the comfortable and the poor should occur on the basis of mutual respect and the expectation of reciprocal benefit marked a new approach. The most widely used method of dispensing urban charity in the late nineteenth century was the Charity Organization Society's two-pronged attack, pioneered in 1877, on poverty and social incompetence. First, each local society established a master file of charity cases in its city and checked each new request for aid against it to see whether the aid was truly needed, whether the recipients would use the aid wisely, and whether the family requesting aid was being simultaneously helped by another agency. The Charity Organization Society did not dispense aid of its own in most cases but, rather, served as a clearing house for all of a city's charitable agencies to prevent them from duplicating their efforts and giving money to unworthy poor. Second, the Charity Organization Societies encouraged "friendly visiting" to provide personal contact between the givers and receivers of charity and to perform some of the functions of a modern caseworker (there were no professional social workers until the twentieth century). Visitors were usually middle- or upper-middle-class women who volunteered to visit a group of families on relief each week or each month. This system was supposed to have a number of advantages over the earlier plan of dispensing outdoor relief in an impersonal manner. Friendly visiting encouraged contact between the rich and the poor, but the friendly visitors believed the benefits went all in one direction—toward the poor. Of course, the friendly visitors felt they were accumulating good marks in heaven for their pains but received no benefit from the poor themselves. The families on relief, however, were to receive contact with superior people whom they could emulate in their drive for self-sufficiency. The friendly visitors would also demonstrate to the poor how kind and charitable the well-to-do classes were and how interested they were in the plight of the poor. Such understanding would relieve social conflict. Friendly visiting also took the place of monetary relief. Many welfare experts felt that the poor required charity because they were too indolent and ignorant to live on the pittance they received in wages. The Charity Organization Societies hoped that the rich, educated, economically efficient middle-class women would teach the poor how to live on what they made.

Essentially, friendly visiting was another attempt to use a missionary approach to remold the poor according to the values of the middle class.

[16] Jane Addams, *Twenty Years at Hull House* (New York, 1910), 72.

The visitor was to be the poor family's model and teacher, but more significantly its disciplinarian and goad, for the friendly visitor had the final say whether the family went down on the rolls of the Charity Organization Society as "worthy" or "unworthy." The visitor may have been supposed to be friendly, a benevolent and helpful representative from the upper reaches of society, but the poor family could never forget that she was a judge of whether they were spending their relief money wisely and whether they were acting morally.

The societies and the volunteers were motivated largely by a desire to impose social control on the poor. The New York Charity Organization Society warned that "if we do not furnish the poor with elevating influences, they will rule us by degrading ones." A Boston Brahmin, president of that city's Society, argued that charity organization and the friendly visitors were the "only hope of civilization against the gathering curse of pauperism in great cities."[17] Charity Organization was an attempt to employ scientific and efficient methods and face-to-face missionary or educational activity to remold the character of the poor.

Settlements assumed that such imposition of value systems was the wrong way to dispense urban charity. Instead they sought to unite people of different social classes on the basis of mutual respect, understanding, and tolerance. Addams intended her efforts to add the "social function to democracy." It was not enough for all Americans to go through the common ritual of voting at the same time for the same candidates. Democracy was more significantly a matter of economic cooperation and a common social life. Jane Addams had been born into the rural Illinois gentry after the Civil War—her father was a mill owner and state representative from his district. She attended a girls' academy and then embarked on the Grand Tour where she discovered both the abysmal poverty of England's industrial cities—she seems to have been unfamiliar with similar conditions in her own land—and the emptiness and insignificance of the socially respectable lady's functions of homemaking and attending "society" affairs. She founded Hull House so that she could work to reduce both urban squalor and the vacuity of the young middle-class lady's life. At Hull House she sought to recapture some of what she recalled of the open community spirit of the small town in which she was raised. Social classes were to be close to each other and knowledgeable about and understanding of each other. On Halsted Street the community was considerably more diverse than that of the Illinois prairie town, including middle-class old-stock Americans, fairly prosperous second-generation Irish-Americans, and poor first-generation Italians, Jews, and Bohemians. That they all could live and work to-

[17] Roy Lubove, *The Professional Altruist: The Emergence of Social Work as a Career, 1880–1930* (Cambridge, Mass., 1965), 5.

gether in a mutually respectful community was the essence of social democracy.

The settlement's main function was educational—both in the larger sense of teaching the community to work together and informing it on political and social issues of particular importance and in the sense of teaching children and adults specific skills and virtues. Hull House sponsored a number of social and study clubs and sought to mobilize the community in several campaigns to demand better city enforcement of sanitation codes. Like the other settlement houses, Hull House provided a nursery school and kindergarten for neighborhood children; adult education classes; instruction for girls in dietetics and the use of American prepackaged foods and cooking facilities—skills the settlement workers hoped the girls would pass on to their immigrant parents—; playgrounds and other recreational facilities for youngsters cooped up in factories or stores all day; trade training for boys unable or unequipped to find decent jobs; and health examinations and health education for neighborhood residents always threatened by disease from poor sanitation and overcrowded conditions. Public school systems assumed nearly all these burdens in the twentieth century, just as the settlement leaders had wanted them to do. That they did so was one of the great triumphs of educational reform in the Progressive era. Jane Addams and other progressives argued that the school could not fill all the needs of children and their community unless they conceived their task as broader than simply providing skill training in cultural subjects. In response, the public schools did greatly broaden their concerns—to the physical, vocational, and social needs of children, to adult education, to out-of-school recreation. They added school nurses to their staffs and examined the children's teeth, provided hot lunches and free milk, built playgrounds and appointed recreation directors, broadened the curriculum to include cooking and sewing, business English, metal stamping, and healthy home life. They opened their doors during the day to children, at night to adults, and on weekends and in the summer to the whole community.

Yet all these reforms and additions did not quite add up to "socialized" education as the liberal progressives like Jane Adams defined it. The additional school activities captured the form but not the spirit of what the settlements were seeking to accomplish in their communities. Jane Addams thought community strength depended on mutual respect between members of the community, not on the submissiveness with which each community member performed his social responsibilities. A community school should facilitate that sense of mutual respect. Her work with the immigrant groups in the Halsted Street neighborhood illustrated her goals. She was concerned both about conflict among groups and between immigrant children and their parents. For example, she persuaded a group of Irish-American ladies to give a party for a group of Italian women, and she thought it especially successful because one Irish-American woman told her that she had changed her plans to leave the neighborhood because some "Dagoes" had moved in next door. The problem of the conflict between the generations within immigrant families was perhaps even more complicated and poignant. The children of immigrants sought to assimilate, or at least appear to assimilate, as rapidly as possible to American ways which they found in the schools, in the streets, in whatever "mass media" were available. In their craving for peer approval they tried especially hard to copy other American children, and young as they were, they adapted rapidly. Soon they found that they were embarrassed by and ashamed of their parents who did not adapt (often psychologically could not adapt) as rapidly, clung to the old ways, wore different clothing, enforced or tried to enforce different standards of discipline, and spoke English poorly if at all. Their shame led many immigrant children to reject their parents and their ethnic culture. This rejection pleased most American social reformers for it hastened the assimilation process. The more rapidly the immigrants could be separated from their former ways, the better for American society, was an important tenet of conservative progressive belief.

Addams did not agree. She saw, and tried to get others to see, the immigrant as something more than a lump of clay to be remolded and inculcated with American middle-class values. To counteract the conflict between the immigrant generations she established the Labor Museum at Hull House, where she gathered examples of the arts and crafts that neighborhood immigrants had practiced as European peasants. She set the immigrant craftsmen to work in the museum using their native tools to make further examples of peasant handicrafts. At the same time she brought the children and others into the museum in an attempt to generate respect among them for the culture and skills of the Old World that, though they might be irrelevant to industrialization in the United States, produced lovely items and gave great satisfaction to the craftsmen. Addams also established Old Settlers Day on which the neighborhood honored the immigrants from each ethnic group who had come to Chicago earliest. She tried to engender respect between the generations by associating the heroism and courage of these immigrant pioneers with that of the native American trans-Appalachian pioneers. These ventures illustrated what Addams meant by socialized education and the school's duty to encourage community unity based upon mutual respect. The ideal school, the socialized school, would be just like a settlement house. It would be directed by residents of the neighborhood and its staff would be in constant contact with all the social dimensions of the community. Schoolwork would constantly be adapted to the needs and desires of the residents. School and community could be one; school would not seek to separate the child from his community, or his family, or the culture he had inherited. She hoped that the school would enrich the life of the community and that the community would enrich the curriculum and spirit of the school. In "socializing" education, she hoped—perhaps too romantically—to make the school a pivot around which a community could form and an instrument through which the community could fulfill itself.

V

The public schools were not very responsive to the spirit behind the settlement movement. When "socialized education" reached the schools, its basic thrust had been changed; it had been "captured" by the conservative progressives. This is evident in the small but significant visiting teacher movement that began in New York and several other cities after 1905. Although most visiting teachers were trained as social caseworkers and performed the functions now handled by school social workers, they avoided calling themselves social workers until 1942, for fear that their work would be impeded by the aura of charity surrounding "social work." Settlement houses on the Lower East Side began the visiting teacher movement in New York when in 1906 they assigned social workers from their staffs to work with difficult children in the schools. The following year the Public Education Association (PEA) of New York City, with aid from the Junior League, assumed responsibility for financing and directing the effort. The wives of the wealthy and intellectual elite of the city had formed the PEA in 1895 to support legislation that would improve the public schools. By 1907 it had become a coeducational organization that represented the most powerful reform interests in the city and it was dedicated to keeping control of the public schools out of the hands of Tammany Hall politicians and in the hands of the city's elite. The elite wished both to maintain high-quality instruction in the public schools and to employ them to stem the tide of social disorder threatening to well up from the immigrant and pauper hordes crowded into the ever burgeoning slums.

The Public Education Association spoke as if the visiting teacher were assuming the leading role in socializing the schools, not only through the social services she brought to bear upon the individual child but also through her influence upon the regular school teachers. Before World War I the visiting teacher movement was not large: in 1913, when New York City's public school system assumed financial responsibility for some visiting teachers, private agencies were supporting only ten in the whole city. Their supporters did not really expect visiting teachers to reach large numbers of children and solve large numbers of learning problems; rather, they hoped that the visiting teachers' attitudes toward the relation of social problems to school problems would encourage the schools to widen their concern from the intellectual and physical welfare of children to their social welfare as well. Educating the schools to assume wider social responsibilities was what the New York reformers meant by socializing education through the visiting teacher.

On that superficial level, Jane Addams would have been in whole-hearted agreement. When we explore more deeply into what the visiting teacher and her supporters thought her responsibilities were, a vast gap appears between their ideas and those of the liberal progressives like Jane Addams. The chairwoman of the PEA's Committee on Visiting Teachers, also the founder of the Junior League in New York, wrote in 1916:

> The Visiting Teacher experiment was undertaken . . . in the belief that, if the school could extend its reach into the homes of the children, better citizens could be developed, many failures prevented, and future expenditures thereby saved to New York City. When a child grows up to be a public charge or falls below his or her possibilities as a citizen, whether the failure be attributable to the school because it did not meet his needs, or to adverse conditions in the home, the State suffers as well as the individual and it is the State that pays the cost. The State, therefore, in the interest of its own future and for the sake of the economy, must adapt its instrument, the school, to meet the problems of these failures.

The experiment was a success, she continued, because visiting teachers demonstrated that "by obtaining cooperation in the child's home and by giving the school, at the same time, a better understanding of his environment so that it can adapt its methods to his particular needs, the most unpromising child can not only be kept from the courts but may be developed into a potential good citizen."[18] Julia Richman, a district superintendent on the Lower East Side, was the public school official most supportive of visiting teachers in the early years of the experiment. "Many leading educators," she wrote in 1910, pleading for money for the experiment, "realize that every national evil or weakness should be traced to its primary cause, and that such weakness should be controlled in future generations by the proper training of the children now in the schools. National extravagance can," she pointed out as an example, "be reduced if the millions of children now in schools be taught habits of economy and thrift."[19] Jane Addams had seen the socializing of education as a means of bringing the strengths of the community into the school for children to explore; Julia Richman thought that socializing education meant convincing the school to begin to identify and cure social weakness just as it had accepted its duty to identify and treat

[18] Natalie Henderson Swan, "Introduction" to Harriet M. Johnson, *The Visiting Teacher in New York City: A Statement* (New York, 1916), xi.

[19] Julia Richman, "A Social Need of the Public School," *Forum*, XLIII (February, 1910), 161.

physical weaknesses in schoolchildren. In schools where visiting teachers were assigned, the teacher "is being trained to look for what is wrong with the child *socially,* just as in the last few years she has learned to look for what is wrong with the child *physically.* When the time comes that every teacher shall be able to detect the social needs of each child, and the special school and home visitor shall follow up each case until social disabilities shall have been removed from the life of the child, then, and not till then, can we feel that rescue is possible for all school children."[20]

Visiting teachers spent most of their time adjusting the child to the school rather than the other way around. Most realized that there should be a reciprocal relation and wrote of their duty to make adjustments in the schools, but it is clear that adjusting the school in any fundamental sense was not part of their social purpose. The few such adjustments that they reported were of a rather minor and temporary sort. Teachers were asked to cooperate and tolerate certain habits in an immigrant child to save the child embarrassment while the visiting teacher worked with the family to eradicate the habits. A visiting teacher discovered that a non-achieving child had a bent for music and encouraged his teacher to allow him to use it in class whenever possible. Visiting teachers often discovered learning problems in children that the latter had been too embarrassed or too frightened to discuss with their teachers; the visiting teacher then told the classroom teacher and improvement followed. Only occasionally were there glimmerings of a view that socialized education might require schools to change rather fundamentally in order to serve the needs and develop the strengths of the people in their neighborhoods. "The need for sufficient flexibility to enable each school to meet the requirements of the children in its district is becoming generally recognized," the chairwoman of the PEA's Committee on Visiting Teachers wrote in 1916. "In this connection the visiting teacher can be of signal assistance. She not only knows the individual families, but she knows the social and industrial life of the district, which knowledge, combined with her experience in teaching, enables her to help the principal in adapting the school to the needs of the neighborhood."[21] Some visiting teachers did organize club work among students and parents outside the school, in a manner much like that of the settlement house. In 1916 visiting teachers were reported to "have assisted in organizing parents' associations and in conducting child's [*sic*] study clubs, some in arranging food exhibits with special emphasis on diet for children, exhibits of handwork done by children in their homes which have been illuminating to teachers and mothers—as to capabilities of the children and the lacks in the curriculum and which have also enabled the school to show its approval of

20 *Ibid.,* 168–169.
21 Swan, "Introduction," xiv–xv.

homework. One visiting teacher carried out an experiment in giving school credit for home helping which led to additions to the curriculum."[22]

More typically the visiting teachers were concerned with imposing values on the children with school difficulties, much in the manner of the friendly visitors. In her plea for financial support Julia Richman summarized several cases. One fourteen-year-old girl was compelled by her mother and older brother to peddle after school, which was apparently affecting her schoolwork adversely. "The brother is an idler, the father is dead, the mother is in ill health, and they are trying to throw the burden of support upon the child. These people have been in America only a few months, and will be brought to terms upon the threat that this is a violation of the law, and that if we report it to the courts, the family may be deported. It will, however, be necessary for the social worker to do some missionary work with the brother, and possibly even to secure some position for him, in order to place this family on its feet." The visiting teacher found the problem "of the girl of fourteen or fifteen who is just beginning to enter the life that leads to moral degradation" most difficult and time consuming.

> When a girl of this age is beginning to associate with vicious companions and to frequent low places of amusement, it takes infinite tact, much time and considerable money for the visitor to win the girl back to the paths of rectitude. In these cases it is only by means of personal friendship and personal attention, of taking her to concerts and other forms of pure entertainment, of an occasional day spent in the country, of frequent visits to the home and of personal effort of the most tactful kind, that the visitor can succeed in saving such a girl, body and soul.[23]

Such a vision of having a representative of the school extend her personal supervision over the morals and habits of children even when they were out of the grasp of the school itself was central to the concept of socializing education through the visiting teacher. Such extended supervision would increase the school's social efficiency, its ability to keep children out of jail and off the welfare rolls and to make them good citizens. The chairwoman of the PEA's visiting teacher committee pointed out that children in New York City attended school only one ninth of the time. "This record might be allowable for village life or for the countryside, but it does not belong to the teeming, distracting life of a metropolis whose perils and temptations beset the child at every turn. That vital thing called character cannot be shaped and determined in

[22] Jane F. Culbert (of the Public Education Association of New York), "Visiting Teachers and Their Activities," *Proceedings of the National Conference of Charities and Corrections* (Boston, 1916), 598.

[23] Richman, "Social Need," 166–168.

one-ninth of the child's time."[24] Socializing education for these reformers meant broadening the school's capacity to "rescue" children by imposing on them the values institutionalized in the American public school. Socialized education had become part of the conservative progressive program.

The schools' employment of social casework in socializing education was partly responsible for the conservative course which that reform followed in the public schools. Roy Lubove has argued quite cogently that social work's professionalization on the basis of the caseworkers' supposed expertise in dealing with single individuals led it to ignore issues of social reform and social structure. The casework approach took those social conditions as given and thought that the only way the worker could effect improvement was to adjust the individual to the social conditions surrounding him.[25] This habitual routine of adjusting the individual to social conditions without questioning those conditions led the caseworker to see social problems lodged in the individual rather than in the social structure. The normal, expected, indeed professional way for the visiting teacher to look at school problems or learning problems was to see them as evidence of the child's failure to adjust to the school. The individual, not the institution, was at fault. The casework view and the conservative progressive view reinforced each other. Improve the child by adjusting him to the given social structure so that he could play the part assigned to him in it.

VI

Jane Addams believed that the socialized educational institution, modeled on the settlement house, should serve the community as a cultural and political focus. "So far as a Settlement can discern and bring to local consciousness neighborhood needs which are common needs, and can give vigorous help to the municipal measures through which such needs shall be met, it fulfills its most valuable function."[26] At Hull House, Addams and the people of the neighborhood fought a series of political campaigns to secure better municipal services and to throw off boss rule. She encouraged neighborhood residents to stand up to the citywide administration and to work together for political ends in order to experience a vital sense of community. Such a community would enable men to overcome some of the sense of personal insignificance in relation to

[24] Swan, "Introduction," xv.
[25] Roy Lubove, in *The Professional Altruist,* has also suggested that as professionalization among social workers advanced, they began to avoid social reform.
[26] Addams, *Twenty Years at Hull House,* 225.

massive governmental and economic institutions in the urban complex. Hers was a typical liberal progressive solution to the problem of bigness, a part of the movement for direct democracy. The public schools appeared very inviting as potential loci of such community organization. At least one public school stood in every neighborhood, an ongoing institution with which community residents, especially the majority who were parents and children, were already familiar and involved. Liberal progressives like Jane Addams saw the school as a potential focus of community interest, participation, and power. Although neither she nor the other liberal progressives used the term "community control," their thinking resembled that of the community control advocates of the 1970s.

The reformers' desire to employ the public schools to build such local community spirit, autonomy, and power came into constant conflict with the desires and actions of the conservative progressive reformers. The latter sought to rationalize city government and to make it more efficient and sought to systematize the schools in order to make them inculcate more effectively the social values they thought necessary for social control. The conservative progressives thought of community in much larger terms than did the liberals. The liberals wished to make a vital community of the neighborhood; the conservatives to make the whole city and the whole nation a single efficient rational community. This difference in point of view was clear in the struggles to reform and reorganize the governance of urban school systems around the turn of the century.

In 1890 almost every major city governed its schools through some sort of district school system or through large school boards to which each district or ward within the city elected representatives. The influence of the early-nineteenth-century district school organization remained strong. Some centralization had, of course, occurred over the century. Citywide school administrators—superintendents and their subordinates—appeared in the 1840s, districts were consolidated from time to time, and school boards—which sometimes numbered over 100 members because so many districts in the city had to be represented—were reduced in size. These tentative moves toward more centralization still left power over educational decisions dispersed through the districts. New York City in the 1890s is a case in point. The mayor appointed a 21-person central school board, which in turn appointed 5 residents from each of the 24 wards (Brooklyn was not a part of New York at the time) as trustees of the schools in that ward. The trustees had the power to hire and fire all the personnel in their ward and to contract for all maintenance and construction work. To compound the confusion of responsibility, the mayor also appointed a group of three school inspectors in each locale, and they were expected to oversee the work of the trustees. The inspectors did not fulfill their centralizing function. They had little power and failed to use even that; the posts were generally regarded as well-paying political sinecures.

The decentralization of school governance paralleled the decentralization in urban government in general. The mayor's power was scant and that of the assembled councilmen or aldermen, representatives of local wards, strong. City politics was essentially a process of bargaining and logrolling among politicians representing local interests. Around the turn of the century upper-middle-class and upper-class businessmen, professionals, and reformers fought to revise this system of urban government. They found that it hampered their interests and their desires for citywide cohesion, economic development, and social control. They identified it as a source of vast corruption in urban government. Without a strong executive with citywide vision and centralized planning offices, the only way to secure authorization from the city government for development projects affecting the whole city was to bribe enough of the locally oriented politicians—whose constituencies would not support a citywide project unless it benefited their ward directly—to vote for it. Many of the reformers understood that the boss system had developed in cities for just this reason; the boss assembled enough local politicians to control the city government, agreed to get passed proposals whose proponents paid him the required bribe, and then used that money—or what he did not use for personal pleasure—to reward the local politicians in his coalition. The upper- and upper-middle-class reformers disliked this corruption—even when they were involved in it, or perhaps because they were—and the inefficiency that it imposed on the city's development.

These classes had a particular interest in citywide projects as opposed to merely local ward interests because they increasingly chose to live in newer, more secluded, more sheltered sections of the city far from their places of business and the cultural institutions which their forefathers had constructed in the center of the city. For them all parts of the city were increasingly interdependent. The businessman wanted his factory protected by a strong and honest police force while he was away; he needed rapid transit facilities so that he and his workers could get to work quickly and cheaply. Doctors interested in improving the public health needed citywide arenas in which to work: measures to improve sanitation facilities would prevent disease only if they were uniformly applied over the whole urban area. These men were also urban boosters who wanted to increase the city's capacity to attract more people and more business. To make the city more attractive required massive commitments by city government to public works—more streets, sewers, streetcars, parks, schools, land fill, and so on. Localism within urban government hindered all these efforts. When the boss system worked effectively—and, for all their power, the bosses were frequently unable to deliver on their promises—it was needlessly expensive and slow. When it did not, there was chaos. Localistic aldermen blocked project after project for the improvement of the whole city. Neighborhood businessmen did not want rapid transit that would speed people out of the neighborhood so that they could buy conveniently downtown. Aldermen wanted new streets and sewers but each fought tenaciously and at great length to assure himself that his ward got its share of the new facilities and of the jobs that went with them. Since the neighborhood was the source of the local politician's power, he sought to enhance its importance and to keep it cohesive; the reformers and centralizers, on the other hand, wanted to deemphasize the neighborhoods so that the city could be viewed and its development planned as a single unit.

Reformers' efforts to solve these problems of fragmented control over urban services through centralizing city government took a variety of forms. Whenever possible, they fostered the establishment of commission or city manager forms of city government. The first plan vested strong executive powers in a small group of men elected at-large from the city; in the second a commission, elected in a similar manner, appointed a professional city manager—an urban "expert"—who held the bulk of the ongoing executive power. In both cases the reformers succeeded in breaking the power of local politics: individual wards were no longer represented in city government and, especially with the city manager, the administration and much of the day-to-day policy making was separated from partisan political considerations. In larger cities, where the power of localism and machine politicians was stronger, the best the reformers could hope to achieve were reductions in the size of the city councils or boards of aldermen, at-large rather than representative council or aldermanic elections, and increases in the power of the mayor's office. In this way the reformers tried and to some extent succeeded in centralizing power.

With schools the situation was quite similar. The conservative progressives wished to impose a centralized control over the public schools in order to make them serve the interests of the whole city more effectively. They thought that local control of schools caused corruption that was expensive and that impeded high-quality instruction. Most school appointments were political ones, including that of teacher. School janitors, frequently the brokers of school politics of the day, placed maintenance contracts which generally brought poor workmanship to the schools at ridiculously high prices. The elite reformers also thought, at least in some cities, that local control prevented some children from having a chance to learn true American values because Catholic districts and immigrant districts encouraged their schools to preserve "foreign" values. It is very difficult to judge the accuracy of the conservative progressives' assessments of the effects of localism on schools in the late nineteenth century. There is very little evidence to suggest, for example, that local control actually did encourage schools to respond creatively to the particular cultures of their neighborhoods—local political control was hardly likely to break the habits and attitudes that principals and teachers had learned at normal school. The ward boss did have to clear all prospective teachers before they were appointed but the bosses cleared almost all. Political favoritism was probably most important in determining which teachers became principals and which principals, assistant superintendents. Even here, however, it is difficult to interpret the many charges of political favoritism—whether they represent truth or just the frustrations of those who did not get promoted. There was corruption in the school system—schools often bought coal at twice the rate that other institutions did. How widespread and how costly it was, however, is unknown. In short, it appears that local control in the late nineteenth century was neither the abyss that the conservative reformers depicted nor a source of much encouragement for the liberal reformers' dreams of the school as a community center.

The conservative reformers, nonetheless, were convinced that destruction of local control was necessary to making schools more efficient social institutions. Business paid a considerable portion of the school taxes and wanted the most for its money. Businessmen and elite reformers wanted the schools to foster social order—to make the city streets safe to walk—and to build a stable and industrious population. They wanted schools to impose uniform values of honesty, respect for authority, thrift, and Americanism. Reformers distrusted local control because it placed power in the hands of the non-elite: local businessmen, politicians, saloonkeepers, perhaps even workingmen. Such a pattern violated what the elite felt was its proprietary right to control intellectual and cultural institutions, to control the instrument of reform that they had done so much to create since the common school movement began. Supervising educational institutions was their responsibility, not the local politician's. The elite sensed that they were, in a democracy, losing their traditional control over urban politics—that the immigrant working-class vote was too powerful to overcome. They did hope, however, that they might retain control over society's future and its political health by controlling education—which even in a democracy could be reserved for the elite who were expert in matters of culture and intelligence. By controlling the institutions which were to mold future generations, the elite hoped to halt the social deterioration which they saw resulting from their loss of political power.

This desire explains the efforts they have made continuously since 1890 to "take the schools out of politics." These elite reformers have struggled to centralize control of the schools in single, citywide, small school boards, appointed either by the mayor (often with the advice of a group of leading citizens who provided a list of "acceptable" candidates for each vacant position) or sometimes the governor (considered less subject to the pressures of local city politics) or elected at-large rather than from individual districts. Reformers have sought to make school elections nonpartisan, thus protecting them from boss or party influence and giving independent citizens, not interested in political advancement, a chance to run. In almost every city around the turn of the century the city's elite banded together in citizens' committees to wrest control from the politicians. The Public Education Association in New York, formed originally to fight Tammany's control of the city schools, did succeed in destroying the ward trustee system and placing all control in the hands of the central board appointed by the mayor. Unfortunately for the reformers, the city's voters frequently elected mayors from Tammany whose appointments rarely satisfied reform wishes. Nonetheless, in New York and other cities, the establishment of small centralized boards, however chosen, served to further the conservative reformers' ends. Since the small school boards had neither the time nor the administrative capacity to supervise the day-to-day activities of the schools, they had to delegate more responsibility to professional administrators—experts in school management who because of their professional training and aspirations shared the values of the elite more than they shared those of local politicians and local neighborhoods. Although the elite never successfully freed schooling from "politics" so that they could dominate it, they did, by curtailing the influence of political parties and local politicians in education and by enhancing the power of the expert administrators, maintain their values in public school systems which served populations with class and political orientations quite different from theirs.

To get the schools to meet the needs of the larger city community, the elite felt it necessary to insulate them from the city's smaller communities and their people. As the elite reformers of Pittsburgh stated during one campaign to "take the schools out of politics": "Employment as ordinary laborer and in the lowest class of mill work would naturally lead to the conclusion that such men did not have sufficient education or business training to act as school directors. . . . Objection might also be made to small shopkeepers, clerks, workmen at many trades, who by lack of educational advantages and business training, could not, no matter how honest, be expected to administer properly the affairs of an educational system, requiring special knowledge, and where millions are spent each year."[27] Jane Addams had hoped to arouse precisely this kind of person to social action through socialized schools.

[27] Samuel P. Hays, "The Politics of Reform in Municipal Government in the Progressive Era," *Pacific Northwest Quarterly*, LV (October, 1964), 163.

VII

The programs that progressive reformers like Dewey and Addams outlined had promised a great deal but, although the reformers did inspire changes in the schools that did broaden the education and improve the lives of millions of Americans, the more significant and far reaching of the promises Dewey made went unfulfilled because the conservative progressives captured the impetus of school reform. Their vision of the purposes and proper organization of the public schools came to dominate by World War I. Their success resulted from their control of or alliance with the dominant economic powers in the country and from their successful appeal to the middle class. The liberal progressives' vision of community and socialized education appeared too radical and mystical to most Americans. Efficiency, rationality, social control, and national unity appealed to the businessman's and professional's economic self-interest and to the middle class' vision of social reform. Moreover, the conservatives were able to identify community control and localism with political corruption—thus appealing further to the moralism of the middle class and the interests of the large taxpayers. War xenophobia after 1915 made Americans even less tolerant of the "different" values and cultures that liberal progressives hoped community control would enhance. Furthermore, as the Progessive era waned, conservative progressive reform doctrine provided many Americans growing tired of struggling to improve society a means of maintaining a rhetorical commitment to reform while withdrawing from the actual struggle. School reform, as envisioned by the conservative progressives, allowed people to assume a middle ground between the more radical position that condemned American institutions for contributing to poverty and slums and personal dehumanization and the reactionary (or completely nonprogressive) position that argued there was nothing wrong with America at all. Yes, people could say, something is wrong with American life, but the schools, efficient, progressive, socially oriented, will improve it in the future. The nature of the improvement that conservative progressives sought can be understood more clearly by an analysis of the development of progressive reform in the American high school, subject of the next chapter.

GUIDE TO FURTHER READING

Educational change after 1880 is introduced in LAWRENCE CREMIN, *The Transformation of the School: Progressivism in American Education, 1876–1957* (New York, 1961), an optimistic and historiographically significant interpretation of the subject and one which concludes with an excellent bibliography. In response to Cremin's generous hypotheses, and based upon recent research on American social and intellectual history on the postbellum era, revisionist interpretations of educational progressivism have been developed. The most popular revisionist studies are JOEL SPRING, *Education and the Rise of the Corporate State* (Boston, 1972), CLARENCE KARIER et al., *Roots of Crisis: American Education in the Twentieth Century* (Chicago, 1973), EDWARD KRUG, *The Shaping of the American High School, 1880–1920* (Madison, Wis., 1964), and MARVIN LAZERSON's excellent study, *Origins of the Urban School: Public Education in Massachusetts, 1870–1915* (Cambridge, Mass., 1971). PATRICIA GRAHAM, *Community and Class in American Education, 1865–1918* (New York, 1974), TIMOTHY SMITH, "Progressivism in American Education, 1880–1900," *Harvard Educational Review*, XXXI (Spring, 1961), 168–193, SOL COHEN, *Progressives and Urban School Reform: The Public Education Association of New York City, 1895–1954* (New York, 1964), and WILLIS RUDY, *Schools in an Age of Mass Culture* (Englewood Cliffs, N. J., 1965), focus on educational progressivism from several perspectives and offer useful bibliographies.

Our discussion of educational progressivism is based upon these important interpretations of the larger issues of the Progressive era: ROBERT H. WIEBE, *The Search for Order, 1877–1920* (New York, 1967), ROLAND BERTHOFF, *An Unsettled People: Social Order and Disorder in American History* (New York, 1971), Part IV, DAVID NOBLE, *The Progressive Mind, 1890–1917* (Chicago, 1970), WILLIAM A. WILLIAMS, *The Contours of American History* (Cleveland, 1961), RICHARD HOFSTADTER, *The Age of Reform: From Bryan to F.D.R.* (New York, 1955), ERIC GOLDMAN, *Rendezvous with Destiny: A History of Modern American Reform* (New York, 1952), SAMUEL P. HAYS, *The Response to Industrialism, 1885–1914* (Chicago, 1957), GILMAN OSTRANDER, *American Civilization in the First Machine Age: 1890–1940* (New York, 1970), CLYDE GRIFFEN, "The Progressive Ethos," in STANLEY COBEN and LORMAN RATNER, eds., *The Development of an American Culture* (Englewood Cliffs, N. J., 1970), 120–149, SIDNEY FINE, *Laissez Faire and the General Welfare State* (Ann Arbor, Mich., 1956), MORTON WHITE, *Social Thought in America: The Revolt Against Formalism* (New York, 1957), CHARLES FORCEY, *The Crossroads of Liberalism: Croly, Weyl, Lippmann, and the Progressive Era, 1900–1925* (New York, 1961), JERRY ISRAEL, ed., *Building the Organizational Society: Essays on Associational Activities in Modern America* (New York, 1972), HAROLD U. FAULKNER, *The Quest for Social Justice, 1898–1914* (New York, 1931), GABRIEL KOLKO, *The Triumph of Conservatism: A Reinterpretation of American History, 1900–1916* (New York, 1963), JAMES WEINSTEIN, *The Corporate Ideal in the Liberal State: 1900–1918* (Boston, 1968), DANIEL LEVINE, *Varieties of Reform Thought* (Madison, Wis., 1964), THOMAS R. HASKELL, "Safe Havens for Sound Opinion: The American Social Science Association and the Professionalization of Social Thought in the United States, 1865–1909" (Unpublished Dissertation, Stanford University, 1973), MARY O. FURNER, *Advocacy and Objectivity: A Crisis in the Professionalization of American Social Science, 1865–1905* (Lexington, Ky., 1975), and SAMUEL HABER, *Efficiency and Uplift: Scientific Management in the Progressive Era* (Chicago, 1964). Two central primary documents of progressive ideology are WALTER LIPPMANN, *Drift and Mastery* (New York,

1914), and HERBERT CROLY, *The Promise of American Life* (New York, 1911); both have been reprinted recently in paperback editions.

JOHN DEWEY's philosophy, policies, and influence is currently undergoing reinterpretation. CLARENCE KARIER's excellent examination of liberalism under stress, "Liberal Ideology and the Quest for Orderly Change," in KARIER, *Roots of Crisis* (Chicago, 1973), 84–107, recalls a significant weakness in Dewey's pragmatism. JEAN B. QUANDT, *From the Small Town to the Great Community: The Social Thought of Progressive Intellectuals* (New Brunswick, N. J., 1970), suggests that Dewey's Protestant background in a small community influenced his image of the ideal learning environment considerably. RICHARD HOFSTADTER, *Anti-Intellectualism in American Life* (New York, 1963), Parts III–V, MORTON WHITE, *The Origins of Dewey's Instrumentalism* (New York, 1943), MERLE CURTI, *The Social Ideas of American Educators* (New York, 1935), GEORGE DYKHUIZEN, *The Life and Mind of John Dewey* (Carbondale, Ill., 1973), and OSCAR HANDLIN, *John Dewey's Challenge to Education: Historical Perspectives on the Cultural Context* (New York, 1959), remain useful. DEWEY elaborates his educational philosophy in *Democracy and Education* (New York, 1916), *The School and Society* (1900; Chicago, 1915), *The Child and the Curriculum* (Chicago, 1902), *Experience and Education* (New York, 1938), REGINALD D. ARCHAMBAULT, ed., *Dewey on Education: Appraisals* (New York, 1966), PAUL A. SCHILPP, ed., *The Philosophy of John Dewey* (Evanston, Ill., 1939). Southern Illinois University Press is currently publishing John Dewey's collected works; two useful guides have appeared from that project: JO ANN BOYDSTON, ed., *Guide to the Works of John Dewey* (Carbondale, Ill., 1970), and BOYDSTON and KATHLEEN POULOS, *Checklist of Writings about John Dewey, 1887–1973* (Carbondale, Ill., 1974).

While PAUL VIOLAS, "Jane Addams and the New Liberalism," in KARIER, *Roots of Crisis* (Chicago, 1973), 66–83, an intellectual sketch, argues that conservative goals, such as social control, inspired Addams' involvement with humanitarian reform, ALLEN DAVIS, *American Heroine: The Life and Legend of Jane Addams* (New York, 1973), DANIEL LEVINE, *Jane Addams and the Liberal Tradition* (Madison, Wis., 1971), and LEVINE, *Varieties of Reform Thought* (Madison, Wis., 1964), suggest that ideology and philosophy were rather irrelevant to Addams' work. CHRISTOPHER LASCH has interpreted Addams' life in *The New Radicalism in America [1889–1963]: The Intellectual as a Social Type* (New York, 1965), and collected a useful anthology, *The Social Thought of Jane Addams* (Indianapolis, 1965).

The Americanization movement has been examined in ROBERT A. CARLSON, *The Quest for Conformity: Americanization Through Education* (New York, 1975), EDWARD G. HARTMANN, *The Movement to Americanize the Immigrant* (New York, 1948), GERD KORMAN, *Industrialization, Immigrants and Americanizers: The View from Milwaukee, 1866–1921* (Madison, Wis., 1967), JOHN HIGHAM, *Strangers in the Land: Patterns of American Nativism, 1860–1925* (New Brunswick, N. J., 1955), and OSCAR HANDLIN, *The Uprooted* (Boston, 1951).

The centralization movement in the 1890s that reduced working-class and ethnic influence on urban boards of education is treated in DAVID TYACK, *The One Best System: A History of American Urban Education* (Cambridge, Mass., 1974), WILLIAM ISSEL, "Modernization in Philadelphia School Reform, 1882–1905,"

Pennsylvania Magazine of History and Biography, XCIV (July, 1970), 358–383, ELINOR M. GERSMAN, "Progressive Reform of the St. Louis School Board, 1897," *History of Education Quarterly,* X (Spring, 1970), 3–21, DIANE RAVITCH, *The Great School Wars: New York City, 1805–1973* (New York, 1974), chs. 8–16, SAMUEL P. HAYS, "The Politics of Reform in Municipal Government in the Progressive Era," *Pacific Northwest Quarterly,* LV (October, 1964), 157–169, JOSEPH M. CRONIN, *The Control of Urban Schools: Perspectives on the Power of Educational Reformers* (New York, 1973), and SOL COHEN, *Progressives and Urban School Reform* (New York, 1964).

CHAPTER 10

The High School in the Progressive Era

I

In 1890 THE AMERICAN HIGH SCHOOL WAS A RATHER MINOR SEGMENT of the public educational effort more closely allied with the colleges than with the public schools; by 1920 the high school enjoyed a reputation as not yet the biggest but the most important and progressive segment of the American educational enterprise. Its image changed from that of an elite institution to that of the most important agent of mass training for life. The change is clear in two major reports published by committees of the National Education Association, one in 1893 and the other in 1918. The earlier report, written by the Committee of Ten, demanded that all instructional efforts in the secondary school be directed toward "training the powers of observation, memory, expression, and reasoning." The report of the Commission on the Reorganization of Secondary Education, published twenty-five years later, listed seven objectives, the famous Cardinal Principles of Secondary Education, by which the report was identified: "Health, command of fundamental processes, worthy home-membership, vocation, citizenship, worthy use of leisure, and ethical character." In the quarter century between the two reports, the high school in America had moved from sharing the concerns of higher education to sharing the concerns and purposes of common school education. In the process the high school became an agent of conservative progres-

288

sive reform. This transformation had three basic causes: the enormous increase in high school enrollments over the period, the concomitant increase in the number and variety of educators directly concerned with high school operation, and the relevance of conservative progressive doctrine to the professional and status needs of this group of public educators.

Between 1890 and 1920 the American public high school experienced an almost ninefold increase in enrollments—from 200,000 in 1890 to over 1 million by 1912 to almost 2 million by 1920.[1] If we combine the figures for public and private secondary school enrollments, we find both kinds of secondary schooling enrolling 6.7 percent of the 14–17 age group in 1890; 10.2 percent in 1900; 15.4 percent in 1910; and 32.3 percent in 1920. By 1910 the overwhelming majority of these children attended public high schools rather than private secondary schools. Urban areas experienced the greatest increase in attendance (sometimes 50 to 60 percent of a city's high-school age children were enrolled in high school by 1920). Scattered population and the continued need for adolescent labor that rendered child labor laws ineffective in the rural areas retarded high school development there. The percentage figures combined with the urban concentration reveal that the character of high school students changed dramatically, becoming more diverse in background and social class and requiring, it appeared, a profoundly different program than had been appropriate for the students of the 1890s. Then the high school had been an institution of elite schooling; by 1920 it was closer to being an agency of mass education.

Historians are unable to explain completely the reasons for this remarkable increase in high school attendance over the thirty-year period. Enrollments in public high schools increased gradually throughout the second half of the nineteenth century, but why that secular trend accelerated sharply when it did remains something of a mystery. Changes in the economy surely had a lot to do with it. Around the turn of the century industries mechanized many of the simple routine operations on which they had previously employed children. What unskilled labor remained was more likely to be heavy labor that only strong adults could perform. Therefore, many children who would have worked in factories in the nineteenth century were unable to find jobs and chose to attend high school instead. Since child labor laws passed in this period did not cause but merely confirmed the drop in the employment of children, they may not be cited as having caused the upsurge in high school attendance. A second economic change contributed to increased enrollments. Sharp increases in per capita income in many social classes after 1900 allowed

---

[1] Our discussion in this chapter has relied heavily on Edward Krug's study of *The Shaping of the American High School, 1880–1920* (Madison, Wis., 1964).

more families to let their children forego earnings and continue in school. Third, the number of white-collar jobs increased abruptly after 1890. Widespread business adoption of the typewriter and the duplicator created literally thousands of new secretarial and paper-pushing jobs—the ability to type and copy documents created a need for more typed documents and more copies of them. As the economy's emphasis shifted from basic industries to consumer industries, the need for service personnel—especially salesmen and salesclerks—grew sharply. This kind of job became reserved for the person who had some high school education. Why this happened is difficult to explain; much historical investigation of this point remains to be done. In many cases the skills taught in the high school were not necessary to the performance of the job, but employers may have felt (or educators may have led them to feel) that the student who remained in school demonstrated perseverance, ambition, and a willingness to follow directions and put up with rigid routines that made him more qualified for white-collar work than the person who had left school. In any case, high school enrollments rose because it became increasingly evident to those interested in the status and income accompanying white-collar occupations that a high school education was a valuable—perhaps *the* most valuable—guarantee of securing such positions. Anxiety about decreasing opportunity in America and intensified job competition may have caused many to want the insurance of added education—an insurance that in the nineteenth century few had thought it necessary to obtain. Much of this reasoning is speculative; definitive answers must await further research.

Increased enrollment brought an increase in the number of persons employed in the high school setting. The number of public high schools increased sixfold from 1890 to 1920—from 2,526 to 14,326. There were less than 10,000 high school teachers in 1890; over 100,000 in 1920. Other high-school-related occupations grew at an even faster rate—there were more superintendents and assistant superintendents, assistant principals, recreation directors, school psychologists, and vocational guidance counselors. Since prospective high school teachers had to receive more advanced and more specialized training than the common school teachers, teacher training institutions had to upgrade themselves (many claiming college and university status). They needed larger faculties and more facilities in order to offer training in all the specialized subjects and nonclassroom tasks of the high school. Thus, the growth of the high school spurred the development of a whole class of educators who were neither teachers nor superintendents.

This increase in size and specialization of function among those working in the public high school led them to seek a professional identity and status of their own—separate from that of the college teacher and from that of the elementary school teacher. The conservative progressives' desire to impose social control, to use the schools to prepare children to fit into the society and to perform their appointed roles in it efficiently, seemed tailored to the needs of the high school personnel's professional aspirations. Conservative progressivism suggested a basic distinction between elementary and secondary mass education. The former taught general values and skills; the latter taught different values and skills to different children according to the specialized roles they would assume as adults. This distinction made the high school educators most responsible for the social engineering function of the schools, for supervising the distribution of human resources in the society. In this way the high school developed a function of its own and its personnel developed a professional identity and purpose all their own. We can understand this process, a rather subtle and perhaps only half-conscious one at the time, by examining carefully the change in the aspirations of the high school between 1893 and 1918.

II

In the 1890s the public high school was not very different from the college in curriculum, student body, or staff. Both institutions trained the elite. The high school's major purpose was to teach the cultural skills to the children of the elite and to prepare them for college. Latin remained the most important part of the public high school curriculum. In most cases the families who could afford to let their children attend were already fairly well-to-do; the high school was not primarily an institution for social mobility in the 1890s. This was especially true of those who remained beyond the tenth grade. Throughout the nineteenth century a not insignificant percentage of students consisted of girls who attended for a year or two in order to qualify themselves as elementary school teachers. Many of those girls were undoubtedly using the high school to prepare themselves to rise from the working class to the genteel middle class. These girls, whatever their numbers, did not set the tone or purpose of the high school, whose teachers were more professionally distinct from elementary teachers than from college professors. Before 1900 a good many people served both as college professors and high school teachers at different times in their careers, even moving from college teaching to secondary teaching or administration without demonstrable loss in status or self-esteem. High school teachers were often called professors, and before 1900 presented papers at meetings of the scholarly organizations dedicated to academic research. Furthermore, the lack of clear distinction between secondary and tertiary levels of schooling that appeared in the antebellum period continued through the end of the nineteenth century. Although the elite colleges had well established rules requiring all matriculants to be secondary school graduates, the majority of colleges still operated secondary departments and made eleventh- and twelfth-grade material part of the college curriculum. The 1890s would see several efforts to clarify the confused relations between the high school and the college; the Committee of Ten's was the most famous.

In 1892 the National Education Association—urged by James H. Baker, former principal of the Denver High School and newly elected president of the University of Colorado; Nicholas Murray Butler, a young philosophy professor at Columbia who had visions of becoming an important school reformer in New York and in the rest of the nation (he was instrumental in the founding of the Public Education Association in New York); and Harvard's President Charles W. Eliot, to expand its interests from elementary education to higher education—appointed the Committee of Ten on Secondary School Studies to investigate and recommend changes in the college admissions structure and the curriculum of the secondary school. The two problems were closely intertwined, for most public high schools and private academies determined their curricula according to what the colleges required entering students to know. However, each college had somewhat different admissions standards—Harvard expected its applicants to know different things than Columbia expected its applicants to know, for example. Each college had precise admissions requirements and each ran its own admissions examinations. Harvard would list six or seven novels on which each applicant should be prepared to write an essay, three Latin works that the student should be able to translate on sight, and certain history texts that the student should be able to summarize. The admissions examinations were not very different from the normal classroom recitation—they tested the student's memory much more than his ability to think or use ideas. Such precise requirements placed great burdens on schoolmasters attempting to prepare a class whose students wished to enter more than one college.

Midwestern state universities solved this problem through the so-called accreditation method, whereby university professors would visit any high school seeking accreditation within their state and, if they found its curriculum rigorous enough and its teachers able enough, would certify that all students who graduated from that high school in good standing or above a certain grade average could automatically enter the university. Although Michigan had started this method in 1869–1870, it did not become generalized in the Midwest until the 1890s when other colleges began to accept the state university certifications in lieu of their own admissions examinations. In 1902 the North Central Association of Colleges and Secondary Schools took over the accreditation function for all midwestern colleges and universities and that single agency certified all schools in the region. Accreditation also appeared in some of the western and southern states. In New England and the mid-Atlantic states another solution emerged. A central examination board would test all college applicants in a variety of subjects and submit each student's grades on the examinations to the college to which he wished admission. Each college could use and interpret those tests as it wished, setting whatever grade level it chose as a minimum and requiring the applicants to take tests in whatever subjects its faculty thought important. The tests themselves, however, were standard for all colleges—all students who needed Latin for admission would have to study the same texts in order to pass the Latin examination regardless of the college they wished to enter. This plan made the schoolmaster's task considerably easier. Butler seems to have been the first to broach the idea of an examination board. He suggested it in 1891 and in 1893 tried to get the Columbia faculty to open correspondence with other colleges to begin such an organization; but he failed, as did Eliot when he proposed similar action by the Association of Colleges of New England in 1894. Finally, in 1899, the Association of College and Preparatory Schools of the Middle States and Maryland resolved to sponsor such an examination board, and the first tests were given in 1901. In that year the organization called itself the College Entrance Examination Board, dropping its association with the mid-Atlantic region, and by 1905 a number of colleges and universities throughout the nation were using its facilities.

The Committee of Ten was formed while debate on these issues was intense but before any likely solution had gained much headway among the nation's institutions of higher education. Accreditation had many friends, but a majority of those concerned with college admissions argued that although it had many advantages it was not really adequate as a means of regulating college admissions. Most considered the method too easy in that the visitations for certification were infrequent and often cursory and the method treated all students in a school as equal—when colleges wished to know which few students in a high school merited admission, the accreditation method made either all or none of its graduates eligible. Butler may have sought to involve the NEA with the problem in order to further his specific alternative to accreditation; at any rate, others looked to the Committee of Ten for imaginative recommendations for reducing the chaotic relations between high school preparation and college admission.

The association appointed the presidents of Harvard, Michigan, Missouri, Colorado, and Vassar, and a professor from Oberlin (who would soon become president there) to the committee along with William Torrey Harris, then Commissioner of Education, the headmaster of the Lawrenceville School, the principal of the Girls High and Latin School in Boston, and the principal and professor of mental and moral science at the Albany Public High School. Two of the college presidents had once been high school teachers. Only Harris had experience with education at the elementary school level. The committee in turn appointed nine subcommittees, each of which was to study the specific problems of a major category of subjects: Latin; Greek; English; other modern languages; mathematics; physics, astronomy, and chemistry; natural history, including botany, physiology, and zoology; history, civil government, and political economy; and geography and geology. The subjects picked for subcommittee consideration demonstrate that the committee viewed secondary education in strictly academic terms with special emphasis on the cultural, elite subjects—two of the nine subcommittees were concerned with the classical languages. The full committee reviewed the nine individual reports, added their own ideas, and wrote (Eliot was the major author) a report recommending general curriculum policy for the secondary schools, to which they added the reports of the nine subcommittees.

The Committee of Ten's major recommendation was that the secondary school should not distinguish between students who were ending their educational careers in the high school and those who intended to go on to college. All should take the same courses and receive the same kind of teaching. The committee argued, it must be noted, not that a college preparatory course was the best education for everyone at the high school level but, rather, that the best preparation for life was also the best preparation for college. An education good enough for the terminal student was also good enough for those planning to enter college. The committee wished to enable students to postpone their decision about attending college as long as possible. Because most colleges required at least four years of Latin for admission, a student had to choose to prepare for college early or not at all. If he chose the latter course, he could not change his mind. The college men on the committee surely hoped that easing this requirement for an early decision would bring more students into the colleges.

But their major concern was the fate of the terminal student, always a problem for the secondary school. In 1890 high schools and academies were training 6.7 percent of the age group; colleges, perhaps 1.5 percent of the 18–22 age group. Only one quarter, therefore, of the high school population was continuing on to college. Some of the remaining three quarters, of course, left high school after the first or second year or took a teacher training course and thus did not very much concern the high school administrators. But a significant number remained who did not intend to go to college, and the heavy concentration on Latin and Greek in the college preparatory program seemed inappropriate. High school leaders sought to develop alternative programs—English and science tracks—but inevitably, since the high school's primary concern was with college preparation, these alternatives turned out to be poorly staffed and second rate. The Committee of Ten sought to eliminate the problem altogether by deemphasizing the high school's responsibility for college preparation. Instead, the secondary school's "main function," the committee wrote, "is to prepare for the duties of life that small proportion of all the children in the country—a proportion small in number, but very important to the welfare of the nation—who show themselves able to profit by an education prolonged to the eighteenth year, and whose parents are able to support them while they remain so long at school."[2] If a child was properly prepared to assume the "duties of life" as a member of the elite, the committee's report concluded, he was properly prepared for college admission.

The committee went on to argue that proper preparation of those few members of the society with the leisure, money, and ability to profit from prolonged schooling for the duties they would assume in life entailed disciplining their minds rather than preparing them for jobs. The committee also recommended, somewhat tentatively, four different programs of study which combined the high school subjects in different ways. Each would be sufficiently rigorous to qualify a student for college admission. Considering various academic subjects equivalent for admissions purposes marked a significant break with the past because it regarded the quality and depth of instruction as more important than the specific subject matter in determining eligibility for college. The committee proposed a classical, a Latin-scientific, a modern languages, and an English program. Each would prepare a student adequately either for life or for college. The programs were quite similar: each required the student to take four years of English, four of mathematics, and three of history. Each contained four to nine years of foreign language and at least three years of natural science. The committee spent considerable time juggling the number of class hours assigned to each one of these subjects—trading, for example, the fifth hour of Latin in the third year for one more hour of science in that year, and so on. The committee found that it wanted students to study too many subjects in too great depth and constructed programs of such difficulty that few high schools in the nation could implement them.

It is important to recognize—as the high school reformers of the first quarter of the twentieth century failed to do—that the Committee of Ten did not seek to impose "class" education on the masses or to impose college standards on the secondary schools. The committee members knew that the high schools were not then, and they did not expect them to become, mass institutions. They believed that high schools would continue to train the elite to assume elite positions in the society. They thought that discipline of the mind, training of the powers of "observa-

[2] The *Committee of Ten Report* is conveniently reprinted in Theodore R. Sizer, *Secondary Schools at the Turn of the Century* (New Haven, Conn., 1964); our quotation is from p. 261.

tion, memory, expression, and reasoning," was vital to such preparation. The committee members recognized the validity, indeed the necessity, of manual and vocational training, but thought that those activities belonged in the mass institutions—the elementary schools and vocational training institutions which might be created as extensions of them. The committee was not antiprogressive. Instead, it viewed the high school and college as one unit of the educational system and elementary and vocational schools as another. Its aim was to keep the two units separate, in institutional form and purpose. It sought to distinguish higher education from common education.

The committee also sought to clarify the articulation between the high school and the college—to define precisely where one's responsibility ended and the other's began. It argued firmly that only a four-year high school curriculum was adequate college preparation. Its members, especially President Eliot, hoped to stop colleges from recruiting students out of the tenth and eleventh grades of high schools and high schools from claiming the title of college on the strength of a few elementary-level college courses they offered in the eleventh and twelfth grades. In the nineteenth century a student could enter college whenever he convinced the college he was ready by passing an examination which tested his ability to memorize a few books. This examination was not likely to be very difficult when colleges competed for fee-paying students. It was not coincidental that Eliot chaired both the Committee of Ten and the Board of Trustees of the Carnegie Foundation for the Advancement of Teaching at the time that foundation defined the Carnegie Unit, which in 1906 finally did succeed in regularizing the relation between colleges and high schools. In seeking to establish a pension system for college teachers in private nondenominational colleges, the foundation had to define a "college"—how big, what kind of courses should it offer, and what kind of students should it have? The Carnegie planners determined that a college must have at least six professors, offer a four-year liberal arts program, and admit only students who had graduated from secondary school. The last standard raised additional questions. The foundation's planners defined "graduation" in terms of the number of hours of classroom instruction at the secondary level a student had received. They established the "unit" as a measure of five hours of classroom work in a subject each week during one school year; courses that met less than the required five hours per week received fractional units. In order to "graduate," the student had to accumulate at least fourteen units, with no more than four taken in any single year. This definition made the four-year high school course mandatory for all students going on to college and bound the high schools to a four-year curriculum. A second-rate college could no longer take students from the midst of their high school studies or its faculty would lose their pensions; high schools had to offer a four-year program or their students would be ineligible to attend any college which wanted pensions for its faculty. The Committee of Ten had also sought to establish such structural distinctions so that the colleges and secondary schools could divide their responsibilities and the limited supply (at least in the 1890s) of postelementary school students.

An even more important motive behind the Committee of Ten's recommendations was its desire to impose on secondary schools and, through them, on other colleges the reforms that had changed the leading universities and colleges since 1870. The committee urged secondary schools to establish a limited elective system in which students could choose among four programs and among some elective courses within each program, and it sought to open the high school curriculum to modern subjects like science, history, and English. Although two of its nine subcommittees studied the problems of the classics, the committee was probably less concerned with Latin and Greek than most of the leading high schools of the day. That five of the nine committees dealt with science, history, and modern languages testified to the committee's interest in broadening the high school curriculum. Few of the nearly 4,000 public and private secondary schools had introduced modern subjects and electives in any serious way by 1890. As discussed in Chapter 8, the introduction of new subjects to the curriculum depended on an elective system which made room for all the important subjects to be treated in more than a superficial manner. Members of the committee desired the introduction of science, history, and modern languages because they considered their information—but, more important, the methods of reasoning and the faculties of judgment they demonstrated—vital to the training of educated leaders in a democracy. Since it realized that most high school students were not going to continue to college, the committee wished to insure that the high school focused on these leadership preparing subjects and reduced its concentration on the classical languages.

Elective reform and the introduction of modern subjects to the curriculum proceeded apace at the nation's leading colleges and universities after 1870, but by 1890 those reforms had not affected the vast majority of America's 574 colleges. These reforms required colleges to expand staff, laboratories, and research facilities and most simply did not have the money. The Committee of Ten hoped to speed the adoption of these reforms in the remaining traditional colleges indirectly by changing the high school curriculum. It was impossible for Harvard, Columbia, Johns Hopkins, and Michigan to influence small colleges directly. But leading colleges and universities could, through their admissions requirements, exert considerable pressure on the secondary schools. Since a high school's proudest boast was that its graduates could enter the nation's finest colleges, the important high schools had to follow what the colleges established as admissions standards. Therefore, by offering relaxed college admissions standards, the Committee of Ten hoped to persuade the secondary schools to adopt broader and more modern curricula. When that happened and secondary school students received this broadened training, which the committee members were convinced they would see as better training, high school graduates would refuse to attend those colleges which offered only the narrow classical curriculum, thus forcing the traditional colleges to change or go out of business.

The Committee of Ten's recommendations received mixed reviews, and they made little evident difference in the secondary school curriculum of the 1890s. Implementing the programs of study and additional instruction in science and modern languages that the committee recommended was beyond the financial and staff capability of the majority of secondary schools. During that period the majority of secondary schools were large enough to employ only one or two teachers and could not teach the variety of subjects recommended. Many educational leaders endorsed the report, especially its argument that terminal and continuing students should receive the same training because courses that prepared for life also prepared for college. A good deal of criticism came from educators who failed to comprehend the report's meaning. Some objected that it made all studies of equivalent value while the report actually recommended that all the programs it outlined count equally toward college admission. Others, especially superintendents of common school systems, objected to the committee's meddling in elementary school affairs, which it did by recommending that some subjects traditionally reserved for high school, like Latin, algebra, and physics, be introduced to the already crowded seventh- and eighth-grade curricula. Elementary school men bristled that college presidents and high school principals sought to dictate to the common school. Some objected because the report was not as stirring as those of Horace Mann and would not, therefore, provide an "inspiring trumpet call" for the "headless host" of American educators.[3] Some felt that the committee's plan of twenty hours of instruction per week was too heavy a load for students. Calvin Woodward objected that manual training was not included in the committee's recommendations but found few supporters among the high school establishment.

The most vigorous objections came from the other side, from the classicists in the colleges and the secondary schools who thought that the committee's desire for more modern subjects in the secondary school

[3] Superintendent John Kennedy of Batavia, N. Y. (1894), is quoted in Krug, *Shaping the American High School, 1880–1920,* 73.

threatened both the future of their subjects and the future of culture and civilization in the United States. The president of Bowdoin intoned somewhat confusedly: "Latin is the Thermopylae, where the modern Greeks must take their stand, determined to withstand the Barbarians or perish in the attempt."[4] Classical teachers at all levels, presidents of small colleges, and secondary school principals echoed this refrain all through the 1890s. The specific points at issue were the committee's recommendations that students should not begin Greek, even in the Classical Program, until the third year of high school and that juniors and seniors should study Latin for only four (rather than five) hours per week, thus making more room for the modern subjects. The classicists thought the committee had "sold out" to the soft pedagogy which sought to tailor the curriculum to student interests. They charged that it favored utility over culture. The classicists contended that higher education's chief purpose should be to inculcate values higher than materialism and ambition. Americans lacked taste and self-discipline; the classics were the best antidote. The classicists were strong enough and mustered enough support among other secondary school men to get an 1899 NEA committee on secondary school studies to recommend three years of Greek and five hours of Latin in all four years. The widespread support for this "conservative" position cannot be explained only in terms of cultural values, however. The classicists spoke for the small colleges and the small secondary schools which could not afford to introduce the modern subjects the committee recommended and which feared that if the report's recommendations were implemented they would, just as Eliot hoped, lose out in the competition for students. The desire to preserve civilization and the desire to save their institutions went hand in hand. Status concerns also motivated some of the high school support for the classicists' position. In the nineteenth century the high school teacher, like the college teacher, was a symbol of high culture. He taught the same subjects as the most educated college professor and enjoyed a status not far different from the average college professor's. Heavy concentration on the classics assured him a higher self-esteem. Happily for the classicists, for the status-conscious high school teachers, and for the economically marginal colleges, the Committee of Ten's recommendations had little effect on the secondary schools in the 1890s or thereafter. The debate over the committee's report was far more vociferous than the report's practical influence would have warranted—as such, however, the report offers the historian especially good insight into the ideology of the high schools before 1900.

[4] William De Witt Hyde, "Educational Values as Assessed by the Committee of Ten," *School Review*, II (December, 1894), 640, quoted in Krug, *Shaping the American High School, 1880–1920*, 65.

III

After 1900 the nature of the criticism of the Committee of Ten changed radically, signaling the beginnings of a profound shift in the thinking of men closely associated with the high school in America. After 1900 the high school leaders castigated the committee as an aristocratic, college-dominated, conservative group bent on strangling the proper democratic development of the American high school and of the American adolescent. They charged that the committee sought to insure college domination of the high school by imposing programs which restricted the teaching in high schools to subjects needed for college preparation. Where the committee had in fact sought to broaden the secondary school curriculum of the 1890s, the post-1900 high school leaders criticized it for trying to narrow it. They condemned the committee for seeking to enforce mental discipline when the high school ought to prepare students for life by giving them information and needed vocational skills. They constantly pointed out that the committee included only one representative of a typical public high school—conveniently forgetting that Baker of Colorado had spent most of his career as a high school educator.

These criticisms can be understood only as manifestations of an attempt by a new generation of high school leaders to define a new role for themselves and for the institutions in which they worked. As the number of high school teachers and administrators soared and as the university ideals of research and publishing became more widely accepted throughout the college system, the close links between college and secondary school educators dissolved. High school teachers found themselves increasingly unwelcome at scholarly meetings of university researchers; job interchangeability between levels was impossible when college teachers held doctorates and high school teachers earned only bachelor's degrees. The Carnegie Foundation excluded high school personnel from its pension plan. High school teachers resented the fact that, although they far outnumbered college professors, their status was distinctly second class. It was evident that this situation would change only when high school educators separated themselves from the college teachers and erected an independent professional identity. Condemnation of the Committee of Ten and its policy of "college domination" was one very good way of effecting that separation. The condemnation implied that college educators were not competent to advise on secondary school policy because secondary education was an enterprise totally separate in purpose and method from college education. Secondary school educators could handle their own affairs, with no help from meddlesome college presidents, thank you.

Between 1900 and 1910 the high school educators began to identify more closely with the common school than with the colleges. The published statements of high school men after 1900 reveal an increasing concern with the high school as an institution that offered all children a democratic education. This quite radical change in ideology or assumption occurred despite the fact that by 1910 it was serving only a little over 15 percent of the high-school-age population (although that figure may have been twice as high in cities, where most high school leaders worked).

Numbers alone cannot explain the abruptness of the change. The high school did not cease to be an elite institution and become an agent of mass schooling when it passed some enrollment figure between 6 and 15 percent. Its ideology came to resemble that of the common school because high school educators thought such a change would aid them in professionalizing secondary education as a separate branch of education. This effort to professionalize secondary education was not a formalized or programmatic one. Rather, it was an only partially conscious movement that resulted from thousands of personal and group decisions throughout the world of the American high school. The most influential decisions, perhaps, were those made by thousands of secondary school men as they shaped their careers in the rapidly growing and somewhat loosely defined high school where careers were quite susceptible to individual control. How these men elected to build their reputations, whom they sought to emulate, which aspects of their work they chose to emphasize profoundly shaped the new profession. Many who came to fill the burgeoning ranks of high school teachers and administrators had begun their careers in the elementary schools and brought with them the commitment to mass schooling and the professional identity of the common school teacher. High school men began to claim the leadership of the whole common school movement. Their qualifications for leadership compared favorably to those of the common school teachers. They were better educated, more specialized (they taught subjects rather than grades), and performed more complex tasks (they taught advanced subjects rather than the "easy" elementary ones).

The key to the high school leaders' efforts to separate themselves from college educators, identify a special province in which they alone could be expert, and establish themselves as leaders of the common school movement depended upon their ability to professionalize. Many factors define a profession and the high school educators did not consider all of them. For example, a profession usually has control over who receives the right to practice the profession and, traditionally in the United States, there has been a direct fee-for-service relation between the professional and his client. Restriction of access was difficult to achieve in a rapidly growing field and, of course, the public high school teacher could never establish a private economic relationship with his clients. The high school leaders had better prospects of claiming professional status through the creation of a body of knowledge and technique, of expertise, unique to the profession and somewhat mysterious to all outside the profession; of training facilities where the expertise could be transmitted effectively; and of a reward structure by which the profession could demonstrate its approval or disapproval of the individual professional's conduct. Most important to their claim was their ability to identify a public need which the profession's unique expertise could serve.

Conservative progressive doctrine was extraordinarily useful to high school leaders in their efforts to define their special expertise and its special social function. Preparing children for life in such a way that the society, the national community, would operate more efficiently, more smoothly, more quickly became the special function of the high school and the ability to fulfill these ends became the special expertise of the high school teacher. Possession of this special expertise differentiated the high school educator from all others in the society. Conservative progressives called on the schools to foster social order, to make the society run more smoothly, to eliminate conflict within the society. The high school leaders accepted this function, made it the basis of the identity and expertise of their group. It became their special function, clothed with immense social significance and with the mystery that every profession employs to free itself from the control of the people it promises to serve. Incidentally, or perhaps not so incidentally, their identification with the conservative wing of progressivism helped their personal self-esteem and status as well because that wing included the more elite and higher status reformers.

The development of professional schools of education early in the twentieth century furthered the secondary educators' concern with professional identity and the development of expertise. Secondary school leaders—the men most likely to attend university departments of education at the time—took many of their professional ideas and aspirations from the professors of education under whom they studied. Teachers College opened its doors in 1887 and allied with Columbia University in 1893, it is true, and other university centers for the study of education flourished at Chicago, Michigan, and Stanford before the end of the nineteenth century. The real burst of professionalism in the training of educators came, however, at the beginning of the twentieth century when departments and schools of education appeared throughout the nation and when already established ones sought to emulate the other disciplines assembled in the university by expanding their function from training teachers to doing research that would serve the public interest. Just as economics departments sought to train experts in economic policy and political science departments to train experts in political procedures, education departments or schools sought to produce experts in educational policy. Just what constituted educational expertise was an open question at the beginning of the twentieth century. Educators had persistently hunted a science of education but were no closer to finding it at the end than at the beginning of the nineteenth century. Psychology appeared to be one discipline or "science" around which educators could professionalize—teachers, after all, sought to influence the mind and the emotions and psychology was the discipline that dealt specifically with mind and feeling. Many university professors of education chose that avenue. In an era which acclaimed "social" in every context, however, the social role of the school appeared an even more fruitful area for the putative educational expert. The very word social promised that such experts would be closely involved in major policy determination, a fact which would enhance their personal and group prestige. Conservative progressivism, with which many university professors of education had contact through their colleagues in other departments of the university, seemed to present a ready-made doctrine for the man who wished to make himself an expert in the social role of education. The conservative progressives recommended a form of social organization and the school expert found it relatively easy to step in and claim that the school, properly designed, could further that organization.

In adopting the rhetoric and goals of conservative progressivism, the secondary school educators tended, if anything, to overemphasize the conservatives' call for social order. An educational sociologist writing during World War I spoke for many newly professionalized educators identified with the unprecedented growth of the high school when he criticized John Dewey for being too individualistic and too soft. "While it is true that citizens of a democracy need to be taught to think, it is even more important, especially in the present crisis, that they be trained to revere and obey."[5] His desire to use the schools to control and manipulate was typical: it was more baldly stated because of war xenophobia. The very pretentiousness of its claim that the contrast it discussed was a black-and-white affair demonstrated the zeal of the convert and the absolutism of the missionary. Here we also see how the schoolmen took the conservative progressives' broad program of institutional and individual reform aimed at making society operate more smoothly and with less conflict and narrowed it to a concern with shaping individuals to fulfill their social roles as defined by existing institutions. The conservative progressives had been concerned, as much as anything, with shaping efficient social institutions; the schoolmen tended to ignore the possibility or the desirability of shaping institutions and concentrated instead on shaping individuals to fit efficiently into the system.

[5] Ross L. Finney, "Sociological Principles Fundamental to Pedagogical Method," *Educational Review*, LV (February, 1918), 109, quoted in Krug, *Shaping the American High School, 1880–1920*, 422.

This process can be most clearly understood by analyzing the development of industrial and vocational education at the high school level after 1905 and the ideas which appeared in the report of the Commission on the Reorganization of Secondary Education in 1918.

IV

Before 1900 vocational education, although it appeared in some public high schools, had not been a concern of high school leaders—it was clearly on the periphery of the high school's mission. All that changed abruptly in the new century. Like the shift in identification from college to common school orientation, the secondary school men's interest in vocational training was a sudden and surprisingly pervasive one. The report of the Massachusetts Commission on Industrial and Technical Education (the Douglas Commission), published in 1906, touched off this interest in vocational education among regular schoolmen. The report announced the results of an investigation of the condition of fourteen- and fifteen-year-old children in the state who did not attend school. The Commission determined that 25,000 children fit that classification and that most of them worked in industrial jobs without hope of advancement because they lacked the skills required for any more specialized tasks. The report also noted that those who employed these children found them to be poor workers. The Commission's investigator also interviewed the parents of some of the youngsters employed in the factories and found that in most cases the parents had wanted the children to remain in school. The investigator reported that thirty-five or forty superintendents and principals told her that they felt the students left school not because of economic necessity but because they found school unattractive and uninteresting. These men reported that they felt the youngsters' leaving meant the schools had failed them.

The Commission concluded from this investigation that the state's child-rearing system was wasteful and inefficient. The schools were not equipping either the children who left school or those who stayed with what the report called "industrial intelligence." Therefore, industries had to rely on chance and on a rapidly weakening apprenticeship system to find either skilled workers or young men prepared to profit from technical training. Consequently, Massachusetts industry incurred increased production costs, its output was more limited and of lower quality than it should have been, and the state's competitive economic position was undermined. "The State needs a wider diffusion of industrial intelligence as a foundation for the highest technical success," the report concluded.[6] To fill this need, the Commission urged the state's schools to

---

[6] *Report of the Massachusetts Commission on Industrial and Technical Education* (Boston, 1906), 18–19, quoted in Krug, *Shaping of the American High School, 1880–1920,* 220.

introduce more manual training at all levels and to change its orientation from cultural to vocational training. In a more controversial vein it recommended that the state establish and finance from state tax revenue a separate vocational and technical high school in each of the larger cities and towns. These schools were to be entirely independent of the local public school systems.

At the same time that the Douglas Commission circulated its report, two educationists established the National Society for the Promotion of Industrial Education "to unite the many forces making toward industrial education the country over."[7] The inculcation of industrial intelligence was the prime topic at the NEA's 1907 annual meeting and was the subject of a large number of the articles and discussions devoted to secondary education that appeared in the next few years. This sudden popularity of industrial training as a central rather than peripheral concern of the secondary school is explained in part by the fact that secondary school men found it a conspicuous symbol of their independence from college domination. As part of their rebellion, they stressed the subject matter most antithetical to the liberal subjects of the college and college preparatory curricula. Industrial education's popularity also evidenced the concern that schoolmen shared with conservative progressives for the competitive position of American industry vis-à-vis that of Germany. By 1905 Americans recognized Germany as the rising economic and political power on the continent and a serious threat to Anglo-American domination of world commerce. Germany's industrial success, many believed, rested on her early development of a system of mandatory vocational and technical education for all students not deemed worthy of college preparation. Many secondary school men urged America to follow the German example in order to remain industrially strong. The popularity of industrial education also resulted from a concern with the dropout. Under twentieth-century conditions of diminishing opportunity and increasing technological sophistication of industry, dropouts faced a greater problem in finding jobs that promised an adequate wage than they had in the nineteenth century. The dropout's lot was a hard one but one that could easily be relieved, the educators thought, by additional years of schooling. Moreover, as educators assumed more and more responsibility for imposing social order and rested their professional prestige on their ability to do so, the dropout was a constant source of embarrassment. Like the common school reformers of the previous century, the secondary school men realized that they could accomplish what they promised only if they got or kept the children in school where the high school educators' professional skills could affect them. Their prestige suffered whenever students resisted their efforts and left school.

[7] National Society for the Promotion of Industrial Education, *Proceedings of the Organizational Meeting,* Bulletin No. 1 (New York, 1907), quoted in Lawrence Cremin, *The Transformation of the School* (New York, 1961), 39.

Vocational training would, the schoolmen hoped, make high school so attractive and interesting that potential dropouts would remain within its purview so that the educators could prepare them to render efficient social service. Vocational training was also popular because educators saw it as a way of dealing with the less bright students who appeared more and more frequently as the high school expanded. Vocational training, besides being useful, was, they thought, considerably easier than the liberal academic subjects.

The most important source of its popularity, however, was the fact that vocational training appeared a clear and direct implementation of the injunction to prepare students for life. We can distinguish three ways in which educators interpreted that injunction between 1890 and 1920. The Committee of Ten urged high schools to prepare students for life by teaching them methods of thinking and information which they must employ in their future lives as social leaders. When Dewey urged the schools to prepare children for life, he wanted them to teach skills that would enable the student to participate fully in all aspects of social life at whatever level of the social hierarchy he was to occupy. For the leaders of the vocational training movement, preparing for life meant preparing for work. This latter meaning was the one that professionalizing high school educators chose to emphasize.

The injunction to prepare future adults while they were children for the work they would do as adults led the secondary educators to discard traditional doctrines about democratic opportunity and about the importance of a common education for everybody. They envisioned an educational system much like the European ones in which the state assigned children at an early age to training schools which would prepare them for specific jobs and disqualify them for all other jobs. Since jobs ranked on a social hierarchy according to salary and prestige, European schools sorted children at age ten, eleven, or twelve into the social stations they would occupy as adults. The vocational training enthusiasts did not recognize their doctrine as apostasy; indeed, they praised it as an extension of democracy. They argued that the liberal subjects were not meant to prepare a child to think for himself or discipline his mind so that he would have a variety of career options open when he left school but were meant to prepare the student to begin special training for the learned professions. Since, in this view, the liberal arts were vocational subjects, the traditional system was undemocratic because it required those not expecting to enter the elite professions to study the liberal arts. It would be more democratic, the dean of Teachers College argued in 1906, to train everyone for his or her profession—in that way every child would derive equal benefit from the public schools.[8] By arguing that all possible

8 James Russell, "The Trend in American Education," *Educational Review*, XXXII (June, 1906), 28–41.

high school curricula were vocationally oriented—that any high school training, however conceived, was intimately connected to future work roles—the secondary school leaders made vocational education fit democratic theory. Indeed, they made vocational education sound more democratic than the "class" education provided by the liberal arts curriculum.

The decision that preparation for life meant preparation for work forced a host of new decisions upon the schools. If children of high school age—or even pre-high school age—were to be prepared for different work roles, some agency of the school had to decide which students were fitted for which roles and guide (or force) them to prepare for these chosen roles. It was not coincidental, therefore, that the vocational guidance movement appeared soon after 1906. Frank Parsons, founder of the Vocation Bureau in Boston in 1908 and author of *Choosing a Vocation* (published posthumously in 1909), is generally regarded as the founder of the vocational guidance movement, although there have been, inevitably, other claimants, especially Jesse B. Davis, of Grand Rapids, Michigan. The Vocation Bureau, financed by Mrs. Quincy Shaw, the same Boston philanthropist who had supported kindergartens and manual training classes, was originally intended to help immigrants in Boston's North End become productive and economically self-sustaining as fast as possible by helping them find, on the first try, the line of work at which each one of them could succeed.

Parsons was something of a maverick progressive. In 1895 he ran for mayor of Boston on a combined Prohibition, Socialist, and Populist ticket. He had a reputation as something of a radical, teaching at the University of Kansas when a Populist state administration sought to make that university a Populist stronghold. Parsons demanded both liberal progressive reforms like public ownership of natural monopolies and conservative reforms like monopoly planning and immigration restriction. He carried the conservative progressives' desire for social order to radical extremes. He was a social engineer. "Life can be moulded," he asserted, "into any conceivable form. Draw up your specifications for man . . . and if you will give me control of the environment and time enough, I will clothe your dreams in flesh and blood."[9] He was an efficiency expert who wished to codify human values. He liked to write about the "mathematical demonstrability of the wisdom of righteousness"; his biographer wrote that he laughed little himself, but lectured often on the "laws of laughter." It was a "moral duty," Parsons wrote, "to perspire at least once every day."[10] He reacted against the waste of modern capitalism—against railroad competition which raised prices and lowered

[9] Frank Parsons, quoted in Arthur Mann, *Yankee Reformers in the Urban Age: Social Reform in Boston, 1880–1900* (Cambridge, Mass., 1954), 134.

[10] Quoted in *ibid.*, 127.

the quality of service for no rational reason. Public ownership and monopoly planning would solve these problems. He reacted similarly to the inefficiency and waste involved in the traditional processes of preparing men for their lifework. As early as 1894 he wrote that "the training of a race-horse, and the care of sheep and chickens have been carried to the highest degree of perfection that intelligent planning can attain. But the education of a child, the choice of his employment, are left very largely to the ancient haphazard plan—the struggle for existence, and the survival of the fittest."[11] Parsons saw vocational guidance as a means of rectifying these traditional, inefficient habits. Vocational guidance would help the child have a more successful life and help society use its manpower resources more efficiently.

Within a year Parsons' bureau was training counselors that the Boston public schools employed to determine which elementary school graduates should attend the city's commercial and technical high schools. The idea was widely imitated; the First National Conference on Vocational Guidance, held in Boston in 1910, attracted delegates from forty-five cities, and a National Vocational Guidance Association was formed in 1913. Vocational guidance quickly spread to public high schools throughout the nation. Its concern was, in the early years, exclusively with guiding people to the proper vocational decisions. Only after 1920 did the mental hygiene movement and Freudian psychology turn guidance in the school to a concern with the adjustment of the whole personality.

V

High school men began to have second thoughts about industrial education when its most vocal advocates insisted that vocational training should occur in institutions separate from the high school. In 1917 Congress passed the Smith-Hughes Act to provide federal money for training and salaries for teachers and supervisors of trade, industrial, and agricultural subjects in secondary schools which devoted half their time to these vocational subjects, in part-time schools for young workers, and in evening schools for adult workers. Vocational education developed rapidly but in a way that did not help the high school educators enhance their own or their institution's prestige and importance as contributors to social efficiency. Those educators had to look elsewhere to define the high school's function. They remained committed to building their professional identity on their ability to foster social efficiency, but they had to define more precisely just how the high school accomplished this

[11] Quoted in Willis Rudy, *Schools in an Age of Mass Culture* (Englewood Cliffs, N. J., 1965), 18.

end. This was the function of the Commission on the Reorganization of Secondary Education (CRSE).

The history of the CRSE, appointed by the Board of Directors of the National Education Association in 1913, exemplified how the careerist aspirations of high school educators shaped the very definition of the high school. Clarence D. Kingsley conceived and lobbied for the appointment of the CRSE, chaired it, and wrote most of its report. Kingsley began his educational career as an instructor of mathematics at Colgate, then earned a master's degree in education at Teachers College in 1904 and while studying there served as an agent of the Charity Organization Society. He went on to teach mathematics at the Brooklyn Manual Training High School and, having chosen secondary over higher education, began to work his way up in the secondary school hierarchy. He became an active leader in the Brooklyn High School Teachers Association, which he persuaded to endorse his proposal for another study of the articulation between the college and the high school (several such studies, of greater and lesser interest, had been completed since the Committee of Ten made its report). On the strength of the Brooklyn endorsement, Kingsley got the NEA's Department of Secondary Education to appoint in 1910 a committee of nine to study high school–college relations and to appoint Kingsley chairman. In 1912 this committee reported but was not dissolved. Kingsley convinced the Department of Secondary Education to establish, under the nine-man committee, a series of subcommittees on each of the high school subjects—like those under the Committee of Ten except that in 1912 separate subcommittees investigated the place of the vocational subjects. (Meanwhile a friend appointed Kingsley to a state high school inspectorship in Massachusetts, a soft job which left him plenty of time to run these national committees.) In 1913, at Kingsley's behest, the central board of the NEA merged the Department of Secondary Education's committee of nine with its subcommittees into a larger committee charged with recommending the proper shape of the secondary school curriculum. When Kingsley received the chairmanship of this body, he had achieved a position of leadership in his profession from which he could shape that profession and build his own reputation. Unfortunately, he died young, before he could benefit from his carefully nurtured reputation and power. He lived long enough, however, to oversee the writing and publication of the reports of the CRSE and its various subject-matter subcommittees. He was mainly responsible for choosing and defining the seven Cardinal Principles of Secondary Education.

Kingsley, like so many high school leaders, identified the fostering of social efficiency as the function which would set the high school apart from other educational institutions and make it the most important educational institution in America. His contribution lay in broadening the high school's role from serving social efficiency simply by preparing students to work efficiently to fostering social efficiency by preparing children to perform all of their life functions efficiently and in a manner that would serve the state. For Kingsley vocational efficiency was only a small part of social efficiency. The historian can get a good sense of what Kingsley wanted from his definition of the "New Aims of the Modern High School," published in 1914. He called for investigations which would determine what kinds "of boys and girls of eighteen society needs." The high school must set out to provide such people. If "certain attitudes toward life" make for progress, then the high school ("we") must figure out methods of giving boys and girls "those attitudes toward life." The high school must train the "rank and file" for its responsibilities. Its aims must include "the inculcation of health habits, health ideals, and health knowledge; the development of civic pride, and intelligent interest in movements for human betterment; appreciation of good music, art, and literature; and right standards of conduct in the home, in the community, and in the vocation."[12] Notice here the confusion as to who decides what kind of young people the society needs. A growing body of opinion among educators, especially among those in schools of education who sought to emulate the research ideal of the universities, held that educators were responsible for such determinations. Their expertise was so great that they were capable both of serving social needs and of defining those needs as well. This was an extravagant and arrogant claim, but it would certainly have added to the educators' status and prestige had they succeeded in convincing others that they truly possessed such foresight. David Snedden, a friend of Kingsley and one of the most outspoken advocates of social efficiency in secondary education, established the sociology of education as a field where educators would investigate the needs of society and define for society the kind of young people it needed. He also wanted sociologists of education to establish a set of indices which would enable practicing educators to know, from examining a child's mental capacity and social background, just what kind of vocation to prepare him to follow.

Kingsley, like any man who makes a career of chairing committees, was something of a compromiser whose support of social efficiency was not quite as extreme as Snedden's. Nonetheless, the quest for social efficiency dictated the terms of the report Kingsley's committee published in 1918. "The purpose of democracy is so to organize society that each member may develop his personality primarily through activities designed for the well-being of his fellow members and of society as a whole." In order to work, democracy must operate at "a high level of efficiency" and each individual within it must choose "that vocation and

[12] Clarence Kingsley, "New Aims of the Modern High School," *Journal of Education* (Boston), LXXIX (23 April, 1914), 458.

those forms of social service in which his personality may develop and become most effective." Schools should develop in each student "the knowledge, interest, ideals, habits, and powers whereby he will find his place and use that place to shape both himself and society toward ever nobler ends."[13] An efficient democracy was one in which the needs of the group determined the development of the individual. Like Dewey, Kingsley hoped that individual interest and social interest were always harmonious and mutually fulfilling. But, when a conflict did arise between them, Kingsley believed that individual fulfillment was definitely secondary to group or social fulfillment. Here is where Kingsley, like so many other school reformers of the period, parted company with Dewey, who made the relation of the individual and society somewhat ambiguous and the matter of priorities in the infrequent cases of conflict between them, a matter that depended on the specific situation of each conflict. In the specific case Dewey nearly always championed the individual's right to resist social coercion. Kingsley neglected these ambiguities and Dewey's advice to treat all conflicts on a case-by-case basis in favor of making the relation of the individual and society unequivocal. For Kingsley and for the other advocates of social efficiency, the needs of the group, the nation's efficiency, nearly always superseded the individual's needs.

Two suggestions from the pens of leading educational sociologists of the period illustrate the growing tendency toward viewing the high school as an institution which molded individuals to fit society. Charles A. Ellwood, a sociologist at the University of Missouri much interested in educational questions, saw the high school serving an important eugenics function in the United States. Many reform-minded Americans in this pre-Hitlerian era advocated improving the nation's racial stock by keeping the unfit from breeding future generations of equally unfit people. In contrast to the somewhat heady environmentalism that some progressive reformers espoused, other progressives argued that certain social incompetencies were inherited and no amount of environmental change could eliminate them from the genes of the affected families. The most extreme followers of this point of view were the eugenists. The problem they faced was to find ways to identify the unfit who should be prevented from procreating. The insane, the mentally incompetent, and the criminals were fairly easy to spot as unfit—although keeping them from procreating was a more difficult issue. Separating the fit from the unfit among the population that was not institutionalized was less easy. Ellwood thought he saw a solution in compulsory education laws that were based on achievement rather than age. The state should determine how much learning a person should have to be a worthy citizen. "Then,"

---

[13] Commission on the Reorganization of Secondary Education, *Cardinal Principles of Secondary Education* (U. S. Bureau of Education, Bulletin No. 35 [Washington, D. C., 1918]), 9.

Ellwood wrote in 1914, "let every child in the state be 'sentenced,' as it were, by a rational compulsory education law, to complete this minimum requirement of education in our public schools." Every person would remain in school until he passed an examination that qualified him for citizenship or until he was sent to an institution for the feebleminded. In neither place could he marry or have a family. Ellwood found this an ideal way of improving the country's racial stock and the country itself; he did not, unfortunately, discuss the policy's possible effects on the schools themselves.[14]

David Snedden's dissertation written at Teachers College in 1907 was strangely reminiscent of Horace Mann's Seventh Report. Snedden studied juvenile reform schools—his adviser was the executive officer of the New York Charity Organization Society—and found in them, just as Mann had found in the Prussian reform schools, excellent models for the regular public schools to emulate. The reform school's constant institutional control over the individual child most impressed Snedden. The "work represented by these institutions has represented more fully the idea of state education than has the work of any other part of the educational system" because the reform school must encompass "the entire round of educational effort."[15] Educators in the reform school had to be concerned not only with the intellectual but with the vocational, social, and moral development of their charges. Snedden urged the high schools to adopt this comprehensive attitude.

Kingsley's Commission on the Reorganization of Secondary Education shared Snedden's concern with making the high school and its curriculum shape all aspects of the student's present and future life so that he would become an efficient member of society. Since an efficient society was one free of conflict, its members must share common values and common ideals. The commission's 1918 report claimed that since the elementary school "alone" could not develop the common knowledge, ideals, and interests "essential to American democracy," high schools had to see to the development of these common values in children. It should teach social studies and English so as to promote common social commitment. "History should so treat the growth of institutions that their present value may be appreciated. Geography should show the interdependence of men while it shows their common dependence on nature. Civics should concern itself less with constitutional questions and remote governmental functions, and should direct attention to social agencies close at hand and to the informal activities of daily life that

[14] Charles A. Ellwood, "Our Compulsory Education Laws and Retardation and Elimination in Our Public Schools," *Education*, XXXIV (May, 1914), 575–576, quoted in Krug, *Shaping the American High School, 1880–1920*, 254.

[15] David Snedden, *Administration and Educational Work of American Juvenile Reform Schools* (New York, 1907), 7–8, quoted in Krug, *Shaping the American High School, 1880–1920*, 265.

regard and seek the common good. Such agencies as child-welfare organizations and consumers' leagues afford specific opportunities for the expression of civic qualities by the older pupils." English "should kindle social ideals and give insight into social conditions and into personal character as related to these conditions."[16] Beyond assigning specific subjects the function of furthering common social values, the report listed ways in which the high school's very structure particularly fitted it for the role of common school. It "has a unique opportunity . . . because it includes in its membership representatives from all classes of society and consequently is able through social relationships to establish bonds of friendship and common understanding that can not be furnished by other agencies." The report called for "the social mingling of pupils through the organization and administration of the school" and "the participation of pupils in common activities" which included games, social activities, and student councils. "Among the means of developing attitudes and habits important in a democracy are the assignment of projects and problems to groups of pupils for cooperative solution and the socialized recitation whereby the class as a whole develops a sense of collective responsibility. Both of these devices give training in collective thinking. Moreover, the democratic organization and administration of the school itself, as well as the cooperative relations of pupil and teacher, pupil and pupil, and teacher and teacher, are indispensable."[17] These, of course, were prescriptions for the development of the comprehensive high school.

But the development of common values and ideals through the social studies, English, and the extracurriculum was apparently not enough, in the Commission's eyes, to insure a smooth-running and efficient society. Like the conservative progressives generally, Kingsley's group thought that efficiency required the imposition of direction, goals, and unity itself from the top. Such, finally, was the recommendation of the CRSE, a recommendation which was to govern the bulk of the thinking and policy making for the public high school for nearly three decades. Despite all of its employment of John Dewey's and Jane Addams' liberal rhetoric about school reform—the use of cooperative projects and socialized recitations, democracy within the classroom and within the school's administration, close relations between the school and the child's home and neighborhood, the indivisibility of the child, the understanding of the interdependence of all men—the report finally elected to impose a commitment to social service on the child, to put the group first and the individual a rather poor second. In describing how it determined which seven principles were the most important, the Commission listed the kind

[16] CRSE, *Cardinal Principles*, 14.
[17] *Ibid.*, 15, 23, 14.

of criteria it employed in determining how to build the good high school curriculum. The language speaks for itself.

> In order to determine the main objectives that should guide education in a democracy it is necessary to analyze the activities of the individual. Normally he is a member of a family, of a vocational group, and of various civic groups, and by virtue of these relationships he is called upon to engage in activities that enrich the family life, to render important vocational services to his fellows, and to promote the common welfare. It follows, therefore, that worthy home-membership, vocation and citizenship, demand attention as three of the leading objectives.
>
> Aside from the immediate discharge of these specific duties, every individual should have a margin of time for the cultivation of personal and social interests. This leisure, if worthily used, will recreate his powers and enlarge and enrich life, thereby making him better able to meet his responsibilities. The unworthy use of leisure impairs health, disrupts home life, lessens vocational efficiency, and destroys civic-mindedness. . . .
>
> To discharge the duties of life and to benefit from leisure, one must have good health. The health of the individual is essential also to the vitality of the race and to the defense of the Nation.[18]

Thus did conservative progressivism come to the American high school.

GUIDE TO FURTHER READING

We have drawn extensively on EDWARD KRUG, *The Shaping of the American High School*, 2 vols. (Madison, Wis., 1964, 1972), and JOEL SPRING, *Education and the Rise of the Corporate State* (Boston, 1972), for our analysis of the high school in the Progressive era. The literature on the history of educational progressivism cited in our bibliography for chapter 9 was also very useful. Research into the changing occupational structure and its effect on school attendance has just begun; most of it remains unpublished. SELWYN K. TROEN's paper presented at the American Historical Association convention (Chicago, 1975), for example, suggests that technological improvements such as the cash register and telephone reduced substantially the employment opportunities for children ten to fifteen in department stores in large cities and thus contributed to increased attendance; see also TROEN, *The Public and the Schools: Shaping the St. Louis System, 1838–1920* (Columbia, Mo., 1975).

Increasing educational professionalism and the identification of educators around the high school is evident in KRUG's studies of the high school and in RAYMOND CALLAHAN, *Education and the Cult of Efficiency* (Chicago, 1962), and ROY LUBOVE, *The Professional Altruist: The Emergence of Social Work as a Career, 1880–1930* (Cambridge, Mass., 1965). A good example of an emerging professional educator is David Snedden; see WALTER DROST, *David Snedden and Education for Social Efficiency* (Madison, Wis., 1967). Most of the evidence,

[18] *Ibid.*, 9–10.

however, lies inert in professional educational periodicals and in materials in teacher training institutions.

For evidence on the differentiating function of the high school, consult SPRING, *Education and the Rise of the Corporate State,* MARVIN LAZERSON, *Origins of the Urban School: Public Education in Massachusetts, 1870–1915* (Cambridge, Mass., 1971), LAZERSON and NORTON GRUBB, eds., *American Education and Vocationalism: A Documentary History* (New York, 1974), SOL COHEN, "The Industrial Education Movement, 1906–17," *American Quarterly,* XX (Spring, 1968), 95–110, ARTHUR WIRTH, *Education in the Technological Society* (Scranton, Pa., 1971), PAUL H. DOUGLAS, *American Apprenticeship and Industrial Education* (New York, 1921), and BRIAN SIMON, "Classification and Streaming: A Study of Grouping in English Schools, 1860–1960," in PAUL NASH, ed., *History and Education* (New York, 1970), 115–159. On the vocational guidance movement see W. RICHARD STEPHENS, *Social Reform and the Origins of Vocational Guidance* (Washington, D. C., 1970), and ARTHUR MANN, *Yankee Reformers in the Urban Age: Social Reform in Boston, 1880–1900* (Cambridge, Mass., 1954), chapter 6.

THEODORE R. SIZER, *Secondary Schools at the Turn of the Century* (New Haven, Conn., 1964), is the most extensive examination of the Committee of Ten and conveniently includes a copy of the report. Charles W. Eliot's involvement in high school reform is outlined in HUGH HAWKINS, *Between Harvard and America: The Educational Leadership of Charles W. Eliot* (New York, 1972), chapter 8, and Eliot's reply to critics of the report, "The Fundamental Assumptions in the Report of the Committee of Ten," *Educational Review,* XXX (November, 1905), 325–343, has been reprinted in EDWARD KRUG, ed., *Charles W. Eliot and Popular Education* (New York, 1961), 147–166.

CHAPTER 11

Progressivism and the Kindergarten, 1870–1925

THE KINDERGARTEN, AT THE OTHER END OF THE EDUCATIONAL SPECTRUM from the high school, serves as an excellent illustration of how the various reform impulses of the late nineteenth and early twentieth centuries interacted. The kindergarten was born out of the educational idealism so eagerly imported from Europe in the nineteenth century by American educators and out of the intense American interest in using schooling to moralize and to assimilate the urban poor. Its institutional origins as a privately financed and often reformist effort to provide services not offered by the public schools also characterized several other post–Civil War educational innovations. Like those other innovations, it was eventually absorbed by the public schools, a process that profoundly affected the underlying purposes of the kindergarten movement. Followers of G. Stanley Hall's child study movement and of John Dewey's emphases on social education and the necessary interaction of the child with his environment helped to redirect the kindergarten after 1910 from its early idealism to a more "progressive" stance. But, like other levels of education, by 1920 the kindergarten was more influenced by Edward Lee Thorndike's psychological theories of connectionism and by the increasing demands for setting precise and measurable goals for each kind of learning experience. These pressures combined to lead the kindergarten to an emphasis on habit formation—a form of social efficiency—that almost totally crowded out Dewey's learning theory.

316

I

Friedrich Froebel organized the first kindergarten in Germany in 1837; it initially appeared in the United States in 1856. Earlier, of course, there had been many schools devoted to educating small children but the kindergarten, as conceived and established by Froebel and imported into the United States, was a very special kind of school for young children. "Kindergarten" was essentially a trade name which, throughout the remainder of the nineteenth century, denoted only those schools that were run on the Froebelian model. Only in the twentieth century did kindergarten become a generic name for all schools for four- and five-year-olds. Froebel had very definite beliefs as to what schooling for little children should accomplish and an even more precise method of achieving those ends. Unfortunately, he was unable to clothe his beliefs in words precise enough for others to understand clearly, but he succeeded in inventing a series of objects and exercises which employed the objects—Froebel called them "gifts" and "occupations"—that were so concrete and comprehensible that they dominated kindergarten practice for years. They dominated even, or perhaps especially, the practice of those "kindergartners" (the term for the teacher of a kindergarten) who least understood the Froebelian philosophy that lay behind the gifts and occupations.

Froebel's philosophy blended German idealism, Rousseau's naturalism, Pestalozzi's "sense realism"—the root of the object method—and mysticism in a unique way. His philosophy was (and is) difficult to understand. A brief review of five facets of his thought will enable us to see the purpose of his kindergarten rules. First, he believed that within the mind of the newborn child were contained all the capacities and ideals that the child would ever reveal. These capacities and ideas existed in an undeveloped state in the infant, of course, and education's primary purpose was to affect the child in such a way that these inborn ideas would develop naturally. This is the essence of German idealist epistemology: the categories of human thought are inborn rather than constructs based on associations composed of sensory impressions. Truth, and the standard of truth, is thus inherent; it is in the mind and simply needs to be realized by mental development. A second facet of Froebel's thought involved the relation between the mind and the sense impressions, which stimulated the potentialities of the mind and drew out the ideas already existent there. A child had to develop his inner potential by expressing those ideas behaviorally: he had to display externally his "inner" self. Sense impressions, in Froebel's view, stimulated that expression of the inner. Third, he did not believe that just any expression of the inner was the most efficient way to draw out the child's mental capacities. Rather, Froebel prescribed a certain set of "creative activities" which the child was to perform by following his teacher's commands. These activities were to structure precisely the child's expression of the inner, and thus to develop it fully. Because as an idealist he believed that all human minds contained identical ideas and categories, Froebel could prescribe the same precise activities for each child. He did not recognize individual differences. Fourth, Froebel identified developmental stages in childhood and, for each stage, identified a "best" way of expressing the inner. For children under six, this best way was through play, and Froebel structured the kindergarten around what he called "creative play" or "creative activity." His use of "creative" appears today somewhat peculiar because he believed that proper play meant children participating in games and toy construction, all facets of which were rigidly prescribed. Fifth, Froebel strongly believed that all ideas, people, and things were parts of a unity, and that the proper drawing out of a child's inner potential also involved connecting each child's inner with the unity of the universe. He stressed, for instance, that playing with spheres would suggest to young children both perfection and unity. He emphasized social cooperation rather than competition in his kindergarten in an effort to teach children that the unity and harmony of mankind demonstrated the higher unity of the universe. Similarly, group singing and circle games were mainstays of his curriculum because they emphasized unity. Although this kind of summary does a great injustice to the subtleties of Froebel's thought, it rather accurately portrays its ambiguities and the difficulties of communicating it to large numbers of potential kindergartners.

On the other hand, Froebel's methods were quite clear and precise. He defined ten gifts—gifts because God gave them to help children—and four occupations. Six of the gifts were solids, each with surfaces, lines, points, and "reconstruction." The four occupations were solids, surfaces, lines, and points. The child was supposed to start with the unified solid: the first gift consisted of "six colored worsted balls about one inch and a half in diameter" to be manipulated in a certain way by the child. Then in the seventh, eighth, and ninth gifts he was to break down the solids into surfaces, lines, and points, and in the tenth he was to reconstruct the idea of a surface and a solid with straight sticks using softened peas or wax pellets as glue. The occupations correlated with the gifts. While the child dealt with the solid gifts (variously shaped blocks) he also modeled clay or carved wood in prescribed manner and sequence; while exploring the gift of surface (squares, triangles, and their parts) he folded, cut, and painted paper; while dealing with the gift of line (straight splints of wood and circular rings of metal or paper) he drew, wove threads, and interlaced; while exploring the gift of points (beans, lentils, seeds, and pebbles) he strung beads or perforated paper or cardboard according to a set pattern. Froebel was nothing if not prescriptive in his directions to the kindergartners. Here are his directions for the fifth gift, a three-inch cube which consisted of 27 one-inch cubes,* three bisected and three quadrisected diagonally.

> Lay four times two whole cubes in an oblong before you; place perpendicularly upon them again four times two whole cubes. Over these two cubes lay two half cubes, so that they touch in the middle by their sharp edges; with the last two cubes, each of the two half cubes yet required is represented by two quarters. In the long hollow thus made sink four whole cubes. What have you made which now stands before each of you? "A house with an overhanging roof, four cubes high and two cubes broad."[1]

Froebel just as rigidly laid out the drill on the circle games and wrote a number of songs and poems for group participation.

Devotees transferred Froebel's methodological prescriptions whole to the United States and it was half a century before reformers successfully broke down those rigidities. The Froebelian system was extraordinarily ossified from the start; its custodians would not allow the least tampering with the procedures the master had laid out. It is hard to understand exactly why the Froebelian method retained such exceptional rigidity in the transfer—why some significant modifications did not occur due to changing experiences and the changing cultural environment into which it was transferred. Part of the explanation probably lies, as Evelyn Weber has suggested,[2] in the nature of Froebel's thought. His emphasis on unity encouraged the feeling that his method must be treated as a whole and respected as a single entity. The very limited understanding which most of Froebel's American disciples had of the reasoning behind his method led them to eschew tampering with it for fear of destroying some vital but unrecognized facet of the scheme. Insecure in their comprehension of the whole, they feared that to change one part of the plan would lay them open to pressures for change in the others, against which they did not feel equipped to argue. They could defend their commitment to the whole better than to the parts taken separately.

II

The Froebelian kindergarten (and for the Froebelians a kindergarten was not a kindergarten if it was not Froebelian) came to the United States

---

* The size was important. If too small, the cubes would seem trivial. If too large, the child could not visualize their general meaning. Kindergarten literature of the late nineteenth century is full of dazzling pedantry involving the sizes of gifts and the extreme dangers that would accompany deviation from those ideal sizes.

[1] Friedrich Froebel, *Pedagogics of the Kindergarten*, trans. Josephine Jarvis (New York, 1895), 223.

[2] Evelyn Weber, *The Kindergarten: Its Encounter with Educational Thought in America* (New York, 1969), 17.

first to serve the children of the liberal and progressive upper middle class. Social reformers quickly adopted it as an important tool for assimilating lower-class children to middle-class values and ideals. During its first forty years in the United States the kindergarten was almost exclusively a private venture, supported by parents whose children attended or by philanthropists concerned with helping the poor. Only late in the nineteenth century did it become generally accepted as part of the urban public school system.

The pioneer kindergartens, mostly short lived, in the United States were German-speaking ones, established by liberal and upper-middle-class German refugees of the abortive revolution of 1848. Mrs. Carl Schurz founded the first one on her front porch in Watertown, Wisconsin, in 1856. Mrs. Schurz and other founders of German-speaking kindergartens had studied with Froebel himself and commonly used their kindergartens as advertisements for Froebel's design and as training schools in which they passed on Froebel's principles and techniques to American women. A chance meeting in 1859 brought Mrs. Schurz together with Elizabeth Peabody of Boston, Horace Mann's and Nathaniel Hawthorne's sister-in-law and one of the famous Peabody sisters of Salem. In 1860, deeply impressed by the kindergarten ideal, Peabody organized in Boston the first English-speaking program in the United States. With her sister, Mary Mann, she wrote a book advocating the kindergarten's adoption throughout the United States as an alternative means of introducing children to the world of learning and as the best means of expanding their potentialities.

The German influence quickly caught on among native Americans and soon upper-middle-class communities throughout the United States were sending to Germany for trained kindergartners to conduct classes for the children of the rich. Kindergartens were begun in West Newton in 1864, Gramercy Park in New York City in 1872, San Francisco in 1873, and Los Angeles in 1876. To reduce the dependence on Germany as a source of supply for kindergartners, advocates made some effort to establish training schools where American women could learn the method. In most cases, however, American women learned it by assisting imported teachers or, like Peabody herself, by studying the method in Germany.

Froebelian idealism struck a responsive chord among many genteel Americans—perhaps especially genteel American women—in the mid-nineteenth century. People who had been nurtured on the romantic idealism of transcendentalist and other philosophic alternatives to Enlightenment rationalism found appealing Froebel's emphasis on inner potentiality, on unity, and on cooperation rather than competition. Elizabeth Peabody herself had been an Emersonian transcendentalist; she reflected in extreme form a point of view shared by much of her social class after the Civil War. Froebel also presented these people with what appeared to be a useful way of softening the discipline of very young children. The contemporary theory of child nurture, that children were different from adults and that they had a natural propensity for good rather than a natural tendency toward willful evil, which we have earlier identified as a major ingredient in the reform philosophies of men like Horace Mann, was very popular among the upper social classes. These classes contributed the majority of early supporters of the kindergarten. These new theories of child nurture, however, had not effectively altered public school practice by the end of the Civil War. Froebel's kindergarten seemed to embody just these changed attitudes. Members of the upper middle class appear to have initially imported the kindergarten as a means of keeping their children out of the early grades of the public school where parents thought the discipline too harsh and the skill training too rigid. Originally, the kindergarten could serve as an alternative to the first three grades rather than as an experience that necessarily preceded the first grade. However rigid Froebel's methods may appear to us, his emphasis on play, on singing, on creativity (no matter how peculiarly defined), was welcomed as a reduction in rigidity relative to the program offered in the public schools. Parents of the upper middle and upper classes that were influenced by the liberalism of 1848, transcendentalism, or nonfundamentalist Protestantism, and who shared the romantic view of the child (or at least of their own children), were the first supporters of the kindergarten. They supported it because it suggested a "freer" educational experience than any other known in the United States at the time.

Just as Horace Mann had believed that liberal methods of child nurture could also be applied effectively to poor children and greatly improve their behavior, kindergarten advocates shifted their focus from serving the well-to-do to educating the children of the poor. Although the fortunate classes continued to support and patronize kindergartens established for their children, the thrust of the movement shifted to an effort to establish kindergartens in slum districts. Kindergartners, reformers, and educators quickly grasped the kindergarten's great potential as an agent for Americanizing immigrant children. In 1903 an influential magazine editor recognized the kindergarten as "our earliest opportunity to catch the little Russian, the little Italian, the little German, Pole, Syrian, and the rest and begin to make good American citizens of them."[3]

This shift in focus resulted in a spectacular growth period for the kindergarten in the United States. Evelyn Weber, in her excellent study of the institution, estimated that there was fewer than 12 kindergartens

[3] Quoted in Marvin Lazerson, *Origins of the Urban School: Public Education in Massachusetts, 1870–1915* (Cambridge, Mass., 1971), 47.

in the United States in 1870 but over 400 by 1880. Growth continued at a similar rate up until World War I. The kindergarten's shift from the rich neighborhoods to the ghettos began in the early 1870s. Mrs. Quincy Adams Shaw, a wealthy Boston widow of established family whose philanthropies would include industrial schools and vocational guidance bureaus in the Boston area, initiated in 1871 a charity kindergarten in Boston's North End—where new immigrants were most heavily concentrated. By the end of the decade she was supporting thirty-one such kindergartens in the Boston area, spending well over $200,000 on them in the years before the Boston School Committee assumed responsibility for most in 1888. Even more spectacularly, perhaps, Susan Blow, with the enthusiastic support of Superintendent William Torrey Harris, convinced the board of education in St. Louis to assume responsibility for kindergartens in the poorer sections of that city in 1873. Few other such systematic efforts occurred in the seventies and public acceptance of responsibility for kindergartens waited much longer in most cities. Most of the efforts in the seventies were individual ones—a philanthropist joined with a single teacher to open a small kindergarten in a neglected portion of the city. But the popularity of kindergartens was growing rapidly. Milton Bradley, the toy manufacturer, began marketing the Froebelian kindergarten equipment in 1871; the National Education Association endorsed the entire Froebelian program in 1873 and urged that public school systems establish kindergartens. Like all other interest groups, kindergartners and their supporters in the late seventies began to organize. Elizabeth Peabody founded the American Froebel Union in 1878, which was reorganized in Detroit in 1882, marking the movement's penetration of the Midwest. Two years later the kindergartners' organization merged with the NEA and formed a kindergarten department within that larger organization. But in 1892 the International Kindergarten Union (IKU) split off from the Kindergarten Department of the NEA to form a separate organization within which kindergartners could concentrate on their own affairs. In 1900 the IKU had 65 branches and over 6,000 members; by 1918 its 132 branches enrolled 18,000 members.

As kindergartners organized after 1880, efforts spread to establish kindergartens throughout the lower-class sections of America's cities and towns. By 1897, 400 associations of philanthropic women had been organized in urban America to provide financial support for extending the kindergarten experience to all poor children and their mothers. In the largest cities the so-called Free Kindergarten Associations established networks of kindergartens and even financed training schools for kindergarten teachers. These associations were also instrumental in convincing public school systems to assume responsibility for kindergartens. They lobbied to change laws that prohibited expenditure of tax money on the education of children under six, and kindergartens established by these associations most often became the nucleus for the public kindergarten system. The Women's Christian Temperance Union, hoping to protect future generations from lowly and evil appetites by educating children in self-discipline, established and maintained a number of kindergartens in the United States. Settlement houses were also important to the maturing kindergarten movement, although perhaps not as quantitatively influential as the disproportionate amount of publicity they generated and received would make us think. Relations between the kindergarten and the settlement house were very close. Many settlements had begun as kindergarten efforts, almost all settlements maintained kindergartens, and settlement workers were often kindergartners.

With this shift in the prospective clientele for the kindergarten went a subtle change in the rhetoric concerning its goals. For well-to-do children, kindergartners had stressed children's natural goodness and their right to freedom and play; they stressed moral training and discipline for the children of the poor. Like any school concerned with young children, the kindergarten sought to facilitate the socialization of youngsters—to bring them out of the selfishness of their homes into the world of social responsibilities where each child would have to wait his turn and defer to the wishes of others. Kindergartens for the affluent concentrated on making the child's transition from being the egotistical center of the home to being one of many children in the classroom as easy and as flexible as possible. The kindergarten was ultimately supposed to socialize the rich child, to instill self-discipline and order, but it was to do so gradually and gently. It purpose was to moderate the intensity of that socialization process.

Goals for the slum child were far different. Their kindergarten was supposed to accelerate the socialization process, to get these difficult clients into school (and away from the unfortunate influence of their improper home lives and the ghetto street) as soon as possible. The 1880s and 1890s witnessed a proliferation of child-oriented welfare agencies and a growing conviction among welfare workers that the child was the most important object of reform effort. The child was to be rescued from the evils of his environment—from what Jacob Riis called the slum child's Hobson's choice between the overcrowded home and the corrupting and anarchic street. The kindergarten would offer an alternative, a place where young children could come that was clean, that provided space for wholesome and structured exercise, and that furnished, in the person of the teacher, good moral influences very different from those supposedly transmitted by their parents. One principal avowed to the St. Louis kindergarten supervisor that kindergartens led "the children of the poor . . . into useful habits of thought and conduct which their home environment could never develop[.]" A prominent Boston philanthropist said, "Let us take the little child in the future from its possibly ignorant, filthy, careless mother, as soon as it can walk . . . and give it three hours daily in the kindergarten, where during that time it will be made clean, will enjoy light, color, order, music, and the sweet influence of a living and self-controlled voice."[4] Very much as Charles Loring Brace had believed the country to be a more conducive environment for children than the city, the kindergarten movement also contained a rural bias—as suggested in its very name, translated literally as "children's garden." The kindergarten was an alternative to the slum where the child could begin to learn the moral habits that, the kindergartners assumed, he could not learn at home. Reformers like Felix Adler, as we have noted in an earlier chapter, viewed the kindergarten as an early introduction to habits of industriousness and industrial training.

Many reformers saw in the kindergarten the hope of influencing not only the unfortunate children of the slum environment but also the homes from which the children came. Toward this end, early kindergartens established for poor children were organized in such a way that teachers had half of each day free to visit children's families in order to bring them advice on hygiene, diet, and cultural and moral habits. (Home visits were abandoned, as an economy measure, when kindergartens were absorbed by the public school systems after 1890.) Settlement workers found the kindergarten a significant tool in their effort to improve the environment of the urban poor. Organizing the small children into groups, into little communities, was a significant and relatively easy first step toward organizing at least some of the neighborhood families into a community. Settlement workers intended to work with the children and through them reach and change the behavior of their families. The kindergarten seemed an ideal way of entering the households which were otherwise inaccessible to the social reformers. The alliance was symbolized by the founding of Elizabeth Peabody House in Boston in 1896 on the anniversary of Froebel's birthdate. That social settlement adopted the motto, "A Little Child Shall Lead Them," and asked whether "the moral life of a neighborhood [could] be elevated by work concentrated upon the youngest children and mothers?"[5] The resounding answer was "yes." Lucy Wheelock, the founder of one of the more successful kindergarten training schools, wrote a very popular story among kindergartners entitled "The Lily's Mission," which portrayed the manner in which kindergartners and settlement workers hoped their work with children would affect adults.

Two "ragged, dirty children" bring a flower home to their dingy tenement apartment. The mother has failed to keep the house clean; the father is out

[4] Quoted in Susan Blow, "Kindergarten Education," Nicholas M. Butler, ed., *Education in the United States* (Albany, N.Y., 1899), II, 33; Annie A. Fields is quoted in Lazerson, *Origins of the Urban School,* 49.

[5] The Annual Report of the Elizabeth Peabody House is quoted in *ibid.,* 51.

drinking. Overjoyed at seeing the flower, the mother places it on a windowsill only to discover that dirt prevents any sunlight from shining through the window to the flower. With the window clean, sunlight reveals the filth of the apartment, which is then quickly cleaned, the mother is washed and dressed, and father, overcome by his new environment upon his return home, vows to give up the bottle.[6]

Such was the kindergarten's social reform mission. By teaching the child, reformers taught—or thought they taught—the parents.

In its transformation into an agency for social reform, the kindergarten began to lose some of its belief in the inherent goodness of children and its commitment to natural growth as the best means of development. When seeking to reform slum children, kindergartners as a rule became more concerned with shaping, molding, and directing them in particular ways, and became less subtle in their efforts. None of the early kindergartners believed in anarchy, of course, and no followers of Froebel advocated real spontaneity in the classroom, but they did believe that order and self-discipline would come as a natural result of free growth. Kindergartners working with slum children came to believe more and more that character, order, and discipline had to be inculcated. Surprisingly, what did not change in this shift to a slum clientele was the adherence to Froebelian principles and techniques. Kindergartners in settlement houses continued to work with the gifts and occupations as rigidly as did their colleagues in the best neighborhoods. Although many were not surprised by the difficulty in making Froebelian methods interest hungry, filthy, and alienated children from immigrant ghettos, they continued almost to a woman to believe that if only they tried harder, the traditional methods would work. Lower-class kindergartens did give more attention to marching, and rigidly supervised group activities in which children had to obey orders in unison became prevalent. Kindergartners in the slums also increased their emphasis on Bible readings and prayers.

In the environment of the slum, moreover, the kindergarten became an agent of the school. This arrangement was often formalized when the public schools in many cities made available to reformers schoolrooms for kindergarten classes, even though the public schools played no formal part in conducting the programs. Kindergartners themselves sought to bring middle-class values to those children who had not benefited from such a background. Gradually, the kindergarten came to be seen as an extension downward of, rather than an alternative to, formal schooling. As the New Bedford School Committee said in 1902, "The great majority of children who do not attend school between five and seven are unfortunately those of foreign parentage, and, as a rule, often of the most ignorant kind. They are the very children who should be in school at the

---

[6] *Ibid.*, 55.

earliest permissible age, as they, as a rule, are the first to leave school to go to work."[7] Their solution, of course, was to establish kindergartens which would catch these children early. Although it began as an alternative to the early years of public schooling, by 1900 the kindergarten had adopted the public schools' purposes and had become an appendage to the regular school.

III

This interest in using the kindergarten as an agent of urban social reform or as a way of saving poor children from their evil and corrupt environment by facilitating their entrance into school did not change the Froebelian principles and methods of the kindergarten. Although it is true that the most sympathetic and sensitive settlement kindergartners recognized that the personality and style of the teacher was perhaps the kindergarten's most effective influence on children, gifts and occupations remained the central tools with which the kindergartner approached her charges. Just as their colleagues in higher levels of schooling attacked the rigidities of late-nineteenth-century public education in the Progressive era, reformers in the kindergarten carried the spirit of progressive reform into an attack on the rigidities of the Froebelian kindergarten.

The first phase of the attack came from G. Stanley Hall and the child study movement he so enthusiastically initiated. Hall pointed out that in several ways Froebel had misunderstood the meaning and uniqueness of childhood. Hall objected to Froebel and his followers' refusal to adjust their theory to empirical evidence about the nature of the child. Froebel built his philosophy of the kindergarten on an idealist, preconceived notion of childhood and neither he nor his followers had closely examined real children in real classrooms to see if those principles and methods made sense. Hall's child study movement, of course, was heavily committed to just this kind of empirical study of actual children. In his work, Hall found that Froebel had made several mistakes. The gifts and objects Froebel had prescribed were far too small to profit children. One-inch cubes and other small items required children to use their accessory muscles instead of exercising their fundamental muscles which, study showed, had to be developed before the accessory muscles. Hall was among the first to suggest that kindergartners use large toys rather than small detailed ones. Hall also criticized Froebelian methods because they required children to sit and work with little objects rather than to move around. Even those Froebelian techniques which called for children to move were too regulated and allowed for none of the spontaneous play

[7] Quoted in *ibid.*, 48.

movement so important, according to Hall, for children of that age. He charged that the Froebelians failed to recognize that children's minds were different from adult minds and that, if Froebel's gifts and occupations had any meaning at all, they had meaning only for the rational adult mind. Children from four to eight, Hall contended, where in a stage of growth where emotions played a far greater role than intellect. Froebel's intellectualized idealism meant nothing to such children; a more appropriate experience would include opportunities for spontaneous play with a wide variety of materials enabling them to fulfill their need for fantasy and mythmaking.

At the superficial, rhetorical level, Hall and the kindergartners were in agreement. Both sought to allow the natural development of children and warned teachers not to interfere with this process. Both emphasized that play was more natural than the pedagogical drill and practice of the public schools. All agreed that knowing the child was crucial to the success of any teaching effort. It is symptomatic of the fact that times were changing, however, that underneath that rhetorical similarity Hall and the Froebelians agreed on almost nothing. Froebelians thought they encouraged the natural and playful development of children; Hall thought them manipulative and rigid. His way of understanding the child differed completely from theirs. Although the child study movement carried out a great deal of research on kindergartens, Hall and his ideas had little influence on the kindergarten before the turn of the century. His attack on Froebelian principles was too severe for the devotees to accept. When he suggested in a lecture to the International Kindergarten Union in 1895 that Froebelian methods needed basic modification, thirty-three of the thirty-five members of the audience walked out of the room in protest.[8]

John Dewey was no more successful in his attempts to effect fundamental changes in the kindergarten curriculum and the dominant conceptions of method. Dewey agreed with Hall that activities should be correlated more with increasing knowledge about the child's physical and emotional development, and that the child's spontaneous activities were often more important than his acting out the intellectual forms of his teacher.[9] But Dewey disagreed rather fundamentally with Hall's conception of what kindergarten-age children should be learning. For both Hall and Froebel, the young child's natural development followed some inner logic based upon qualities inherent in his mind or emotional makeup. Dewey contended, instead, that how the person developed was determined in large part by external stimuli; that the mind was shaped accord-

---

[8] *Ibid.*, 44–45.

[9] John Dewey, "The Kindergarten and Child Study," *Addresses and Proceedings*, National Education Association (1897), 585–586.

ing to the problems it had to solve. Hall and Froebel conceived of kindergarten activities in a sort of timeless and placeless continuum: children in Germany reenacted the same intellectual and emotional developments as did children in New York or Peking. Dewey contended that the child in different circumstances should and would learn differently because each environment called upon him to respond to unique problems. Dewey wanted the kindergarten to stress social learning, and to engage the child's mind with the issues and qualities typical of his own immediate environment.

Dewey considered the kindergarten child capable of more than fantasizing and emotional development; he could learn a good deal of intellectual content and, even more important, begin to get a sense of himself as a social being. Dewey, as we have seen, wished to make the schoolroom, including the kindergarten, into a community where children could learn the spirit and habits of cooperation and come to understand their place in the social order. A kindergartner was to facilitate her children's growth as social beings by exercising their intelligence in solving social problems that grew out of the classroom's community environment. Dewey thought that only purposeful learning was effective. Learning something, usually by memorization, because a teacher or a curriculum required it was not effective. Purposeful learning occurred only when the student had a use for what he was learning. Such purposes or uses for learning grew out of the child's social environment, both inside the school and out, and the most productive pedagogy would be one that recognized and developed that alliance between schooling and the real world surrounding the child. Dewey criticized Froebelian methods precisely because they did not engage the child in purposeful activity. Instead, they set before the student tasks that may have seemed purposeful at the time Froebel conceived them, but were surely not so for the turn-of-the-century child in the urban slum. The gifts and occupations had little or nothing to do with such a child's goals or purposes and thus, according to Dewey, could not be effective learning aids.

Neither Dewey nor Hall directly influenced the kindergarten movement significantly. They were important because they supplied ammunition to the few prominent reformers within the kindergartners' ranks, such as Anna E. Bryan of Louisville, who after 1887 began giving children a chance to carry on purposeful activity in the kindergarten; Bryan's student, Patty Smith Hill, who became a leading reformer at Teachers College after 1900 and instituted a number of reforms based on Hall's insights (including the introduction of the oversized kindergarten blocks now so familiar); and Alice Putnam of Chicago, whose training school (first at Cook County Normal under Francis W. Parker and then at Hull House) emphasized social learning and introduced kindergartners to the environment of the slum child. These women were voices in the wilderness for some time; as late as 1913 an IKU report demanded that Froebelian principles and methods be retained as a unified whole. Yet by 1920 the era of the Froebelian kindergarten was over; the reformers began to be heard and change came quickly. For all its tenacity, Froebelian theory disappeared rapidly once in began to crumble—perhaps confirming the conservatives' notion that unless the program were retained as a whole no part of it could survive.

IV

The change (between 1910 and 1920) that did occur in kindergarten theory did not represent any triumph of rhetorical or liberal progressivism as embodied in the ideas of reformers like John Dewey or Jane Addams. Their Liberal ideas were finally no more effective at this level of education than they were in the secondary schools. The transformation of the kindergarten resulted from several factors, including the educational ideas of Dewey and Hall, already reviewed, the assumption of responsibility by the public schools for the kindergarten, the connectionist psychology of Edward Lee Thorndike, and the project method of William Heard Kilpatrick. This combination of factors worked together to introduce to the public kindergarten the same concern with social efficiency which we pointed out was influential at other levels of education during the Progressive era. "Efficiency" was not a word often or easily applied to the kindergarten. The combination of efficiency and small children probably grated on the ears of even the efficiency advocates of the period. Kindergartners substituted "habit formation" for efficiency; the two concepts can be thought of as synonymous.

When private philanthropic kindergartens became part of public school systems, they found themselves in competition with every other area of public education for the limited financial resources available. Kindergartens were particularly expensive. Teacher/pupil ratios were considerably lower than in the regular primary classes (kindergartners seldom taught more than twenty-five students), kindergartens required more varied equipment than the normal schoolroom, and kindergartners worked in the classroom for only half a day, a policy that left them time for home visits and other social reform work. School superintendents, school boards, and taxpayers began to ask, after 1900, whether kindergartens were worth the extra money spent on them.

To this classic question of educational efficiency, one which was being asked of every level in the educational system at the time, the Froebelian kindergartners had a fairly weak answer. On the one hand, they argued that their program, by segregating the slum child and introducing him to healthier moral values, was particularly relevant to the urban school.

On the other hand, they admitted that Froebelian principles and methods had not been changed to meet the needs of the slum child; that kindergartens were alike for both the wealthy and the impoverished child. Nor could the Froebelians demonstrate that their work had been particularly effective with slum children, especially in terms that would appeal to other educators whose primary interest lay in making the work of the regular grades more efficient.

When pressed, however, the more agile and acute kindergartners told the educational budgetmakers what they wanted to know—that, yes, the kindergarten did make the public schools as a whole more effective by preparing children (especially slum children) to enter the first grade more easily. Kindergartens, they pointed out, socialized these children to the routines and expectations of the school. First-grade teachers could get right down to academic learning as soon as the year began because the kindergarten teachers had already trained the children to be neat and punctual, to listen to the teacher, to sit quietly, and to grow accustomed to the sound of English (which was especially important to immigrant children). Several elementary school principals reported in the late 1890s that the pupils entering the first grade after completing a kindergarten program knew "better how to handle themselves. They have been trained to control their activities, and can begin school work at once." "They [were] cleaner, neater and better mannered," the reports continued, and gained significantly with regard to the following points: "The formation of good habits, the development of freedom and activity, the power to understand directions, the social element, and last, but not the least, the attention paid to cleanliness."[10] These benefits sounded good to school administrators and they urged the kindergartners to deliver on them. But why was it necessary, if socialization to school routines was the purpose of the kindergarten, to allow teachers a half day out of the classroom to visit families? Why should kindergartners have smaller classes than primary teachers? (Many cities eliminated these features of the charity kindergarten.) If kindergartens were most effective in preparing children for the first grade, why not absorb them as the first rung on the educational ladder?

Kindergartners were not able to argue effectively for maintaining a kindergarten that was distinct and different from the regular school. Educators, instead, forced them to view the kindergarten as the introduction to the regular school and urged them to deemphasize play and spontaneity in favor of early drill and practice in speaking English and learning obedience and order. Several cities eliminated the kindergarten and established preprimary or subprimary classes. These new programs made no pretense at offering recreational routines or a distinct kind of

[10] Quoted in Blow, "Kindergarten Education," 34–36.

education and, instead, concentrated on preparing children to advance into the first grade. Under the unification scheme, the first grade was to incorporate kindergarten elements of play and games, drawing, construction, and nature study, while the kindergarten was going to set its charges to work on reading and numbers. "The reading which is taught, however," protested one advocate of unification, "is not the 'scourge of infancy,' as Rousseau called it in 1762. Instead, the reading methods are so playful and delightful that the children find in them the same pleasure that they experience in listening to nursery rimes [sic] and fairy tales, and such methods quickly open the road to the fairyland of children's books."[11] This compromise testified to the fact that the kindergarten movement did influence at least the early grades of the schools to change somewhat, but it also showed how profound was the public schools' influence on the kindergarten. In most cities the kindergarten became part of the primary department and its activities and goals were coordinated with those of the first three grades. Both major kindergarten curriculum studies of the 1920s recommended that the curriculum of the first grade and of the kindergarten be planned as a whole.[12] Before 1910 kindergarten teachers were almost always trained separately; by 1930, 80 percent of the training departments trained kindergarten and primary teachers together. By 1920 the public kindergarten had lost its role as an agency of social reform, and instead had become an arm of the public schools. As such, it concentrated as much on preparing the child for promotion as on attending to his current educational needs.

Within this framework, the seemingly scientific ideas of Thorndike and Kilpatrick became important to the development of the revised conception of the kindergarten because they were very useful in resolving the institutional difficulties that arose out of the public schools' absorption of the kindergarten as part of the educational ladder. In the nineteenth century the kindergarten had been, on the whole, an independent institution with independent sources of income. Kindergartners were special teachers with their own training schools,* and the kind of teaching they did was supposed to differ from that done by other teachers. The public schools' takeover of the kindergarten was something of a trauma for these teachers, therefore, because now they found themselves competing for prestige and money with the rest of the teaching profession and, as a minority within that company, found that they were measured

---

* In 1906 there were 137 private kindergarten training schools and only 54 kindergarten training departments in teachers colleges or normal schools; by 1920 only 31 private training schools remained while 109 training departments were located in teachers' colleges.

[11] Samuel Chester Parker and Alice Temple, *Unified Kindergarten and First Grade Teaching* (Boston, 1925), 1.

[12] Agnes Burke et al., *A Conduct Curriculum for the Kindergarten and First Grade* (New York, 1923), and Parker and Temple, *Unified Kindergarten.*

against the standards of the larger profession. As education in general was embracing the standards of science during this era, the kindergartners found themselves forced to abandon Froebelian idealism in favor of rationales for their work that appeared more scientific, and thus more convincing, to their colleagues in education. Thorndike and Kilpatrick provided those rationales.

Edward Lee Thorndike was important because he defined educational outcomes in ways that were immediately and easily applied to the situation of teaching young children. Thorndike's learning theory, usually identified as "connectionism" or "stimulus-response" psychology, was a fully atomized version of British associationism and had close parallels to the phrenological movement of an earlier era. Connectionism was related to the more famous contemporary school of behaviorism, associated with the name of John B. Watson, but is different enough that the student must be sure not to confuse the two. Phrenology, connectionism, and behaviorism all sought to determine how inputs into the human senses effected behavioral outcomes. In some sense, of course, this is the concern of all psychologies that are not idealist (those which contend, like Froebel, that the mind's inherent qualities and potentialities shape its performance far more significantly than does information or stimulus which the mind receives through the senses). But phrenology, connectionism, and behaviorism were unique in breaking down behavior into thousands of distinct and separate events. Moral behavior, or being good, was a sufficiently meaningful category of analysis for most psychologists before the twentieth century; for the phrenologists, Thorndike, and Watson, such a concept of behavior was scientifically incomprehensible. They set out to distinguish and identify all the distinct, discrete human actions or emotions that fell under the general heading of moral behavior. The phrenologist would include loyalty, honesty, love, industriousness, and self-control among the behaviors. A century later connectionism and behaviorism would require even more atomistic categories. Washing behind the ears, saying thank you, offering a woman a seat, rising early to get to work on time, and resisting alcohol might be among the specific traits that Thorndike and Watson would identify. In the realm of learning, where Thorndike did most of his work, connectionism abandoned the logic of mental discipline, the common nineteenth-century theory that argued that learning was a single behavior which was facilitated in all cases by disciplining and exercising the mind. Thorndike, in a paper he published in 1901 with Robert S. Woodworth entitled "The Influence of Improvement in One Mental Function upon the Efficiency in Other Functions,"[13] made his initial reputation in the educational world by denying emphatically that learning one subject was exactly like learning

---

[13] *Psychological Review*, VIII (May, July, November, 1901), 247–261, 384–395, 553–564.

another. He denied the accompanying pedagogical theory which concluded that, since learning was a single behavior, training received in the extensive study of a few of the more difficult subjects would "transfer" to the mastery of all other subjects. Thorndike believed that his experimental work had proved that the ability to master Latin did not facilitate a person's ability to master the slide rule or any other skill. Over the remainder of his career, Thorndike elaborated instead an alternative theory which held that the mastery of a complex subject involved a whole series of distinct behaviors that were usually specific to the mastery of that single subject. In reading, for example, the recognition of each letter in the alphabet was a distinct behavior, as was the recognition of each syllable's sound. Reading required the combination of literally hundreds of these different behaviors. On this point Thorndike and the behaviorists were in agreement. Differences appeared in the manner in which connectionists and behaviorists set out to explain how behavior could be influenced.

Thorndike's pedagogical theory rested on the assumption that each of the required behaviors came about as the result of an equally discrete stimulus and that learning occurred when the connection between a stimulus and the proper behavior became automatic or habitual in the child. Since each of the behaviors involved in the mastery of a complex task like reading was separate, and because there was no transfer of training (learning to recognize one letter did not facilitate learning another), Thorndike argued that each of the behaviors involved had to be taught separately, and that each had to be connected to a specific stimulus. The child had to be taught by being presented with a specific stimulus and rewarded when he responded correctly. Thorndike thought the child had learned when he became habituated to saying "r" each time he saw the letter *r*. Learning, was nothing but correct "habit formation," or the imprinting of the correct stimulus-response bonds.

Connectionism and behaviorism agreed substantially on this point. Thorndike and Watson differed, however, in their search for precisely how these connections within the mind, the connections between a stimulus and a response, were made. Behaviorists were willing to accept and work with the fact that rewarding consistently a particular response to a constant stimulus made that response habitual to that stimulus. As Watson pointed out, it was impossible to see and measure that which went on within the brain. He was not interested in such activity. Behaviorists defined psychology as a hard science, and defined science as a mode of thought that dealt with what could be seen and measured. Thorndike was less rigid and more interested in the mind itself. Therefore, he outlined his famous laws of learning—basically, the law of exercise and the law of effect—as explanations of how habituation occurred within the mind. A stimulus had to be repeated and the proper response secured often to insure that the stimulus-response bonds would grow and remain strong; and the brain learned habits more effectively when those habits brought extrinsic or intrinsic rewards or satisfactions to the learner. Thorndike went on to define the stimulus-response connection as a neural bond strengthened by the repeated electrical impulses across a synapse which occurred each time the proper response was made. The learned habit was, in effect, an imprinted electrical bond between nerves in the brain. It seemed to have become imprinted, like an electrical circuit, by repeated use. In this sense a learned behavior became an involuntary habit for Thorndike.

For all its simplistic qualities,* Thorndike's learning theory has been immensely influential in modern educational thought. Much of modern theory about operant conditioning rests on the insights and the viewpoints that were first Thorndike's. A good deal of the rationale underlying the development of educational technology is based on Thorndike's model of learning, or at least on similar ones developed by his followers. Much of our contemporary concern with specifying exact goals for the educational process, a concern which is both stultifying and healthy, stems from his concern with breaking down learning into its constituent parts.

Thorndike became the most influential voice in educational science after 1910. Those, like the public kindergartners, seeking a place for themselves in the educational establishment, had to justify their claims in terms of his ideas. Thorndike's ideas were peculiarly appropriate for the kindergarten. By demonstrating that the overall "goal" of learning was more reasonably thought of as a whole series of proximate goals, that the ultimate goal of schooling was really only a combination of smaller goals, he made it somewhat easier for kindergartners to defend their place in the system. Reducing learning to its incremental steps was important to kindergartners who taught preliterate children little in the way of intellectual content or finished skills but, rather, prepared children to learn the content and skills at another level of the educational system. On the basis of Thorndike's insights they could talk scientifically about the preparatory behaviors they were inculcating; thus they legitimized their place in the public schools. It should be noted, however, that while facilitating the kindergartners' search for a place in the public school system, Thorndike's rationale also bound, as an integral part, the kindergarten to the public school. The kindergarten was no longer an alternative to public schooling but merely the introductory step in the public school's efforts to train the young.

* Learning is considerably more complex than Thorndike made it seem; the brain can master certain subjects without prior familiarity with them; and modern psychologists think that considerable evidence exists to support the proposition that some transfer of training does occur.

If Thorndike provided the kindergartners with a perspective in which to indentify significant educational goals for their institution, Kilpatrick and his "project method" helped them define just how those goals were to be achieved. In Chapter 12 a fuller discussion of Kilpatrick's project method will appear. Kilpatrick's purpose was to outline a program which stressed social learning while it catered to the individual desires and personalities of the children. Because thorough learning resulted when the learner was involved and interested, Kilpatrick believed that children in groups should recommend the "projects" upon which they wished to work. The teacher would then help the students draw out the lessons inherent in the project and emphasize particularly the "social" lessons offered in the experience. In this way the interests of the children could be drawn upon to deepen their appreciation of social responsibility and the rewards of cooperation and group activity. Larger social purposes, ones which appeared to be supported by the public, were coupled with the popular argument that the interests and desires of the students played an important role in their education.

In an era when educational efficiency was the watchword and when educators at all levels felt that every policy had to be justified precisely and concretely, Kilpatrick's concern with building correct social habits often overshadowed his discussion of purposeful learning. Most efforts at implementing his program quietly discarded its essence: that it was the individual child or group of children who were to propose a project because in their motivation to complete the project lay the key to effective learning. Too often Kilpatrick's program offered the children preplanned projects instead of asking them to choose and plan their own. Certain projects—often prepackaged by textbook publishers—were supposed to build specific habits and were assigned, just like textbooks, in order to accomplish these learning goals. Spontaneity and self-direction were sacrificed to habit formation. In the search for curricular justification, the creation of proper habits—which could be specified in great detail—was more convincing than claims of teaching self-direction or commitment to social living. Specific skills were stressed more often than were general skills, not because specific skills were thought to be more important but because, in the Thorndikean view, specific skills comprised the general skills. Educators, to improve their work, had to concentrate on teaching these specific skills. In this schema, concern with detail began to crowd concern with larger goals; habit formation began to be considered the ultimate, rather than the proximate, goal of teaching.

Such a reversal of priorities can be seen rather clearly in the development of kindergarten theory in the early 1920s. How the interaction of Deweyan ideals, institutional changes, and the need for justification led to the elevation of habit formation as the central goal of the kindergarten can be seen in the experiences of the reformer Patty Smith Hill, one of the most influential of the new students of kindergarten theory, as she described them in the introduction to *A Conduct Curriculum for the Kinder-garten and First Grade* (1923). Hill had been trained in Louisville with Anna Bryan, one of the first kindergartners to trade strict Froebelianism for spontaneous and creative activity. In 1905 Hill joined the faculty at Teachers College, Columbia University, where in her first year she tangled quite successfully in an alternating lecture series with Susan Blow, the doughty champion of Froebelianism. Before coming to Teachers College, Patty Hill had studied with Dewey, Francis Parker, and G. Stanley Hall; at Teachers College she met and worked with Thorndike and Kilpatrick. As director of the kindergarten and primary department at Teachers College (the first such department to be affiliated with a university in the United States) and as director of an experimental unit at various schools in the city, she wielded immense authority among kindergartners in the United States.

Patty Hill brought to Teachers College some of the ideas about curriculum that she and her mentor had employed in the philanthropic kindergarten in Louisville. She sought to conduct an experiment which tried "to apply the principles of democracy to school organization" in a New York public kindergarten. Seeking to teach "the beginnings of self-government," the experimental school encouraged the children to learn from each other, through their own experience, emphasis being laid upon the initiation and execution of their purposes and plans." Students were, whenever possible, "without waste of time and effort," to make their own decisions and choices. Hill urged a "new conception of the teacher as a guide rather than as a dictator."[14] Her experiment seemed far too radical, however, and few bothered to pay it any heed. Teachers College dropped the experiment in the public school but later revived it in the college's own experimental school. Here the experiment caught on and even convinced teachers and parents that several of its features should be instituted in the first grade. But, calling the experiment "radical and wasteful," conservatives still resisted. To counter this view, "in order, therefore," she explained, "to justify the results of such training through some more convincing evidence than the mere enthusiasm of those who were conducting the experiment, it was realized that some method of recording daily work must be devised."[15] The teachers chose to keep track of several outcomes that they thought came from the freer organization of the kindergarten, including "initiative, independence, perseverance, concentration, and social-cooperation." They expected the children they sent on to the first grade to demonstrate "ability to initiate purposes and plans, ability to persevere or 'stick to one's job' in spite of difficulties, ability to lead and follow intelligently, ability to work alone or in a group, ability to know when one needs help and when and

[14] Burke et al., *Conduct Curriculum*, xi.
[15] *Ibid.*, xii.

where such help is to be secured, ability to give fair criticism to self and others and finally to profit by such criticism."[16]

The kindergartners diligently recorded the outcomes of their work in this fashion, but found that their categories were considered hopelessly vague. In 1921, hoping to profit from outside criticism and advice, they called in a number of psychologists, all of whom claimed that they could be of little help because the categories "under which the records were made dealt almost exclusively with non-measurable qualities, those not sufficiently objective to induce psychologists to attempt to scale or measure them. While the qualities, as such, were approved and acknowledged as of unquestioned worth, they were too vague, too indefinite, to warrant attempts at scientific measurement. It was agreed," she wrote, "that some more objective outcomes must be found before further attempts could be made to measure the progress of young children."[17]

Hill then secured the aid of Agnes Rogers, a psychologist who broke up "the captions of our previous records into the more specific abilities and habits involved." She published a "habit inventory"—a compendium of hundreds of specific behaviors which were important to young children in accelerating their later learning.

> As this inventory was used, the observers noted, not only the obvious improvement and acceleration of habit-formation with the children, but also that the supervisors and class-room teachers began to think of all instruction in terms of desirable changes in thought, feeling, or conduct; in other words, in terms of changed behavior due to a changed nervous system. As was but natural, changes in behavior were appreciated first in the realm of moral and social conduct. But as the study proceeded, the conception of behavior grew to include, not only those technical activities listed as conduct, but all those changes in thought and feeling, directly or indirectly, immediately or remotely, leading to and influencing behavior.[18]

Soon teaching habits—not only those concerned with social conduct, but those which aided cognitive development—became the pivot of the curriculum. "Thus the proper conduct of the three R's or the correct technique of the fine and industrial arts became as evident as the so-called moral or social conduct. Each school subject was studied from the viewpoint of the desirable improvements in thought, feeling, and conduct which might thereby be stimulated and established in habits of behavior. Thus the activities of each subject were listed in one column; opposite were listed the desired changes which should grow out of these activities."[19] The effort was to establish "definite aims and objectives [for] the teachers of young children, laying the emphasis, not on knowledge or

[16] *Ibid.*, xii–xiii.
[17] *Ibid.*
[18] *Ibid.*, xiv.
[19] *Ibid.*, xv.

appreciation as such, but on desirable changes or improvements in these —in the changed nervous system which leads to habits of behavior, finally culminating in character." No single part of the curriculum was to be considered "a formal school subject, but as a social situation rich in activities and experiences leading to the formation of desirable habits." The influence of Kilpatrick here becomes clear. Habits acquired because they were needed as part of a social situation were more likely to be effectively learned because the child would derive a sense of satisfaction from the exercise of the habit. Habits were supposed to be learned in real situations which required them, rather than in artificial situations; only in the real situation would the child derive satisfaction from solving a worthwhile problem. The "proper technique or conduct of crossing the street, a habit of tremendous importance in safeguarding the lives of little children in large cities," was to be taught in action rather than in the abstract. The excursions about the city taken by the children would be the "best social situation for teaching the child 'Safety First.' "[20]

Nothing inherent in the concept of habit formation dictated that its widespread adoption would have a deleterious effect on schooling; the quest for specificity and self-consciousness and scientific understanding upon which habit formation rested is extremely important to the development and delivery of effective educational services. But institutional arrangements made it almost inevitable that habit formation would come to dominate kindergarten goals to the exclusion of more important but less specific ones. Given the institutional situation, it was unlikely that habit formation would have been left to serve just as a convenient and accurate measure of pedagogical effectiveness and as a means of identifying proximate educational goals. Teachers tend to "teach to the tests" and, when habit formation was identified as the measurable outcome of kindergarten training, teachers began to concentrate on insuring that they achieved those outcomes. Second, in their fight for status and security in the educational establishment, kindergartners sought consecration from the day's leading educational thinkers. These men (almost all were men) valued most highly strategies promising precise and measurable results. The kindergartners obliged by stressing their involvement with habit formation. Third, in the transmission of the conduct curriculum (which Hill admitted could more accurately be called a curriculum of behaviors or habits) to thousands and thousands of kindergartners, the spontaneity, the idea of student decision and choice, the idea of the social situation determining the habits learned, all of which were prominent in Patty Hill's formulation, tended to get buried under the more precise, more delimited, more identifiable discussion of specific habits and the specific stimuli that led to each of them. It was far

20 *Ibid.*, xv–xvii

easier to communicate successfully what is codified than that which is abstract and generalized. It is easier to convey to others a pedagogical method's details and its apparatus than to get people to understand the spirit behind the method. How enticing the conduct curriculum with its columns of habits and outcomes must have been to the kindergartner seeking a way to improve and justify her work is clear from a glance at almost any page of *A Conduct Curriculum*. The accompanying chart deals with the results to be expected from playing in a sandbox during the work period.[21] How reassuring for the teacher to learn from this chart that among the purposes of the kindergarten was to teach children to keep the floor clean, to sweep without raising dust, and to share materials. The habits to be formed gave the teacher a series of benchmarks against which to measure her performance; unfortunately, they too often became her only goals.

Hill apparently recognized this problem, noting that "in school practice it makes a vast difference whether the teacher views a habit as something to be taught at any time, or under any conditions, or as a form of activity organically related to an experience or situation in which the *raison d'être* for learning arises."[22] The situation, the purposefulness of the project, rather than the teacher's predetermined objectives, must determine the way the class should develop. She seemed to argue that the establishment of "definite aims and objectives" must become a means of achieving "wider freedom" for the child. "The objectives must not curtail the child's opportunities for orginality and initiative. On the contrary, we must make habit serve as a means to a more productive creativity."[23] But Patty Hill, with her heritage of efforts to reform the kindergarten and to implement some of Dewey's ideals, took a far different perspective on the meaning of habit formation than did hundreds and thousands of kindergartners who, from a background of Froebelian methodological rigidity, read guides like the *Conduct Curriculum*. Froebel and the habit formers were strangely alike in the way they precisely defined the pedagogical process and its goals. Indeed, as Evelyn Weber has perceptively suggested, the theory of habit formation served, in many instances at least, to give scientific sanction to the same effort to impose middle-class values on children of other backgrounds that had motivated the earlier generation of Froebelians so enthusiastically to bring the kindergarten into the slums.[24] As the authors of the *Conduct Curriculum* put it, "For the child of this age moral training is largely social adaptation. The teacher should be conscious of the opportunities for such training

[21] *Ibid.*, 29–30.
[22] *Ibid.*, xvii.
[23] *Ibid.*, xix.
[24] Weber, *Kindergarten*, 146–147.

| | Desirable Changes in Thought, |
Typical Activities	Feeling, and Conduct

GROUP I (age 2½–4)

Manipulating sand with no definite purpose in view:
Patting.
Pounding.
Piling.
Digging.
Making cakes and pies, tracks, etc.
Using molds.
	Sharing materials.
	Trying to keep sand in box to prevent waste; learning not to throw sand.
	Keeping floor clean under sand box.
	  Learning to use broom and dust pan.
	  Sweeping with care to avoid raising dust.
	  Putting sand which has been swept from floor in waste receptacle (not back in sand box).
	Keeping sand toys in place.
	Pleasure in using sand.

GROUP II (4–5)

Manipulation is still in evidence. Making tracks, tunnels for train, fences for animals, caves for animals. (Problems are largely individual.)	Sharing space as well as materials. Increasing skill in handling tools and keeping floor clean. Tendency to formulate some plan before beginning to work. Increased realization of the fact that materials are common property and must be used by taking turns. Growing interest in result.

GROUP III (5–6)

Less interest in mere manipulation. Working with definite plan. Beginning cooperative problems, using entire space for one scheme, such as: Railroad system. Farm. City. River system. Fort and castle. Hills and lakes. Noah's Ark Play. Using measuring cups (comparison of amounts).	Learning to play cooperatively. Assuming responsibility for certain part of the general scheme. Respecting ideas of other children. Increasing ability to plan a large scheme. Ability to decide upon the best arrangement and space for things to be made. Ability to select the most essential parts to be made. Gaining elementary ideas about measure.

and of the necessity for the formation of habits and attitudes such as obedience, consideration for others, respect, and reverence."[25] "Habit" became a way of objectifying value; habit formation, in the last analysis, was most often value training or inculcation rather than, as some of the theorists claimed, the introduction of students to independence and decision making. The rigidities and teacher centeredness (or even theory centeredness) which had characterized the Froebelian movement, came to characterize the kindergarten of the twenties and thirties, but now the rigidities had become those of scientific psychology and measurement.

GUIDE TO FURTHER READING

Two important and excellent studies of the kindergarten have informed our chapter substantially. We relied heavily on EVELYN WEBER's internal analysis of the kindergarten movement in discussing the ideological and philosophical changes which the movement underwent before 1930; see *The Kindergarten: Its Encounter with Educational Thought in America* (New York, 1969). MARVIN LAZERSON, *Origins of the Urban School: Public Education in Massachusetts, 1870–1915* (Cambridge, Mass., 1971), includes a superb discussion on the external relations between the kindergarten movement and those larger social pressures influencing educational innovation before 1915. Both volumes include thorough bibliographies.

The clearest expression of Froebelianism and its American tradition can be found in: WILLIAM H. KILPATRICK, *Froebel's Kindergarten Principles Critically Examined* (New York, 1916); and the work of SUSAN BLOW, particularly *Educational Issues in the Kindergarten* (New York, 1908), and "Kindergarten Education," Nicholas M. Butler, ed., *Education in the United States* (Albany, N.Y., 1899), vol. II. The International Kindergarten Union's defense of conservative Froebelianism was collected in the Committee of Nineteen, *The Kindergarten* (Boston, 1913); the idealism of the nineteenth-century kindergarten and its continuity with the activities of Horace Mann is emphasized in ELIZABETH PEABODY and MARY MANN, *Guide to the Kindergarten and Moral Culture of Infancy* (New York, 1877).

G. Stanley Hall is the subject of an excellent biography by DOROTHY ROSS, *G. Stanley Hall: The Psychologist as Prophet* (Chicago, 1972). Hall's writings have been excerpted in CHARLES E. STRICKLAND and CHARLES BURGESS, eds., *Health, Growth, and Heredity: G. Stanley Hall on Natural Education* (New York, 1965). The shock HALL experienced when he learned that many children knew nothing of cows or the origins of milk and butter can be seen in his essay, "The Contents of Children's Minds," *Princeton Review*, XI (May, 1883), 249–253. Also useful are R. JACKSON WILSON, *In Quest of Community: Social Philosophy in the United States, 1860–1920* (New York, 1968), chapter 5, and CHARLES BURGESS and MERLE BORROWMAN, *What Doctrines to Embrace?* (Glenview, Ill., 1969), chapters 3, 4. GERALDINE JONCICH [CLIFFORD]'s sampling of THORN-

---

[25] Burke et al., *Conduct Curriculum*, 10.

DIKE'S writings, *Psychology and the Science of Education: Selected Writings of Edward L. Thorndike* (New York, 1962), should be supplemented with her study of *The Sane Positivist: A Biography of Edward L. Thorndike* (Middletown, Conn., 1968). "The Project Method," *Teachers College Record,* XIX (September, 1918), 319–335, by WILLIAM H. KILPATRICK is the best discussion of that topic. The clearest expressions of DEWEY's theories on early childhood education remain his *The School and Society* (Chicago, 1900; revised in 1915) and *The Child and the Curriculum* (Chicago, 1902). For the emergence of the flexible view of the child see BERNARD WISHY, *The Child and the Republic* (Philadelphia, 1968), and the other literature cited in our bibliography for chapter 4.

The post-Froebelian kindergarten is presented in AGNES BURKE et al., *A Conduct Curriculum for the Kindergarten and First Grade* (New York, 1923) (especially the preface by PATTY HILL), SAMUEL CHESTER PARKER and ALICE TEMPLE, *Unified Kindergarten and First Grade Teaching* (Boston, 1925), and JOHN and EVELYN DEWEY, *Schools of Tomorrow* (New York, 1915), chapter 5.

CHAPTER 12

American Education Between the Wars, 1918–1940

I

On the surface, at least, the Cardinal Principles of Secondary Education continued to control the rhetoric of the high school for the next two decades. It was the U.S. Bureau of Education's most popular publication to date, and sold over one hundred thousand copies by 1928. Yet, as was typical of the vast poorly articulated educational establishment in the United States at that time, when 1,228 superintendents were polled in 1928 about their knowledge of the report, only 225 had heard of it—although, presumably, many more were familiar with its ideas. In the two decades following the war, high schools continued to offer the new services they had so eagerly introduced prior to 1917. More and more adopted tracking systems in which students prepared for different futures in different curricula, ranging from college preparatory to commerical and industrial ones. The rhetoric of social efficiency and progressivism remained. Educators continued to attract more children into high school; while the high schools enrolled only 28 percent of the eligible age group in 1920, the figure climbed to more than 47 percent by the end of that decade. By 1940, despite the dislocations of depression, over 80 percent of the age group attended high school.[1]

Beneath these similarities, however, a subtle but profound shift occurred. The purpose and perspectives of the high school and of public education in general adopted a more provincial cast than they had before World War I. Before 1917 educational reform was infused with national purpose; the schools were regarded as vital social institutions. Increasingly, in the twenties and thirties, each school or school system became the creature of its local community and set out to perform functions directed at improving local conditions or solving local problems. During the Progressive era, reformers of all stripes had seen the schools as part of the cutting edge of social change—schools were crucial to increasing efficiency or enhancing the sense of national community. The importance of schools then lay in the fact that so much of the progressive reform effort was predicated on the notion that social improvement would occur only by increasing the intelligence of the population. Bedeviling social problems could be eliminated through the application of science or rationality. These solutions would occur more quickly with the diffusion of rationality among the people. Reformers expected that an informed and educated electorate would force improvement on society. Many of the more public and popular reform efforts of the Progressive era were, as Richard Hofstadter has pointed out, preeminently educational movements: the muckraking journalists set out to "educate" the public about the evils in its midst; politicians like Theodore Roosevelt sought to lead by instructing the people through countless lectures on the nation's problems and the preferred solutions to them. If the people were informed, they would inevitably demand and secure needed changes by voting for better leaders and by taking their community responsibilities more seriously. Thus, schooling had a vital role to play in national improvement.

The experience surrounding World War I diminished many reform leaders' faith in the people and their potential for rational behavior. Indeed, this period saw concepts such as "popular" and "rational" become identified as polar opposites, and "masses" and irrationality became nearly synonymous. Developments in psychology after 1915 helped undermine the intellectual and social leaders' faith in education as an important tool of social betterment. John B. Watson's behaviorism, Freud's recognition of the importance of the unconscious and emotional factors in behavior, and the success of propaganda during the war and of the advertising business afterward greatly reduced faith in rationality and in the belief that appeals to reason could meaningfully affect men's

[1] Statistics from Edward Krug, *The Shaping of the American High School: II, 1920–1941* (Madison, Wis., 1972), 218.

behavior. Progressive reformers had assumed that the public, when informed, would see evil for what it was and all citizens, by exercising their reasoning capacities, would arrive at the same or similar solutions to those evils. Our inherent reasoning capacity guaranteed that, ultimately, correct reactions to social problems would be implemented. The force of Watson's behaviorism was to empty man of all inherent capacities and to argue that, because human behavior was determined entirely by outside stimuli, men and their behavior were at the mercy of those who manipulated these stimuli. Watson created the "hollow man" who when stimulated in certain ways would act accordingly. The hollow man did nothing with the stimulus—did not reason on it or choose his reaction.* Under these theories it was hard to retain much faith in the supremacy of reason or in the human capacity for reasoned choice.

The theories of Sigmund Freud were, of course, quite different from those of Watson but in many ways they carried the same message for Americans around 1920. Instead of emptying the human mind of all power of reason and choice, Freud described other forces in the psyche, principally emotional and unconscious forces, that were far more powerful than reason. For Freud reason was a fragile element in the human psyche which fought desperately to keep the emotional and unconscious forces in check—through repression and sublimation. Freud, who hoped his theories would help men to understand better how to use their reason to cope with unconscious drives and motivations, believed that reason could remain dominant. His followers and especially his popularizers in America emphasized instead the weakness of reason and the consequent power of irrational, emotional behavior. Appeals to reason would seldom be effective, they argued, since the unconscious drives consistently overwhelmed reason.

America's reformers and thinkers saw the most powerful and immediate demonstration of the accuracy of psychology's emerging belief in irrationality's dominance over reason in determining human behavior in the triumph of war propaganda and in the rise of the advertising industry. Sober second thoughts about the war made it clear how successfully Allied propaganda had deluded Americans into thinking that the Germans committed all the atrocities and that justice lay entirely with the Allies. The ability of pictorial and written descriptions of German in-

---

* Behaviorism was an extension of Ivan Pavlov's work with the salivating dog. The experimenter rang a bell each time he put food before a dog so many times that the dog formed the habit of salivating each time he heard a bell ring. The experimenter then rang the bell but did not place the food before the dog and the dog continued to salivate at the sound of the bell. Watson posited that the same techniques would work with humans—that the experimenter could manipulate the stimuli in such a way as to imprint habits of any kind upon the human's action. What was so important and so frightening was that the experimenter could produce behaviors in the human subject that had no more rational relation to the stimulus than did the dog's salivating at the sound of a bell.

humanities to move the American population from its adopted stance of neutrality toward firm support of the Allied cause convinced many that reason and judgment played a relatively minor role in forming opinion. In George Creel's Committee on Public Information, the United States government, after our entry into the war, formed its own propaganda arm. Appealing to the emotions of fear and patriotism through the manipulation of symbols, "the Creel committee succeeded in goading most Americans including intellectuals into a frenzy of loyalty."[2] The Creel committee recommended renaming sauerkraut "liberty cabbage" and the hamburger, "liberty sandwich." It organized groups to press neighbors to buy Liberty bonds and to force those suspected of disloyalty to kiss the flag, and it inspired citizens to hound German-Americans and others who did not support the war vocally enough. By picturing the German as the stereotypical "blond beast" or "Hun," the Committee on Public Information succeeded in changing people's minds without appealing to their reason. Business quickly adopted similar techniques in massive advertising campaigns after the war. Advertising turned from its traditional function of passing on information about products and their uses to an emphasis on relating products to the positive emotions of potential buyers. Thus grew the habit, with which we are all familiar, of associating cars with beautiful girls and cigarettes with luxurious surroundings. Because such appeals attracted more customers than truthful information about the product, it was difficult to argue for the old faith that in the realm of politics and social reform appeals to reason might still be effective.

The experiences of the war provided hundreds of examples of mass irrationality, of the readiness of people to succumb to emotion. Many reformers and intellectual leaders were disillusioned by the outcome of the crusade to "make the world safe for democracy"—frustrated that "peace without victory" was an empty slogan after the European powers had "put the Treaty of Versailles over" on Woodrow Wilson. Intellectuals and reformers came face to face with the problems inherent in the concept of mass reform. The "people" in whom they had placed their faith attempted to impose mass conformity on American society as war hysteria mounted after 1917. The people set out to suppress pacificism and to eliminate the teaching of German in the public schools (they were largely successful). The people suspected all German-Americans and were eager to humiliate them and demand gestures of fealty previously unheard of in America; they drove the German-born conductor of the Boston Symphony Orchestra from the stage. The people spontaneously formed flying squads of patriots who forced their neighbors to buy bonds or have their houses spattered with yellow paint. A young teacher in Iowa,

[2] Roderick Nash, *The Nervous Generation, 1917–1930* (Chicago, 1970), 51.

suspected of disloyalty, was stripped to the waist by a mob, painted yellow, and marched about the public square while carrying an American flag. This popular war jingoism spilled over into vilification of all dissent, whether related to the war or not. This frenzy of conformity fueled the Red Scare of 1919 when the attorney general of the United States teamed with numbers of "patriotic" groups to identify and deport suspected socialists and communists on the assumption that all such people must be aliens. The attorney general and the people were surprised to find that many of these suspects were in fact citizens, some even native Americans.[3]

The two major pieces of social reform legislation which were passed during and after the war also sought to impose conformity on the society. Ratification of the Eighteenth Amendment to the Constitution prohibiting the sale of alcholic beverages and passage of the Volstead Act enforcing it in 1919 put the United States' grandest attempt to legislate moral conformity on the books. A movement to restrict immigration in the United States, which had sought to tighten immigration policy since 1890, finally achieved its discriminatory goals in the National Origins Act of 1924, which restricted the inflow of immigrants from any country to a small percentage of their proportion of the population in 1890. Since in 1890 the population was as yet little affected by massive immigration from southeastern Europe, the act discriminated against immigrants who differed most from the Anglo-Saxon ideal of an American citizen. All in all, these experiences shattered the faith of intellectuals and reformers who had felt that the people could be a source of positive reform and, instead, led them to feel that the people were to be feared by those who valued individual freedom and rationality. The reformers felt that it was vain to try to educate the people to support reform.

Now reformers and intellectuals of the Progressive era had been interested in conformity, at least to the extent that conformity contributed to a sense of community, a pattern of obligations and responsibilities which they sought to resurrect. (Agitation for Prohibition and immigration restriction had been very much a part of the Progressive era, after all.) In some sense the mass conformity of a war-hysterical nation simply carried the progressive desire for a revitalized community to one of its logical extremes. Nevertheless, in the twenties the people's impulse toward conformity disillusioned those who had depended so much on education to build community in the previous decades. Experience with these problems made them suspect the goal of community and made them more receptive to the idea that individuality and community were mutually exclusive, even opposite concepts, that the individual had to be protected

[3] William Preston, Jr., *Aliens and Dissenters: Federal Suppression of Radicals, 1903–1933* (New York, 1963), chapters 7, 8.

from the community. This was a dichotomy that would have been completely foreign to the earlier era when reformers believed that true individuality was reached only through service to the community. The achievement of community—to which educational reform in the Progressive era was dedicated—came to seem, for many, no longer an admirable goal.

The reforms of the Progressive era are justly characterized as "middle-class" reforms, products of a remarkable alliance between intellectuals, reformers, radicals, and the great urban middle class. When Jane Addams or John Dewey demanded a greater sense of community in the United States, they were articulating a need felt and longed for by millions of Americans. There is every reason to believe that the middle class supported movements to clean up the slums, to educate the poor, to eliminate corruption, and to curb economic monopoly. After 1915 that alliance between the intellectuals and the middle class was eroded. Just how and why it deteriorated is a long and complex story which cannot be treated here. Intellectuals sensed themselves a separate alienated class,[4] in part because since 1915 they saw themselves increasingly as targets of radical baiting in the society. It became fashionable in intellectual circles to debunk American middle-class values, the values of the small town, the business ethos, and the debased Puritan ethic—a mixture of Victorian prudery and a self-interested work ethic. Now intellectuals, following H. L. Mencken, spoke of the typical citizen of the United States as a member of the species, "boobus Americanus." After the world war, intellectual and social reformers saw that the concerned middle-class citizen with whom they had worked and of whom they had expected so much had turned into a reactionary stuffed shirt. The man "who aspired to overturn Society," Walter Weyl wrote of the "tired radicals," "ends by fighting in a dull Board of Directors of a village library for the inclusion of certain books." The intellectuals convinced themselves that alliances with such bigoted, irrational, and small-minded people could effect no useful change. Adopting that attitude toward the middle class tended to cut these intellectual leaders off from the rest of the country. "What will you say to a man who believes in hell, or that the Pope of Rome wants to run this country, or that the Jews caused the War?" Ludwig Lewisohn asked. "How would you argue with a Methodist minister from an Arkansas village, with a Kleagle of the Klan, with a 'this-is-a-white-man's-country' politician from central Georgia?"[5] The point, of course, is that Lewisohn and his fellows would not have thought of arguing with such

[4] Christopher Lasch, *The New Radicalism in America [1889–1963]: The Intellectual as a Social Type* (New York, 1965).

[5] Mencken quoted in Nash, *Nervous Generation*, 59; Weyl in William E. Leuchtenburg, *The Perils of Prosperity, 1914–1932* (Chicago, 1958), 125; and Lewisohn in *ibid.*, 147.

types either before or after the war. Neither would they have thought to characterize prewar American society as one consisting mainly of such types. Their growing sense of a separate identity, their need to debunk values which they held directly responsible for the enforced conformity of the war years and the rampant materialism and anti-intellectualism of the postwar decade made them react against the middle class and the average American.

Intellectuals and social leaders were all to some degree disillusioned with the results of the world war and with the behavior of the middle class and the masses. A very few of their number were alienated from American society as a whole and went into actual or virtual exile—some in Paris, others in Greenwich Village, some in the isolated bohemias they imagined for themselves. Despairing of the possibilities for reform, they settled instead for trying to protect the few true individualists (such as themselves) from conformist pressure. The majority did not follow this course and continued to think of ways of making the United States a better place to live, to strive to fulfill the dream of founding a society based on respect for the individual, on community self-determination, and on the fair distribution of justice and material goods. But, unlike their prewar predecessors, they seldom sought to involve the great bulk of the population in the process of developing or implementing plans for a better society. Neither mass education nor mass involvement in a reform crusade would effect society's improvement; rather, it would come through the application of expert knowledge to social problems. The expert was to work behind the scenes, out of the glare of publicity or public oversight, choosing solutions to problems from alternatives so complex that the average man was unable to understand them. Experts implemented their favored choices not through appeals to a mass audience but by persuading a relatively small group of decision makers in the political arena—senators and representatives or their aides and, more important as the decade of the twenties closed, cabinet officers, presidential advisers, and the president himself. Experts in tariffs, foreign trade, business regulation, railroad finance, conservation, agriculture, public works, and so forth became increasingly prominent between the wars. Leonard White has shown that in the field of economics and political science there were only 25 "experts" involved at the federal level in 1896 but there were 848 by 1931, an increase which was paralleled in other fields and at other levels of government.[6] The United States was becoming what some have dubbed the "expert society."

The growing importance of the expert after World War I—indeed, it was the experts' very useful service during that war that made the

[6] Leonard White, *Trends in Public Administration* (New York, 1933), 271–272.

concept so convincing—was clearly an extension of the Progressive era's earlier concern for encouraging the disinterested and scientific scrutiny of controversial issues. The idea of taking controversial issues out of politics and submitting them for resolution to disinterested experts who were trained to apply the findings of science to political and social problems was a crucial aspect of political reform in that earlier era. But by the 1920s the social meaning of the expert had changed in important respects. The Progressive era had experienced something of a conflict between the urge toward expertise and one toward popular involvement in public decision making, but that conflict was largely papered over by the belief that the common or average man could understand the processes of scientific analysis in which the expert engaged. Like the expert, the common man was rational and capable of being persuaded by rational arguments. The expert could be, in some sense, both an expert and a mass educator. As the belief in the rationality of the common man faded, the conflict between expert management and popular opinion became more obvious. Popular opinion connoted emotional debate and irrational decisions; expertise, scientific and rational judgment of the issues. As social leaders and reformers grew convinced that applying expertise to social problems was the way to solve them, they no longer shared the progressives' perception of popular education as a tool of social change and social improvement. Schooling was no longer on the cutting edge of reform.

The New Deal provides perhaps the best example of the lowered estimation of schooling among those dedicated to improving society. One can note first that the New Deal, for all its concern with welfare in the United States, did surprisingly little to improve public schooling.[7] An era of reform which did so much to alter relations among American institutions and was so concerned with the distribution of wealth effected virtually no change in the distribution of educational opportunity or in the manner in which education was financed or administered. The New Deal's two major educational thrusts were aimed not at improving or changing education so much as at reducing unemployment and distributing welfare funds. The Civilian Conservation Corps (1933–1942) placed unemployed city youth in quasi-military camps where they studied traditional subjects briefly but concentrated on learning the skills useful to them in fulfilling assigned public service jobs, mostly in improving the national parks and other recreational and conservation areas in the countryside. The National Youth Administration (1935–1943) distributed weekly grants to high school and college students encouraging them to complete their schooling rather than to seek jobs in an already

---

[7] We have relied heavily on the brilliant discussion of this point in Rush Welter, *Popular Education and Democratic Thought in America* (New York, 1962), 310–314.

saturated labor market. It is important to note further that the federal government undertook both these efforts with little input from or coordination with the country's educational institutions or leaders. They were conceived as temporary supplements to traditional patterns of schooling and were intended to have no impact on those traditional patterns. When they were dismantled during World War II, they left no mark on the way in which education was delivered in the United States.

More important, political reform and political reformers during the New Deal era paid far less attention to building public support for the reforms implemented than had their counterparts during the Progressive era. Most symbolic, perhaps, is the famous "hundred days" of legislation that opened the presidency of Franklin Roosevelt. Presidential aides and their expert advisers prepared a multitude of bills on a crash basis and rushed them through Congress with a minimum of debate and almost no attempt to explain them or build support for them among the larger public. These bills—including the Emergency Banking Act, the establishment of the Civilian Conservation Corps, the Federal Emergency Relief Act, the Agricultural Adjustment Act, the Tennessee Valley Authority Act, and the National Industrial Recovery Act—affected the most basic aspects of the economy and social life of the United States and yet they became law with almost no public discussion. Here the concept of an educated citizenry prepared to understand and judge political alternatives had no place. Roosevelt's first hundred days symbolized the fact that reformers and social leaders had found a way of achieving their ends without needing to involve the masses—an involvement which had always required extensive efforts to educate those masses to new ways of thinking.

That schooling ceased to be the kind of pressure point for the effecting of reform that it had been earlier did not mean that schools closed or that educational thought and method did not continue to develop. Indeed, schools expanded their enrollments, and the application of scientific analysis to pedagogy and the professionalization of educators continued apace. It did mean that schooling ceased to be the matter of national debate that it had been before the war. Since education was not an important device for social improvement, those with a national vision, a national audience, a sense of making a difference at the national level paid it little attention. Spokesmanship for education passed to members of the educational establishment and to the various local political establishments which bore responsibility for maintaining schools under the American system of local control. Americans heard about schools in the twenties and thirties largely from educators themselves or from local social leaders instead of from national leaders. This change in the focus of advocacy brought with it the subtle but significant shift toward provincialism noted at the opening of this chapter.

The shift was not, of course, total. Some national leaders still regarded education as important; nearly all paid lip-service to its importance for schooling, like motherhood, has always been a "good thing" in the United States. But educational thought and practice shifted from a national emphasis which focused on the role of the school in increasing the national good to a local or provincial and individualistic emphasis which concentrated on the role of the school in increasing the strengths of the local community, in reasserting traditional mores, and in increasing personal happiness. There was an increased provincialism about education after 1920, a definite sense that schooling was vital less for the changes it encouraged than for its role in maintaining traditional values and for guarding against social change.

Historians of American society have often characterized the 1920s as a period of fundamental conflict between two points of view, two Zeitgeists—one urban, cosmopolitan, heterogeneous, and adventuresome; the other rural, homogeneous, fundamentalist, and traditional. Several dramatic confrontations symbolized this underlying conflict: the fundamentalist-modernist debates within the Protestant sects, the Scopes trial in Tennessee in which William Jennings Bryan fought, successfully, against the great liberal lawyer Clarence Darrow and the barbs of the metropolitan press to uphold that state's ban on the teaching of evolution in the public schools; the fight in the Democratic Convention of 1924 over whether to include a platform plank repudiating the Ku Klux Klan; the various conflicts over Prohibition between the "urban wets" and the "rural drys," culminating in 1928 when Al Smith, an immigrant's son from the Lower East Side of New York City, sought the presidency on a platform promising to repeal Prohibition against Herbert Hoover, born on an Iowa farm and trained as a mining engineer in California, who stood for the traditional values of self-help and individual responsibility and promised to retain laws against drinking. This conflict is often characterized as one between urban and rural values, but one should not assume that all urbanites stood on one side against all residents of rural areas.

Yet the conflict was closely associated with the fact that the increasing urbanization of the United States appeared to threaten traditional values. The 1920 census revealed that for the first time more Americans lived in communities of 2,500 people or more than lived in smaller ones. The very distinction between rural and urban locations began to disintegrate as the automobile and the improved roads that accompanied its use broke down the isolation of the rural folk and made the spread of urban ideas and urban products more complete. But the rural, fundamentalist, independent, White Anglo-Saxon Protestant cast of mind, though embattled, remained intact, even among large segments of the urban population. Urbanization's threat to that cast of mind's hegemony produced the militant demands for the institutionalization of those values made by such organizations as the Klan and the fundamentalist church.

The 1920s, then, saw two value systems struggle for supremacy and for public adherence. It was a desperate fight—between an older set of values that had become increasingly rigid and sour in the face of powerful challenges to their survival and a newer set that were trying to fit themselves to a changing world and social structure but which were not as yet clearly defined. The hypothesis of this chapter is that the schools became the creatures, willingly or unwillingly, of the spokesmen for the first set of values. Schools between the world wars stood principally on the side of transmitting traditional values and confirming the older, more rural persuasion.

Gathering evidence on the practice of individual schools and individual school systems and on the "messages" they conveyed to their students is woefully difficult—schooling has, on the whole, been too normal and routine a business for writers to have described it carefully or even for school systems to have kept adequate records of courses and of student activities and pedagogical methods from which historians can reconstruct local practice. To prove the hypothesis with which we closed the last paragraph is impossible, given the present state of knowledge about the history of education during that period. What we will do here is describe some developments that we find particularly suggestive of the tone that permeated most public schools in the era and which appear to be particularly fruitful as areas for further research.

II

One such suggestive indication involves the reception of intelligence testing following the discovery during the war that psychologists could accurately test large numbers of people simultaneously. Interest in the capabilities of the intelligence scale as a device for sorting and guiding young people precisely and efficiently had been high since 1905 when Theodore Simon and Alfred Binet introduced the idea of using a battery of standardized tests to identify the mentally retarded child in France. American psychologists and welfare workers quickly adopted and refined Binet's methods and the individual administration of the IQ test became a very popular and important aspect of social service institutions, including schools, in the period before the war. But the individual test was cumbersome—it was supposed to be (although it often was not) administered by a trained psychologist and could be given to only one child at a time. Because of this inefficient process, intelligence testing was limited before the war to those with special problems. At the time of America's entry into the war, however, a group of psychologists volunteered their expertise to the army to construct a version of the intelligence test which could be administered to large groups of men simultaneously. The psychologists promised the army that these group tests could identify recruits who were mentally unfit to profit from the training offered by the army. The psychologists created the test and over the course of the war administered it—in two versions, one for illiterates—to 1.7 million servicemen. Test results were used to identify men with the talents to become officers, those needing special training to fit them for the infantry, and those so intellectually retarded that they had to be separated from the service. The psychologists and the military commanders agreed that the IQ test had been a great help in making the training programs of the army more effective and more efficient; the psychologists were pleased to see that the group test ranked people just as accurately as had the individual tests.

Many educational reformers quickly understood that what had worked so well in channeling men into their proper places in the military hierarchy would work just as well in helping the schools fulfill their promise of sorting students and guiding them into their proper lifework. Right after the war there was a flurry of interest in the test's potential contribution to the schools' mission to smooth the transition to the world of work and to individualize instruction by tailoring curricular expectations to the intellectual capacity of the student. With the group IQ test, the schools had all the tools they needed to fulfill their promise of adjusting their offerings to the child's needs and of propelling each child to the career for which he was best fit. The IQ test would be the most accurate predictive device; since it could now successfully be given to large groups, it would be efficient.

What is noteworthy, however, about the educational atmosphere of the 1920s and 1930s is that public and much educational interest in the IQ test quickly waned; the device that provided the capstone to the progressive desire for ordering, efficiency, guidance, and individualization was suddenly rather out of date. This does not mean that psychologists and measurement people did not continue work on developing tests, increasing their accuracy, and training others to interpret their results. But the public interest in testing as the leading edge of educational reform disappeared; testing quickly became just another one of the emerging specialties within the educational establishment. The initial use of the group IQ tests in schools inspired a number of passionate criticisms of the testing methods and of the implications for democracy of ranking people so precisely on a single scale of merit; indeed, there is little in the current reaction against the IQ test that was not being said in the late teens and early twenties. But the public controversy soon died down and, although professional testers and psychometricians continued to debate the same and much more esoteric issues concerning the tests, the public seemed uninterested. Tests continued to be in widespread use all through the period—although just how wide is unclear—and, so far as we can tell, people pretty much accepted them as part of schooling without being worried about their accuracy or their implications. The conclusion to be drawn from that phenomenon may be that because the tests were not perceived at the time as having much in the way of consequences, they did not attract much attention—positive or negative. Investigating further why that may have been so will give us some deeper insights into the differences in educational atmosphere between the pre- and postwar years.

During the Progressive era, people counted on the intelligence test to help improve society—not unexpectedly, given the high value the era placed on reason or intellect as the key to right living. American psychologists began to translate Binet's tests into English in 1908 and began developing their own versions of the scales in that same year. Several different tests were used until 1916 when Lewis Terman of Stanford University published the Stanford version of the Simon-Binet test. (Revised in 1937 and 1960, it continued to dominate the field through the 1960s.) Most of the early tests in the United States were administered to the mentally defective and the delinquent in order to determine proper training programs for them. Partly because several of them worked for institutions for delinquents and partly because such institutions were convenient places to pursue research, the early testers worked mostly with already institutionalized delinquents or feeble-minded children rather than testing randomly in the population. Testers struggled to differentiate among morons, imbeciles, and idiots and to distinguish the effects of environment from those of heredity. Psychometricians played a significant role in the nature-nurture debate which was raging even then. They generally agreed that nature was more important, especially in determining mental capability and achievement. The testers were very interested in the relation between low intelligence and crime. When they brought their batteries to prisons and reformatories, they found most of the criminals or potential criminals to be retarded—by which they meant that the individual's mental age was two or more years below his chronological age. This rather startling statistic led them to "explain" crime as caused by low intelligence. Not until widespread testing of people not already incarcerated in institutions revealed an almost equal incidence of "retardation" among the general population did testers revise their belief that low intelligence led to crime. It was a natural theory to which to adhere in an era which valued highly the social functions of reason.

Their concentration on the defective and the deviant, their finding that low intelligence caused people to act out against society, and their belief that mental defects (and thus criminal tendencies) were inherited determined the nature of the reforms the intelligence testers would support. Theirs was a difficult reform position. The theory underlying mental testing held that intellectual capacity did not change over a person's lifetime: you could assign an IQ to a four-year-old and expect it to be an accurate portrayal of his capacity when he was eighteen or twenty-six. Thus, those who dealt with mental defectives could not seek significant social reform through improving those people because their charges were essentially unchangeable. These psychologists most often resolved their dilemma by joining the eugenics movement. Eugenics is a science that deals with improving the hereditary or genetic material of a breed or a race; eugenists try to breed the best offspring from an available population. The eugenics movement that appeared in the 1890s in the United States illustrated a growing concern that America's Anglo-Saxon heritage was being seriously diluted by the massive waves of southern and eastern European immigrants, who along with native blacks appeared to be considerably more fecund than were native whites. According to eugenists, those with the best genes to pass on to their offspring were having fewer children while those with less adequate genetic endowment were having more and more children. So long as such a breeding pattern was allowed to continue, the quality of the American population would deteriorate. The movement to restrict immigration grew out of these same fears and shared the same supporters as the eugenics movement. Some advocated tightening immigration in the early part of the century by using intelligence tests to keep mental defectives out of the country. In the first two decades of the twentieth century eugenists sought to encourage the "better" people to reproduce more and the poor and deviant to reproduce less. Some urged that the bearers of the poorest genes be forceably prevented from reproducing at all. They wanted the state to sterilize habitual offenders, and many states did pass and enforce such laws during the teens and twenties. The mental testers promised to contribute to this effort to strengthen America by identifying those among the apparently deviant who should and those who should not reproduce. The IQ test promised to introduce some degree of objectivity to the process of determining the most valuable and, more importantly before 1915, the least valuable people in the society. Yet the great extent to which the testers' results simply confirmed the biases of the period suggest that they were far from achieving objectivity with their tests. The fact that they did confirm already held opinions probably accounts for the popularity of the IQ test in the prewar years.

It may be difficult for us to believe that progressive Americans thought high intelligence correlated so highly with other desirable social traits. It now seems very clear that high intelligence is no barrier to criminal activity and that low intelligence does not prevent a person from leading a full and useful life. But the Progressive era thought otherwise. E. L.

Thorndike, the nation's most influential educational psychologist between 1900 and 1940, found that "the correlations between the divergences of an individual from the average in different desirable traits are positive, that the man who is above the average of his race in intellect is above rather than below it in decency, sanity, even in bodily health." He believed that "scholarship is prophetic of success out of school; [that] a good mind means a better than average character."[8] There are several reasons for this faith in IQ scores as accurate measures of all facets of personal worth. This faith was, in part, a product of the period's considerable respect for rationality and reason. In part, it derived from the period's naïve faith in the quantifiable; in part, from a desire for precise methods of sizing up people that were capable of replacing the traditional means of judging others being undermined by social rootlessness and the declining power of organized religion. The IQ score offered a society nervous about establishing mutual expectations a much appreciated, if spurious, precision that could be applied to the very difficult business of judging others. Most important, the intelligence testers' formulae gained widespread acceptance because they confirmed the judgments that most people made anyway. Historians have made much of the hereditarian bias of the early intelligence testers—revealed in their belief that intelligence was an inherited trait or combination of traits (intelligence testers were never very clear as to what it was they were measuring; intelligence, they admitted when pressed, was the ability to do well on their tests; they rested their argument for the validity and utility of the tests on the "fact" that those who did well on the tests also did well in life). But their hereditarian bias matched that of the society for which they wrote. When the tests indicated that blacks and "swarthy" immigrants had inherited a relatively deficient mental capacity, they merely confirmed what most people of the era believed anyway. When they stated that poor people and criminals acted as they did because of defective mental inheritance, most people did not find that point arguable. Indeed, much of what people saw as the virtue of intelligence tests was that they gave scientific support and respectability to the judgments that most people already made about the deviants in their midst.

Thus intelligence testing found a ready audience in the years before 1917 and, when the testers said that their product would contribute to the betterment of society, most believed them. By the early twenties that confidence in the findings and in the importance of intelligence tests had waned. Society devalued rationality and reason because of changing psychological views as to the sources of human behavior. The correlation between intellect and character was far less clear in an era of Freud and Watson than it had been earlier.

[8] Edward Lee Thorndike, "Eugenics: With Special Reference to Intellect and Character," *Popular Science Monthly*, LXXXIII (April, 1913), 131–132.

The waning of interest was also an unintended result of the application of mass testing in the army. Here at the moment of its greatest triumph the intelligence test overstepped the bounds of credibility and seemed to threaten the mass of Americans. The army tested almost 2 million men and found the average mental age of those men to be around 14. Because these recruits were all at least 18 chronologically, the test results meant that the average American was retarded. For the first time the mental testers began to say negative things about the mass of Americans and to do so in an uncomfortable way. Previously, they had spoken negatively only of the few whom most Americans already judged deviant. Now the psychologists implied that the average American was deviant, defective, and, according to the logic of those like Thorndike who believed intellect correlated with morality, lacking in virtue. That was too much for the average person to accept, and he did not. Much like his contemporary counterpart who happily continues to watch commercial situation comedies while cultural leaders condemn him for it, the average American ignored those who thought that a test could measure a man's worth. They may have thought it a good way of confirming other judgments about who was a genius and who seriously defective, but by and large it appeared another attempt by the urban elite to use modern science as a means of deprecating the character of the average, upstanding, God-fearing American citizen.

The lessening public interest in testing also came about because people did not, after 1920, believe that intelligence rankings would play an important role in ordering the American social structure. Intelligence testers had attracted much attention when they convinced people that they had a valid method for ranking and channeling individuals in society. But, by the 1920s, the public did not believe that intelligence was a standard of merit that had much relevance to their society and economy. Intellectual merit was a universal measure of worth, applicable to all people in all situations regardless of background and place. Such universal values were devalued in the twenties and thirties in favor of more local provincial values. As we shall explore later in this chapter, personality, sociability, character, and "who you knew" were considered, and quite possibly were, more important in determining success in life than academic ability or the ability to do well on the intelligence tests. Whether the public's perception of the relevance of intellectual competition was accurate or not, it appears to have felt that way and urged the schools to reflect their beliefs. We see running through the educational rhetoric and practice of the interwar period an effort to deemphasize academic competition, to eliminate failure, to include in the schools as many different routes to success as possible. We contend that the fact that the reaction to the testers' condemnation of the average man did not take the form of protest against the method indicates that most Americans did not believe the use of intelligence tests had serious implications for themselves, their children, or the society in general. When, in the 1960s and 1970s, people did sense that the testers' determinations of their children's intellectual merit did significantly affect their children's future, protests were long and vociferous. But the 1920s did not seem to share the later period's belief that intellectual merit—however determined—played a vital role in determining relative social status.

Another indication of the provincial tone of public education after 1920 was the success of the Ku Klux Klan in convincing the voters of Oregon to pass an initiative petition in 1922 which required that all children aged eight to sixteen attend the public schools. The United States Supreme Court struck down this law in 1925 and confirmed the right of parents to choose private schools for their children—so long as they were accredited by the state. In describing the background of this case, historian David Tyack called attention to the kinds of attitudes toward schooling which arose out of the conflict between the two casts of mind that we have described above.[9] Atlanta, Georgia, in 1914, witnessed the rebirth of the Klan, an organization which little resembled its predecessor of the reconstruction era in ideology or personnel. By the early 1920s, at the height of its appeal, it claimed over 1.5 million members, who lived in urban as well as rural areas, both north and south. The enemies of the Klansmen in the twentieth century included not only blacks but Jews, Catholics, immigrants, the rich, and the cosmopolitan urbanite. Indeed, the Klan was more concerned with attitudes and values than with proscribing particular ethnic groups as a whole. They feared any value which seemed to abandon securely rooted traditions. The typical Klansman was a blue-collar worker or a farmer of marginal economic status in a society that had suddenly begun to celebrate "making money" as one of its chief virtues. He felt that he was stuck in his economic and social position while the rest of the society passed him by, that his status and values were being humiliated by members of minority groups, city slickers, and those whose success depended on guile more than on hard work. He lashed out at any changes that threatened to elevate other values and standards of worth above those to which he clung. Thus his anger focused on the newcomer, minority group members, and the bearer of urban values—these types symbolized deviations from the old American stock and from the old American values to which the unhappy and insecure Klansman adhered rigidly in hopes of deriving some sense of worth and dignity. Unlike the intellectuals and social leaders discussed above, Klansmen specified a quite important role for the school in their fight against change. Schools would socialize newcomers and social devi-

[9] David B. Tyack, "The Perils of Pluralism: The Background of the Pierce Case," *American Historical Review*, LXXIV (October, 1968), 74–98.

ants to the values from which the typical Klansman drew his sense of worth. In joining the Klan the new member swore, among other things, that he believed "that our Free Public School is the cornerstone of good government and that those who are seeking to destroy it are enemies of our Republic and are unworthy of citizenship." Klan policy supported (1) compulsory English in elementary schools, (2) "education of the alien population, by federal aid, not only in cultural and vocational subjects, but especially in the principles of American institutions," (3) separation of church and state, (4) equal educational opportunities for all (As David Tyack has reminded us, the Klan apparently did not mean by this phrase quite what it has come to mean today—as the Klan was virulently anti-black.), and (5) "inculcation of patriotism, love of the flag, respect for law and order, and undying loyalty to constitutional government."[10]

In Oregon the Klan campaigned vigorously, largely through front and semifront organizations, to defend the public school and its mission to inculcate a common set of values against the Catholics who maintained their own schools, immigrants who supported a number of Lutheran parochial schools (instruction in which was often carried out in German), and the rich who maintained their separate elitist schools. By demanding that all children between eight and sixteen attend only public schools, the Klan planners hoped that the law would destroy all but the vestiges of the state's various independent school systems. One Klan pamphlet painted an apocalyptic vision. A terrified schoolmaster pulls on the bell rope of the school calling for help while an episcopal bishop (representing rich private schooling), a methodist elder, and a seventh-day adventist minister stand at the corners of the building and a Catholic priest comes running toward the school with crucifix held high and a torch in the other hand. No help came. "Our Old Cedar School House, next in my heart to Mother's grave, was tumblin' to the ground, in flames, the crushed and shriveled form . . . of the teacher for mor'n fifty years, lay dead with his snow-white head hangin' out of the open front door, his thin, bony old hand aholdin' tight to the bell rope, the swayin' bell pealin' its final call, and the burnin' flag on the tall spire, The Last Torch of Liberty, Fadin' from the World."[11] Such emotional appeals were apparently effective for, to the surprise of nearly all political prognosticators, the initiative passed by a vote of 105,000 to 103,000. The law never took effect because it was immediately appealed by representatives of the parochial schools and was finally struck down in 1925 by the United States Supreme Court in *Pierce* v. *Oregon.* But the law's effects are not the question here. Rather, the important thing to note is that a majority of the voters of the state of Oregon favored this kind of restrictive legislation and apparently agreed

[10] *Ibid.,* 79.
[11] *Ibid.,* 82.

with the Klan that the role of the public school was to inculcate values so special and so narrowly interpreted that they could not be provided in private schools. Historians are baffled that such an initiative should pass in a state like Oregon, which contained few blacks, few Catholics, few immigrants, and almost no southeastern European immigrants.* (Unsuccessful attempts to pass similar laws occurred in Washington and Michigan.) But that it did pass in a state where the threat of deviance was low makes it all the more significant. It is further significant that local educational organizations were either neutral on the issue or supported the initiative—apparently Oregon's educators were willing to accept a law which enhanced their purpose and their public support, however it might tamper with the freedoms and rights of particular citizens. Clearly, they did not disagree with an interpretation of their purpose as the inculcation of narrow patriotism and traditional values.

Oregon's successful initiative was bizarre and so clearly a violation of civil liberties that national civil libertarian leaders and a number of national educational leaders spoke out against it and a well-organized campaign to invalidate it began immediately. But the Oregon incident was merely the tip of an iceberg and patriots, Klansmen, and other conservative traditionalists undoubtedly pressed thousands of petty harassments against suspected deviance in the schools. These harassments were never written into law and seldom received enough publicity to come to the attention of the national press or influential civil libertarians. Howard K. Beale has collected evidence of thousands of such cases. He recalled the announcement of the disciplining in 1934 of six radical teachers in Toledo, Ohio. Informal charges of radicalism were brought before the six as a result of reports from student spies who had been placed in their classes to gather incriminating evidence. The president of the school board assured Toledo that the six would "mend their ways." Immediate punishment consisted of transferring the teachers to classes far removed from their competence and interests. An economics teacher was forced to teach auto mechanics, a civics teacher was transferred to the mathematics department, and a member of the social science faculty was required to teach English and assume janitorial duties. "Their radicalism won't amount to much" in these new fields, the board president pointed out perceptively. "These teachers will be living examples of what will happen to others if radicalism isn't stopped." After a lengthy appeal and the ultimate intervention of the Toledo Federation of Teachers, the six were reinstated in the courses from which they had been transferred. Upton Sinclair reported that in Butte, Montana, the school board purged the high school library of "the standard works on history, economics, soci-

---

* Perhaps because Oregon was dominated by a white, Protestant, Anglo-Saxon constituency that segment sought to confirm symbolically its social authority and status, much as the New York Protestants did in the 1840s.

ology, and ethics, which have any tendency toward democracy in industry or even in politics."[12] The message and its implications were clarified in town after town. In these cases harassment was often successful as there was no national hue and cry to rescue the victims. The same generalization can be drawn from the Scopes trial—an incident too famous to warrant description here. In that case national civil libertarians convinced John T. Scopes to teach evolution in one of his biology classes so that his trial could serve as a test case for the Tennessee law banning such instruction. A famous team of lawyers was brought in to defend Scopes. They fought vigorously against this political and religious interference with the freedom of the schools to teach. Even so, they lost the case, and Tennessee's law against the teaching of evolution stood until 1967 when it was repealed by the state legislature. Again, there were undoubtedly thousands of cases of political and religious interference with public education that did not come to the attention of the kind of men that supported the Scopes test case. Schools and teachers quickly and quietly bowed to public pressure in these incidents. In the public schools Bible reading was made compulsory in locality after locality during this period.

Robert and Helen Lynd's sociological study of Muncie, Indiana, *Middletown* (1929), also gives insight into the traditional, rigid, and "safe" role assumed by the public schools in the 1920s. Social studies or civics in the Muncie schools stressed the common and fundamental principles of the American way so as to protect children from radicalism, bohemianism, excessive individualism, modern religion, and the lures of urbanization. One teachers' guide in Muncie listed the "fundamental institutions of society" as "private property, guaranteed privileges, contracts, personal liberty, [and the] right to establish private enterprises." In 1921 the Indiana state teachers' manual threw out the right of revolution. It "does not exist in America. We had a revolution 140 years ago which made it unnecessary to have any other revolution in this country. . . . One of the many meanings of democracy is that it is a form of government in which the right of revolution has been lost. . . . No man can be a sound and sterling American who believes that force is necessary to effectuate the popular will. . . . Americanism . . . emphatically means . . . that we have repudiated old European methods of settling domestic questions, and have evolved for ourselves machinery by which revolution as a method of changing our life is outgrown, abandoned, outlawed." One Muncie high school teacher told the sociologists that "in class discussion I try to bring out minor points, two ways of looking at a thing and all that, but in examinations I try to emphasize important principles and group the main facts that they have to remember around them. I always

[12] Quoted in Howard K. Beale, *Are American Teachers Free?* (New York, 1936), 117; and Upton Sinclair, *The Goslings: A Study of the American Schools* (Pasadena, Calif., 1924), 151.

ask simple fact questions in examinations. [The students] get all mixed up and confused if we ask questions where they have to think, and [they] write all over the place."[13] Such confusion had to be avoided at all costs in a school system dedicated to anchoring traditional values in young people firmly enough to withstand all the pressures of a changing world. Periodicals carried such opinions as the following:

> It is notorious that our public school system, which is the strongest bulwark of Americanism, is being viciously attacked from without and from within, by papists and anti-Christian Jews, of the Bolshevik Socialist stripe. Thousands of Roman Catholics, trained in parochial schools, and thousands of subversive protocol Jews are "boring from within," while ostensibly serving as public school teachers. The appointment of papists or anti-Christian Jews, to teach American children in our public schools, should be absolutely prohibited. National security can sanction no other course.[14]

The traditionalists who exerted primary control over the schools wanted their own value system left intact and believed that children should be educated away from changing values. If the schools could throw the right of revolution out of the civics texts, perhaps the threat of revolutionary change that beset these traditionalists on every side would also vanish.

On the whole it appears that most of the nation's educators—researchers, administrators, and teachers—were pleased to see their institutions support the rural, traditionalist point of view. Historians find so little extant evidence regarding the conflict over political and religious interference with schools in part because schools in most cases put up little resistance to such interference—indeed, one could even say that in most instances the educators welcomed it. In part, this may have occurred because large numbers of educators found themselves in a position similar to that of the Klansman: they were stuck in relatively low-paying and unglamorous, unsuccessful jobs in an era when material achievement appeared to be everybody's measure of personal success. During the Progressive era, education had had a certain status and glamour because it was part of a drive for national greatness; being an educator made one part of that effort. Only the low pay remained when, as the energy went out of education's national drive after 1920, the glamour and status disappeared. Educators were happy to be included among the important supporters of the American way by the provincial forces of the day. Perhaps more important, however, was that influential educators in the period tended to come from rural, white Anglo-Saxon backgrounds— backgrounds different from those of the majority of the schools' clientele

[13] Robert S. and Helen M. Lynd, *Middletown: A Study in Modern American Culture* (New York, 1929), 198–199.
[14] Quoted in Beale, *Are American Teachers Free?*, 115.

by 1920. One notes also an important shift in the center of educational research away from Teachers College on the east coast and Stanford on the west toward the Midwest—especially Minnesota, Michigan, Wisconsin, and Ohio State. The eastern and western private universities were not eclipsed, by any means, but the rise of the midwestern land grant schools in educational research diluted the cosmopolitan, nationalistic thrust given to educational thought by the coast schools. In 1931 the Department of Superintendence of the National Education Association publicly endorsed Prohibition at the time it was increasingly discredited across the nation. One study of 850 school superintendents done in the early 1930s showed that the typical one was "a native, of long established American ancestry and tradition, 44 years old, reared in a large family on a farm by parents with a common school education who were church members and regular attendants." The superintendent was "a member, active worker, and regular attendant of the church" and belonged to five professional and six community organizations. Only 16 of the 850 superintendents had Catholic parents and only 6 were Catholics themselves. Two hundred and sixty-four were Methodists.[15] Provincialism and protection of the status quo sat easy with such men.

Another characteristic feature of the 1920s was the so-called attack upon the village and its consequent counterattack. Some of the decade's best and most popular literature, such as Sherwood Anderson's *Winesburg, Ohio* (1919) or Sinclair Lewis' *Main Street* (1920), attacked the American small town—commonly thought to be the repository of American values and character—as ugly, bigoted, conformist and suffocating to the creative mind, and full of twisted, unhappy, unfulfilled people. This was a common attitude among intellectuals and social leaders of the day. They continually reminded their readers that the small town was not a utopia but, rather, that it was sexually and intellectually repressive. They believed that progress and freedom in the United States depended upon the eradication of that village atmosphere and on the promotion of the more open, stimulating, cosmopolitan urban culture.

The defenders of the older values mounted a counterattack on the social critics' portrait of the small town. One means that they selected and promoted vigorously was the use of the public school to inculcate a sense of patriotism toward the local community. They wanted to protect their children from the lure of the city and from the propaganda of social critics who threatened to convince young people that a better life awaited those who moved away from the local community. The Lynds, in their two investigations of Muncie, *Middletown* and *Middletown in Transition* (1937), reported that in 1924 only 3 of the 80 high school graduates who went to college attended schools outside of Indiana or its contiguous states. Sixty-six went to college in Indiana: 12 to the state universities,

15 Krug, *Shaping of the American High School, 1920–1941*, 186–187.

44 to the small local teachers college (Ball State Teachers College), and the other 10 to nearby small colleges. In the early thirties, due partly to the Depression and partly to the improved reputation and expanded facilities of Ball State, the number of young people going to a college at any distance from their local community was even smaller. Sixty-five high school graduates on the average applied to college each year. Annually, only one applied to a major state university outside Indiana; one every other year applied to an endowed university; between two and six sought entrance to the University of Indiana or Purdue. The remainder —approximately 60 out of the 65—stuck closer to home in small colleges. In fact, between 70 and 80 percent of the high school graduates attending college enrolled at Ball State—a college of approximately 1,000 students. In other words, even among the elite of this town—those having money enough to keep their children in school—education was a means of sticking close to home. Muncie seemed proud that its children went to these small colleges which, the local newspaper wrote, "give something besides the ability to feel at home in evening clothes."[16] Such colleges kept the kids acclimated to the values of the local community. The revitalization of the neighboring normal school into Ball State in 1918 through the financial intervention of Muncie's most prominent local family reinforces the point. The move to build Muncie's own college had all the elements of the booster college movement of the nineteenth century; the opposition was reminded that the college would enhance the town's economy by bringing more students. It would also raise the town's fame and reputation. But, just as important, it would keep more local children at home for their college years. It was a way for townsfolk to provide low-level professional training for their children without any risk that they would absorb alien, urbane values as they might in schools far from home. Although the college was technically a normal school administered by the state, the Ball family had a good deal of influence over its policy and the family was widely believed to have ordered the removal of certain books—including John Dos Passos' *1919* (1932)—from the library shelves and to have vetoed the college's inviting certain radical speakers. Although, as the Lynds point out, Ball State was, relative to the rest of the town, a liberalizing influence, and its faculty was on a far longer intellectual and behavioral "tether" than were teachers at the high school, the local college displayed a very muted liberalism relative to that found on other, more cosmopolitan campuses. It served, therefore, to protect Muncie's young adults from these undermining influences. Ball State was what Christopher Jencks and David Riesman have called a "safe" college.[17]

[16] Robert S. and Helen M. Lynd, *Middletown in Transition: A Study in Cultural Conflicts* (New York, 1937), 434.

[17] *The Academic Revolution* (Garden City, N. Y., 1968), 50 ff.

In this period the schools also took a more positive attitude toward community. With a nod toward the old-time district school, they sought, especially through organized athletics and the extracurriculum, to become the foci of their communities. With the steadily increasing pressure for more schooling, a larger and larger segment of a town's population was engaged in the act of going to school and consequently more and more families were concerned with schooling for a longer period of time. In Muncie, during the 1920s and 1930s, almost 20 percent of the population attended school. The numbers attending high school between 1900 and 1940 increased rapidly. In 1889–1890, 1 of every 67 people in Muncie attended high school; in 1923–1924, 1 of every 21 persons was enrolled. If one counts the parents and siblings of these students, one recognizes that in the 1920s the high school touched a very large percentage of the town's population. These statistics encouraged the high school to become a natural focus of community affairs. In Muncie, in 1925, the Lynds found that more "civic loyalty centers around [high school] basketball than around any other one thing."[18] Hundreds of people of all ages stood outside the newspaper office getting the phoned-in play-by-play of an "away game" and shouted themselves hoarse cheering a team too far away to hear. Although only five or ten boys could play for the high school, the whole school and indeed the whole town could become involved in pep rallies and cheering. A. B. Hollingshead found high school football and basketball, especially the latter, serving much the same function when he studied *Elmtown's Youth* (1949) in 1940–1941. He pointed out how important winning teams were felt to be to the preservation of community cohesion. Evidence from several sources indicates that rarely was there a situation in which high school athletics was just plain fun and sport. Almost from the day that high school intramural sports were organized in the late teens and early twenties, the emphasis was on maintaining the town's reputation by winning. Beating the neighboring town's teams in football and basketball reaffirmed Elmtowners' conviction that their town was morally superior to its rival. Coaches unable to produce teams capable of winning those important games were certain to lose their jobs. "To put it mildly," wrote a principal in the early twenties, "a teacher in many a small West Virginia high school who attempted honestly to enforce the rules laid down by the State High School Athletic Association would be blacklisted. He would suffer indignities. Littleton High School was of this sort, and the villagers of Littleton wanted teams that could win." When D. H. Pierce, the principal, interrupted a girls' basketball game because, "under instructions from the coach," the team was "playing as 'foul' a game as it knew how," he was nearly fired. He recognized that basketball games during the week interfered with the

18 Lynds, *Middletown*, 485.

academic work of the school and therefore eliminated them. The coach, who also taught at the junior high, responded that that "ain't the way we do them things in this section."[19] In Elmtown and elsewhere local businessmen gave star players money and merchandise as rewards; players received inordinate social prestige in the town; and in the school they were excused from academic work. Not the game but the winning of the game became the cement which maintained community solidarity and morale.

The enhancement of community pride became, indeed, the predominant rationale for most of the extracurriculum in small town high schools during this period. Hollingshead found much emphasis on the role of the extracurriculum in entertaining "students, parents, and Elmtowners in their leisure time." The board of education, the administrators, teachers, and students all shared this point of view. "They want their athletic teams to win games, their musical organizations to perform publicly at all possible times in a creditable manner, and their dramatics group to produce plays that will not be criticized but enjoyed. Extra-curricular activities without spectator appeal or broad public relations value, such as girls' athletics, student government, and departmental clubs, receive little active support from the Board or the community."[20] Here the educators were clearly responding to the community's demand that the school stimulate the community's self-pride. This "community-focus function" of the high school in the twenties and thirties differs from the community-focus function of the district school of a hundred years earlier. The twentieth-century experience seems characterized by an artificial quality. In the earlier instance the community function seemed to derive naturally from activities that were part of an ongoing community. The school—often the village's only public building—was the natural place where public meetings were held, where the natural sociability and community spirit of those isolated towns and villages could find expression. The spelling bees and the public readings, the political debates and the parties in the district school were not contrived and the emphasis was on the content of the activities or on the social interaction of the experience. In the latter instance, however, contrivance seems the dominant characteristic. Towns sought in the activities of a very few the symbols of community solidarity that would help restore the sense of unity despite the assaults of the mass media and an expanded communication and transportation network which brought the outside world to the doorstep of the town. The high school extracurriculum was not an outgrowth of natural community activities, nor did it reflect the kind of natural sociability of the old-time village. The essence of the important extracurricular

[19] Quoted in Beale, *Are American Teachers Free?*, 593.
[20] A. B. Hollingshead, *Elmtown's Youth* (New York, 1949), 192–193.

activities was that a few participants represented and entertained a largely passive community. The community's activities were restricted to a largely impersonal form of group cheering or clapping, as at a musical event. The emphasis on winning and on successful performance demonstrated how the focus had shifted from expressing natural community spirit to sustaining community pride.

By the twenties most of the natural spirit of community solidarity in the towns had largely disappeared. Entrepreneurs shared a booster spirit and large numbers of townspeople insisted, rather defensively, that their town and others like it were better than the big cities where the critics of the small towns lived. But the district school had served what Robert H. Wiebe has labeled the "island community," in which almost all of a person's vital relations were comprehended within his small community. By 1920 members of the community had extensive business and social contacts beyond the borders of the town. Businessmen and bankers dealt with and represented regional and national firms and central banks. Because markets for the town's goods lay far beyond its borders, the economic status of the community depended on outsiders. Social distance within the town increased as industrialization widened the gap between fewer and fewer employers and more and more employees, the gradations between workingman and businessman became more distinct, and the coming of the electric trolley and the automobile allowed the small town to spread out over more space which further encouraged neighborhood segregation. Improved public transportation and the automobile allowed for far more frequent contact between the local community and other neighboring towns as people found it easier and easier to travel away from home. Furthermore, the increased speed of communication between metropolitan areas and smaller communities, the movies and then the radio, all broke down the barriers between the island community and the larger world. Members of the local community became almost full-fledged citizens of the regional hinterland or national community created by the mass media. Given this situation, people in the small town had less reason to think of themselves as a community.

And yet, so fearful were they of the changes occurring all around them, changes rooted in the urbanization and cosmopolitanism of their country, that they desperately sought to recreate a sense of community behind which they could protect themselves, and more especially their children, from the undesirable aspects of these changes. The school was central to this effort. As we have seen, the athletic and extracurricular spectaculars of the school served as a focus for community pride and solidarity—at least so long as the teams won and the activities were "successful." As important, the schools were designed to protect kids from the dangerous ideas emanating from outside the community, from the temptations to take part in the modern, radical, urban culture. We have already suggested that schoolmen used the social studies curriculum to inculcate traditional status quo ideals in students as a means of protecting them from the alien and radical beliefs of America's critics. Just as important as saving them from the ideological taint of alien and modern thought was saving them from the subversive influences of modern culture and modern behavior which were also spawned in metropolitan America and Europe and flooded into the small town through the expanding mass media. The twenties and thirties offered youth a variety of role models to follow, all equally frightening to those parents and adults most concerned with maintaining the status quo. In the twenties a youth could model himself on the flapper, on the alienated members of the lost generation, or on the sheiks and queens of the movies. Whatever variety of flaming youth he became, he would turn toward sex, booze, "creativity," and independence and away from hard work and responsible citizenship. In the thirties the models that young adults threatened to follow were even worse. Kids made heroes of the hoodlums and their molls who were staples of the 1930s movies; American youths, frustrated by their unemployment and superfluousness to the society, were thought to look with too uncritical an eye toward European youth movements that contributed so much to the rise of fascism and nazism. In both cases the society called upon the schools to do something, and the educators responded as best they could.

Through this period the schools became concerned with issues such as dress codes; whether or not girls should wear stockings or lipstick to school, or how dressed up they should be for school-sponsored parties and dances. Many schools required girls to wear uniform clothes to school. In Stevens Point, Wisconsin, the boys gathered into a secret organization to rid their classes of "sheiks," whose appearance and dress imperiled the schools' conservative image. Schools were also very concerned with managing the social life of their charges, partly because the extensive socializing of the era was alleged to cut sharply into the students' study and sleep time (and thus accounted for a high number of school failures), and because it was in their social activities that students most often got caught up in the rituals of the flaming youth culture. Schools faced a dilemma here. On the one hand, they thought their students' taste in dances and parties excessive and really did not want to encourage it. On the other, they felt that only by sponsoring these events could the school exert a necessary control over party length and the kind of music offered. In some sense sex, or its suggestion, was to be guarded against most. In the second half of this century the schoolmen's victorian concerns seem ludicrous and their estimation of the danger farfetched. But they saw the suggestive rhythms of jazz, the physical intimacy of the fox trot, and the lewd gyrations of the Charleston as the entering wedge of a social revolution and fought back as best they could. Liquor was another problem with which schools sought to deal, but on this issue they were very ineffective. Drinking could be prohibited from school-sponsored events and innocuous punches substituted, but the school could exert no control over what the students did in the parking lot during the party or what they did afterward.

In their search for effective means of protecting young people in the twenties from the influences of the youth culture, the schools focused on two outside threats to their power—the high school fraternity and sorority and the students' homes. Educators viewed fraternities and sororities as nests of the youth culture which took time from students' schoolwork and emphasized far different achievement criteria than those encouraged by the school. In the social organizations students learned to stress dress, independence, popularity, sex, and drinking. The schools perceived a threat so great that they moved vigorously—if not terribly successfully—to suppress these organizations. Some states and many local systems summarily forbade fraternities and sororities; the seriousness with which they viewed these rules is evident in the fact that 22 cities (of 171 studied) promised to expel any students found to be members of these illegal groups and 15 others promised to suspend the students.[21] Other cities promised to withhold credits, to ban students from extracurricular activities, or to punish students with fines. Against the home and the laxness of parental discipline, the schools could do little but protest. But protest they did, and vigorously. Students were more interested in popularity and having fun because parents encouraged them to be popular, because parents refused to make them work hard, and because parents did not discipline their children. The work ethic started at home, the schoolmen contended, and American homes in the twenties were failing to instill that ethic. The parents' failure left the school with a task that it could not accomplish alone.

In the thirties the schools continued to worry about student social life, sex, drinking, and lack of application to studies. But their primary concern now focused on the problem of youth's frustration with an economy in which there was no place for young people. Schools spent even more time and effort on teaching patriotism and respect for the status quo, discouraging students from questioning the system even more than they had in the twenties—as is reflected in the upsurge of loyalty oaths required of teachers in this period. Schools had to be even more careful to guard against radical ideas creeping into the curriculum at a time when student frustration encouraged their receptiveness to those radical doctrines. The public saw as evidence of this radicalism the growing number of student demonstrations in support of the demands of labor and the campaigns for peace. Americans had begun to ask fearfully whether there

[21] Krug, *Shaping of the American High School, 1920–1941*, 135.

was going to be a real "student movement" in the United States; it was the task of the school to see that there was not.

The adolescent crime rate was another problem of the thirties which the schools were expected to solve. The alienated, independent bank robber became something of a culture hero among the young. Americans were justifiably afraid that frustrated and unemployed youths would follow similar patterns. Crime statistics bore out their fears. Dorothy Canfield Fisher reported in 1939 that only 10 percent of those held for major crimes in the country were over 30 years of age.[22] The number of arrests among those under 20 was growing alarmingly. Relative to their actual and reputed activities in the thirties, the "sins" of youth in the twenties appeared more and more innocent to Americans during the Depression.

Unemployment lay behind the threat of youthful radicalism and adolescent crime. The figures were tragically appalling. In 1935 more than 4 million youths (aged 16 to 24) were neither employed nor in school. In 1940 one third of the unemployed were under 25 years of age even though that age group comprised but 22 percent of the available work force and these years covered only one fifth of the average work career. In several cities the unemployment rate among youth soared to more than 50 percent; the average was around 40 percent.[23] Although nearly everyone recognized that the economy and not the schools was responsible for this state of affairs, educators, as well as the larger society, thought that the schools should respond to protect young people and society against the dangers portended. For those schoolmen who had been seeking since the beginnings of the social efficiency movement in the prewar years to bring more and more young people under the auspices of the schools, to insure a smooth transition from youth to adulthood and from dependence to productivity, the existence of hundreds of thousands of idle youths provided a golden opportunity to claim an added responsibility for the schools. Schools would hold more and more young people in "custody" for a longer period of time, thereby easing the transition into adulthood. Keeping these youths under the control of the school would protect them from alienation, radicalism, and the lure of crime until they were old enough to find jobs and become productive workers. Such moves would at once enhance the role of the school and reduce the number of people seeking jobs by shrinking the labor force to match the decreased number of jobs provided by a stagnant economy.

Educators and citizens alike criticized the schools for their inability to prepare young people for the world of work. The vocational education pioneered around World War I had been too specific, the critics felt, too

[22] Dorothy Canfield Fisher, *Our Young Folks* (New York, 1943), 27.

[23] Krug, *Shaping of the American High School, 1920–1941*, 310, and Fisher, *Our Young Folks*, 27.

closely tied to the learning of a single skill. Schooling had failed to train adaptable workers who were able, in response to the availability of jobs, to employ a variety of skills. As the nation's understanding of the industrial economy increased, it was recognized that most jobs were semiskilled, for which training need take no more than a few weeks. Vocational education had concentrated on training craftsmen, a type of preparation unimportant to an economy dominated by semiskilled laborers. It offered no solution to the unemployment problems encountered during the Depression. Because of these criticisms, vocational education lost much of the luster it had acquired in the years since 1900, and although it continued as a relatively small facet of the educational establishment, it ceased to be a focal point for educational innovation or influence until its rhetorical revitalization as "career education" during the 1970s. Instead, educators focused increasingly on a form that could be called "general prevocational education." This approach, one which was never really clarified, sought to train youth in the habits of work and personality adjustment which would equip them with the general skills useful in a variety of occupations and prepare them to learn the specifics of a particular job when it became available to them.[24]

Complex machinery had usurped the rudimentary tasks in the factory and, because young people had neither the maturity nor the judgment to tend these machines, social commentators and educators agreed that modern industrialism could provide no useful work for youth. "What are we to do with our youth up to the age of eighteen or twenty when the best technical engineers and industrial experts are agreed that they cannot be used in the industry and agriculture of the future?" asked one NEA staff member in 1934.[25] One answer was to keep them in school until they matured enough to handle complex industrial jobs. Such a reconception of the purposes of secondary education required a curriculum far different from the one that had predominated up to that time. Book learning, concentration on intellectual processes, or even traditional vocational skill training was insufficient. They bored young people and kept them away from the institutions in which they should have spent their time. As a custodial institution, the school had to do something else; it had to prepare young people for adulthood in a more general way. Again, the prescription was vague, but most agreed that somehow this custodial institution had to provide what one member of the American Youth Commission called "the irreplaceable vitamin of work and responsibility."[26] In earlier times youth had acquired this vitamin through chores around the home or by finding useful work in a preindustrial or early

[24] Krug, *Shaping of the American High School, 1920–1941,* 311, 313.
[25] *Ibid.,* 311.
[26] Fisher, *Our Young Folks,* 83.

industrial economy. Such opportunities were no longer available in the urban home stocked with modern conveniences, in an economy where buying finished goods was far more efficient than making them at home, and in which machines had taken over the simple tasks that young people had previously performed in the factory. Schools had to recreate, artificially, an environment in which young people could absorb this vitamin. The public seemed to agree with the educational commentators that young people were soft, that they lacked industriousness and a commitment to the work ethic. In a word, young people lacked "character," and the only way that character was instilled was through the performance of useful work. Many of these analysts shared an almost mystical belief that physical manual labor would restore certain primitive and essential values in youth—values which had been seriously undermined during the 1920s and 1930s. As a result these analysts turned, perhaps inevitably, to the experience of the CCC and NYA. Particularly appealing to those who longed for the schools to assume a custodial role for all children was the practice of combining education with paid public service jobs. Many advocated compulsory participation in residential work camps for men and women between 18 and 20.[27] The idea of the universal and compulsory CCC-type camps which kept youth off the labor market and obliged them, through enforced work schedules, to develop their loyalty to the work ethic, was an extreme manifestation of the less radical dreams of the majority of educators who sought to use the schools in an attempt to solve the youth problem of the 1930s.

Such an extreme proposal—although it received a respectful hearing—got nowhere in the end. Both the political and logistic problems appeared too grave. The fact that the CCC and NYA spent substantially more per enrollee than the regular public schools made this proposal economically impossible. No one had outlined how the schools were going to find enough useful work for all their older students when the economy could not provide it naturally. The hopes and the directions were very vague. The problems appeared vast and unresolvable. Educators and their critics were as uncertain about solutions to the youth problems of the thirties as were the economic planners about solutions for the economic riddle of the Depression. In both cases the advent of total war solved their problems at least temporarily. War made the economy hum; war production needs and the military draft eliminated the problem of idle and uncommitted youth. The vast economic expansion of the postwar years allowed educators to forget those earlier questions, but economic developments, technological change, and the problems of poverty and unemployment in the seventies have raised many of them once again.

[27] Krug, *Shaping of the American High School, 1920–1941*, 320.

During the twenties and thirties the schools were constantly called upon to redress the failures of the family, culture, and economy, areas over which the schools exercised no significant control. The educational establishment was continually asked to protect and guard American youth from forces far stronger and more influential than the schools could realistically hope to be. Schools were supposed to resist the results of urbanization, to protect children's minds from the messages and values omnipresent in the pervasive mass media, and to prevent them from feeling frustrated, angry, and alienated over an economic situation which was inherently frustrating and alienating. Rapid change brought rising expectations for schools to maintain traditional values in the face of altered circumstances.

III

It is ironic that this educational effort to preserve the status quo was carried out under the banner of curricular and pedagogical progressivism and modernism. What progressive or modern meant in that context was not entirely clear. No important breakthrough occurred in the twenties and thirties which could be said to reorient pedagogical theory in a way characteristic of those decades. Instead, what pedagogical change appeared was principally derivative of developments in the previous two decades. Individuals and school systems tended to use these ideas eclectically and in many cases to accept clichéd rhetoric without paying particular attention to the actual meanings. Since curricular and pedagogical decisions were increasingly decentralized, it is difficult to reconstruct what children were taught and how. Curriculum development in the twenties and thirties encouraged the involvement of teachers in deciding what they taught. Hundreds and thousands of systems turned to their own staffs to work up their curricula. Although national movements and ideas influenced these local initiatives, each one developed its own unique combination of ideas and pattern of offerings. Perhaps the central educational concept at this time was "social," which, as Edward Krug has suggested, was thought to have a good deal of scientific precision, but was actually an obscurant which, through its constant repetition and application to processes quite different from each other, served only to cloud over what appear on hindsight to have been significant differences in method or point of view. Unfortunately for the historian who requires clarity and precision in expression to identify and outline differences, educational theorists and commentators resorted to repeating "social," again and again, which only muddied the waters.

It is clear what the so-called modernists were against during the twenties and thirties. They opposed all emphasis on the traditional academic curriculum. Thus they continued the attack on college admission requirements which were thought to force high schools to emphasize history, English, mathematics, and foreign languages. They objected to the emphasis on learning from books and the suggestion that, since most knowledge was contained there, the school's principal task was to aid children in extracting that knowledge. They opposed the rote memorization thought to have characterized earlier education, the isolation of students within the traditional school, and the isolation of the traditional school and its curriculum from the real world, from "life," as they said. Modernists wanted the schools to help the child learn from experience, rather than from lifeless books. The bookish curriculum was to be sacrificed to one which built learning experiences around actual and simulated "real life" experiences. The modern school was to replace academic disciplines with subjects—such as vocational training and civics—that prepared the child not for college, but for real living. On this point the pedagogues of the twenties and thirties were saying nothing more than had educational reformers in the previous two decades.

Educational theory of the period contained the same confusion that we have noted in Dewey's thought: that confusion between education that stresses individual development and fulfillment and education which prepares the child to contribute to society. Educators spoke often of their responsibility to help the student realize his full potential and to develop his creative impulses, but at the same time spoke of the school's power and its duty to equip children to find a role in which they could be useful to the society either in preserving or changing the status quo. Some historians have argued that the impulse toward using schools to increase personal fulfillment and freedom was the dominant mode of the twenties and that the impulse to use schools as social agents was the ruling doctrine of the 1930s. Such a division assumes that there was far more order and coherence in educational beliefs than there actually was.

The Progressive Education Association (PEA), founded in 1919 by a group of parents and educators connected almost exclusively with private schools or public schools in wealthy suburbs, became the repository—until 1940—of the mantle of progressive reform and as such mirrored much of the era's conflicting and confusing pedagogical thought. Historians have noted that in the twenties the PEA seemed to favor the child-centered approach to education. Advocates believed that the interests of the child rather than arbitrary curricular guidelines should determine what was taught. They emphasized that teachers should recognize the child as a "free personality" and teach accordingly.[28] Educators connected with the PEA in its early years helped introduce work in creative

[28] The phrase is George Counts' and can be found in *Dare the School Build a New Social Order?* (New York, 1932), quoted in Lawrence Cremin, *The Transformation of the School: Progressivism in American Education, 1876–1957* (New York, 1961), 259.

writing and artistic and musical expression to the schools. Of all the educators of the period, they were probably the most concerned with invigorating the "individual self-fulfillment" band of the progressive spectrum. Schools represented in the PEA introduced the most radical pedagogy of the period. Characteristic of these schools was the increased amount of movement within the individual classroom—children were not tied to their desks as in the traditional school. Classroom equipment, books, supplies, games, and artistic tools were far more plentiful than in the average school. The curriculum tended to be organized around topics rather than subjects or disciplines. There was far more contact between community and the classroom. These schools were praised and described in great detail in Agnes de Lima, *Our Enemy the Child* (1926), and Harold Rugg and Ann Shumaker, *The Child-Centered School* (1928). But, except for the emphasis in several schools on creative expression, they represent little that had not been outlined and implemented in the previous period (as is indicated by a comparison of John and Evelyn Dewey's *Schools of Tomorrow* [1915] with the two volumes mentioned above). The PEA provided these initiatives with a sense of esprit as parts of a movement, a corporate indentity, and the beginnings of a public relations thrust to generalize their efforts to a wider realm, but it failed to introduce precision into the thinking of progressive educators or to establish anything like a progressive orthodoxy.

The PEA's point of view appears as coherent as it does to us largely because in the thirties a group of educational thinkers, most of whom were associated with Teachers College, sought to "take over" the PEA in the interest of enlisting its imprimatur in favor of education for social change or what some called "social reconstruction." As part of their effort, they attacked the PEA of the twenties as a nest of individualists whose emphasis on the individual child blinded them to the need for social learning. George Counts of Teachers College led the attack on the PEA and its upper-middle-class members. In *Dare the Schools Build a New Social Order?* (1932) he argued that teachers must decide what the new and better society should look like, and then teach this vision of the better society to their students. Teachers must abandon their fears of indoctrination or imposition, he argued, and inculcate in children what they thought was right. "The weakness of Progressive Education thus lies in the fact that it has elaborated no theory of social welfare, unless it be that of anarchy or extreme individualism." Counts wrote:

> In this, of course, it is but reflecting the viewpoint of the members of the liberal-minded upper middle class who send their children to the Progressive schools—persons who are fairly well-off, who have abandoned the faiths of their fathers, who assume an agnostic attitude towards all important questions, who pride themselves on their open-mindedness and tolerance, who favor in a mild sort of way fairly liberal programs of social reconstruction,

who are full of good will and humane sentiment, who have vague aspirations for world peace and human brotherhood, who can be counted upon to respond moderately to any appeal made in the name of charity, who are genuinely distressed at the sight of *unwonted* forms of cruelty, misery, and suffering, and who perhaps serve to soften somewhat the bitter clashes of those real forces that govern the world; but who, in spite of all their good qualities, have no deep and abiding loyalties, possess no convictions for which they would sacrifice over-much, would find it hard to live without their customary material comforts, are rather insensitive to the accepted forms of social injustice, are content to play the role of interested spectator in the drama of human history, refuse to see reality in its harsher and more disagreeable forms, rarely move outside the pleasant circles of the class to which they belong, and in the day of severe trial will follow the lead of the most powerful and respectable forces in society and at the same time find good reasons for so doing. These people have shown themselves entirely incapable of dealing with any of the great crises of our time—war, prosperity, or depression. At bottom they are romantic sentimentalists, but with a sharp eye on the main chance. That they can be trusted to write our educational theories and shape our educational programs is highly improbable.[29]

Teachers must not take their direction from this class but must instead recognize the "stark reality" of the world, reestablish an "organic relation with the community," develop "a compelling and challenging vision of human destiny" which includes a picture of an increasingly collectivized economy and a far more just distribution of economic goods, and agree to teach that vision, fully aware and proud of the fact that they are imposing their beliefs on their charges. "Agnosticism, skepticism, or even experimentalism" when divorced from a particular program "constitutes an extremely meager spiritual diet for any people." Intellectuals, "a queer breed of man at best," may find it satisfactory, especially in view of their "sheltered" lives, but most people "will always demand something more solid and substantial. Ordinary men and women crave a tangible purpose towards which to strive and which lends richness and dignity and meaning to life."[30] Counts wanted the educational profession to find and transmit such a tangible purpose suited to a society characterized by technological and material abundance as well as spiritual poverty.

Counts' attacks on the individualism of the early PEA attracted widespread enthusiasm and debate in the profession. Counts and others who stressed the social functions of progressive education rose to power in the PEA. The organization broadened its appeal and membership to more educators stirred by the promise of finding a significant role for their profession during the great national crisis of the thirties. Continued attacks on the early PEA as a supporter of individualism, selfishness, and

[29] Counts, *New Social Order,* 7–8.
[30] *Ibid.,* 9, 38–39.

privilege attracted the enthusiastic support of others. Isaac L. Kandel, a colleague of Counts at Teachers College, laid America's current problems at the door of the excessive individualism inherent in the pedagogy of the PEA in the twenties. Progressives should "recognize the consequences of their own doctrines," Kandel wrote, "and concern themselves not with a new social order but with the removal of those causes of social disorder which were, until recently, inherent in their philosophy of education."[31]

But, as Edward Krug has wisely pointed out, such criticism confused pedagogical method with economic theory: to teach to individual differences has really nothing to do with making children into selfish or economically self-centered adults.[32] Nor, indeed, were the attacks on the individualism of the early PEA essentially accurate. The social reconstructionists distorted and oversimplified the thought of their predecessors, presumably to gather support for their views among other educators. In the twenties the PEA manifested the same tensions between advocacy of self-fulfillment and social service that had characterized educational reform since 1890. The introductory plank of the PEA's first platform, "Freedom to Develop Naturally," typified the problem: "The conduct of the pupil should be self-governed according to the social needs of his community, rather than by arbitrary laws."[33] Individual teachers and schools might adjust their emphasis according to the demands of their community or clientele—and it is probable that the more middle class and private the school was, the more support (at least rhetorical) individual freedom received—but it was rare for educators to focus on one while neglecting the other. Similarly, the attempt to work out a neat historical division between the twenties and the thirties on the basis of differing emphases on individualism and collectivism in education does not work out. Rather, emphases on child-centeredness, on social control, on social adjustment, on social reform were mixed together eclectically throughout the era, with the mixture varying both geographically and chronologically.

The philosophical debates of the Progressive Education Association were both distant and rather rarified for the average American teacher or educational administrator and the urgings of George Counts, no matter how interesting, were impossible to implement by a profession as tightly controlled as teaching. In the average school the distinctions that were so heatedly debated in New York easily blurred before the realities of classroom teaching. The progressive or modern pedagogy that was

[31] Quoted in Krug, *Shaping of the American High School, 1920–1941*, 221.
[32] *Ibid.*, 221–224.
[33] Quoted in Cremin, *Transformation of the School*, 243, from *Association for the Advancement of Progressive Education* (Washington, D. C., n.d.).

most likely to be practiced in the schoolroom was not the product of a doctrinaire focus on the child or on society but, rather, some variation of the project method. This method, inextricably associated with the name of William Heard Kilpatrick, professor of the philosophy of education at Teachers College throughout this period, offered teachers both a rather precise teaching method and a supportive theory that wove together almost all the strands of progressive thinking about schooling since 1900. Kilpatrick described the "project method" in an essay written in 1918 and elaborated his ideas in a later volume, *Foundations of Method* (1925). The project method, disseminated through 60,000 reprints of the article distributed between the wars, through *Foundations of Method*, and through Kilpatrick's tremendous magnetism as a teacher of large classes (he is said to have had 35,000 students from all parts of the United States during his career at Teachers College and to have deeply affected the practice of an extraordinarily large number of them), became perhaps the most characteristic device of modern or progressive pedagogy in this era.

The project method, which Kilpatrick first outlined in print in 1918 although he had taught similar conceptions for many years previously, sought to build the school curriculum around "wholehearted purposeful activity in a social situation." By this he meant for children themselves, guided in their choice by the teacher, to "purpose" to do something—be it constructive, so as "to embody some idea or plan in external form" such as building a boat or writing a letter; be it appreciative, as when the child "purposed" to listen to music or appreciate a picture; be it problem solving, as when a child sought to determine "whether or not dew falls"; or be it the obtaining of some degree of skill, as in writing or reading a foreign language. Each project—the activity centered around the carrying out of the child's or children's (for Kilpatrick hoped that there would be many group activities) purpose—was to be chosen by children and to bring results which they desired. Such activity on the part of children would make them learn more efficiently for modern behaviorist learning theory argued that a stimulus-response bond is more firmly imprinted when the learner derives satisfaction from his response (Edward Lee Thorndike's law of effect). There was no better way to insure satisfaction for the learner than to have him choose his own goal. Compelling a child to learn or accomplish something always creates some annoyance in the child which interferes with the effective imprinting of the desired stimulus-response bond. No such annoyance will deter a child who is learning something because he wants to. The boy who carries out his own purpose in school "looks upon his school activity with joy and confidence and plans yet other projects"; the boy who is coerced into learning "counts his school a bore and begins to look elsewhere for the expression there denied. To the one the teacher is a friend and comrade; to the other, a taskmaster and enemy. The one easily feels himself on the side of the school and other social agencies, the other with equal ease considers them all instruments of suppression."[34]

This concern with the social effects of education and with the superior social learning that could derive from purposeful activity in school underlay Kilpatrick's strategy. Kilpatrick sought to marry child-centeredness and social efficiency[35] and, although the marriage was sometimes awkward, he did succeed in effecting a seemingly compatible coupling which convinced thousands of educators that social learning and social efficiency could be achieved through catering to the desires of the individual child. The very process of letting a child "purpose" a project created moral and social good.

> The worthy life consists of purposive activity and not mere drifting [Kilpatrick wrote]. We scorn the man who passively accepts what fate or some other chance brings to him. We admire the man who is master of his fate, who with deliberate regard for a total situation forms clear and far-reaching purposes, who plans and executes with nice care the purpose so formed. A man who habitually so regulates his life with reference to worthy social aims meets at once the demands for practical efficiency and of moral responsibility. Such a one presents the ideal of democratic citizenship. It is equally true that the purposeful act is not the unit of life for the serf or the slave. . . .
>
> As the purposeful act is thus the typical unit of the worthy life in a democratic society, so also should it be made the typical unit of school procedure.[36]

Kilpatrick assured his readers that he was advocating "no scheme of subordination of teacher or school to childish whim." Guidance, sometimes even coercion, would be necessary and only worthy purposes would be implemented. But Kilpatrick insisted that "no necessary conflict in kind between the social demands and the child's interests" existed. "It is the special duty and opportunity of the teacher to guide the pupil through his present interests and achievement into the wider interests and achievement demanded by the wider social life of the older world." The project method would have a significant positive moral influence on children precisely because it stressed social rather than selfish ends.

> Moral character is primarily an affair of shared social relationships, the disposition to determine one's conduct and attitudes with reference to the welfare of the group. . . . To [achieve this] can we conceive of a better way than by living in a social *milieu* which provides, under competent supervision, for shared coping with a variety of social situations? In the school procedure here

[34] William H. Kilpatrick, "The Project Method," *Teachers College Record,* XIX (September, 1918), 334, 332–333, 327, *passim.*

[35] See Cremin, *Transformation of the School,* 217, for a slightly different analysis of Kilpatrick's attempt to reconcile the competing theories.

[36] Kilpatrick, "Project Method," 324–325.

advocated children are living together in the pursuit of a rich variety of purposes, some individually sought, many conjointly. . . . Under the eye of the skillful teacher the children as an embryonic society will make increasingly finer discriminations as to what is right and proper. Ideas and judgment come thus. Motive and occasion arise together: the teacher has but to steer the process of evaluating the situation. The teacher's success—if we believe in democracy—will consist in gradually eliminating himself or herself from the success of the procedure.[37]

Proper purposeful activity in the school would teach not only judgment but also proper "response bonds." Social projects would instill "the necessary habits of give and take." Because children were so dependent on peer approval, the law of effect would insure that they would learn those habits and responses which brought such approval and the personal satisfaction attendant on it.

Kilpatrick sought to take Dewey's general ideas about learning by doing and social learning and make them definite or specific enough for application in the classroom. Kilpatrick sought alternatives to the fixed, a priori curriculum. Because society changed rapidly, no curriculum could be designed that would meet the needs of each new wave of students. The curriculum at any given moment must be constructed out of the purposes and needs of the students then attending school. Furthermore, Kilpatrick thought that the project method would make schooling more lifelike—"the only way to learn to live well is to practice living well" he wrote in 1925—and his program provided just such practice.[38] "The purposeful act prepares best for life while at the same time it constitutes the present worthy life itself.[39] Kilpatrick envisioned an ongoing, fluid process of education in which the individual teacher was continually adapting her teaching to match the ever changing ideals and reality of the worthy life.

The project method was widely disseminated and employed in schools throughout the country but Kilpatrick's vision was impossible to maintain. As with almost all educational ideas that demand flexibility, fluidity, constant modifying of response on the part of the institution, the more widely it was disseminated, the more inflexible the method became. Projects, supposedly the response to individual or group purposes, became totally preplanned by textbook writers, methods teachers, curriculum specialists, and the educational materials companies. The accompanying illustration of a unit or project from the third grade of one of the best progressive schools—the Lincoln School attached to Teachers College—shows what inevitably happened, even in the best of circum-

[37] *Ibid.*, 329–330.
[38] Kilpatrick, *Foundations of Method* (New York, 1925), 109.
[39] Kilpatrick, "Project Method," 323.

A UNIT OF STUDY RELATED TO
BOATS
THIRD GRADE

SUBJECT MATTER CONTENT WHICH HELPED SOLVE THE PROBLEMS

PROBLEMS- QUESTIONS

STIMULATION

In the spring of last year many of the boys of this group were interested in trains and other means of travel.

Many summer experiences with boats.

Wood in supply box cut in shapes suggestive of boats.

Bulletin prepared by the teacher.

Trip to see Half-Moon.

Trip to see boat models.

To construct boats that will look like a certain kind and with which children can play.

How do boats "go"?

Who first thought of making a sailboat?

How did people get the idea for different shapes for boats?

To know more about the people who traveled on the seas in early times.

To find out about the making of boats.

How many different kinds of boats do we have today and how is each kind used?

How did early people use their ships?

To find out about the different parts of a boat.

How do people know how much to put into a boat before it will sink?

INDUSTRIAL ARTS
Construction of boats: Making pattern, shaping hull, making sail, making keel, casting weight for keel, making rack for boat, and testing boat.
How boats developed from early times to the present day.
The difficulty involved in building a toy boat so it will balance in water.
Different kinds of sail boats.
The need for a keel on a boat.
Different methods of propelling a boat.
Modern inventions in connection with the propulsion of boats.
What makes boats float.
Different uses of boats today.

HISTORY
The Half-Moon directed interest to Hendrick Hudson and his ship.
Historic ships: Santa Maria, Mayflower.
Reference work, reading and discussions about:
Vikings: What color and kinds of clothing did they wear? What did they eat? What kind of houses did they have? What were their boats like? Did Vikings have stores? How did Viking writing look? Story of Lief Erickson. The gods of the Vikings. Their beliefs.
Phoenicians: Scenery, boats, people, trade, beliefs, clothing, cities, industries, etc.
Egyptians: Scenery, country, boats, beliefs, tools, writing, etc. Story of the building of Solomon's Temple.
Early Mediterranean peoples.

GEOGRAPHY
Pictures of boat from newspaper which interested children in world geography.
Geography related to countries studied.
Norway: Country, climate, people and occupations.
Phoenicia: Country, climate, people, trading routes, daily life of early people compared with that of today.
Egypt: Country, climate, trading, etc.
Map interest: Norway, showing ancient home of the Vikings.
The Mediterranean countries, showing cities of Phoenicia and routes on which the King of Tyre sent materials for Solomon's Temple.
Plasticene map of Mediterranean Sea and surrounding countries on which children sailed card-board models of early boats.
Globe in frequent use to locate places mentioned.
Outline world map, locating countries.
Interest in determining distances (reading scales on map).
How far is it from Norway to Phoenicia?
How far is it from Norway to America?
Building Lower Manhattan on floor with blocks to exhibit boats.
Map was drawn on floor; buildings in New York City that helped most with sea travel.

ARITHMETIC
Measuring for boat patterns and measurements in boat making.
Figuring the number of board feet used by class in building boat racks.
Arithmetic problems in connection with science experiment of water displacement and floating objects.
What is a gram?
What is a cubit?
Dimensions of Solomon's Temple compared with dimensions of the Lincoln School.
Children saw a cubit measure at the Museum.

FINE ARTS
Sketching and painting pictures of Half-Moon.
Sketching and painting boat models.
Drawing blackboard frieze showing history of boats.
Ten easel pictures showing story of Lief Erickson.
Cut paper pictures of boats.
Painting Egyptian boats seen at Museum.
Painting Viking pictures showing clothing.
Painting modern boats.
Making clay tablet.

COMPOSITION—LITERATURE
Stories written about the trip to see Half-Moon.
Stories of other trips by individual children.
Original poems about boats and the sea.
Labels and invitations for boat exhibit.
Written and oral reports about boats, Vikings, Phoenicia and Egypt.
Stories for bulletin, room paper, council news, or absent class members, telling of class interest and study.

READING
Reference material pertaining to topics under discussion, found in school library or at home.
Children's reading material: Lief and Thorkle, Viking Stories, Early sea people, Boat Book prepared by other Third Grade, material prepared by student teachers.

SCIENCE
How can we tell if our boats will float and balance? Try out in delta table.
Three experiments: Why do some objects float and why do some sink?
How do people know how much to put into boat before it will sink?

DRAMATIZATION
Play-Story of Lief Erickson, spontaneously prepared by class.

MUSIC
Old Gaelic Lullaby. Volga Boat Song. Sail Bonnie Boat.

PROBABLE OUTCOMES

DESIRABLE HABITS AND SKILLS

Better skill in sketching.
Better skill in handling brush and paints.
A beginning of the development of how to sew.
Developing the habit of making a pattern before constructing an article.
Developing skill in shaping wood by means of plane and spokeshave.
Developing skill in using gouge and mallet.
Developing skill in reading distances on map.
Rapid growth in map drawing.
Developing habit of reading the newspaper.
Better skill in measuring.
Ability to gather information on a certain subject and reporting to class.
Increased ability in writing.

ATTITUDES AND APPRECIATIONS

Economic:

An appreciation of the use of weights and measures.
What it means to construct a real boat that will float and balance properly.
Appreciation of the change in the lives of the people caused by the discovery of iron and the use of sails.
Appreciation of paper as a writing material.
Appreciation of the modern inventions in connection with the propulsion of ships.

Social:

What the early people contributed to the world.
The number of people and industry it takes to supply materials for the construction of one building.
Comparison of the ideas of fairness of the early people with the present day.

Recreational:

Developing a joy in painting, sketching and drawing.
Growing interest in reading books about historical peoples, inventions or boats.
Playing with boats made.
Interest in the construction of a toy-boat.
Interest in the construction of a real boat.
The pleasure in making maps.
The pleasure of playing with maps.

Aesthetic:

Appreciation of the beauty in line and construction of boats.
The adventure of the ship.

INFORMATION

Knowledge of the development of the boat from raft to steamship.
Who Hendrick Hudson was.
General idea of historic ships.
An interesting acquaintance with Vikings, Phoenicians, and Egyptians.
General geographical knowledge of the world.
What a cubit measure is.
Knowledge of how to draw maps.
Some idea of what makes objects float.
Some idea of how to make boats balance in water.
Some idea of how to construct a toy-boat.
How the early people made their clay tablets.
How to make a clay tablet.
The need for molds in casting metals.
Some idea of how iron is made into different shapes.

NEW INTERESTS LEADING TOWARD FURTHER ACTIVITIES

Interest in world geography and travel.
Maps and actual distances between given places.
The time it takes to get to certain places.

Interest in silk through answering the questions: What kind of clothing did the Vikings wear?
How is velvet made?

Interest in what clay is: How it is prepared for our use and how it was prepared by early people for making clay tablets.

Interest in the Egyptian and Phoenician alphabet and how our alphabet was developed from it.
The materials the Egyptians used for writing.

Interest in metals.
Interest in weight of different metals through casting of lead for keels.
How metals are shaped.

Interest in the construction of modern buildings through reading about Solomon's Temple and comparing it with the construction of the Lincoln School.

Interest in other phases of transportation.

TOTAL PERSONALITY AS MODIFIED BY THE FOREGOING EXPERIENCES

stances.[40] Here was a project on boats, designed hopefully to grow out of interests and activities that the students had had during vacation and stimulated subtly by a few class activities, which involved making model boats, studying how boats worked, reading about the history of boats and the economic significance of water travel. The educator outlined in advance the stimulation, the problems, the activities, and the outcomes and expected the student to fit into this previously designed scheme. Kilpatrick's requirement for spontaneity was lost, but other parts of his idea were well preserved and became the selling points for this particular and very popular modern method. Projects were generally social in nature, in that students worked together on activities that supposedly grew out of their life experiences and interests and that were designed to familiarize them in a very direct and concrete way with their social and economic environment. Thus the project method embodied the modern reaction against the abstract, irrelevant academic discipline as it solved, in the interests of training children for social living, the problem of overcoming the traditional isolation of the individual learner.

How does the historian explain the popularity of progressive or modern pedagogy—especially the emphasis on group learning and social activity—in a society which sought to use its schools to protect the status quo and protect its children from the threats of modernism? Why did educators and the communities they served seek to adopt the pedagogical strategies that were pioneered in the United States by a group of progressives who had in mind quite different ends and held a significantly different position on that great debate between the two sets of values that characterized the twenties and the early years of the thirties? There are at least three somewhat overlapping explanations which help us resolve this apparent contradiction.

First, progressive or modern education became a counter in the boosteristic competition among communities that so characterized the speculative, growth-oriented 1920s. In something of the same way in which budding towns in the antebellum period bid for colleges and institutions of higher education in order to attract settlers and investment, towns of the 1920s sought to garner a progressive image for their school system in order to establish the fact that their town was a "live" one, that its leaders and its institutions had a lot of "pep." Such a reputation, it was hoped, would attract industry and a labor force to the town. James M. Shield's fictional account of the coming (and waning) of progressivism in a small southern city in this period rings quite true. That tobacco processing community decided—or at least the businessmen on its board of education decided—in the mid-twenties that they could do a good deal for the city and undoubtedly for their businesses by putting, in the super-

[40] Cremin, *Transformation of the School,* 284–285.

intendent's words, "more—er—ah—pep into our school system." One member of the board committed $10,000 toward that goal and the city literally went out and bought progressivism—in this case a Ph.D. from Teachers College with a reputation as a progressive educator who was to serve the schools as a curriculum director or specialist. The board apparently gave little thought to developing better schools for the children but, rather, sought to "advertise the schools . . . [and] put Nugget City on the map!" A good portion of the $10,000 gift from the board member was to go for "special publicity purposes" in connection with the hiring of the noted progressive educator. The businessmen were convinced that news of its progressive school system would put Nugget City a jump ahead of its competitors in recruiting new residents and new industry. It is instructive here to follow the plot to its conclusion. Nugget City was not really prepared for a progressive educator from Teachers College. That community, like so many others of the day, expected its teachers not to drink, its female teachers not to smoke, not to play cards, not to joyride, not to go to movies. Teachers were expected, nay required, to attend church and to teach Sunday school. The new curriculum specialist instituted the project method and introduced a more "relevant" social studies curriculum that focused on group study of local political and economic institutions. While the city prospered in the late twenties, the community was willing to look the other way when the newcomer violated community mores and instituted these somewhat suspicious programs. When the Depression reduced the likelihood of growth and made the natives of the city more defensive and more concerned with protecting their way of life from outside criticism and threats of change, the community's attitude toward progressivism, Teachers College style, changed. The business leaders found that relevant social studies included the study of excess profits gathered by the tobacco companies and, coincidentally, they found both the curriculum specialist and the kinds of curricula he recommended too expensive. Therefore, the leaders, with substantial support from the community, hounded the progressive out of town, dashing his hopes of improving the schools according to his ideals just as the Depression had dashed Nugget City's hopes of achieving substantial growth. The search for "progressive" ways of schooling had not changed the town; when progressivism looked like a useful advertising device, it was employed; when it did not, it was discarded.[41]

When the Lynds returned to Middletown in the early thirties, they described much the same trend. In the late twenties, a revitalized Ball State Teachers College worked closely with the public school administrators to devise a plan for making that city's schools more "progressive."

[41] James Shields, *Just Plain Larnin'* (New York, 1934).

The plan announced two somewhat conflicting goals: teaching for "individual differences" and increasing the efficiency of the school system. Muncie and Ball State established a laboratory school to serve as a yardstick for the other schools in the city. There the emphasis was on small classes, counseling and guidance, and exploratory teaching—moving from a factually based curriculum to one based on "discovery." The community seems to have greeted with enthusiasm these moves in the direction of individual differences and teaching that would allow students to answer questions for themselves rather than demanding that they accept the answer on the basis of some outside authority. What the "progressives" at the teachers college identified as progressive, the city's businessmen viewed similarly. With the advent of the depression and its accompanying onslaught of pessimism, the leaders of the city came to a different set of conclusions. The progressive ideas of the teachers college were expensive and dangerous. The necessity of shoring up the status quo by teaching community solidarity, unquestioning obedience to accepted values, and the virtue of hard work—and the necessity of doing this cheaply—overwhelmed earlier commitments to individual differences and student exploration. In the thirties the community began to police the ideas of its teachers more closely, class sizes were increased, the interference of the progressives in the college with the city's schools decreased, and the emphasis placed on inculcating basic values was revitalized, symbolized by the 1935 state requirement that all schools teach compulsory courses on the state and federal constitutions. As the local newspaper put it—revealing the peripheral impact that "progressivism" had had on Muncie—"fads" would give way to "common-sense" education. An up-and-coming city like Muncie wanted the best for itself in the twenties and wanted all the trappings of careful modernity. The rhetoric of progressivism, at least, offered them those trappings and they embraced it. But, when it seemed that even rhetorical commitments to progressivism might further threaten a status quo and value system already disturbed by depression, the city was quick to scuttle progress in favor of common sense. One reason, then, for progressivism's popularity —at least in the twenties—is that it appeared to offer communities committed to maintaining the status quo a chance to appear up to date.[42]

The second reason for the popularity of progressive pedagogy—especially its concern with group activity and social learning—was that it seemed to offer a perfect training strategy to fit youngsters for "business success" as defined in the twenties and thirties. The predominant image of the successful businessman prior to World War I had characterized him as a self-made man, somewhat lonely and imperious, an entrepreneur who had won his place by being tougher than any other in his

[42] Lynds, *Middletown in Transition*, 216–226, 226 n.

field. These successful men had made their mark in production—of steel, oil, textiles, and automobiles—or in the creation of transportation empires. Although they generally admired individual businessmen who conquered the system, people also regarded—and this was especially true during the Progressive era—business as something of a social menace. Businessmen were selfish, cruel, hard driving, and socially unconcerned, especially for their own workers and the larger public of consumers.

All these characteristics of business changed, or seemed to change, with World War I. A concerted public relations drive by business set out to convince the public that business was indeed quite service oriented. An often cited example was that businessmen devoted themselves to government service for a "dollar-a-year" during the war. Businessmen and their public relations firms (John D. Rockefeller was probably the first to hire a public relations expert, Ivy Lee in 1914) created the United Fund as a symbol of business' community concern. Public relations men touted business' growing concern for employee welfare, for company hospitals and picnics and recreation programs, and for various profit-sharing schemes. All of these devices had had an earlier existence as part of businessmen's efforts to win the support of their employees and to keep them from radical, militant unions or socialist parties. In the twenties business made every effort to tell the public of their efforts. But business' greatest public service, it claimed, was insuring economic growth and a higher standard of living for the American people. Without a vital business sector Americans would not have the world's highest living standard. There was no greater public service than the creation and maintenance of those standards.

Business' contribution to a higher standard of living had much more impact as a rallying cry after the war because the nature of business' relations with the consumers had changed vitally. In 1920, 1 in 20 of the largest firms in the United States dealt directly with the public; by 1929, 9 of 20 did so. The automobile industry and major appliance manufacturers had now joined the ranks of big business and they sold directly—through franchised dealerships—to the consumer. When Henry Ford was able to produce and sell over half a million Model T's in 1916 (the United States had produced only 65,000 automobiles in 1908), he changed the nature of business-consumer relations in the United States. Ford created an impact on the average American's standard of living unparalleled to that date—at least, since the advent of ready-to-wear clothing in the mid-nineteenth century. Obviously, Carnegie's work in steel, Rockefeller's in oil, or Huntington's in railroads had a significant impact on the average American, but it was indirect. The Ford Motor Company directly gave the individual American the opportunity to purchase geographic independence and mobility and social status for $360 in the form of a Model T. The contributions of big business to the standard of living of the average man seemed much clearer. The shift from the production of durable goods to consumer goods signified a profound change in the image of business.

The advent of the assembly-line-produced automobile illustrates the change inherent in the increased contact between industry and the consumer. Before the war demand for cheap cars was so high that the auto companies could not produce enough to meet it. By 1920, however, the perfection of the modern assembly line solved the production problem. Now companies could produce more cars than consumers "naturally" demanded. What was true of automobiles was true of most industries producing consumer goods. Companies turned from problems of production to problems of marketing. The twenties and thirties were predominantly decades of the development of marketing skills in business. As we have seen, the twenties saw the development of advertising that sought not only to inform potential customers about the features of a product but to "create" a demand among potential consumers for that product. Sales efforts became so important that businessmen promoted the adoption of consumer credit—turning "going into debt," which had once been regarded as sinful, into an act that was regarded as socially useful, a way of increasing demand, maintaining production, and keeping the standard of living high. As the emphasis on sales increased, the successful businessman was increasingly seen as the effective salesman. New economic empires were built, according to the new belief, not on the ability to produce goods but on the ability to create and tap markets.

Another significant change in business in the twenties was the attentiveness of industrial psychology and personnel management to the social organization of the workplace. Psychologists and business school professors advised businessmen that they could get more out of their employees by treating them with respect, by engaging them in the process of decision making, by being receptive to their ideas, and by creating a warm and supportive environment rather than by driving their workers as the older businessmen had reportedly done. Employees should feel that they were members of a team, working together to solve problems under the supportive leadership of an affable, yet forceful and inspiring leader. The successful manager had to encourage rather than coerce his employees if he was to be successful. Cooperation, not hierarchical bureaucracy, became the watchword of the era. How much the psychologists' admonitions actually affected business practice is hard to tell; they certainly did, however, affect the image of the businessman.

This shift in the focus of business—toward public service, toward face-to-face relations with the ultimate consumer, toward salesmanship, toward personnel management—created, it was thought, a need for a new kind of businessman. The lonely, self-made, imperious businessman was superseded by the personable leader, the glad-hander, the team manager, the community leader, the persuasive salesman. The successful businessman needed personality—in order successfully to manage men and sell himself as well as his product. Bruce Barton described the keys to business success in a book he wrote in 1924 to update the image of Jesus Christ for the 1920s. Barton, president of Barton, Durstine, and Osborn, a very successful advertising firm, noted how he could never get to like the "sissified" Jesus he learned about in Sunday school. As an adult, he was amazed to see how differently Jesus came across in the Bible and wrote *The Man Nobody Knows* (1924) to share his amazement with others. Barton had been brought up to think Christ a "kill-joy!" Yet "he was the most popular dinner guest in Jerusalem! The criticism which proper people made was that he spent too much time with publicans and sinners (very good fellows, on the whole, the man thought) and enjoyed society too much." Barton had once thought Christ a "failure!" Yet "he picked up twelve men from the bottom ranks of business and forged them into an organization that conquered the world." According to Barton, Christ's success derived largely from the fact that Jesus was what Barton called a "sociable Man." The trouble with all the prophets before Jesus was that they were excessively forbidding, full of moral grandeur, but not very pleasant all the same. "They are not," as Barton summed it up, "the kind of men whom you would choose as companions on a fishing trip." Not so Christ. He was a convivial man who liked a good party and a little fun. His ability to make the people love him accounted for his success. Christ devoted the Last Supper to personnel management, talking to his disciples in order "to lift up their hearts, to make them think nobly of themselves, to fill their spirits with a conquering faith."[43]

Barton contended that Christ was "The Founder of Modern Business." Christ's words, "whosoever will be great among you, shall be your minister, and whosoever of you will be the chiefest, shall be servant of all[,]" had been ignored until twentieth-century American businessmen picked them up. "You will hear that discovery proclaimed in every sales convention as something distinctly modern and up to date. It is emblazoned in the advertising pages of every magazine." The automobile advertisements cried: "We are great because of our service. . . . We serve; therefore we grow."[44] The desire to serve and the personality capable of getting people to like you (and your product) were in Barton's, as well as the popular, view the keys to business success. The prevalence of this view can be gathered from an early statement in the Lynds' study where they justify their twofold division between the working and the business classes by arguing that members of the working class "address their activities in getting their living primarily to *things,* utilizing material tools

[43] Bruce Barton, *The Man Nobody Knows* (New York, 1924), Preface, 66, 87–88.
[44] *Ibid.,* 164–165.

in the making of things and the performance of services, while the members of the [business class] address their activities predominantly to *people* in the selling or promotion of things, services, and ideas." People of higher status worked with people.[45]

This view of business and social success had obvious implications for explaining the popularity of progressive pedagogy, especially in the twenties when "business" was so popular. What better educational preparation for this kind of business world than a curriculum and extracurriculum that stressed social learning, group projects, teamwork in the classroom and on the playing field, than a school which stressed well-roundedness and the ability to get along, to be popular, to take part constantly in group activities? A pedagogy which attacked the idea of the individual child selfishly pursuing his own learning in isolation from other children appeared better able to turn out successful team workers and leaders than had the older academic curricula which seemed insistent on creating the lonely, imperious, self-reliant person. Group learning of any subject and participation in the extracurriculum became the vocational education of the era. Progressive or modern pedagogy which constantly litanized about group projects and social learning had vast appeal—for reasons very different from those motivating its founders—to communities whose schools were directed by businessmen and whose citizens wished to participate in a consumer-oriented economy.

The third reason for the popularity of modern or progressive pedagogy in the twenties and thirties is more speculative. Modern pedagogy's constant reiteration of "social" and "group" and "cooperation" suggested its support of the idea of community. This was most important in an era when urbanization and social change seemed rapidly to be undermining the community spirit of an earlier era. Surely the idea that it was important for schools to *teach* young adults how to get along with people indicated a declining confidence in the strength of community in America, for in a real community getting along with people was learned naturally through continual and personal interaction. Only when people thought that their children were not experiencing such interaction did it become necessary to include training in these skills in the formal activities of the school. As we have seen, declining confidence in community cohesion was characteristic of the period. Desperate to revitalize an older sense of community in the face of social and cultural change, people turned to the progressive emphasis on group activity and social learning as a means of teaching community skills. The analysis can go one step further. The impact of urbanization, the communications revolution, and social change had made community members—despite all their protests in support of community solidarity—lose confidence in their community

---

[45] Lynds, *Middletown*, 22.

and lose confidence in each other. These people were no longer totally sure of their community or why they clung to its values. But the alternative to community was a resurrection and reliance upon independent individualism—an alternative too frightening for most. One recalls George Babbitt's failing attempt to divorce himself from the booster values of his community and go it alone and his immediate realization that he could not. An even more compelling document is Dale Carnegie's *How to Win Friends and Influence People*, first published in 1936, which interprets this fear of individualism and offers a solution clearly dependent upon a school which uses progressive pedagogical methods. Purportedly, Carnegie set out to teach people how to cultivate their personal magnetism; his advice, smile. If one smiled, and smiled sincerely, all the time, one could win over people. Smiling works because smiling at people sincerely makes them feel important, worthwhile. But Carnegie is clear that one must smile sincerely rather than smile as an actor might in playing a role or smile cynically knowing that one is manipulating another person. Carnegie does not claim that you should love everyone or that sincere concern for others should make you happy. No, Carnegie seems to be saying that you should smile sincerely at another person so that when he, also having read Carnegie's advice, smiles at you, you can still believe that he is doing so sincerely, and thus feel important yourself. It is sort of a bluff, put up to make dealing with an impersonal and cynical world possible. If you smile sincerely at others, they will smile sincerely at you. This minimizes the possibility of feeling rejected. Dale Carnegie did not believe in a world of community or social unity. "People," he wrote in 1937, "are not interested in you. They are not interested in me. They are interested in themselves—morning, noon, and after dinner."[46] The sociability that Carnegie called for provided, he hoped, a way to survive in that kind of world of individualism, distrust, and disinterest. The world of self-centered individualism was a frightening and ugly world. He hoped to create, as an alternative, a false community of smiles.

Many of the leaders and constituents of the public schools in the twenties and thirties, although they supported the old-line values and the virtues of the small community against urban cosmopolitanism, shared, if not so articulately, Carnegie's despair about the strength of the spirit of community in the United States. But no more than Carnegie could they succumb to that despair. Like him, their concern became that of developing some kind of artificial sense of community—especially among the young—so that the traditional values could survive. For this purpose the progressive pedagogical stress on social learning and group activities, on teaching children to get along, was crucial. Ironically, progressive pedagogy—invented as a means of trying to adjust young people to a new and

---

[46] Quoted in Donald Meyer, *The Positive Thinkers* (New York, 1965), 185.

rapidly changing world—became employed by the supporters of the status quo, who had disproportionate influence on the school during these decades, to bolster, somewhat artificially, a status quo which these supporters sensed was rapidly waning under pressures greater than those with which the schools could deal.

GUIDE TO FURTHER READING

The most useful introductions to American society between the wars are WILLIAM E. LEUCHTENBURG'S *The Perils of Prosperity, 1914–1932* (Chicago, 1958), and *Franklin D. Roosevelt and the New Deal, 1932–1940* (New York, 1963). These volumes trace the important social and political trends and episodes of the two decades and have thorough, if dated, bibliographies. Also useful, particularly on the politics and personalities of the era, are ARTHUR M. SCHLESINGER, JR., *The Age of Roosevelt,* 3 vols. (Boston, 1957–1961), and RICHARD HOFSTADTER, *The Age of Reform: From Bryan to F. D. R.* (New York, 1955). Intellectual historians have recently broadened our understanding of social thought during the twenties and thirties; their bibliographies are the most current available. RODERICK NASH, *The Nervous Generation: American Thought, 1917–1941* (Chicago, 1970), is especially good on the alienated intellectuals; ROBERT M. CRUNDEN, *From Self to Society, 1919–1941* (Englewood Cliffs, N. J., 1971), examines individualism and collectivism among a group of social theorists traditionally assumed to be too obscure or peripheral to warrant attentive study; and RICHARD H. PELLS, *Radical Visions and American Dreams: Culture and Social Thought in the Depression Years* (New York, 1973), is very good on the challenges to liberalism after the Crash.

Schooling in general is best introduced by EDWARD KRUG, *The Shaping of the American High School, 1920–1941* (Madison, Wis., 1972). Krug's work is systematic and thorough, and yet, in it can be found the germs of hundreds of needed research projects. RUSH WELTER, *Popular Education and Democratic Thought in America* (New York, 1962), chapters 17-18, contains a perceptive analysis of New Deal educational policy. CHARLES O. BURGESS and MERLE BORROWMAN, *What Doctrines to Embrace* (Glenview, Ill., 1969), is very speculative and the final chapter in particular offers many exciting insights into the relationship between the schools and the world of work. LAWRENCE CREMIN, *The Transformation of the School: Progressivism in American Education, 1876–1957* (New York, 1961), Part II, remains the standard guide to progressive education after World War I, and has an excellent guide to the important primary sources.

The American experience of mass irrationality that surrounded World War I has been examined in LEUCHTENBURG, *Perils of Prosperity,* and NASH, *Nervous Generation,* both of which treat the Creel Committee. More specifically, the involvement of the federal government in suppressing dissent is thoroughly detailed in WILLIAM PRESTON, *Aliens and Dissenters: Federal Suppression of Radicals, 1903–1933* (New York, 1963), ROBERT K. MURRAY, *Red Scare: A Study in National Hysteria, 1919–1920* (New York, 1955), and STANLEY COBEN, "A Study in

Nativism: The American Red Scare of 1919–1920," *Political Science Quarterly*, LXXIX (1964), 52–75.

The history of psychology is best introduced in two standard works, GARDNER MURPHY, *An Historical Introduction to Modern Psychology*, rev. ed. (New York, 1949), and EDWIN G. BORING, *A History of Experimental Psychology*, 2nd ed. (New York, 1950). Behaviorism is intelligently interpreted by JOHN C. BURNHAM, "The New Psychology: From Narcissism to Social Control," in JOHN BRAEMAN et al., eds., *Change and Continuity in Twentieth-Century America: The 1920s* (Columbus, Ohio, 1968), 351–398, "On the Origins of Behaviorism," *Journal of the History of the Behavioral Sciences*, IV (April, 1968), 143–151, and "Psychiatry, Psychology, and the Progressive Movement," *American Quarterly*, XII (Winter, 1960), 457–465; also useful are DAVID BAKAN, "Behaviorism and American Urbanization," *Journal of the History of the Behavioral Sciences*, II (January, 1966), 5–28, and LUCILLE BIRNBAUM, "Behaviorism in the 1920s," *American Quarterly*, VII (1955), 15–30. The literature on educational psychology and its disinterest in social reform is discussed in ROBERT L. CHURCH, "Educational Psychology and Social Reform in the Progressive Era," *History of Education Quarterly*, XI (Winter, 1971), 391–405. Freud's experience in the United States is the subject of NATHAN HALE's excellent *Freud and the Americans: The Beginnings of Psychoanalysis in the United States, 1876–1917* (New York, 1971), and is treated in FREDERICK HOFFMAN, *The Twenties* (New York, 1955). The advertising industry's shifting strategies are outlined in OTIS PEASE, *The Responsibilities of American Advertising: Private Control and Public Interest, 1920–1940* (New Haven, Conn., 1958), MERLE CURTI, "The Changing Concept of 'Human Nature' in the Literature of American Advertising," *Business History Review*, XLI (Winter, 1967), 335–367, DANIEL BOORSTIN, *The Americans: The Democratic Experience* (New York, 1973), and MICHAEL MCMAHON, "An American Courtship: Psychologists and Advertising Theory in the Progressive Era," *American Studies*, XIII (Fall, 1972), 5–18.

The literature on the intelligence testing movement is accumulating rapidly, but few have done more than critique the values and biases of the personalities involved. Many of these critiques, however, are very capable and have contributed significantly to our understanding of the issues and decisions faced by testing advocates early in the twentieth century. The best is CLARENCE J. KARIER's "Testing for Order and Control in the Corporate Liberal State," conveniently reprinted in KARIER et al., *Roots of Crisis* (Chicago, 1973), 108–137, which locates the testing movement in the larger world of class and racial prejudice, business involvement, and philanthropic support. His inclusion of sample questions, drawn from early intelligence tests, demonstrates clearly the cultural biases of the movement's pioneers. RUSSELL MARKS, "Race and Immigration: The Politics of Intelligence Testing," in KARIER, ed., *Shaping the American Educational State: 1900 to the Present* (New York, 1975), 316–342, is also useful.

The contribution of World War I to the maturing testing movement and a revealing analysis of the content and goals of the tests developed by the army are included in DANIEL J. KEVLES, "Testing the Army's Intelligence: Psychologists and the Military in World War I," *Journal of American History*, LV (December, 1968), 565–581, and JOEL SPRING, "Psychologists and the War: The Meaning of Intelligence in the Alpha and Beta Tests," *History of Education Quarterly,* XXI (Spring, 1972), 3–15. The most useful primary source for examining the wartime experience is ROBERT M. YERKES, ed., *Psychological Examining in the United States Army: Memoirs of the National Academy of Sciences,* XV (Washington, D. C., 1921).

In a series of exchanges published in the *New Republic* between 25 October, 1922, and 17 January, 1923, journalist WALTER LIPPMANN pointed out that the army tests had been designed simply to categorize and rank individuals and that popularizers distorted this initial purpose by claiming that the tests measured inherited capability and potential—intelligence—and argued with psychologist LEWIS TERMAN over the possible abuses of the tests. Opposition to immigration, based on studies of intellectual inheritance, can be found in C. C. BRIGHAM, *A Study of American Intelligence* (Princeton, N. J., 1923).

Anthropological and racial theory played an important role in forcing upon Americans their unfortunate response to statistics on inheritance and intelligence. The ease with which even "scholars" accepted the equation of character and tested mental ability can be seen in the two famous studies of criminality and heredity, RICHARD LOUIS DUGDALE, "Hereditary Pauperism, as Illustrated in the 'Jukes' Family," *Proceedings of the National Conference on Charities and Corrections* (1877), 81–95, expanded and revised as *The Jukes: A Study in Crime, Pauperism, and Heredity* (New York, 1887), and HENRY HERBERT GODDARD, *The Kallikak Family: A Study in the Heredity of Feeble-Mindedness* (New York, 1912). The eugenics movement, to which these studies by Dugdale and Goddard provided ammunition, has been well researched. The best introduction remains MARK HALLER's general survey, *Eugenics: Hereditarian Attitudes in American Thought* (New Brunswick, N. J., 1963). HALLER and RUDOLPH VECOLI, "Sterilization: A Progressive Measure?," *Wisconsin Magazine of History,* XLIII (Spring, 1960), 190–202, outline the politics of positive and negative eugenics. Recently, historians of science and medicine have examined the changes in genetics, anthropological theory, and the biological sciences which first encouraged, and then discouraged, the acceptance of hereditarian doctrine among professional scientists. HAMILTON CRAVENS, "American Scientists and the Heredity-Environment Controversy, 1883–1940" (Unpublished Dissertation, University of Iowa, 1969), is the most elaborate discussion. Drawing on Cravens' work, KENNETH LUDMERER has treated the history of genetics more generally in *Genetics and American Society: An Historical Appraisal* (Baltimore, 1972). Evolutionary theory in the late nineteenth century was important to the eugenics movement, especially as it was applied to specific racial and ethnic groups. The best discussion can be found in JOHN S. HALLER, *Outcasts from Evolution: Scientific Attitudes of Racial Inferiority, 1859–1900* (Urbana, Ill., 1971). An excellent discussion of hereditarianism in nineteenth-century America is CHARLES S. ROSENBERG, "The Bitter Fruit: Heredity, Disease, and Social Thought in Nineteenth-Century America," *Perspectives in American History,* VIII (1974), 189–235.

Experts and professionals have played an increasingly important role in American society since 1910; their influence and the public's acceptance of the legitimacy of expertise can be seen in LEONARD WHITE, *Trends in Public Adminis-*

tration (New York, 1933); BARRY DEAN KARL, "Presidential Planning and Social Science Research: Mr. Hoover's Experts," in *Perspectives in American History*, III (1969), 347–409, and *Executive Reorganization and Reform in the New Deal: The Genesis of Administrative Management, 1900–1939* (Cambridge, Mass., 1963), are both excellent studies; RICHARD HOFSTADTER, *Anti-Intellectualism in American Life* (New York, 1963), Part III, and ROBERT H. WIEBE, *The Segmented Society: An Introduction to the Meaning of America* (New York, 1975), offer brilliant observations about the American acceptance of expert advice.

American responses to urbane cosmopolitanism can be seen in several separate episodes. An excellent overview of the religious hostilities is DAVID REIMERS, "Protestantism's Response to Social Change: 1890–1930," in FREDERICK C. JAHER, ed., *The Age of Industrialism in America: Essays in Social Structure and Cultural Values* (New York, 1968), 364–383, which should be supplemented with PAUL CARTER, "The Fundamentalist Defense of the Faith," in JOHN BRAEMAN et al., eds., *Change and Continuity in America: The 1920s*, 179–214. GILMAN M. OSTRANDER, "The Revolution in Morals," *ibid.*, 323–350, is also useful. The Scopes trial is covered thoroughly in RAY GINGER, *Six Days or Forever?: Tennessee v. John Scopes* (Boston, 1958), and LAWRENCE W. LEVINE, *Defender of the Faith, William Jennings Bryan: The Last Decade, 1915–1925* (New York, 1965), chapter 9. DON KIRSCHENER, *City and Country: Rural Responses to Urbanization in the 1920s* (Westport, Conn., 1970), opens a topic that requires much more research. Immigration restriction, as a topic, has been dominated by JOHN HIGHAM, *Strangers in the Land: Patterns of American Nativism, 1860–1925* (New York, 1955). HOWARD K. BEALE collected information on thousands of examples of community reaction to a number of facets of "modern" culture in *Are American Teachers Free? Analysis of Restraints upon the Freedom of Teaching in American Schools* (New York, 1936).

The educational involvement of the Ku Klux Klan in the twentieth century is the topic of DAVID TYACK, "The Perils of Pluralism: The Background of the Pierce Case," *American Historical Review*, LXXIV (October, 1968), 74–98. The larger significance of the Klan and the best introduction to its urban membership can be found in KENNETH T. JACKSON, *The Ku Klux Klan in the City, 1915–1930* (New York, 1967), and DAVID M. CHALMERS, *Hooded Americanism: The First Century of the Ku Klux Klan* (Garden City, N. Y., 1965). An excellent essay on the Klan in the 1920s is ROBERT COATS MILLER, "The Ku Klux Klan," in JOHN BRAEMAN et al., eds., *Change and Continuity in America: The 1920s*, 215–256.

The Prohibition movement has attracted widespread historical interest. Our discussion has drawn most heavily on the work of JOSEPH R. GUSFIELD, because his interpretation of the tensions surrounding the status concerns of the middle class offers much to the history of education. For an illuminating and persuasive application of Gusfield's work to another aspect of educational history, see DAVID TYACK's forthcoming work on the history of compulsory schooling. GUSFIELD's *Symbolic Crusade: Status, Politics, and the American Temperance Movement* (Urbana, Ill., 1963), should be supplemented with his article, "Prohibition: The Impact of Political Utopianism," in JOHN BRAEMAN et al., eds., *Change and Continuity in America: The 1920s*, 257–308. Also useful are JAMES H. TIMBERLAKE, *Prohibition and the Progressive Movement, 1900–1920*

(Cambridge, Mass., 1963), ANDREW SINCLAIR, *Prohibition: The Era of Excess* (New York, 1962), and JOHN C. BURNHAM, "New Perspectives on the Prohibition Experiment," *Journal of Social History,* II (1968), 51–68.

Our discussion of education during the 1930s relied heavily on RUSH WELTER, *Popular Education and Democratic Thought in America* (New York, 1962); the sociological work of ROBERT S. and HELEN M. LYND, *Middletown* (New York, 1929) and *Middletown in Transition* (New York, 1937); EDWARD KRUG, *Shaping of the American High School, 1920–1941;* JAMES SHIELDS' novel, *Just Plain Larnin'* (New York, 1934); AUGUST B. HOLLINGSHEAD, *Elmtown's Youth: The Impact of Social Classes on Adolescents* (New York, 1949); and W. LLOYD WARNER et al., *Democracy in Jonesville* (New York, 1949). New Deal policies and the public schools are examined specifically in Krug's study of the American high school, and several publications of the Educational Policies Commission: *Federal Activities in Education* (Washington, D. C., 1939), *The Purposes of Education in American Democracy* (Washington, D. C., 1938), *The Unique Function of Education in American Democracy* (Washington, D. C., 1937), and *Research Memorandum on Education in the Depression* (Social Science Research Council Bulletin, No. 28 [New York, 1937]).

Youth culture and juvenile criminality are best approached through the following sociological observations: a fascinating document of the pressures exerted by the juvenile peer group is the autobiographical study, *The Jack-Roller: A Delinquent Boy's Own Story* (Chicago, 1930), by CLIFFORD R. SHAW; DOROTHY CANFIELD FISHER, *Our Young Folks* (New York, 1943), and BEN LINDSEY and WAINRIGHT EVANS, *The Revolt of Modern Youth* (New York, 1925), are also excellent sources.

Educational radicalism in the thirties and the "reconstructionist" program are examined in C. A. BOWERS, *The Progressive Educator and the Depression: The Radical Years* (New York, 1969), and PAUL C. VIOLAS, "The Indoctrination Debate and the Great Depression," in CLARENCE KARIER et al., *Roots of Crisis* (Chicago, 1973), 148–162. The pivotal documents are representative of the trend in general. Most important are the three essays by GEORGE COUNTS collected and published as *Dare the School Build a New Social Order?* (New York, 1932). The details of the feuds within educational radicalism during the Depression can be followed in that reconstructionist forum, *The Social Frontier,* the first issue of which appeared in October, 1934.

The evolution of extracurricular activities can be followed in EDWARD KRUG, *Shaping of the American High School, 1920–1941,* and JOEL SPRING, *Education and the Rise of the Corporate State* (Boston, 1972).

The Progressive Education Association is treated in Part II of CREMIN'S *Transformation of the School.* As a national movement it is the subject of PATRICIA A. GRAHAM, *Progressive Education: From Arcady to Academe—A History of the Progressive Education Association, 1919–1955* (New York, 1967).

Changes in the reputation and image of businessmen after 1900 that followed changes in the production and distribution of goods, and the effort businessmen made to affect their reputation and image, can be seen most clearly in the following: LOREN BARITZ, *The Servants of Power: A History of the Use of Social*

Science in American Industry (Middletown, Conn., 1960), THOMAS C. COCHRAN, *Business in American Life: A History* (New York, 1972), Part IV, JAMES WEINSTEIN, *The Corporate Ideal in the Liberal State, 1900–1918* (Boston, 1968), JOEL SPRING, *Education and the Rise of the Corporate State* (Boston, 1972), MILTON DERBER, "The Idea of Industrial Democracy in America, 1915–1935," *Labor History,* VIII (Winter, 1967), 3–29, MORRELL HEALD, *The Social Responsibilities of Business: Company and Community, 1900–1960* (Cleveland, 1970), SIGMUND DIAMOND, *The Reputation of the American Businessman* (Cambridge, Mass., 1955), DONALD MEYER, *The Positive Thinkers* (New York, 1965), and JOHN G. CAWELTI, *Apostles of the Self-Made Man: Changing Concepts of Success in America* (Chicago, 1965).

PART V

Redefining Commonality, 1940–1975

CHAPTER 13

The Reaction Against Progressivism, 1941–1960

SCHOOLING IN THE UNITED STATES UNDERWENT A VAST CHANGE AFTER World War II. Society let it be known that it expected schools to accomplish certain social tasks which had never been expected of them or which had been clearly subordinate or even rhetorical parts of their earlier mission. This reform movement in education was equal in intensity (it is too early to know whether it has had equivalent results) to the reform movement in the first two decades of this century. Like that earlier movement, it was initiated not by educators but by others making demands that educators were not initially ready to fulfill. In the first instance, the outsiders consisted of college professors, people engaged in maintaining America's world hegemony during the cold war, and middle- and upper-middle-class parents interested in college preparatory schooling for their children. They demanded a return to the academic emphasis that had supposedly characterized schools before the advent of modernism, or progressivism, early in the century. In a later instance, the pressure came from first the blacks and then from other ethnic and racial groups among the poor, and their supporters throughout the society, who demanded that schools teach them successfully the educational skills necessary to compete on equal terms with more privileged groups—in short, that the schools offer compensatory education so good that it would enable these people to achieve economic and social equality despite the handicaps of their initial social situation. Indeed, the demands made on schools in the

401

fifties and sixties began to seem so extravagant to some in the early seventies that it became quite fashionable to emphasize education's limited power to effect changes in the social structure. In this chapter we will deal with the demands for "a return to academic standards" in the schools; in the next, with the demands for equality through the schools—demands, it should be noted despite the chapter division, that were not unconnected to those of the 1950s.

I

American schoolmen emerged from the pressures of World War II in much the same mood and with many of the same ideas that had characterized their work in the thirties. Although they had participated in the total involvement of the war—running trade training schools around the clock which offered brief training courses in defense industry skills, accelerating the educational pace to enable boys to get into uniform faster—and saw the problem of unemployed superfluous youth which had plagued them through the thirties disappear overnight, schoolmen seemed fully to expect those or similar conditions to reappear after the war and planned accordingly. As we have seen, the glamour had vanished from the type of vocational education so respected in the teens and twenties. More and more people realized that most industrial jobs required nothing more than a few hours or a few weeks of preparation and that a two- to four-year vocational course was a waste of time. College preparation, on the other hand, appeared peripheral to the major problems of educating adolescents. Since most would not attend college (schoolmen seem to have been unprepared for the tremendous growth in colleges after 1950), they should not be saddled with a college preparatory course in high school. This, of course, had been good doctrine since the turn of the century. Increasingly, in the thirties and then after the war, schoolmen focused on those for whom they considered neither college preparation nor vocational education appropriate.

Essentially, the educators' point of view seems to have been a negative one. They saw themselves and their schools, especially the high schools, as primarily custodial institutions which kept kids off the labor market and kept them busy because, in the words of a much earlier generation, idle hands did the devil's work. Demands that every young adult between 18 and 21 should spend time in school under adult supervision and proposals for CCC-like work camps surfaced in the late thirties and again after the war as part of this promise by schoolmen to elaborate the custodial function of their institutions in order to protect society from the sort of social unrest which had been threatened by idle youths in both the United States and Europe during the thirties.

Educators tried, of course, to put a positive face on their proposals. They were not simply offering to incarcerate youngsters until there was room for them in the labor market. Schoolmen pledged to prepare them for life. But in this context "life" referred less to earning a living and more to areas of concern like family, childrearing, spending habits, and leisure-time activity. In these claims, educators were elaborating a tradition that had begun with the advent of the mass high school. The Seven Cardinal Principles of 1918 assumed the duties of every well-rounded high school to include preparation in family living and worthy use of leisure. As schools emphasized the development of personality and social skills during the twenties and thirties, these areas of school responsibility grew more prominent. But the "life adjustment" movement of the forties and early fifties saw these responsibilities take on a new urgency that came to dominate the thinking of the schoolmen.

Schools focused on teaching personal relations and the strategies of everyday living rather than academic or vocational skills. In 1938 the Educational Policies Commission, created in 1935 by the NEA and its Department of Superintendence to study and pronounce upon the proper social role for the schools, boiled "The Purposes of Education in American Democracy" down to four: self-realization, human relations, civic efficiency, and economic competence. The members of the commission apparently regarded this as an amplification of the Cardinal Principles; the direction of amplification is clear in a skit presented to the American Association of School Administrators in 1940, and reported by Edward Krug.[1] Eighty-five local high school students acted out the four purposes. Economic competence was presented "thru the adventures of Fay and Bob, just graduated and deeply in love, who face life haunted by nightmares of employers, advertisers, and loan sharks. But education comes to their aid, and the scene ends optimistically and tunefully." Economic competence no longer meant how to do a job, but how to get and hold one, how to get along with employers and fellow workers, and how to spend one's earnings as wisely as possible.

This trend culminated in the work of the Commission on Life Adjustment Education for Youth, established through the Office of Education in 1946 in response to demands of schoolmen committed to developing a rationale for the high school's custodial function. Charles Prosser, one of the leading advocates of vocational education since 1910, had suggested the commission's function a year earlier. He reminded his audience that vocational schools would prepare approximately 20 percent of youth for "desirable skilled occupations" and that the academic high school would equip another 20 percent for college entrance. Programs

[1] Edward Krug, *The Shaping of the American High School: II, 1920–1941* (Madison, Wis., 1972), 249, 253–254.

already existed for these two groups. However, he continued, "we do not believe that the remaining 60 percent of our youth of secondary school age will receive the life adjustment training they need and to which they are entitled as American citizens—unless and until the administrators of public education with the assistance of the vocational education leaders formulate a similar program for this group."[2] The commission recommended that programs for this 60 percent emphasize physical, mental, and emotional health, help youth resolve both present adolescent problems and anticipated adult ones, provide work experience that would teach industrious habits rather than specific job skills, and develop activity skills that could lead to personal achievement and satisfaction during one's leisure time. The commission made major reports in 1951 and 1954 and speeded the adoption of life adjustment training programs in thousands of schools throughout the land. Life adjustment became the symbol of modern education, the embodiment of the progressive reforms of the previous four decades (however much it may have distorted the meaning of those reforms). As such, it became the image of modernism against which lay critics reacted so vigorously after 1950. We must note carefully the underlying theme of life adjustment: that a majority of young people were destined for such a marginal place in the American economy and the American power structure that the schools had no real role in preparing them either for productive work or productive leadership and, rather, should seek to prepare them to garner whatever personal satisfaction they could during their lives. The primary thrust of innovation in schooling in this period, then, was directed toward the marginal rather than toward those who promised to assume a major productive or leadership role in the society. Reformers would attack that set of priorities most bitterly.

II

A torrential volley of criticism of the public schools as they were—which meant censure of what the critics thought was modern and progressive in the schools—began around 1950. Mortimer Smith published *And Madly Teach* in 1949; Bernard Bell's *Crisis in Education* appeared the same year. In 1953 a group of books summarized several years of journal criticism: Albert Lynd's *Quackery in the Public Schools,* Arthur Bestor's *Educational Wastelands,* Robert Hutchin's *The Conflict in Education.* In 1954 Smith published *The Diminished Mind,* and Hyman G. Rickover's *Education and Freedom* appeared in 1959. The gentlest, and partly for that reason the most influential, of the critics of progressive education was James

[2] U.S. Office of Education, *Life Adjustment Education for Every Youth* (Washington, D.C., n.d.), 15; quoted in Lawrence Cremin, *The Transformation of the School* (New York, 1961), 334.

Bryant Conant. His *American High School Today* (1958) and *The Education of American Teachers* (1963) chided the educational profession but also proposed reforms that did not require the kind of basic reorientation called for by some of the rougher critics.

The critics, although very different from each other, agreed on a number of points. They all criticized what they called the aimlessness of public education. Progressive reforms had given too much weight to adjustment, to encouraging kids to pursue their own interests, to social activities, to personality development, and to the project method which watered down the basic academic or disciplinary skills. The schools, in short, were not exacting enough because they neglected the important, academic, intellectual, and difficult subjects. Some called the typical modern school more a circus than an academic institution. All called for a return to the basics—to more grammar, more mathematics and more required work in algebra and trigonometry, more reading of classical literature, more work in languages, more history and less civics. Established in 1956 in response to the prodding of Bestor and Mortimer Smith, the Council on Basic Education advocated the philosophy that "schools exist to provide the essential skills of language, numbers, and orderly thought, and to transmit in a reasoned pattern the intellectual, moral, and aesthetic heritage of civilized man."[3] The tone of the criticisms and proposals for reform implied support for the concept of mental discipline—that a return to the basic academic subjects and hard drill and practice would exercise the students' minds and thus cultivate the "ability to think." Implicitly, they supported the transfer theory of training* —which Thorndike had thought he had discredited years earlier.

Virtually all of the critics indicted the professional educational establishment and its teacher training and teacher certification processes. Lynd argued that the profession had adopted a jargon with which to mystify laymen and to prevent them from interfering with the profession's management of the schools. Many noted that schools of education were the weakest units in higher education, with poor students and soft courses often devoid of intellectual content. Teacher training institutions put far too much emphasis on training teachers how to teach and far too little on training them what to teach. Meanwhile, the profession had accumulated enough power to organize certification requirements for teachers in such a way that only those who had taken many "soft" education courses could get jobs teaching in the schools while people far better prepared in the basic disciplines (and thus supposedly more qualified to teach those disciplines) were excluded. Some did not hesitate to see in

[3] *The Main Job of the Schools* (Washington, D.C., n.d.), quoted in Cremin, *ibid.*, 346n.

* If a student learned to think by studying language or trigonometry, he would then be prepared to transfer those thinking skills to any subject or problem presented to him in later life.

these developments evidence of a conspiracy among teachers' colleges and their faculties to subvert the academic or intellectual mission of the public schools. Nor was it difficult to connect, if ever so subtly, the social radicalism evinced by a man like Counts at Teachers College with the communist conspiracy so feared in the 1950s. The connection was even clearer when critics noted the "fact" that the schools, in their concern for life adjustment, had failed to produce scientifically trained manpower to help America vanquish its cold war enemies. At any rate, the villains in the piece were the teacher trainers and the educational theorists and researchers who produced the jargon, the textbooks for teacher training, and the watered-down curricula of the schools. In short, the critics of the era mounted the same kind of full-scale attack on the educational establishment that had shaken the classical, traditional educators in the Progressive era. As Lawrence Cremin has pointed out, the criticisms had come full circle—turn-of-the-century critics had summoned a new group of scientific professionals to take control of education away from the traditionalists and direct it toward new goals; those in the fifties attacked that very group of professionals and demanded that education be returned to the control of those most competent in the intellectual disciplines.

The critics of the fifties were not alike, however, in their prescriptions for an adequate public educational system. All sought trained minds but were divided over what goals such training was to serve. The critics ranged, in the terms developed by Merle Borrowman and Charles Burgess, across a spectrum from those with "humanistic" goals to those with "efficiency" ones. The humanists—including Bestor and Smith, for example—rejected Dewey's pragmatism which they contended justified the schools' emphasis on utilitarian, functional, immediately useful activity. They cited permanent values which transcended the immediate worldly functions and claimed that the schools owed their students a relationship with these values through instruction in history (both Bestor and Smith were historians), philosophy, and even religion.

Although these critics are often remembered as holding the public schools responsible for graduating students inadequately prepared for college, they claimed to be equally concerned with those for whom high school was a terminal institution. That student, in particular, needed more than training in good grooming, in developing saleable skills, or in spending money. He required instead, in Smith's words, "an education that will enable him to live in the world as an intelligent citizen, and . . . that will provide him with some inner resources so that he can live with himself without being swept along by the currents of mass superstition and mass custom."[4] The liberal arts could, they thought, transmit

---

[4] Mortimer Smith, ed., *The Public Schools in Crisis: Some Critical Essays* (Chicago, 1956), 7.

such a sense of values. They urged an education that produced trained minds and, more importantly, that produced independent, intellectually self-sufficient people with a firm sense of values.

At the other end of the scale were James B. Conant and Admiral Rickover, both concerned about the need for trained (especially scientifically trained) minds for the country's scientific and defense establishments. These men valued the liberal arts—the appreciation of art and literature. But it was far more important to them to have youth trained to handle scientific concepts and higher math, minds trained to do work desperately needed by a technological society. This concern with efficiency links them with those who held the schools responsible for vocational efficiency in the earlier part of the century; America in 1950 needed scientists as in 1900 it had needed skilled craftsmen.[5] Admiral Rickover, who created and supervised the building of the first nuclear submarines, is a good example. In public speeches and in frequent testimony before eager congressmen, he began his caustic review of the deficiencies of modern public education with a story of how hard it had been for him to assemble competent development and production teams for the building of the *Nautilus*. The American school system had not turned out enough capable scientists and engineers. Colleges were not at fault, he contended, for they had only high school graduates with which to work. American secondary education, because of the aimless nature of its curriculum and its failure to challenge students with serious problems of math and science, was responsible for the country's inability to produce capable scientists and engineers. Good teaching in the high school could encourage the capable into those needed fields and could accelerate their training so that they could master needed skills at a reasonable age. Manpower was wasted—something unaffordable in an era of cold war and technological competition. Rickover's early warnings were confirmed by the U.S.S.R.'s successful launching of the first satellite in 1957—proof positive, doomsayers claimed, that the dreaded Russians were technologically superior to the United States. Educational critics quickly pointed out that Sputnik did not reveal any fundamental flaw in the American system or the American character, but simply the costs of an educational system that neglected intellectual training. One should realize, however, that the criticisms of the progressive public schools antedated the Sputnik crisis of confidence by nearly a decade and that the concern with scientific and technical training existed long before America's deficiencies were so dramatically exposed.

The developing interest of James Bryant Conant in American public education makes this point very clearly. Since Conant so well represents

[5] Merle Borrowman and Charles Burgess, *What Doctrines to Embrace?: Studies in the History of American Education* (Glenview, Ill., 1969), chapter 5.

the efficiency concerns of the educational critics, since those concerns appear to have been most influential in changing American schooling patterns, and since Conant was himself the most influential of the critics, we can profitably examine his views in detail. Conant, after serving as a major in the Chemical Warfare Service in World War I and briefly manufacturing explosives in the postwar years, returned to Harvard, where he had earned his Ph.D. in chemistry at age 23. He rose quickly at Harvard, became department chairman at age 38, and two years later, in 1933, was inaugurated president. While president of Harvard he was one of the earliest to recommend United States preparedness for possible war with the Axis Powers; during the war he was instrumental in organizing scientific and engineering talent in support of the war effort; he played an important role in facilitating work on the atomic bomb; he helped establish the National Science Foundation; and he advised the government on instituting the military draft and establishing national manpower objectives through it. He was also becoming involved as a critic of modern education. He mounted the platform as spokesman for educational standards always available to the president of Harvard; he moved on to join the Educational Policies Commission in the early forties, chaired it for a time, and later chaired the American Council of Education. In the late fifties he received several substantial grants from the Carnegie Foundation to study the American high school and later American teacher training institutions and to disseminate his findings to the nation.

From these platforms Conant made two main arguments for the central role of education in the American system. First, taking a Jeffersonian stance, he claimed that the public schools should identify each generation's intellectual elite and insure that that elite was well prepared educationally to assume positions of political and technological leadership. Schools functioning in this manner would guarantee the continuation of the social fluidity which Americans felt had characterized their society. This fluidity, Conant contended, did not mean that at any given time there would be no differentiations in status or power but, rather, that distinctions were not passed from generation to generation. Maintenance of such classlessness depended on rearranging the makeup of social classes at the passing of each generation. Here the schools, by testing and sorting each generation of youngsters to identify the intellectually talented, could play a vital role. Like his revered Jefferson, Conant called for an intellectual meritocracy with a vengance. Unlike Jefferson, Conant lived in an era when such ideas were likely to be taken seriously. Social leaders were those individuals who merited such position and responsibility on the basis of their intelligence; it was the school's job to select those who had such merit. This formula allowed Conant to maintain an elitist perspective for himself and his university while still believing in the basic classlessness and fluidity of his society. Indeed, he first enunciated this position in proposing that Harvard initiate a special scholarship program for promising youths from regions outside New England and from social classes seldom represented at the university. In this way Harvard could better assume its responsibility for sponsoring a meritocratic elite and thereby help create a national community of the intellectually meritorious. Conant seemed to harken back to proposals for a national university, and to Jefferson's ideal of a single university atop a pyramidal educational structure where the graduates of all the top colleges could gather and form a community.

In the thirties Conant saw his proposals for employing the schools to identify and rake out each new generation's elite as a mechanism for keeping youngsters from joining alien movements such as fascism or communism, and for preventing them from being alienated from a society in which there were not enough jobs. Conant argued that society through its schools should hold out to each young person the chance to become a member of the new elite. Such an offer would convince them that the American system was best. Alienation could not take root if all realized that they had the opportunity to prove themselves. After the war Conant expanded these claims for the importance of the public school as symbol and guarantor of the democratic American way. By then he was seeking, not the loyalty of young adults at home, but the attention and support of the nonaligned world in the ideological struggle between the United States and the forces of communism. For Conant, the redistributive role played by the public school became one important proof of American superiority.

It is crucial to note how significant a step Conant had taken here. Most educators of the late thirties and forties were concerned with the 60 percent preparing neither for college nor for skilled jobs; they judged the school's most important function to be creating a viable educational experience for the average child. Conant shifted the focus entirely. Schools should concentrate on the best; they should abandon their custodial role in favor of sorting the children out and identifying those capable of advance, challenging them to their fullest potential to prepare them for possible advancement into the elite. The schoolmen of the period felt it "democratic" to be concerned with the poorer student, with the average or mass student. Conant made it permissible to concentrate on the better students without feeling that one was deserting democratic tenets. He was disturbed that he might be interpreted to mean that the schools should focus exclusively on those with potential and ignore the others and sought desperately for ways that schools could make the "also-rans"—those without sufficient intellectual merit—useful to society. He wrote a good deal of unconvincing rhetoric to the effect that the social prestige attached to those with college educations was unwarranted because a man should not receive prestige just because his particular occupation required a longer period of schooling. To relieve this problem Conant advocated community junior colleges which would offer "advanced training" in a great variety of general, technical, and vocational fields. These colleges, he hoped rather wistfully, would help equalize social status among the occupations as more and more occupations required "college" training for entrance. Conant was a man genuinely concerned with the plight of the losers in the meritocratic society, as his later volume, *Slums and Suburbs* (1960), makes clear. But many of the movements that he initiated in the schools after World War II tended to ignore the plight of those judged as lacking intellectual merit in order to focus directly on the "best" students.

Obviously, Conant's Jeffersonian view of the school's function in a democracy pointed toward such a focus, but even more important in this regard was his oft-repeated concern for the production of highly trained manpower for the United States. As organizer of manpower for the war effort, Conant experienced none of that sense of there being too many people for the work that needed doing, which had gripped many social critics and educators before the war. He found that highly trained, competent people were in short supply during the war and expected them to be in short supply afterward. Because schools no longer had to keep youngsters off the labor market, he saw no usefulness in the prewar educational programs designed for just such a purpose. There were many positions for which to prepare men. Society had neglected many things and this work now had to be done. He shared much of the sense of urgency that had marked the vocational education leaders around the time of World War I; to maintain the nation's powers the schools had to prepare young people to work hard. Conant brought the language of efficiency back into education. "In a competitive world, society must indicate the opportunities that are open to those of varying talents. With a maximum of persuasion and a minimum of compulsion, we can, in education as in public health, direct the lives of many to the better advantage of both the individual and the state."[6] In *The American High School Today* he argued that it was the social duty of every child with intellectual potential to enroll only in the challenging courses which would prepare him for leadership, and to shun courses which were soft or irrelevant to that preparation. Educational thought in the thirties and in the later life adjustment movement had concentrated on developing programs addressed to the child's supposed needs or to that which the youngster would find enjoyable. Conant sought to reverse this emphasis and urged school programs tailored to social needs. For him, the nation's needs were largely in the fields of science and engineering—rather than

[6] James B. Conant, "The University and a Free Society," *School and Society,* LIII (25 January, 1941), 101.

in the skilled trades, as they had been for efficiency spokesmen of the earlier era. These needs required American schools to emphasize the basic skills—in mathematics, in science, in foreign languages, and in communication. Conant angrily reported that many capable students could not even get four years of math or science or language in their high schools. He called for all high schools to offer a curriculum which would provide, at minimum for their better students, full coverage of the basic areas. He thought the curriculum should be enriched for the best students by including elementary college work in the high school, perhaps under the aegis of the Advanced Placement Program. He firmly believed that a more challenging high school program in math and the sciences would recuit more youngsters to pursue those fields in college, that one cause of America's dearth of scientific manpower was that schools held potentially valuable people back until it was too late for them to prepare for such careers.

But Conant did not rely simply on the power of well-taught and challenging subjects to attract youngsters to the most socially useful fields. Like his predecessors in the efficiency movement, he recommended an intensified guidance system* which would identify the talented and "persuade" them to do their social duty by fulfilling their potential. Such a system would also help those with lesser talent find their appropriate niche in the occupational structure as early as possible, while wasting as little effort as practicable and avoiding unrealistic expectations. Conant was quite disturbed that, because social status depended so much on educational level, many wished to go on to college who were unsuited for occupational roles requiring a college education. He was particularly concerned that parents would push their children into college in order to maintain for their children the social status the parents merited but which the children might not be capable of earning for themselves. A guidance system that directed children to areas dictated by their merit would insure the redistributive effects of the educational system that Conant so valued. A successful guidance system, he hoped, would persuade children to choose the appropriate path, thus obviating any need to compel people to stay where they belonged. In this way the nation could preserve maximum individual freedom with maximum rationality and meritocracy. America could prepare itself to compete against totalitarianism without dictating to its citizens the roles they should play.

* As Borrowman and Burgess have pointed out, Conant sought a guidance system quite like that developed before 1920. He did not wish to expand the guidance system that existed in the forties which stressed counseling young people about their personal adjustments and emotional problems. Although he made guidance a central part of his scheme, his proposals seem to have affected that part of the educational establishment far less than any other part.

Although critical of the educational profession, Conant displayed great sympathy for its problems and support for some of the goals it had set for itself. Unlike some of the other critics, he did not dismiss the need for democratic schooling as unimportant. While Rickover proposed that the United States model its school system on those of Britain or France by segregating the best students into elite institutions at an early age, Conant defended the comprehensive high school as a means of creating a necessary sense of community across classes. More important, his criticisms extended an invitation to educators to mend their ways and to step into a role that made them more important and crucial to attaining national goals than they had been since World War I. In this way Conant also suggested a strategy through which educators could shift away from the localistic emphasis of the interwar years. He told educators that schools adopting his proposals would become responsible for maintaining the equality of opportunity which was basic to democracy and for channeling young people into future roles in a way that would make the nation strong. This seemed a far cry from the tired rhetoric of social learning and custodial function that the educational profession recited after the war. Conant developed quite a large following among professional educators and his combination of gentle criticism and support made the educational profession far more willing to change than it would have been had someone of his diplomatic skills not been present. Educators would probably have resisted proposals for change much more vigorously, even desperately, had they been couched only in the antiprofessional, conspiratorial, accusatory phrases of men like Bestor and Rickover. Conant served as a kind of mediator between those critics, and an ever widening public supportive of those criticisms, and the educational profession. He proposed ways in which the educators could satisfy their critics without admitting a great deal of error, while maintaining control of the educational processes, and while increasing their sense of worth because they played a vital function in the nation. Conant's achievement made possible the rapid spread of reform after 1950.

III

The influence of Conant and the other critics and their many, many allies within and without the educational profession was widespread. It was evident in three ways. First, the fifties and sixties saw a major effort to revamp school curricula in such a way as to stress the academic disciplines and to redefine these disciplines as methods of thinking rather than as bodies of fact. Not surprisingly, given the concerns voiced by men like Conant and Rickover, the curriculum revision movement began in physics (1956) and mathematics (1958). Planning groups of university professors in education and in the subject fields and school teachers, organized in response to their sense that what was then being taught in the schools under the guise of math and science, was grossly inferior. These groups sought to replace general or applied science with "real" physics, math, or biology. They had a distinctly college preparatory focus and sought to make the teaching of math and physics reflect the most recent models of interpretation—that is, Einstein's relativity rather than Newton's mechanics—and introduce youngsters at an early age to the methods of thought employed by skilled researchers in those fields—thus, little children were taught set theory and probability. The curriculum developers wished to emphasize that disciplines were not finished bodies of information but changed and grew as a result of an ongoing process of inquiry. To master a discipline was to master its way of thought. There was no point, they argued, in teaching children a lot of information about math or physics that would be obsolete by the time they grew up. The process of thinking, of knowing, of inquiry—one of the period's most fashionable, if least understood, terms—was to be taught so that as a student matured he would know how to approach those problems which had not yet existed when he had been a student. A curriculum that prepared youngsters in this fashion was certainly a better way to recruit and to train needed scientific manpower than was the older, "modern" way of teaching snippets of each discipline as it related to a specific project or organizing theme for the year. Teaching physics as physicists approached it would surely contribute to the nation's manpower needs far more efficiently than teaching about physics' applications to "the problems of life."

Curriculum revision of this kind occurred in math, physics, biology, chemistry, and social science; the so-called inquiry method spread into almost every field taught in the public schools. Curriculum reform reached into both the elementary and the high schools. These projects sprang not from the needs of any particular school system or from any particular locale but were rather national in scope, designed to serve the nation's needs and financed by the federal government or the great foundations. This wave of curriculum revision marked a great change from the habits of the previous decades. Earlier revisions had been local or at most statewide efforts to create curricula that met the needs of a particular community. These efforts rested on the assumption that life conditions varied from community to community enough to require localized curricula to prepare youth properly for adulthood, and on the assumption, which the later reformers did not dispute, that the more involved people on the local level became with curriculum revision, the more likely it was that the revisions would be implemented.

The curriculum revision projects of the fifties and sixties took a long time to complete, as the project leaders had first to agree on their field's most important methods of inquiry and then search out ways of making those methods concrete enough to be taught to all age levels. The project then developed an extensive battery of teaching materials—texts, films, laboratory kits, and simulation games—tried them out in various schools, and revised them accordingly. The projects also faced the problem of training teachers who had learned physics or math in the old way to handle and teach the new materials correctly. Teachers who had been taught that their role was to inculcate a body of fact relating to physics or biology had to be retrained to teach the inquiry method, where questions and problems were posed to encourage children to find answers for themselves. Although the curriculum reformers talked much about the possibilities of "teacher proof" curricula, all recognized that reform would stand or fall according to the teachers' ability to grasp the new focus of learning. The curriculum projects, therefore, were eager to establish and maintain various forms of teacher institutes, in-service training projects, and summer school training sessions to try to retool public school faculties. And, lastly, the projects sought to disseminate their materials widely—either through the project itself or by turning its products over to an experienced commercial publisher. Receptivity to the new curricula was highest in the elite suburban schools, but by the middle sixties the "new" math and the "new" physics and biology and social studies were widely spread throughout the American public school system. Spurred by the critics of progressivism and the support they had gathered among the public, the curriculum revisions had succeeded in a relatively short time in redefining what was "new" in American education.

The second major influence of the educational critics of the fifties was their impact on the pattern of financing public education. By elevating the national purposes of schooling above local purposes and by stressing the school's relation to national defense, the critics and their supporters made the federal government a natural source of financial support for educational improvement. The federal government responded to this newly felt responsibility first through the National Science Foundation (which Conant was influential in creating) which directed millions of dollars to curriculum revision projects in the natural and social sciences and supported thousands of teacher retraining institutes. More important, perhaps, was the National Defense Education Act in 1958, which symbolized explicitly the period's conviction that good education and strong defense were related and committed the federal government to support many different educational efforts—including scholarships for students in the sciences and engineering, the development of university programs in those fields as well as in those areas of foreign language and social science that prepared students and researchers to know more about democracy's enemies, and upgrading public school programs in natural and social sciences. Federal financial support, coming as a bonus rather than as a substitute for local taxes, made manifest how important national politicians felt improved schools were to the national good.

The critics of education had major influence in a third area. They were in large part responsible for the growing popularity and influence of cognitive psychology, especially that which argued that children could learn complex intellectual skills at an early age. Obviously, the critics did not produce new ideas in the psychological community; behavioral science seldom invents new ideas to respond to current fashion. The beginnings of cognitive psychology and several descriptions of the early potential for learning had long been available in the literature but, until the critics were heard from, these points of view had been ignored, disbelieved, and/or rejected by those responsible for applying the discoveries of science to education. Researchers in a behavioral science pursue fruitfully a number of different ideas and thrusts simultaneously. These various ideas and thrusts may conflict with one another or they may simply point in different directions—as different researchers feel different areas are more important than others. But, in studying the influence of psychological ideas on an institution such as education, one is concerned not with all the ideas that may be extant at a given moment but with the ones which get through, as it were, to the educational institutions, which get taught in the schools of education, which inform textbook creation, and which form the base upon which guides to children's behavior are written for parents and teachers. Only those ideas that coincide with the prejudices of the society or with those of the educational establishment get taught or popularized and in turn shape the popular and educational attitudes which were at first receptive to them. In the behavioral sciences, unlike the natural sciences, proofs of the correctness of one's findings are seldom overwhelmingly convincing. Evidence in the behavioral sciences is almost always open to doubt, to qualification, to interpretation. Research into human behavior is simply not as definite as that in the natural realm and findings of behavioral science are seldom provable to the extent that they can overcome, at least in the short term, any popular prejudices against them. This is particularly true when, as is nearly always the case, there are conflicting findings. Thus, learning theorists and cognitive psychologists were saying in the thirties that little children of three or four could be taught to read without damage to their psyches and that such early training would truly accelerate their advancement in school. But popular and educational prejudice sided with the findings of other psychologists to the effect that children were not "ready" to read until they were six or six and one half, and that any attempt to teach a child to read before he was ready was just so much wasted motion. A child might, at great labor to himself and his teacher, learn to read but he would not use the skill until he was "ready"; at which point he could virtually teach himself to read in a few months because he "wanted to." Children learned better when they were interested, and interest most often developed according to natural processes rather than through the initiative of adults. This theory of learning was most influential in the twenties, thirties, and forties and accounts for some of what later critics termed the softness and slow pacing of "progressive" schools and those schools' emphasis on teaching to the child's interests. Furthermore, once committed to practices based on this learning theory, educators tended to listen almost exclusively to psychological theories that supported those practices.

The criticisms of the fifties enhanced the popular appeal of psychological findings that emphasized the very young child's ability and desire to learn complex skills. Such theories got a much more respectful hearing than formerly and received a great deal more support, institutional and financial, than they had in the previous decades. The critics suggested that the country was experiencing a crisis in trained intelligence about which something had to be done. The public then welcomed psychologists who promised that this crisis could be effectively eased by speeding up and deepening the learning process. These psychologists lent support to the criticisms that the schools were stifling the country's intellectual potential by holding children back. As attention, support, and interest in that kind of theory grew, more and more psychologists initiated studies of cognition and of ways to enhance it through the schools. Lee Cronbach, J. McVicker Hunt, and Jerome Bruner were just a few of the many who codified the new ideas and supervised their application. In sum, they argued that children could learn more than had been previously thought, they could learn it better, and, perhaps most important, they could learn it earlier. They claimed not only that there was no bar to early learning, but also that children possessed a natural curiosity and a desire for order and mastery driving them to try to comprehend the processes that underlay the academic disciplines and other rational modes of thought and communication. These claims discredited earlier strategies which instructed teachers to introduce the subject disciplines only indirectly by connecting them with extrinsic topics which might be interesting to the student—by, for example, teaching the physics of buoyancy through a project on boats which might appeal to student interest in boats. The newer view held that the child's natural curiosity about his universe motivated him to learn about physics qua physics. In view of this, psychologists urged schools to get on with the job of teaching the disciplines from the very beginning. An extreme, but at the same time widely influential, statement of this view appeared in Jerome Bruner's *The Process of Education* (1960): "Any subject can be taught effectively in some intellectually honest form to any child at any stage of development." Such a statement makes very clear the important influence that cognitive psychologists like Bruner had on inspiring the great curriculum projects' interest in teaching schoolchildren the same processes of inquiry and discovery that real scientists followed. The cognitive psychologists' ideas had wide influence in shifting popular attitudes toward the role of intellectual or cognitive stimulation in early childhood—the tremendous popularity of so-called "educational" toys is a case in point.

All in all, the fifties and sixties saw as profound a shift in thinking about education as had been seen at least since the Progressive era. The schools refocused on subject matter and on intellectual discipline. They became, once more, very interested in efficiency, although they defined it quite differently from their predecessors. Schooling returned to the center of the national effort and became the beneficiary of awesome amounts of money, now increasingly gathered and spent nationally. Educators turned to efforts at speeding up learning and at increasing the continuity between the earliest school experiences and those that followed. Educational critics from Bestor to Conant were influential in helping to turn schooling in these directions, but no handful of critics, however convincingly they wrote, could have turned the situation around by themselves. Their effectiveness resulted from their ability to articulate and mobilize a vast reservoir of public discontent with the schools. American society had changed enough since the 1930s to make many people very receptive to the critics' denunciation of the schooling popular in the thirties and forties and to their proposals for educational reform. As no definitive social history of a period so recent as the 1950s and 1960s yet exists, the remainder of this discussion must be somewhat speculative as we seek to identify some of the social developments which made possible this popular change in the thinking about mass schooling in the United States.

IV

One of the most important, and at the same time obvious, developments was the effect of the baby boom of the fifties and sixties on the schools. Even in the twenties, but especially in the depression conditions of the thirties, the United States experienced a very low birth rate—every thousand women aged 15 to 44 gave birth to about 118 live children in 1920, 89.2 in 1930, 75.8 in 1936, and 80 in 1940. With the growing prosperity brought on by the war and the boom which followed it, young people married and established households earlier and began to raise larger families than had their predecessors during the depression. Birth rates rose to 102 per thousand in 1946, 106.2 in 1950, and 118 in 1955. Economics is not the only explanation of the baby boom—the increased value placed on the idea of the family and an increasing child-centered-ness also explain some of it—but it was probably the most important determinant. The products of the baby boom began streaming into the first grade by the middle forties and became a flood by 1950, first in the lower grades and then in the high schools. The public school system of the United States suddenly found itself overtaxed. While the number of schoolchildren rose because of wartime and postwar conditions, these same conditions made the schools even less prepared to cope with the flood. Wartime economic mobilization meant that few new schools were built between 1940 and 1945. Thus the baby boom hit an antiquated and inadequate plant. Moreover, during the war and in the boom times that followed, large numbers of teachers left their profession for more lucra-tive jobs elsewhere in the economy. The demand for higher teachers' salaries contained in virtually all writings about education in the fifties, whether critical or supportive, was a recognition that, for probably the first and only time in American history, the schools had to compete with other institutions to recruit a labor force.

Thus by 1950 the products of the baby boom were streaming into a school system short on buildings and especially short on staff. The cus-todial rhetoric of the thirties and early forties no longer made any sense. A school system that could not find room for the children aged 5 to 16 could hardly contend that it should assume responsibility for occupying the time of, or adjusting to life, children aged 16 to 21. Keeping older kids off the labor market could at best be a minor task for an institution unable to find space and staff to teach the basic common skills to younger children. With the baby boom, the focus of educators and of laymen interested in education inevitably turned toward the lower grades and to the more traditional tasks of the school. There was no longer much interest in offering nontraditional, new, and extra services to older youth. (In the seventies and eighties, as the public school system experiences a shortage of regular students [due to declining birth rates], it will be interesting to see whether educators return to some of the custodial interests of the prebaby boom era as a means of utilizing overbuilt facili-ties and an abundant supply of teachers.) The flood of schoolchildren who had to be taught the basic common skills accounts in part also, we believe, for the renewed emphasis on efficiency, on getting the taxpayers' money's worth, that motivated educators and their critics alike in the fifties.*

---

* Merle Borrowman and Charles Burgess have pointed out an extremely suggestive relation between the ratio of dependency in American society (i.e., the percentage of the popula-tion below 18 and over 65 compared to the percentage of the population in the produc-tive years 18 to 65) and the shifting focus of educational effort from what they term "social productivity values" to what they call "consummatory values." When dependency is high, as it was during the Progressive era and during the fifties and sixties, educators and the public emphasize matters of efficiency, of training youngsters to move quickly into pro-ductive work. Emphasis is on social need, on making children quickly conform to the

Cold war propaganda and fears also helped convince Americans of the need for a more efficient and intellectually stimulating school system. Educational historians who cite it as the primary cause for the demise of progressivism make too much of the cold war. But we must recognize the cold war as a stimulator and powerful reinforcer of the attitudes which led to the changing educational focus of these years. The cold war maintained wartime concerns for manpower development, defense, and preparedness at a high pitch for two decades after the end of World War II. As the nature of warfare changed, the concept of preparedness altered accordingly. Wars would no longer be fought by traditional infantry, where the primary need was for cannon fodder, but required instead highly trained personnel to operate complicated and expensive machinery (a military technology invented and built by other brainy and highly skilled people). The public demanded and educators claimed that the schools should train youngsters to develop the kind of technological skills needed to defend the country. Futhermore, the cold war required the United States to compete on all fronts—military, scientific, economic, cultural. Almost any project could gain public support if it could be construed as helping the United States do something "better" than the communist bloc. Here again education was a pivotal effort. Schools must train scientists, engineers, and businessmen so that the United States could maintain its technological supremacy over the Russians or, after Sputnik, catch up with the USSR. A healthy technology stimulated the economy by "spinning off" ideas for ever newer consumer products to improve the "American standard of living"—proof positive in many eyes that the United States was better than the Soviet Union—and to keep the national economy, symbolized by the Gross National Product, larger and more robust than that of the Soviets. The exploitation and marketing of these technological breakthroughs required the cooperation of scientists, engineers, and businessmen. The latter, because they were working with such complicated material and technologies and needed to communicate so closely with highly intellectual scientists, had to be better trained.

The cold war also entailed a cultural, spiritual, and social battle with the Soviet Union in an effort to win over to democracy the nonaligned peoples of the world. It was popular to argue that the two superpowers were vying to win the allegiance of the other nations to either democracy or communism. Victory would not go to those who "conquered" the nonaligned people, but to those who demonstrated the superiority of their "way of life." American education was expected to play a vital role

---

values of the society and to understand that their duty is to contribute to that society. In periods of low dependency—when more workers support fewer non-workers—like the thirties and the seventies, there is more concern with nonproductive values, training for leisure, and home life. More emphasis falls on teaching appreciation of art and music, on personality development, and on training to ease psychological and emotional problems.

in proving that the American way was better. First of all, the American educational system was to prepare the agents of American culture to deal with these nonaligned and enemy countries. Since the cultural conflict required personnel who could speak the languages and understand the cultures of communist and non-Western peoples, educators were expected to help young people overcome traditional American parochialism or isolationism by stressing foreign languages and the study of foreign cultures—through history and social studies, literature and language. At the collegiate level, this emphasis culminated in foundation- and government-supported "foreign area study programs."

Second, and probably more important, the idea of cultural conflict and of the need to sell the American way to other nations led to a revitalized emphasis on the peculiar virtues of democratic mass schooling as practiced in the United States. Most attractive to foreigners was the system of free, universal, comprehensive schooling through the high school years and the increasing availability of a college education to a substantial portion of the population without formal career tracking such as that found in almost all other industrialized nations. Thus only in America, the salesmen argued, did every child have the chance to prove himself through the age of sixteen or beyond, and to reap, after he had proven himself, the advantages of a society that encouraged open social mobility. Only in America was there a commitment to rearranging the class structure every generation and to an educational system designed to fulfill this ideal. The schools' role as sustainer of Jeffersonian democracy, as Conant construed that ideology, was a major propaganda tool in the United States' fight against the Soviet bloc for the support of other countries.

The postwar era differed essentially from the previous decades in the attitude or spirit which pervaded the society. In the twenties and thirties American society was badly split between the values of an urban culture and the more traditional values of an earlier rural and small town culture, and during the Depression it was beset by a lassitude born of a despair about the possibility of improving either the economy or the society. Despite the sound and fury of the New Deal, the country was in a state of drift, seeking to shore up threatened institutions but not really knowing where it was heading or why. The postwar era was, in contrast, marked by a great display of purposefulness. Without adequately answering the questions of where or why, the society claimed to be going somewhere and doing so with rapidity and determination. The economy and the population grew enormously and the standard of living rose steadily. The nation had grown used to, if not completely happy with, urbanism and its attendant values. The cold war, in a way, became the focus of this purpose, so important and primary that it served to paper over, or seemed to answer, the questions of where and why, to resolve any lingering conflicts over rural and urban values. The nation's purpose was to maintain its premier status as the international leader in politics, war, economics, and culture, to maintain its world hegemony in the face of the growing threat of international communism. Since the country relied on science, technological skills, and trained brain power to achieve its purpose, schooling lay very near the center of society's attention.

There seem to have been other more subtle influences—about which the state of current research into the era allows us only to hypothesize. The society seemed to develop a sense of unified purpose in the face of the communist threat, but there was also an element of insecurity lying behind the prosperity and show of confidence in America's future. Much of the popularity of the educational changes of this era might be attributable to the efforts of Americans, especially middle-class Americans, to assuage their insecurity through securing the "best" schooling for their children. Signs of insecurity were everywhere. It was a wonderfully prosperous era—at least for those citizens to whom the media paid attention—but the memory of the Depression still haunted many; there seemed no way to get enough money to protect oneself from that kind of disaster, no way that the national economy could definitely insure continuing prosperity. For many the era was one of expanding opportunity and mobility, of making the long-awaited move out of the congested city to the suburban home with a white picket fence around its quarter acre. But much of the mobility seemed tenuous and acquiring the symbols of higher status strained the budget. Downward mobility was always possible—without the expected raise or promotion, or with the loss of a job. Nor did the rising members of the middle class usually accumulate the money or security to insure that they could pass their new-found status on to their children. Expanded opportunity also meant expanded competition and a potentially rapid change in relative status—if your chance to rise was greater, so was that of the person below you, and he might seize the chance to pass you by. There was no rest from the competition.

Furthermore, the era was unceasingly discomforted by the cold war and the threat of the "bomb." From the Berlin airlift of 1948 to the Cuban Missile Crisis of 1962, the cold war constantly threatened to turn hot. The bomb seemed so imminent that people built shelters in their suburban yards. For the first time in the twentieth century the prospect was real that the weapons of total war might be used on the United States; that Americans might suffer atomic devastation was deeply frightening, casting a shadow of insecurity over the suburban dream. Senator Joseph McCarthy, and the furor he raised through his accusations that dozens of communists had penetrated the State Department and other branches of the federal government, illustrated the national insecurity. The popularity of McCarthy's technique of attributing all the country's problems to the existence of spies and treasonous individuals who gnawed at American institutions from within, betrayed Americans' discomfiture at some aspects of their situation and their need to create an artificial national unity. Nonconformity and serious questioning of national norms, goals, or behavior were felt to be intolerable. Americans were not so secure in their recent prosperity and sense of national purpose to feel comfortable with dissent, with any questioning of social justice, the distribution of wealth, or foreign policy. Insecurity required assurance that America was the best country in the world; all criticism was rejected.

The people that appear to have felt this particular pattern of insecurity most keenly were suburbanites of the upper middle and middle classes. They sought schools that would push youngsters to their potential and prepare them for demanding colleges to protect their own children from much of this economic and social insecurity. In order to achieve those ends, however, they had to change the educational system rather drastically, and to do that they had to gain more control over their schools. As Nathan Glazer and others have pointed out, the first call for community control of the schools in this century was not voiced by inner city black communities in the late sixties. Rather, that first demand came from middle-class residents of the cities who voted for community control with their feet by moving to the suburb where they could exert far more direction over that smaller community's institutions—especially schools —than they could in the bureaucratized cities. The suburbs, which underwent vast expansion when prosperity accommodated the demand for new housing and new environments which had been pent up for fifteen years by depression and war, offered as one of their great attractions good schools and the chance for parents to take a real hand in controlling what happened in them.

With this rapid suburbanization went a groundswell of antiprofessionalism against the educationists, fed by the critics of education whose work we have reviewed. One of the fifties' most popular books on education, Lynd's *Quackery in the Public Schools,* grew out of a parent's experience as a school board member in a small Massachusetts town that was changing from a self-contained community into a bedroom suburb of Boston. Lynd viciously attacked the cant and jargon of the educationists. He deplored the training that the teachers had been forced to undergo in order to meet the requirements for certification written into law by powerful educationists in teachers colleges who sought to create a market for the training their teachers colleges offered. He laughed at the quality of the texts that the children used; and he bewailed the almost inarticulate, illiterate, uneducated students that the educators succeeded in graduating from the public schools. Lynd's charges were not new, even then, but what was interesting about his book was that he contended that a normal citizen like himself could do something to change all this by getting on the school board—at least in a small suburb—, learning about the system and then voting to change those things that needed change. There was no need to be mystified by the jargon of the educationists or to maintain a hands-off attitude toward the schools because the training of children was so complicated. People with a normal liberal arts or engineering degree or even a business degree were better trained than educationists were—Lynd and his fellow critics never tired of pointing out that those preparing to teach ranked lower on aptitude and achievement tests than any other group of college students. Well-educated parents knew as much if not more about kids and how to teach them than did the average teacher or principal. Parents should use that knowledge to change their schools and to give their kids a better deal. Lynd was not an average American citizen at the time—he was well educated, a professional writer and businessman, and lived in a community where his voice could be heard—but he was not untypical of the suburban middle class. Many were college- and often graduate school-trained professionals or managers living in fairly homogeneous suburbs where there was substantial agreement on the goals of good schooling and where parents exerted effective power over local institutions. Whatever their proportion in the general population, people of this kind provided the largest cadre of support for the changes in education during this period and exerted an influence at the "grass roots" level to see that changes were implemented.

It can also be useful to view the ferment of the fifties and sixties as another chapter in the continuing conflict between the liberal arts colleges and universities and the teachers colleges. Ever since they began to attack the Committee of Ten after 1900, teachers colleges and the educators they trained had been declaring themselves more and more independent from the colleges and the colleges' efforts to define public school curricula and standards of educational success. In the fifties the pendulum swung back. University scholars, not educators, dominated curriculum revision. The bulk of the criticism of the public schools came from college presidents, professors, or journalists very sympathetic to their views. They constantly drew invidious comparisons between themselves and the educationists. The university was the home of scientific research and advanced technological training—the great hopes of the United States in its drive to maintain its worldwide hegemony. Therefore, it was most capable of defining the goals of schooling. In the educational universe of this era the universities were the stars. They received the bulk of federal and foundation money. The primary goal of the public schools became to prepare students for success in the universities. Since educationists and their training institutions lay outside that scientific mainstream, engaging at best in a pseudoscience adorned with inpenetrable but essentially meaningless jargon, they had no skills in defining the proper education for those who would live in the nuclear age.

Or so it appeared to university people and to the middle-class suburban residents. University criticism of the public schools received respectful hearings from suburban residents whose social and economic insecurity made them especially determined that their children get into good colleges that would insure, or at least go far in the direction of insuring, their future in a technological society. As advanced education had been so crucial to the parents' achievement of suburban middle-class status, most were concerned that their children receive similar advantages with results at least as good. When university scholars argued that the public schools must change their ways in order to prepare youngsters adequately for college, suburban parents immediately demanded that their schools follow that advice.

The upper middle class found the advice to return to the subject matter disciplines and to the traditional intellectual values of schooling congenial in other ways as well. The public schools' continuing stress on education for community and for adjusting kids to the local life made no sense to this essentially transient population in the new suburbs. That focus fit better a population that was rooted in the same community for generations or at least decades. The suburban middle class displayed an entirely different pattern. Frequent moves from community to community came to signify success. One moved from city to suburb as a symbol of higher social status and most contemplated or dreamed of moving from their first suburban community to another one of larger homes and higher social status. Successful corporate managers moved around not only within a single metropolitan region but from region to region as they worked their way up the corporate hierarchy by apprenticing themselves in their company's far-flung branch operations. Remaining in the same place came to symbolize failure—having reached a dead end. These parents did not want education that stressed the virtues of the local community, that socialized the students primarily to that community, that urged the student to stay in the same place. The focus of education should be national—the same in Scarsdale, Shaker Heights, Winnetka, or Palo Alto. Thus, in the suburbs, schools turned from the community focus advocated by educators in the thirties and forties to a focus on national manpower needs, on the products of national curriculum revision projects, and on the entrance requirements of the better colleges, demonstrated in the College Entrance Examination Board tests. They eagerly sought advice from admissions officers in these institutions about the best combination of test scores, athletic prowess, and extracurricular activities that would secure a student's admission to these schools.

Advocates of a return to the basics also hoped that such a change would stimulate a resurgence of individualism in the United States. Suburbanites of the fifties and sixties are generally remembered as some of the most conformist and "other-directed" people that our nation has known. They all, reputation has it, wore gray flannel suits, carried identical attaché cases, bought ranch wagons, held neighborhood barbecues, and joined a church for social reasons. They were "organization men," more dependent upon the approval of others than on their personal achievements as a criterion of success. It is difficult to make historical comparisons about the degree of conformity or individualism among groups of people at different historical moments; the urge to conform and the urge to rebel both run deep and each individual follows his unique pattern in resolving those two conflicting pressures. Thus it is not so clear that the fifties were more conformist than earlier, or later, eras. What is clear, however, is that Americans worried more about the conformity and other-directedness displayed in their society than they had before.

One reason we remember the fifties as being conformist is that academics and the media were constantly bewailing that fact. Two of the era's most popular serious books were David Riesman's *The Lonely Crowd* (1950) and William H. Whyte's *The Organization Man* (1956), both of which lamented the loss of individualism in America and the attendant overemphasis on harmony and cooperation and growing dependence on the opinions of others to assess one's own success. The popularity of these books suggests that the reading public, much of which lived in the new suburbs, was deeply concerned about redressing the balance between individualism and conformity. A natural place to begin to adjust that balance was the schools, which were reputed to emphasize teaching children how to get along together and how to adjust. Whyte's interpretation of the social ethic he was criticizing sounded like a definition of the purposes of progressive education in the early twentieth century. It is "that contemporary body of thought which makes morally legitimate the pressures of society against the individual. Its major propositions are three: a belief in the group as the source of creativity; a belief in 'belongingness' as the ultimate need of the individual; and a belief in the application of science to achieve the belongingness."[7]

The emphasis on the group project, on cooperative endeavors, on stressing the social rather than the personal utility and function of every act had characterized the efforts of the public schools for many years. The conclusion was easily drawn that such training was at least partially responsible for what these writers and their audience believed to be an excess of conformity. Returning to the basics promised a return to individualism and inner-directedness by stressing individual rather than group achievement and by exercising and disciplining the mind—here sentiment was returning to the mental discipline approach of the nineteenth century—which in turn would strengthen the person's will power

[7] William H. Whyte, *The Organization Man* (New York, 1956), 7.

to resist group demands. Such discipline would instill backbone or spine in the person in a way that the progressive or modern school never did. Finally, the study of the traditional disciplines—especially the humanities which received a very good press, if little money, during this era—would provide the future adult with perspectives on life, society, and people with which he could establish his own values independent of the group or situation in which he happened to find himself. Some undoubtedly hoped that reversing the trends of modern education would not only redress the balance between individualism and conformity but would also undermine the habits and attitudes which were in part responsible for the problems of the twenties and thirties. Raising children differently would eliminate the nightmare of the Depression, improve society, and possibly prevent the kinds of adolescent irresponsibility that had characterized the decades between the wars. Reversing the direction of educational change would help the society achieve some of the stability, rectitude, and respect for individuality that had characterized America in the period before World War I, before modernism had made a serious impact on the educational scene.

The educational changes proposed in the fifties and sixties promised to assuage the insecurity of the suburban middle class in one other way. Those changes pointed toward establishing intellectual merit as the central criterion of success in the United States. The schools of the twenties and thirties had elaborated a number of different tracks—academic, extracurricular, vocational, and athletic—in which students could excel. Meanwhile, the economy still offered some paths—principally sales and inventing—through which the uneducated could achieve success. The educational critics of the fifties pushed schools to focus more and more narrowly on the academic track, and the economy increasingly closed off paths of opportunity for those without advanced education. Success depended on one's ability to communicate articulately in a complex industrial society and on one's ability to understand and manipulate the advancing technology of the era, technology that pervaded everything from the defense industry to retailing. Advanced education was absolutely crucial, therefore, to those career paths that led to positions of leadership, power, and high or even upper-middling social status. The middle classes recognized this and saw that the critics of the fifties were suggesting changes in the public schools which would make them better preparatory schools for advanced education. Hoping to secure entry for their children into an important career, they moved swiftly to implement the suggestions of the critics, the new curriculum makers, and cognitive psychologists in their local schools.

James Bryant Conant had recognized the coming of meritocracy and had welcomed, even heralded, its arrival. Yet his essential Jeffersonianism called for the wholesale rearrangement of the social classes within each generation by selecting from all of the nation's children those who displayed the greatest intellectual potential. They were to be schooled to assume leadership positions in the future. What happened, unfortunately, was that his suggestions for improving schooling in these ways were not evenly implemented across society and across the social classes. Upper- and middle-class suburbs moved far more quickly to adopt the new education than did rural or urban systems. Various causes account for this uneven implementation; there is no need to attribute evil motives either to the critics or to those who benefited so much from the changes. First of all, suburban middle-class parents, who so often owed their social position to their demonstrated academic capabilities, understood the important relation of precollege education to later success. They naturally moved to protect their children, to give them all the security they could, by using the public schools for college preparation. Second, the size of suburbs was more conducive to change; smaller communities were more responsive to parental pressures than were the large urban systems in which educationists were more firmly entrenched. Third, the pattern of financing public schools through local property taxes made the well-to-do suburbs more able to adopt new (and usually expensive) curricula, to pay salaries high enough to attract the best teachers, and to build the facilities and enlarge the staffs to cope with the baby boom. Although not without their financial troubles and strains, suburbs found themselves with a steadily increasing tax base as more homes were built and the value of existing property rose. Suburban middle-class parents had a vital stake in improved schooling and were therefore willing to tax themselves fairly heavily to improve their educational facilities. Rural districts found their populations falling, their tax bases shrinking somewhat, with far less community interest in education and thus less willingness to tax themselves for improved education. Urban districts began to suffer shrinking tax bases as industry moved to the suburban ring and large areas of the city became blighted. The cities' property tax rolls included businessmen whose children were schooled in the suburbs, old people whose children were out of school, and apartment house operators whose tenants had little interest in the local schools. None of these urban taxpayers displayed the suburbanites' interest in paying to improve public schools. Furthermore, while other city services demanded ever more of the urban tax dollar, suburbs, which enjoyed a kind of parasitic relation to the city, could allocate the bulk of local tax money to schools. City tax money had to support not only schools but police and fire protection, sanitation for the manufacturing, retailing, entertainment, and public areas of the city that were used by city and suburban residents alike, welfare payments for the growing numbers of poor people who were clustering in the cities, and museums, libraries, and other such public institutions used by the residents of the entire region. In the cities, in other words, there was less willingness to seek better schools and far fewer resources with which to improve them. Yet, even had there been a groundswell of interest, there existed in the huge urban educational bureaucracies a far more entrenched opposition to educational change.

The suburbanites did not create the growing emphasis on intellectual merit, but they recognized it and moved quickly to take advantage of it. They fought to improve their schools in order to improve their children's chances for success in a meritocratic system. In doing so, for the reasons outlined above, they succeeded also in using education to separate their children from other children in the society, to give their children a chance that other children did not have. They did not deliberately exclude other children from the advantages so much as they moved quickly to secure for their children the opportunities while largely ignoring the plight of children who did not live in the suburbs (and for whom private education was unavailable). As a result, the suburban high school became a college preparatory school while urban and rural high schools generally did not. College attendance had become more important than ever as a determinant of success in the United States. One report revealed that in 1961 "of the nation's 26,500 high schools, a mere 5000 produce 82 percent of all college students."[8] Thus, the reforms of the fifties and sixties served, somewhat fortuitously, to allocate educational services unevenly across the social spectrum—in a pattern strangely reminiscent of that planned by the social efficiency educators of four decades earlier. Despite Conant's Jeffersonianism and the celebration of the comprehensive high school, the public school system came to offer different social classes different educations based upon their presumed future status. Growing recognition of this situation and growing horror at the social cost such a system would ultimately exact in a democracy led to the next great era of educational reform—the effort to secure equal educational opportunity for all Americans, especially for the poor and the black.

GUIDE TO FURTHER READING

The best chronicles of the decades after World War II are WILLIAM E. LEUCHTEN-BURG, *A Troubled Feast: American Society Since 1945* (Boston, 1973), WALTER K. NUGENT, *Modern America* (New York, 1973), ERIC F. GOLDMAN, *The Crucial Decade—and After: America 1945–1960* (New York, 1961), and ROLAND BERTH-OFF, *An Unsettled People: Social Order and Disorder in American History* (New York, 1971), Epilogue. The McCarthy era and the American experience with extremism during the 1940s and 1950s are outlined in MICHAEL PAUL ROGIN, *The Intellectuals and McCarthy* (Cambridge, Mass., 1967), ROBERT GRIFFITH, *The Politics of Fear* (Lexington, Ky., 1970), and RICHARD HOFSTADTER, *The Paranoid*

---

[8] Patricia Sexton, *Education and Income: Inequalities of Opportunity in Our Public Schools* (New York, 1961), 187.

Style in American Politics and Other Essays (New York, 1965). DAVID P. GARDNER, *The California Oath Controversy* (Berkeley, 1967), concentrates on these influences on education. LAWRENCE A. CREMIN, *The Transformation of the School* (New York, 1961), Part II, remains the standard work on the collapse of the Progressive Education Association. ROBERT H. WIEBE, "The Social Function of Public Education," *American Quarterly*, XXI (Summer, 1969), 147–164, and MARTIN TROW, "The Second Transformation of American Public Education," *International Journal of Comparative Sociology*, II (September, 1961), 144–166, are two excellent essays which place the debate of the 1950s in historical perspective.

The most important contributions of the educational critics of the 1950s were MORTIMER SMITH, *And Madly Teach* (Chicago, 1949), BERNARD BELL, *Crisis in Education* (New York, 1949), ALBERT LYND, *Quackery in the Public Schools* (Boston, 1953), ARTHUR BESTOR, *Educational Wastelands* (Urbana, Ill., 1953), and *The Restoration of Learning* (New York, 1955), ROBERT M. HUTCHINS, *The Conflict in Education in a Democratic Society* (New York, 1953), MORTIMER SMITH, *The Diminished Mind: A Study of Planned Mediocrity in Our Public Schools* (Chicago, 1954), VIVIAN THAYER, *Public Education and Its Critics* (New York, 1954), and HYMAN G. RICKOVER, *Education and Freedom* (New York, 1959). JAMES B. CONANT offered more friendly criticism in *The American High School Today* (New York, 1959), *The Comprehensive High School* (New York, 1967), *Education and Liberty: The Role of the Schools in a Modern Democracy* (Cambridge, Mass., 1953), *Slums and Suburbs* (New York, 1961), and *The Education of American Teachers* (New York, 1963). ROBERT M. WEISS, *The Conant Controversy in Teacher Education* (New York, 1969), THOMAS GRISSOM, "Education and the Cold War: The Role of James B. Conant," in CLARENCE J. KARIER et al., *Roots of Crisis* (Chicago, 1973), 177–197, MERLE BORROWMAN and CHARLES BURGESS, *What Doctrines to Embrace* (Glenview, Ill., 1969), chapter 5, and JAMES B. CONANT, *My Several Lives: Memoirs of a Social Inventor* (New York, 1970), are useful secondary accounts.

Important documents in the history of cognitive psychology after World War II are JEROME S. BRUNER, *The Process of Education* (Cambridge, Mass., 1960), which should be supplemented with his reassessment, *"The Process of Education* Revisited," *Phi Delta Kappan*, LIII (September, 1971), 18–21, BENJAMIN S. BLOOM, *Stability and Change in Human Characteristics* (New York, 1964), J. MCVICKER HUNT, *Intelligence and Experience* (New York, 1961), JEROME S. BRUNER et al., *A Study of Thinking* (New York, 1956), and BRUNER et al., *Contemporary Approaches to Cognition* (Cambridge, Mass., 1957).

JEAN PIAGET's most relevant publications are *The Psychology of the Child*, trans. HELEN WEAVER (New York, 1969), *The Origins of Intelligence in Children* (New York, 1952), *The Construction of Reality in the Child* (New York, 1954), and *Six Psychological Studies* (New York, 1967), edited by DAVID ELKIND, who has interpreted Piaget's work for his American audience in *Children and Adolescents: Interpretive Essays on Jean Piaget* (New York, 1970), and *Studies in Cognitive Development: Essays in Honor of Jean Piaget* (1969; New York, 1970). Also useful are BARRY J. WADSWORTH, *Piaget's Theory of Cognitive Development* (New York, 1971), and JOHN L. PHILLIPS, *The Origins of Intellect: Piaget's Theory* (San Francisco, 1969).

An exciting approach to the function of schooling in American society after World War II is through the examination of adolescent culture and family life. Several excellent pieces of research which were completed during the 1950s proved very useful. EDGAR Z. FRIEDENBERG, *The Vanishing Adolescent* (New York, 1959), and particularly *Coming of Age in America: Growth and Acquiescence* (New York, 1963), are very good; JULES HENRY, *Culture Against Man* (New York, 1963), Part II, explores family life and the public schools; and KENNETH KENISTON, *The Uncommitted: Alienated Youth in American Society* (New York, 1960), should be supplemented by his study of *Young Radicals: Notes on Committed Youth* (New York, 1968), and "Youth as a Stage of Life," in *Youth and Dissent* (New York, 1971), 3–21.

Our discussion of middle-class aspirations and activities has drawn heavily on the best sociological literature of the post–World War II era. Most useful are DAVID RIESMAN, *The Lonely Crowd* (1950; New Haven, Conn., 1969), WILLIAM H. WHYTE, *The Organization Man* (New York, 1956), C. WRIGHT MILLS, *White Collar: The American Middle Classes* (New York, 1951), AUGUSTE SPECTORSKY, *The Exurbanites* (Philadelphia, 1955), and HERBERT J. GANS, *The Levittowners* (New York, 1967), the research for which was conducted in the late 1950s. JOHN KENNETH GALBRAITH, *The New Industrial State* (Boston, 1967), remains valuable.

CHAPTER 14

Changing Definitions of Equality of Educational Opportunity, 1960–1975

I

IN THE 1950s AMERICANS DEMANDED THAT SCHOOLS ADOPT AN ACADEMIC emphasis that would strengthen the United States in its fight against the forces of international communism and provide greater security for the children of the newly burgeoning affluent suburbs. Americans in the 1960s demanded that schools attack the problems of poverty and racial and ethnic discrimination. In the broad, and therefore imprecise, categorization and periodization of his trade, the historian of education can identify the fifties as a time when schools enlisted in the cold war and the sixties as an era when they enlisted in the "War on Poverty." The change did not constitute a rejection of earlier concerns but, rather, an elevation of newer interests to positions of primacy. Foundations, the federal government, and the public considered different tasks more worthy of attention and financial support. The concern with academic achievement and collegiate preparation did not cease; indeed, much of the work of the curriculum reformers came to fruition only in the sixties. But by then the "action" had shifted elsewhere—to problems that seemed far more pressing than that of raising the intellectual capacities of the children of affluence.

In the early sixties large numbers of Americans awoke to the fact that the fruits of their society's tremendous postwar prosperity had bypassed a considerable segment of the population. Some said as much as one third of the country's population lived in dire poverty despite the record-breaking growth of the Gross National Product, and all agreed that this figure was at least 20 to 25 percent. Through books like Michael Harrington's *The Other Americans* (1962), and high-impact media journalism like Edward R. Murrow's television documentary about migrant farm workers, "Harvest of Shame" (1960), Americans learned of the "invisible poor" living in the midst of affluence. Psychologically isolated in their apparent lack of aspiration and hope, the poor remained physically quarantined in their monstrous urban ghettos, in authoritarian migrant labor camps, or in beautiful but economically-depressed Appalachian mountain communities. These revelations spawned a flood of interest in poverty and its elimination. They inspired the Democratic administrations of John Kennedy and Lyndon Johnson to declare in 1963 and 1964 the so-called War on Poverty—a congeries of federal efforts to subsidize low-income housing, job retraining programs, improved inner city schools, regional planning in depressed areas such as Appalachia, improved health care, and expanded welfare services which culminated in the creation of the Office of Economic Opportunity in 1964. Scholars eagerly set out to analyze and explain "poverty amidst plenty," and their concepts of the "culture of poverty" and the "cycle of poverty" became the era's conventional wisdom. According to such an analysis, poverty passed from parents to children to grandchildren in a seemingly endless cycle of poor jobs which led to poor housing and poor food which contributed to poor health which in turn held the person in a poor job. This cycle also led to a loss of hope and energy, to the formation of a "culture" of poverty characterized by passivity, isolation, broken homes, residential instability, and lack of aspiration. The children of poverty came to school nutritionally deprived, in poor health, and with aspirations already circumscribed. Consequently, they learned little in school, which meant, in turn, that they could get only the poorest jobs and the cycle repeated itself. Commentators often contrasted the postwar poor with their counterparts in earlier eras, sometimes invidiously, but other times with a real understanding of the problems faced by the weak, the dark skinned, and the technologically handicapped in an affluent and industrial society. Earlier, the poor had typically been immigrants on the way up, so the story went, who, despite their grinding poverty and the foul conditions of their tenements, built a sense of community in their ghettos, maintained family and group stability, and taught their children the value of achievement. In contrast, the postwar poor were society's rejects, without the skills or aspirations to find a useful place in their communities, and too deeply embedded in a culture of hopelessness and passivity to force their children ahead. The poor lacked any sense that they could take effective action to improve their situation. They were weak, frightened, passive, and hopeless, and these characteristics were so deeply ingrained that they were passed on directly to the children—insuring that they too would remain in the culture of poverty.

But the poor, especially the urban poor, did not remain invisible or forgotten in the 1960s. Massive riots—some called them rebellions—broke out in the black ghettos of almost all of America's larger cities between 1964 and 1968—most spectacularly in Harlem (1964), Watts (1965), and Detroit (1967). The rioters' penchant for attacking white-owned businesses, the wanton disregard for life and property displayed during the riots, and the civil authorities' inability to restore control over an unwilling population demonstrated the depth of despair and alienation among the black urban poor and the social dangers posed by such a condition. Growing evidence of an epidemic of urban street crime and the flourishing of the deadly and crime-inspiring hard drug trade in the poorest parts of the nation's largest cities made the lessons even clearer. As Americans became more concerned with events in the ghettos, they became aware of the pervasiveness and rapidity of the decay of their cities. Alienation, drugs, crime, and urban decay were by no means new in the 1960s, but social leaders and the media aroused greater public interest in them than had ever existed before. It should be noted that, although poverty was widespread in both rural and urban areas, public awareness focused on urban poverty—largely, one suspects, because of the fear of, and the fascination with, the urban violence that was a symptom of that poverty.

The affluent grew concerned with relieving or, indeed, with eliminating the conditions that gave rise to urban violence and alienation among the poor. As in almost all reform movements of this kind, the public interest combined humanitarian concerns for suffering individuals caught in the culture of poverty with fear for the future of a society which contained such danger at the very hubs of its civilized existence. Could the United States continue to be strong and respected if a cancer of alienation and violence raged at its very core? Most answered in the negative and looked for ways of excising the disease.

As was their wont when faced with social crises, public leaders and opinion makers demanded that the schools take a major part in achieving justice for the poor. Schooling in America has always attracted those concerned with social problems because it promised to relieve the situation without in any way threatening to upset the current social structure. Using schools as an engine of social reform nearly always assumes that change will occur only after the students grow up. By its very nature it is gradualist, suggesting that nothing sudden needs to be done to readjust the social order. Education's inevitable emphasis on individual development implies that individual faults rather than social injustices lie at the root of the problem. Since schools can play some role in changing the individual and almost none in directly changing the social structure, they concentrate on making individuals conform to the needs or demands of the surrounding society rather than seeking to change society to fit the needs of individuals. Another of education's advantages as a reform mechanism is that society can provide it relatively easily and cheaply for the disadvantaged without reducing the amount offered to everyone else. In this, education contrasts rather sharply with other more immediately effective strategies of reducing poverty through some form of direct redistribution of wealth—from the top fifth of the population which receives almost 50 percent of the nation's income, to the bottom fifth, which earns only about 5 percent. In the short run, at least, redistribution resembles something of a zero-sum-game in which, because there is a finite sum of income, raising the income of one person demands that another's be lowered. Education, on the other hand, is infinite—in the short run, no one has to receive less schooling because the poor receive more. (One major mistake made by educational strategists in this period, however, was to appear to be raising the educational expenditures for the poor without increasing them for the working class, whose educational needs and facilities were nearly as desperate as those of the poor. Thus, educators made it seem as if one group were being awarded educational advantages at the expense of another; as if, in the context of the time, working-class whites were being sacrificed to provide better schools for poor blacks.)

Educational expansion seemed a particularly apt solution in this case, moreover, because of the supposed cyclical nature of poverty. If the school could be made to serve as an antidote rather than as a reinforcer of the culture of poverty, the cycle might be broken. Schools should help children overcome the negative influences of their environment and parentage, give them a sense of hope and achievement, and teach them marketable skills. Analysts discovered that poor children absorbed the culture of poverty from the schools as they were. Just as the poor received the poorest services in other areas—from garbage collection to social security payments—so they received the poorest educational services. Buildings were older, teachers were less experienced, and expenditures on books and equipment were lower than those in schools in better neighborhoods. Moreover, the poor schools tended to reinforce the children's negative self-images which had been acquired at home and on the streets. Teachers and administrators shared the parental view that the children's futures were more or less hopeless, that they would do poorly in school and in life afterward. Many observers described the tragic way in which the children of the poor who began school so enthusiastically were quickly benumbed and discouraged by their poor performance and by the deadening effect of an irrelevant curriculum taught by teachers who thought the students incapable of learning.

Schooling was also attractive because it concentrated on children. Reformers feared that adults were so deeply rooted in the culture of poverty, that they were so inured to failure, that nothing could change them. Their children, on the other hand, were young and malleable enough for schools to liberate them from their circumstances. Educational facilities would have to be better, schools would have to expect more of the children and teach marketable skills. Schools had to begin their fight with the debilitating circumstances surrounding their students at a time when the children were young enough to respond and their roots in the culture of poverty shallow enough to be disengaged.

Leaders of the educational profession responded eagerly to society's demand that they commit their institutions to eliminating poverty. Since in their eagerness to serve they promised that schools could do far more than in fact they were capable of doing, it is useful at this point to speculate about the reasons for this eagerness. Some of it, surely, manifested solicitude for suffering individuals forced to endure grinding, debilitating poverty in an affluent culture. Indeed, one might suggest, although it could never be proven, that educators as professionals committed to teaching and working with people felt this humanitarian concern with somewhat greater intensity than most Americans. Surely, educators shared their fellow citizens' fear that the continued alienation and despair among the poor and the concomitant rise in violence and crime threatened the very bases of social stability and progress. James Bryant Conant spoke for educators as well as for the rest of society in warning that conditions in the American slums constituted a kind of "social dynamite."[1]

There appear, however, to have been some special motives that impelled the educational profession to get so enthusiastically involved in the elimination of poverty—motives rooted in the continuing conflict between "educationists," based in schools of education, and subject-matter specialists, based in colleges and universities, over the control of educational research and the direction of educational reform. In the fifties, the university-based or -trained subject-matter specialists regained something closely resembling the dominant position they had held in educational affairs before the turn of the century. They did so, of course, at the expense of the professional educators based in schools of education. Shifting the focus of the educational effort from the suburbs to the central cities, from teaching inquiry-based mastery of the scientific method to teaching marketable skills, was a way in which the education-

[1] James B. Conant, *Slums and Suburbs* (New York, 1961), 10.

ists could reclaim the dominant position in precollegiate education that they had held for most of the century. What occurred was not simply a replay of the educationists' fight against the Committee of Ten, but there were striking resemblances. The educational literature of the sixties included references to "collegiate domination" quite reminiscent of the Progressive era. Professional educators identified themselves as defenders of the nonelite, noncollegebound, just as they had earlier. The subject-centered approach was subordinated to a student-centered approach in a change quite similar to that which occurred during the first three decades of this century. Concentrating on poverty allowed educators to stress those aspects of the educational situation which were more in their bailiwick than they were in that of the subject-matter specialists. They shifted emphasis from the curriculum to the learner and the problems that he brought to school. The first educational step in breaking the poverty cycle was to counteract the influences of poverty which followed the child to school and which would, unless dealt with, prevent him from succeeding with a curriculum, of whatever type. Furthermore, the fight against poverty committed educators to stress teaching children who were not going to college rather than those who were—again, somewhat isolating the subject-matter specialists. The injunction that schoolchildren should learn to investigate material in the various fields just as real scholars did seemed less relevant to the war on poverty than it had to the cold war. The new science and math curricula seemed all a bit esoteric when the problems of education in the ghetto so often revolved around teaching adolescents to read and youngsters to make change.

Of course, educators did not turn their backs on the advances of the fifties. Especially important to the efforts to eliminate poverty were psychology's findings about the preschool child's cognitive potential and the importance of early learning to the future capabilities of children (these findings were applied in the massive Head Start program). Nor did the cooperation and mutual stimulation that had characterized the relations between the better schools of education and major universities cease. Educators did walk a little taller on the campus than they had in the previous decade, and they received a higher percentage of the available research money. Fields of educational study dismissed as soft and silly during the academically oriented fifties gathered new respect. Pedagogy, counseling, and humanistic psychology were taken a great deal more seriously when education was required to counteract the culture of poverty. A reform program that would not only help the society but could also help educators recover some of their dignity, so badly damaged in the antieducationist fifties, held, therefore, a special attractiveness to American educationists. They rushed, perhaps too eagerly, to commit themselves to that program.

By assuming responsibility for playing such a major role in eliminating poverty in the United States, educationists—probably unwittingly—opened to challenge some of the most fundamental assumptions about the role of schools as agents of democracy and equality in American society. The commitment to eliminating poverty was a commitment to a goal unabashedly economic and materialistic. It was, as well, a goal capable of precise measurement. This was a radical move for education. Previously schools had promised to improve the morals and intellects of children, to make them more efficient as workers, to make them conform to some definition of American values, and to make them more curious and scientifically literate. These were significant goals, but they were of a vague quality that made it difficult to tell whether or not the schools had been successful in their fulfillment. It is difficult to measure conformity, morality, or efficiency. Success or failure was a matter of opinion, and one man's opinion was as accurate as another's. The opposite was true of a goal such as the elimination of poverty. The amount of poverty in the society was a relatively precise, calculable quantity about which there could be little argument. The schools' success in eliminating poverty was easily measured. Until the sixties schools had been hesitant in committing themselves to improving the material status of their students. A school might point with pride to one or two of its successful graduates, but no school thought of doing a statistical analysis of the careers of all its alumni to test the relationship between education and success. Such an argument was not employed until the 1960s when, indeed, educators began to advertise openly to parents and young people, particularly dropouts, that remaining in school would substantially increase one's lifetime earnings. Everyone was included in this promise. The commitment to ending poverty promised the same thing, of course: that schools could have an important effect on the material futures of all their students. The notoriety of a few successful graduates was ignored; now statisticians surveyed the poor in order to determine the differences made by education. Promises made by the schools had a similar effect on the poor. Traditionally, poor and immigrant communities perceived the success of a few of their educated members as evidence that the group as a whole was rising in status, that opportunity existed for all of them in American society, and that formal education made a difference in later life. The 1960s witnessed the serious undermining of that tradition. Among the poor and ethnic minorities a developing sense of group consciousness turned their attention to the progress made by the entire group, rather than to that made by a few individuals, as an index of their status in American society. They increasingly held the educational system responsible for bettering their circumstances. Neither statisticians nor the poor found that schools were very successful in achieving such results.

Poverty failed to recede before the educational onslaught and school leaders drifted from confusion to desperation and finally to frustration over the whole business of deploying the school as an agency of social change. They faced the tasks of reassessing the school's capacity to insure equality and of redefining the meaning of equality of educational opportunity. Early in the decade, educators had been confident that providing equal educational facilities to all groups would guarantee that ultimately the distribution of goods among these groups would be equal. This was the assumption so seriously undermined during the 1960s. This long-standing—and rarely examined—assumption held that "equal opportunity" was guaranteed when all children received the same educational opportunities. It was provided when, in the words of the later "input-output" analysts, a child received teachers as competent, buildings as new, books as up to date, materials as plentiful, school sessions as long, and expenditures as great as every other child in the country. With these opportunities he had an equal chance to display his merit or potential, and thus to achieve the degree of success he deserved. Although all children might encounter the same facilities, some would use them more effectively than would others, a circumstance that simply reflected their differing merit. This was the definition of equal educational opportunity upon which Jefferson's pyramidal scheme for schooling in Virginia had rested. It remained the accepted wisdom through the early 1960s.

Poor children and those of certain minority groups consistently failed to make as effective use of their equal facilities as did the children of more privileged groups. This was the dilemma faced by educators in the 1960s. The genetic theories of intelligence so popular in America before 1940 had explained the differential in academic achievement and material success between the privileged groups and the disadvantaged and minority groups admirably. The performance of the poor and the blacks was worse because they were inherently inferior. Schools offered them an equal chance, of which they were unable to take advantage because of inherited deficiencies. This argument had been roundly rejected as a result of psychological and genetic research in the twenties and thirties and because of popular horror at the implementation of such a theory by Hitler's Germany. By 1960 this hereditarian theory was no longer available to explain why equal facilities failed to produce a society in which success was equally and proportionately distributed among social classes and ethnic groups. Education in the sixties, then, had to explain why equal opportunities failed to produce equal results. Educators had promised to find better ways of organizing educational institutions and services so that equality would result. Because education failed to solve this problem successfully by 1970, a mounting frustration and defeatism within the educational establishment has occurred, to complement the increasing disappointment, anger, and disinterest in the schools among parents and taxpayers.

II

Just as the effort to bring the common school to black freedmen after the Civil War highlighted so many of the contradictions in the common school philosophy, so the effort to extend racial equality and justice to blacks after World War II sharply revealed the inadequacies of the assumption that equal educational facilities could effect a more equal distribution of justice and material success in American society. Understanding these developments requires a brief excursion into educational developments in the black community since the 1890s.

Despite the second-class education to which blacks, north and south, were relegated in the decades after the Civil War, they remained optimistic that schooling would better their social and economic position. They attended school in great numbers and spent a high proportion of their relatively meager supply of material goods to provide institutions of education. This continued interest in education can be explained in several ways. One popular explanation is that blacks found it the most promising area on which to concentrate their efforts simply because whites denied meaningful roles to blacks in politics and in business more effectively than they cut off access to meaningful education. Southern blacks could not get skilled jobs because of discrimination; state legislatures had deprived them of the right to vote and hold political office. From that perspective, schools looked relatively promising. Inferior as they might be, and not all of them were, they at least remained open to blacks. In a relatively bleak situation, schools held out all sorts of prospects for future advancement. With better education, succeeding generations of blacks could break down prejudice or insure the independence and self-sufficiency of the black community. There was nothing better in sight.

Another explanation, perhaps more persuasive, is that blacks, like any other ambitious group of people in the United States, had a kind of folk faith in the power of education to advance their group. America was the land of opportunity and in it those who demonstrated their ability could find success. School was the place to begin to demonstrate that ability. This, of course, was Booker T. Washington's message and, whatever Washington's current reputation, at the turn of the century his message struck a responsive chord. Millions of blacks agreed with him that high educational attainment was proof against prejudice and that the practice of the virtues learned in school would ease significantly relations between blacks and whites and pave the way for the individual's and the race's rise from the bottom. Blacks, like immigrants and native whites, sensed the power and esteem that was associated with being an educated man in America.[2]

A third explanation for the tremendous black investment in education since the Civil War has been the ability of education, as a concept and an ideal, to serve as a common denominator in the black community, an ideal upon which almost all members of that community could agree. Separationists and integrationists, race men and accommodators, moderates and militants (at least in the pre-1960 version of that term) all agreed on the pressing need for more education among blacks. There was some disagreement over the means or the kind of education. The most famous of these disagreements, that between Washington and DuBois (whether the emphasis in black education should fall on providing the most advanced education available to the "talented tenth" of the black population to insure leadership at that level or on providing better education at lower levels for the bulk of the black population so as to improve their chances for self-help, economic comfort, and a decent standard of living), has been emphasized out of proportion to its real importance as a source of disagreement among the antagonists or among blacks in general. Both men recognized that in order to advance, their race must secure better education at both levels. Their antagonism was far more deeply rooted in issues of power and attitudes toward accommodation than it was in differences in educational philosophy. Education was a cause broad enough to include both men comfortably. Education had other virtues as a unifier. The long-standing split in black communities between integration and separation could easily be papered over in educational matters. Holders of either philosophy could agree that more education would be valuable—either for learning the ways of the white so as to hasten integration or as a way of learning skills that would enhance the race's prospects for success in independence. Further, the separatist could as easily argue for integrated education (as he often did) on the theory that only in an integrated classroom would blacks receive the best education because the parents of the white students in the class would not tolerate for their children the inferior education that blacks received in segregated classrooms. The integrationist, in turn, could argue for a separate education in order to provide black children with the necessary background for integration. This is not to say that these various positions did not involve substantial differences of philosophy, but that these differences were easily muted in the period before World War II when all such

[2] Timothy L. Smith, "Native Blacks and Foreign Whites: Varying Responses to Educational Opportunity in America, 1880–1950," *Perspectives in American History,* VI (1972), 309–337, and Timothy Smith, "Immigrant Social Aspirations and American Education, 1880–1930,"*American Quarterly,* XXI (Fall, 1969), 523–543.

discussions were necessarily abstract. Because integration was so far from being a realistic prospect and adequate opportunities for advanced professional education were so far from implementation, the debaters never had to face the hard choices that some of their ideological conflicts might have forced upon them. In the 1960s and 1970s, when educational prospects for blacks seemed to have improved, at least on paper, these choices caused serious conflicts within black communities. Until recently, however, blacks commonly agreed that more education was a good thing, and because it was in such short supply they embraced it in any form offered. Thus education became a central focus for black aspirations, and it was noncontroversial enough to serve as a unifying factor within black communities.

No one of these three explanations can entirely explain the black commitment to education. All three, and probably others, coalesced to foster this commitment to schooling among blacks. The commitment was immense, as Timothy L. Smith has pointed out. White support for black schools in the South since the Civil War has been important, perhaps even crucial, to whatever success those schools have had. But financially strapped southern blacks contributed as much, or more, to the effort for schooling as northern white churches or white charitable foundations. As we have previously pointed out, southern states regularly gave five, ten, and even fifteen times as much money per capita to white public schools as they did to black schools—despite explicit laws to the contrary.[3] Blacks desperately and repeatedly raised money among themselves to try to keep their "public" schools operating somewhere near the level at which the states maintained the white public schools. Before the 1920s, when the southern states began to provide some public secondary education for Negroes, black efforts combined with white philanthropy to support hundreds of private secondary schools and colleges for young black people.

Black commitment to education was even more dramatic in the northern cities, to which southern blacks began to stream after 1910. Timothy L. Smith has compared the enrollment figures for blacks, children of native whites, and children of foreign-born whites aged 14 through 18—in other words, ages at which youngsters were no longer compelled to stay in school and were likely to seek work instead. He found that in 1910, in seven of the nation's eight largest cities, blacks enrolled in higher percentages than did the children of immigrants; in the eighth city this pattern was true of children 14 through 16. In some cases higher proportions of black children of a certain age were enrolled than children of native whites. Any number of cities in the northern and border states in

[3] Louis Harlan, *Separate and Unequal: Public School Campaigns and Racism in the Southern Seaboard States, 1901–1915* (New York, 1968).

1910 show similar figures. Statistics from the 1930 census demonstrate the continuing black interest in education. Even though migrants from the rural South constantly disrupted the black communities in northern cities and the immigration laws of 1921 and 1924 had allowed immigrant communities to achieve a growing stability, blacks in several cities sent a higher proportion of their teenagers to school than did immigrants and, when it did not exceed them, the percentages of black teenage enrollment came very close to matching those for immigrants and native whites.[4]

These figures demonstrate an extraordinary belief in the effectiveness of education in the face of circumstances that seemingly would have disheartened the most optimistic souls. The schools openly discriminated against blacks, placed them in old overcrowded buildings, gave them the most aged and out-of-date materials, and gerrymandered district boundaries to keep blacks out of white schools. Schools constantly pushed blacks into tracks that would prepare them for their "place" in society. The schoolmen's dilemma in this situation must be recognized: Should they prepare blacks for jobs from which their race was currently excluded and risk having the youngsters unable to find employment suited to the skills they had mastered, or should they prepare their black students to perform the sorts of tasks that society allowed them to perform? The schools had not created the economic discrimination in the labor market, nor was anything they were likely to do in the way of job or skill training likely to change that pattern in the short run. Most educators resolved the dilemma in favor of preparing blacks for jobs known to be open to them. The curriculum usually stereotyped black behavior—blacks were forever happy and humble, smiling and singing and serving whites. White (as well as a number of black) teachers subtly and not so subtly—in word and deed, in their very dedication to instilling genteel manners and middle-class moralisms in black children—indicated their belief that blacks were inferior. Despite these discriminatory and humiliating aspects of the public schools, black families kept their older children enrolled in those schools in surprisingly large numbers.

The blacks' faith in education as a means of individual and group "betterment" is also evident in their heroic and, for many years, lonely legal battle against segregated schooling. The blacks' decision, through the national office of the National Association for the Advancement of Colored People, to invest so much time, energy, and money in the fight for integrated educational facilities in the southern states indicates that they perceived education to be one of the most vital aspects of their eventual progress toward equality—ranking alongside voting rights, fair employment, and access to decent housing. In some minds education had

[4] Smith, "Native Blacks and Foreign Whites," 309–319, 327–328.

first priority because, as they argued, adequate education would insure that blacks received those further rights of full citizenship. The NAACP began its assault on separate schools in 1935. There is no particular need to describe this long and arduous but ultimately successful campaign in detail. Segregated education rested on the Supreme Court's decision in *Plessy* v. *Ferguson* (1896) that, so long as blacks received absolutely equal facilities, the fact that the facilities were separate constituted no violation of their civil rights. "Separate but equal" became the formula for justifying all segregated institutions in the South—from drinking fountains and railroad cars to schools. The NAACP lawyers first attacked educational segregation by seeking to enroll qualified black students in all-white public medical, law, or pharmacy schools in states where no such professional training was available to blacks. The states were accused of violating black civil rights if they refused to enroll the applicants. The NAACP did not intend to force the states to create a network of separate professional schools for blacks in each of the states but, by focusing on the most expensive level of education, sought to point out the absurd, really impossible, expense involved in maintaining the truly equivalent "dual system" that *Plessy* v. *Ferguson* demanded.[5] In attacking segregation at the graduate and professional level, the NAACP lawyers deliberately exploited a peculiarity of southern racial sentiment. Racial mixing among the adults at this level of education was less dangerous than integration in the primary and secondary schools. There was less conviction and emotion in southern resistance to this entering wedge. Thurgood Marshall argued the case for the NAACP, and later recalled the strategy of his organization. "Those racial supremacy boys somehow think that little kids of six or seven are going to get funny ideas about sex and marriage just from going to school together, but for some equally funny reason youngsters in law school aren't supposed to feel that way. We didn't get it but we decided that if that was what the South believed, then the best thing for the moment was to go along."[6] The most famous and influential case, *Sweatt* v. *Painter,* decided finally by the Supreme Court in 1950, involved a black prevented from attending the law school at the University of Texas (the state's only public law school) because of his race. To meet its obligations under the separate but equal doctrine, Texas established an off-campus tutorial in which the black applicant could prepare for the bar. He in turn filed suit alleging that he was being denied equal protection of the law because the two institutions were unequal. The Supreme Court agreed, contending that equality of facilities was probably impossible at the level of advanced professional education because,

---

[5] The president of Oklahoma University, George L. Cross, remarked: "You can't build a cyclotron for one student." Quoted in Alfred Kelly, "The School Desegregation Case," in John Garraty, ed., *Quarrels That Have Shaped the Constitution* (New York, 1962), 254.

[6] Quoted in *ibid.*

even if monetary input were equivalent, there was no way of equalizing "those qualities which are incapable of objective measurements but which make for greatness in a law school."[7] In other words, things like colleagueship of superior students and reputation, which were so important in getting a sound legal education and even more important in securing a job afterward, could not be duplicated from one school to the next simply by duplicating the pattern of monetary and curricular inputs. The reputation of the law school at the University of Texas was just as important as any other consideration, and the black had as much right as anyone to the school's degree. No separate facility, no matter how equal in objective measures, could compensate for that lack of reputation. Therefore, relegating blacks to separate professional schools prevented them from receiving the same quality of education available to whites in the same state, and this clearly violated the blacks' civil rights. Although the Court's decision was heartening to the plaintiffs, it was very narrow and fell far short of fundamentally challenging educational segregation. The Court had not challenged the "separate but equal" doctrine at all; it had merely said that it was impossible to create schools that were both separate and equal at that particular level of education. The Court was silent regarding the application of separate but equal at the levels of education at which most blacks and whites were enrolled.

The NAACP decided to challenge the very concept of separate but equal education in its next series of suits. Several of these suits, which by now had accumulated a good deal of white support, reached the Supreme Court's docket in 1952, and in 1954 the Court issued its famous decision in the case of *Brown* v. *Board of Education of Topeka,* handed down on 17 May, 1954—"Black Monday" to many—in which it nullified the Plessy doctrine as it applied to schools by arguing that separate schools were inherently unequal. Segregation in and of itself had a "detrimental effect" on black children, the Court held, "for the policy of separating the races is usually interpreted as denoting the inferiority of the Negro group."[8] One interesting aspect of this decision was that the Court relied far less on legal precedents—what the framers of the Constitution had meant or the validity of *Plessy* v. *Ferguson*—than it did on the sociological and psychological evidence outlining the effect of segregation on children. Because of the breadth of its decision's impact, the Court heard additional arguments from interested parties concerning the relief to be granted the plaintiffs, and in 1955 ordered all southern segregated districts to desegregate their public schools "with all deliberate speed." With agonizing slowness and a good deal of foot-dragging and a number of attempts to circumvent the law, southern districts seemed to have

[7] *Sweatt* v. *Painter*, 339 U. S. 629 (1950).
[8] *Brown* v. *Board of Education*, 347 U. S. 483 (1954).

moved to comply. In law, blacks now had access to the same educational institutions as whites, in which they could begin to demonstrate their true capacity and merit and compete equally for success and power. Blacks, legally, seemed to have secured equal educational opportunity.

The *Brown* decision should have been a climax to decades of educational aspiration among American blacks, proof that their tenacity had paid off and that they had achieved parity. Instead, it turned out to be but another source of frustration for the black community and the beginning of a startlingly rapid deterioration of the blacks' faith in education's power to improve their lot. A number of factors account for this reversal in black attitudes toward education. First, the nation's unwillingness to implement the Court's demand for integration deeply disappointed the blacks. Southern school districts fought to frustrate the law at every turn. In 1955 and 1956 the southern states adopted the policy of "massive resistance," which was in fact an agglomeration of strategies designed to annul or render ineffective the new "law of the land." The editor of the Richmond, Virginia, *Newsleader* voiced a popular southern opinion in early 1955. "When the court proposes that its social revolution be imposed upon the South 'as soon as practicable,' " he wrote, "there are those of us who would respond that 'as soon as practicable' means never at all."[9] In the aftermath of the *Brown* decision there was a revival of the Ku Klux Klan, the founding of the White Citizen's Council, and the *Birth of a Nation* reappeared at local theaters. Southern lawyers strained to find constitutional support for the right of states to override Supreme Court decisions, especially on "local" matters like education. States passed laws and constitutional amendments that required segregated schools, or guaranteed white parents the right to have their children educated in all-white schools even if their local school was integrated, or made local referenda totally binding with regard to the racial composition of the local public schools. State and local school authorities sought to delay action by fighting each desegregation petition brought by the NAACP through every legal avenue of appeal. Some localities and states tried to convert their public schools into private institutions and then established, with tax money, enough scholarships to cover tuition for all the district's children. But since the schools were technically private, they argued, race could be used as a criterion of admission without violating the Supreme Court's edict against that practice in the public schools. Prince Edward County in Virginia simply shut down its public school system for four years (1959–1964) and limped along with a halfhearted private school effort rather than carry out court-ordered integration. But the federal courts ultimately struck down each of these strategies. Legal massive

[9] Richmond, Va., *Newsleader* (May, 1955).

resistance did not succeed in stopping integration in the South, although it slowed its progress considerably.

Some southerners employed actual or threatened violence to stem the tide of integration. Whites murdered several civil rights workers, harassed and intimidated parents and children who sought to integrate public educational facilities, and at times sought physically to prevent black children from entering "white" schools. Again, violence slowed but did not stop integration in the South. The White Citizen's Council conducted a well-coordinated program of financial pressure, christened "economic thuggery" by a liberal southern newspaper editor. "The white population in this county controls the money," a council member pointed out. "We intend to make it difficult, if not impossible, for any negro who advocates desegregation to find and hold a job, get credit or renew a mortgage." The council employed "boycotts instead of bullwhips." They also sponsored essay contests in which handsome cash awards were given youngsters who best defended the topic: "Why I Believe in Segregation."[10]

This resistance, both legal and violent, brought a series of dramatic confrontations between federal authorities who sought to enforce the law and local police forces and private citizens determined to obstruct it. The legal battles continued, of course; in 1956, in an attempt to get the legislative and judicial branches to tangle, eighty-two representatives and nineteen senators introduced the "Southern Manifesto" denouncing the Supreme Court into both houses of Congress. Countless physical confrontations occurred also—most dramatically in 1957 when President Eisenhower sent federal troops to Little Rock to insure that black students were safely enrolled, over the objections of the state's governor, in Central High School; in 1962 when large numbers of federal marshals were required to force James Meredith's enrollment at the University of Mississippi over the objections of the state authorities, an incident in which two lives were lost; and in 1963 when President Kennedy nationalized the Alabama National Guard to enforce the integration at the state university. In each of these confrontations, those enforcing the federal court orders ultimately prevailed. Positive action in accord with the *Brown* decision was painfully slow in coming, but in fact each year saw a slightly higher proportion of black children going to school with whites in the South.

In the North, however, the exact opposite occurred. Public schools in northern cities grew more segregated, rather than less, as urban whites fled to the suburbs just as fast as, if not faster than, blacks migrated to and within the cities. The overall proportion of blacks attending school

[10] Quoted in John Martin, *The Deep South Says "Never"* (New York, 1957), 25; *New York Times* (21 November, 1954), 52.

with whites has actually decreased fractionally nationwide since 1955. Although in some cases northern school systems had gerrymandered district boundaries to segregate blacks into schools of their own, in most cases racial segregation in northern schools simply reflected racial segregation in housing. Such de facto segregation—segregation in fact but not segregation created by explicit law, or de jure, as was segregation in the South—fell entirely outside the scope of the *Brown* decision. That decision declared it unconstitutional to separate deliberately schoolchildren by race but said nothing about segregation that occurred because of residential patterns or political boundaries. For almost two decades civil rights advocates and educators have sought legal redress for the victims of this kind of scholastic deprivation. It is clear that if segregation imposed by law hurts a child, he is equally damaged by de facto segregation, even though the kinds of segregation are quite legally distinct.

Until the 1970s aggressive federal courts attempted to force urban school systems to eliminate de facto segregation. The courts argued that, since any segregation deprives black children of their right to equal educational opportunity, school systems must take positive action to eliminate it if they are not to violate the blacks' civil rights. In effect, they argued that not to seek to reduce racial imbalance, however caused, was to accept and support it. Until Richard Nixon's inauguration in 1969, the Office of Education threatened some urban school systems with the loss of federal school funding—a substantial amount of money by the 1960s—if they failed to move to eliminate or a least reduce racial imbalance in their schools. Some smaller cities, usually suburbs within a metropolitan core, like Evanston, Illinois, or Berkeley, California, have moved to eliminate segregation through extensive cross-town busing of black children to schools in white neighborhoods and white children to schools in black districts. But central cities and many suburbs have been unable to comply, partly because white parents have resisted fiercely and partly because cities like Baltimore, St. Louis, Cleveland, Detroit, Washington, and Newark have too few white children left in their schools to balance all the predominantly black schools. Moreover, evidence accumulated that attempts to relieve racial imbalance in cities with large black populations persuaded more and more white parents to leave the city or to send their children to private schools. In the face of these demographic problems, integrationists have suggested more wide-ranging solutions. The most popular are programs calling for busing white children from the suburbs into the central city schools while transporting blacks to suburban schools, or for melding city and suburbs into a single school system ("metropolitanism") in order to provide a larger and more stable supply of white children with which to achieve racial balance. Since a majority of suburban whites are violently opposed to these suggestions and since the Nixon and Ford administrations reduced the Office of Education's and the federal courts' pressure on cities to end discriminatory practices, de facto segregation promises to remain the rule rather than the exception for some time to come and the pace of integration should remain excruciatingly slow. In sum, the *Brown* decision did not lead to widespread integration of white and black children; rather, it precipitated a reaction that starkly revealed white revulsion at the prospect of sending their children to school with blacks. Such revulsion suggested that revisions in the statute books and in educational organization were unlikely to alter racial injustice as much as blacks had hoped.

Another factor in the blacks' wavering faith in education was a growing realization that increased education simply did not "pay off" for blacks as it did for whites. The extraordinary black perseverance in schools in the urban North in the first three or four decades of this century did not lead to the promised access to material security and improved social status. Blacks continued to be excluded wholesale from the skilled trades. In one job category after another they were the last hired and the first fired—as the Depression made bitterly clear. Blacks with advanced education did not find the jobs to which their preparation entitled them in business but ended up far too often as postal clerks, redcaps, and Pullman car porters. Three or four generations of adherence to the maxims of Booker T. Washington had not produced any noticeable rise in the blacks' relative social position. If anything, blacks probably sensed something of a downward trend—vivified by the increasingly pathological, slumlike quality of the black ghettos in the urban North. As more and more blacks moved from the South to the northern cities, ghettos grew larger and more separate from the rest of the city and its suburban rings. To their residents and to analysts of the black situation, inner cities seemed to be forgotten enclaves of unemployment, underemployment, violence, broken homes, drug abuse, and shattered dreams. This picture was clearly too bleak, however, for the bulk of ghetto families continued to adhere to middle-class values and to strive for a better life with some success, and the relative socioeconomic position of blacks in America had not turned downward since the thirties (it had not improved very much either). Yet the appalling suffering everywhere visible in the ghettos and their staggeringly rapid increase in size after World War II seemed to cry out for immediate solutions, solutions too pressing to depend upon the palliatives of education. Access to better housing outside the ghetto, to better jobs and to political power was required—immediately. Schooling had proven unable to assure any large number of blacks access to these rights in previous decades and, in view of the desperate situation in the northern ghettos, many blacks and white supporters of the black pursuit of equality asserted that equal access to schools was not enough.

This rising dissatisfaction with schools as a means of bettering the blacks' place in American society coincided with the growth of a new kind of civil rights movement that used nonviolent tactics to demand immediate changes in the blacks' legal and social status. The success of these demands for immediate change further undermined black reliance on education, which presented a thoroughly gradualist approach to reform. In 1955 Martin Luther King electrified the black community by leading a successful year-long boycott of public buses in Montgomery, Alabama, in protest of statutes which forced blacks to sit at the back of the buses. That venture's success in eliminating one Jim Crow practice launched a raft of peaceful demonstrations by blacks and their white sympathizers against all kinds of Jim Crow regulations requiring separation in restaurants, public facilities, and politics. In 1959 "freedom riders" began testing Jim Crowism on interstate public transportation. In 1961 black college students began occupying all the seats—thus, "sitting in"—at lunch counters in Greensboro, North Carolina, which refused to serve blacks. This nonviolent economic pressure worked and white businesses rather quickly ended their practice of racial separation.

The nonviolent civil rights movement, ironically aided by the violent response of many southerners to it—typified by the actions of Birmingham police chief Eugene "Bull" Connor in 1963—prompted public opinion and the federal government to take dramatic steps to support the blacks' drive for equality. Civil rights leaders were able to demonstrate mass support—as in the huge March on Washington in 1963—for federal action in the fields of voter, job, and housing discrimination. The government responded by prohibiting voter discrimination in 1957, 1960, and 1965, by restricting housing discrimination in 1962 and 1968, and by forbidding job discrimination in 1964 in the great civil rights bill of that year, a significant legislative act which also outlawed discrimination in any public accommodations. Race-conscious blacks learned, they thought, many things from the successes of the nonviolent civil rights movement, but the most significant lesson relating to education was their recognition that the tactics of demand and demonstration did far more to remove legal and customary impediments to racial progress than did decades of education. The accomplishments came far more quickly as well. Booker T. Washington's educational gradualism appeared a poor strategy. Blacks could demand and get their rights rather than having to prove that they "deserved" them.

As was the case with school desegregation efforts, the civil rights movement's attack on legal discrimination brought both victories and frustrations. The desegregation of public accommodations and especially the expansion of voting opportunities surely changed the lives of southern blacks. Civil rights groups and the Justice Department cooperated assiduously to enforce the prohibitions against voter discrimination and to mount voter registration drives at the grass roots level. As a result, for the first time since Reconstruction, blacks were able to exert some influence in southern politics. They became the electoral majority in a few southern towns and counties. By the early 1970s blacks had registered in massive numbers in the South and had begun to hold important positions in the region's governmental structures—although the number of black officeholders was still not proportionate to the size of the black population. By mid-decade, indeed, a black was elected mayor of Atlanta, the South's second largest city.

Despite its success, the nonviolent civil rights movement failed to touch many areas important in the South and neglected issues vital to blacks in northern urban ghettos. In the North overt legal discrimination (Jim Crow laws) had not really been much of a problem for blacks in the twentieth century. Northern whites had discriminated against blacks almost as severely and rigidly as had their southern counterparts, but they did so less openly and as a matter of custom rather than law. This discriminatory pattern was a great deal more difficult to combat than was the legal discrimination in the South. In the North thousands of informal arrangements and deeply ingrained assumptions about black inferiority restricted blacks to poor jobs and to poor neighborhoods. Achieving equality and justice between blacks and whites came to seem less and less a legal problem and far more a problem of "white racism"—far less susceptible to change through boycott or demonstration.

The successes and failures of the civil rights movement highlighted the shortcomings of the educational approach to elevating the blacks' social position. The gradualism implied in the educational solution to the race problem had shown itself to be slower and much less effective than the tactics of demand and demonstration. Moreover, the recognition that virulent, irrational, and often unconscious "white racism" rather than legal discrimination was the pattern against which blacks had to fight made Washington's injunction to get an education and win the respect of whites seem largely fatuous. Better manners and improved skills seemed unlikely to shake racist beliefs or to prove to whites that blacks "deserved" full citizenship rights. The overwhelmingly bleak situation in the ghettos suggested that the promise that more education would enable blacks to improve their social status and economic security was a chimera. And the persistence of poverty among large numbers of blacks, north and south, mocked the public schools' promise that they could increase opportunity and social equality for all groups. In short, many blacks and many of their supporters in the white community, as well as a growing number of social analysts, no longer believed that more schooling or a more equal distribution of schooling was capable of ending racial injustice in the United States. Thus did the black experience undermine the schools' claim that they could expand democracy and equality in the society.

Another challenge to the assumption that equal educational opportunity (defined as access to equal educational facilities) guaranteed groups equal access to wealth and power in the society came in 1966 with the publication of Professor James Coleman's report on the "Equality of Educational Opportunity." This study, up to that time the largest statistical survey of the process of education, had been mandated by Congress in the Civil Rights Act of 1964. Coleman apparently set out to document what the legislators and educators expected him to find: that blacks had unequal access to educational facilities in the United States, and that such unequal access explained their unequal achievement in the schools. Coleman measured inputs into schooling—training of teachers, quality of school books, age and condition of physical plant, and the like—and a group of variables relating to the background of children in various kinds of schools. When he compared these variables to school achievement (the output of his input-output analysis), he did not find what everyone had expected. First of all, Coleman found that black and white schools in the United States were not as unequal as most people had assumed. Second, he discovered that differences in relative school achievement were not closely tied to differences in the measurable educational inputs. (Such research has its problems: many school qualities that educators think quite crucial to the learning process are not susceptible to quantification—thus one might find two schools essentially equal in "objective," measurable aspects but quite different in attitudes, spirit, and aspirations.) What Coleman was saying, in effect, was that spending even unlimited amounts of money on improving teacher training or revising curricula or building new schools, for example, would not significantly reduce the relative differences between the achievement levels of poor children and other students. Schooling could not overcome the effects of the culture of poverty. This challenged the very strategy of the war on poverty's educational thrust. Just as blacks were beginning to point out, more of the same was not going to work.

What did correlate most highly with differences in achievement among poor children was the socioeconomic status of the children with whom they attended school. Thus, the poor child of low socioeconomic status achieved more if he attended a middle-class school than did the child of low socioeconomic background who attended a school made up largely of children from a similar background. Or, in the racial context, black children from impoverished backgrounds were likely to achieve more if they attended school with whites—for, statistically, going to school with blacks meant going to school with lower-class children, while going to school with whites was more likely to mean being in school with middle-class kids. It was not, Coleman argued, what the schools were able to teach the child but, rather, the influence of the peer group in the school on that child that accounted for differential rates of educational progress.

Coleman's message was disheartening to educators and social planners, and at first they tried to ignore it as much as possible. Indeed, Daniel P. Moynihan suspects that the government—which was deeply committed to alleviating poverty by pouring money into ghetto schools so that they would be just as good as those in the suburbs—was so embarrassed by the findings that it made Coleman's report public on the July 4th weekend when it would get little publicity, and seemed deliberately to limit its circulation.[11] Most dishearteningly, the report did not show educators how to keep the promises they had made to break the cycle of poverty. Instead, it catalogued what the schools could not do. They could not remain passive purveyors of equal educational facilities from which all children could reap benefits according to their merit. Such an even-handed distribution of services would simply continue the cruel situation which already existed. The report also indicated the futility of spending more money on schools in pockets of poverty and ghettos: one could not "buy" facilities capable of solving the problem. Further, the report discounted the effectiveness of "educational" inputs of all kinds in determining students' eventual academic and social success. What the student learned from his peers was more crucial to his future social position than what he gathered from his teachers and his books. Racial and social class integration in schools, which Coleman suggested as the most viable solution to the problem of teaching youngsters to escape the culture of poverty, was, for the demographic, political, and ideological reasons discussed above, difficult to effect. The schools could not accomplish such integration alone, and yet many in the late sixties hoped that somehow the schools could integrate the social classes even though more powerful social institutions refused to do anything of the sort.

The clearest message embodied in the Coleman report and in black demands in the middle sixties was that traditional assumptions about education's responsibilites were inadequate. Educational researchers and blacks—joined somewhat haltingly by Puerto Ricans and Latinos—agreed that breaking the poverty cycle and eliminating racial discrimination in the society required more than providing the poor with school facilities of a quality equal to those possessed by the rich (although all agreed, of course, that equal facilities should be provided as a base upon which further efforts could be built). Those responsible for these findings and demands did not feel that the schools could accomplish nothing to break the poverty cycle, but thought that they would have to work harder to do it. They urged schools to provide unequal inputs in order to guar-

[11] Daniel P. Moynihan, "Sources of Resistance to the Coleman Report," *Harvard Educational Review*, XXXVIII (Winter, 1968), 23–36.

antee equal outputs. The important equality with which schools were to be concerned was equality of results, not of facilities. The measure of equality was not how much money a school spent on a child but how much it taught him. Schools served the interests of equality and democracy only when they succeeded in teaching all their citizens the skills necessary to live in and compete in the modern world. This new definition did not reject Jeffersonian notions of competition and meritocracy so much as it demanded that the competitive, meritocratic selection process be postponed to the post school years. The school years should be used to bring all children up to a level that would allow all to enter the competitive, meritocratic selection process of adult life equally well prepared.

The theory held that, because the disadvantages or inequalities with which children came to school resulted from environmental or social adversities, society was responsible for compensating for those disadvantages. Schools were to redress the balance so that the children of each social and ethnic group could begin adult life on an equal footing with other groups. Only in this way could "equality of opportunity" be assured in American society.

This new definition of what constituted equality of opportunity focused on groups rather than on individuals—no one on either side thought that every child should, or could, be made to have equal capabilities. This point was, rather, that the distribution of skills, potential, and merit within any particular socioeconomic, racial, or ethnic group ought closely to approximate the distribution of those characteristics in any other socioeconomic, racial, or ethnic group. The equality in question was not equality of skills or material success between any two randomly chosen individuals but equality in skills and material success between the children (considered as groups) of any two social classes or racial or ethnic groups. Indeed, this new definition of how the schools should serve the democratic goal of equality of opportunity matured only with the emergence of a new group consciousness in American society, especially among the "disinherited"—the blacks, the Latinos, and the poor as a social class.

In the face of the researchers' evidence concerning the irrelevance of traditional concepts of equality of opportunity and minority group demands for a new one, educators, seeking to maintain their promise to help eliminate poverty, embarked on a search for mechanisms with which they could assure "equality of results." A bevy of possibilities did emerge as schools throughout the nation introduced new programs with great fanfare. In many cases the fanfare was more significant than the actual reform; the claims of novelty were far newer than were the strategies themselves. In other cases, however, the efforts were sincere, well financed, and imaginatively carried out. These programs can best be discussed under five headings.

"Compensatory education" was one major effort. The most well-known and typical example of this approach was the Head Start program, begun as a massive effort by the Office of Economic Opportunity (not the Office of Education) in 1965 and 1966. The Head Start program was a summer preschool program designed to involve professional educators, community workers, guidance counselors, and parents in an effort to stimulate the cognitive powers of poor children. In many ways, as Marvin Lazerson has argued, Head Start resembled the earlier kindergarten movement during the Progressive era in its focus on preparing youngsters considered to be from deprived backgrounds to fit into the culture of the public school. At that time, however, the kindergartners stressed inculcation of routines and good manners; in the 1960s the emphasis fell upon "learning to learn." Research on learning—especially that of Martin Deutsch, J. McVicker Hunt, and Benjamin Bloom—was finding that the first few years of life were terribly significant in determining the child's later capacity to learn. Some psychologists thought the child's learning experience in those years determined half or more of his later achievement in cognitive tasks. And yet, reformers urged, those were the years when society's agencies had the least control over children, and when their parents and neighborhoods had the most. Parents in the culture of poverty were "obviously" incapable of providing proper stimulation for their youngsters. Overwhelmed by life and by too many children, they were unable or unwilling to pay the kind of close attention to the individual child that middle-class parents did through constant talking to and game playing with their children. Inured in poverty, they could afford only the drabbest surroundings and, psychologists reported, even the dullness of a tenement's kitchen floor deprived the ghetto child of the cognitive stimulus provided by the bright geometry of the middle-class kitchen floor. Head Start would compensate for such deprivation by providing children from poor environments with games and materials to arouse their curiosity, challenge their imaginations, and allow them to solve problems that would build their sense of mastery. Head Start teachers and volunteers—there was supposed to be one adult for every five children—would act like middle-class mothers to stimulate the children through talking, questioning, helping, and guiding. The Head Start experience would help the children build cognitive capacity and give them a "leg up" when they went off to public school after the summer's adventure.

Initially, the program did give the children that head start, allowing "graduates" of the program to progress through the tasks of the first few months of school much more successfully than children of a similar background who had not had the Head Start experience. Subsequent research soon discovered, however, that these relative advantages did not persist for more than six months or so, that children from deprived backgrounds without the Head Start experience caught up within a relatively short period. Although some argued that this finding demonstrated the regular school's failure to teach the advantaged children in such a way that their gains would continue—and the Office of Education designed Operation Follow Through in 1968 to test ways of enriching and individualizing the work of the primary grades so as to make the Head Start gains more lasting—most concluded that the Head Start compensatory program had failed to accomplish its primary goal. It did not improve the cognitive achievement of poor children. Head Start was far from being a total failure, of course, for it accomplished a number of significant things: it called much needed attention to the health and nutritional needs of poor children and created a mechanism through which some of those needs could be satisfied; it drew attention to the importance of early childhood education as never before; its involvement of poor parents in the program gave them much needed experience in ways of encouraging their children to achieve in school; and it gave participating school teachers a valuable added perspective on the needs and capabilities of poor children. Nonetheless, Head Start failed to make demonstrable progress in eliminating academic differentials between poor and middle-class children.

Head Start was by no means the first of the compensatory programs. Urban educators sensed early in the civil rights movement the need for schools to compensate for cultural deprivation among poor children. In 1956 New York City began a pilot project that eventually became the Higher Horizons program. Higher Horizons provided smaller classes, specially prepared teachers, extra guidance services, psychological counseling, social workers who helped coordinate home and school efforts, enrichment programs and trips to cultural events, extra work in English, and extensive small group tutoring for disadvantaged children (64,000 in 1963). Other cities tried similar efforts. Most projects sought to lengthen the school day, or to use weekends and summers to give students extra help. Some included more emphasis on vocational preparation; others emphasized enrichment; some basic communication and computation skills. Many used paraprofessionals or volunteers to provide the extra individualized instruction which lay at the foundation of the programs. By the mid-sixties, dozens of projects were functioning and the number expanded enormously after 1965 because much of the money granted the school districts with concentrations of disadvantaged children under Title I of the Elementary and Secondary Education Act (1965) was spent on compensatory programs. Assuredly, in most of these programs, students gained much—broader perspectives, more sense of worth, more intellectual challenges, more fun. But, as with Head Start, almost all of the programs failed in their principal mission of improving the cognitive achievements of the children of poverty. Because the cognitive skills, especially reading, were assumed to be the most critical in enabling kids to break out of the cycle of poverty, the compensatory approach or strategy did not seem to be an effective one for achieving equality of educational results.

These failures are not surprising for compensatory programs sought essentially to direct more money, more expensive educational inputs, at poor children. As the Coleman report, the U. S. Commission on Civil Rights' study of "Racial Isolation in the Public Schools" (1967), and much subsequent research have revealed, extra spending on educational services cannot erase the results of cultural differences between the poor and the middle class. It was a hard lesson to learn, partly because Americans were habituated to the belief that money could solve any problem, partly because educators wanted desperately to believe that the traditional tools of their trade, if used profusely enough, would succeed in effacing the effects of poverty. But gradually the public and the educators began to recognize that successful achievement of equality of results—if it could be achieved at all, an important caveat by the mid-sixties—would require far more imaginative programs than yet devised, programs that offered different and specialized advantages to the children of the poor.

The second category of efforts designed to produce equal results sought to go beyond mere compensatory programs by making the school curriculum "relevant" to ghetto children. One of the great "discoveries" of the sixties was the fact that materials used in the public schools, like the programs on television, contained a middle-class outlook and focused on problems and situations relevant only to the middle class. Elementary school readers included pictures of suburban homes with white picket fences but hardly ever showed urban homes like those in which poor children lived. They spent an inordinate amount of space describing farms and farm animals in ways totally foreign to children in the central city (or, indeed, foreign even to the experience of migrant farm laborers). Policemen in the readers were always friendly and jovial and helpful; never like the hostile, frightened, bullying policemen ghetto youngsters had learned to fear even before they began school. These readers hardly ever portrayed a black face (or, when they did, they placed it in a totally white environment). History and civics books were little better. Ghetto youngsters deserved, reformers argued, a curriculum that honed their cognitive skills on stories and problems about things that they knew. Furthermore, reformers thought that such a curriculum, which demonstrated that the problems experienced in their lives warranted as much attention as those of the suburban middle class, would enhance the self-image of the central city students, enrich their lives, and help them to feel less isolated from the mainstream of American society. The movement to teach English as a second language, intially applied to Spanish-speaking students from Puerto Rico and Latin America and later to blacks whose southern or ghetto dialects (or what some have come to call "black English") were considered their "first" language, was one result of the drive for relevance. Using the attitudes and pedagogical devices found to be effective in teaching English-speaking children European languages had several advantages. First, because the teacher assumed that the child's current speech patterns represented a separate tongue rather than simply misspoken English, he no longer found it necessary to tell the child that he must unlearn the speech habits he brought with him in order to master proper English. No longer was the student's manner of speaking "wrong," or that of the teacher "right"; rather, the child's was right for some occasions and the teacher's for others. The child's job was to learn the teacher's so that he could use it when appropriate. This reconceptualization of the teaching of English to minority students allowed such a student to value his background while learning new communication skills useful outside the minority community—especially in job interviews.

The black studies movement was another effort to create more relevant curricula for the children of poverty. By focusing more heavily on the great achievements of blacks in the American and African past, the public school curriculum could give poor black children some idea of the breadth and distinction of their people's history, reinforce the blacks' positive self-image, make them more interested in the history or civics they were studying, and, not least, teach them more accurate history. Some of its black advocates believed, and apparently many whites feared, that black studies would stress values that conflicted with those of white society and would teach separatism and black superiority. In fact, black studies, and later Latino and American Indian (or "native American") studies, sought to increase a student's interest in what he was studying and to enhance his image of himself to the point where he could develop a sense of control or mastery. He would then be able to perform more successfully on the cognitive tests that were critical in determining his economic future. Black studies suffused the curriculum. Areas besides history and civics were affected. Readers contained more and more black faces (at the beginning publishers tried to get by with coloring Dick and Jane brown, but gradually real blacks in believable situations were included). Some of the most militant supporters of this approach called for arithmetic problems geared to black circumstances. Many educators hoped to attract poorly motivated blacks to reading by substituting Piri Thomas and Malcolm X for Shakespeare, George Eliot, and Hemingway in literature classes. They bypassed the great traditional literature in favor of fiction about blacks in the urban ghetto—about racial injustice, black athletes, drugs, gangs, and welfare. By the late sixties, Chicano, Puerto Rican, and American Indian groups were demanding and getting literature and history courses that dealt with their experiences. The black,

Latino, and American Indian studies movements—and the group power movements of which they were a part—sparked a new interest in ethnic identity and cultural pluralism in the United States and led, in the late sixties and early seventies, to a new interest in the problem of cultural pluralism in the schools. Can the schools turn away from their traditional efforts to instill homogeneous values and attitudes in children and to teach children that one set of values and one way of doing things is superior to all others and, instead, try to teach children to value cultural differences and to respect those of different backgrounds and beliefs? Many educators hope that if the schools can adopt a multicultural approach in which children could learn to value both their own and other cultures without concern for ranking one above the other, they will be far more successful in paving the way for equal achievement among young people of different backgrounds.

Another area of effort designed to increase the schools' effect on the achievement of poor children was the drive to recruit more and more teachers from a background roughly similar to that of the children having difficulty. For some years the profession had sought to recruit teachers from minority groups, but after the mid-sixties recruiting efforts focused on those who were both black or Chicano and who also had come up from the culture of poverty. Such recruits were believed to understand the children of poverty better than other teachers and to serve as the best possible ego models to inspire poor children. At the same time, educators came to realize how important it was that all teachers destined to teach the children of the poor should make every effort to overcome their cultural bias. So that future teachers would understand and empathize with the cultural background of the urban child, teacher training institutions throughout the country developed more and more courses in urban sociology, in black studies, and in minority psychology. At the graduate level, the Office of Education began in 1968 the so-called Triple T Project (for Training of Teachers of Teachers) in dozens of institutions. Designed to train future teachers college professors in such a way that they would be thoroughly familiar with inner-city problems and their manifestation in the schools and thoroughly prepared to pass their knowledge and experience on to the teachers they would ultimately train, the TTT program required each project to include significant and continuing representation of the inner-city community on its board of directors. The program assigned trainees to extensive internships in the inner city under the supervision of the graduate faculty, members of the community, and especially competent regular teachers from the inner-city schools.

The three efforts so far discussed gained near universal support among the opinion makers in the field of education (although this does not mean that they were adequately financed). None stirred much debate;

none produced any startling results. The other two categories of effort to achieve equal results stirred considerable debate over how best to organize the educational effort to break poverty's hold on the children of the poor. Supporters of integration fought bitterly with those who thought "community control" the most effective means of reaching these same goals. This vigorous and still inconclusive debate and its ramifications have been at the very core of educational thinking for a decade and show no sign of abating. Integration carries a somewhat different connotation than desegregation in this context: the latter is negative, the former positive. *Desegregation* referred to the process of breaking down legal barriers which kept children who lived near one another racially separated in their schools. Largely a problem of the South, the fight for desegregation was a fight to return to the natural racial mixing of the schools in which explicit laws artificially separated the races. On the other hand, *integration* was an attempt to establish, artificially, conditions of racial—and, less important, of class—mixture which did not exist naturally. In the heavily segregated residential pattern of the North (and increasingly in urban areas in the South), de facto segregation was the governing pattern. Supporters of integration sought to overcome this pattern imposed by residential segregation by creating racially mixed institutions through such means as busing and metropolitanism.

Much of the support for racial and, to a lesser extent, class integration grew out of a feeling among people on both sides of the poverty line that American society was becoming too fragmented. Because ethnic, racial, and class groups were cut off from each other, they misunderstood, feared, and resented one another. These were conditions likely to produce bitter conflict, as in Watts and Harlem. Racial and social class integration promised to increase understanding among groups and thus reduce social tensions. Some of the most optimistic thought that racial integration would even encourage the United States toward a genuinely interracial society where the races respected each other and where group affiliation had no influence on an individual's social opportunity.

Others supported integration because they believed that sending the poor and the black to school with the white and the affluent was the surest way of breaking the poverty cycle. The Coleman report, as we have pointed out, lent immense credence to this belief. Poor children, and especially black children in Coleman's context, showed significant gains in academic achievement relative to their more affluent peers only when they attended school with children wealthier than themselves—children more middle class, more motivated to learn, better able to concentrate, and more readily adjusted to the routines of schooling. Coleman's research clearly outlined the need for social class integration in the schools, but his findings became a goad to racial rather than class integration.

Coleman was concerned to see poor children of whatever color attend school with middle-class children of whatever color. Mixing poor blacks and poor whites would not help. Yet interpretations of his findings concentrated on race and left the class aspects of his research strangely muted. Why this should have been so is an interesting question. Part of the answer surely lies in the fact that the report's findings that black achievement was enhanced most by integrated schools, coming at the time of the emergence of the black power movement, was the most immediately controversial. The narrowed focus on racial integration resulted because many thought that the blacks, because of the added burden of race, represented the least tractable part of the problem of poverty—if you solved that part of it, the rest would be easy. One can further speculate that educational reformers and planners were as unconsciously blind to the differences between blackness and poverty as was the mass of Americans, who against all the evidence persisted in assuming that all poor people were black (as in the belief that all welfare clients are black), just as an earlier generation of Americans believed that all poor people were immigrants. One might even wonder whether focusing on racial rather than class integration in some way reflected a sense that racial integration, despite all the resistance to it, was politically more palatable than class integration among affluent Americans. At any rate, a widely held prointegration theory developed which concluded that achieving equality of results was largely a matter of mixing the races. In the longer perspective, it will probably come to be realized that this theory focused on the wrong aspect of the problem. Poverty, after all, was a class, not a race, problem. The stress on racial integration tended to obscure that point.

The "white hostage" approach to improving schools for blacks provided additional support for integration. No white parents, the reasoning went, would put up with the school conditions that black children endured every day. Therefore, if all black children could be placed in schools with white children, the latter's parents, in protecting their own children, would also procure better facilities, and consequently better results, for black children. This approach apparently generated the most support for integration in the black community; it promised concrete, immediate advantages.

A great deal of white prointegration rhetoric contained more than a trace of condescension which, naturally, infuriated many blacks. Many, both black and white, interpreted Coleman to be saying that blacks could succeed only if they went to school with whites, that they could learn only bad habits from their black peers, their parents, and their culture. A group of black parents in Detroit interpreted this viewpoint to be suggesting that "quality education cannot be provided in inner city schools because if you mix Black with Black you can only get stupidity."[12] Coleman did not mean to suggest this, but his findings could easily be read to reinforce existing white attitudes to this effect. Whites seemed to support school integration in order to rescue blacks from their poor environments, their inadequate parents, and their deprived culture. This attitude was not far different from the one Horace Mann and other antebellum reformers displayed toward the neglected children. of the industrial classes. Education was a missionary effort to bring poor children much needed culture and a knowledge of the right way of doing things.

It is still too early to achieve full historical perspective on the integration movement of the sixties. The nature of its support is complex and its attitudes and covert goals are masked in language with which we are so familiar that we cannot yet perceive many of the true meanings behind those familiar words. But some aspects of the movement are suggestive. Until the late sixties most white supporters pictured integration as upward. The image usually focused on a few blacks moving into good white schools or black and white children in laboratory "magnet" schools (schools so innovative and successful that, even though located in black ghettos, they would attract white parents and their children). The image pictured busing black children to the suburbs—one thinks immediately of the voluntary and private METCO system in metropolitan Boston or the limited busing experiments in Hartford and a host of other cities. Integration was popularly viewed as bringing blacks to the white middle-class culture. The controversy over busing that broke out in earnest after 1968 put a very different face on the matter. By then federal courts had come to agree with a number of planners in the Office of Education and in civil rights groups that the only way effectively to desegregate urban schools was through some sort of enforced busing, often across city boundaries since the schools in the major black population centers were losing whites so quickly that there remained too few with whom to integrate. The contemplated enforced busing in cities like Detroit and Richmond meant that not only would blacks be taken to white suburbs and integrated "up" but whites would be bused from the suburbs into the black neighborhood schools—integrated "down," as it were. When this became clear, a great popular resistance developed to enforced integration through busing of a kind politicians and school boards could not ignore. When integration began to be seen as more than a missionary effort to the deprived, its support among opinion makers and governmental leaders suddenly dropped. The Nixon administration reversed

[12] From "Detroit Schools—A Blueprint for Change," by the Inner City Parents Council, quoted in Leonard Fein, *The Ecology of the Public Schools: An Inquiry into Community Control* (New York, 1971), 10.

the federal government's record of supporting civil rights and desegregation compiled since 1954 and, instead, supported legislation to prohibit the spending of federal monies to finance busing for integration purposes. Many states passed laws prohibiting school boards from busing children out of their home districts or out of their neighborhood schools without parental consent.

Modern urban racial demography makes it clear that any attempts to break the cycle of poverty among blacks through integration is going to require extensive busing, but the current popular and political resistance to such busing guarantees that progress in that direction is sure to be slow. The situation is further confused by growing scholarly debate as to whether integration of blacks into middle-class white schools has been particularly effective in improving the academic performance or the self-esteem of the black children bused into such schools. The debate is far too complex to be discussed here except to point out that the opponents of busing are not without some evidence that busing is not worth the costs, at least in terms of improving black children's chances in later life. Here is one place that the confusion of racial and class integration is regrettable. Residential and educational segregation according to race is both wrong and wrongheaded. On that basis, surely, every effort should be made to eliminate it. But the fight of the sixties was made on other grounds—that segregation caused, and desegregation would eliminate, poverty—and by 1970 when much of the interest in eliminating poverty seemed to be flagging, when integration seemed harder to accomplish, and when integration's influence on the culture of poverty came into question, much of the steam inevitably drained out of the movement for racial balance in the schools.

The sixties saw another, opposing strategy for employing schools in the effort to eliminate poverty and the culture that it bred—the movement for community control. The movement was born out of the confluence of four separate sets of ideas and experiences. First, many influential social scientists and their audience in the federal government advanced the idea that perhaps the greatest cause of hopelessness and passivity among those caught in the culture of poverty was the fact that poor people in the United States lacked any power over the institutions which most affected their lives. They argued that the improvement of welfare services, better education, and better housing all treated the symptoms while doing little to affect the basic causes of dependence, passivity, and hopelessness. Redistributing power in such a way that poor people gained some control over their lives and over the forces that impinged upon them would make the poor a different people—independent, active, achieving. The wide influence of this point of view was evident in the requirement for "maximum feasible participation" of community residents in the programs included in the Economic Opportunity Act of

1964, and in the Model Cities and Community Action programs. (Its failure to convince completely is evident in the spotty enforcement of this requirement.) Each of these programs made provisions for planning to be carried out jointly among the federal government, local authorities, and residents of the affected communities. Community residents were to vote for representatives to these bodies and, often, to approve or disapprove of specific reform proposals. Although community control of schools was a part of no particular federal program or suggested proposal, the idea of community control was in the air and the schools, often considered the last bastion of local control in the United States anyway, seemed natural institutions in which to test the theory. Each community already contained one or more schools with some localized administrative apparatus. Although authority over schools had been flowing to central offices in urban areas since the Progressive era, it did not appear so difficult to return it to local neighborhoods. Furthermore, schools were important institutions affecting the lives of every poor child, and because they affected all the children, they touched the majority of adults in the community. Thus they seemed an ideal place upon which to focus efforts for community control.

A second source of support for the notion of community control of the schools was the growing fashionableness of proposals for the decentralization of the unwieldy educational bureaucracies that delivered educational services in urban America. Overbureaucratization and overcentralization became increasingly modish explanations for the supposed failure of innovation to improve urban systems, for city schools' failure to match the quality of their much smaller surrounding suburban school systems. The theory held that smaller, decentralized systems could adopt new strategies and adjust to new problems far more rapidly and effectively than larger systems with their endless miles of red tape, their hierarchies of middle management employees more concerned with protecting their power and their jobs than with improving education, and their requirements to balance so many competing interests that the safest course was to continue without change. David Rogers' popular *110 Livingston Street* (1968) exposed these problems as they appeared in the central headquarters of the huge New York City system, which employed over 50,000 teachers and sought to serve over 1 million children. Books like Rogers' increased the popularity of "decentralization" as a means of overcoming bureaucratic resistance to reform. Proposals for decentralization had been formulated as early as the 1930s. But prior to the mid-sixties efforts at implementation were restricted to turning over authority to local districts within the system. This was an administrative reform only. Professional educators at the local level received more opportunity to control the educational services under their direction, but such decentralization did not imply any additional participation in school affairs by the local community. By the mid-sixties, however, educational reformers and the concerned public began to see decentralization as a means of generating greater public participation in educational decisions. The report of the Mayor's Advisory Panel on the Decentralization of the New York City Schools (the Bundy report), entitled "Reconnection for Learning" (1967), was a particularly important document of this period. It called for both administrative reform (the creation of thirty near autonomous districts within the city) and vastly increased community participation—locally elected school boards were to control each of the new districts. Several other steps were to be taken to "reconnect" members of the community with the schools that served them.

A third development which fed the popularity of community control was the rise of the "black power" movement beginning in 1963 or 1964. In those years increasing numbers of young black civil rights leaders turned their backs on the interracial alliances formed to achieve desegregation and the nullification of Jim Crow laws. These leaders identified the next step in bettering conditions for blacks as building black political strength through developing a voting bloc strictly representative of black interests. To effect this independence these leaders began to place far more emphasis on black identity, on those qualities which made blacks different from (and in some cases superior to) whites. They glorified the black experience, past and present. Some black power advocates sought a black separatism resembling that espoused by Marcus Garvey in the 1920s, some described a separate black state within the United States, others a separate black economy within American society. But most envisioned no such ultimate goals. Rather, black power sprang from a feeling that the time for the strategies of challenging discrimination legally and cooperating with whites to achieve black goals had passed. Now blacks must depend upon themselves to achieve their rightful social status and must develop political power to do so. Separatism was not the ultimate goal of the black power movement so much as it was a device for creating unity and a sense of responsibility and independence within the black community. Black power sought to build among blacks an identity as a group capable of determining its own place in the society through concerted effort. Gaining control over the schools to which their children went was to be part of that effort.

The fourth element or experience from which the community control movement sprang was, in the context of the history of American education, the most extraordinary. In the major cities of the northern United States, a grass roots realization matured among black parents that the public schools were failing to teach black children adequately because the schools rather than the children were incompetent. When black parents and the black community began, perhaps for the first time, to review the achievement of black children in predominantly black schools relative to the achievement of white children in predominantly white schools (a process much facilitated when urban school systems were forced to publish school-by-school test results), they were incensed to see how poorly their children were doing. Instead of assuming the blame for these poor scores themselves, the blacks condemned the public schools for failing to teach their children. This reaction was a radical departure from the manner in which minority groups had traditionally reacted to the public schools. Historically, minority groups seem to have accepted the educators' rationales that their children did poorly in school because they were less talented or motivated than other children or because their backgrounds did not fit them adequately to succeed in school. Parents and children, not the schools, were responsible for poor academic performance. Such explanations had protected the schools from criticism "from below" for generations, but they failed to satisfy black parents in the 1960s. Nothing but professional incompetence, they argued, could account for the fact that blacks as a group should be learning so much less in school than whites as a group. Out of pride and anger and frustration, black parents refused to accept the blame for their children's failure to learn to read and compute.

Instead, they faulted the schools and set out to pressure them to change. The process of "demanding" better performance from the schools brought them face to face with the people occupying powerful school and municipal offices who, the blacks discovered with some surprise, revealed themselves as deceptive, foot-dragging, deliberately myopic, hostile, racist, and incapable. The confrontation served, in Carolyn Eisenberg's phrase, to "demythologize," for the blacks, urban politicians, liberal do-gooders, and professional educators. As a result, parents gained the confidence to argue that, since those controlling the schools in poor neighborhoods were unqualified, the parents of the children forced to attend those schools should take control. They could hardly make the schools worse, and there was great hope that they could make them much better.

This hope rested upon no theoretical foundation or upon any detailed empirical research such as that accumulated by Coleman in support of integration efforts. Empirical data was unavailable because no real experiments in community control had been conducted. Community control accumulated what theoretical justification it did only after the demands were made. Community control initially rested on political rather than educational imperatives. Because the movement's first focus was on asserting black prerogatives in a society that consistently denied those prerogatives, specific promises that it would improve educational achievement were not critical to its early popularity. Furthermore, community control can be said to have gained followers not so much because of its persuasiveness as a theory as because of the desperation in the black community. By the mid-sixties, white migration to the suburbs made any form of desegregation, integration, or racial balance in urban areas more and more illusory. They would come, if at all, only after years, perhaps generations, of struggle. Yet, at the same time, the sense of crisis that pervaded the black communities—deteriorating housing, spiraling rates of drug addiction and unemployment among black youths, and the belief that the government was building internment camps for blacks—made it impossible to contemplate waiting generations or even years for relief from the curse of inferior schooling. Something had to be done about the atrocious conditions in ghetto schools immediately and the doctrine of community control offered hope.

Support for community control also grew because of the perceived condescension toward blacks in the Coleman report and among so many of integration's supporters. Blacks felt terribly insulted by Coleman's apparent assurance that their children could not do well in schools populated mostly by other blacks. That conclusion was especially inflammatory in 1966 because advocates of black power, in their struggle to build a sense of identity and positive self-image in the black community, wished to dispel the idea that the only hope for relieving the black's economic and racial plight lay in making him more and more like the white. They stressed that blacks had a unique heritage and culture to pass on to their children. Black children did not need to learn white culture in white schools at the cost of losing their own. Blacks wanted to be independent and responsible in their own right, not objects of missionary attention. Community control embodied just such independence and responsibility.

As the movement progressed, advocates of community control of schools in black neighborhoods came to offer two broad theoretical explanations of why such a scheme of educational organization and pupil distribution would improve the educational advantages of black children. One theory grew out of the condescension perceived in the integration approach. Blacks increasingly viewed as a form of cultural imperialism demands that they be measured against middle-class white standards of acceptable educational achievement. Blacks appeared to do worse in school than whites, the argument went, because standards of success were too narrowly construed and were tailored to the abilities of middle-class white children. A broader definition of success should include areas in which blacks excelled more than whites. Theorists seldom bothered to describe this broadened definition very explicitly, but they claimed that such a broadening of the definition of academic success would occur only when black people gained control over their school systems. Community control, of course, would assure them that dominion. Because they would be directed by local citizens, ghetto schools could develop curricula more relevant to the lives and aspirations of black children than was possible in an integrated setting or in a system in which schools were controlled from a central office.

The second broad area of theoretical support for community control emerged from a growing body of educational research that purported to show that a student's self-concept and the teacher's concept of the student largely determined the student's degree of academic success. Schools controlled by the community would eliminate teachers and administrators whose racism made them expect little of black students. The local citizens governing the schools would also serve as positive ego models for black children. Attending schools in which their parents and community helped determine policy and select teachers would enhance the black students' achievement, both by improving their self-concepts and by providing them with teachers who thought they could learn.[13]

Despite the fact that the issue of community control has generated a vast amount of controversy in education since the mid-sixties, such a program has yet to be implemented in a way demanded by its advocates; consequently, examples of community control from which empirical data could be gathered are sparse, and evaluation of the doctrine's effectiveness as a solution to the problems of poverty and racism in American society is impossible. Various schemes of dividing urban systems into more or less self-governing smaller units have been devised and implemented, but no city has satisfactorily resolved the problem of how to give those who do not raise and pay the taxes sufficient power over their schools to change them substantially. Conflicts with central boards over the distribution and use of funds and with teacher organizations over the authority to choose and discipline teachers have constantly bedeviled community control experiments. The very essence of community control is localizing power to select school employees and to allocate monies among programs. Without these powers, control cannot meaningfully exist. And yet the larger community rightfully demands some power over local behavior. It demands that the local district spend the tax resources of the whole community wisely and that it judge employees equitably according to agreed-upon criteria. The inability to find precisely the right formulae for balancing the interests of the local and the larger communities has prevented the implementation of valid systems of community control.

Evaluation of community control is also hampered by the fact that, of all the solutions to poverty suggested in the 1960s, community control of schools has inspired the loudest objections and the most bitter ideological battles. Community control appeared to reject the goal of interracial harmony in favor of racial separatism. This especially angered liberals who had been the blacks' greatest allies in the immediate past. As Leon-

[13] Robert Rosenthal and Lenore Jacobson, *Pygmalion in the Classroom* (New York, 1968).

ard Fein points out, a basic aspect of liberal ideology in the United States has been the rejection of localized pluralism or the "village community" in favor of a more universalized society which dissolves the petty prejudices and parochialisms of the ethnic, religious, or local group. Liberals, who most often appeal to rationality as a means of determining what is good and bad, believe that those who cling to groups formed around ethnic, racial, religious, or local ties tend to do so for irrational, affective reasons, and to judge questions of right and wrong on the same basis. Thus liberals felt that blacks were deserting their joint commitment to rationality and universalism as alternatives to prejudice in American society, returning instead to the irrational, emotional community loyalty which, according to liberal ideology, helped to create prejudice. The situation in New York City, the showcase of battles over community control, further exacerbated the ideological conflict between old allies. There blacks were pitted against the heavily Jewish teachers' union—a confrontation that led to three bitter strikes and which left embittered large segments of the nation's Jewish community, a community which had provided many of the most vigorous white advocates of integration and racial justice. Thus it is difficult to find accounts of community control and its educational effects that are not badly biased by the writer's particular ideological position on the issue of whether the strategy is a good one. We are far from understanding the relative effectiveness of community control and racial balance as strategies for improving education or the possible ramifications of their implementation on the larger society. Nor will we learn more by judging them before they are understood.

III

It is really far too early to assess the schools' performance in the effort to break the cycle of poverty in the United States. New curricula, bicultural and multicultural approaches, integration, and community control have hardly had time to be implemented and their strengths and weaknesses identified so that they could be revised further. In very few instances has any one of these strategies been applied fully and wholeheartedly. The educational questions remain too entangled with the emotional and ideological questions of race and prejudice to admit an objective perspective. Yet educators and the public alike are already engaged in pronouncing judgments on the schools' success in fulfilling their promise to eliminate poverty. This process of quick, premature judgment has put the educational profession in a somewhat perilous position.

The judgments receiving the greatest amount of public attention have been those which point out that new school efforts have not yet reversed the effects of poverty in the United States. Moreover, many of these judgments clearly imply that the schools will never contribute to the eradication of poverty. Yet there have been real gains in the percentages of minority group students attending college, for example, and evidence that the income gap between well-educated blacks under age thirty-five and whites of similar education has been greatly reduced. These gains, however, seem less significant than the statistics showing that reading scores in most ghetto schools remain well below those in other urban schools and that for black families in the urban ghettos—whose percentage in the total population is not falling—income differentials and other measures of "success" remain nearly as discouraging as they did in 1960.

These negative findings discouraged and confused educators and their supporters. They had enthusiastically promised in the early sixties that schools would help eradicate poverty. And, as the problems began to appear more difficult, the educators seemed to promise even more. One must recognize the magnitude of that promise; they not only agreed to improve education but also to insure that better education would effect definite social change. Education would not only provide equal facilities in which students could demonstrate their potential; it would teach children so equally that they could enter adult life from substantially equal positions. Black and other minority demands, the optimistic reformism of the sixties, the modern demand for immediate and total results, and their own desire to serve society combined to cause educators to bite off more than they could chew. By 1975 it seemed clear that the schools had yet to fulfill the promises they had made, and the temper of the times dictated not that the schools counsel patience in order to give the reforms of the sixties a fair test, but that they scramble to find new solutions. One result of this desperate search for effective innovation was the short-lived experiment of subcontracting the teaching function to various industrial concerns which promised, in "performance contracts," to raise reading and math scores to certain levels in a certain period of time or receive no payment for their services. Nothing could demonstrate more graphically the schools' sense of their own impotence than this effort to turn over their teaching function to outsiders.

Even more disturbing is that the sense of failure was so pervasive that when some scholars with an interest in learning and education began explaining away the failures of the schools, they received wide public support and acclaim. Arthur Jensen's "How Much Can Schooling Boost I.Q.?" (1969)[14] argued that the failure of various compensatory strategies "proved" that blacks in the United States really did have an inherently inferior capacity for abstract reasoning. Jensen's complex statistical argument was not very satisfying to the majority of psychologists, learning

---

[14] Arthur Jensen, "How Much Can Schooling Boost I.Q.?", *Harvard Educational Review*, XXXIX (Winter, 1969), 1–123.

theorists, and geneticists who reviewed it, but it clearly struck a responsive chord in American society. It was much discussed and often cited as a rationale for spending less money on compensatory education. Jensen's arguments provided a vent for many latent feelings that blacks were inferior and many, both educators and laymen, used his findings, or a tempered version of them, to explain what they understood to be the blacks' lack of school success despite a decade's best efforts to help them. In a longer perspective, it may appear that Jensen's work was the beginning of a resurrection of the educators' traditional explanation of why certain groups did poorly in school—that the students and their racial inheritance, rather than the schools, were at fault. His work may signal the beginning of a rejection of environmental explanations of poverty and failure, and a return to an hereditarian or genetic explanation which had been submerged since the thirties.[15]

In *Inequality: A Reassessment of the Effect of Family and Schooling in America* (1972) Christopher Jencks and his associates argued that the assumed correlation between educational advantages and future success in the society was far more tenuous than people had realized when they enlisted the schools in the effort to eliminate poverty. "Luck," and aspects of personality having little or nothing to do with cognitive ability, seemed far more important than academic success in determining a person's future in the economic structure. Jencks sought to deemphasize group inequality as a measure of social pathology and substituted individual inequality in its place. He was far more concerned with eliminating the differences in wealth between the richest fifth of the population and the poorest fifth than between blacks and whites. The average black worker earns 50 percent less than the average white worker, but the average member of the richest fifth of the population earns 600 percent more than those in the poorest fifth. "We would, of course, like to see a society in which everyone's opportunities for advancement were equal. But we are far more interested in a society where the extremes of wealth and poverty are entirely eliminated than in a society where they are merely uncorrelated with skin color, economic origins, sex, and other such traits."[16] In a sense, then, Jencks was taking the war on poverty more seriously than were the educational reformers of the sixties, who tended to confuse poverty with blackness and to see programs aimed specifically at blacks as a means of eliminating poverty throughout the society. Jencks concluded that education played a relatively marginal role in determining that pattern of grossly unequal distribution and, consequently had little

[15] Michael B. Katz develops the hereditarian-environmentalist cycle in *Class, Bureaucracy, and Schools* (New York, 1971), 111–113, and in *The Irony of Early School Reform* (Cambridge, Mass., 1968), 207–208.

[16] Christopher Jencks et al., *Inequality: A Reassessment of Family and Schooling in America* (New York, 1972), 14.

power to change it. Educators had promised something that they could not, by the very nature of the problem, achieve. Poverty would have to be eliminated directly through the redistribution of income, through new patterns of compensation for work, and the like. Jencks did not criticize education for its failure so much as he relegated it to a very peripheral role in affecting this major social problem. Education was not the mighty engine of social reform that its proponents had claimed in the years after 1960.

Jensen and Jencks and their many amplifiers have challenged education's power to achieve the social changes which it had promised, and their popularity reveals education's exposed and precarious position in society today. Education had been at the center of public attention since World War II, as a crucial guardian of American hegemony during the cold war and as a vital lever of social reform in the sixties. Education had gained that central position—and the prestige and financial support that accompanied it—by promising much. Educators had to continue to do so in order to retain that position, prestige, and support. By the 1970s those promises rang at least somewhat hollow. Educators themselves were rapidly losing confidence in the ability of schools to succeed in fulfilling the pledges that they had made or that society continued to demand of them. At the same time society, sensing the hollowness of some of the promises, began to demand that schools justify the money poured into them by proving their social utility. Consequently, the schools are casting about in every direction for new ways to serve the public. By 1975 the educational enterprise seemed to lack leadership, a focus, a sense of social vitality, and a sense of spirit. Indeed, the schools seemed to be acting in a somewhat rudderless manner, buffeted one way by one set of demands and in a second direction by another, responding to none of the demands very well and disappointing everyone in the process.

As a result the nation has grown increasingly short tempered with its schools. The honeymoon period between the society and its schools, which developed in the few years after the introduction of the new curricula in the fifties, has come to an end. In part, this is an aspect of the general cynicism and distrust of government that has grown in the United States because of the unpopular war in Indo-China and Watergate, and in part it reflects disappointment with the schools' performance. Poor and minority groups continue to demand that schools insure the success of their children; the schools fail to make demonstrable strides in that direction; and the poor and minority groups get even angrier with them. The working class and the lower middle class are also enraged because they feel they have been neglected in the effort to prepare the well-to-do for college, on the one hand, and to save the poor from poverty, on the other. Their educational needs have been ignored and formal education has failed to teach the simple values of obedience, respect, patriotism, and mastery of the three Rs demanded by the working class. Parents in every social class are incensed because the schools have not protected their children from drugs. Parents of the upper classes are increasingly upset that the inquiry method of education so popular in their schools seems regularly to lead their children to question sacrosanct values and to rebel against established traditions. Even colleges have lost some of their aura of popularity and respect because of the riotous behavior of college students in the late sixties and early seventies. That the best educated and most privileged in the best institutions should act in such a manner made it seem to many that schools were a corrupting influence rather than a valuable one. The society resents the high cost of schools. Where in the late fifties and early sixties, communities competed with each other to spend more money to insure little Johnny the best education, taxpayers and parents in the seventies are taking a jaundiced view of school expenditures and demanding an accounting of every dollar spent. There are concerted efforts to eliminate fads and frills—although, as always, one person's frill is another's necessity—and programs in art, music, foreign languages, and special remedial classes get dropped. Voters turn down school bond issues and school tax increases with surprising regularity and yet demand more and more from their schools. They seek to resolve the paradox by demanding more efficiency and accountability: schools should spend money only on those programs and materials which clearly can be shown to make a difference in the students' academic achievement. But, by and large, the public does not understand the complexities of these issues and expects from the schools quick, simple, and demonstrably effective responses to its requests, but the schools cannot adequately respond. For educational institutions, schools have done a surprisingly poor job of informing the general public of what they are doing and of the problems they face.

In one sense the schools have created this problem for themselves. Since the turn of the century and especially since World War II, they have sold the American public on the notion that they are a key institution in solving social problems. The public has believed them. Schools have prided themselves on being social service institutions and the public has consequently come to expect the schools to respond to their demands. Clearly, the schools are institutions which can and should help improve the society, institutions which can and should respond to societal needs. These functions, however, are but a part of the schools' role. It has enduring obligations to new generations of young people to pass on and criticize the culture of man, and an obligation to serve as a moral exemplar of what is best in that tradition. They have, furthermore, an obligation to teach all children those rudimentary intellectual skills which will enable them to continue to learn for themselves. These primary obligations of schools in our society override any responsibility they may feel to do the immediate bidding of the society and various groups within it. Until educators make this fact clear by defining the schools' obligations publicly and precisely, they will continue to be buffeted by the conflicting appeals of various social groups. Relinquishing their claim to be primarily concerned with solving social problems will not be easy for schools. Since the founding of the common schools in Horace Mann's day, schools have sought the limelight of public attention by promising to be effective agencies of social control and/or social change. Relinquishing that role will mean relinquishing the limelight, and that is always hard to do. But unless it is done schools can only continue to scurry in response to these conflicting demands. In doing so they will satisfy no one, their students least of all.

GUIDE TO FURTHER READING

WILLIAM E. LEUCHTENBURG, *A Troubled Feast: American Society Since 1945* (Boston, 1973), WALTER K. NUGENT, *Modern America* (New York, 1973), ANDREW HACKER, *The End of the American Era* (New York, 1970), RONALD BERMAN, *America in the Sixties: An Intellectual History* (New York, 1968), and WILLIAM L. O'NEILL, *Coming Apart: An Informal History of America in the 1960s* (New York, 1971), concentrate on recent American domestic policies and activities. MICHAEL B. KATZ offers his sobering thoughts on educational reform in the sixties in *Class, Bureaucracy, and Schools: The Illusion of Educational Change in America* (1971; New York, 1975), chapter 3. GODFREY HODGSON surveys the recent literature on the contribution of schooling to mobility in his excellent essay, "Do Schools Make a Difference?", *Atlantic Monthly* (March, 1973), 35–46.

Black Power: The Politics of Liberation in America (New York, 1967), by STOKELY CARMICHAEL and CHARLES V. HAMILTON, remains the central document of that movement. ANTHONY LEWIS interprets the civil rights movement during the 1950s and 1960s in his comprehensive *Portrait of a Decade: The Second American Revolution* (New York, 1964), and C. ERIC LINCOLN examines *The Black Muslims in America* (1964; rev. ed., Boston, 1973). The white support extended to the black movement is reflected in CHARLES SILBERMAN, *Crisis in Black and White* (New York, 1964). The culture of poverty and its debilitating influence is analyzed in CHARLES A. VALENTINE, *Culture and Poverty: Critiques and Counter-Proposals* (Chicago, 1968), ELEANOR LEACOCK, ed., *Culture of Poverty: A Critique* (New York, 1971), OSCAR LEWIS, *La Vida: A Puerto Rican Family* (New York, 1966), LEE RAINWATER and WILLIAM L. YANCEY, *The Moynihan Report and the Politics of Controversy* (Cambridge, Mass., 1967), MICHAEL HARRINGTON, *The Other America* (New York, 1962), and DANIEL P. MOYNIHAN, *Maximum Feasible Misunderstanding: Community Action in the War on Poverty* (New York, 1969). A series of exposés alerted reformers to urban educational problems: among the most influential were JONATHAN KOZOL, *Death at an Early Age* (Boston,

474 EDUCATION IN THE UNITED STATES

1967), and HERBERT KOHL, *36 Children* (New York, 1967). KENNETH CLARK'S *Dark Ghetto* (New York, 1965), and ELLIOT LIEBOW'S *Tally's Corner: A Study of Negro Streetcorner Men* (Boston, 1967), are excellent portraits of ghetto life. For evidence that urban schools in white working-class or ethnic communities are similarly unattractive, see PETER BINZEN, *Whitetown, U.S.A.* (New York, 1970).

Southern resistance to desegregation and integration was organized on several fronts. The legal environment within which opponents of desegregation found themselves is outlined in ALFRED KELLY, "The Desegregation Case," in JOHN GARRATY, ed., *Quarrels That Have Shaped the Constitution* (New York, 1962), ALBERT BLAUSTEIN and CLARENCE FERGUSON, *Desegregation and the Law: The Meaning and Effect of the Desegregation Cases* (1957; rev. ed., New Brunswick, N. J., 1962), and DAVID FELLMAN, ed., *The Supreme Court and Education* (1960; rev. ed., New York, 1969), which contains the relevant Court decisions. The parameters of legal and extralegal "massive resistance" to the edicts of the Supreme Court can be found in ROBBINS L. GATES, *The Making of Massive Resistance: Virginia's Politics of Public School Desegregation, 1954–1956* (Chapel Hill, N. C., 1964), BOB SMITH, *They Closed Their Schools: Prince Edward County, Virginia, 1951–1964* (Chapel Hill, N. C., 1965), BENJAMIN MUSE, *Virginia's Massive Resistance* (Bloomington, Ind., 1961), JOHN B. MARTIN, *The Deep South Says "Never"* (New York, 1957), NUMAN V. BARTLEY, *The Rise of Massive Resistance: Race and Politics in the South during the 1950s* (Baton Rouge, La., 1969), I. A. NEWBY, *Challenge to the Court: Social Scientists and the Defense of Segregation, 1945–1966* (Baton Rouge, La., 1969), JAMES J. KILPATRICK, *The Southern Case for School Segregation* (New York, 1962), and THOMAS P. BRADY, *Black Monday* (Winona, Miss., 1955). HODDING CARTER, III, *The South Strikes Back* (New York, 1959), and BROOKS HAYS, *A Southern Moderate Speaks* (Chapel Hill, N. C., 1959), promote the cause of moderation. ANNE MOODY, *Coming of Age in Mississippi* (New York, 1968), CARL T. ROWAN, *Go South to Sorrow* (New York, 1957), and PAT WATTERS, *The South and the Nation* (New York, 1969), are personal documents worth consulting.

Desegregation in the urban North is examined in ROBERT L. CRAIN, *The Politics of School Desegregation* (Garden City, N. Y., 1969), RAYMOND W. MACK, ed., *Our Children's Burden: Studies in Desegregation in Nine American Communities* (New York, 1968), and GORDON FOSTER, "Desegregating Urban Schools: A Review of Techniques," *Harvard Educational Review*, XLIII (February, 1973), 5–36. Integration through busing is portrayed rather pessimistically in LILLIAN B. RUBIN'S fascinating volume on *Busing and Backlash: White Against White in a California School District* (Berkeley, 1972); a case study of more successful integration efforts is CAROLYN RALSTON, "Desegregation in Berkeley, California," in FRANCIS A. J. IANNI, ed., *Conflict and Change in Education* (Glenview, Ill., 1975).

Community control of public education in the United States is best introduced by LEONARD FEIN in his brilliant analysis, *The Ecology of the Public Schools: An Inquiry into Community Control* (New York, 1971). Other useful interpretations are DAVID K. COHEN, "The Price of Community Control," *Commentary*, (July, 1969), 23–32; and MARIO FANTINI et al., *Community Control and the Urban School* (New York, 1970). Scholarly attention has focused on the New York City situation in the late 1960s; the best discussions are MARTIN MAYER's general chronicle, *The Teachers Strike: New York, 1968* (New York, 1969), LOUIS KUSH-NICK, "Race, Class, and Power: The New York Decentralization Controversy," *Journal of American Studies,* III (December, 1969), 201–219, DIANE RAVITCH, *The Great School Wars: New York City, 1805–1973* (New York, 1974), SOL STERN, " 'Scab' Teachers," *Ramparts,* VII (17 November, 1968), 17–25, the anthology edited by MARILYN GITTELL and MAURICE BERUBE, *Confrontation at Ocean Hill–Brownsville: The New York School Strikes of 1968* (New York, 1969), and CAROLYN EISENBERG, "The Parents' Movement at IS 201: From Integration to Black Power, 1958–1966" (Unpublished Dissertation, Columbia University, 1971), an excellent study which is not yet conveniently available.

DAVID ROGERS, *110 Livingston Street: Politics and Bureaucracy in the New York City School System* (New York, 1968), and PETER SCHRAG, *Village School Downtown: Politics and Education—A Boston Report* (Boston, 1967), expose bureaucratic inadequacies in two major cities.

MARVIN LAZERSON suggests the parallels between the recent Head Start movement and late nineteenth-century kindergarten promotion efforts in "Social Reform and Early Childhood Education: Some Historical Perspectives," *Urban Education,* II (April, 1970), 84–102. The Westinghouse Learning Corporation and Ohio University provide evidence that the positive influences of the Head Start program were only temporary in *The Impact of Head Start* (Springfield, Va., U. S. Department of Commerce, 1969), which is questioned by ALICE M. RIVLIN, "Forensic Social Science," *Harvard Educational Review,* XLIII (February, 1973), 61–75.

One of the most important documents of the 1960s was the report by JAMES S. COLEMAN et al., *Equality of Educational Opportunity* (Washington, D. C., 1966). Scholars from every policy discipline were moved to respond; their analyses have been collected in two volumes: the *Harvard Educational Review,* XXXVIII (Winter, 1968), issue on "Equality of Educational Opportunity," and FREDERICK MOSTELLER and DANIEL P. MOYNIHAN, eds., *On Equality of Educational Opportunity* (New York, 1972).

Disillusion with the effectiveness of schooling as a means of alleviating poverty and enhancing individual and group mobility has drawn on the Coleman report and the recent analysis by CHRISTOPHER JENCKS and his associates, *Inequality: A Reassessment of the Effect of Family and Schooling in America* (New York, 1972), an interpretation that reminds us of the importance of "luck" to individual advancement. A collection of responses, and a reply by JENCKS, was included in the *Harvard Educational Review,* XLIII (February, 1973).

For the reemergence of hereditarianism in the 1960s, and the debate it spawned, the central document is ARTHUR JENSEN, "How Much Can We Boost IQ and Scholastic Achievement?", *Harvard Educational Review,* XXXIX (Winter, 1969), 1–123, which has been elaborated and refined in *Genetics and Education* (London, 1972). The initial publication of Jensen's work provoked a collection of responses and replies which were reprinted in the *Harvard Educational Review,* XXXIX (Spring and Summer, 1969). RICHARD HERRNSTEIN has contributed "I.Q.," *Atlantic Monthly,* CCXXVIII (September, 1971), 43–64, an historical examination of intelligence testing in the twentieth century, and a larger interpretive essay on *I.Q. in the Meritocracy* (Boston, 1973). Scholarly critiques of Herrnstein and Jensen have been collected by ALAN GARTNER, COLIN GREER, and FRANK RIESSMAN and published as *The New Assault on Equality: I.Q. and Social Stratification* (New York, 1974); the best essay included is SAMUEL BOWLES and HERBERT GINTIS, "IQ in the United States Class Structure," 7–84. Also useful are the concluding sections of CLARENCE KARIER, ed., *Shaping the Educational State* (New York, 1975).

Index

Abbott, Martin, 131-33
Abolitionism, 117, 123, 141, 233, 253
Academies, 11, 13, 23-50, 184
Accreditation method, 292-93
Adams, Charles F., 233, 237
Adams, Henry, 232, 233
Addams, Jane, 278, 283-84, 313, 329, 348; educational views of, 269-75
Adler, Felix, 219-24, 324
Adult education, 272; of blacks during Reconstruction, 132
Advanced Placement Program, 411
Advertising, 344-46
Age-grading, 59, 187
Age of college students, 35
Albany Regency, 164
Alvord, J. W., 131
American Bible Society, 43
American Council on Education, 408
American Education Society, 35, 43
American Froebel Union, 322
American High School Today, The, 410
American Home Missionary Society, 43
American Indians, 457, 458
American Missionary, The, 134
American Missionary Association, 132, 204
American Philosophical Society, 4, 5
American Revolution, 3, 4, 6, 8, 63
American Sunday School Union, 43, 78
American System, 63-65
American Tract Society, 43
American Youth Commission, 372
Americanization movement, 126, 162, 166, 199-200, 259, 260, 321
Amherst College, 29
Anderson, Sherwood, 364
Anna Jeannes Fund, 214
Anti-tobacco movement, 131
Applied research stations, 229
Apprenticeship, 68, 171, 193, 196, 197, 219, 304
Aristocrats, 120, 122, 124, 143, 144
Armstrong, Samuel C., 125; program for black industrial education, 204-10
Association for Improving the Condition of the Poor, 198
Association of College and Preparatory Schools of the Middle States and Maryland, 293
Association of Colleges of New England, 293
Associationism, 332
Asylums, 88, 117
Athletics, 16, 24. *See also* Extracurriculum
Atlanta University, 132, 213
Attendance, 192, 351; common school goal of increase in, 56-58; antebellum, 57; high school, 289-90
Aycock, Charles B., 149

Baby boom, 417-18, 427
"Badges of Status," 48, 171, 173, 182-83. *See also* Differentiation
Baker, James H., 292, 300
Baldwin, William H., 211
Ball State Teachers College, 365, 385-86
Bank of the United States, 64
Baptists, 89

Barnard, Henry, 36, 38, 61, 127, 135
Beard, Charles, 266
Beale, Howard K., 361
Behaviorism, 94, 332-34, 344-45
Bell, Bernard, 404
Benevolent societies, 77-78
Benson, Lee, 62-63
Bestor, Arthur, 404-406, 412, 417
Bethel Baptist School Society, 158
Bible, 19, 43, 77, 90, 91, 172, 173, 176, 210, 325; in Catholic School Controversy, 161-69
Bidwell, Charles, 172-73
Binet, Alfred, 353, 355
Birth of a Nation, 445
Black belt, 144, 149
Blacks, 156, 216-17, 232-34, 356, 357, 359, 361, 401, 428, 445; during reconstruction, 119-52 *passim;* duties of educators toward, 124; Freedmen's Bureau, 128-29; colleges established for, 131-32; adult education for, 132; and northern teachers in South, 137-38; contributions to education, 137-38; blamed for failures, 138-39; and redeemer governments, 143; in North Carolina, 144-45; opposition to education for, 152; industrial education for, 204-17; 1960's and, 433-73 *passim;* commitment to education, 439-45; integration, 443-51; Coleman Report, 451-53; "black English," 457; black studies movement, 457-58; community control, 463-68; black power movement, 464-66
Blair, Henry, 127-28
Blair, Bill, 127-28
Bloom, Benjamin, 454
Blow, Susan, 203, 322
Boorstin, Daniel, 40
Boosterism, 40-42, 45, 49, 57, 63, 66, 121, 280, 384
Bosses, urban, 280-82. *See also* Tweed, William Marcy; Tammany Hall
Boston Charity Organization Society, 271

Boston Children's Aid Society, 198
Boston Educational Commission for Freedmen, 129
Boston English Classical High School, 183, 184
Boston House of Reformation, 194
Boston Latin School, 183
Boston Manufacturing Company, 173
Boston School Committee, 92, 322
Boston Schoolmasters, 97-104
Boston Symphony Orchestra, 346
Bowdoin College, 299
Brace, Charles L., 205, 220-22, 324; industrial training and juvenile reform programs, 196-201
Bradley, Milton, 322
Brown, John, 134
Brown University, 230, 231
Brown v. *Board of Education of Topeka*, 444-48
Bruner, Jerome, 416, 417
Bryan, Anna E., 328, 336
Bryan, William Jennings, 251, 352
Bull Moose Party, 252
Bundy Report, 464
Bureaucratization, 118, 154, 186-89, 422, 428, 463. *See also* Oswego Movement
Burgess, Charles O., 406, 411, 418-19
Bushnell, Horace, 86-88
Busing, desegregation by, 447, 459, 461-62
Butler, Nicholas M., 292-93

Calvinism, 86
Cambridge University, 7, 26
Cardinal Principles of Secondary Education, 288, 309-14, 343, 403
Carnegie, Andrew, 387
Carnegie, Dale, 391-92
Carnegie Foundation, 300, 408
Carnegie Foundation for the Advancement of Teaching, 296
Carnegie unit, 296
Catholics, 60, 84, 107, 128, 154, 156, 172-73, 199-200, 233, 359-61, 363; anti-Catholicism, 43-44, 159; immi-

gration of, 57, 123; as threat to
Whigs, 74; Bible reading and, 90,
165; Catholic School Controversy,
157-69; in challenge to Public School
Society, 159; William Seward and,
161; Democrats and, 164

Centralization, 10, 127, 161, 167-69;
goal of common school movement,
56; to restore social control, 58;
Whig and Democrat positions on, 61,
70; at Oswego, New York, 108; in
early twentieth century, 279-84

Certification requirements, 405

Charity Organization Society, 270-74,
309

Charity schools, 60, 78, 106

Chartering process: definition of, 27-
29; for academies and colleges, 36;
Whig and Democrat positions on, 63

Child, Lydia M., 134

Chapter of Erie, A, 233

Child and the Curriculum, The, 260-
69

Child-Centered School, The, 376

Child labor legislation, 182, 258, 289

Child nature, 86

Child study movement, 316, 326-27

Choosing a Vocation, 307

Christian Nurture, 86-89, 92

Civil Rights Act of 1964, 451

Civil rights movement, 449-51

Civil service reform, 235, 244

Civil War, 125, 141

Civilian Conservation Corps, 350, 373,
402

Classical curriculum, 30-34, 133, 184-
85, 205, 238; role in differentiating
students, 47-48; Committee of Ten
Report on, 294-300

Clay, Henry, 63-66, 73, 74

Codification of educational practices,
186, 189, 338; of object method,
109-11; of project method, 381-84

Cognitive psychology, 415-17, 426,
436

Cold War, 401, 406, 407, 419, 421

Coleman Report, 451-53, 456, 459-

61, 465, 466

Colgate University, 309

College Entrance Examination Board,
293, 424

Colleges, 3, 7, 77, 156, 384, 401, 402,
407, 428, 436; in early nineteenth
century, 23-50 *passim;* education to
differentiate and distinguish students
in, 23-24; student violence in, 24;
women and, 25-26; local control and,
26-27; nature of governance of, 26-
27; chartering process for, 27-29;
public function of, 29; classical curriculum in, 30-36; antebellum founding of, 36-50; overbuilding of, 38-
50; fund-raising for, 42-43; influence
of denominationalism on, 43-45;
maintenance of class distinctions in,
47; importance of student organizations in, 49-50; citizen interest in,
49-50; founded in late nineteenth
century, 228-29; Committee of Ten
on, 288-305 *passim. See also* Universities

Colonial era, 8, 9, 24, 28, 37, 56, 85,
120, 183; finishing schools for women in, 26

Columbia University, 229, 292, 293,
297. *See also* Teachers College,
Columbia University

Commission on Life Adjustment Education for Youth, 403

Committee of Ten, 288, 292-304,
306, 309, 423, 436

Committee on Public Information, 346

Committee on the Reorganization of
Secondary Education, 288, 304, 309-
14. *See also* Cardinal Principles of
Secondary Education

Common school movement, 3, 12, 55-
81, 111, 120, 154, 187-89, 230-32,
282; to overcome problems of district school system, 10; character of,
55; goals of, 55-56; effort to increase
attendance in, 56-58; length of
school year increased by, 57; for social control and reform, 58-61; com-

pulsory education and, 59; age grading in, 59; establishment of free
school system, 60-61; Whigs and,
61-70; Democrats and, 61-65; role
of education in economic growth,
65-70; imposition of values and
morality in, 69-70; social control
undermined, 70-76; attempts to restore social control, 76-81; in South,
118-27
Community control: of district
schools, 10; of academies and colleges, 26; in 1960s, 284, 422, 462-
68
Compensatory education, 401; in
1960s, 454-56; criticism of, 469-
70
Comprehensive high school, 313, 412
Compulsory education legislation, 154,
156, 201, 235, 311; nineteenth century attitude toward, 59
Conant, James B., 404-405, 407-12,
414, 417, 420, 426-28, 435
Conduct Curriculum, A, 336-41
Congregationalism, 89, 172
Connectionism, 94, 316, 332-33
Connor, Eugene, 449
Conservation movement, 254
Constitution, U. S., 6, 28, 126, 444;
Fourteenth and Fifteenth Amend-
ments to, 137; Eighteenth Amend-
ment to, 347
Cook County Normal School, 261,
328
Cornell University, 227
Corporal punishment, 98-100, 102
"Cottage system," 88
Council on Basic Education, 405
Counts, George, 375n; 376-78, 406
Coxey's Army, 222
Credit Moblier Scandal, 232
Creel, George, 346
Cremin, Lawrence A., 380n, 406
Crime rate, adolescent, 371
Cross, Barbara, 88
Cross, George L., 443
Cronbach, Lee J., 416

"Cult of true womanhood," 179
Cultural pluralism, 260, 458
Curricular relevance movement, 456-
58
Curricular revision movement, 401-
28 *passim*
Curry, J. L. M., 133, 213
Custodial institutions, schools as, 371,
372, 402-403, 418

"Dame schools," 79
Dangerous Classes of New York, The,
197
*Dare the Schools Build a New Social
Order?,* 376-77
Darrow, Clarence, 352
Dartmouth College, 28-29
Darwin, Charles, 139
Davis, Jesse B., 307
Decentralization, 9-10, 463-64. *See
also* Local control
Deference in social structure, 6, 21, 73,
102
Deism, 89
De Lima, Agnes, 376
Democratic Party, 128, 142-44, 151,
352, 432; in opposition to common
school movement, 61-65; as re-
deemers in South, 143; in Catholic
School controversy, 164-69
Denominationalism: college overbuild-
ing and, 44-45; in Reconstruction
educational philanthropy, 129-30
Department of Education, 127
Department of the Interior, 127
Dependency rate, 146
Depression of the 1930s, 371-73, 385,
420, 421, 426, 448, 464
Desegregation of public schools, 459-
62
Deutsch, Martin, 454
Dewey, Evelyn, 376
Dewey, John, 85, 221, 252, 284, 303,
306, 311, 313, 316, 329, 335-36,
339, 348, 375-76, 381, 406; educa-
tional views of, 260-69; in opposition
to Froebelian kindergarten, 327-28

Dickens, Charles, 110, 178
Differentiation, 118, 154, 155, 183–86, 193, 428
District, 10, 13; defined as legal entity, 9
District committee, 10, 11
District school, 8-21, 56, 57, 60, 66, 120, 168, 279, 366-68; Thomas Jefferson's plan for, 4; local and community control of, 9-10; schoolmasters in, 11-12; intellectual inefficiency of, 12-13; limited objectives of, 13; limited pedagogy of, 14-16; spelling bees in, 16-20; as introduction to deferential social structure, 20-21
Dos Passos, John, 365
Douglas Commission, 304-305
Du Bois, John, 163
Du Bois, W. E. B., 217, 440
Dwight, Timothy, 73

Economic growth, 123, 185
Economic Opportunity Act of 1964, 463
Educational Policies Commission, 403, 408
Efficiency, 257-58, 284. *See also* Social efficiency
Eggleston, Edward, 104
Eisenberg, Carolyn, 465
Eisenhower, Dwight D., 446
Elective reform movement, 240-42, 252, 297-98
Eliot, Charles W., 227, 292, 293, 296, 299
Ellwood, Charles, 311-12
Elmtown's Youth, 366, 367
Emerson, Ralph Waldo, 320
Emory University, 213
Emulation, 100-102
Enrollment. *See* Attendance
Environmentalism, 117, 311, 355, 357, 470
Equal educational opportunity, 117, 148, 445, 447, 451-53, 460; redefined in 1960s, 438

Equality, 141, 401-402, 412, 469-71
"Equality of Educational Opportunity," 451-53
Eugenics, 311, 356
European universities, 7
Everett, Edward, 237
Examination boards, 293
Expertise, 244-45, 256-58, 262, 281, 283, 302-304, 349-51
Extracurriculum, 35, 48, 228, 313, 366, 367n, 390; in early nineteenth century colleges, 34; in public schools, 367-68

Faculty psychology, 32, 93, 94
"Family plan," 88, 199
Farley, Harriet, 176-81
Federal government, 126-29, 414-15, 431, 438, 447
Federal Reserve System, 64
Federalist Party, 62
Feebleminded, 355
Fein, Leonard, 467-68
Female teachers, 26; economic reasons for, 79; Christian Nurture and, 88; social status in nineteenth century and, 181
Financing of education, 414-15
Fisher, Dorothy C., 371
Fishlow, Albert, 37, 57, 58
Fisk, Jim, 233
Fisk University, 132, 213
Fleming, Donald, 238
Ford, Gerald R., 447-48
Ford, Henry, 387
Foregone income, 290; as barrier to attendance, 61
Foundations of Method, 379
Franklin, Benjamin, 30, 31, 175
Fraternities, 370
Free Kindergarten Association, 322
Free school, 60, 61, 120
Freedmen, 117-52 *passim*
Freedmen's Bureau, 128-29, 131, 132, 138, 204, 205, 215
Freedmen's Union Commission, 131
French Canadian immigrants, 106

French Revolution, 3, 4, 96

Freud, Sigmund, 344, 345, 357

Freudian psychology, 308

"Friendly visiting" movement, 270-74, 277

Froebel, Friedrich, 222, 261; philosophy of, 317-19

Froebelian kindergarten, 317-32; opposition to, 326-29

Fulton, Robert, 66

German universities, 245-46

"Gifts and occupations," 317-19, 325-26

Glazer, Nathan, 422

Gould, Jay, 233

Grading. *See* Age-grading

Graduate school, 228, 241

Grant, Ulysses S., 119, 134, 232, 235

Greek language. *See* Classical curriculum

Gross National Product, educational expenditures as percentage of, 58

"Gross Regional Product," 121

Habit formation, 316, 335; in kindergarten, 336-41

Hale, Edward E., 133-34, 137-38

Hall, G. Stanley, 316, 329, 336; opposed Froebelian kindergarten, 326-28

Hampton, Wade, 143-44

Hampton Institute, 125, 132, 204, 207-209, 212, 219

Handlin, Oscar, 160

Hanson, Harriet, 177

Harlan, Louis, 146

Harper, Francis R. W., 134

Harrington, Michael, 432

Harris, William T., 85, 218, 293-94, 322

Harvard College and University, 46, 177, 227, 229-30, 235, 237, 240, 292-93, 297, 408, 409; in colonial era, 26, 27, 29

"Harvest of Shame, The," 432

Haywood, Atticus, 213

Head Start program, 436, 454-56

Herbart, Johann, 261

Hereditarianism, 117, 139, 355, 357, 438, 470

High schools, 3; in mid-nineteenth century, 154-56, 181-86; in Progressive era, 288-314; Committee of Ten recommendations for, 293-300; professionalization of staff of, 300-303; vocational and industrial education in, 304-308

Higher education. *See* Colleges; Universities

Higher Horizons program, 455

Hill, Patty Smith, 328, 335-41

Hofstadter, Richard, 344

Hollingshead, A. B., 366, 367

Home and Colonial Infant and Juvenile Society of London, 109

Hoosier Schoolmaster, The, 10, 11, 19, 104

Hoover, Herbert, 352

"How Much Can Schooling Boost I.Q.?," 469-70

How to Win Friends and Influence People, 391

Howard University, 132-33, 213

Hughes, John, 162-69

Hull House, 269, 271-72, 278, 328

Human nature, 117

Hunt, J. McVicker, 416, 454

Hutchins, Robert, 404

Illiteracy rate, 121

Immigrants, 125-27, 156, 159-60, 163, 165, 175, 196, 199, 202-203, 233, 235, 253, 259, 260, 272, 273, 281, 307, 321, 322, 325, 330; foregone income and, 61; Whig Americanization program for, 162

Immigration, 74-77, 232, 258-59, 356, 357, 359, 361, 432, 437, 440-42, 460; in southern cities, 123; restrictions on, 347

Industrial education and training, 126, 193-203, 217-25, 304-309, 324; in South, 152; definition of, 193; as central role of education, 305; to increase attendance, 306; as extension of democracy, 309. *See also* Manual training; Vocational education

Industrial psychology, 388

Industrial Revolution, 159

Industrialization, 106, 120, 170, 173, 193, 273; as threat to Whigs, 70-71

Inequality: A Reassessment of the Effects of Family and School in America, 470-71

In loco parentis, 24, 77

Inquiry method, 413, 414, 417, 435

Integration, 142, 440-52, 456-62, 465, 468. *See also* Segregation

International Kindergarten Union, 322, 327, 329

I. Q. testing, 353-59

Irish immigrants, 74, 106, 123, 125, 175, 272-73; characterized, 159-60; German immigrants threatened by, 163

Jackson, Andrew, 64, 73

Jacksonians, 62-64

Jefferson, Thomas, 4-8, 40, 408-10, 420, 426, 428, 438, 453

Jencks, Christopher, 365, 470-71

Jensen, Arthur, 469-71

Jews, 200, 237, 359, 363, 468

Jim Crow, 449, 450, 464

Johns Hopkins University, 228, 229, 297

Johnson, Andrew, 128-29

Johnson, Lyndon B., 432

Julius Rosenwald Fund, 214

Junior colleges, 410

Junior League in New York City, 275

Juvenile delinquency, 194, 201

Kaestle, Carl, 188

Kandel, Isaac, 378

Katz, Michael B., 102, 103, 117, 182, 470*n*

Kennedy, John F., 432, 446

Kilpatrick, William H., 329, 331, 332, 335, 336; project method of, 379-84

Kindergarten, 232, 272, 307, 454; in Progressive era, 316-41; Froebelian, 317-32; transformation of, 329-41; habit formation and, 336-41

King, Martin Luther, Jr., 449

Kingsley, Clarence, 309-13

Knights, Peter, 187

Knox College, 40

Krug, Edward, 374, 378

Ku Klux Klan, 137, 141, 348, 352, 353, 359-61, 363, 445

Labor unions, 214-22

Laissez faire, 251, 255

Lafayette College, 46-47

Land grant colleges, 230

Land Ordinance of 1785, 122

Larcom Lucy, 176-81

Latin. *See* Classical curriculum

Latin Grammar Schools, 37

Latinos, 452, 453, 457, 458

Lawrence, Abbott, 69, 123; on education and economic growth, 65-66

Lawrence Scientific School, 230

Lazerson, Marvin, 454

"Learning by doing," 15, 97

Lee, Ivy, 387

Lewis, Sinclair, 364

Lewisohn, Ludwig, 348-49

Life adjustment movement, 403-404, 406, 410

"Lily's Mission, The," 324-25

Lincoln, Abraham, 65, 118

Lincoln National Temperance Association, 131

Lincoln School, 381-84

Literacy test, 149

Local control, 7, 26, 161, 162, 167-69, 280-82, 284, 351-53; opposed by common school movement, 10; colleges and academies and, 23; Democratic ideology and, 63; interfered with by American System, 65; in 1960s, 462-68. *See also* Centralization; Community control

Locke, John, 87, 108
L'Ouverture, Toussaint, 134
Lowell Experiment, 76-68, 88, 154, 173-81
Lowell Offering, The, 175-81
Loyalty oaths, 370
Lubove, Roy, 278
Lutherans, 360
Lyceums, 78, 174, 176
Lynd, Albert, 404, 422-23
Lynd, Robert and Helen, 362, 364, 365, 385, 389
Lyon, Mary, 25

McCarthy, Joseph, 421
MacClay, William, 168
McGuffey, William H., 85, 91, 133
Mackie, Mary F., 209, 210
McKinley, William, 251
Magnet schools, 461
Man Nobody Knows, The, 389
Mann, Horace, 60, 61, 89-110, 123, 203, 213, 234, 298, 312, 321, 461, 473; centralization and, 56; on education and economic growth, 66-70; nonsectarian morality sought by, 89-90; on Bible reading, 90-91; on vocal music, 91-93; on phrenology, 93-95; Pestalozzianism and, 95-97; Boston Schoolmasters controversy with, 97-104
Mann, Mary, 320
Manual training, 217-25, 298; John Dewey's views on, 265-68. *See also* Industrial education and training; Vocational education and training
Manual Training School, Washington University, 218
March on Washington, 449
Marshall, Thurgood, 443
Mass literacy training, 5
Massachusetts Board of Education, 56, 68, 70, 90
Massachusetts Commission on Industrial and Technical Education, 304-305
Mechanics institutes, 78

Memorization, rote, 110, 375. *See also* Recitation
Mencken, H. L., 348
Mental discipline, 32, 85, 98, 300, 332
Mental hygiene movement, 308
Meredith, James, 446
Meritocracy, 5, 358, 408-10, 426-28, 453
Methodism, 130, 158, 164
"Metropolitanism," 447, 459
Meyers, Marvin, 64-65
Middle class, 181; desire to differentiate children of, 155; defined and characterized, 169-73; in 1950s, 422-24
Middletown, 362, 364-65, 385
Middletown in Transition, 364
Milton, John, 30
Missionary societies, 130-31
Mobility, 155, 173, 182, 228, 291, 421; noneducational routs to, 6-7; function of district school to restrict, 20-21; as purpose of colleges and academies, 23; classical curriculum and, 30-31
Morality. *See* Values, imposition of
Morgan, Edmund, 8
Morgan, J. P., 253
Morrill Act, 205, 230, 231
"Moving school," 9
Moynihan, Daniel P., 452
Murphy, Edgar G., 211
Murrow, Edward R., 432

Nation, The, 235
National Youth Administration, 350-51, 373
National Association for the Advancement of Colored People, 442-45
National Association of Manufacturers, 219
National Defense Education Act, 414
National Education Association, 109, 288, 293, 305, 309, 364, 372, 403; Committee of Ten, 292-314; kindergarten department, 322
National Origins Act of 1924, 347

National Science Foundation, 408-414

National Society for the Promotion of Industrial Education, 305

National Teachers Association, 109, 119, 125

National Vocational Guidance Association, 308

Nativism, 156

Natural state of goodness, 4, 97

Neef, Joseph, 95

"Negative liberalism," 62-63, 164, 165

New Deal, 128, 350-51, 420

New England Freedmen's Aid Society, 129

New Freedom, 252

New Nationalism, 252, 258

New York Catholic Protectory, 199

New York Charity Organization Society, 271, 312

New York Children's Aid Society, 197-201

New York City, 10, 40, 61, 75, 94, 122, 130, 156, 157-69, 182, 194, 197, 199, 200, 205, 222, 232, 274, 279, 283, 292, 320, 352, 378, 455, 463, 468

New York Common Council, 167

New York Ethical Culture Society, 219

New York House of Refuge, 194, 195

New York Juvenile Society, 198

Nixon, Richard M., 447, 461-62

Normal schools, 11, 105, 143, 204, 212, 213, 282, 290, 302-303, 320, 322, 331, 405-406, 408, 413, 415, 423; antebellum college founding and, 33; common school movement and, 56; at Oswego, New York, 109; in 1960s, 435-36. *See also* Professionalism in education

North American Review, 235

North Central Association of Colleges and Secondary Schools, 293

Northwestern University, 38

Norton, Charles E., 233-36, 241

Oberlin College, 25, 293

Object method: Pestalozzian version of, 97-98; Oswego version of, 104-11

Office of Economic Opportunity, 432, 456

Office of Education, 447, 454, 455, 458, 461

Ohio State University, 364

Oklahoma University, 443

Operation Follow Through, 455

Organized athletics, 16, 24. *See also* Extracurriculum

Organized labor, 256, 258, 260; industrial education and, 214-22

Original sin, 87

Orphanages, 99

Oswego Movement, 104-11, 186, 222, 223

Oswego Normal School, 104, 109

Other Americans, The, 432

Oxford University, 7, 26

Parker, Francis W., 261, 328, 336

Parkman, Francis, 237

Parsons, Frank, 307-308

Peabody, Elizabeth, 320, 322, 324

Peabody Fund, 212-13

Perfectionism, 117

"Perpetual scholarship," 38

Pestalozzi, Johann H., 15, 96-97

Pestalozzianism, 103, 219, 222; Horace Mann and, 95-97; attempted implementation in Oswego Movement of, 104-11

Phelps-Stokes Fund, 214

Philadelphia House of Refuge, 194

Philanthropy, 43, 78, 120, 141, 142, 147-49, 152, 199-201, 203, 234, 307, 316, 320, 322, 329, 423, 431, 441; Reconstruction and, 129-39; at black schools, 212-17

Phillips, Wendell, 119, 134

Phillips Academies, 46-48

Phrenology, 93-95, 332

Pierce, D. H., 366

Pierce v. *Oregon*, 360-61

Plessy v. *Ferguson*, 443-44

Poor whites, 120, 123-26, 130
Populism, 254-56
Port Royal Experiment, 130
Port Royal Relief Association of Pennsylvania, 130
Porter, James M., 46-47
"Positive liberalism," 62, 164
Poverty, 432-39, 451, 452, 458, 462
Presbyterianism, 123
Princeton University, 24
Prisons, 88, 117
Process of Education, The, 416
Professionalism in education, 103, 111, 169, 192, 289-91, 299, 305, 306, 351, 405, 412, 465, 471-73; as goal of common school movement, 55-56; high school and, 300-304; War on Poverty and, 435-37
"Progressive education," 252, 374-87, 390, 401
Progressive Education Association, 252, 274-83, 293, 375-78
Progressivism, 111, 117, 225, 251-341, 344, 347, 348, 350, 351, 355, 356, 363, 387, 417, 436, 454, 463; economic growth and, 253-55; liberal and conservative, 255-60; of John Dewey, 260-69; in settlement house movement, 269-74; urban public schools and, 274-83; high schools and, 288-314; college curriculum and, 297-99; professionalism of educators and, 302-303; vocational education and, 304-308; kindergarten and, 316-41
Prohibition movement, 259, 347
Project method, 329, 335, 379-84
Prosser, Charles, 403
Protestants, 43, 60, 84, 107, 123, 171-73, 199, 321, 352, 361; philanthropy during Reconstruction, 130-33; preservation of values of, 155; schools populated by, 156; Catholic School Controversy and, 157-69
Prussian reform schools, 312
Psychology, 344-45. *See also* Behaviorism; Connectionism; Faculty psychology; Habit formation
Public School Society, 157-69
Puerto Ricans, 452, 456, 457
Purdue University, 365
Puritans, 85-86, 120
Puritan Dissenting Academies, 30
Putnam, Alice, 328

Quakers, 157
Quackery in the Public Schools, 422-23

Radical Reconstruction governments, 136-38, 141-46
Rantoul, Robert, 173
Rates, school. *See* School taxes
Reading, 415-16
Recitation method, 240, 263, 292; in district schools, 11, 14; understanding retarded by, 14-15; higher education and, 15, 34; opposed by Benjamin Franklin, 31. *See also* Rote memorization
Reconstruction, 119, 126, 138, 141, 143, 147, 148, 216, 253, 450
Red Scare of 1919, 347
Redeemer governments, 143-44
Reform schools, 99, 232, 312; cottage plan, 88; model for industrial education, 194-201
Religious instruction, 43-44. *See also* Catholics; Protestants
Rensselaer Polytechnic Institute, 33
Republican Party, 62, 65, 126, 128, 139, 142, 144, 151
Research. *See* Scientific research
Residential segregation, 71-72, 156, 459, 462
Revivals, 25
Ricardo, David, 28
Richman, Julia, 275-278
Rickover, Hyman, 404, 407, 412
Riesman, David, 365, 425
Riis, Jacob, 323
Robber barons, 233
Rockefeller, John D., 387
Rogers, Agnes, 337

Rogers, David, 463

Roosevelt, Franklin D., 351

Roosevelt, Theodore, 220, 252, 256, 257, 344

Rose, Willie Lee, 130

Rote memorization, 110, 375. *See also* Recitation

Rousseau, Jean Jacques, 96, 317, 331

Rudolph, Frederick, 25, 34, 44

Rugg, Harold, 376

Russian Revolution, 3

Scholarship, professional, 228-30. *See also* Scientific research

Scholarships, 157

School and Society, The, 260-69

School taxes, 9, 60, 61, 142, 147, 149, 150, 156, 157, 162, 167, 168, 415; in Reconstruction, 143-45; in Progressive era in South, 151

Schoolhouses, 10, 11, 12, 95, 137, 138, 143, 146

Schoolmasters in district schools, 11-15

Schools of Tomorrow, 376

Schurz, Mrs. Carl, 320

Scientific research, 228-30, 237-39, 241, 300, 302; as new purpose of universities, 242-46

Scopes, John T., 362

Scopes Trial, 352, 361-62

Sectarianism, 89, 90, 159, 162, 168

Segregation, 142, 211, 459-62; in South, 442-51. *See also* Integration

"Separate but equal," 443-45

Settlement house movement, 269-74, 276, 278; kindergarten work in, 323-25

Seward, William, 161-69

Shaw, Mrs. Quincy Adams, 203, 307, 322

Sheffield Scientific School, 230

Sheldon, Edward A., 60, 105-11, 186

Sherman, William T., 128

Shields, James M., 384-85

Shumaker, Ann, 376

Sigourney, Lydia, 95

Silliman, Benjamin, 34

Simon, Theodore, 353

Sinclair, Upton, 364

Slater Fund, 212-13

Slavery, 120, 234-35, 253; common school movement and, 123

Slums and Suburbs, 410

Smalls, Robert, 134

Smith, Adam, 28, 251

Smith, Al, 352

Smith, Henry Nash, 41

Smith, Mortimer, 404-406

Smith, Timothy L., 441

Smith College, 25

Smith-Hughes Act, 308

Snedden, David, 310, 312

Social cohesion, restoration of, 185

Social control, 70, 76, 80, 88, 104, 119, 122, 155, 201, 252, 279, 280, 284, 291, 303, 329, 378, 473; common school movement and, 58-61; undermined, 71-74; Whig efforts to restore, 77-79; at Oswego, New York, 105; in South, 123; kindergarten and, 325-26. *See also* Values, imposition of

Social Darwinism, 139, 255

Social efficiency as function of high school, 309-11, 407, 408, 410, 411, 417

Social reform, 102, 118-24, 343, 431-73 *passim*, 433, 437, 468, 471-73; required reformed pedagogy, 84; at Oswego, New York, 105-11

Social reconstruction movement, 376-77

Social workers, 72, 278. *See also* Settlement house movement

Society for the Protection of Destitute Roman Catholic Children in the City of New York, 199

Sororities, 370. *See also* Extracurriculum

Southern Education Board, 147, 211

"Southern Manifesto," 446

Special education, 142, 189, 192-225 *passim*, 227, 232

Special Field Order Number 15, 128

Spelling bee, 100, 367; in district
  school, 16-20
Spelman College, 213
Spencer, Herbert, 255
Spencer, John, 167-69
Spoils system, 232, 244
Standardization, 188. *See also* Bureau-
  cratization; Codification
Stanford University, 228, 302, 355,
  364
State literary funds, 142-43
State school fund, 157-59, 162
States rights doctrine, 65, 126
Stone, Lucy, 25
Student violence, 24
Sunday School Movement, 43, 78
Supreme Court: Dartmouth College
  Case of 1819, 28; integration deci-
  sions in, 443-46
Sweatt v. *Painter*, 443-44
Swint, Henry Lee, 131-33

TTT Project, 458
Tammany Hall, 164, 283
Tariffs, 63-64, 128, 232
Taxes. *See* School taxes
Teachers: in South during Reconstruc-
  tion, 133-36, 141; certification of,
  405. *See also* Female teachers; Pro-
  fessionalism in education
Teacher-training institutions. *See*
  Normal schools
Teachers College, Columbia University,
  302, 306, 309, 312, 328, 336, 364,
  376, 378, 379, 385, 406
Technical schools, 33
Temperance movement, 117, 131
Tennessee Coal and Iron Company,
  213, 216
Terman, Lewis, 355
Terminal students, 294-95
Tewksbury, Donald, 37
Textbook publishers, 109, 335, 381
Textbooks, 12, 19-20, 59
Thernstrom, Stephan, 187
Thorndike, Edward Lee, 316, 329,
  331, 336, 356-57, 379, 405; learn-

ing theory of, 332-35
Tracking, 343, 409
Transfer of training, 32, 239, 333-34,
  405
Treaty of Versailles, 346
Tuition, 38, 39, 157, 158; in colleges
  and academies, 24; in elementary
  schools, 60-61
Tulane University, 149
Turner, Frederick J., 254
Tuskegee Institute, 210-11, 217
Tutors, 120-21
Tweed, William Marcy, 232-33, 235
Tweed Ring, 232
Tyack, David, 187-89, 359, 360

Unitarianism, 89, 91, 172
United Fund, 387
United States Bureau of Education,
  343
United States Commission on Civil
  Rights, 456
United States Military Academy, 33
United States Steel Corporation, 253
Universities, 126, 156, 375, 384, 401,
  402, 407, 428, 436; in Progressive
  era, 227-46; curricular reform in,
  238-42; Committee of Ten on, 288-
  305; admissions to, 292-95. *See
  also* Colleges
University of California, 228
University of Chicago, 228, 302; La-
  boratory School of, 260, 266
University of Colorado, 292, 293, 300
University of Edinburgh, 7
University of Indiana, 365
University of Kansas, 307
University of Leyden, 7
University of Michigan, 228, 229, 293,
  297, 302, 364
University of Minnesota, 364
University of Missouri, 41, 293, 311
University of Pennsylvania, 30
University of Texas, 443-44
University of Virginia, 5, 8, 45
University of Wisconsin, 228, 229,
  364

Urbanization, 120, 170, 220, 368; in
mid-nineteenth century, 71-75; at
Oswego, New York, 106; in 1920s,
352-53; communities and, 390-91
Urban poverty, 74-76

Values, imposition of, 81, 85, 88, 118,
135-36, 154, 186, 196, 201, 219-
20, 222, 223, 259, 273, 282, 316,
323, 325, 330, 341, 361; in Whig
ideology, 69-70, 160-61; through
vocal music, 93; at Oswego, New
York, 105; Protestantism and, 165;
Catholicism and, 166; in industrial
education, 193-94; in reform schools,
195. *See also* Social control
Vanderbilt, Cornelius, 233
Vassar College, 25, 293
Visiting teacher movement, 274-78
Vocal music, 91-93
Vocation Bureau, 307
Vocational education and training,
371-72, 375, 402, 403. *See also* In-
dustrial education; Manual training
Volstead Act, 347

War Hawks, 63
War on Poverty, 431-32
Ward, Lester Frank, 255
Washington, Booker T., 142, 208-17
passim, 439-40, 448-50
Washington, George, 7, 232
Washington University, 217
Watergate, 471
Watson, John B., 332, 344-45, 357
Wayland, Francis, 34, 47, 230, 231
Weber, Evelyn, 319, 324, 339
Webster, Noah, 16-20, 40, 47, 133

Wellesley College, 25
Western Home Missionary Society, 78
Westward expansion, 73-74, 76
Weyl, Walter, 348
Wheelock, Lucy, 324
Whigs, 84, 88, 100, 102, 105-106,
118, 119, 121-22, 140, 147, 168,
185; characterized, 61-65; reforms
of, 65-70; threats to ideology of,
70-74; personal compromise and,
79-80; on purpose of education,
161; centralization and, 162-63;
Public School Society and, 164-66
White, Leonard, 349
White Citizen's Council, 445-46
"White hostages," 460
Whitney, Eli, 66
Whyte, William H., 425
Wiebe, Robert H., 368
Wilson, Woodrow, 252, 256, 346
"Whole word" reading method, 97
Willard, Emma, 25
Williams College, 29, 204
Women, 320; in higher education, 25-
26; in common school movement,
79; in Lowell Experiment, 174-81;
charity work by, 270-71. *See also*
Female teachers
Women's Christian Temperance Union,
323
Women's rights movement, 131
Woodward, Calvin, 217-21
Woodworth, Robert, 332
World War I, 344-46, 354, 387
World War II, 351, 373, 402, 418

Yale Report of 1828, 31-35, 85, 238
Yale University, 27, 34, 230, 235